OCP
Oracle® Certified Professional
Java® SE 21 Developer
Study Guide

OCP

Oracle® Certified Professional
Java® SE 21 Developer

Study Guide

Exam 1Z0-830

Jeanne Boyarsky

Scott Selikoff

A Wiley Brand

Published by John Wiley & Sons, Inc., Hoboken, New Jersey.
Published simultaneously in Canada and the United Kingdom.

ISBNs: 9781394286614 (paperback), 9781394286638 (ePDF), 9781394286621 (ePub)

For general information on our other products and services, please contact our Customer Care Department within the United States at (800) 762-2974, outside the United States at (317) 572-3993. For product technical support, you can find answers to frequently asked questions or reach us via live chat at https://sybexsupport.wiley.com.

Wiley also publishes its books in a variety of electronic formats. Some content that appears in print may not be available in electronic formats. For more information about Wiley products, visit our web site at www.wiley.com.

Library of Congress Control Number: 2024941967

Cover image: © Jeremy Woodhouse/Getty Images
Cover design: Wiley

SKY10087578_101124

To the GearMasters (FIRST Tech Challenge Team 8365) 2014–2024.
You inspired me and so many others!
—Jeanne

For my daughter, Elysia, your intelligence, sense of humor, endless energy, and
perseverance make you a force to be reckoned with. May you continue to grow
into the powerful woman I know you're destined to be.
—Scott

Acknowledgments

Jeanne and Scott would like to thank numerous individuals for their contributions to this book. Thank you to Caroline Define and Archana Pragash for guiding us through the process and making the book better in many ways. Thank you to Janeice DelVecchio for being our technical editor as we wrote this book. Janeice pointed out many subtle errors in addition to the big ones. Thank you to Elena Felder for being our technical proofreader and finding the errors that we managed to sneak by Janeice. And a special thank-you to our copy editor Kim Wimpsett for finding subtle errors that everyone (including us!) missed. This book also wouldn't be possible without many people at Wiley, including Kenyon Brown, Pete Gaughan, Ashirvad Moses, and many others.

Jeanne would personally like to thank Dani, Janeice, Kim, Norm, Scott, and Shweta during a difficult month that overlapped with book writing. She also wants to thank Victor for his patience as Jeanne worked on two books simultaneously. (this one and *Real-World Java: Helping You Navigate the Java Ecosystem*). A big thank-you to Scott for being a great co-author while honoring Jeanne's request to not think about the book until FIRST Robotics Championships was over. A big thank-you to everyone at CodeRanch.com who asked and responded to questions and comments about our books. Finally, Jeanne would like to thank all of the new programmers at CodeRanch.com and FIRST robotics teams FRC 694 and FTC 310/479 for the constant reminders of how new programmers think.

Scott could not have reached this point without his wife, Patti, and family, whose love and support make this book possible. He would like to thank his twin daughters, Olivia and Sophia, and youngest daughter, Elysia, for their patience and understanding and bringing Daddy a cup of cappuccino when it was "time for Daddy to work in his office!" Scott would like to extend his gratitude to his wonderfully patient co-author, Jeanne, on this, their tenth book. He doesn't know how she puts up with him, but he's glad she does and is thrilled at the quality of books we produce. Finally, Scott would like to thank his mother, Barbara Selikoff (a retired teacher), for teaching him the value of education, and his father, Mark Selikoff, for instilling in him the benefits of working hard.

Both of us would like to give a big thank-you to the readers of our books. Hearing from all of you who enjoyed the book and passed the exam is a great feeling. We appreciate the 7Up sorting tip from Anil Philip that you'll see in the book along with Venkat Subramaniam for the restaurant analogy for concurrency. We'd also like to thank those who pointed out errors and made suggestions for improvements to the Java 17 book. As of July 2024, the top two were Guillaume Bailly and Albert Attard.

About the Authors

Jeanne Boyarsky was selected as a Java Champion in 2019 and is a leader of the NYJavaSIG. She has worked as a Java developer for more than 22 years at a bank in New York City where she develops, mentors, and conducts training. Besides being a senior moderator at `CodeRanch.com` in her free time, she works on the forum code base. Jeanne also mentors the programming division of a FIRST robotics team, where she works with students just getting started with Java. She also speaks at several conferences each year.

Jeanne got her bachelor's degree in 2002 and her master's degree in computer information technology in 2005. She enjoyed getting her master's degree in an online program while working full time. This was before online education was cool! Jeanne is also a Distinguished Toastmaster and a Scrum Master. You can find out more about Jeanne at `www.jeanneboyarsky.com` and follow her on social media at `x.com/jeanneboyarsky` or `mastodon.social/@jeanneboyarsky`.

Scott Selikoff is a professional software developer and author with almost 25 years of experience developing full-stack database-driven systems. Skilled in a plethora of software languages and platforms, Scott currently works as a staff software engineer at Google, specializing in architecture and cloud services.

A native of Toms River, New Jersey, Scott earned his bachelor's degree from Cornell University in mathematics and computer science in 2002 after three years of study. In 2003, he received his master's degree in computer science, also from Cornell University. As someone with a deep love of education, Scott has always enjoyed teaching others new concepts. Scott is a leader of the Garden State Java User Group, helping to facilitate discussions and exchange of ideas within the community. He has also taught lectures at multiple universities and conferences.

Scott lives in New Jersey with his loving wife, Patti; three amazing daughters, twins Olivia and Sophia and little Elysia; a very playful dog, Georgette; and three silly cats, Snowball, Sugar, and Minnie Mouse. In his spare time, he plays violin in the Toms River Multigenerational Orchestra. You can find out more about Scott at `www.linkedin.com/in/selikoff` or follow him on social media at `x.com/ScottSelikoff`.

Jeanne and Scott are both moderators on the `CodeRanch.com` forums and can be reached there for question and comments. They also co-author a technical blog called Down Home Country Coding at `www.selikoff.net`.

In addition to this book, Jeanne and Scott are the authors of nine best-selling Java books:

- *OCP Java 17 Practice Tests* (Sybex, 2022)
- *OCP Java 17 Developer Study Guide* (Sybex, 2022)
- *OCP Java 11 Practice Tests* (Sybex, 2021)
- *OCP Java 11 Developer Complete Study Guide* (Sybex, 2020)
- *OCP Java 11 Programmer II Study Guide* (Sybex, 2020)
- *OCP Java 11 Programmer I Study Guide* (Sybex, 2019)
- *OCA/OCP Java 8 Practice Tests* (Sybex, 2017)
- *OCP: Java 8 Programmer II Study Guide* (Sybex, 2016)
- *OCA: Java 8 Programmer I Study Guide* (Sybex, 2015)

About the Technical Editor

Janeice DelVecchio has been a professional Software Developer for 14 years, and has had a lifelong love of programming and computers. Editing technical books is a fun task for her because she likes finding and fixing defects of all types.

In her day job she uses a very broad range of skills with technologies including cloud computing, process automation, advanced unit testing and devops. She also volunteers at CodeRanch.com where she runs the Java class known as the Cattle Drive.

She is an expert with the Java programming language. If you ask her which language is the best, she will tell you that languages are tools and to pick the one that fits your use case. The first language she learned was BASIC, and one day she hopes to learn gaming development.

In her spare time, she enjoys cooking, solving puzzles, and playing video games. She loves eating sushi, drinking craft beer, and petting dogs—her guilty pleasure is 80's pop music. She lives in Litchfield County, Connecticut with her dog, Desmond and her cat, Suki.

About the Technical Proofreader

Elena Felder got into Java development back when the language lacked even generics, and has been delighted that the language, its tooling and community have continued to grow and adapt to successfully keep up with the ever-changing world.

Elena got into proofreading Jeanne and Scott's books because one day a very long time ago she got Jeanne to spend way longer than planned revising a single slide on lambda syntax by pointing out everything that could go wrong, which then lead to proofreading one of Jeanne and Scott's first Java 8 certification book chapters for fun (as one does). She's been proofreading the Wiley Java certification books professionally ever since.

After 20 years of real-world Java experience, including four years of maintaining Google Cloud's Spring Framework integrations, Elena switched to writing code and chasing bugs in what feels like every language imaginable. Java, however, remains a personal favorite!

Currently Elena leads the ecosystem integrations team at MotherDuck, a DuckDB-powered serverless data warehouse.

She lives in Brooklyn, NY with her husband, two children, two cats, and countless plants.

Contents at a Glance

Contents

Introduction

This book is for those looking to complete the Java SE 21 Developer Professional exam (1Z0-830) and obtain the Java 21 Developer Certified Professional title. This exam is commonly referred to as the OCP (Oracle Certified Professional) 21 exam. This book is also for those looking to gain a deeper understanding and appreciation of Java. Not only do we want you to pass your exams, but we want to help you to improve yourself and become a better professional software developer.

The book provides detailed preparation for the following Oracle certification exam:

1Z0-830 Exam: Java SE 21 Developer Professional The Developer Professional exam covers a wide variety of core topics in Java 21 including classes, interfaces, streams, collections, concurrency, and modules.

In this introduction, we start by covering important information about the various exams. We then move on to information about how this book is structured. Finally, we conclude with an assessment test so you can see how much studying lies ahead of you.

Understanding the Exam

At the end of the day, the exam is a list of questions. The more you know about the structure of the exam, the better you are likely to do. For example, knowing how many questions the exam contains allows you to better manage your progress and time remaining. In this section, we discuss the details of the exam, along with some history of previous certification exams.

Choosing Which Exam to Take

Java is now about 30 years old, celebrating being "born" in 1995. As with anything that age, there is a good amount of history and variation between different versions of Java. Over the years, the certification exams have changed to cover different topics. The number of exams and names of certifications have also changed.

Oracle has simplified things over time. Becoming an Oracle Certified Professional now requires passing only one exam, not two, and there are no Java 21 upgrade exams. Regardless of the previous certifications you hold, everyone takes the same Java 21 exam to become an Oracle Certified Professional.

There's another less popular exam called the Java Foundations exam. Our advice is to only take the Java Foundations exam if your employer has specifically asked you to as it is not meant for professionals who work with Java every day. Our book page explains how to use this book to study for the Java Foundations exam:

www.selikoff.net/ocp21

Differences Between the Java 21 Exam and Previous Java Exams

If you're certified with an older version of Java, you might expect the Java 21 exam to be a lot like the exams you took in the past. While there are some similarities, the exam also contains some major differences that you should be aware of.

- Questions are generally longer, have more code to read, and contain a lot more answer options (up to 10).

- Questions often span multiple, independent objectives.

- You're more likely to run out of time on this exam.

- There is no longer an exam software feature to right-click and cross out options you've eliminated.

In our experience, we found this to be a more challenging exam than some of the Java exams of the past, so it's important to allot an appropriate amount of time to study for the exam.

Taking an Online Exam

In the past, the exam was offered both at a physical testing center and online via a remote proctor. Oracle now *only offers the exam online*, which means you'll need to take it remotely.

You'll need a quiet environment, free from interruption for the length of the exam. Prior to taking the exam, you'll also need to install software that monitors your session and ensures the integrity of the exam is not violated. For this reason, we don't recommend taking the exam with a work computer, where installing software may be restricted.

We have posted our experiences taking the exam remotely to give you want an idea of what is involved.

www.selikoff.net/ocp21

Reviewing the Format of the Exam

At the time this book is being published, the exam details are as follows:

- Time limit: **120 minutes**
- Number of questions: **50**
- Passing score: **68%** (34 questions)

Oracle has a tendency to fiddle with the length of the exam and the passing score once it comes out. Oracle also likes to "tweak" the exam objectives over time. It wouldn't be a surprise for Oracle to make *minor* changes to the exam objectives, the number of questions, or the passing score after this book goes to print.

> If there are any changes to the exam after this book is published, we will post them on the book page of our blog: www.selikoff.net/ocp21

Considering the Exam Objectives

Oracle provides a list of objectives to guide you on what to study for the exam. Each objective defines a list of subobjectives providing additional details about the objective. Unfortunately, the objectives don't encompass the full amount of material needed to pass the exam.

So how do you know what to study? By reading this study guide, of course! We've spent years studying the certification exams in all of their forms and have carefully cultivated topics, material, and practice questions that we are confident can lead to successfully passing the exam. For the last 10 years, we've worked directly with Oracle helping to create and refine the objectives and material for the Java 8, Java 11, Java 17, and Java 21 exams. You can even thank us for successfully lobbying to remove JDBC from the Java 21 exam. That's one whole chapter less to study!

As a starting point, you should review the list of objectives presented in this introduction and mark down the ones that are unfamiliar to you. This list, along with the Assessment Test at the end of this introduction, will give you a rough idea of how much you are going to need to study for the exam.

Scope of Objectives

In previous certification exams, the list of exam objectives tended to include specific topics, classes, and APIs that you needed to know for the exam. For example, take a look at an objective for the OCP 8 exam (1Z0-809):

- Use BufferedReader, BufferedWriter, File, FileReader, FileWriter, FileInputStream, FileOutputStream, ObjectOutputStream, ObjectInputStream, and PrintWriter in the java.io package.

Now compare it with the equivalent objective for the OCP 21 exam (1Z0-830):

- Read and write console and file data using I/O streams.

Notice the difference? The older version is more detailed and describes specific classes you need to understand. The newer version is a lot more vague. It also gives the exam writers a lot more freedom to insert a new feature without having to update the list of objectives.

Non-Objective Objectives

Oracle has a habit of adding additional assumptions and requirements outside the scope of exam objectives. For the 1Z0-830, that includes the following two lists of items.

Exam Assumptions

- **Missing package and import statements:** If sample code does not include package or import statements and the question does not explicitly refer to these missing statements, then assume that all sample code is in the same package or that import statements exist to support them.

- **No file or directory path names for classes:** If a question does not state the file names or directory locations of classes, then assume one of the following, whichever will enable the code to compile and run:
  - All classes are in one file.
  - Each class is contained in a separate file, and all files are in one directory.

- **Unintended line breaks:** Sample code might have unintended line breaks. If you see a line of code that looks like it has wrapped and this creates a situation where the wrapping is significant (for example, a quoted String literal has wrapped), assume that the wrapping is an extension of the same line, and the line does not contain a hard carriage return that would cause a compilation failure.

- **Code fragments:** A code fragment is a small section of source code presented without its context. Assume that all necessary supporting code exists and that the supporting environment fully supports the correct compilation and execution of the code shown and its omitted environment.

- **Descriptive comments:** Take descriptive comments, such as "setters and getters go here," at face value. Assume that correct code exists, compiles, and runs successfully to create the described effect.

Exam Expectations

- Understand the basics of Java Logging API.

- Use Annotations such as @Override, @FunctionalInterface, @Deprecated, @SuppressWarnings, and @SafeVarargs.

- Use generics, including wildcards.

Many of these topics fall under the same theme. You can assume external things like imports, file structure, and line breaks are not being tested, unless the exam question is specifically asking about them. Some items include cursory use of things like the Logging API and annotations. Don't worry, we cover what you need to know for the exam in this book!

Choosing the Correct Answer(s)

The exam consists entirely of multiple-choice questions. There are between four and ten possible answers. If a question has more than one answer, the question specifically states exactly how many correct answers there are. This book does not do that. We say *Choose all that apply* to make the questions harder. This means the questions in this book are generally harder than those on the exam. The idea is to give you more practice so you can spot the correct answer more easily on the real exam.

Reading the Exam Code

Many of the questions on the exam are code snippets rather than full classes. Saving space by not including imports and/or class definitions leaves room for lots of other code. You should only focus on `import` statements when the question specifically asks about them.

For example, it is common to come across classes on the exam with `import` statements and portions omitted, like so:

```
public class Zoo implements Serializable {
    String name;
    // Getters/Setters/Constructors omitted
}
```

In this case, you can assume that `java.io.Serializable` is imported and that methods like `getName()` and `setName()`, as well as related constructors, exist. For instance, we would expect this code to compile:

```
var name = new Zoo("Java Zoo").getName();
```

Encountering Out-of-Scope Material

When you take an exam, you may see some questions that appear to be out of scope. *Don't panic!* Often, these questions do not require knowing anything about the topic to answer the question. For example, after reading this book, you should be able to spot that the following does not compile, even if you've never heard of the `java.util.logging.Logger` class.

```
final Logger myLogger = Logger.getAnonymousLogger();
myLogger = Logger.getLogger(String.class.getName());
```

The classes and methods used in this question are not in scope for the exam, but the reason it does not compile is. In particular, you should know that you cannot reassign a variable marked `final`.

See? Not so scary, is it? Expect to see at least a few structures on the exam that you are not familiar with. If they aren't part of your exam preparation material, then you don't need to understand them to answer the question.

Reviewing Question Types

The following list of topics is meant to give you an idea of the types of questions and oddities that you might come across on the exam. Being aware of these categories of questions *can help you get a higher score on an exam!*

Word Problems   A small percentage of questions on the exam do not involve reading code and are instead word problems. These questions are fast to solve. For example, you could get asked which statements are true about I/O.

Code Questions with Extra Information Provided   Imagine the question includes a statement like "XMLParseException is a checked exception." It's fine if you don't know what an XMLParseException is or what XML is, for that matter. (If you are wondering, it is a format for data.) This question is a gift. You know the statement is about exception handling.

Code Questions with Embedded Questions   To answer some questions on the exam, you may have to answer two or three subquestions. For example, the question may contain two blank lines and ask you to choose the two answers that fill in each blank. In some cases, the two answer choices are not related, which means you're really answering multiple questions, not just one! These questions are more difficult and time-consuming because they contain multiple, often independent, questions to answer. Unfortunately, the exam does not give partial credit, so take care when answering questions like these.

Code Questions with Long Options   The hardest questions on the exam have multiple lines of code in each option. For example, some of the questions have 6 possible options and up to 30 lines of code in each! That's a lot of reading. To answer faster, we recommend skimming the answers and identifying the parts that are different. That allows you to more quickly identify syntax and other errors in the different parts and start eliminating choices!

Code Questions with Made-Up or Incorrect Concepts   In the context of a word problem, the exam may bring up a term or concept that does not make any sense, such as falsely saying a record extends another record. In other cases, the exam may use a keyword that does not exist in Java, like struct. For these, you just have to read carefully and recognize when the exam is using invalid terminology to try to trick you.

Questions That Are Really Out of Scope   When introducing new questions, Oracle includes them as unscored questions at first. This allows the exam creators to see how real exam takers do without impacting your score. You will still receive the number of questions the exam lists. However, a few of them may not count. These unscored questions may contain out-of-scope material or even errors. They will not be marked as unscored, so you still have to do your best to answer them. Follow the previous advice to assume that anything you haven't seen before is correct. That will cover you if the question is being counted!

Reading This Book

To get the most out of this book, it might help to have some idea about how this book has been written. This section contains details about some of the common structures and features you find in this book, where to go for additional help, and how to obtain bonus material for this book.

Who Should Buy This Book

If you want to obtain the OCP 21 Java programmer certification, this book is definitely for you. If you want to acquire a solid foundation in Java and your goal is to prepare for the exam, then this book is also for you. You'll find clear explanations of the concepts you need to grasp and plenty of help to achieve the high level of professional competency you need in order to succeed in your chosen field.

This book is intended to be understandable to anyone who has a tiny bit of Java knowledge. If you've never read a Java book before, we recommend starting with a book that teaches programming from the beginning and then returning to this study guide.

This book is for anyone from high school students to those beginning their programming journey to experienced professionals who need a review for the certification.

How This Book Is Organized

This book is divided into 14 chapters, plus supplementary online material: a glossary of important terms, 500+ flash cards, and three practice exams that simulate the real exam.

Unlike the exam objectives, we organize our chapters organically so that each chapter builds on the material of the previous chapters. We also want to make things easier to learn and remember. This means some chapters cover multiple objectives.

The chapters are organized as follows:

- **Chapter 1: Building Blocks** describes the basics of Java, such as how to run a program. It covers variables such as primitives, object data types, and scoping variables. It also discusses garbage collection.

- **Chapter 2: Operators** explains operations with variables. It also talks about casting and the precedence of operators.

- **Chapter 3: Making Decisions** covers core logical constructs such as decision statements, pattern matching with `instanceof` and `switch`, and loops.

- **Chapter 4: Core APIs** works with `String`, `StringBuilder`, arrays, and dates.

- **Chapter 5: Methods** explains how to design and write methods. It also introduces access modifiers, which are used throughout the book.

- **Chapter 6: Class Design** covers class structure, constructors, inheritance, and initialization. It also teaches you how to create abstract classes and overload methods.

- **Chapter 7: Beyond Classes** introduces many top-level types (other than classes), including interfaces, enums, sealed classes, records with and without pattern matching, and nested classes. It also covers polymorphism.

- **Chapter 8: Lambdas and Functional Interfaces** shows how to use lambdas, method references, and built-in functional interfaces.

- **Chapter 9: Collections and Generics** demonstrates method references, generics with wildcards, and Collections. The Collections portion covers many common interfaces, classes, and methods that are useful for the exam and in everyday software development.

- **Chapter 10: Streams** explains stream pipelines in detail. It also covers the Optional class. If you want to become skilled at creating streams, read this chapter more than once!

- **Chapter 11: Exceptions and Localization** demonstrates the different types of exception classes and how to apply them to build more resilient programs. It concludes with localization and formatting, which allow your program to gracefully support multiple countries or languages.

- **Chapter 12: Modules** details the benefits of the new module feature. It shows how to compile and run module programs from the command line. Additionally, it describes services and how to migrate an application to a modular infrastructure.

- **Chapter 13: Concurrency** introduces the concept of platform and virtual threads along with thread-safety. It teaches you how to build multithreaded programs using the Concurrency API and parallel streams.

- **Chapter 14: I/O** introduces you to managing files and directories using the I/O and NIO.2 APIs. It covers a number of I/O stream classes, teaches you how to serialize data, and shows how to interact with a user. Additionally, it includes techniques for using streams to traverse and search the file system.

At the end of each chapter, you'll find a few elements you can use to prepare for the exam:

Summary This section reviews the most important topics that were covered in the chapter and serves as a good review.

Exam Essentials This section summarizes highlights that were covered in the chapter. You should be able to convey the information described.

Review Questions Each chapter concludes with at least 20 review questions. You should answer these questions and check your answers against the ones provided in the Appendix. If you can't answer at least 80 percent of these questions correctly, go back and review the chapter, or at least those sections that seem to be giving you difficulty.

The review questions, assessment tests, practice exams, and other code samples included in this book are *not* derived from the real exam questions, so don't memorize them! Learning the underlying topic not only helps you pass the exam but also makes you a higher-quality programmer in the workplace—the ultimate goal of a certification.

To get the most out of this book, you should read each chapter from start to finish before going to the chapter-end elements. They are most useful for checking and reinforcing your understanding. Even if you're already familiar with a topic, you should skim the chapter. There are a number of subtleties to Java that you could easily not encounter even when working with Java for years. For instance, the following does compile:

```
var $num = (Integer)null;
```

Even an experienced Java developer might be taken aback by this one. The exam requires you to know these kinds of subtleties.

Conventions Used in This Book

This book uses certain typographic styles to help you quickly identify important information and to avoid confusion over the meaning of words, such as on-screen prompts. In particular, look for the following styles:

- *Italicized text* indicates key terms that are described at length for the first time in a chapter. (Italics are also used for emphasis.)
- A `monospaced font` indicates code or command-line text. We often use **bold** to highlight important words or methods within a code sample.
- *`Italicized monospaced text`* indicates a variable.

In addition to these text conventions, which can apply to individual words or entire paragraphs, a few conventions highlight segments of text.

A tip is something to call particular attention to an aspect of working with a language feature or API.

A note indicates information that's useful or interesting. It is often something to pay special attention to for the exam.

Sidebars

A sidebar is like a note but longer. The information in a sidebar is useful, but it doesn't fit into the main flow of the text.

 ### Real World Scenario

A real-world scenario is a type of sidebar that describes a task or an example that's particularly grounded in the real world. This is something that is useful in the real world but is not going to show up on the exam.

Getting Help

Both of the authors are moderators at CodeRanch.com. This site is a quite large and active programming forum that is friendly toward Java beginners. It has a forum just for this exam called *Programmer Certification*. It also has a forum called *Beginning Java* for non-exam-specific questions. As you read the book, feel free to ask your questions in either of those forums. It could be that you are having trouble compiling a class or are just plain confused about something. You'll get an answer from a knowledgeable Java programmer. It might even be one of us!

Remember to check our book page before taking the exam. It contains any recent updates Oracle makes to the exam.

www.selikoff.net/ocp21

Interactive Online Learning Environment and Test Bank

We've put together some really great online tools to help you pass the exams. The interactive online learning environment that accompanies this study guide provides a test bank and study tools to help you prepare for the exam. By using these tools, you can dramatically increase your chances of passing the exam on your first try.

To register and gain access to this interactive online learning environment, please visit this URL:

www.wiley.com/go/Sybextestprep

The online test bank includes the following:

Three Practice Exams   Many sample tests are provided throughout this book and online, including the assessment test, which you'll find at the end of this introduction, and the chapter tests, which include the review questions at the end of each chapter. In addition, there are three bonus practice exams. Use these questions to test your knowledge of the study guide material. The online test bank runs on multiple devices.

500+ Flashcards   The online test bank includes two sets of flashcards specifically written to hit you hard, so don't get discouraged if you don't ace your way through them at first! They're there to ensure that you're really ready for the exam. And no worries—armed with the review questions, practice exams, and flashcards, you'll be more than prepared when exam day comes! Questions are provided in digital flashcard format (a question followed by a single correct answer). You can use the flashcards to reinforce your learning and provide last-minute test prep before the exam.

Additional Resources   A glossary of key terms from this book and their definitions is available as a fully searchable PDF.

Like all exams, the Oracle Certified Professional from Oracle is updated periodically and may eventually be retired or replaced. At some point after Oracle is no longer offering this exam, the old editions of our books and online tools will be retired. If you have purchased this book after the exam was retired or are attempting to register in the Sybex online learning environment after the exam was retired, please know that we make no guarantees that this exam's online Sybex tools will be available once the exam is no longer available.

Studying for the Exam

This section includes suggestions and recommendations for how you should prepare for the certification exam. Rather than just reading this book, we recommend writing and executing programs as part of the study process. How you study can be just as important as what you study.

Creating a Study Plan

Rome wasn't built in a day, so you shouldn't attempt to study for the exam in only one day. Even if you have been certified with a previous version of Java, the new test includes features and components unique to Java 18–21.

Once you have decided to take the test, you should construct a study plan that fits with your schedule. We recommend that you set aside some amount of time each day, even if it's just a few minutes during lunch, to read or practice for the exam. The idea is to keep your momentum going throughout the exam preparation process. The more consistent you are in how you study, the better prepared you are for the exam. Try to avoid taking a few days or weeks off from studying, or you're likely to spend a lot of time relearning existing material instead of moving on to new material.

Creating and Running the Code

Although some people can learn Java just by reading a textbook, that's not how we recommend that you study for a certification exam. We want you to be writing your own Java sample applications throughout this book so that you don't just learn the material but understand the material as well. For example, it may not be obvious why the following line of code does not compile, but if you try to compile it yourself, the Java compiler tells you the problem:

```
float value = 102.0;  // DOES NOT COMPILE
```

A lot of people post the question "Why doesn't this code compile?" on the CodeRanch.com forum. If you're stuck or just curious about a behavior in Java, we encourage you to post to the forum. There are a lot of nice people in the Java community standing by to help you.

Sample Test Class

Throughout this book, we present numerous code snippets and ask you whether they'll compile or not and what their output is. You can place these snippets inside a simple Java application that starts, executes the code, and terminates. You can accomplish this by compiling and running a `public` class containing a `main()` method and adding the necessary `import` statements, such as the following:

```java
// Add any necessary import statements here
public class TestClass {
    public static void main(String[] args) {
        // Add test code here

        // Add any print statements here
        System.out.println("Hello World!");
    }
}
```

This application isn't particularly interesting—it just outputs `Hello World!` and exits. That said, you could insert many of the code snippets presented in this book in the `main()` method to determine whether the code compiles, as well as what the code outputs when it does compile.

 Real World Scenario

IDE Software

While studying for an exam, you should develop code using a text editor and command-line Java compiler. Some of you may have prior experience with integrated development environments (IDEs) such as Eclipse, IntelliJ, and Visual Studio Code. An IDE is a software application that facilitates software development for computer programmers. Although such tools are extremely valuable in developing software, they can interfere with your ability to spot problems readily on an exam.

Identifying Your Weakest Link

The review questions in each chapter are designed to help you hone in on those features of the Java language where you may be weak and that are required knowledge for the exam. For each chapter, you should note which questions you got wrong, understand why you got them wrong, and study those areas even more. After you've reread the chapter and written lots of code, you can do the review questions again. In fact, you can take the review questions over and over to reinforce your learning, as long as you explain to yourself why each answer is correct.

"Overstudying" the Online Practice Exams

Although we recommend reading this book and writing your own sample applications multiple times, redoing the online practice exams over and over can have a negative impact in the long run. For example, some individuals study the practice exams so much that they end up memorizing the answers. In this scenario, they can easily become overconfident; that is, they can achieve perfect scores on the practice exams but may fail the actual exam. If you want more practice questions, see our book page for how to use our Java 17 Developer Practice Tests book in tandem with this book:

`www.selikoff.net/ocp21`

Applying Test-Taking Strategies

This section includes suggestions you can use when you take the exam. If you're an experienced test taker or you've taken a certification test before, most of this should be common knowledge. For those who are taking the exam for the first time, don't worry! We present a number of practical tips and strategies to help you prepare for the exam.

Bringing Your Own Blank Paper

When the exam was offered in person, you would have been provided with writing material in the form of a whiteboard to use to help you answer questions. Writing material can be incredibly helpful on questions involving:

- Numerous options (some questions have 10 options)
- Multiple answers (some questions ask you to pick two or three answers)
- Math and nested loops

Not to mention all questions benefit from process of elimination!

Currently, Oracle doesn't provide any online writing materials, such as a digital whiteboard. In the meantime, they are allowing you to use blank paper as writing material. If you do bring blank paper, make sure to inform your proctor before you start the exam. Your proctor may want to see the paper is blank by holding it to the camera. Be aware, some proctors may not allow blank paper at all.

Whether you use an online whiteboard or you are using paper, the next section covers how to best use it.

Using the Writing Material

For short questions, you can start by first checking whether the code compiles and then move on to understanding what the program does! One of the most useful applications of writing material is tracking the state of primitive and reference variables. For example, let's say you encountered the following code snippet on a question about garbage collection:

```
Object o = new Turtle();
Mammal m = new Monkey();
Animal a = new Rabbit();
o = m;
```

In a situation like this, it can be helpful to draw a diagram of the current state of the variable references, as shown in Figure I.1.

FIGURE I.1 Tracking objects and references

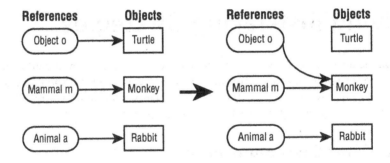

As each reference variable changes which object it points to, you erase or cross out the arrow between them and draw a new one to a different object.

Using the writing material to track state is also useful for complex questions that involve a loop, especially questions with embedded loops. For example, the value of a variable might change five or more times during a loop execution. You should make use of the writing material if permitted to improve your score.

For questions with code in the options, using your writing material for process of elimination is helpful. For example, suppose you get a question asking to choose the record that is compatible with the provided class. You can skip the given class and eliminate options that do not compile.

A.

```
record Calf(int numInches) {
  Calf {
  } }
```

B.

```
record Calf(int numInches) {
  Calf(int numInches) {
     numInches = 1;
  } }
```

C.

```
record Calf(int numInches) {
  Calf(int numInches) {
     super(40);
  } }
```

D.

```
record Calf(int numInches) {
  Calf() {
     this.numInches = 40;
  } }
```

E.

```
record Calf(int numInches) {
  void Calf {
  } }
```

You might approach this question as follows:

- Write A B C D E on your writing material.

- You should be able to eliminate the last option as void indicates the line is a method, but the parentheses are missing, leaving this on your sheet: A B C D ~~E~~

- Next you might observe that options B and D each have an invalid body declaration. See Chapter 7 for details on why these don't compile, leaving you with: A ~~B~~ C ~~D~~ ~~E~~

- You are now down two options left on your paper, A C. You might notice there isn't a defined superclass with a constructor ruling out option C, and giving you option A as the answer. You've answered the question even if don't know what the entire question text was!

Even with options under five lines, you can see how this technique is useful. Now imagine how useful it would be if the options were longer.

While you cannot bring anything written before the exam, you can write down material once the exam starts. For example, if you have trouble remembering which functional interfaces take which generic arguments, it might be helpful to list them at the start of the exam. You can then use this information to answer multiple questions.

Understanding the Question

The majority of questions on the exam contain code snippets and ask you to answer questions about them. For those items containing code snippets, the number-one question we recommend that you answer before attempting to solve the question is this:

Do I need to determine whether the code compiles?

The answer to this question determines your approach to solving the question. If all of the answers to a question are printed values, aka there is no *Does not compile* option, consider that question a gift. It means every line does compile, and you may be able to use information from this question to answer other questions!

Being Suspicious of Strong Words

Many questions on the exam include answer choices with descriptive sentences rather than lines of code. When you see such questions, be wary of any answer choice that includes strong words such as "must," "all," or "cannot." If you think about the complexities of programming languages, it is rare for a rule to have no exceptions or special cases. Therefore, if you are stuck between two answers and one of them uses "must" while the other uses "can" or "may," you are better off picking the one with the weaker word since it is a more ambiguous statement.

Choosing the Best Answer

Sometimes you read a question and immediately spot a compiler error that tells you exactly what the question is asking. Other times, though, you may stare at a method declaration for a couple of minutes and have no idea what the answer is. Unlike some other standardized tests, there's no penalty for answering a question incorrectly versus leaving it blank. If you're nearly out of time or you just can't decide on an answer, select a random option and move on. If you've been able to eliminate even one answer choice, then your guess is better than blind luck.

You should set a hard stop at five minutes of time remaining on the exam to ensure that you've answered each and every question. Remember, if you fail to answer a question, you'll definitely get it wrong and lose points; but if you guess, there's at least a chance that you'll be correct. There's no harm in guessing!

Skipping Difficult or Time-Consuming Questions

The exam software includes an option to "mark" a question and review all marked questions at the end of the exam. If you are pressed for time, answer a question as best you can and then mark it to come back to later.

All questions are weighted equally, so spending 10 minutes answering five questions correctly is a lot better use of your time than spending 10 minutes on a single question. If you finish the exam early, you have the option of reviewing the marked questions as well as all of the questions on the exam, if you choose.

While many of the questions on the exam are long, you may find some require you to spend more time than others. Ones that are time-consuming are good candidates to go back to at the end. Be sure to put something as the answer so you don't risk running out of time and never getting back to the question. After all, a blank answer is guaranteed to be wrong!

Getting a Good Night's Rest

Although a lot of people are inclined to cram as much material as they can in the hours leading up to an exam, most studies have shown that this is a poor test-taking strategy. The best thing we can recommend that you do before taking an exam is to get a good night's rest!

Given the length of the exam and the number of questions, the exam can be quite draining, especially if this is your first time taking a certification exam. You might come in expecting to be done 30 minutes early, only to discover that you are only a quarter of the way through the exam with half the time remaining. At some point, you may begin to panic, and it is in these moments that these test-taking skills are most important. Just remember to take a deep breath, stay calm, eliminate as many wrong answers as you can, and make sure to answer every question. It is for stressful moments like these that being well rested with a good night's sleep is most beneficial!

Taking the Exam

So you've decided to take the exam? We hope so, if you've bought this book! In this section, we discuss the process of scheduling and taking the exam, along with various options for each.

Scheduling the Exam

The exam is administered by Oracle and is taken online. To buy an exam voucher, start on the exam page:

```
education.oracle.com/java-se-21-developer-professional/pexam_1Z0-830
```

If you have any trouble navigating the website, see our tips linked from (yep, you guessed it!):

www.selikoff.net/ocp21

At the time this book is being published, you can reschedule the exam without penalty until up to 24 hours before. This means you can register for a convenient time slot well in advance, knowing that you can delay if you aren't ready by that time. Rescheduling is easy and can be done completely on the website. This may change, so check the rules before paying.

The Day of the Exam

Allow yourself some time to prepare your workspace for the exam. Remember to put away notes, books, etc. The exam requests two forms of ID, including one that is a government-issued photo ID. You may only get asked to show one, but have both handy just in case.

Also make sure to notify any family or roommates that you are taking the exam and encourage them to be "somewhere else" while taking the exam. If someone interrupts your exam, your proctor may invalidate it.

Finding Out Your Score

As soon as you finish, the exam software shows if you passed along with your score. CertView updates shortly after you finish your exam. In addition to your score, you'll also see the objectives for which you got a question wrong. Once you have passed the 1Z0-830 exam and fulfilled the required prerequisites, the OCP 21 title is granted within the hour. CertView is also where you can get an electronic certificate or badge.

Objective Map

This book has been written to cover every objective on the exam.

Java SE 21 Developer (1Z0-830)

The following table provides a breakdown of this book's exam coverage for the Java SE 21 Developer (1Z0-830) exam, showing you the chapter where each objective or subobjective is covered.

Exam Objective	Chapter
Handling Date, Time, Text, Numeric and Boolean Values	
Use primitives and wrapper classes. Evaluate arithmetic and boolean expressions, using the Math API and by applying precedence rules, type conversions, and casting.	1, 2, 4

Exam Objective	Chapter
Manipulate text, including text blocks, using String and StringBuilder classes.	4
Manipulate date, time, duration, period, instant and time-zone objects including daylight saving time using Date-Time API.	4

Controlling Program Flow

Create program flow control constructs including if/else, switch statements and expressions, loops, and break and continue statements.	3

Using Object-Oriented Concepts in Java

Declare and instantiate Java objects including nested class objects, and explain the object life-cycle including creation, reassigning references, and garbage collection.	1, 7
Create classes and records, and define and use instance and static fields and methods, constructors, and instance and static initializers.	5, 6, 7
Implement overloaded methods, including var-arg methods.	5
Understand variable scopes, apply encapsulation, and create immutable objects. Use local variable type inference.	1, 6, 7, 8
Implement inheritance, including abstract and sealed types as well as record classes. Override methods, including that of the Object class. Implement polymorphism and differentiate between object type and reference type. Perform reference type casting, identify object types using the instanceof operator, and pattern matching with the instanceof operator and the switch construct.	3, 6, 7
Create and use interfaces, identify functional interfaces, and utilize private, static, and default interface methods.	7, 8
Create and use enum types with fields, methods, and constructors.	7

Handling Exceptions

Handle exceptions using try/catch/finally, try-with-resources, and multi-catch blocks, including custom exceptions.	11

Working with Arrays and Collections

Create arrays, List, Set, Map and Deque collections, and add, remove, update, retrieve and sort their elements.	4, 9

Working with Streams and Lambda expressions

Use Java object and primitive Streams, including lambda expressions implementing functional interfaces, to create, filter, transform, process, and sort data.	10

How to Contact the Publisher

If you believe you have found a mistake in this book, please bring it to our attention. At John Wiley & Sons, we understand how important it is to provide our customers with accurate content, but even with our best efforts an error may occur.

To submit your possible errata, please email it to our Customer Service Team at wileysupport@wiley.com with the subject line "Possible Book Errata Submission."

Assessment Test

Use the following assessment test to gauge your current level of skill in Java for the 1Z0-830. This test is designed to highlight some topics for your strengths and weaknesses so that you know which chapters you might want to read multiple times. Even if you do well on the assessment test, you should still read the book from cover to cover, as the real exam questions are quite challenging.

1. What is the result of executing the following code snippet?

```
41: final int score1 = 8, score2 = 3;
42: Integer myScore = 7;
43: var goal = switch (myScore) {
44:     case score1, score2, 7 -> "good";
45:     case Integer i when i < 10 -> "better";
46:     case Integer i when i >= 10 -> "best";
47:     default -> { yield "unknown";}
48:     case null -> "nope";
49: };
50: System.out.print(goal);
```

A. good

B. better

C. best

D. unknown

E. nope

F. Line 44 does not compile.

G. Line 45 does not compile.

H. Line 46 does not compile.

I. Line 47 does not compile.

J. Line 48 does not compile.

2. What is the output of the following code snippet?

```
int moon = 9, star = 2 + 2 * 3;
float sun = star > 10 ? 1 : 3;
double jupiter = (sun + moon) - 1.0f;
int mars = --moon <= 8 ? 2 : 3;
System.out.println(sun + ", " + jupiter + ", " + mars);
```

A. 1, 11, 2

B. 3.0, 11.0, 2

C. 1.0, 11.0, 3

D. 3.0, 13.0, 3

E. 3.0f, 12, 2

F. The code does not compile because one of the assignments requires an explicit numeric cast.

3. Which APIs exist for creating or working with virtual threads? (Choose all that apply.)

A. `Executors.newVirtualThread()`

B. `Executors.newVirtualThreadExecutor()`

C. `Executors.newVirtualThreadPerTaskExecutor()`

D. `new VirtualThread()`

E. `Thread.ofVirtual()`

F. `Thread.ofVirtualThread()`

4. What is the output of this code?

```
20: Predicate<String> empty = String::isEmpty;
21: Predicate<String> notEmpty = empty.negate();
22:
23: var result = Stream.generate(() -> "")
24:     .filter(notEmpty)
25:     .collect(Collectors.groupingBy(k -> k))
26:     .entrySet()
27:     .stream()
28:     .map(Entry::getValue)
29:     .flatMap(Collection::stream)
30:     .collect(Collectors.partitioningBy(notEmpty));
31: System.out.println(result);
```

A. It outputs {}.

B. It outputs {false=[], true=[]}.

C. The code does not compile.

D. The code does not terminate.

5. What is the result of the following program?

```
1: public class MathFunctions {
2:     public static void addToInt(int x, int amountToAdd) {
3:         x = x + amountToAdd % -5;
4:     }
5:     public static void main(String[] args) {
6:         var a = 15;
7:         var b = 10;
8:         MathFunctions.addToInt(a, b);
9:         System.out.println(a);    } }
```

A. 10

B. 15

C. 25

D. Compiler error on line 3

E. Compiler error on line 8

F. None of the above

6. Suppose that we have the following property files and code. What values are printed on lines 8 and 9, respectively?

Penguin.properties
```
name=Billy
age=1
```

Penguin_de.properties
```
name=Chilly
age=4
```

Penguin_en.properties
```
name=Willy
```

```
5: Locale fr = Locale.of("fr");
6: Locale.setDefault(Locale.of("en", "US"));
7: var b = ResourceBundle.getBundle("Penguin", fr);
8: System.out.println(b.getString("name"));
9: System.out.println(b.getString("age"));
```

A. Billy and 1

B. Billy and null

C. Willy and 1

D. Willy and null

E. Chilly and null

F. The code does not compile.

7. What is guaranteed to be printed by the following code? (Choose all that apply.)

```
int[] array = {6, 9, 8};
System.out.println("B" + Arrays.binarySearch(array,9));
System.out.println("C" + Arrays.compare(array,
  new int[] {6, 9, 8}));
System.out.println("M" + Arrays.mismatch(array,
  new int[] {6, 9, 8}));
```

A. B1

B. B2

C. C-1

D. C0

E. M-1

F. M0

G. The code does not compile.

8. Which functional interfaces complete the following code, presuming variable r exists? (Choose all that apply.)

```
6: _____ x = r.negate();
7: _____ y = () -> System.out.println();
8: _____ z = (a, b) -> a - b;
```

A. BinaryPredicate<Integer, Integer>

B. Comparable<Integer>

C. Comparator<Integer>

D. Consumer<Integer>

E. Predicate<Integer>

F. Runnable

G. Runnable<Integer>

9. Suppose you have a module named com.vet. Where could you place the following module-info.java file to create a valid module?

```
public module com.vet {
    exports com.vet;
}
```

A. At the same level as the com folder

B. At the same level as the vet folder

C. Inside the vet folder

D. None of the above

10. What is the output of the following program? (Choose all that apply.)

```
15: interface HasTail { default int getTailLength() { return 2; } }
16: abstract class Puma implements HasTail {
17:     int getTailLength() { return 4; } }
18: public class Cougar implements HasTail {
19:     public static void main(String[] args) {
20:         int length = 10;
21:         try {
```

```
22:            var puma = new Puma() {
23:                public int getTailLength() { return length; }
24:            };
25:            System.out.print(puma.getTailLength());
26:        } catch (Exception e) {
27:            length++;
28:        } }
29:    public int getTailLength(int length) { return 2; }
30: }
```

A. 2

B. 4

C. 10

D. Line 15 does not compile.

E. Line 16 does not compile.

F. Line 17 does not compile.

G. Line 20 does not compile.

H. Lines 22–24 do not compile.

I. Line 27 does not compile.

J. None of the above.

11. Which lines in `Tadpole.java` give a compiler error? (Choose all that apply.)

```
// Frog.java
1: package animal;
2: public class Frog {
3:     protected void ribbit() { }
4:     void jump() { }
5: }
```

```
// Tadpole.java
1:  package other;
2:  import animal.*;
3:  public class Tadpole extends Frog {
4:      public static void main(String[] args) {
5:          Tadpole t = new Tadpole();
6:          t.ribbit();
7:          t.jump();
8:          Frog f = new Tadpole();
9:          f.ribbit();
10:         f.jump();
11:     } }
```

A. Line 5.

B. Line 6.

C. Line 7.

D. Line 8.

E. Line 9.

F. Line 10.

G. All of the lines compile.

12. Which of the following statements can fill in the blank to make the code compile successfully? (Choose all that apply.)

```
Set<? extends RuntimeException> mySet = new _____ ();
```

A. `HashSet<? extends RuntimeException>`

B. `HashSet<Exception>`

C. `TreeSet<RuntimeException>`

D. `TreeSet<NullPointerException>`

E. `LinkedHashSet<>`

F. `LinkedHashSet<?>`

G. None of the above

13. Assume that `birds.ser` exists, is accessible, and contains data for a `Bird` object. What is the result of executing the following code? (Choose all that apply.)

```
1:  import java.io.*;
2:  public class Bird {
3:      private String name;
4:      private transient Integer age;
5:
6:      // Getters/setters omitted
7:
8:      public static void main(String[] args) {
9:          try(var is = new ObjectInputStream(
10:             new BufferedInputStream(
11:             new FileInputStream("birds.ser")))) {
12:           Bird b = is.readObject();
13:           System.out.println(b.age);
14:      } } }
```

A. It compiles and prints 0 at runtime.

B. It compiles and prints `null` at runtime.

C. It compiles and prints a number at runtime.

D. The code will not compile because of lines 9–11.

E. The code will not compile because of line 12.

F. It compiles but throws an exception at runtime.

14. How many of the following declarations (lines 14–19) are valid instance members of a class?

```
13: public class Zoo {
14:     var var = 3;
15:     Var case = new Var();
16:     void var() {}
17:     int Var() { var _ = 7; return _;}
18:     String new = "var";
19:     var var() { return null; }
20: }
```

A. 0

B. 1

C. 2

D. 3

E. 4

F. 5

15. Which is true if the contents of path1 start with the text Howdy? (Choose two.)

```
System.out.println(Files.mismatch(path1,path2));
```

A. If path2 doesn't exist, the code prints −1.

B. If path2 doesn't exist, the code prints 0.

C. If path2 doesn't exist, the code throws an exception.

D. If the contents of path2 start with Hello, the code prints −1.

E. If the contents of path2 start with Hello, the code prints 0.

F. If the contents of path2 start with Hello, the code prints 1.

16. Which of the following is the best type to insert into the blank to allow the program to compile successfully?

```
1: import java.util.*;
2: final class Amphibian {}
3: abstract class Tadpole extends Amphibian {}
4: public class FindAllTadpoles {
5:     public static void main(String... args) {
6:         var tadpoles = new ArrayList<Tadpole>();
7:         for (var amphibian : tadpoles) {
8:             _____ tadpole = amphibian;
9: } } }
```

A. List<Tadpole>

B. Boolean

C. Amphibian

D. Tadpole

E. Object

F. None of the above

17. What is the result of compiling and executing the following program?

```
1:  public class FeedingSchedule {
2:      public static void main(String[] args) {
3:          var x = 5;
4:          var j = 0;
5:          OUTER: for (var i = 0; i < 3;)
6:              INNER: do {
7:                  i++;
8:                  x++;
9:                  if (x> 10) break INNER;
10:                 x += 4;
11:                 j++;
12:             } while (j <= 2);
13:         System.out.println(x);
14: } }
```

A. 10

B. 11

C. 12

D. 17

E. The code will not compile because of line 5.

F. The code will not compile because of line 6.

18. When printed, which String gives the same value as this text block?

```
var pooh = """
    "Oh, bother." -Pooh
    """.indent(1);
System.out.print(pooh);
```

A. "\n\"Oh, bother.\" -Pooh\n"

B. "\n \"Oh, bother.\" -Pooh\n"

C. " \"Oh, bother.\" -Pooh\n"

D. "\n\"Oh, bother.\" -Pooh"

E. `"\n \"Oh, bother.\" -Pooh"`

F. `" \"Oh, bother.\" -Pooh"`

G. None of the above

19. A(n) _____ module always contains a `module-info.java` file, while a(n) _____ module always exports all its packages to other modules.

    A. automatic, named

    B. automatic, unnamed

    C. named, automatic

    D. named, unnamed

    E. unnamed, automatic

    F. unnamed, named

    G. None of the above

20. What is the result of the following code?

```
22: SequencedMap<Character,Integer> t = new TreeMap<>();
23: t.put('k', 1);
24: t.put('m', 2);
25: var u = Collections.unmodifiableMap(t);
26: t.put('m', 3);
27: t.putFirst('m', 4);
28: t.putLast('x', 5);
29: t.replaceAll((k, v) -> v + v);
30: u.entrySet()
31:    .stream()
32:    .map(e -> e.getValue())
33:    .forEach(System.out::print);
```

    A. 145

    B. 125

    C. 135

    D. 2468

    E. 2810

    F. 2410

    G. The code does not compile.

    H. The code compiles but line 26 throws an exception at runtime.

    I. None of the above.

21. Which of the following lines can fill in the blank to print `true`? (Choose all that apply.)

```
10: public static void main(String[] args) {
11:    System.out.println(test(_____));
```

```
12: }
13: private static boolean test(Function<Integer, Boolean> b) {
14:     return b.apply(5);
15: }
```

A. i::equals(5)

B. i -> {i == 5;}

C. (i) -> i == 5

D. (int i) -> i == 5

E. (int i) -> {return i == 5;}

F. (i) -> {return i == 5;}

22. How many times is the word true printed?

```
var s1 = "Java";
var s2 = "Java";
var s3 = s1.indent(1).strip();
var s4 = s3.intern();
var sb1 = new StringBuilder();
sb1.append("Ja").append("va");

System.out.println(s1 == s2);
System.out.println(s1.equals(s2));
System.out.println(s1 == s3);
System.out.println(s1 == s4);
System.out.println(sb1.toString() == s1);
System.out.println(sb1.toString().equals(s1));
```

A. Once.

B. Twice.

C. Three times.

D. Four times.

E. Five times.

F. The code does not compile.

23. What is the output of the following program?

```
1: class Deer {
2:     public Deer() {System.out.print("Deer");}
3:     public Deer(int age) {System.out.print("DeerAge");}
4:     protected boolean hasHorns() { return false; }
5: }
6: public class Reindeer extends Deer {
```

```
7:        public Reindeer(int age) {System.out.print("Reindeer");}
8:        public boolean hasHorns() { return true; }
9:        public static void main(String[] args) {
10:          Deer deer = new Reindeer(5);
11:          System.out.println("," + deer.hasHorns());
12: } }
```

A. ReindeerDeer,false

B. DeerAgeReindeer,true

C. DeerReindeer,true

D. DeerReindeer,false

E. ReindeerDeer,true

F. DeerAgeReindeer,false

G. The code will not compile because of line 4.

H. The code will not compile because of line 11.

24. Which of the following are true? (Choose all that apply.)

```
private static void magic(Stream<Integer> s) {
    Optional o = s
        .filter(x -> x < 5)
        .limit(3)
        .max((x, y) -> x - y);
    System.out.println(o.get());
}
```

A. magic(Stream.empty()); runs infinitely.

B. magic(Stream.empty()); throws an exception.

C. magic(Stream.iterate(1, x -> x++)); runs infinitely.

D. magic(Stream.iterate(1, x -> x++)); throws an exception.

E. magic(Stream.of(5, 10)); runs infinitely.

F. magic(Stream.of(5, 10)); throws an exception.

G. The method does not compile.

25. Assuming the following declarations are top-level types declared in the same file, which successfully compile? (Choose all that apply.)

```
record Music(List<String> tempo) {
    final int score = 10;
}
record Song(String lyrics, Music m) {
    Song {
        this.lyrics = lyrics + "Never gonna give you up";
```

```
   } }
sealed class Dance {}
record March() {
   int roll(Song s) {
      return switch (s) {
         case null -> 2;
         case Song(var q, Music(List d)) -> 1;
         default -> 3;
      };
   }
}
sealed class Ballet extends Dance permits NewDance {
   Ballet {
      var d = LocalDate.of(2025, Month.OCTOBER, 20);
      if (d.isAfter(LocalDate.now()))
         System.out.print("say goodbye");
   }
}
abstract class NewDance extends Ballet {}
```

A. Music

B. Song

C. Dance

D. March

E. Ballet

F. NewDance

G. None of them compile.

26. Which of the following expressions compile without error? (Choose all that apply.)

    A. `int monday = 3 + 2.0;`

    B. `double tuesday = 5_6L;`

    C. `boolean wednesday = 1 > 2 ? !true;`

    D. `short thursday = (short)Integer.MAX_VALUE;`

    E. `long friday = 8.0L;`

    F. `var saturday = 2_.0;`

    G. None of the above

27. What is the result of executing the following application?

    ```
    final var cb = new CyclicBarrier(3,
        () -> System.out.println("Clean!"));  // u1
    ```

```
try (var service = Executors.newSingleThreadExecutor()) {
    IntStream.generate(() -> 1)
        .limit(12)
        .parallel()
        .forEach(i -> service.submit(() -> cb.await())); // u2
}
```

A. It outputs Clean! at least once.

B. It outputs Clean! exactly four times.

C. The code will not compile because of line u1.

D. The code will not compile because of line u2.

E. It compiles but throws an exception at runtime.

F. It compiles but waits forever at runtime.

28. Which statement about the following method is true?

```
5:  public static void main(String... unused) {
6:      System.out.print("a");
7:      try (StringBuilder reader = new StringBuilder()) {
8:          System.out.print("b");
9:          throw new IllegalArgumentException();
10:     } catch (Exception e | RuntimeException e) {
11:         System.out.print("c");
12:         throw new FileNotFoundException();
13:     } finally {
14:         System.out.print("d");
15: } }
```

A. It compiles and prints abc.

B. It compiles and prints abd.

C. It compiles and prints abcd.

D. One line contains a compiler error.

E. Two lines contain a compiler error.

F. Three lines contain a compiler error.

G. It compiles but prints an exception at runtime.

Answers to Assessment Test

1. J. The code does not compile. In pattern matching switch statements, the order matters. In this example, line 47 dominates line 48, leading to unreachable code on line 48, and making option J the correct answer. For more information, see Chapter 3.

2. B. Initially, moon is assigned a value of 9, while star is assigned a value of 8. The multiplication operator (*) has a higher order of precedence than the addition operator (+), so it gets evaluated first. Since star is not greater than 10, sun is assigned a value of 3, which is promoted to 3.0f as part of the assignment. The value of jupiter is (3.0f + 9) - 1.0, which is 11.0f. This value is implicitly promoted to double when it is assigned. In the last assignment, moon is decremented from 9 to 8, with the value of the expression returned as 8. Since 8 less than or equal to 8 is true, mars is set to a value of 2. The final output is 3.0, 11.0, 2, making option B the correct answer. Note that while Java outputs the decimal for both float and double values, it does not output the f for float values. For more information, see Chapter 2.

3. C, E. The Executors class has one factory method for working with virtual threads. It is newVirtualThreadPerTaskExecutor(), making option C correct. There is no constructor for virtual threads. There is a factory method Thread.ofVirtual(), making option E the other answer. For more information, see Chapter 13.

4. D. First, this mess of code does compile. However, the source is an infinite stream. The filter operation will check each element in turn to see whether any are not empty. While nothing passes the filter, the code does not terminate. Therefore, option D is correct. For more information, see Chapter 10.

5. B. The code compiles successfully, so options D and E are incorrect. The value of a cannot be changed by the addToInt() method, no matter what the method does, because only a copy of the variable is passed into the parameter x. Therefore, a does not change, and the output on line 9 is 15, which is option B. For more information, see Chapter 5.

6. C. Java will use Penguin_en.properties as the matching resource bundle on line 7. Since there is no match for French, the default locale is used. Line 8 finds a matching key in the Penguin_en.properties file. Line 9 does not find a match in the Penguin_en.properties file; therefore, it has to look higher up in the hierarchy to Penguin.properties. This makes option C the answer. For more information, see Chapter 11.

7. D, E. The array is allowed to use an anonymous initializer because it is in the same line as the declaration. The results of the binary search are undefined since the array is not sorted. Since the question asks about guaranteed output, options A and B are incorrect. Option D is correct because the compare() method returns 0 when the arrays are the same length and have the same elements. Option E is correct because the mismatch() method returns a -1 when the arrays are equivalent. For more information, see Chapter 4.

8. C, E, F. First, note that option A is incorrect because the interface should be BiPredicate and not BinaryPredicate. Line 6 requires you to know that negate() is a convenience

method on `Predicate`. This makes option E correct. Line 7 takes zero parameters and doesn't return anything, making it a `Runnable`. Remember that `Runnable` doesn't use generics. This makes option F correct. Finally, line 8 takes two parameters and returns an `int`. Option C is correct. `Comparable` is there to mislead you since it takes only one parameter in its single abstract method. For more information, see Chapter 8.

9. D. If this were a valid `module-info.java` file, it would need to be placed at the root directory of the module, which is option A. However, a module is not allowed to use the `public` access modifier. Option D is correct because the provided file does not compile regardless of placement in the project. For more information, see Chapter 12.

10. F, H. A method within an abstract class without an access modifier is considered to have package access. The class inherits the `default` method from the interface and is implicitly `public`, which means line 17 reduces the visibility of this access modifier. For this reason, line 17 does not compile and option F is correct. Line 23 also does not compile, as a local class can only access a local variable that is `final` or effectively final, making option H correct. If line 27 were removed, then the variable would be effectively final and lines 22–24 would compile. For more information, see Chapter 7.

11. C, E, F. The `jump()` method has package access, which means it can be accessed only from the same package. `Tadpole` is not in the same package as `Frog`, causing lines 7 and 10 to trigger compiler errors and giving us options C and F. The `ribbit()` method has `protected` access, which means it can only be accessed from a subclass reference or in the same package. Line 6 is fine because `Tadpole` is a subclass. Line 9 does not compile, and our final answer is option E because the variable reference is to a `Frog`, which doesn't grant access to the `protected` method. For more information, see Chapter 5.

12. C, D, E. The `mySet` declaration defines an upper bound of type `RuntimeException`. This means that classes may specify `RuntimeException` or any subclass of `RuntimeException` as the type parameter. Option B is incorrect because `Exception` is a superclass, not a subclass, of `RuntimeException`. Options A and F are incorrect because the wildcard cannot occur on the right side of the assignment. Options C, D, and E compile and are the answers. For more information, see Chapter 9.

13. D, E. The declaration on lines 9–11 includes an unhandled checked `IOException`, making option D correct. Line 12 does not compile because `is.readObject()` must be cast to a `Bird` object to be assigned to b. It also does not compile because it includes two unhandled checked exceptions, `IOException` and `ClassNotFoundException`, making option E correct. If a cast operation were added on line 12 and the `main()` method were updated on line 8 to declare the various checked exceptions, the code would compile but throw an exception at runtime since `Bird` does not implement `Serializable`. Finally, if the class did implement `Serializable`, the program would print `null` at runtime, as that is the default value for the `transient` field `age`. For more information, see Chapter 14.

14. B. Line 14 does not compile because `var` is only allowed as a type for local variables, not instance members. Lines 15 and 18 do not compile because `new` and `case` are reserved words and cannot be used as identifiers. Line 16 compiles, as `var` can be used as a method name. Line 17 does not compile because a single underscore (`_`) cannot be used as an identifier. Line 19 does not compile because `var` cannot be specified as the return type of a

method. Since only one line compiles, option B is the answer. For more information, see Chapter 1.

15. C, F. Option C is correct as `mismatch()` throws an exception if the files do not exist unless they both refer to the same file. Additionally, option F is correct because the first index that differs is returned, which is the second character. Since Java uses zero-based indexes, this is 1. For more information, see Chapter 14.

16. F. The `Amphibian` class is marked `final`, which means line 3 triggers a compiler error and option F is correct. For more information, see Chapter 6.

17. C. The code compiles and runs without issue; therefore, options E and F are incorrect. This type of problem is best examined one loop iteration at a time:

- On the first iteration of the outer loop, `i` is 0, so the loop continues.

- On the first iteration of the inner loop, `i` is updated to 1 and x to 6. The `if` statement branch is not executed, and x is increased to 10 and j to 1.

- On the second iteration of the inner loop (since j = 1 and 1 <= 2), `i` is updated to 2 and x to 11. At this point, the `if` branch will evaluate to `true` for the remainder of the program run, which causes the flow to break out of the inner loop each time it is reached.

- On the second iteration of the outer loop (since i = 2), `i` is updated to 3 and x to 12. As before, the inner loop is broken since x is still greater than 10.

- On the third iteration of the outer loop, the outer loop is broken, as `i` is already not less than 3. The most recent value of x, 12, is output, so the answer is option C.

For more information, see Chapter 3.

18. C. First, note that the text block has the closing `"""` on a separate line, which means there is a new line at the end and rules out options D, E, and F. Additionally, text blocks don't start with a new line, ruling out options A and B. Therefore, option C is correct. For more information, see Chapter 1.

19. C. Only named modules are required to have a `module-info.java` file, ruling out options A, B, E, and F. Unnamed modules are not readable by any other types of modules, ruling out option D. Automatic modules always export all packages to other modules, making the answer option C. For more information, see Chapter 12.

20. I. The code compiles, so option G is incorrect. Line 26 does not throw an exception, as we are modifying the underlying collection, not the unmodifiable map, so option H is incorrect. Lines 27 and 28 each throw an `UnsupportedOperationException` (when run independently). `TreeMap` is a `SequencedMap`, so while it does inherit these methods, it does not support them. Doing so could break the ordering for the `Comparator`. For this reason, option I is correct. For more information, see Chapter 9.

21. C, F. Option A looks like a method reference. However, it doesn't call a valid method, nor can method references take parameters. The `Predicate` interface takes a single parameter and returns a `boolean`. Lambda expressions with one parameter are allowed, but not required, to omit the parentheses around the parameter list, making option C correct.

The return statement is optional when a single statement is in the body, making option F correct. Option B is incorrect because a return statement must be used if braces are included around the body. Options D and E are incorrect because the type is Integer in the predicate and int in the lambda. Autoboxing works for collections, not inferring predicates. If these two were changed to Integer, they would be correct. For more information, see Chapter 8.

22. D. String literals are used from the string pool. This means that s1 and s2 refer to the same object and are equal. Therefore, the first two print statements print true. While the indent() and strip() methods create new String objects and the third statement prints false, the intern() method reverts the String to the one from the string pool. Therefore, the fourth print statement prints true. The fifth print statement prints false because toString() uses a method to compute the value, and it is not from the string pool. The final print statement again prints true because equals() looks at the values of String objects. Since four are true, option D is the answer. For more information, see Chapter 4.

23. C. The Reindeer object is instantiated using the constructor that takes an int value. Since there is no explicit call to the parent constructor, the compiler inserts super() as the first line of the constructor on line 7. The parent constructor is called, and Deer is printed on line 2. The flow returns to the constructor on line 7, with Reindeer being printed. Next, the hasHorns() method is called. The reference type is Deer, and the underlying object type is Reindeer. Since Reindeer correctly overrides the hasHorns() method, the version in Reindeer is called, with line 11 printing , true. Therefore, option C is correct. For more information, see Chapter 6.

24. B, F. Calling get() on an empty Optional causes an exception to be thrown, making option B correct. Option F is also correct because filter() makes the Optional empty before it calls get(). Option C is incorrect because the infinite stream is made finite by the intermediate limit() operation. Options A and E are incorrect because the source streams are not infinite. Therefore, the call to max() sees only three elements and terminates. For more information, see Chapter 10.

25. C, D. Music does not compile because a record cannot contain instance variables that are not declared as part of the record. Song does not compile because a compact record constructor does not allow modifying an instance variable with a this reference. Dance does compile, making option C correct. A permits clause is optional for a sealed class if the associated classes are in the same file. March also compiles, making option D correct. A pattern matching switch can include elements of the record and use var. Ballet does not compile, as it is missing parentheses in the constructor. Remember, only records support compact constructors. NewDance also does not compile as a class that extends sealed classes must be marked final, sealed, or non-sealed. For more information, see Chapter 7.

26. B, D. Option A does not compile, as the expression 3 + 2.0 is evaluated as a double, and a double requires an explicit cast to be assigned to an int. Option B compiles without issue, as a long value can be implicitly cast to a double. Option C does not compile because the ternary operator (? :) is missing a colon (:), followed by a second expression. Option D is correct. Even though the int value is larger than a short, it is explicitly cast to a short, which means the value will wrap around to fit in a short. Option E is incorrect, as you cannot use a decimal (.) with the long (L) postfix. Finally, option F is incorrect, as an underscore cannot be used next to a decimal point. For more information, see Chapter 2.

27. F. The code compiles without issue. The key to understanding this code is to notice that our thread executor contains only one thread, but our `CyclicBarrier` limit is 3. Even though 12 tasks are all successfully submitted to the service, the first task will block forever on the call to `await()`. Since the barrier is never reached, nothing is printed, and the program hangs, making option F correct. For more information, see Chapter 13.

28. F. Line 5 does not compile as the `FileNotFoundException` thrown on line 12 is not handled or declared by the method. Line 7 does not compile because `StringBuilder` does not implement `AutoCloseable` and is therefore not compatible with a try-with-resource statement. Finally, line 10 does not compile as `RuntimeException` is a subclass of `Exception` in the multi-`catch` block, making it redundant. Since this method contains three compiler errors, option F is the correct answer. For more information, see Chapter 11.

Chapter

1

Building Blocks

OCP EXAM OBJECTIVES COVERED IN THIS CHAPTER:

✓ **Handling Date, Time, Text, Numeric and Boolean Values**

- Use primitives and wrapper classes. Evaluate arithmetic and boolean expressions, using the Math API and by applying precedence rules, type conversions, and casting.

✓ **Using Object-Oriented Concepts in Java**

- Declare and instantiate Java objects including nested class objects, and explain the object life-cycle including creation, reassigning references, and garbage collection.

- Understand variable scopes, apply encapsulation, and create immutable objects. Use local variable type inference.

Welcome to the beginning of your journey to achieve a Java 21 certification. We assume this isn't the first Java programming book you've read. Although we do talk about the basics, we do so only because we want to make sure you have all the terminology and detail you need for the exam. If you've never written a Java program before, we recommend you pick up an introductory book on Java 8 or higher. Examples include *Head First Java, 3rd Edition* (O'Reilly Media, 2022) and *Beginning Programming with Java for Dummies* (For Dummies, 2021). Then come back to this certification study guide.

As the old saying goes, you have to learn how to walk before you can run. Likewise, you have to learn the basics of Java before you can build complex programs. In this chapter, we present the basics of Java packages, classes, variables, and data types, along with the aspects of each that you need to know for the exam. For example, you might use Java every day but be unaware that you cannot create a variable called `3dMap` or `this`. The exam expects you to know and understand the rules behind these principles. While most of this chapter should be review, there may be aspects of the Java language that are new to you since they don't come up in practical use often.

Learning About the Environment

The Java environment consists of a number of technologies. In the following sections, we go over the key terms and acronyms you need to know and then discuss what software you need to study for the exam.

Major Components of Java

The *Java Development Kit* (JDK) contains the minimum software you need to do Java development. Key commands include the following:

- `javac`: Converts `.java` source files into `.class` bytecode
- `java`: Executes the program
- `jar`: Packages files together
- `javadoc`: Generates documentation

The `javac` program generates instructions in a special format called *bytecode* that the `java` command can run. Then `java` launches the *Java Virtual Machine* (JVM) before running the code. The JVM knows how to run bytecode on the actual machine it is on. You can think of the JVM as a special magic box on your machine that knows how to run your `.class` file within your particular operating system and hardware.

Where Did the JRE Go?

In Java 8 and earlier, you could download a Java Runtime Environment (JRE) instead of the full JDK. The JRE was a subset of the JDK that was used for running a program but could not compile one. Now, people can use the full JDK when running a Java program. Alternatively, developers can supply an executable that contains the required pieces that would have been in the JRE.

You might have noticed that we said the JDK contains the minimum software you need. Many developers use an *integrated development environment* (IDE) to make writing and running code easier. While we do not recommend using one while studying for the exam, it is still good to know that they exist. Common Java IDEs include Eclipse, IntelliJ IDEA, and Visual Studio Code.

Downloading a JDK

Every six months, Oracle releases a new version of Java. Java 21 came out in September 2023. This means Java 21 will not be the latest version when you download the JDK to study for the exam. However, you should still use Java 21 to study with since this is a Java 21 exam. The rules and behavior can change with later versions of Java. You wouldn't want to get a question wrong because you studied with a different version of Java!

You can download Oracle's JDK on the Oracle website, using the same account you use to register for the exam. There are many JDKs available, the most popular of which, besides Oracle's JDK, is OpenJDK.

Many versions of Java include *preview features* that are off by default but that you can enable. Preview features are not on the exam. To avoid confusion about when a feature was added to the language, we will say "was officially introduced in" to denote when it was moved out of preview.

Check Your Version of Java

Before we go any further, please take this opportunity to ensure you have the right version of Java on your path.

```
javac -version
java -version
```

Both of these commands should include version number 21.

Understanding the Class Structure

In Java programs, classes are the basic building blocks. When defining a *class*, you describe all the parts and characteristics of one of those building blocks. In later chapters, you see other building blocks such as interfaces, records, and enums.

To use most classes, you have to create objects. An *object* is a runtime instance of a class in memory. An object is often referred to as an *instance* since it represents a single representation of the class. All the various objects of all the different classes represent the state of your program. A *reference* is a variable that points to an object.

In the following sections, we look at fields, methods, and comments. We also explore the relationship between classes and files.

Fields and Methods

Java classes have two primary elements: *methods*, often called functions or procedures in other languages, and *fields*, more generally known as variables. Together these are called the *members* of the class. Variables hold the state of the program, and methods operate on that state. If the change is important to remember, a variable stores that change. That's all classes really do. It's the programmer's job to create and arrange these elements in such a way that the resulting code is useful and, ideally, easy for other programmers to understand.

The simplest Java class you can write looks like this:

```
1: public class Animal {
2: }
```

Java calls a word with special meaning a *keyword*, which we've marked bold in the previous snippet. Throughout the book, we often bold parts of code snippets to call attention to them. Line 1 includes the public keyword, which allows other classes to use it. The class keyword indicates you're defining a class. Animal gives the name of the class. Granted, this isn't an interesting class, so let's add your first field.

```
1: public class Animal {
2:     String name;
3: }
```

 NOTE   The line numbers aren't part of the program; they're just there to make the code easier to talk about.

On line 2, we define a variable named name. We also declare the type of that variable to be String. A String is a value that we can put text into, such as "this is a string". String is also a class supplied with Java. Next we can add methods.

```
1: public class Animal {
2:     String name;
```

```
3:      public String getName() {
4:          return name;
5:      }
6:      public void setName(String newName) {
7:          name = newName;
8:      }
9: }
```

On lines 3–5, we define a method. A method is an operation that can be called. Again, public is used to signify that this method may be called from other classes. Next comes the return type—in this case, the method returns a String. On lines 6–8 is another method. This one has a special return type called *void*. The void keyword means that no value at all is returned. This method requires that information be supplied to it from the calling method; this information is called a *parameter*. The setName() method has one parameter named newName, and it is of type String. This means the caller should pass in one String parameter and expect nothing to be returned.

The method name and parameter types are called the *method signature*. In this example, can you identify the method name and parameters?

```
public int numberVisitors(int month) {
    return 10;
}
```

The method name is numberVisitors. There's one parameter named month, which is of type int, which is a numeric type. Therefore, the method signature is numberVisitors(int).

Comments

Another common part of the code is called a *comment*. Because comments aren't executable code, you can place them in many places. Comments can make your code easier to read. While the exam creators are trying to make the code harder to read, they still use comments to call attention to line numbers. We hope you use comments in your own code. There are three types of comments in Java. The first is a single-line comment.

```
// comment until end of line
```

A single-line comment begins with two slashes. The compiler ignores anything you type after that on the same line. Next comes the multiple-line comment.

```
/* Multiple
 * line comment
 */
```

A multiple-line comment (also known as a multiline comment) includes anything starting from the symbol /* until the symbol */. People often type an asterisk (*) at the beginning of each line of a multiline comment to make it easier to read, but you don't have to. Finally, this is a Javadoc comment:

```
/**
 * Javadoc multiple-line comment
 * @author Jeanne and Scott
 */
```

This comment is similar to a multiline comment, except it starts with /**. This special syntax tells the Javadoc tool to pay attention to the comment. Javadoc comments have a specific structure that the Javadoc tool knows how to read. You probably won't see a Javadoc comment on the exam. Just remember it exists, so you can read up on it online when you start writing programs for others to use.

As a bit of practice, can you identify which type of comment each of the following six words is in? Is each a single-line or a multiline comment?

```
/*
 * // anteater
 */

// bear

// // cat

// /* dog */

/* elephant */
/*
 * /* ferret */
 */
```

Did you look closely? Some of these are tricky. Even though comments technically aren't on the exam, it is good to practice looking at code carefully.

OK, on to the answers. The comment containing `anteater` is in a multiline comment. Everything between /* and */ is part of a multiline comment—even if it includes a single-line comment within it! The comment containing `bear` is your basic single-line comment. The comments containing `cat` and `dog` are also single-line comments. Everything from // to the end of the line is part of the comment, even if it is another type of comment. The comment containing `elephant` is your basic multiline comment, even though it takes up only one line.

The line with `ferret` is interesting in that it doesn't compile. Everything from the first /* to the first */ is part of the comment, which means the compiler sees something like this:

```
/* */ */
```

We have a problem. There is an extra */. That's not valid syntax—a fact the compiler is happy to inform you about.

Classes and Source Files

Most of the time, each Java class is defined in its own `.java` file. In this chapter, the only top-level type is a class. A *top-level type* is a data structure that can be defined independently within a source file. For the majority of the book, we work with classes as the top-level type, but in Chapter 7, "Beyond Classes," we present other top-level types, as well as nested types.

A top-level class is often `public`, which means any code can call it. Interestingly, Java does not require that the type be `public`. For example, this class is just fine:

```
1: class Animal {
2:     String name;
3: }
```

You can even put two types in the same file. When you do so, *at most one* of the top-level types in the file is allowed to be `public`. That means a file containing the following is also fine:

```
1: public class Animal {
2:     private String name;
3: }
4: class Animal2 {}
```

If you do have a `public` type, it needs to match the filename. The declaration `public class Animal2` would not compile in a file named `Animal.java`. In Chapter 5, "Methods," we discuss what access options are available other than `public`.

 Noticing a pattern yet? This chapter includes numerous references to topics that we go into in more detail in later chapters. If you're an experienced Java developer, you'll notice we keep the examples and rules simple in this chapter. Don't worry; we have the rest of the book to present more rules and complicated edge cases!

Writing a *main()* Method

A Java program begins execution with its `main()` method. In this section, you learn how to create one, pass a parameter, and run a program. The `main()` method is often called an entry point into the program, because it is the starting point that the JVM looks for when it begins running a new program.

Creating a *main()* Method

The `main()` method lets the JVM call our code. The simplest possible class with a `main()` method looks like this:

```
1: public class Zoo {
2:     public static void main(String[] args) {
```

```
3:        System.out.println("Hello World");
4:    }
5: }
```

This code prints Hello World. To compile and execute this code, type it into a file called Zoo.java and execute the following:

```
javac Zoo.java
java Zoo
```

If it prints Hello World, you were successful. If you do get error messages, check that you've installed the Java 21 JDK, that you have added it to the PATH, and that you didn't make any typos in the example. If you have any of these problems and don't know what to do, post a question with the error message you received in the *Beginning Java* forum at CodeRanch:

```
https://www.coderanch.com/forums/f-33/java
```

To compile Java code with the javac command, the file must have the extension .java. The name of the file must match the name of the public class. The result is a file of byte-code with the same name but with a .class filename extension. Remember that bytecode consists of instructions that the JVM knows how to execute. Notice that we must omit the .class extension to run Zoo.class.

The rules for what a Java file contains, and in what order, are more detailed than what we have explained so far (there is more on this topic later in the chapter). To keep things simple for now, we follow this subset of the rules:

- Each file can contain only one public class.
- The filename must match the class name, including case, and have a .java extension.
- If the Java class is an entry point for the program, it must contain a valid main() method.

Let's first review the words in the main() method's signature, one at a time. The keyword public is what's called an *access modifier*. It declares this method's level of exposure to potential callers in the program. Naturally, public means full access from anywhere in the program. You learn more about access modifiers in Chapter 5.

The keyword *static* binds a method to its class so it can be called by just the class name, as in, for example, Zoo.main(). Java doesn't need to create an object to call the main() method—which is good since you haven't learned about creating objects yet! In fact, the JVM does this, more or less, when loading the class name given to it. If a main() method doesn't have the right keywords, you'll get an error trying to run it. You see static again in Chapter 6, "Class Design."

The keyword void represents the *return type*. A method that returns no data returns control to the caller silently. In general, it's good practice to use void for methods that change an object's state. In that sense, the main() method changes the program state from started to finished. We explore return types in Chapter 5 as well. (Are you excited for Chapter 5 yet?)

Finally, we arrive at the `main()` method's parameter list, represented as an array of `java.lang.String` objects. You can use any valid variable name along with any of these three formats:

```
String[] args
String options[]
String... friends
```

The compiler accepts any of these. The variable name `args` is common because it hints that this list contains values that were read in (arguments) when the JVM started. The characters `[]` are brackets and represent an array. An array is a fixed-size list of items that are all of the same type. The characters `...` are called *varargs* (variable argument lists). You learn about `String` in this chapter. Arrays are in Chapter 4, "Core APIs," and varargs are in Chapter 5.

Optional Modifiers in *main()* Methods

While most modifiers, such as `public` and `static`, are required for `main()` methods, there are some optional modifiers allowed.

```
public final static void main(final String[] args) {}
```

In this example, both `final` modifiers are optional, and the `main()` method is a valid entry point with or without them. We cover the meaning of `final` methods and parameters in Chapter 6.

Passing Parameters to a Java Program

Let's see how to send data to our program's `main()` method. First, we modify the Zoo program to print out the first two arguments passed in.

```java
public class Zoo {
    public static void main(String[] args) {
        System.out.println(args[0]);
        System.out.println(args[1]);
    }
}
```

The code `args[0]` accesses the first element of the array. That's right: array indexes begin with 0 in Java. To run it, type this:

```
javac Zoo.java
java Zoo Bronx Zoo
```

The output is what you might expect.

```
Bronx
Zoo
```

The program correctly identifies the first two "words" as the arguments. Spaces are used to separate the arguments. If you want spaces inside an argument, you need to use quotes as in this example:

```
javac Zoo.java
java Zoo "San Diego" Zoo
```

Now we have a space in the output.

```
San Diego
Zoo
```

Finally, what happens if you don't pass in enough arguments?

```
javac Zoo.java
java Zoo Zoo
```

Reading args[0] goes fine, and Zoo is printed out. Then Java panics. There's no second argument! What to do? Java prints out an exception telling you it has no idea what to do with this argument at position 1. (You learn about exceptions in Chapter 11, "Exceptions and Localization.")

```
Zoo
Exception in thread "main" java.lang.ArrayIndexOutOfBoundsException:
    Index 1 out of bounds for length 1
    at Zoo.main(Zoo.java:4)
```

To review, the JDK contains a compiler. Java class files run on the JVM and therefore run on any machine with Java rather than just the machine or operating system they happened to have been compiled on.

Single-File Source Code

If you get tired of typing both javac and java every time you want to try a code example, there's a shortcut. You can instead run this:

```
java Zoo.java Bronx Zoo
```

There is a key difference here. When compiling first, you omitted the file extension when running java. When skipping the explicit compilation step, you include this extension. This feature is called launching *single-file source-code* programs and is useful for testing or for small programs. The name cleverly tells you that it is designed for when your program is one file.

Understanding Package Declarations and Imports

Java comes with thousands of built-in classes, and there are countless more from developers like you. With all those classes, Java needs a way to organize them. It handles this in a way similar to a file cabinet. You put all your pieces of paper in folders. Java puts classes in *packages*. These are logical groupings for classes.

We wouldn't put you in front of a file cabinet and tell you to find a specific paper. Instead, we'd tell you which folder to look in. Java works the same way. It needs you to tell it which packages to look in to find code.

Suppose you try to compile this code:

```java
public class NumberPicker {
    public static void main(String[] args) {
        Random r = new Random();   // DOES NOT COMPILE
        System.out.println(r.nextInt(10));
    }
}
```

The Java compiler helpfully gives you an error that looks like this:

```
error: cannot find symbol
```

This error could mean you made a typo in the name of the class. You double-check and discover that you didn't. The other cause of this error is omitting a needed *import* statement. A *statement* is an instruction, and import statements tell Java which packages to look in for classes. Since you didn't tell Java where to look for Random, it has no clue.

Trying this again with the import allows the code to compile.

```java
import java.util.Random;  // import tells us where to find Random
public class NumberPicker {
    public static void main(String[] args) {
        Random r = new Random();
        System.out.println(r.nextInt(10));  // a number 0-9
    }
}
```

Now the code runs; it prints out a random number between 0 and 9. Just like arrays, Java likes to begin counting with 0.

In Chapter 5, we cover another type of import referred to as a static import. It allows you to make static members of a class known, often so you can use variables and method names without having to keep specifying the class name.

Packages

As you saw in the previous example, Java classes are grouped into packages. The `import` statement tells the compiler which package to look in to find a class. This is similar to how mailing a letter works. Imagine you are mailing a letter to 123 Main Street, Apartment 9. The mail carrier first brings the letter to 123 Main Street. Then the carrier looks for the mailbox for apartment 9. The address is like the package name in Java. The apartment number is like the class name in Java. Just as the mail carrier only looks at apartment numbers in the building, Java only looks for class names in the package.

Package names are hierarchical like the mail as well. The postal service starts with the top level, looking at your country first. You start reading a package name at the beginning too. For example, if it begins with `java`, this means it came with the JDK. If it starts with something else, it likely shows where it came from using the website name in reverse. For example, `com.wiley.javabook` tells us the code is associated with the `wiley.com` website or organization. After the website name, you can add whatever you want. For example, `com.wiley.java.my.name` also came from `wiley.com`. Java calls more detailed packages *child packages*. The package `com.wiley.javabook` is a child package of `com.wiley`. You can tell because it's longer and thus more specific.

You'll see package names on the exam that don't follow this convention. Don't be surprised to see package names like `a.b.c`. The rule for package names is that they are mostly letters or numbers separated by periods (`.`). Technically, you're allowed a couple of other characters between the periods (`.`). You can even use package names of websites you don't own if you want to, such as `com.wiley`, although people reading your code might be confused! The rules are the same as for variable names, which you see later in this chapter. The exam may try to trick you with invalid variable names. Luckily, it doesn't try to trick you by giving invalid package names.

In the following sections, we look at imports with wildcards, naming conflicts with imports, how to create a package of your own, and how the exam formats code.

Wildcards

Classes in the same package are often imported together. You can use a shortcut to `import` all the classes in a package.

```
import java.util.*;    // imports java.util.Random among other things
public class NumberPicker {
    public static void main(String[] args) {
        Random r = new Random();
        System.out.println(r.nextInt(10));
    }
}
```

In this example, we imported `java.util.Random` and a pile of other classes. The `*` is a wildcard that matches all classes in the package. Every class in the `java.util` package is available to this program when Java compiles it. The import statement doesn't bring in child packages, fields, or methods; it imports only classes directly under the package. Let's say you wanted to use the class AtomicInteger (you learn about that one in Chapter 13, "Concurrency") in the java.util.concurrent.atomic package. Which import or imports support this?

```
import java.util.*;
import java.util.concurrent.*;
import java.util.concurrent.atomic.*;
```

Only the last import allows the class to be recognized because child packages are not included with the first two.

You might think that including so many classes slows down your program execution, but it doesn't. The compiler figures out what's actually needed. Which approach you choose is personal preference—or team preference, if you are working with others on a team. Listing the classes used makes the code easier to read, especially for new programmers. Using the wildcard can shorten the import list. You'll see both approaches on the exam.

Redundant Imports

Wait a minute! We've been referring to System without an import every time we printed text, and Java found it just fine. There's one special package in the Java world called java.lang. This package is special in that it is automatically imported. You can type this package in an import statement, but you don't have to. In the following code, how many of the imports do you think are redundant?

```
 1:  import java.lang.System;
 2:  import java.lang.*;
 3:  import java.util.Random;
 4:  import java.util.*;
 5:  public class NumberPicker {
 6:      public static void main(String[] args) {
 7:          Random r = new Random();
 8:          System.out.println(r.nextInt(10));
 9:      }
10: }
```

The answer is that three of the imports are redundant. Lines 1 and 2 are redundant because everything in java.lang is automatically imported. Line 4 is also redundant in this example because Random is already imported from java.util.Random. If line 3 wasn't present, java.util.* wouldn't be redundant, though, since it would cover importing Random.

Another case of redundancy involves importing a class that is in the same package as the class importing it. Java automatically looks in the current package for other classes.

Let's take a look at one more example to make sure you understand the edge cases for imports. For this example, Files and Paths are both in the package java.nio.file. The exam may use packages you may never have seen before. The question will let you know which package the class is in if you need to know that in order to answer the question.

Which import statements do you think would work to get this code to compile?

```java
public class InputImports {
    public void read(Files files) {
        Paths.get("name");
    }
}
```

There are two possible answers. The shorter one is to use a wildcard to import both at the same time.

```java
import java.nio.file.*;
```

The other answer is to import both classes explicitly.

```java
import java.nio.file.Files;
import java.nio.file.Paths;
```

Now let's consider some imports that don't work.

```java
import java.nio.*;          // NO GOOD - a wildcard only matches
                            // class names, not "file.Files"

import java.nio.*.*;        // NO GOOD - you can only have one wildcard
                            // and it must be at the end

import java.nio.file.Paths.*; // NO GOOD - you cannot import methods
                              // only class names
```

Naming Conflicts

One of the reasons for using packages is so that class names don't have to be unique across all of Java. This means you'll sometimes want to import a class that can be found in multiple places. A common example of this is the Date class. Java provides implementations of java.util.Date and java.sql.Date. What import statement can we use if we want the java.util.Date version?

```java
public class Conflicts {
    Date date;
    // some more code
}
```

The answer should be easy by now. You can write either import java.util.*; or import java.util.Date;. The tricky cases come about when other imports are present.

```java
import java.util.*;
import java.sql.*;    // causes Date declaration to not compile
```

When the class name is found in multiple packages, Java gives you a compiler error. In our example, the solution is easy—remove the `import java.sql.*` that we don't need. But what do we do if we need a whole pile of other classes in the `java.sql` package?

```
import java.util.Date;
import java.sql.*;
```

Ah, now it works! If you explicitly import a class name, it takes precedence over any wildcards present. Java thinks, "The programmer really wants me to assume use of the `java.util.Date` class."

One more example. What does Java do with "ties" for precedence?

```
import java.util.Date;
import java.sql.Date;
```

Java is smart enough to detect that this code is no good. As a programmer, you've claimed to explicitly want the default to be both the `java.util.Date` and `java.sql.Date` implementations. Because there can't be two defaults, the compiler tells you the imports are ambiguous.

If You Really Need to Use Two Classes with the Same Name

Sometimes you really do want to use `Date` from two different packages. When this happens, you can pick one to use in the `import` statement and use the other's *fully qualified class name*. Or you can drop both `import` statements and always use the fully qualified class name.

```
public class Conflicts {
    java.util.Date date;
    java.sql.Date sqlDate;
}
```

Creating a New Package

Up to now, all the code we've written in this chapter has been in the *default package*. This is a special unnamed package that you should use only for throwaway code. You can tell the code is in the default package, because there's no package name. On the exam, you'll see the default package used a lot to save space in code listings. In real life, always name your packages to avoid naming conflicts and to allow others to reuse your code.

Now it's time to create a new package. The directory structure on your computer is related to the package name. In this section, just read along. We cover how to compile and run the code in the next section.

Suppose we have these two classes in the C:\temp directory:

```
package packagea;
public class ClassA {}

package packageb;
import packagea.ClassA;
public class ClassB {
    public static void main(String[] args) {
        ClassA a;
        System.out.println("Got it");
    }
}
```

When you run a Java program, Java knows where to look for those package names. In this case, running from C:\temp works because both packagea and packageb are underneath it.

Compiling and Running Code with Packages

You'll learn Java much more easily by using the command line to compile and test your examples. Once you know the Java syntax well, you can switch to an IDE. But for the exam, your goal is to know details about the language and not have the IDE hide them for you.

Follow this example to make sure you know how to use the command line. If you have any problems following this procedure, post a question in the *Beginning Java* forum at CodeRanch. Describe what you tried and what the error said.

```
https://www.coderanch.com/forums/f-33/java
```

The first step is to create the two files from the previous section. Table 1.1 shows the expected fully qualified filenames and the command to get into the directory for the next steps.

TABLE 1.1 Setup procedure by operating system

Step	Windows	Mac/Linux
1. Create first class.	C:\temp\packagea \ClassA.java	/tmp/packagea /ClassA.java
2. Create second class.	C:\temp\packageb \ClassB.java	/tmp/packageb /ClassB.java
3. Go to directory.	cd C:\temp	cd /tmp

Now it is time to compile the code. Luckily, this is the same regardless of the operating system. To compile, type the following command:

```
javac packagea/ClassA.java packageb/ClassB.java
```

If this command doesn't work, you'll get an error message. Check your files carefully for typos against the provided files. If the command does work, two new files will be created: `packagea/ClassA.class` and `packageb/ClassB.class`.

Compiling with Wildcards

You can use an asterisk to specify that you'd like to include all Java files in a directory. This is convenient when you have a lot of files in a package. We can rewrite the previous `javac` command like this:

```
javac packagea/*.java packageb/*.java
```

However, you cannot use a wildcard to include subdirectories. If you were to write `javac *.java`, the code in the packages would not be picked up.

Now that your code has compiled, you can run it by typing the following command:

```
java packageb.ClassB
```

If it works, you'll see `Got it` printed. You might have noticed that we typed `ClassB` rather than `ClassB.class`. As discussed earlier, you don't pass the extension when running a program.

Figure 1.1 shows where the `.class` files were created in the directory structure.

FIGURE 1.1   Compiling with packages

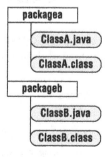

Compiling to Another Directory

By default, the javac command places the compiled classes in the same directory as the source code. It also provides an option to place the class files into a different directory. The -d option specifies this target directory.

> Java options are case sensitive. This means you cannot pass –D instead of –d.

If you are following along, delete the ClassA.class and ClassB.class files that were created in the previous section. Where do you think this command will create the file ClassA.class?

```
javac -d classes packagea/ClassA.java packageb/ClassB.java
```

The correct answer is in classes/packagea/ClassA.class. The package structure is preserved under the requested target directory. Figure 1.2 shows this new structure.

FIGURE 1.2   Compiling with packages and directories

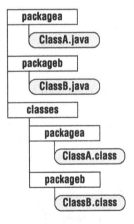

To run the program, you specify the classpath so Java knows where to find the classes. There are three options you can use. All three of these do the same thing:

```
java -cp classes packageb.ClassB
java -classpath classes packageb.ClassB
java --class-path classes packageb.ClassB
```

Notice that the last one requires two dashes (--), while the first two require one dash (-). If you have the wrong number of dashes, the program will not run.

Three Classpath Options
You might wonder why there are three options for the classpath. The -cp option is the short form. Developers frequently choose the short form because we are lazy typists. The -classpath and --class-path versions can be clearer to read but require more typing.

Table 1.2 and Table 1.3 review the options you need to know for the exam. There are *many* other options available! And in Chapter 12, "Modules," you learn additional options specific to modules.

TABLE 1.2   Important javac options

Option	Description
-cp <classpath> -classpath <classpath> --class-path <classpath>	Location of classes needed to compile the program
-d <dir>	Directory in which to place generated class files

TABLE 1.3   Important java options

Option	Description
-cp <classpath> -classpath <classpath> --class-path <classpath>	Location of classes needed to run the program

Ordering Elements in a Class

Now that you've seen the most common parts of a class, let's take a look at the correct order to type them into a file. Comments can go anywhere in the code. Beyond that, you need to memorize the rules in Table 1.4.

TABLE 1.4   Order for declaring a class

Element	Example	Required?	Where does it go?
Package declaration	package abc;	No	First line in the file (excluding comments or blank lines)
import statements	import java.util.*;	No	Immediately after the package (if present)
Top-level type declaration	public class C	Yes	Immediately after the imports (if any)
Field declarations	int value;	No	Any top-level element within a class
Method declarations	void method()	No	Any top-level element within a class

Let's look at a few examples to help you remember this. The first example contains one of each element.

```
package structure;      // package must be first non-comment
import java.util.*;     // import must come after package
public class Meerkat {  // then comes the class
   double weight;       // fields and methods can go in either order
   public double getWeight() {
      return weight; }
   double height;    // another field - they don't need to be together
}
```

So far, so good. This is a common pattern that you should be familiar with. How about this one?

```
/* header */

package structure;



// class Meerkat
public class Meerkat { }
```

Still good. We can put comments anywhere, blank lines are ignored, and imports are optional. In the next example, we have a problem:

```
import java.util.*;
package structure;        // DOES NOT COMPILE
```

```
String name;              // DOES NOT COMPILE
public class Meerkat { }  // DOES NOT COMPILE
```

There are two problems here. One is that the package and import statements are reversed. Although both are optional, package must come before import if present. The other issue is that a field attempts a declaration outside a class. This is not allowed. Fields and methods must be within a class.

Got all that? Think of the acronym PIC (picture): package, import, and class. Fields and methods are easier to remember because they merely have to be inside a class.

Throughout this book, if you see two public classes in a code snippet or question, you can assume they are in different files unless it specifically says they are in the same .java file.

Now you know how to create and arrange a class. Later chapters show you how to create classes with more powerful operations.

Creating Objects

Our programs wouldn't be able to do anything useful if we didn't have the ability to create new objects. Remember that an object is an instance of a class. In the following sections, we look at constructors, object fields, instance initializers, and the order in which values are initialized.

Calling Constructors

To create an instance of a class, all you have to do is write new before the class name and add parentheses after it. Here's an example:

```
Park p = new Park();
```

First you declare the type that you'll be creating (Park) and give the variable a name (p). This gives Java a place to store a reference to the object. Then you write new Park() to actually create the object.

Park() looks like a method since it is followed by parentheses. It's called a *constructor*, which is a special type of method that creates a new object. Now it's time to define a constructor of your own.

```
public class Chick {
    public Chick() {
        System.out.println("in constructor");
    }
}
```

There are two key points to note about the constructor: the name of the constructor matches the name of the class, and there's no return type. You may see a method like this on the exam:

```
public class Chick {
   public void Chick() { }   // NOT A CONSTRUCTOR
}
```

When you see a method name beginning with a capital letter and having a return type, pay special attention to it. It is *not* a constructor since there's a return type. It's a regular method that does compile but will not be called when you write new Chick().

The purpose of a constructor is to initialize fields, although you can put any code in there. Another way to initialize fields is to do so directly on the line on which they're declared. This example shows both approaches:

```
public class Chicken {
    int numEggs = 12;   // initialize on line
    String name;
    public Chicken() {
       name = "Duke";   // initialize in constructor
    }
}
```

For most classes, you don't have to code a constructor—the compiler will supply a "do nothing" default constructor for you. There are some scenarios that do require you to declare a constructor. You learn all about them in Chapter 6.

Reading and Writing Member Fields

It's possible to read and write instance variables directly from the caller. In this example, a mother swan lays eggs:

```
public class Swan {
    int numberEggs;                              // instance variable
    public static void main(String[] args) {
       Swan mother = new Swan();
       mother.numberEggs = 1;                    // set variable
       System.out.println(mother.numberEggs);    // read variable
    }
}
```

The "caller" in this case is the main() method, which could be in the same class or in another class. This class sets numberEggs to 1 and then reads numberEggs directly to print it out.

You can even read values of already initialized fields on a line initializing a new field.

```
1: public class Name {
2:     String first = "Theodore";
3:     String last = "Moose";
4:     String full = first + last;
5: }
```

Lines 2 and 3 both write to fields. Line 4 both reads and writes data. It reads the fields first and last. It then writes the field full.

Executing Instance Initializer Blocks

When you learned about methods, you saw braces ({}). The code between the braces (sometimes called "inside the braces") is called a *code block*. Anywhere you see braces is a code *block*.

Sometimes code blocks are inside a method. These are run when the method is called. Other times, code blocks appear outside a method. These are called *instance initializers*. In Chapter 6, you learn how to use a static initializer.

How many blocks do you see in the following example? How many instance initializers do you see?

```
1: public class Bird {
2:     public static void main(String[] args) {
3:         { System.out.println("Feathers"); }
4:     }
5:     { System.out.println("Snowy"); }
6: }
```

There are four code blocks in this example: a class definition, a method declaration, an inner block, and an instance initializer. Counting code blocks is easy: you just count the number of pairs of braces. If there aren't the same number of open ({) and close (}) braces or they aren't defined in the proper order, the code doesn't compile. For example, you cannot use a closed brace (}) if there's no corresponding open brace ({) that it matches written earlier in the code. In programming, this is referred to as the *balanced parentheses problem*, and it often comes up in job interview questions.

When you're counting instance initializers, keep in mind that they cannot exist inside a method. Line 5 is an instance initializer, with its braces outside a method. On the other hand, line 3 is not an instance initializer, as it is called only when the main() method is executed. There is one additional set of braces on lines 1 and 6 that constitute the class declaration.

Following the Order of Initialization

When writing code that initializes fields in multiple places, you have to keep track of the order of initialization. This is simply the order in which different methods, constructors, or blocks are called when an instance of the class is created. We add some more rules to the order of initialization in Chapter 6. In the meantime, you need to remember the following:

- Fields and instance initializer blocks are run in the order in which they appear in the file.
- The constructor runs after all fields and instance initializer blocks have run.

Let's look at an example:

```
1:  public class Chick {
2:      private String name = "Fluffy";
3:      { System.out.println("setting field"); }
4:      public Chick() {
5:          name = "Tiny";
6:          System.out.println("setting constructor");
7:      }
8:      public static void main(String[] args) {
9:          Chick chick = new Chick();
10:         System.out.println(chick.name); } }
```

Running this example prints this:

```
setting field
setting constructor
Tiny
```

Let's look at what's happening here. We start with the main() method because that's where Java starts execution. On line 9, we call the constructor of Chick. Java creates a new object. First it initializes name to "Fluffy" on line 2. Next it executes the println() statement in the instance initializer on line 3. Once all the fields and instance initializers have run, Java returns to the constructor. Line 5 changes the value of name to "Tiny", and line 6 prints another statement. At this point, the constructor is done, and then the execution goes back to the println() statement on line 10.

Order matters for the fields and blocks of code. You can't refer to a variable before it has been defined.

```
{ System.out.println(name); }  // DOES NOT COMPILE
private String name = "Fluffy";
```

You should expect to see a question about initialization on the exam. Let's try one more. What do you think this code prints out?

```
public class Egg {
    public Egg() {
        number = 5;
    }
    public static void main(String[] args) {
        Egg egg = new Egg();
        System.out.println(egg.number);
    }
```

```
    private int number = 3;
    { number = 4; } }
```

If you answered 5, you got it right. Fields and blocks are run first in order, setting number to 3 and then 4. Then the constructor runs, setting number to 5. You see *a lot more rules and examples* covering order of initialization in Chapter 6. We only cover the basics here so you can follow the order of initialization for simple programs.

Understanding Data Types

Java applications contain two types of data: primitive types and reference types. In this section, we discuss the differences between a primitive type and a reference type.

Using Primitive Types

Java has eight built-in data types, referred to as the Java *primitive types*. These eight data types represent the building blocks for Java objects, because all Java objects are just a complex collection of these primitive data types. That said, a primitive is not an object in Java, nor does it represent an object. A primitive is just a single value in memory, such as a number or character.

The Primitive Types

The exam assumes you are well versed in the eight primitive data types, their relative sizes, and what can be stored in them. Table 1.5 shows the Java primitive types together with their size in bits and the range of values that each holds.

TABLE 1.5 Primitive types

Keyword	Type	Min value	Max value	Default value	Example
boolean	true or false	n/a	n/a	false	true
byte	8-bit integral value	-128	127	0	123
short	16-bit integral value	-32,768	32,767	0	123
int	32-bit integral value	-2,147,483,648	2,147,483,647	0	123
long	64-bit integral value	-2^{63}	$2^{63} - 1$	0L	123L
float	32-bit floating-point value	n/a	n/a	0.0f	123.45f
double	64-bit floating-point value	n/a	n/a	0.0	123.456
char	16-bit Unicode value	0	65,535	\u0000	'a'

Is *String* a Primitive?

No, it is not. That said, `String` is often mistaken for a ninth primitive because Java includes built-in support for `String` literals and operators. You learn more about `String` in Chapter 4, but for now, just remember it's an object, not a primitive.

There's a lot of information in Table 1.5. Let's look at some key points:

- The `byte`, `short`, `int`, and `long` types are used for integer values without decimal points.
- Each numeric type uses twice as many bits as the smaller similar type. For example, `short` uses twice as many bits as `byte` does.
- All of the numeric types are signed and reserve one of their bits to cover a negative range. For example, instead of `byte` covering 0 to 255 (or even 1 to 256), it actually covers −128 to 127.
- A `float` requires the letter f or F following the number so Java knows it is a `float`. Without an f or F, Java interprets a decimal value as a `double`.
- A `long` requires the letter l or L following the number so Java knows it is a `long`. Without an l or L, Java interprets a number without a decimal point as an `int` in most scenarios.

You won't be asked about the exact sizes of these types, although you should have a general idea of the size of smaller types like `byte` and `short`. A common question among newer Java developers is, what is the bit size of `boolean`? The answer is, it is not specified and is dependent on the JVM where the code is being executed.

Signed and Unsigned: *short* and *char*

For the exam, you should be aware that `short` and `char` are closely related, as both are stored as integral types with the same 16-bit length. The primary difference is that `short` is *signed*, which means it splits its range across the positive and negative integers. Alternatively, `char` is *unsigned*, which means its range is strictly positive, including 0.

Often, `short` and `char` values can be cast to one another because the underlying data size is the same. You learn more about casting in Chapter 2, "Operators."

Writing Literals

There are a few more things you should know about numeric primitives. When a number is present in the code, it is called a *literal*. By default, Java assumes you are defining an `int` value with a numeric literal. In the following example, the number listed is bigger than what fits in an int. Remember, you aren't expected to memorize the maximum value for an int. The exam will include it in the question if it comes up.

```
long max = 3123456789;  // DOES NOT COMPILE
```

Java complains the number is out of range. And it is—for an int. However, we don't have an int. The solution is to add the character L to the number.

```
long max = 3123456789L;  // Now Java knows it is a long
```

Alternatively, you could add a lowercase l to the number. But *please* use the uppercase L. The lowercase l looks like the number 1.

Another way to specify numbers is to change the "base." When you learned how to count, you studied the digits 0–9. This numbering system is called *base 10* since there are 10 possible values for each digit. It is also known as the *decimal number system*. Java allows you to specify digits in several other formats.

- Octal (digits 0–7), which uses the number 0 as a prefix—for example, 017.

- Hexadecimal (digits 0–9 and letters A–F/a–f), which uses 0x or 0X as a prefix—for example, 0xFF, 0xff, 0XFf. Hexadecimal is case insensitive, so all of these examples mean the same value.

- Binary (digits 0–1), which uses the number 0 followed by b or B as a prefix—for example, 0b10, 0B10.

Be sure to be able to recognize valid literal values that can be assigned to numbers.

Literals and the Underscore Character

The last thing you need to know about numeric literals is that you can have underscores in numbers to make them easier to read.

```
int million1 = 1000000;
int million2 = 1_000_000;
```

We'd rather be reading the latter one because the zeros don't run together. You can add underscores anywhere except at the beginning of a literal, the end of a literal, right before a decimal point, or right after a decimal point. You can even place multiple underscore characters next to each other, although we don't recommend it.

Let's look at a few examples:

```
double notAtStart = _1000.00;        // DOES NOT COMPILE
double notAtEnd = 1000.00_;          // DOES NOT COMPILE
double notByDecimal = 1000_.00;      // DOES NOT COMPILE
double annoyingButLegal = 1_00_0.0_0; // Ugly, but compiles
double reallyUgly = 1 _____ 2;   // Also compiles
```

Using Reference Types

A *reference type* refers to an object (an instance of a class). Unlike primitive types that hold their values in the memory where the variable is allocated, references do not hold the value of the object they refer to. Instead, a reference "points" to an object by storing the memory address where the object is located, a concept referred to as a *pointer*. Unlike other languages, Java does not allow you to learn what the physical memory address is. You can only use the reference to refer to the object.

Let's take a look at some examples that declare and initialize reference types. Suppose we declare a reference of type `String`.

```java
String greeting;
```

The `greeting` variable is a reference that can only point to a `String` object. A value is assigned to a reference in one of two ways.

- A reference can be assigned to another object of the same or compatible type.
- A reference can be assigned to a new object using the `new` keyword.

For example, the following statement assigns this reference to a new object:

```java
greeting = new String("How are you?");
```

The `greeting` reference points to a new `String` object, `"How are you?"`. The `String` object does not have a name and can be accessed only via a corresponding reference.

Objects vs. References

Do not confuse a reference with the object that it refers to; they are two different entities. The reference is a variable that has a name and can be used to access the contents of an object. A reference can be assigned to another reference, passed to a method, or returned from a method. All references are the same size, no matter what their type is.

An object sits on the heap and does not have a name. Therefore, you have no way to access an object except through a reference. Objects come in all different shapes and sizes and consume varying amounts of memory. An object cannot be assigned to another object, and an object cannot be passed to a method or returned from a method. It is the object that gets garbage collected, not its reference.

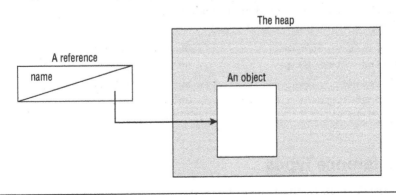

Distinguishing Between Primitives and Reference Types

There are a few important differences you should know between primitives and reference types. First, notice that all the primitive types have lowercase type names. All classes that come with Java begin with uppercase. Although not required, it is a standard practice, and you should follow this convention for classes you create as well.

Next, reference types can be used to call methods, assuming the reference is not null. Primitives do not have methods declared on them. In this example, we can call a method on reference since it is of a reference type. You can tell length is a method because it has () after it. See if you can understand why the following snippet does not compile:

```
4: String reference = "hello";
5: int len = reference.length();
6: int bad = len.length(); // DOES NOT COMPILE
```

Line 6 is gibberish. No methods exist on len because it is an int primitive. Primitives do not have methods. Remember, a String is not a primitive, so you can call methods like length() on a String reference, as we did on line 5.

Finally, reference types can be assigned null, which means they do not currently refer to an object. Primitive types will give you a compiler error if you attempt to assign them null. In this example, value cannot point to null because it is of type int:

```
int value = null;    // DOES NOT COMPILE
String name = null;
```

But what if you don't know the value of an int and want to assign it to null? In that case, you should use a numeric wrapper class, such as Integer, instead of int.

Creating Wrapper Classes

Each primitive type has a wrapper class, which is an object type that corresponds to the primitive. Table 1.6 lists all the wrapper classes along with how to create them.

TABLE 1.6   Wrapper classes

Primitive type	Wrapper class	Wrapper class inherits Number?	Example of creating
boolean	Boolean	No	Boolean.valueOf(true)
byte	Byte	Yes	Byte.valueOf((byte) 1)
short	Short	Yes	Short.valueOf((short) 1)
int	Integer	Yes	Integer.valueOf(1)
long	Long	Yes	Long.valueOf(1)

TABLE 1.6 Wrapper classes *(continued)*

Primitive type	Wrapper class	Wrapper class inherits Number?	Example of creating
float	Float	Yes	Float.valueOf((float) 1.0)
double	Double	Yes	Double.valueOf(1.0)
char	Character	No	Character.valueOf('c')

Converting from *String* Using *valueOf()* Methods

The classes in Table 1.6 include a valueOf(String str) method that converts a String into the associated wrapper class. For example:

```
int primitive = Integer.parseInt("123");
Integer wrapper = Integer.valueOf("123");
```

The first line converts a String to an int primitive. The second converts a String to an Integer wrapper class. On the numeric wrapper classes, valueOf() throws a NumberFormatException on invalid input. For example:

```
System.out.println(Integer.valueOf("five")); // NumberFormatException
```

On Boolean, the method returns Boolean.TRUE for any value that matches "true" ignoring case, and Boolean.FALSE otherwise. For example:

```
System.out.println(Boolean.valueOf("true"));     // true
System.out.println(Boolean.valueOf("TrUe"));     // true
System.out.println(Boolean.valueOf("false"));    // false
System.out.println(Boolean.valueOf("FALSE"));    // false
System.out.println(Boolean.valueOf("kangaroo")); // false
System.out.println(Boolean.valueOf(null));       // false
```

Finally, the numeric integral classes (Byte, Short, Integer, and Long) include an overloaded valueOf(String str, int base) method that takes a base value. As you saw earlier, base 16, or hexadecimal includes the characters 0-9 along with A-Z. The overloaded valueOf() method allows you to pass any of these characters and ignores case. For example:

```
System.out.println(Integer.valueOf("5", 16)); // 5
System.out.println(Integer.valueOf("a", 16)); // 10
```

```
System.out.println(Integer.valueOf("F", 16)); // 15
System.out.println(Integer.valueOf("G", 16)); // NumberFormatException
```

This has been known to show up on exams from time to time, so make sure you understand these examples.

All of the numeric classes in Table 1.6 extend the Number class, which means they all come with some useful helper methods: byteValue(), shortValue(), intValue(), longValue(), floatValue(), and doubleValue(). The Boolean and Character wrapper classes include booleanValue() and charValue(), respectively.

As you probably guessed, these methods return the primitive value of a wrapper instance, in the type requested.

```
Double apple = Double.valueOf("200.99");
System.out.println(apple.byteValue());    // -56
System.out.println(apple.intValue());     // 200
System.out.println(apple.doubleValue());  // 200.99
```

These helper methods do their best to convert values but can result in a loss of precision. In the first example, there is no 200 in byte, so it wraps around to -56. In the second example, the value is truncated, which means all of the numbers after the decimal are dropped. In Chapter 5, we apply autoboxing and unboxing to show how easy Java makes it to work with primitive and wrapper values.

Some of the wrapper classes contain additional helper methods for working with numbers. You don't need to memorize these methods; you can assume any you are given are valid. For example, Integer has the following:

- max(int num1, int num2), which returns the largest of the two numbers
- min(int num1, int num2), which returns the smallest of the two numbers
- sum(int num1, int num2), which adds the two numbers

Defining Text Blocks

Earlier we saw a simple String with the value "hello". What if we want to have a String with something more complicated? For example, let's figure out how to create a String with this value:

```
"Java Study Guide"
   by Jeanne & Scott
```

Building this as a String requires two things you haven't learned yet. The syntax \" lets you say you want a " rather than to end the String, and \n says you want a new line. Both of these are called *escape characters* because the backslash provides a special meaning. With these two new skills, we can write this:

```java
String eyeTest = "\"Java Study Guide\"\n   by Jeanne & Scott";
```

While this does work, it is hard to read. Luckily, Java has *text blocks*, also known as multiline strings. See Figure 1.3 for the text block equivalent.

FIGURE 1.3   Text block

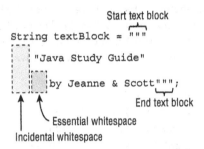

A text block starts and ends with three double quotes ("""), and the contents don't need to be escaped. This is much easier to read. Notice how the type is still `String`. This means any `String` methods you already know or will learn in Chapter 4 apply to text blocks too. It also means you use a text block with a method that takes a `String`. For example:

```java
public String label(String title, String author) {
    return """
           Book:
           """ + title + " by " + author;
}
public void prepare() {
    String labelled = label("""
        Java Study Guide
        For Java 21
        2024 Edition""", "Jeanne & Scott");
    System.out.println(labelled);
}
```

You might have noticed the words *incidental* and *essential whitespace* in the figure. What's that? *Essential whitespace* is part of your `String` and is important to you. *Incidental whitespace* just happens to be there to make the code easier to read. You can reformat your code and change the amount of incidental whitespace without any impact on your `String` value.

Imagine a vertical line drawn on the leftmost non-whitespace character in your text block. Everything to the left of it is incidental whitespace, and everything to the right is essential whitespace. Let's try an example. How many lines does this output, and how many incidental and essential whitespace characters begin each line?

```
14: String pyramid = """
15:    *
16:   * *
17:  * * *
18:  """;
19: System.out.print(pyramid);
```

There are four lines of output. Lines 15–17 have stars. Line 18 is a line without any characters. The closing triple " would have needed to be on line 17 if we didn't want that blank line. There are no incidental whitespace characters here. The closing """ on line 18 are the leftmost characters, so the line is drawn at the leftmost position. Line 15 has two essential whitespace characters to begin the line, and line 16 has one. That whitespace fills in the line drawn to match line 18.

Table 1.7 shows some special formatting sequences and compares how they work in a regular String and a text block.

TABLE 1.7   Text block formatting

Formatting	Meaning in regular String	Meaning in text block
\"	"	"
\"""	n/a – Invalid	"""
\"\"\"	"""	"""
Space (at end of line)	Space	Ignored
\s	Two spaces (\s is a space and preserves leading space on the line)	Two spaces
\ (at end of line)	n/a – Invalid	Omits new line on that line

Let's try a few examples. First, do you see why this doesn't compile?

```
String block = """"doe"""; // DOES NOT COMPILE
```

Text blocks require a line break after the opening """, making this one invalid. Now let's try a valid one. How many lines do you think are in this text block?

```
String block = """
    doe \
    deer""";
```

Just one. The output is doe deer since the \ tells Java not to add a new line before deer. Let's try determining the number of lines in another text block.

```
String block = """
    doe \n
    deer
    """;
```

This time we have four lines. Since the text block has the closing """ on a separate line, we have three lines for the lines in the text block plus the explicit \n. Let's try one more. What do you think this outputs?

```
String block = """
    "doe\"\"\"
    \"deer\"""
    """;
System.out.println("*"+ block  + "*");
```

The answer is:

```
* "doe"""
 "deer"""
*
```

All of the \" escape the ". There is one space of essential whitespace on the doe and deer lines. All the other leading whitespace is incidental whitespace.

Declaring Variables

You've seen some variables already. A *variable* is a name for a piece of memory that stores data. When you declare a variable, you need to state the variable type along with giving it a name. Giving a variable a value is called *initializing* a variable. To initialize a variable, you just type the variable name followed by an equal sign, followed by the desired value. This example shows declaring and initializing a variable in one line:

```
String zooName = "The Best Zoo";
```

In the following sections, we look at how to properly define variables in one or multiple lines.

Identifying Identifiers

It probably comes as no surprise to you that Java has precise rules about identifier names. An *identifier* is the name of a variable, method, class, interface, or package. Luckily, the rules for identifiers for variables apply to all of the other types that you are free to name.

There are only four rules to remember for legal identifiers.

- Identifiers must begin with a letter, a currency symbol, or a _ symbol. Currency symbols include dollar ($), yuan (¥), euro (€), and so on.

- Identifiers can include numbers but not start with them.

- A single underscore (_) is not allowed as an identifier.

- You cannot use the same name as a Java reserved word. A *reserved word* is a special word that Java has held aside so that you are not allowed to use it. Remember that Java is case sensitive, so you can use versions of the keywords that differ only in case. Please don't, though.

Don't worry—you won't need to memorize the full list of reserved words. The exam will only ask you about ones that are commonly used, such as class and for. Table 1.8 lists all of the reserved words in Java.

TABLE 1.8   Reserved words

abstract	assert	boolean	break	byte
case	catch	char	class	const*
continue	default	do	double	else
enum	extends	final	finally	float
for	goto*	if	implements	import
instanceof	int	interface	long	native
new	package	private	protected	public
return	short	static	strictfp	super
switch	synchronized	this	throw	throws
transient	try	void	volatile	while

* The reserved words const and goto aren't actually used in Java. They are reserved so that people coming from other programming languages don't use them by accident—and, in theory, in case Java wants to use them one day.

There are other names you can't use. For example, `true`, `false`, and `null` are literal values, so they can't be variable names. Additionally, there are contextual keywords like `module` in Chapter 12. Prepare to be tested on these rules. The following examples are legal:

```
long okidentifier;
float $OK2Identifier;
boolean _alsoOK1d3ntifi3r;
char __SStillOkbutKnotsonice$;
```

These examples are not legal:

```
int 3DPointClass;      // identifiers cannot begin with a number
byte hollywood@vine;   // @ is not a letter, digit, $ or _
String *$coffee;       // first character * is not a letter, $ or _
double public;         // public is a reserved word
short _;               // a single underscore is not allowed
```

---

camelCase and snake_case

Although you can do crazy things with identifier names, please don't. Java has conventions so that code is readable and consistent. For example, *camelCase* has the first letter of each word capitalized. Method and variable names are typically written in camelCase with the first letter lowercase, such as `toUpper()`. Class and interface names are also written in camelCase, with the first letter uppercase, such as `ArrayList`.

Another style is called *snake_case*. It simply uses an underscore (_) to separate words. Java generally uses uppercase snake_case for constants and enum values, such as `NUMBER_FLAGS`.

The exam will not always follow these conventions to make questions about identifiers trickier. By contrast, questions on other topics generally do follow standard conventions. We recommend you follow these conventions on the job.

Declaring Multiple Variables

You can also declare and initialize multiple variables in the same statement. How many variables do you think are declared and initialized in the following example?

```
void sandFence() {
    String s1, s2;
    String s3 = "yes", s4 = "no";
}
```

Four String variables were declared: s1, s2, s3, and s4. You can declare many variables in the same declaration as long as they are all of the same type. You can also initialize any or all of those values inline. In the previous example, we have two initialized variables: s3 and s4. The other two variables remain declared but not yet initialized.

This is where it gets tricky. Pay attention to tricky things! The exam will attempt to trick you. Again, how many variables do you think are declared and initialized in the following code?

```java
void paintFence() {
   int i1, i2, i3 = 0;
}
```

As you should expect, three variables were declared: i1, i2, and i3. However, only one of those values was initialized: i3. The other two remain declared but not yet initialized. That's the trick. Each snippet separated by a comma is a little declaration of its own. The initialization of i3 only applies to i3. It doesn't have anything to do with i1 or i2 despite being in the same statement. As you will see in the next section, you can't actually use i1 or i2 until they have been initialized.

Another way the exam could try to trick you is to show you code like this line:

```java
int num, String value; // DOES NOT COMPILE
```

This code doesn't compile because it tries to declare multiple variables of *different* types in the same statement. The shortcut to declare multiple variables in the same statement is legal only when they share a type.

 Legal, valid, and compiles are all synonyms in the Java exam world. We try to use all the terminology you could encounter on the exam.

To make sure you understand this, see if you can figure out which of the following are legal declarations:

```java
4: boolean b1, b2;
5: String s1 = "1", s2;
6: double d1, double d2;
7: int i1; int i2;
8: int i3; i4;
```

Lines 4 and 5 are legal. They each declare two variables. Line 4 doesn't initialize either variable, and line 5 initializes only one. Line 7 is also legal. Although int does appear twice, each one is in a separate statement. A semicolon (;) separates statements in Java. It just so happens there are two completely different statements on the same line.

Line 6 is *not* legal. Java does not allow you to declare two different types in the same statement. Wait a minute! Variables d1 and d2 are the same type. They are both of type double. Although that's true, it still isn't allowed. If you want to declare multiple variables in the same statement, they must share the same type declaration and not repeat it.

Line 8 is *not* legal. Again, we have two completely different statements on the same line. The second one on line 8 is not a valid declaration because it omits the type. When you see an oddly placed semicolon on the exam, pretend the code is on separate lines and think about whether the code compiles that way. In this case, the last two lines of code could be rewritten as follows:

```
int i1;
int i2;
int i3;
i4;
```

Looking at the last line on its own, you can easily see that the declaration is invalid. And yes, the exam really does cram multiple statements onto the same line—partly to try to trick you and partly to fit more code on the screen. In the real world, please limit yourself to one declaration per statement and line. Your teammates will thank you for the readable code.

Initializing Variables

Before you can use a variable, it needs a value. Some types of variables get this value set automatically, and others require the programmer to specify it. In the following sections, we look at the differences between the defaults for local, instance, and class variables.

Creating Local Variables

A *local variable* is a variable defined within a constructor, method, or initializer block. For simplicity, we focus primarily on local variables within methods in this section, although the rules for the others are the same.

Final Local Variables

The `final` keyword can be applied to local variables and is equivalent to declaring constants in other languages. Consider this example:

```
5: final int y = 10;
6: int x = 20;
7: y = x + 10;  // DOES NOT COMPILE
```

Both variables are set, but y uses the `final` keyword. For this reason, line 7 triggers a compiler error since the value cannot be modified.

The `final` modifier can also be applied to local variable references. The following example uses an `int[]` array object, which you learn about in Chapter 4.

```
5: final int[] favoriteNumbers = new int[10];
6: favoriteNumbers[0] = 10;
```

```
7: favoriteNumbers[1] = 20;
8: favoriteNumbers = null;  // DOES NOT COMPILE
```

Notice that we can modify the content, or data, in the array. The compiler error isn't until line 8, when we try to change the value of the reference favoriteNumbers.

Uninitialized Local Variables

Local variables do not have a default value and must be initialized before use. Furthermore, the compiler will report an error if you try to read an uninitialized value. For example, the following code generates a compiler error:

```
4: public int notValid() {
5:     int y = 10;
6:     int x;
7:     int reply = x + y;  // DOES NOT COMPILE
8:     return reply;
9: }
```

The y variable is initialized to 10. By contrast, x is not initialized before it is used in the expression on line 7, and the compiler generates an error. The compiler is smart enough to recognize variables that have been initialized after their declaration but before they are used. Here's an example:

```
public int valid() {
    int y = 10;
    int x;  // x is declared here
    x = 3;  // x is initialized here
    int z;  // z is declared here but never initialized or used
    int reply = x + y;
    return reply;
}
```

In this example, x is declared, initialized, and used in separate lines. Also, z is declared but never used, so it is not required to be initialized.

The compiler is also smart enough to recognize initializations that are more complex. In this example, there are two branches of code.

```
public void findAnswer(boolean check) {
    int answer;
    int otherAnswer;
    int onlyOneBranch;
    if (check) {
        onlyOneBranch = 1;
        answer = 1;
    } else {
```

```
    answer = 2;
  }
  System.out.println(answer);
  System.out.println(onlyOneBranch);   // DOES NOT COMPILE
}
```

The answer variable is initialized in both branches of the if statement, so the compiler is perfectly happy. It knows that regardless of whether check is true or false, the value answer will be set to something before it is used. The otherAnswer variable is not initialized but never used, and the compiler is equally as happy. Remember, the compiler is concerned only if you try to use uninitialized local variables; it doesn't mind the ones you never use.

The onlyOneBranch variable is initialized only if check happens to be true. The compiler knows there is the possibility for check to be false, resulting in uninitialized code, and gives a compiler error. You learn more about the if statement in Chapter 3, "Making Decisions."

 On the exam, be wary of any local variable that is declared but not initialized in a single line. This is a common place on the exam that could result in a "Does not compile" answer. Be sure to check to make sure it's initialized before it's used on the exam.

Passing Constructor and Method Parameters

Variables passed to a constructor or method are called *constructor parameters* or *method parameters*, respectively. These parameters are like local variables that have been pre-initialized. The rules for initializing constructor and method parameters are the same, so we focus primarily on method parameters.

In the previous example, check is a method parameter.

```
public void findAnswer(boolean check) {}
```

Take a look at the following method checkAnswer() in the same class:

```
public void checkAnswer() {
  boolean value;
  findAnswer(value);   // DOES NOT COMPILE
}
```

The call to findAnswer() does not compile because it tries to use a variable that is not initialized. While the caller of a method checkAnswer() needs to be concerned about the variable being initialized, once inside the method findAnswer(), we can assume the local variable has been initialized to some value.

Defining Instance and Class Variables

Variables that are not local variables are defined either as instance variables or as class variables. An *instance variable*, often called a field, is a value defined within a specific instance of an object. Let's say we have a Person class with an instance variable name of type String. Each instance of the class would have its own value for name, such as Elysia or Sarah. Two instances could have the same value for name, but changing the value for one does not modify the other.

On the other hand, a *class variable* is one that is defined on the class level and shared among all instances of the class. It can even be publicly accessible to classes outside the class and doesn't require an instance to use. In our previous Person example, a shared class variable could be used to represent the list of people at the zoo today. You can tell a variable is a class variable because it has the keyword static before it. You learn about this in Chapter 5. For now, just know that a variable is a class variable if it has the static keyword in its declaration.

Instance and class variables do not require you to initialize them. As soon as you declare these variables, they are given a default value. The compiler doesn't know what value to use and so wants the simplest value it can give the type: null for an object, zero for the numeric types, and false for a boolean. You don't need to know the default value for char, but in case you are curious, it is '\u0000' (NUL).

Inferring the Type with *var*

You have the option of using the keyword var instead of the type when declaring local variables under certain conditions. To use this feature, you just type var instead of the primitive or reference type. Here's an example:

```
public class Zoo {
    public void whatTypeAmI() {
        var name = "Hello";
        var size = 7;
    }
}
```

The formal name of this feature is *local variable type inference*. Let's take that apart. First comes *local variable*. This means just what it sounds like. You can use this feature only for local variables. The exam may try to trick you with code like this:

```
public class VarKeyword {
    var tricky = "Hello"; // DOES NOT COMPILE
}
```

Wait a minute! We just learned the difference between instance and local variables. The variable tricky is an instance variable. Local variable type inference works with local variables and not instance variables.

Type Inference of *var*

Now that you understand the local variable part, it is time to go on to what *type inference* means. The good news is that this also means what it sounds like. When you type var, you are instructing the compiler to determine the type for you. The compiler looks at the code on the line of the declaration and uses it to infer the type. Take a look at this example:

```
7:  public void reassignment() {
8:      var number = 7;
9:      number = 4;
10:     number = "five";  // DOES NOT COMPILE
11: }
```

On line 8, the compiler determines that we want an int variable. On line 9, we have no trouble assigning a different int to it. On line 10, Java has a problem. We've asked it to assign a String to an int variable. This is not allowed. It is equivalent to typing this:

```
int number = "five";
```

> If you know a language like JavaScript, you might be expecting var to mean a variable that can take on any type at runtime. In Java, var is still a specific type defined at compile time. It does not change type at runtime.

For simplicity when discussing var, we are going to assume a variable declaration statement is completed in a single line. You could insert a line break between the variable name and its initialization value, as in the following example:

```
7:  public void breakingDeclaration() {
8:      var silly
9:          = 1;
10: }
```

This example is valid and does compile, but we consider the declaration and initialization of silly to be happening on the same line.

Examples with *var*

Let's go through some more scenarios so the exam doesn't trick you on this topic! Do you think the following compiles?

```
3:  public void doesThisCompile(boolean check) {
4:      var question;
5:      question = 1;
6:      var answer;
7:      if (check) {
8:          answer = 2;
9:      } else {
```

```
10:        answer = 3;
11:    }
12:    System.out.println(answer);
13: }
```

The code does not compile. Remember that for local variable type inference, the compiler looks only at the line with the declaration. Since question and answer are not assigned values on the lines where they are defined, the compiler does not know what to make of them. For this reason, both lines 4 and 6 do not compile.

You might find that strange since both branches of the if/else do assign a value. Alas, it is not on the same line as the declaration, so it does not count for var. Contrast this behavior with what we saw a short while ago when we discussed branching and initializing a local variable in our findAnswer() method.

Now we know the initial value used to determine the type needs to be part of the same statement. Can you figure out why these two statements don't compile?

```
4: public void twoTypes() {
5:     int a, var b = 3;    // DOES NOT COMPILE
6:     var a, b = 3;        // DOES NOT COMPILE
7:     var n = null;        // DOES NOT COMPILE
8: }
```

Line 5 wouldn't work even if you replaced var with a real type. All the types declared on a single line must be the same type and share the same declaration. We couldn't write int a, int b = 3; either. Line 6 shows that you can't use var to define two variables on the same line.

Line 7 is a single line. The compiler is being asked to infer the type of null. This could be any reference type. The only choice the compiler could make is Object. However, that is almost certainly not what the author of the code intended. The designers of Java decided it would be better not to allow var for null than to have to guess at intent.

> While a var cannot be initialized with a null value without a type, it can be reassigned a null value after it is declared, provided that the underlying data type is a reference type.

Let's try another example. Do you see why this does not compile?

```
public int addition(var a, var b) {  // DOES NOT COMPILE
    return a + b;
}
```

In this example, a and b are method parameters. These are not local variables. Be on the lookout for var used with constructor parameters, method parameters, or instance variables. Using var in one of these places is a good exam trick to see if you are paying attention. Remember that var is used only for local variable type inference!

There's one last rule you should be aware of: var is not a reserved word and allowed to be used as an identifier. It is considered a reserved type name. A *reserved type name* means it cannot be used to define a type, such as a class, interface, or enum. Do you think this is legal?

```java
package var;

public class Var {
   public void var() {
      var var = "var";
   }
   public void Var() {
      Var var = new Var();
   }
}
```

Believe it or not, this code does compile. Java is case sensitive, so Var doesn't introduce any conflicts as a class name. Naming a local variable var is legal. Please don't write code that looks like this at your job! But understanding why it works will help get you ready for any tricky exam questions the exam creators could throw at you.

 Real World Scenario

var in the Real World

The var keyword is great for exam authors because it makes it easier to write tricky code. When you work on a real project, you want the code to be easy to read.

Once you start having code that looks like the following, it is time to consider using var:

```java
PileOfPapersToFileInFilingCabinet pileOfPapersToFile =
   new PileOfPapersToFileInFilingCabinet();
```

You can see how shortening this would be an improvement without losing any information:

```java
var pileOfPapersToFile = new PileOfPapersToFileInFilingCabinet();
```

If you are ever unsure whether it is appropriate to use var, we recommend "Local Variable Type Inference: Style Guidelines," which is available at the following location:

```
https://openjdk.org/projects/amber/guides/lvti-style-guide
```

Managing Variable Scope

You've learned that local variables are declared within a code block. How many variables do you see that are scoped to this method?

```
public void eat(int piecesOfCheese) {
    int bitesOfCheese = 1;
}
```

There are two variables with local scope. The bitesOfCheese variable is declared inside the method. The piecesOfCheese variable is a method parameter. Neither variable can be used outside of where it is defined.

Limiting Scope

Local variables can never have a scope larger than the method they are defined in. However, they can have a smaller scope. Consider this example:

```
3: public void eatIfHungry(boolean hungry) {
4:     if (hungry) {
5:         int bitesOfCheese = 1;
6:     } // bitesOfCheese goes out of scope here
7:     System.out.println(bitesOfCheese);  // DOES NOT COMPILE
8: }
```

The variable hungry has a scope of the entire method, while the variable bitesOfCheese has a smaller scope. It is only available for use in the if statement because it is declared inside of it. When you see a set of braces ({}) in the code, it means you have entered a new block of code. Each block of code has its own scope. When there are multiple blocks, you match them from the inside out. In our case, the if statement block begins at line 4 and ends at line 6. The method's block begins at line 3 and ends at line 8.

Since bitesOfCheese is declared in an if statement block, the scope is limited to that block. When the compiler gets to line 7, it complains that it doesn't know anything about this bitesOfCheese thing and gives an error.

Remember that blocks can contain other blocks. These smaller contained blocks can reference variables defined in the larger scoped blocks, but not vice versa. Here's an example:

```
16: public void eatIfHungry(boolean hungry) {
17:     if (hungry) {
18:         int bitesOfCheese = 1;
19:         {
20:             var teenyBit = true;
21:             System.out.println(bitesOfCheese);
```

```
22:        }
23:     }
24:     System.out.println(teenyBit);   // DOES NOT COMPILE
25: }
```

The variable defined on line 18 is in scope until the block ends on line 23. Using it in the smaller block from lines 19 to 22 is fine. The variable defined on line 20 goes out of scope on line 22. Using it on line 24 is not allowed.

Tracing Scope

The exam will attempt to trick you with various questions on scope. You'll probably see a question that appears to be about something complex and fails to compile because one of the variables is out of scope.

Let's try one. Don't worry if you aren't familiar with if statements or while loops yet. It doesn't matter what the code does since we are talking about scope. See if you can figure out on which line each of the five local variables goes into and out of scope.

```
11: public void eatMore(boolean hungry, int amountOfFood) {
12:     int roomInBelly = 5;
13:     if (hungry) {
14:        var timeToEat = true;
15:        while (amountOfFood > 0) {
16:            int amountEaten = 2;
17:            roomInBelly = roomInBelly - amountEaten;
18:            amountOfFood = amountOfFood - amountEaten;
19:        }
20:     }
21:     System.out.println(amountOfFood);
22: }
```

This method does compile. The first step in figuring out the scope is to identify the blocks of code. In this case, there are three blocks. You can tell this because there are three sets of braces. Starting from the innermost set, we can see where the while loop's block starts and ends. Repeat this process as we go on for the if statement block and method block. Table 1.9 shows the line numbers that each block starts and ends on.

TABLE 1.9   Tracking scope by block

Line	First line in block	Last line in block
while	15	19
if	13	20
Method	11	22

Now that we know where the blocks are, we can look at the scope of each variable. hungry and amountOfFood are method parameters, so they are available for the entire method. This means their scope is lines 11 to 22. The variable roomInBelly goes into scope on line 12 because that is where it is declared. It stays in scope for the rest of the method and goes out of scope on line 22. The variable timeToEat goes into scope on line 14 where it is declared. It goes out of scope on line 20 where the if block ends. Finally, the variable amountEaten goes into scope on line 16 where it is declared. It goes out of scope on line 19 where the while block ends.

You'll want to practice this skill a lot! Identifying blocks and variable scope needs to be second nature for the exam. The good news is that there are lots of code examples to practice on. You can look at any code example on any topic in this book and match up braces.

Applying Scope to Classes

All of that was for local variables. Luckily, the rule for instance variables is easier: they are available as soon as they are defined and last for the entire lifetime of the object itself. The rule for class, aka static, variables is even easier: they go into scope when declared like the other variable types. However, they stay in scope for the entire life of the program.

Let's do one more example to make sure you have a handle on this. Again, try to figure out the type of the four variables and when they go into and out of scope.

```
1:  public class Mouse {
2:      final static int MAX_LENGTH = 5;
3:      int length;
4:      public void grow(int inches) {
5:          if (length < MAX_LENGTH) {
6:              int newSize = length + inches;
7:              length = newSize;
8:          }
9:      }
10: }
```

In this class, we have one class variable, MAX_LENGTH; one instance variable, length; and two local variables, inches and newSize. The MAX_LENGTH variable is a class variable because it has the static keyword in its declaration. In this case, MAX_LENGTH goes into scope on line 2 where it is declared. It stays in scope until the program ends.

Next, length goes into scope on line 3 where it is declared. It stays in scope as long as this Mouse object exists. inches goes into scope where it is declared on line 4. It goes out of scope at the end of the method on line 9. newSize goes into scope where it is declared on line 6. Since it is defined inside the if statement block, it goes out of scope when that block ends on line 8.

Reviewing Scope

Got all that? Let's review the rules on scope.

- *Local variables*: In scope from declaration to the end of the block
- *Method parameters*: In scope for the duration of the method
- *Instance variables*: In scope from declaration until the object is eligible for garbage collection
- *Class variables*: In scope from declaration until the program ends

Not sure what garbage collection is? Relax, that's our next and final section for this chapter.

Destroying Objects

Now that we've played with our objects, it is time to put them away. Luckily, the JVM takes care of that for you. Java provides a garbage collector to automatically look for objects that aren't needed anymore.

Remember, your code isn't the only process running in your Java program. Java code exists inside of a JVM, which includes numerous processes independent from your application code. One of the most important of those is a built-in garbage collector.

All Java objects are stored in your program memory's *heap*. The heap, which is also referred to as the *free store*, represents a large pool of unused memory allocated to your Java application. If your program keeps instantiating objects and leaving them on the heap, eventually it will run out of memory and crash. Oh, no! Luckily, garbage collection solves this problem. In the following sections, we look at garbage collection.

Understanding Garbage Collection

Garbage collection refers to the process of automatically freeing memory on the heap by deleting objects that are no longer reachable in your program. There are many different algorithms for garbage collection, but you don't need to know any of them for the exam.

As a developer, the most interesting part of garbage collection is determining when the memory belonging to an object can be reclaimed. In Java and other languages, *eligible for garbage collection* refers to an object's state of no longer being accessible in a program and therefore able to be garbage collected.

Does this mean an object that's eligible for garbage collection will be immediately garbage collected? Definitely not. When the object actually is discarded is not under your control, but for the exam, you will need to know at any given moment which objects are eligible for garbage collection.

Think of garbage-collection eligibility like shipping a package. You can take an item, seal it in a labeled box, and put it in your mailbox. This is analogous to making an item eligible for garbage collection. When the mail carrier comes by to pick it up, though, is not in your control. For example, it may be a postal holiday, or there could be a severe weather event. You can even call the post office and ask them to come pick it up right away, but there's no way to guarantee when and if this will actually happen. Ideally, they will come by before your mailbox fills with packages!

Java includes a built-in method to help support garbage collection where you can suggest that garbage collection run.

```
System.gc();
```

Just like the post office, Java is free to ignore you. This method is not *guaranteed* to do anything.

Tracing Eligibility

How does the JVM know when an object is eligible for garbage collection? The JVM waits patiently and monitors each object until it determines that the code no longer needs that memory. An object will remain on the heap until it is no longer reachable. An object is no longer reachable when one of these two situations occurs:

- The object no longer has any references pointing to it.
- All references to the object have gone out of scope.

Realizing the difference between a reference and an object goes a long way toward understanding garbage collection, the new operator, and many other facets of the Java language. Look at this code and see whether you can figure out when each object first becomes eligible for garbage collection:

```
1: public class Scope {
2:     public static void main(String[] args) {
3:         String one, two;
4:         one = new String("a");
5:         two = new String("b");
6:         one = two;
7:         String three = one;
8:         one = null;
9:     } }
```

When you are asked a question about garbage collection on the exam, we recommend that you draw what's going on. There's a lot to keep track of in your head, and it's easy to make a silly mistake trying to hold it all in your memory. Let's try it together now. Really. Get a pencil and paper. We'll wait.

Got that paper? OK, let's get started. On line 3, write **one** and **two** (just the words—no need for boxes or arrows since no objects have gone on the heap yet). On line 4, we have our first object. Draw a box with the string **"a"** in it, and draw an arrow from the word one to that box. Line 5 is similar. Draw another box with the string **"b"** in it this time and an arrow from the word two. At this point, your work should look like Figure 1.4.

FIGURE 1.4 Your drawing after line 5

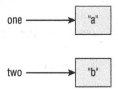

On line 6, the variable one changes to point to "b". Either erase or cross out the arrow from one and draw a new arrow from one to "b". On line 7, we have a new variable, so write the word **three** and draw an arrow from three to "b". Notice that three points to what one is pointing to right now and not what it was pointing to at the beginning. This is why you are drawing pictures. It's easy to forget something like that. At this point, your work should look like Figure 1.5.

FIGURE 1.5 Your drawing after line 7

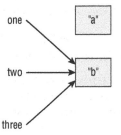

Finally, cross out the line between one and "b" since line 8 sets this variable to null. Now, we were trying to find out when the objects were first eligible for garbage collection. On line 6, we got rid of the only arrow pointing to "a", making that object eligible for garbage collection. "b" has arrows pointing to it until it goes out of scope. This means "b" doesn't go out of scope until the end of the method on line 9.

Code Formatting on the Exam

Not all questions will include package declarations and imports. Don't worry about missing package statements or imports unless you are asked about them. The following are common cases where you don't need to check the imports:

- Code that begins with a class name
- Code that begins with a method declaration

- Code that begins with a code snippet that would normally be inside a class or method

- Code that has line numbers that don't begin with 1

You'll see code that doesn't have a method. When this happens, assume any necessary plumbing code like the main() method and class definition were written correctly. You're just being asked if the part of the code you're shown compiles when dropped into valid surrounding code. Finally, remember that extra whitespace doesn't matter in Java syntax. The exam may use varying amounts of whitespace to trick you.

Summary

Java begins program execution with a main() method. The most common signature for this method run from the command line is public static void main(String[] args). Arguments are passed in after the class name, as in java NameOfClass firstArgument. Arguments are indexed starting with 0.

Java code is organized into folders called packages. To reference classes in other packages, you use an import statement. A wildcard ending an import statement means you want to import all classes in that package. It does not include packages that are inside that one. The package java.lang is special in that it does not need to be imported.

For some class elements, order matters within the file. The package statement comes first if present. Then come the import statements if present. Then comes the class declaration. Fields and methods are allowed to be in any order within the class.

Primitive types are the basic building blocks of Java types. They are assembled into reference types. Reference types can have methods and be assigned a null value. Numeric literals are allowed to contain underscores (_) as long as they do not start or end the literal and are not next to a decimal point (.). Wrapper classes are reference types, and there is one for each primitive. Text blocks allow creating a String on multiple lines using """.

Declaring a variable involves stating the data type and giving the variable a name. Variables that represent fields in a class are automatically initialized to their corresponding 0, null, or false values during object instantiation. Local variables must be specifically initialized before they can be used. Identifiers may contain letters, numbers, currency symbols, or _. Identifiers may not begin with numbers. Local variable declarations may use the var keyword instead of the actual type. When using var, the type is set once at compile time and does not change.

Scope refers to that portion of code where a variable can be accessed. There are three kinds of variables in Java, depending on their scope: instance variables, class variables, and local variables. Instance variables are the non-static fields of your class. Class variables are the static fields within a class. Local variables are declared within a constructor, method, or initializer block.

Constructors create Java objects. A constructor is a method matching the class name and omitting the return type. When an object is instantiated, fields and blocks of code are initialized first. Then the constructor is run. Finally, garbage collection is responsible for removing objects from memory when they can never be used again. An object becomes eligible for garbage collection when there are no more references to it or its references have all gone out of scope.

Exam Essentials

Be able to write code using a *main()* method.   A main() method is usually written as public static void main(String[] args). Arguments are referenced starting with args[0]. Accessing an argument that wasn't passed in will cause the code to throw an exception.

Understand the effect of using packages and imports.   Packages contain Java classes. Classes can be imported by class name or wildcard. Wildcards do not look at subdirectories. In the event of a conflict, class name imports take precedence. Package and import statements are optional. If they are present, they both go before the class declaration in that order.

Be able to recognize a constructor.   A constructor has the same name as the class. It looks like a method without a return type.

Be able to identify legal and illegal declarations and initialization.   Multiple variables can be declared and initialized in the same statement when they share a type. Local variables require an explicit initialization; others use the default value for that type. Identifiers may contain letters, numbers, currency symbols, or _, although they may not begin with numbers. Also, you cannot define an identifier that is just a single underscore character. Numeric literals may contain underscores between two digits, such as 1_000, but not in other places, such as _100_.0_.

Understand how to create text blocks.   A text block begins with """ on the first line. On the next line begins the content. The last line ends with """. If the ending """ is on its own line, a trailing line break is included.

Be able to use *var* correctly.   A var is used for a local variable. A var is initialized on the same line where it is declared, and while it can change value, it cannot change type. A var cannot be initialized with a null value without a type, nor can it be used in multiple variable declarations.

Be able to determine where variables go into and out of scope.   All variables go into scope when they are declared. Local variables go out of scope when the block they are declared in ends. Instance variables go out of scope when the object is eligible for garbage collection. Class variables remain in scope as long as the program is running.

Know how to identify when an object is eligible for garbage collection.   Draw a diagram to keep track of references and objects as you trace the code. When no arrows point to a box (object), it is eligible for garbage collection.

Review Questions

The answers to the chapter review questions can be found in the Appendix.

1. Which of the following are legal entry point methods that can be run from the command line? (Choose all that apply.)

   A. `private static void main(String[] args)`

   B. `public static final main(String[] args)`

   C. `public void main(String[] args)`

   D. `public static final void main(String[] args)`

   E. `public static void main(String[] args)`

   F. `public static main(String[] args)`

2. Which answer options represent the order in which the following statements can be assembled into a program that will compile successfully? (Choose all that apply.)

   `X: class Rabbit {}`

   `Y: import java.util.*;`

   `Z: package animals;`

   A. X, Y, Z

   B. Y, Z, X

   C. Z, Y, X

   D. Y, X

   E. Z, X

   F. X, Z

   G. None of the above

3. Which of the following are true? (Choose all that apply.)

   ```
   public class Bunny {
      public static void main(String[] x) {
         Bunny bun = new Bunny();
   } }
   ```

   A. `Bunny` is a class.

   B. `bun` is a class.

   C. `main` is a class.

   D. `Bunny` is a reference to an object.

   E. `bun` is a reference to an object.

   F. `main` is a reference to an object.

   G. The `main()` method doesn't run because the parameter name is incorrect.

4. Which of the following are valid Java identifiers? (Choose all that apply.)

A. `_`

B. `_helloWorld$`

C. `true`

D. `java.lang`

E. `Public`

F. `1980_s`

G. `_Q2_`

5. Which statements about the following program are correct? (Choose all that apply.)

```
2:   public class Bear {
3:       private Bear pandaBear;
4:       private void roar(Bear b) {
5:           System.out.println("Roar!");
6:           pandaBear = b;
7:       }
8:       public static void main(String[] args) {
9:           Bear brownBear = new Bear();
10:          Bear polarBear = new Bear();
11:          brownBear.roar(polarBear);
12:          polarBear = null;
13:          brownBear = null;
14:          System.gc(); } }
```

A. The object created on line 9 is first eligible for garbage collection after line 13.

B. The object created on line 9 is first eligible for garbage collection after line 14.

C. The object created on line 10 is first eligible for garbage collection after line 12.

D. The object created on line 10 is first eligible for garbage collection after line 13.

E. Garbage collection is guaranteed to run.

F. Garbage collection might or might not run.

G. The code does not compile.

6. Assuming the following class compiles, how many variables defined in the class or method are in scope on the line marked on line 14?

```
1:   public class Camel {
2:       { int hairs = 3_000_0; }
3:       long water, air=2;
4:       boolean twoHumps = true;
5:       public void spit(float distance) {
6:           var path = "";
7:           { double teeth = 32 + distance++; }
```

```
 8:        while(water > 0) {
 9:            int age = twoHumps ? 1 : 2;
10:            short i=-1;
11:            for(i=0; i<10; i++) {
12:                var Private = 2;
13:            }
14:            // SCOPE
15:        }
16:    }
17: }
```

A. 2

B. 3

C. 4

D. 5

E. 6

F. 7

G. None of the above

7. Which are true about this code? (Choose all that apply.)

```
public class KitchenSink {
    private int numForks;

    public static void main(String[] args) {
        int numKnives;
        System.out.print("""
            "# forks = " + numForks +
            " # knives = " + numKnives +
            # cups = 0""");
    }
}
```

A. The output includes # forks = 0.

B. The output includes # knives = 0.

C. The output includes # cups = 0.

D. The output includes a blank line.

E. The output includes one or more lines that begin with whitespace.

F. The code does not compile.

8. Which of the following code snippets about var compile without issue when used in a method? (Choose all that apply.)

A. `var spring = null;`

B. `var fall = "leaves";`

C. `var evening = 2; evening = null;`

D. `var night = Integer.valueOf(3);`

E. `var day = 1/0;`

F. `var winter = 12, cold;`

G. `var fall = 2, autumn = 2;`

H. `var morning = ""; morning = null;`

9. Which of the following is correct?

A. An instance variable of type `float` defaults to 0.

B. An instance variable of type `char` defaults to `null`.

C. A local variable of type `double` defaults to `0.0`.

D. A local variable of type `int` defaults to `null`.

E. A class variable of type `String` defaults to `null`.

F. A class variable of type `String` defaults to the empty string `""`.

G. None of the above.

10. Which of the following expressions, when inserted independently into the blank line, allow the code to compile? (Choose all that apply.)

```
public void printMagicData() {
    var magic = _____;
    System.out.println(magic);
}
```

A. `3_1`

B. `1_329_.0`

C. `3_13.0_`

D. `5_291._2`

E. `2_234.0_0`

F. `9___6`

G. `_1_3_5_0`

11. Given the following two class files, what is the maximum number of imports that can be removed and have the code still compile?

```
// Water.java
package aquarium;
public class Water { }
```

```
// Tank.java
package aquarium;
import java.lang.*;
import java.lang.System;
import aquarium.Water;
import aquarium.*;
public class Tank {
    public void print(Water water) {
        System.out.println(water); } }
```

A. 0

B. 1

C. 2

D. 3

E. 4

F. Does not compile

12. Which statements about the following class are correct? (Choose all that apply.)

```
1: public class ClownFish {
2:     int gills = 0, double weight=2;
3:     { int fins = gills; }
4:     void print(int length = 3) {
5:         System.out.println(gills);
6:         System.out.println(weight);
7:         System.out.println(fins);
8:         System.out.println(length);
9: } }
```

A. Line 2 generates a compiler error.

B. Line 3 generates a compiler error.

C. Line 4 generates a compiler error.

D. Line 7 generates a compiler error.

E. The code prints 0.

F. The code prints 2.0.

G. The code prints 2.

H. The code prints 3.

13. Given the following classes, which of the following snippets can independently be inserted in place of INSERT IMPORTS HERE and have the code compile? (Choose all that apply.)

```
package aquarium;
public class Water {
   boolean salty = false;
}
```

```
package aquarium.jellies;
public class Water {
   boolean salty = true;
}
```

```
package employee;
INSERT IMPORTS HERE
public class WaterFiller {
   Water water;
}
```

A. import aquarium.*;

B. import aquarium.Water;
import aquarium.jellies.*;

C. import aquarium.*;
import aquarium.jellies.Water;

D. import aquarium.*;
import aquarium.jellies.*;

E. import aquarium.Water;
import aquarium.jellies.Water;

F. None of the above

14. Which of the following statements about the code snippet are true? (Choose all that apply.)

```
3: short numPets = 5L;
4: int numGrains = 2.0;
5: String name = "Scruffy";
6: int d = numPets.length();
7: int e = numGrains.length;
8: int f = name.length();
```

A. Line 3 generates a compiler error.

B. Line 4 generates a compiler error.

C. Line 5 generates a compiler error.

D. Line 6 generates a compiler error.

    E. Line 7 generates a compiler error.

    F. Line 8 generates a compiler error.

15. Which of the following statements about garbage collection are correct? (Choose all that apply.)

    A. Calling `System.gc()` is guaranteed to free up memory by destroying objects eligible for garbage collection.

    B. Garbage collection runs on a set schedule.

    C. Garbage collection allows the JVM to reclaim memory for other objects.

    D. Garbage collection runs when your program has used up half the available memory.

    E. An object may be eligible for garbage collection but never removed from the heap.

    F. An object is eligible for garbage collection once no references to it are accessible in the program.

    G. Marking a variable `final` means its associated object will never be garbage collected.

16. Which are true about this code? (Choose all that apply.)

```
var blocky = """
    squirrel \s
    pigeon   \
    termite""";
System.out.print(blocky);
```

    A. It outputs two lines.

    B. It outputs three lines.

    C. It outputs four lines.

    D. There is one line with trailing whitespace.

    E. There are two lines with trailing whitespace.

    F. If we indented each line five characters, it would change the output.

17. What lines are printed by the following program? (Choose all that apply.)

```
1:  public class WaterBottle {
2:      private String brand;
3:      private boolean empty;
4:      public static float code;
5:      public static void main(String[] args) {
6:          WaterBottle wb = new WaterBottle();
7:          System.out.println("Empty = " + wb.empty);
8:          System.out.println("Brand = " + wb.brand);
9:          System.out.println("Code = " + code);
10:     } }
```

    A. Line 8 generates a compiler error.

    B. Line 9 generates a compiler error.

    C. `Empty =`

    D. `Empty = false`

    E. `Brand =`

    F. `Brand = null`

    G. `Code = 0.0`

    H. `Code = 0f`

18. Which of the following statements about `var` are true? (Choose all that apply.)

    A. A `var` can be used as a constructor parameter.

    B. The type of a `var` is known at compile time.

    C. A `var` cannot be used as an instance variable.

    D. A `var` can be used in a multiple variable assignment statement.

    E. The value of a `var` cannot change at runtime.

    F. The type of a `var` cannot change at runtime.

    G. The word `var` is a reserved word in Java.

19. Which are true about the following code? (Choose all that apply.)

```
var num1 = Integer.parseInt("11");
var num2 = Integer.valueOf("B", 16);
System.out.println(Integer.max(num1, num2));
```

    A. The output is 11.

    B. The output is B.

    C. The code does not compile.

    D. num1 is a primitive.

    E. num2 is a primitive.

    F. A `NumberFormatException` is thrown.

20. Which statement about the following class is correct?

```
1: public class PoliceBox {
2:     String color;
3:     long age;
4:     public void PoliceBox() {
5:         color = "blue";
6:         age = 1200;
7:     }
8:     public static void main(String []time) {
9:         var p = new PoliceBox();
```

```
10:        var q = new PoliceBox();
11:        p.color = "green";
12:        p.age = 1400;
13:        p = q;
14:        System.out.println("Q1="+q.color);
15:        System.out.println("Q2="+q.age);
16:        System.out.println("P1="+p.color);
17:        System.out.println("P2="+p.age);
18: } }
```

A. It prints Q1=blue.

B. It prints Q2=1200.

C. It prints P1=null.

D. It prints P2=1400.

E. Line 4 does not compile.

F. Line 12 does not compile.

G. Line 13 does not compile.

H. None of the above.

21. What is the output of executing the following class?

```
1:  public class Salmon {
2:      int count;
3:      { System.out.print(count+"-"); }
4:      { count++; }
5:      public Salmon() {
6:          count = 4;
7:          System.out.print(2+"-");
8:      }
9:      public static void main(String[] args) {
10:         System.out.print(7+"-");
11:         var s = new Salmon();
12:         System.out.print(s.count+"-"); } }
```

A. 7-0-2-1-

B. 7-0-1-

C. 0-7-2-1-

D. 7-0-2-4-

E. 0-7-1-

F. The class does not compile because of line 3.

G. The class does not compile because of line 4.

H. None of the above.

22. Given the following class, which of the following lines of code can independently replace
INSERT CODE HERE to make the code compile? (Choose all that apply.)

```
public class Price {
    public void admission() {
        INSERT CODE HERE
        System.out.print(amount);
    } }
```

- **A.** `int Amount = 0b11;`
- **B.** `int amount = 9L;`
- **C.** `int amount = 0xE;`
- **D.** `int amount = 1_2.0;`
- **E.** `double amount = 1_0_.0;`
- **F.** `int amount = 0b101;`
- **G.** `double amount = 9_2.1_2;`
- **H.** `double amount = 1_2_.0_0;`

23. Which statements about the following class are true? (Choose all that apply.)

```
1:  public class River {
2:      int Depth = 1;
3:      float temp = 50.0;
4:      public void flow() {
5:          for (int i = 0; i < 1; i++) {
6:              int depth = 2;
7:              depth++;
8:              temp--;
9:          }
10:         System.out.println(depth);
11:         System.out.println(temp); }
12:     public static void main(String... s) {
13:         new River().flow();
14: } }
```

- **A.** Line 3 generates a compiler error.
- **B.** Line 6 generates a compiler error.
- **C.** Line 7 generates a compiler error.
- **D.** Line 10 generates a compiler error.
- **E.** The program prints 3 on line 10.
- **F.** The program prints 4 on line 10.
- **G.** The program prints 50.0 on line 11.
- **H.** The program prints 49.0 on line 11.

Operators

OCP EXAM OBJECTIVES COVERED IN THIS CHAPTER:

✓ **Handling Date, Time, Text, Numeric and Boolean Values**

- Use primitives and wrapper classes. Evaluate arithmetic and boolean expressions, using the Math API and by applying precedence rules, type conversions, and casting.

The previous chapter talked a lot about defining variables, but what can you do with a variable once it is created? This chapter introduces operators and shows how you can use them to combine existing variables and create new values. It shows you how to apply operators to various primitive data types, including introducing you to operators that can be applied to objects.

Understanding Java Operators

Before we get into the fun stuff, let's cover a bit of terminology. A Java *operator* is a special symbol that can be applied to a set of variables, values, or literals—referred to as *operands*—and that returns a result. The term *operand*, which we use throughout this chapter, refers to the value or variable the operator is being applied to. Figure 2.1 shows the anatomy of a Java operation.

The output of the operation is simply referred to as the *result*. Figure 2.1 actually contains a second operation, with the assignment operator (=) being used to store the result in variable c.

FIGURE 2.1 Java operation

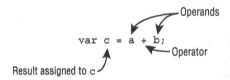

We're sure you have been using the addition (+) and subtraction (−) operators since you were a little kid. Java supports many other operators that you need to know for the exam. While many should be review for you, some (such as the compound assignment operators) may be new to you.

Types of Operators

Java supports three flavors of operators: unary, binary, and ternary. These types of operators can be applied to one, two, or three operands, respectively. For the exam, you need to know a specific subset of Java operators, how to apply them, and the order in which they should be applied.

Java operators are not necessarily evaluated from left-to-right order. In this following example, the second expression is actually evaluated from right to left, given the specific operators involved:

```
int cookies = 4;
double reward = 3 + 2 * --cookies;
System.out.print("Zoo animal receives: "+reward+" reward points");
```

In this example, you first decrement `cookies` to 3, then multiply the resulting value by 2, and finally add 3. The value then is automatically promoted from 9 to 9.0 and assigned to `reward`. The final values of `reward` and `cookies` are 9.0 and 3, respectively, with the following printed:

```
Zoo animal receives: 9.0 reward points
```

If you didn't follow that evaluation, don't worry. By the end of this chapter, solving problems like this should be second nature.

Operator Precedence

When reading a book or a newspaper, some written languages are evaluated from left to right, while some are evaluated from right to left. In mathematics, certain operators can override other operators and be evaluated first. Determining which operators are evaluated in what order is referred to as *operator precedence*. In this manner, Java more closely follows the rules for mathematics. Consider the following expression:

```
var perimeter = 2 * height + 2 * length;
```

Let's apply some optional parentheses to demonstrate how the compiler evaluates this statement:

```
var perimeter = ((2 * height) + (2 * length));
```

The multiplication operator (*) has a higher precedence than the addition operator (+), so the *height* and *length* are both multiplied by 2 before being added together. The assignment operator (=) has the lowest order of precedence, so the assignment to the *perimeter* variable is performed last.

Unless overridden with parentheses, Java operators follow *order of operation*, listed in Table 2.1, by decreasing order of operator precedence. If two operators have the same level of precedence, then Java guarantees left-to-right evaluation for most operators other than the ones marked in the table.

We recommend keeping Table 2.1 handy throughout this chapter. For the exam, you need to memorize the order of precedence in this table. Note that you won't be tested on some operators, like the shift operators, although we recommend that you be aware of their existence.

TABLE 2.1   Order of operator precedence

Operator	Symbols and examples	Evaluation
Post-unary operators	*expression++, expression--*	Left-to-right
Pre-unary operators	*++expression, --expression*	Left-to-right
Other unary operators	-, !, ~, +, *(type)*	Right-to-left
Cast	(Type)reference	Right-to-left
Multiplication/division/ modulus	*, /, %	Left-to-right
Addition/subtraction	+, -	Left-to-right
Shift operators	<<, >>, >>>	Left-to-right
Relational operators	<, >, <=, >=, instanceof	Left-to-right
Equal to/not equal to	==, !=	Left-to-right
Logical AND	&	Left-to-right
Logical exclusive OR	^	Left-to-right
Logical inclusive OR	|	Left-to-right
Conditional AND	&&	Left-to-right
Conditional OR	||	Left-to-right
Ternary operators	*boolean expression ? expression1 : expression2*	Right-to-left
Assignment operators	=, +=, -=, *=, /=, %=, &=, ^=, |=, <<=, >>=, >>>=	Right-to-left
Arrow operator	->	Right-to-left

The arrow operator (->), sometimes called the arrow function or lambda operator, is a binary operator that represents a relationship between two operands. Although we won't cover the arrow operator in this chapter, you will see it used in switch expressions in Chapter 3, "Making Decisions," and in lambda expressions starting in Chapter 8, "Lambdas and Functional Interfaces."

Applying Unary Operators

By definition, a *unary* operator is one that requires exactly one operand, or variable, to function. As shown in Table 2.2, they often perform simple tasks, such as increasing a numeric variable by one or negating a boolean value.

TABLE 2.2   Unary operators

Operator	Examples	Description
Logical complement	!a	Inverts a boolean's logical value
Bitwise complement	~b	Inverts all 0s and 1s in a number
Plus	+c	Indicates a number is positive, although numbers are assumed to be positive in Java unless accompanied by a negative unary operator
Negation or minus	-d	Indicates a literal number is negative or negates an expression
Increment	++e f++	Increments a value by 1
Decrement	--f h--	Decrements a value by 1
Cast	**(String)**i	Casts a value to a specific type

Even though Table 2.2 includes the casting operator, we postpone discussing casting until the "Assigning Values" section later in this chapter, since that is where it is commonly used.

Complement and Negation Operators

The *logical complement operator* (!) flips the value of a boolean expression. For example, if the value is true, it will be converted to false, and vice versa. To illustrate this, compare the outputs of the following statements:

```
boolean isAnimalAsleep = false;
System.out.print(isAnimalAsleep);  // false
isAnimalAsleep = !isAnimalAsleep;
System.out.print(isAnimalAsleep);  // true
```

Next, the *bitwise negation operator* (~) turns all the zeros into ones and vice versa. You can figure out the new value by negating the original and subtracting one. For example:

```java
int number = 70;
int negated = ~number;
System.out.println(negated);    // -71
System.out.println(~negated);  // 70
```

Next, the *negation operator* (-) reverses the sign of a numeric expression, as shown in these statements:

```java
double zooTemperature = 1.21;
System.out.println(zooTemperature);  // 1.21
zooTemperature = -zooTemperature;
System.out.println(zooTemperature);  // -1.21
zooTemperature = -(-zooTemperature);
System.out.println(zooTemperature);  // -1.21
```

Notice that in the previous example we used parentheses, ( ), for the negation operator, -, to apply the negation twice. If we had instead written --, then it would have been interpreted as the decrement operator and printed -2.21. You will see more of that decrement operator shortly.

Based on the description, it might be obvious that some operators require the variable or expression they're acting on to be of a specific type. For example, you cannot apply a negation operator (-) to a boolean expression, nor can you apply a logical complement operator (!) to a numeric expression. Be wary of questions on the exam that try to do this, as they cause the code to fail to compile. For example, none of the following lines of code will compile:

```java
int pelican = !5;         // DOES NOT COMPILE
boolean penguin = -true;  // DOES NOT COMPILE
boolean parrot = ~true;   // DOES NOT COMPILE
boolean peacock = !0;     // DOES NOT COMPILE
```

The first statement will not compile because in Java you cannot perform a logical inversion of a numeric value. The second and third statements do not compile because you cannot numerically negate or complement a boolean value; you need to use the logical inverse operator. Finally, the last statement does not compile because you cannot take the logical complement of a numeric value, nor can you assign an integer to a boolean variable.

Keep an eye out for questions on the exam that use numeric values (such as 0 or 1) with boolean expressions. Unlike in some other programming languages, in Java, 1 and true are not related in any way, just as 0 and false are not related.

Increment and Decrement Operators

Increment and decrement operators, (++) and (--), respectively, can be applied to numeric variables and have a high order of precedence compared to binary operators. In other words, they are often applied first in an expression.

Increment and decrement operators require special care because the order in which they are attached to their associated variable can make a difference in how an expression is processed. Table 2.3 lists each of these operators.

TABLE 2.3 Increment and decrement operators

Operator	Example	Description
Pre-increment	++w	Increases the value by 1 and returns the *new* value
Pre-decrement	--x	Decreases the value by 1 and returns the *new* value
Post-increment	y++	Increases the value by 1 and returns the *original* value
Post-decrement	z--	Decreases the value by 1 and returns the *original* value

The following code snippet illustrates this distinction:

```
int parkAttendance = 0;
System.out.println(parkAttendance);        // 0
System.out.println(++parkAttendance);      // 1
System.out.println(parkAttendance);        // 1
System.out.println(parkAttendance--);      // 1
System.out.println(parkAttendance);        // 0
```

The first pre-increment operator updates the value for parkAttendance and outputs the new value of 1. The next post-decrement operator also updates the value of parkAttendance but outputs the value before the decrement occurs.

For the exam, it is critical that you know the difference between expressions like parkAttendance++ and ++parkAttendance. The increment and decrement operators will be in multiple questions, and confusion about which value is returned could cause you to lose a lot of points on the exam.

Working with Binary Arithmetic Operators

Next, we move on to operators that take two operands, called *binary operators*. Binary operators are by far the most common operators in the Java language. They can be used to perform mathematical operations on variables, create logical expressions, and perform basic variable assignments. Binary operators are often combined in complex expressions with other binary operators; therefore, operator precedence is very important in evaluating expressions containing binary operators. In this section, we start with binary arithmetic operators; we expand to other binary operators in later sections.

Arithmetic Operators

Arithmetic operators are those that operate on numeric values. They are shown in Table 2.4.

TABLE 2.4   Binary arithmetic operators

Operator	Example	Description
Addition	a + b	Adds two numeric values
Subtraction	c - d	Subtracts two numeric values
Multiplication	e * f	Multiplies two numeric values
Division	g / h	Divides one numeric value by another
Modulus	i % j	Returns the remainder after division of one numeric value by another

You should know all but modulus from early mathematics. If you don't know what modulus is, though, don't worry—we'll cover that shortly. Arithmetic operators also include the unary operators, ++ and --, which we covered already. As you may have noticed in Table 2.1, the *multiplicative* operators (*, /, %) have a higher order of precedence than the *additive* operators (+, -). Take a look at the following expression:

```
int price = 2 * 5 + 3 * 4 - 8;
```

First, you evaluate the 2 * 5 and 3 * 4, which reduces the expression to this:

```
int price = 10 + 12 - 8;
```

Then, you evaluate the remaining terms in left-to-right order, resulting in a value of `price` being 14. Make sure you understand why the result is 14 because you will likely see this kind of operator precedence question on the exam.

> All of the arithmetic operators may be applied to any Java primitives, with the exception of `boolean`. Furthermore, only the addition operators `+` and `+=` may be applied to `String` values, which results in `String` concatenation. You will learn more about these operators and how they apply to `String` values in Chapter 4, "Core APIs."

Adding Parentheses

You might have noticed we said "Unless overridden with parentheses" prior to presenting Table 2.1 on operator precedence. That's because you can change the order of operation explicitly by wrapping parentheses around the sections you want evaluated first.

Changing the Order of Operation

Let's return to the previous `price` example. The following code snippet contains the same values and operators, in the same order, but with two sets of parentheses added:

```
int price = 2 * ((5 + 3) * 4 - 8);
```

This time you would evaluate the addition operator `5 + 3`, which reduces the expression to the following:

```
int price = 2 * (8 * 4 - 8);
```

You can further reduce this expression by multiplying the first two values within the parentheses.

```
int price = 2 * (32 - 8);
```

Next, you subtract the values within the parentheses before applying terms outside the parentheses.

```
int price = 2 * 24;
```

Finally, you would multiply the result by 2, resulting in a value of 48 for `price`.

Parentheses can appear in nearly any question on the exam involving numeric values, so make sure you understand how they are changing the order of operation when you see them.

> When you encounter code in your professional career in which you are not sure about the order of operation, feel free to add optional parentheses. While often not required, they can improve readability, especially as you'll see with ternary operators.

Verifying Parentheses Syntax

When working with parentheses, you need to make sure they are always valid and balanced. Consider the following examples:

```
long pigeon = 1 + ((3 * 5) / 3;        // DOES NOT COMPILE
int blueJay = (9 + 2) + 3) / (2 * 4;   // DOES NOT COMPILE
```

The first example does not compile because the parentheses are not balanced. There is a left parenthesis with no matching right parenthesis. The second example has an equal number of left and right parentheses, but they are not balanced properly. When reading from left to right, a new right parenthesis must match a previous left parenthesis. Likewise, all left parentheses must be closed by right parentheses before the end of the expression.

Let's try another example:

```
short robin = 3 + [(4 * 2) + 4];       // DOES NOT COMPILE
```

This example does not compile because Java, unlike some other programming languages, does not allow brackets, [], to be used in place of parentheses. If you replace the brackets with parentheses, the previous example will compile just fine.

Division and Modulus Operators

As we said earlier, the modulus operator, %, may be new to you. The modulus operator, sometimes called the *remainder operator*, is simply the remainder when two numbers are divided. For example, 9 divided by 3 divides evenly and has no remainder; therefore, the result of 9 % 3 is 0. On the other hand, 11 divided by 3 does not divide evenly; therefore, the result of 11 % 3 is 2.

The following examples illustrate this distinction:

```
System.out.println(9 / 3);   // 3
System.out.println(9 % 3);   // 0

System.out.println(10 / 3);  // 3
System.out.println(10 % 3);  // 1

System.out.println(11 / 3);  // 3
System.out.println(11 % 3);  // 2

System.out.println(12 / 3);  // 4
System.out.println(12 % 3);  // 0
```

As you can see, the division results increase only when the value on the left side goes from 11 to 12, whereas the modulus remainder value increases by 1 each time the left side is increased until it wraps around to zero. For a given divisor y, the modulus operation results in a value between 0 and (y - 1) for positive dividends, or 0, 1, 2 in this example.

Be sure to understand the difference between arithmetic division and modulus. For integer values, division results in the floor value of the nearest integer that fulfills the operation, whereas modulus is the remainder value. If you hear the phrase *floor value*, it just means the value without anything after the decimal point. For example, the floor value is 4 for each of the values 4.0, 4.5, and 4.9999999. Unlike rounding, which we'll cover in Chapter 4, you just take the value before the decimal point, regardless of what is after the decimal point.

You can also use modulus with negative numbers. If the divisor is negative, then the negative sign is ignored. Negative values do change the behavior of modulus when applied to the dividend, though. For example, if the divisor is 5, then the modulus value of a negative number is between –4 and 0. The following examples show how this works:

```
System.out.println(2 % 5);    // 2
System.out.println(7 % 5);    // 2
System.out.println(2 % -5);   // 2
System.out.println(7 % -5);   // 2

System.out.println(-2 % 5);   // -2
System.out.println(-7 % 5);   // -2
System.out.println(-2 % -5);  // -2
System.out.println(-7 % -5);  // -2
```

 The modulus operation may also be applied to floating-point numbers although that is out of scope for the exam.

Numeric Promotion

Now that you understand the basics of arithmetic operators, it is vital to talk about primitive *numeric promotion*, as Java may do things that seem unusual to you at first. As we showed in Chapter 1, "Building Blocks," each primitive numeric type has a bit-length. You don't need to know the exact size of these types for the exam, but you should know which are bigger than others. For example, you should know that a long takes up more space than an int, which in turn takes up more space than a short, and so on.

You need to memorize certain rules that Java will follow when applying operators to data types.

Numeric Promotion Rules

1. If two values have different data types, Java will automatically promote one of the values to the larger of the two data types.

2. If one of the values is integral and the other is floating-point, Java will automatically promote the integral value to the floating-point value's data type.

3. Smaller data types, namely, `byte`, `short`, and `char`, are first promoted to `int` any time they're used with a Java binary arithmetic operator with a variable (as opposed to a value), even if neither of the operands is `int`.

4. After all promotion has occurred and the operands have the same data type, the resulting value will have the same data type as its promoted operands.

The last two rules are the ones most people have trouble with and the ones likely to trip you up on the exam. For the third rule, note that unary increment/decrement operators are excluded. For example, applying `++` to a `short` value results in a `short` value.

Let's tackle some examples for illustrative purposes.

▪ What is the data type of x * y?

```
int x = 1;
long y = 33;
var z = x * y;
```

In this case, we follow the first rule. Since one of the values is `int` and the other is `long` and since `long` is larger than `int`, the `int` value x is first promoted to a `long`. The result z is then a `long` value.

▪ What is the data type of x + y?

```
double x = 39.21;
float y = 2.1;
var z = x + y;
```

This is actually a trick question, as the second line does not compile! As you may remember from Chapter 1, floating-point literals are assumed to be `double` unless postfixed with an `f`, as in `2.1f`. If the value of y was set properly to `2.1f`, then the promotion would be similar to the previous example, with both operands being promoted to a `double`, and the result z would be a `double` value.

▪ What is the data type of x * y?

```
short x = 10;
short y = 3;
var z = x * y;
```

On the last line, we must apply the third rule: that x and y will both be promoted to `int` before the binary multiplication operation, resulting in an output of type `int`. If you were to try to assign the value to a `short` variable z without casting, then the code would not compile. Pay close attention to the fact that the resulting output is not a `short`, as we'll come back to this example in the upcoming "Assigning Values" section.

▪ What is the data type of w * x / y?

```
short w = 14;
float x = 13;
double y = 30;
var z = w * x / y;
```

In this case, we must apply all of the rules. First, w will automatically be promoted to int solely because it is a short and is being used in an arithmetic binary operation. The promoted w value will then be automatically promoted to a float so that it can be multiplied with x. The result of w * x will then be automatically promoted to a double so that it can be divided by y, resulting in a double value.

When working with arithmetic operators in Java, you should always be aware of the data type of variables, intermediate values, and resulting values. You should apply operator precedence and parentheses and work outward, promoting data types along the way. In the next section, we'll discuss the intricacies of assigning these values to variables of a particular type.

Assigning Values

Compilation errors from assignment operators are often overlooked on the exam, in part because of how subtle these errors can be. To be successful with the assignment operators, you should be fluent in understanding how the compiler handles numeric promotion and when casting is required. Being able to spot these issues is critical to passing the exam, as assignment operators appear in nearly every question with a code snippet.

Assignment Operator

An *assignment operator* is a binary operator that modifies, or *assigns*, the variable on the left side of the operator with the result of the value on the right side of the equation. Unlike most other Java operators, the assignment operator is evaluated from right to left.

The simplest assignment operator is the (=) assignment, which you have seen already:

```
int herd = 1;
```

This statement assigns the herd variable the value of 1.

Java will automatically promote from smaller to larger data types, as you saw in the previous section on arithmetic operators, but it will throw a compiler exception if it detects that you are trying to convert from larger to smaller data types without casting. Table 2.5 lists the first assignment operator that you need to know for the exam. We present additional assignment operators later in this section.

TABLE 2.5 Simple assignment operator

Operator	Example	Description
Assignment	int a = 50;	Assigns the value on the right to the variable on the left

Casting Values

Seems easy so far, right? Well, we can't really talk about the assignment operator in detail until we've covered casting. *Casting* is a unary operation where one data type is explicitly interpreted as another data type. Casting is optional and unnecessary when converting to a larger or widening data type, but it is required when converting to a smaller or narrowing data type. Without casting, the compiler will generate an error when trying to put a larger data type inside a smaller one.

Casting is performed by placing the data type, enclosed in parentheses, to the left of the value you want to cast. Here are some examples of casting:

```java
int fur = (int)5;
int hair = (short) 2;
String type = (String) "Bird";
short tail = (short)(4 + 10);
long feathers = 10(long);  // DOES NOT COMPILE
```

Spaces between the cast and the value are optional. As shown in the second-to-last example, it is common for the right side to also be in parentheses. Since casting is a unary operation, it would only be applied to the 4 if we didn't enclose 4 + 10 in parentheses. The last example does not compile because the type is on the wrong side of the value.

On the one hand, it is convenient that the compiler automatically casts smaller data types to larger ones. On the other hand, it makes for great exam questions when they do the opposite to see whether you are paying attention. See if you can figure out why none of the following lines of code compiles:

```java
float egg = 2.0 / 9;       // DOES NOT COMPILE
int tadpole = (int)5 * 2L;  // DOES NOT COMPILE
short frog = 3 - 2.0;       // DOES NOT COMPILE
```

All of these examples involve putting a larger value into a smaller data type. Don't worry if you don't follow this quite yet; we cover more examples like this shortly.

In this chapter, casting is primarily concerned with converting numeric data types into other data types. As you will see in later chapters, casting can also be applied to objects and references. In those cases, though, no conversion is performed. Put simply, casting a numeric value may change the data type, while casting an object only changes the reference to the object, not the object itself.

Reviewing Primitive Assignments

See if you can figure out why each of the following lines does not compile:

```java
int fish = 1.0;           // DOES NOT COMPILE
short bird = 1921222;     // DOES NOT COMPILE
int mammal = 9f;          // DOES NOT COMPILE
long reptile = 192_301_398_193_810_323;  // DOES NOT COMPILE
```

The first statement does not compile because you are trying to assign a double 1.0 to an integer value. Even though the value is a mathematic integer, by adding .0, you're instructing the compiler to treat it as a double. The second statement does not compile because the literal value 1921222 is outside the range of short, and the compiler detects this. The third statement does not compile because the f added to the end of the number instructs the compiler to treat the number as a floating-point value, but the assignment is to an int. Finally, the last statement does not compile because Java interprets the literal as an int and notices that the value is larger than int allows. The literal would need a postfix L or l to be considered a long.

Applying Casting

We can fix three of the previous examples by casting the results to a smaller data type. Remember, casting primitives is required any time you are going from a larger numerical data type to a smaller numerical data type, or converting from a floating-point number to an integral value.

```
int fish = (int)1.0;
short bird = (short)1921222;  // Stored as 20678
int mammal = (int)9f;
```

What about applying casting to an earlier example?

```
long reptile = (long)192301398193810323;  // DOES NOT COMPILE
```

This still does not compile because the value is first interpreted as an int by the compiler and is out of range. The following fixes this code without requiring casting:

```
long reptile = 192301398193810323L;
```

 Real World Scenario

Overflow and Underflow

The expressions in the previous example now compile, although there's a cost. The second value, 1,921,222, is too large to be stored as a short, so numeric overflow occurs, and it becomes 20,678. *Overflow* is when a number is so large that it will no longer fit within the data type, so the system "wraps around" to the lowest negative value and counts up from there, similar to how modulus arithmetic works. There's also an analogous *underflow*, when the number is too low to fit in the data type, such as storing −200 in a byte field.

This is beyond the scope of the exam but something to be careful of in your own code. For example, the following statement outputs a negative number:

```
System.out.print(2147483647+1);  // -2147483648
```

Since 2147483647 is the maximum int value, adding any strictly positive value to it will cause it to wrap to the smallest negative number.

Let's return to a similar example from the "Numeric Promotion" section earlier in the chapter.

```
short mouse = 10;
short hamster = 3;
short capybara = mouse * hamster;  // DOES NOT COMPILE
```

Based on everything you have learned up until now about numeric promotion and casting, do you understand why the last line of this statement will not compile? As you may remember, short values are automatically promoted to int when applying any arithmetic operator, with the resulting value being of type int. Trying to assign a short variable with an int value results in a compiler error, as Java thinks you are trying to implicitly convert from a larger data type to a smaller one.

We can fix this expression by casting, as there are times that you may want to override the compiler's default behavior. In this example, we know the result of 10 * 3 is 30, which can easily fit into a short variable, so we can apply casting to convert the result back to a short:

```
short mouse = 10;
short hamster = 3;
short capybara = (short)(mouse * hamster);
```

By casting a larger value into a smaller data type, you instruct the compiler to ignore its default behavior. In other words, you are telling the compiler that you have taken additional steps to prevent overflow or underflow. It is also possible that in your particular application and scenario, overflow or underflow would result in acceptable values.

Last but not least, casting can appear anywhere in an expression, not just on the assignment. For example, let's take a look at a modified form of the previous example:

```
short mouse = 10;
short hamster = 3;
short capybara = (short)mouse * hamster;      // DOES NOT COMPILE
```

So, what's happening on the last line? Well, remember when we said casting was a unary operation? That means the cast in the last line is applied to mouse, and mouse alone. After the cast is complete, both operands are promoted to int since they are used with the binary multiplication operator (*), making the result an int and causing a compiler error.

What if we changed the last line to the following?

```
short capybara = 1 + (short)(mouse * hamster);  // DOES NOT COMPILE
```

In the example, casting is performed successfully, but the resulting value is automatically promoted to int because it is used with the binary arithmetic operator (+).

Casting Values vs. Variables

Revisiting our third numeric promotional rule, the compiler doesn't require casting when working with literal values that fit into the data type. Consider these examples:

```
byte hat = 1;
byte gloves = 7 * 10;
```

```
short scarf = 5;
short boots = 2 + 1;
```

All of these statements compile without issue. On the other hand, neither of these statements compiles:

```
short boots = 2 + hat;   // DOES NOT COMPILE
byte gloves = 7 * 100;   // DOES NOT COMPILE
```

The first statement does not compile because hat is a variable, not a value, and both operands are automatically promoted to int. When working with values, the compiler had enough information to determine the writer's intent. When working with variables, though, there is ambiguity about how to proceed, so the compiler reports an error. The second expression does not compile because 700 triggers an overflow for byte, which has a maximum value of 127.

Compound Assignment Operators

Besides the simple assignment operator (=), Java supports numerous *compound assignment operators*. For the exam, you should be familiar with the compound operators in Table 2.6.

TABLE 2.6 Compound assignment operators

Operator	Example	Description
Addition assignment	a += 5	Adds the value on the right to the variable on the left and assigns the sum to the variable
Subtraction assignment	b -= 0.2	Subtracts the value on the right from the variable on the left and assigns the difference to the variable
Multiplication assignment	c *= 100	Multiplies the value on the right with the variable on the left and assigns the product to the variable
Division assignment	d /= 4	Divides the variable on the left by the value on the right and assigns the quotient to the variable

Compound operators are really just glorified forms of the simple assignment operator, with a built-in arithmetic or logical operation that applies the left and right sides of the statement and stores the resulting value in the variable on the left side of the statement. For example, the following two statements after the declaration of camel and giraffe are equivalent when run independently:

```
int camel = 2, giraffe = 3;
camel = camel * giraffe;   // Simple assignment operator
camel *= giraffe;          // Compound assignment operator
```

The left side of the compound operator can be applied only to a variable that is already defined and cannot be used to declare a new variable. In this example, if camel were not already defined, the expression camel *= giraffe would not compile.

Compound operators are useful for more than just shorthand—they can also save you from having to explicitly cast a value. For example, consider the following. Can you figure out why the last line does not compile?

```
long goat = 10;
int sheep = 5;
sheep = sheep * goat;   // DOES NOT COMPILE
```

From the previous section, you should be able to spot the problem in the last line. We are trying to assign a long value to an int variable. This last line could be fixed with an explicit cast to (int), but there's a better way using the compound assignment operator:

```
long goat = 10;
int sheep = 5;
sheep *= goat;
```

The compound operator will first cast sheep to a long, apply the multiplication of two long values, and then cast the result to an int. Unlike the previous example, in which the compiler reported an error, the compiler will automatically cast the resulting value to the data type of the value on the left side of the compound operator.

Return Value of Assignment Operators

One final thing to know about assignment operators is that the result of an assignment is an expression in and of itself equal to the value of the assignment. For example, the following snippet of code is perfectly valid, if a little odd-looking:

```
long wolf = 5;
long coyote = (wolf = 3);
System.out.println(wolf);   // 3
System.out.println(coyote); // 3
```

The key here is that (wolf=3) does two things. First, it sets the value of the variable wolf to be 3. Second, it returns a value of the assignment, which is also 3.

The exam creators are fond of inserting the assignment operator (=) in the middle of an expression and using the value of the assignment as part of a more complex expression. For example, don't be surprised if you see an if statement on the exam similar to the following:

```
boolean healthy = false;
if(healthy = true)
    System.out.print("Good!");
```

While this may look like a test if healthy is true, it's actually assigning healthy a value of true. The result of the assignment is the value of the assignment, which is true, resulting in this snippet printing Good!. We'll cover this in more detail in the upcoming "Equality Operators" section.

Comparing Values

The last set of binary operators revolves around comparing values. They can be used to check if two values are the same, check if one numeric value is less than or greater than another, and perform Boolean arithmetic. Chances are, you have used many of the operators in this section in your development experience.

Equality Operators

Determining equality in Java can be a nontrivial endeavor as there's a semantic difference between "two objects are the same" and "two objects are equivalent." It is further complicated by the fact that for numeric and boolean primitives, there is no such distinction.

Table 2.7 lists the equality operators. The equals operator (==) and not equals operator (!=) compare two operands and return a boolean value determining whether the expressions or values are equal or not equal, respectively.

TABLE 2.7   Equality operators

Operator	Example	Apply to primitives	Apply to objects
Equality	a == 10	Returns true if the two values represent the same value	Returns true if the two values reference the same object
Inequality	b != 3.14	Returns true if the two values represent different values	Returns true if the two values do not reference the same object

The equality operator can be applied to numeric values, boolean values, and objects (including String and null). When applying the equality operator, you cannot mix these types. Each of the following results in a compiler error:

```
boolean monkey = true == 3;       // DOES NOT COMPILE
boolean ape = false != "Grape";   // DOES NOT COMPILE
boolean gorilla = 10.2 == "Koko"; // DOES NOT COMPILE
```

Pay close attention to the data types when you see an equality operator on the exam. As mentioned in the previous section, the exam creators also have a habit of mixing assignment operators and equality operators.

```
boolean bear = false;
boolean polar = (bear = true);
System.out.println(polar);  // true
```

At first glance, you might think the output should be `false`, and if the expression were (`bear == true`), then you would be correct. In this example, though, the expression is assigning the value of `true` to `bear`, and as you saw in the section on assignment operators, the assignment itself has the value of the assignment. Therefore, `polar` is also assigned a value of `true`, and the output is `true`.

For object comparison, the equality operator is applied to the references to the objects, not the objects they point to. Two references are equal if and only if they point to the same object or both point to `null`. Let's take a look at some examples:

```
var monday = new File("schedule.txt");
var tuesday = new File("schedule.txt");
var wednesday = tuesday;
System.out.println(monday == tuesday);    // false
System.out.println(tuesday == wednesday); // true
```

Even though all of the variables point to the same file information, only two references, `tuesday` and `wednesday`, are equal in terms of `==` since they point to the same object.

Wait, what's the `File` class? In this example, as well as during the exam, you may be presented with class names that are unfamiliar, such as `File`. Many times you can answer questions about these classes without knowing the specific details of these classes. In the previous example, you should be able to answer questions that indicate `monday` and `tuesday` are two separate and distinct objects because the new keyword is used, even if you are not familiar with the data types of these objects.

In some languages, comparing `null` with any other value is always `false`, although this is not the case in Java.

```
System.out.print(null == null);  // true
```

In Chapter 4, we'll continue the discussion of object equality by introducing what it means for two different objects to be equivalent. We'll also cover `String` equality and show how this can be a nontrivial topic.

Relational Operators

We now move on to *relational operators*, which compare two expressions and return a `boolean` value. Table 2.8 describes the relational operators you need to know for the exam.

TABLE 2.8   Relational operators

Operator	Example	Description
Less than	a < 5	Returns true if the value on the left is strictly *less than* the value on the right
Less than or equal to	b <= 6	Returns true if the value on the left is *less than or equal* to the value on the right
Greater than	c > 9	Returns true if the value on the left is strictly *greater than* the value on the right
Greater than or equal to	3 >= d	Returns true if the value on the left is *greater than or equal* to the value on the right
Type comparison	e `instanceof` String	Returns true if the reference on the left side is an instance of the type on the right side (class, interface, record, enum, annotation)

Numeric Comparison Operators

The first four relational operators in Table 2.8 apply only to numeric values. If the two numeric operands are not of the same data type, the smaller one is promoted, as previously discussed.

Let's look at examples of these operators in action:

```
int gibbonNumFeet = 2, wolfNumFeet = 4, ostrichNumFeet = 2;
System.out.println(gibbonNumFeet < wolfNumFeet);       // true
System.out.println(gibbonNumFeet <= wolfNumFeet);      // true
System.out.println(gibbonNumFeet >= ostrichNumFeet);   // true
System.out.println(gibbonNumFeet > ostrichNumFeet);    // false
```

Notice that the last example outputs false, because although gibbonNumFeet and ostrichNumFeet have the same value, gibbonNumFeet is not strictly greater than ostrichNumFeet.

instanceof Operator

The final relational operator you need to know for the exam is the instanceof operator, shown in Table 2.8. It is useful for determining whether an arbitrary object is a member of a particular class or interface at runtime.

Why wouldn't you know what class or interface an object is? As we will get into in Chapter 6, "Class Design," Java supports polymorphism. For now, all you need to know is objects can be passed around using a variety of references. For example, all classes inherit from java.lang.Object. This means that any instance can be assigned to an Object reference. For example, how many objects are created and used in the following code snippet?

```
Integer zooTime = Integer.valueOf(9);
Number num = zooTime;
Object obj = zooTime;
```

In this example, only one object is created in memory, but there are three different references to it because `Integer` inherits both `Number` and `Object`. This means you can call `instanceof` on any of these references with three different data types, and it will return `true` for each of them.

Where polymorphism often comes into play is when you create a method that takes a data type with many possible subclasses. For example, imagine that we have a function that opens the zoo and prints the time. As input, it takes a `Number` as an input parameter.

```
public void openZoo(Number time) {}
```

Now, we want the function to add `O'clock` to the end of output if the value is a whole number type, such as an `Integer`; otherwise, it just prints the value.

```
public void openZoo(Number time) {
   if (time instanceof Integer)
      System.out.print((Integer)time + " O'clock");
   else
      System.out.print(time);
}
```

We now have a method that can intelligently handle both `Integer` and other values. A good exercise left for the reader is to add checks for other numeric data types such as `Short`, `Long`, `Double`, and so on.

Notice that we cast the `Integer` value in this example. It is common to use casting with `instanceof` when working with objects that can be various different types, since casting gives you access to fields available only in the more specific classes. It is considered a good coding practice to use the `instanceof` operator prior to casting from one object to a narrower type.

For the exam, you only need to focus on when `instanceof` is used with classes and interfaces. Although it can be used with other high-level types, such as records, enums, and annotations, it is not common.

Invalid *instanceof*

One area the exam might try to trip you up on is using `instanceof` with incompatible types. For example, `Number` cannot possibly hold a `String` value, so the following causes a compilation error:

```
public void openZoo(Number time) {
   if(time instanceof String) // DOES NOT COMPILE
      System.out.print(time);
}
```

If the compiler can determine that a variable cannot possibly be cast to a specific class, it reports an error.

null and the *instanceof* operator

What happens if you call `instanceof` on a `null` variable? For the exam, you should know that calling `instanceof` on the `null` literal or a `null` reference always returns `false`.

```
System.out.print(null instanceof Object);           // false
```

```
String noObjectHere = null;
System.out.print(noObjectHere instanceof String);   // false
```

The preceding examples both print `false`. It almost doesn't matter what the right side of the expression is. We say "almost" because there are exceptions. This example does not compile, since `null` is used on the right side of the `instanceof` operator:

```
System.out.print(null instanceof null);  // DOES NOT COMPILE
```

 Although it may feel like you've learned everything there is about the instanceof operator, there's a lot more coming! In Chapter 3, we introduce pattern matching with the instanceof operator, and in Chapter 7, "Beyond Classes," we apply it to record patterns and also see how it impacts polymorphism.

Logical Operators

If you have studied computer science, you may have already come across logical operators before. If not, no need to panic—we'll be covering them in detail in this section.

The logical operators, (&), (|), and (^), may be applied to both numeric and `boolean` data types; they are listed in Table 2.9. When they're applied to `boolean` data types, they're referred to as *logical operators*. Alternatively, when they're applied to numeric data types, they're referred to as *bitwise operators*, as they perform bitwise comparisons of the bits that compose the number.

TABLE 2.9   Logical operators

Operator	Example	Description
Logical AND	a & b	The value is `true` only if both values are `true`.
Logical inclusive OR	c | d	The value is `true` if at least one of the values is `true`.
Logical exclusive OR	e ^ f	The value is `true` only if one value is `true` and the other is `false`.

You should familiarize yourself with the truth tables in Figure 2.2, where x and y are assumed to be boolean data types.

FIGURE 2.2 The logical truth tables for &, |, and ^

AND (x & y)

	y = true	y = false
x = true	true	false
x = false	false	false

INCLUSIVE OR (x | y)

	y = true	y = false
x = true	true	true
x = false	true	false

EXCLUSIVE OR (x ^ y)

	y = true	y = false
x = true	false	true
x = false	true	false

Here are some tips to help you remember this table:

- AND is only true if both operands are true.
- Inclusive OR is only false if both operands are false.
- Exclusive OR is only true if the operands are different.

Let's take a look at some examples:

```
boolean eyesClosed = true;
boolean breathingSlowly = true;

boolean resting = eyesClosed | breathingSlowly;
boolean asleep = eyesClosed & breathingSlowly;
boolean awake = eyesClosed ^ breathingSlowly;
System.out.println(resting);  // true
System.out.println(asleep);   // true
System.out.println(awake);    // false
```

You should try these yourself, changing the values of eyesClosed and breathingSlowly and studying the results.

Bitwise Operators

Bits are the 0 and 1 that you would see if you looked at a number in binary. For example, the number 2 is represented as 10 in binary. Table 2.10 includes three bitwise operations that compare the 0s and 1s of a number, and return a new number based on these comparisons. For the exam, you don't need to do a lot of bitwise conversions, but you do need to know some basics.

TABLE 2.10   Bitwise operators

Operator	Example	Description
Bitwise AND	a & b	Compares the bits of two numbers, returning a number that has a 1 in each digit in which *both* operands have a 1, and 0 otherwise.
Bitwise OR	c | d	Compares the bits of two numbers, returning a number that has a 1 in each digit in which *either* operand has a 1, and 0 otherwise.
Bitwise exclusive OR	e ^ f	Compares the bits of two numbers, returning a number that has a 0 in each digit that *matched*, and 1 otherwise.

First, we have the bitwise AND operator (&) and the bitwise OR operator (|). These operators return 1 when both or either corresponding binary digits are 1, respectively. First, you need to know that the original number is returned if both operands are the same.

```
int number = 70;
System.out.println(number);           // 70
System.out.println(number & number);  // 70
System.out.println(number | number);  // 70
```

You also need to know how bitwise operations work on a number and its negation, which returns 0 for bitwise AND (&), and –1 for bitwise OR (|).

```
int negated = ~number;
System.out.println(negated);            // -71

System.out.println(number & negated);  // 0
System.out.println(number | negated);  // -1
```

Finally, we have the binary exclusive OR operator (^). It works like the boolean version except with 0 as false, and 1 as true. However, it checks at each position in the number. You should know that it returns 0 if both numbers are the same (bits are all 0s), and –1 (bits are all 1s) for a value with its negation.

```
System.out.println(number ^ number);   // 0
System.out.println(number ^ negated);  // -1
```

Conditional Operators

Next, we present the conditional operators, && and ||, in Table 2.11.

TABLE 2.11   Conditional operators

Operator	Example	Description
Conditional AND	a && b	The value is true only if both values are true. If the left side is false, then the right side will not be evaluated.
Conditional OR	c || d	The value is true if at least one of the values is true. If the left side is true, then the right side will not be evaluated.

The *conditional operators*, often called short-circuit operators, are nearly identical to the logical operators, & and |, except that the right side of the expression may never be evaluated if the final result can be determined by the left side of the expression. For example, consider the following snippet:

```
int hour = 10;
boolean zooOpen = true || (hour < 4);
System.out.println(zooOpen);   // true
```

Referring to the truth tables, the value zooOpen can be false only if both sides of the expression are false. Since we know the left side is true, there's no need to evaluate the right side, since no value of hour will ever make this code print false. In other words, hour could have been −10 or 892; the output would have been the same. Try it yourself with different values for hour!

Avoiding a *NullPointerException*

A more common example of where conditional operators are used is checking for null objects before performing an operation. In the following example, if duck is null, the program will throw a NullPointerException at runtime:

```
if(duck != null & duck.getAge() < 5) { // Could throw a NullPointerException
    // Do something
}
```

The issue is that the logical AND (&) operator evaluates both sides of the expression. We could add a second if statement, but this could get unwieldy if we have a lot of variables to check. An easy-to-read solution is to use the conditional AND operator (&&):

```
if(duck != null && duck.getAge()<5) {
    // Do something
}
```

In this example, if duck is null, the conditional prevents a NullPointerException from ever being thrown, since the evaluation of duck.getAge() < 5 is never reached.

Checking for Unperformed Side Effects

Be wary of short-circuit behavior on the exam, as questions are known to alter a variable on the right side of the expression that may never be reached. This is referred to as an *unperformed side effect*. For example, what is the output of the following code?

```java
int rabbit = 6;
boolean bunny = (rabbit >= 6) || (++rabbit <= 7);
System.out.println(rabbit);
```

Because rabbit >= 6 is true, the increment operator on the right side of the expression is never evaluated, so the output is 6.

Making Decisions with the Ternary Operator

The final operator you should be familiar with for the exam is the conditional operator, (? :), otherwise known as the *ternary operator*. It is notable in that it is the only operator that takes three operands. The ternary operator has the following form:

```java
booleanExpression ? expression1 : expression2
```

The first operand must be a boolean expression, and the second and third operands can be any expression that returns a value. The ternary operation is really a condensed form of a combined if and else statement that returns a value. We cover if/else statements in a lot more detail in Chapter 3, so for now we just use simple examples.

For example, consider the following code snippet that calculates the food amount for an owl:

```java
int owl = 5;
int food;
if(owl < 2) {
    food = 3;
} else {
    food = 4;
}
System.out.println(food);  // 4
```

Compare the previous code snippet with the following ternary operator code snippet:

```java
int owl = 5;
int food = owl < 2 ? 3 : 4;
System.out.println(food);  // 4
```

These two code snippets are equivalent. Note that it is often helpful for readability to add parentheses around the expressions in ternary operations, although doing so is certainly not required. It is especially helpful when multiple ternary operators are used together, though. Consider the following two equivalent expressions:

```
int food1 = owl < 4 ? owl > 2 ? 3 : 4 : 5;
int food2 = (owl < 4 ? ((owl > 2) ? 3 : 4) : 5);
```

While they are equivalent, we find the second statement far more readable. That said, it is possible the exam could use multiple ternary operators in a single line.

For the exam, you should know that there is no requirement that second and third expressions in ternary operations have the same data types, although it does come into play when combined with the assignment operator. Compare the two statements following the variable declaration:

```
int stripes = 7;
```

```
System.out.print((stripes > 5) ? 21 : "Zebra");
```

```
int animal = (stripes < 9) ? 3 : "Horse";   // DOES NOT COMPILE
```

Both expressions evaluate similar boolean values and return an int and a String, although only the first one will compile. System.out.print() does not care that the expressions are completely different types, because it can convert both to Object values and call toString() on them. On the other hand, the compiler does know that "Horse" is of the wrong data type and cannot be assigned to an int; therefore, it does not allow the code to be compiled.

Ternary Expression and Unperformed Side Effects

As we saw with the conditional operators, a ternary expression can contain an unper-formed side effect, as only one of the expressions on the right side will be evaluated at run-time. Let's illustrate this principle with the following example:

```
int sheep = 1;
int zzz = 1;
int sleep = zzz<10 ? sheep++ : zzz++;
System.out.print(sheep + "," + zzz);   // 2,1
```

Notice that since the left-hand boolean expression was true, only sheep was incre-mented. Contrast the preceding example with the following modification:

```
int sheep = 1;
int zzz = 1;
int sleep = sheep>=10 ? sheep++ : zzz++;
System.out.print(sheep + "," + zzz);   // 1,2
```

Now that the left-hand `boolean` expression evaluates to `false`, only `zzz` is incremented. In this manner, we see how the expressions in a ternary operator may not be applied if the particular expression is not used.

For the exam, be wary of any question that includes a ternary expression in which a variable is modified in one of the expressions on the right-hand side.

Summary

This chapter covered a wide variety of Java operator topics for unary, binary, and ternary operators. Ideally, most of these operators were review for you. If not, you need to study them in detail. It is important that you understand how to use all of the required Java operators covered in this chapter and know how operator precedence and parentheses influence the way a particular expression is interpreted.

There will likely be numerous questions on the exam that appear to test one thing, such as NIO.2 or exception handling, when in fact the answer is related to the misuse of a particular operator that causes the application to fail to compile. When you see an operator involving numbers on the exam, always check that the appropriate data types are used and that they match each other where applicable.

Operators are used throughout the exam, in nearly every code sample, so the better you understand this chapter, the more prepared you will be for the exam.

Exam Essentials

Be able to write code that uses Java operators.   This chapter covered a wide variety of operator symbols. Go back and review them several times so that you are familiar with them throughout the rest of the book.

Be able to recognize which operators are associated with which data types.   Some operators may be applied only to numeric primitives, some only to `boolean` values, and some only to objects. It is important that you notice when an operator and operand(s) are mismatched, as this issue is likely to come up in a couple of exam questions.

Understand when casting is required or numeric promotion occurs.   Whenever you mix operands of two different data types, the compiler needs to decide how to handle the resulting data type. When you're converting from a smaller to a larger data type, numeric promotion is automatically applied. When you're converting from a larger to a smaller data type, casting is required.

Understand Java operator precedence. Most Java operators you'll work with are binary, but the number of expressions is often greater than two. Therefore, you must understand the order in which Java will evaluate each operator symbol.

Be able to write code that uses parentheses to override operator precedence. You can use parentheses in your code to manually change the order of precedence.

Review Questions

The answers to the chapter review questions can be found in the Appendix.

1. Which of the following Java operators can be used with `boolean` variables? (Choose all that apply.)

    A. `==`

    B. `+`

    C. `--`

    D. `!`

    E. `%`

    F. `-`

    G. Cast with (`boolean`)

2. What data type (or types) will allow the following code snippet to compile? (Choose all that apply.)

    ```
    byte apples = 5;
    short oranges = 10;
    _____ bananas = apples + oranges;
    ```

    A. `int`

    B. `long`

    C. `boolean`

    D. `double`

    E. `short`

    F. `byte`

3. What change, when applied independently, would allow the following code snippet to compile? (Choose all that apply.)

    ```
    3: long ear = 10;
    4: int hearing = 2 * ear;
    ```

    A. No change; it compiles as is.

    B. Cast `ear` on line 4 to `int`.

    C. Change the data type of `ear` on line 3 to `short`.

    D. Cast `2 * ear` on line 4 to `int`.

    E. Change the data type of `hearing` on line 4 to `short`.

    F. Change the data type of `hearing` on line 4 to `long`.

4. What is the output of the following code snippet?

```
3: boolean canine = true, wolf = true;
4: int teeth = 20;
5: canine = (teeth != 10) ^ (wolf=false);
6: System.out.println(canine+", "+teeth+", "+wolf);
```

    A. true, 20, true
    B. true, 20, false
    C. false, 10, true
    D. false, 20, false
    E. The code will not compile because of line 5.
    F. None of the above.

5. Which of the following operators are ranked in increasing or the same order of precedence? Assume the + operator is binary addition, not the unary form. (Choose all that apply.)

    A. +, *, %, --
    B. ++, (int), *
    C. =, ==, !
    D. (short), =, !, *
    E. *, /, %, +, ==
    F. !, ||, &
    G. ^, +, =, +=

6. What is the output of the following program?

```
1: public class CandyCounter {
2:     static long addCandy(double fruit, float vegetables) {
3:         return (int)fruit+vegetables;
4:     }
5:
6:     public static void main(String[] args) {
7:         System.out.print(addCandy(1.4, 2.4f) + ", ");
8:         System.out.print(addCandy(1.9, (float)4) + ", ");
9:         System.out.print(addCandy((long)(int)(short)2, (float)4)); } }
```

    A. 4, 6, 6.0
    B. 3, 5, 6
    C. 3, 6, 6
    D. 4, 5, 6
    E. The code does not compile because of line 9.
    F. None of the above.

7. What is the output of the following code snippet?

```
int ph = 7, vis = 2;
boolean clear = vis > 1 & (vis < 9 || ph < 2);
boolean safe = (vis > 2) && (ph++ > 1);
boolean tasty = 7 <= --ph;
System.out.println(clear + "-" + safe + "-" + tasty);
```

A. true-true-true

B. true-true-false

C. true-false-true

D. true-false-false

E. false-true-true

F. false-true-false

G. false-false-true

H. false-false-false

8. What is the output of the following code snippet?

```
4: int pig = (short)4;
5: pig = pig++;
6: long goat = (int)2;
7: goat -= 1.0;
8: System.out.print(pig + " - " + goat);
```

A. 4 - 1

B. 4 - 2

C. 5 - 1

D. 5 - 2

E. The code does not compile due to line 7.

F. None of the above.

9. What are the unique outputs of the following code snippet? (Choose all that apply.)

```
int a = 2, b = 4, c = 2;
System.out.println(a > 2 ? --c : b++);
System.out.println(b = (a!=c ? a : b++));
System.out.println(a > b ? b < c ? b : 2 : 1);
```

A. 1

B. 2

C. 3

D. 4

E. 5

F. 6

G. The code does not compile.

10. Which is not an output of the following code snippet?

```
short height = 1, weight = 3;
short zebra = (byte) weight * (byte) height;
double ox = 1 + height * 2 + weight;
long giraffe = 1 + 9 % height + 1;
System.out.println(zebra);
System.out.println(ox);
System.out.println(giraffe);
```

A. 2

B. 3

C. 6

D. 6.0

E. The code does not compile.

11. What is the output of the following code?

```
11: int sample1 = (2 * 4) % 3;
12: int sample2 = 3 * 2 % -3;
13: int sample3 = 5 * (1 % 2);
14: System.out.println(sample1 + ", " + sample2 + ", " + sample3);
```

A. 0, 0, 5

B. 1, 2, 10

C. 2, 1, 5

D. 2, 0, 5

E. 3, 1, 10

F. 3, 2, 6

G. The code does not compile.

12. The _____ operator increases a value and returns the original value, while the _____ operator decreases a value and returns the new value.

A. post-increment, post-increment

B. pre-decrement, post-decrement

C. post-increment, post-decrement

D. post-increment, pre-decrement

E. pre-increment, pre-decrement

F. pre-increment, post-decrement

13. What is the output of the following code snippet?

```
boolean sunny = true, raining = false, sunday = true;
boolean goingToTheStore = sunny & raining ^ sunday;
boolean goingToTheZoo = sunday && !raining;
```

```
boolean stayingHome = !(goingToTheStore && goingToTheZoo);
System.out.println(goingToTheStore + "-" + goingToTheZoo
    + "-" +stayingHome);
```

A. true-false-false

B. false-true-false

C. true-true-true

D. false-true-true

E. false-false-false

F. true-true-false

G. None of the above

14. Which of the following statements are correct? (Choose all that apply.)

A. The return value of an assignment operation expression can be `void`.

B. The inequality operator (`!=`) can be used to compare objects.

C. The equality operator (`==`) can be used to compare a `boolean` value with a numeric value.

D. During runtime, the & and | operators may cause only the left side of the expression to be evaluated.

E. The return value of an assignment operation expression is the value of the newly assigned variable.

F. In Java, 0 and `false` may be used interchangeably.

G. The logical complement operator (`!`) cannot be used to flip numeric values.

15. Which operator takes three operands or values?

A. =

B. &&

C. *=

D. ? :

E. &

F. ++

G. /

16. How many lines of the following code contain compiler errors?

```
int note = 1 * 2 + (long)3;
short melody = (byte)(double)(note *= 2);
double song = melody;
float symphony = (float)((song == 1_000f) ? song * 2L : song);
```

A. 0

B. 1

C. 2

D. 3

E. 4

17. Given the following code snippet, what are the values of the variables after it is executed? (Choose all that apply.)

```
int ticketsTaken = 1;
int ticketsSold = 3;
ticketsSold += 1 + ticketsTaken++;
ticketsTaken *= 2;
ticketsSold += (long)1;
```

A. ticketsSold is 8.

B. ticketsTaken is 2.

C. ticketsSold is 6.

D. ticketsTaken is 6.

E. ticketsSold is 7.

F. ticketsTaken is 4.

G. The code does not compile.

18. Which of the following can be used to change the order of operation in an expression?

A. [ ]

B. < >

C. ( )

D. \ /

E. { }

F. " "

19. What is the result of executing the following code snippet? (Choose all that apply.)

```
3: int start = 7;
4: int end = 4;
5: end += ++start;
6: start = (byte)(Byte.MAX_VALUE + 1);
```

A. start is 0.

B. start is -128.

C. start is 127.

D. end is 8.

E. end is 11.

F. end is 12.

G. The code does not compile.

H. The code compiles but throws an exception at runtime.

20. Which of the following statements about unary operators are true? (Choose all that apply.)

A. Unary operators are always executed before any surrounding numeric binary or ternary operators.

B. The – operator can be used to flip a `boolean` value.

C. The pre-increment operator (++) returns the value of the variable before the increment is applied.

D. The post-decrement operator (--) returns the value of the variable before the decrement is applied.

E. The ! operator cannot be used on numeric values.

F. None of the above.

Chapter

3

Making Decisions

OCP EXAM OBJECTIVES COVERED IN THIS CHAPTER:

✓ **Controlling Program Flow**

- Create program flow control constructs including if/else, switch statements and expressions, loops, and break and continue statements.

✓ **Using Object-Oriented Concepts in Java**

- Implement inheritance, including abstract and sealed types as well as record classes. Override methods, including that of the Object class. Implement polymorphism and differentiate between object type and reference type. Perform reference type casting, identify object types using the instanceof operator, and pattern matching with the instanceof operator and the switch construct.

Like many programming languages, Java is composed primarily of variables, operators, and statements put together in some logical order. In the previous chapter, we covered how to create and manipulate variables. Writing software is about more than managing variables, though; it is about creating applications that can make intelligent decisions. In this chapter, we present the various decision-making statements available to you within the language. This knowledge will allow you to build complex functions and class structures that you'll see throughout this book.

Creating Decision-Making Statements

Java operators allow you to create a lot of complex expressions, but they're limited in the manner in which they can control program flow. Imagine you want a method to be executed only under certain conditions that cannot be evaluated until runtime. For example, on rainy days, a zoo should remind patrons to bring an umbrella, or on a snowy day, the zoo might need to close. The software doesn't change, but the behavior of the software should, depending on the inputs supplied in the moment. In this section, we discuss decision-making statements including if and else, along with pattern matching.

Statements and Blocks

As you may recall from Chapter 1, "Building Blocks," a Java statement is a complete unit of execution in Java, terminated with a semicolon (;). In this chapter, we introduce you to various Java control flow statements. *Control flow statements* break up the flow of execution by using decision-making, looping, and branching, allowing the application to selectively execute particular segments of code.

These statements can be applied to single expressions as well as a block of Java code. As described in Chapter 1, a block of code in Java is a group of zero or more statements between balanced braces ({}) and can be used anywhere a single statement is allowed. For example, the following two snippets are equivalent, with the first being a single statement and the second being a block containing the same statement:

```java
// Single statement
patrons++;
```

```java
// Statement inside a block
```

```
{
    patrons++;
}
```

A statement or block often serves as the target of a decision-making statement. For example, we can prepend the decision-making if statement to these two examples:

```
// Single statement
if (ticketsTaken > 1)
    patrons++;

// Statement inside a block
if (ticketsTaken > 1) {
    patrons++;
}
```

Again, both of these code snippets are equivalent. Just remember that the target of a decision-making statement can be a single statement or block of statements. For the rest of the chapter, we use both forms to better prepare you for what you will see on the exam.

While both of the previous examples are equivalent, stylistically using blocks is often preferred, even if the block has only one statement. The second form has the advantage that you can quickly insert new lines of code into the block, without modifying the surrounding structure.

The *if* Statement

Often, we want to execute a block only under certain circumstances. The if statement, as shown in Figure 3.1, accomplishes this by allowing our application to execute a particular block of code if and only if a boolean expression evaluates to true at runtime.

FIGURE 3.1   The structure of an if statement

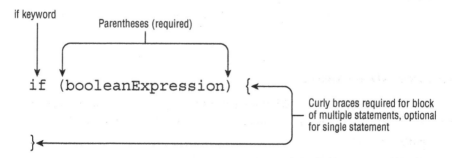

For example, imagine we had a function that used the hour of day, an integer value from 0 to 23, to display a message to the user:

```
if (hourOfDay < 11)
    System.out.println("Good Morning");
```

If the hour of the day is less than 11, then the message will be displayed. Now let's say we also wanted to increment some value, morningGreetingCount, every time the greeting is printed. We could write the if statement twice, but luckily Java offers us a more natural approach using a block:

```
if (hourOfDay < 11) {
    System.out.println("Good Morning");
    morningGreetingCount++;
}
```

Watch Indentation and Braces

One area where the exam writers will try to trip you up is if statements without braces ({}). For example, take a look at this slightly modified form of our example:

```
if (hourOfDay < 11)
    System.out.println("Good Morning");
    morningGreetingCount++;
```

Based on the indentation, you might be inclined to think the variable morning GreetingCount is only going to be incremented if hourOfDay is less than 11, but that's not what this code does. It will execute the print statement only if the condition is met, but it will *always* execute the increment operation.

Remember that in Java, unlike some other programming languages, tabs are just whitespace and are not evaluated as part of the execution. When you see a control flow statement in a question, be sure to trace the open and close braces of the block, ignoring any indentation you may come across.

The *else* Statement

Let's expand our example a little. What if we want to display a different message if it is 11 a.m. or later? Can we do it using only the tools we have? Of course we can!

```
if (hourOfDay < 11) {
    System.out.println("Good Morning");
```

```
}
if (hourOfDay >= 11) {
    System.out.println("Good Afternoon");
}
```

This seems a bit redundant, though, since we're performing an evaluation on hourOfDay twice. Luckily, Java offers us a more useful approach in the form of an else statement, as shown in Figure 3.2.

FIGURE 3.2   The structure of an else statement

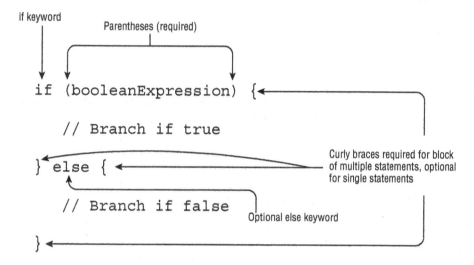

Let's return to this example:

```
if (hourOfDay < 11) {
    System.out.println("Good Morning");
} else System.out.println("Good Afternoon");
```

Now our code is truly branching between one of the two possible options, with the boolean evaluation happening only once. The else operator takes a statement or block of statements, in the same manner as the if statement. Similarly, we can append additional if statements to an else block to arrive at a more refined example:

```
if (hourOfDay < 11) {
    System.out.println("Good Morning");
} else if (hourOfDay < 15) {
    System.out.println("Good Afternoon");
} else {
    System.out.println("Good Evening");
}
```

In this example, the Java process will continue execution until it encounters an `if` statement that evaluates to `true`. If neither of the first two expressions is `true`, it will execute the code of the final `else` block.

Verifying That the *if* Statement Evaluates to a Boolean Expression

Another common way the exam may try to lead you astray is by providing code where the boolean expression inside the `if` statement is not actually a `boolean` expression. For example, take a look at the following lines of code:

```java
int hourOfDay = 1;
if (hourOfDay) {  // DOES NOT COMPILE

   ...

}
```

This statement may be valid in some other programming and scripting languages, but not in Java, where 0 and 1 are not considered `boolean` values.

Shortening Code with Pattern Matching

Pattern matching is a technique of controlling program flow that only executes a section of code that meets certain criteria. In this section, we perform pattern matching with the `if` statement, along with the `instanceof` operator, to improve program control.

 If pattern matching is new to you, be careful not to confuse it with the Java `Pattern` class or regular expressions (*regex*). While pattern matching can include the use of regular expressions for filtering, they are unrelated concepts.

Pattern matching is a useful tool for reducing boilerplate code in your application. *Boilerplate code* is code that tends to be duplicated throughout a section of code over and over again in a similar manner.

To understand why this feature was added, consider the following code that takes a `Number` instance and compares it with the value 5. If you haven't seen `Number` or `Integer`, you just need to know that `Integer` inherits from `Number` for now. You'll see them a lot in this book!

```java
void compareIntegers(Number number) {
   if (number instanceof Integer) {
      Integer data = (Integer)number;
```

```
        System.out.print(data.compareTo(5));
    }
}
```

The cast is needed since the `compareTo()` method is defined on `Integer`, but not on `Number`.

Code that first checks if a variable is of a particular type and then immediately casts it to that type is extremely common in the Java world. It's so common that the authors of Java decided to implement a shorter syntax for it:

```
void compareIntegers(Number number) {
    if (number instanceof Integer data) {
        System.out.print(data.compareTo(5));
    }
}
```

The variable `data` in this example is referred to as the *pattern variable*. Notice that this code also avoids any potential `ClassCastException` because the cast operation is executed only if the `instanceof` operator returns `true`.

Figure 3.3 shows the anatomy of pattern matching using the `instanceof` operator and `if` statements. Adding a variable after the type is what instructs the compiler to treat it as pattern matching. Figure 3.3 also shows an optional conditional clause, which is a useful feature that we will cover in the next section.

FIGURE 3.3   Pattern matching with `if`

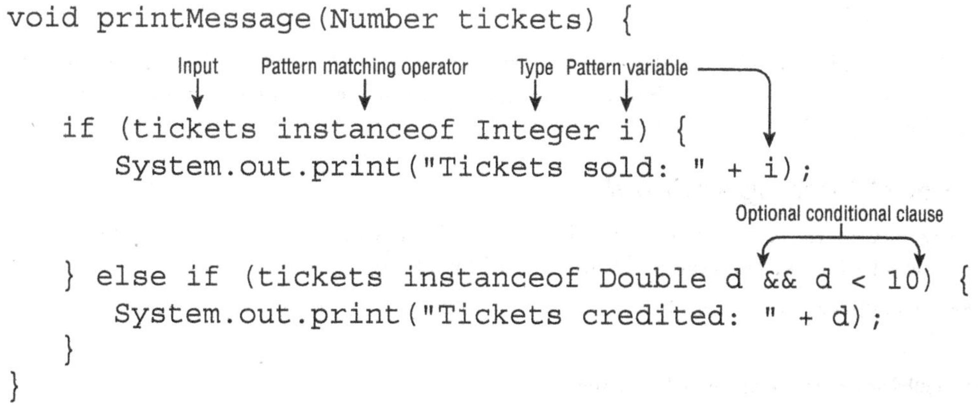

```
void printMessage(Number tickets) {

          Input    Pattern matching operator   Type  Pattern variable

    if (tickets instanceof Integer i) {
        System.out.print("Tickets sold: " + i);

                                          Optional conditional clause

    } else if (tickets instanceof Double d && d < 10) {
        System.out.print("Tickets credited: " + d);
    }
}
```

Reassigning Pattern Variables

While possible, it is a bad practice to reassign a pattern variable since doing so can lead to ambiguity about what is and is not in scope.

```
if (number instanceof Integer data) {
   data = 10;
}
```

The reassignment can be prevented with a final modifier, but it is better not to reassign the variable at all.

```
if (number instanceof final Integer data) {
   data = 10;  // DOES NOT COMPILE
}
```

Pattern Variables and Expressions

Pattern matching supports an optional conditional clause, declared as a boolean expression. This can be used to filter data out, such as in the following example:

```
void printIntegersGreaterThan5(Number number) {
   if (number instanceof Integer data && data.compareTo(5) > 0)
      System.out.print(data);
}
```

We can apply a number of filters, or patterns, so that the if statement is executed only in specific circumstances. Notice that we're using the pattern variable in an expression in the same line in which it is declared.

Pattern Matching with *null*

As saw in Chapter 2, "Operators," the instanceof operator always evaluates null references to false. The same holds for pattern matching.

```
String noObjectHere = null;

if(noObjectHere instanceof String)
   System.out.println("Not printed");

if(noObjectHere instanceof String s)
   System.out.println("Still not printed");

if(noObjectHere instanceof String s && s.length() > -1)
   System.out.println("Nope, not this one either");
```

As shown in the last example, this also helps avoid any potential NullPointerException, as the conditional operator (&&) causes the s.length() call to be skipped.

Supported Types

The type of the pattern variable must be a compatible type, which includes the same type, a subtype, or a supertype of the reference variable. If the reference variable does not refer to a final class or type, then it can also include an unrelated interface for reasons we'll go into more detail about in Chapter 7, "Beyond Classes." Consider the following two examples, in which Integer is a subtype of Number:

```
11: Number bearHeight = Integer.valueOf(123);
12:
13: if (bearHeight instanceof Integer i) {}
14: if (bearHeight instanceof Number n) {}
15: if (bearHeight instanceof String s) {} // DOES NOT COMPILE
16. if (bearHeight instanceof Object o) {}
```

The first example uses a subtype, while the second example uses the same type as the reference variable bearHeight. On line 15, the compiler recognizes that a Number cannot be cast to an unrelated type String and throws an error. Line 16 is permitted but not particularly useful, since every Object except null will return true.

> When pattern matching was first introduced in Java, the type had to be a strict subtype of Number (and not Number itself). For this reason, lines 14 and 16 would not compile. Starting with Java 21, this rule was removed to allow the same or broader types to be used.

Flow Scoping

The compiler applies flow scoping when working with pattern matching. *Flow scoping* means the variable is only in scope when the compiler can definitively determine its type. *Flow scoping is unlike any other type of scoping*, in that it is not strictly hierarchical. It is determined by the compiler based on the branching and flow of the program.

Given this information, can you see why the following does not compile?

```
void printIntegersOrNumbersGreaterThan5(Number number) {
    if (number instanceof Integer data || data.compareTo(5) > 0)
        System.out.print(data);
}
```

The key thing to notice is that we used OR (||) not AND (&&) in the conditional statement. If the input does not inherit Integer, the data variable is undefined. Since the compiler cannot guarantee that data is an instance of Integer, the code does not compile.

What about this example?

```
void printIntegerTwice(Number number) {
   if (number instanceof Integer data)
      System.out.print(data.intValue());
   System.out.print(data.intValue());  // DOES NOT COMPILE
}
```

Since the input might not have inherited Integer, data is no longer in scope after the if statement. Oh, so you might be thinking that the pattern variable is then only in scope inside the if statement block, right? Well, not exactly! Consider the following example that does compile:

```
void printOnlyIntegers(Number number) {
   if (!(number instanceof Integer data))
      return;
   System.out.print(data.intValue());
}
```

It might surprise you to learn this code does compile. Eek! What is going on here? The method returns if the input does not inherit Integer. This means that when the last line of the method is reached, the input must inherit Integer, and therefore data stays in scope even after the if statement ends. Understanding why this example compiles and the one before it does not, is the key to understanding flow scoping.

Flow Scoping and *else* Branches

If the last code sample confuses you, don't worry: you're not alone! Another way to think about it is to rewrite the logic to something equivalent that uses an else statement:

```
void printOnlyIntegers(Number number) {
   if (!(number instanceof Integer data))
      return;
   else
      System.out.print(data.intValue());
}
```

We can now go one step further and reverse the if and else branches by inverting the boolean expression:

```
void printOnlyIntegers(Number number) {
   if (number instanceof Integer data)
      System.out.print(data.intValue());
   else
      return;
}
```

Our new code is equivalent to our original and better demonstrates how the compiler was able to determine that data was in scope only when number is an Integer.

Make sure you understand the way flow scoping works. In particular, it is possible to use a pattern variable outside of the if statement, but only when the compiler can definitively determine its type.

> But wait, there's more pattern matching fun coming! In the next section, we'll use pattern matching with switch statements, and in Chapter 7, we'll apply pattern matching to records and sealed classes.

Building *switch* Statements and Expressions

An if/else statement can get really difficult to read if there are a lot of branches. Take a look at the following:

```
String getAnimalBad(int type) {
    String animal;
    if (type == 0)
        animal = "Lion";
    else if (type == 1)
        animal = "Elephant";
    else if (type == 2 || type == 3)
        animal = "Alligator";
    else if (type == 4)
        animal = "Crane";
    else
        animal = "Unknown";
    return animal;
}
```

Every time we add a new animal, that code gets longer and more difficult to maintain. Luckily, Java includes switch to help simplify this code.

Introducing *switch*

A switch is a complex decision-making structure in which a single value is evaluated and flow is redirected to one or more branches. In Java, there are two flavors: a switch statement and a switch expression. The primary difference between the two (aside from a lot of syntax differences!) is that a `switch` expression must return a value, while a `switch` statement does not.

Let's begin by rewriting our previous method to one that uses a `switch` statement.

```
String getAnimalBetter(int type) {
    String animal;
    switch (type) {
        case 0:
            animal = "Lion";
            break;
        case 1:
            animal = "Elephant";
            break;
        case 2, 3:
            animal = "Alligator";
            break;
        case 4:
            animal = "Crane";
            break;
        default:
            animal = "Unknown";
    }
    return animal;
}
```

That's certainly better than our `if`/`else` version in terms of keeping things organized, but it's still really long. We're assigning `animal` four times, and what's with all the `break` statements? We'll cover all of these details shortly, but for now let's try using a `switch` expression instead.

```
String getAnimalBest(int type) {
    return switch (type) {
        case 0     -> "Lion";
        case 1     -> "Elephant";
        case 2, 3  -> "Alligator";
        case 4     -> "Crane";
        default    -> "Unknown";
    };
}
```

Wow, that is a lot shorter and easier to read! In Java, `switch` expressions were introduced more recently than `switch` statements, resulting in a greater emphasis on reducing boilerplate.

As you might remember from Chapter 1, extra whitespace doesn't matter in Java. That said, whitespace can be used to align text and help improve readability. When writing many of the examples in this chapter, we added extra whitespace to make `switch` statements and expressions easier to read.

Structuring *switch* Statements and Expressions

While `switch` statements and expressions may look different, they share many common rules that we cover in this section. Afterward, we'll cover the specifics of each type.

Defining a *switch*

First off, both types start with a `switch` keyword and a variable wrapped in parentheses.

```
String name = "123";

switch (name) {                        // Switch statement
   case "Sancha":        System.out.print(1);   break;
   case "Jacob", "Jake": System.out.print(2);   break;
   default:              System.out.print(999); break;
}

System.out.println(switch (name) { // Switch expression
   case "Sancha"        -> 1;
   case "Jacob", "Jake" -> 2;
   default              -> 999;
});
```

As you can see, both types of `switch` support zero or more `case` clauses. Each `case` clause includes a set of matching values split up by commas (,). It is then followed by a separator, which can be a colon (:) or the arrow operator (->). Finally, each clause then defines an expression, or code block with braces ({}), for what to execute when there's a match.

Using the Arrow Operator with *switch* Statements

While `switch` statements support both colons and arrow operators, you're likely to see them used with colons more often in practice. This is because the colon syntax has been around a lot longer in Java. If you do use the arrow operator, then you must use it for all clauses. For example, the following `switch` statement does not compile:

```
switch (type) {
   case 0 :  System.out.print("Lion");
   case 1 -> System.out.print("Elephant");
}
```

This would compile if both clauses used the same operator.

Both `switch` types support an optional `default` clause. With `switch` expressions, a `default` clause is often required, as the expression must return a value. More on that shortly.

Without further ado, Figure 3.4 shows the structure of a `switch` statement. While `switch` statements can use the arrow operator, they are more commonly written with colons.

FIGURE 3.4   A `switch` statement

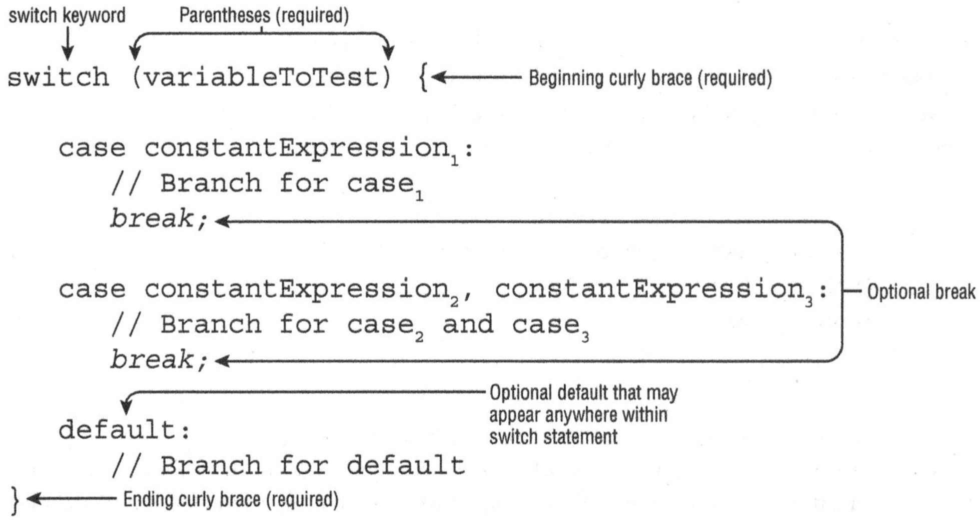

Figure 3.5 shows the structure of a `switch` expression, which returns a value that is assigned to a variable. Compare it with Figure 3.4 and make sure you understand the differences between the two.

Unlike a `switch` statement, a `switch` expression often requires a semicolon (`;`) after it, such as when it is used with the assignment operator (`=`) or a `return` statement. This has more to do with *how* the `switch` expression is used than the `switch` expression itself.

A `switch` expression also requires a semicolon (`;`) after each `case` expression that doesn't use a block. For example, how many semicolons are missing in the following?

```
var result = switch (bear) {
```

```
   case 30 -> "Grizzly"
   default -> "Panda"
}
```

The answer is three. Each `case` or `default` expression requires a semicolon as well as the assignment itself. The following fixes the code:

```
var result = switch (bear) {
   case 30 -> "Grizzly";
   default -> "Panda";
};
```

FIGURE 3.5   A `switch` expression

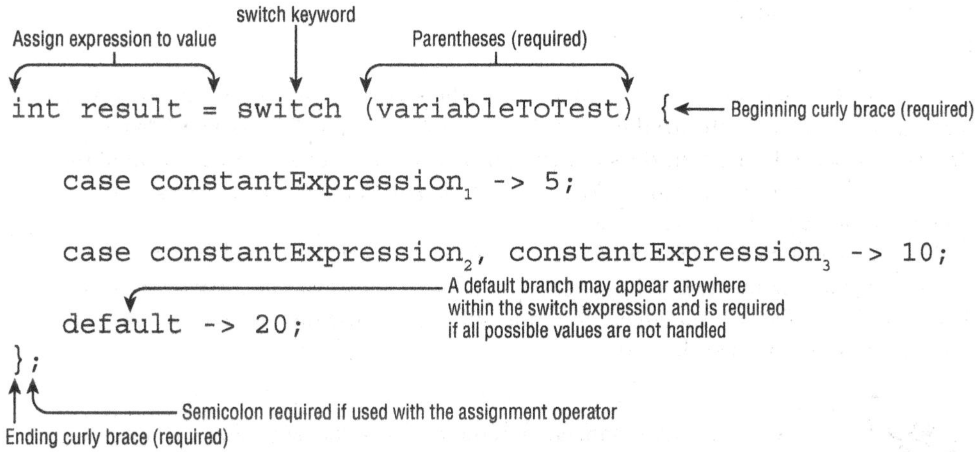

Challenge time! See if you can figure out which of these compiles:

```
int food = 5, month = 4, weather = 2, day = 0, time = 4;

String meal = switch food { // #1
   case 1  -> "Dessert"
   default -> "Porridge"
};

switch (month) // #2
   case 4: System.out.print("January");

switch (weather) { // #3
   case 2: System.out.print("Rainy");
```

```
   case 5: {
      System.out.print("Sunny");
   }
}

switch (day) { // #4
   case 1: 13: System.out.print("January");
   default    System.out.print("July");
}

String description = switch (time) { // #5
   case 10 -> "Morning";
   default -> "Late";
}
```

The first statement does not compile because the switch expression is missing parentheses around the switch variable, as well as semicolons after the case and default clauses. The second statement does not compile because it is missing braces around the switch body. The third statement does compile. Notice that a case clause can use an expression or a code block with braces.

The fourth statement does not compile for two reasons. The case clause should use a comma (,) to separate two values, not a colon (:). It's also missing a colon after the default clause. The last statement does not compile because the assignment operator (=) is missing a semicolon (;) at the end.

A switch statement is not required to contain any case clauses. This is perfectly valid:

```
switch (month) {}
```

Selecting the *switch* Variable

As shown in Figures 3.4 and 3.5, a switch has a target variable that is not evaluated until runtime. The following is a list of all data types supported by switch:

- int and Integer
- byte and Byte
- short and Short
- char and Character
- String
- enum values

- All object types (when used with pattern matching)
- var (if the type resolves to one of the preceding types)

 Notice that boolean, long, float, and double are not supported in switch statements and expressions.

If you've never worked with enums, don't panic! For this chapter, you just need to know that an enumeration, or *enum*, is a type in Java that represents a fixed set of constants, such as the following:

```java
enum Season { SPRING, SUMMER, FALL, WINTER }

enum DayOfWeek {
    SUNDAY, MONDAY, TUESDAY, WEDNESDAY, THURSDAY, FRIDAY, SATURDAY
}
```

If it helps, think of an enum as a class type with predefined object values known at compile time. We cover enums in detail in Chapter 7, including showing how they can define variables, methods, and constructors. For now, you just need to think of them as a list of values.

Starting with Java 21, switch statements and expressions now support pattern matching, which means *any object type* can now be used as a switch variable, provided the pattern matching is used. We'll be covering switch with pattern matching shortly.

Determining Acceptable Case Values

Not just any values can be used in a case clause. First, the values in each case clause must be *compile-time constant values*. This means you can use only literals, enum constants, or final constant variables.

By final constant, we mean that the variable must be marked with the final modifier and initialized with a literal value in the same expression in which it is declared. For example, you can't have a case clause value that requires executing a method at runtime, even if that method always returns the same value.

For these reasons, see if you can figure out why only the first and last case clauses compile:

```java
final int getCookies() { return 4; }
void feedAnimals() {
    final int bananas = 1;
    int apples = 2;
    int numberOfAnimals = 3;
    final int cookies = getCookies();
    switch (numberOfAnimals) {
        case bananas:
        case apples:          // DOES NOT COMPILE
```

```
        case getCookies():  // DOES NOT COMPILE
        case cookies :       // DOES NOT COMPILE
        case 3 * 5 :
   } }
```

The bananas variable is marked final, and its value is known at compile time, so the first case clause is valid. The apples variable in the second case clause is not marked final, so it is not permitted. The next two case clauses, with values getCookies() and cookies, do not compile because methods are not evaluated until runtime, so they cannot be used as the value of a case clause, even if one of the values is stored in a final variable. The last case clause, with value 3 * 5, does compile, as expressions are allowed as case values, provided the value can be resolved at compile time.

Remember, the data type for case clauses must match the data type of the switch variable. See if you can spot why the following does not compile:

```
String cleanFishTank(int dirty) {
    return switch (dirty) {
        case "Very" -> "1 hour";  // DOES NOT COMPILE
        default     -> "45 minute";
    };
}
```

The switch variable is of type int, while the case clause is of type String.

Using Enum Values with *switch*

When the switch variable is an enum type, then the case clauses must be the enum values.

```
enum Season { SPRING, SUMMER, FALL, WINTER }

boolean shouldGetACoat(Season s) {
    return switch (s) {
        case SPRING -> false;
        case Season.SUMMER -> false;
        case FALL -> true;
        case Season.WINTER -> true;
    };
}
```

For an enum value, you can specify just the value, as shown with SPRING and FALL. Starting with Java 21, you can optionally specify the name with the value, such as Season.SPRING and Season.FALL.

Working with *switch* Statements

Taking a look at the earlier getAnimalBetter() method, you might remember there were a lot of break statements at the end of each case. A break statement terminates the switch statement and returns flow control to the enclosing process. Put simply, it ends the switch statement immediately.

While break statements are optional, they tend to be used frequently in switch statements. Without break statements, the code continues to execute the next branch it finds, in order.

What do you think the following prints when printSeasonForMonth(2) is called?

```
void printSeasonForMonth(int month) {
    switch (month) {
        case 1, 2, 3:      System.out.print("Winter-");
        case 4, 5, 6:      System.out.print("Spring-");
        default:           System.out.print("Unknown-");
        case 7, 8, 9:      System.out.print("Summer-");
        case 10, 11, 12: System.out.print("Fall-");
    } }
```

It prints everything!

```
Winter-Spring-Unknown-Summer-Fall-
```

It matches the first case clause and executes all of the branches in the order they are found, including the default clause. Remember when working with switch statements, the *order of the branches is important*! We can fix this to just print Winter- with the same input, by adding break statements.

```
void printSeasonForMonth(int month) {
    switch (month) {
        case 1, 2, 3:      System.out.print("Winter-");  break;
        case 4, 5, 6:      System.out.print("Spring-");  break;
        default:           System.out.print("Unknown-"); break;
        case 7, 8, 9:      System.out.print("Summer-");  break;
        case 10, 11, 12: System.out.print("Fall-");      break;
    } }
```

The last case clause does not actually require a break, as the switch statement is over, but we add it for consistency.

The exam creators are fond of switch examples that are missing break statements! When you spot a switch statement on the exam, always consider whether multiple branches may be visited in a single execution.

Contrast this with a switch expression that matches only a single branch at runtime and therefore does not require break statements.

```
void printSeasonForMonth(int month) {
    String value = switch (month) {
        case 1, 2, 3    -> "Winter-";
        case 4, 5, 6    -> "Spring-";
        default         -> "Unknown-";
        case 7, 8, 9    -> "Summer-";
        case 10, 11, 12 -> "Fall-";
    };
    System.out.print(value);
}
```

When Is a *switch* Expression Not a *switch* Expression?

As stated earlier, a switch expression always returns a value, regardless of the syntax used. What about the following?

```
void printWeather(int rain) {
    switch (rain) {
        case 0 -> System.out.print("Dry");
        case 1 -> System.out.print("Wet");
        case 2 -> System.out.print("Storm");
    }
}
```

Since the return type of System.out.print() is void, this statement does not return a value. This is actually a switch statement that uses the arrow operator syntax. Since it doesn't return a value, it is not a switch expression. It's a little confusing, we know!

Working with *switch* Expressions

Congratulations, you're now an expert on switch statements! Unfortunately, switch expressions have a lot more features and rules we still need to cover. We cover them (one at a time) in this section.

Returning Consistent Data Types

Just as case values have to use a consistent data type, the switch expression must return a consistent value. Simply put, when assigning a value as the result of a switch expression, a branch can't return a value with an unrelated type.

```java
int measurement = 10;
int size = switch (measurement) {
   case 5  -> Integer.valueOf(1);
   case 10 -> (short)2;
   default -> 3;
   case 20 -> "4";    // DOES NOT COMPILE
   case 40 -> 5L;     // DOES NOT COMPILE
   case 50 -> null;   // DOES NOT COMPILE
};
```

The switch expression is being assigned to an int variable, so all of the values must be consistent with int. The first case clause compiles without issue, as the Integer value is unboxed to int. We'll cover autoboxing and unboxing in Chapter 5, "Methods." The second and third case clauses are fine, as they can be stored as an int. The last three case expressions do not compile because each returns a type that is incompatible with int.

Exhausting the *switch* Branches

Unlike a switch statement, a switch expression must return a value. Why? Let's try an illustrative example.

```java
void identifyType(String type) {
   Integer reptile = switch (type) { // DOES NOT COMPILE
      case "Snake"  -> 1;
      case "Turtle" -> 2;
   };
}
```

What is the value of reptile if type is not equal to Snake or Turtle? Does it throw an exception? Return null or -1? The answer is "None of the above." Java decided this behavior would be unsupported and triggers a compiler error if the switch expression is not exhaustive.

A switch is said to be *exhaustive* if it covers all possible values. All switch expressions must be exhaustive, which means they must handle all possible values. As we'll see shortly, there are times a switch statement must be exhaustive too. There are three ways to write an exhaustive switch:

1. Add a default clause.
2. If the switch takes an enum, add a case clause for every possible enum value.
3. Cover all possible types of the switch variable with pattern matching.

In practice, the first solution is the one most often used. You can try writing `case` clauses for all possible `int` values, but we promise it doesn't work! Even smaller types like `byte` are not permitted by the compiler, despite there being only 256 possible values.

The second solution applies only to `switch` expressions that take an enum. For example, consider the following:

```
enum Season { SPRING, SUMMER, FALL, WINTER }

String getWeatherMissingOne(Season value) {
    return switch (value) {  // DOES NOT COMPILE
        case WINTER -> "Cold";
        case SPRING -> "Rainy";
        case SUMMER -> "Hot";
    };
}
```

This code does not compile because FALL is not covered. The fix is either to add a `case` for FALL or add a `default` clause (or both).

```
String getWeatherCoveredAll(Season value) {
    return switch (value) {
        case WINTER -> "Cold";
        case SPRING -> "Rainy";
        case SUMMER -> "Hot";
        case FALL   -> "Warm";
        default     -> throw new RuntimeException("Unsupported Season");
    };
}
```

Since all possible values of `Season` are covered, the `default` branch is optional.

 When writing `switch` expressions, it may be a good idea to add a default branch, even if you cover all possible values. This means that if someone modifies the enum with a new value, your code will still compile.

The third solution for writing an exhaustive `switch` requires some explanation. We'll cover this in an upcoming section, as it only applies to pattern matching.

Using the *yield* Statement

Up until now, the `switch` expression examples we've shown use `case` expressions. Time to expand your knowledge to `case` blocks! A `switch` expression supports both `case` expressions and `case` blocks, the latter of which is denoted with braces ({}). Figure 3.6 shows examples of both.

FIGURE 3.6   A `switch` expression with a `case` block and `yield` statement

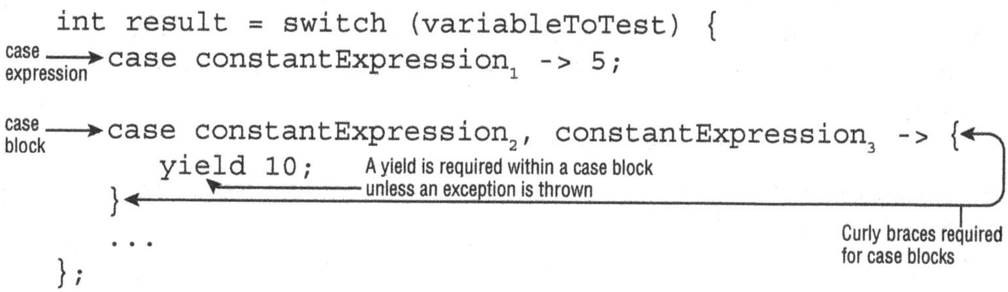

```
    int result = switch (variableToTest) {
case ──▶case constantExpression₁ -> 5;
expression

case ──▶case constantExpression₂, constantExpression₃ -> {◀─
block        yield 10;    A yield is required within a case block
    }◀──────────────────── unless an exception is thrown

    ...                                     Curly braces required
                                            for case blocks
    };
```

In the previous section, we said that a `switch` expression must return a value. But how do you return a value from a `case` block? You could use a `return` statement, but that ends the method, not just the `switch` expression!

Enter the `yield` statement, shown in Figure 3.6. It allows the `case` clause to return a value. For example, the following uses a mix of `case` expressions and `case` blocks:

```
int fish = 5;
int length = 12;
var name = switch (fish) {
   case 1 -> "Goldfish";
   case 2 -> { yield "Trout"; }
   case 3 -> {
      if (length > 10) yield "Blobfish";
      else yield "Green";
   }
   case 4 -> {
      throw new RuntimeException("Unsupported value");
   }
   default -> "Swordfish";
};
```

Think of the `yield` keyword as a `return` statement within a `switch` expression. Because a `switch` expression must return a value, a `yield` is often required within a `case` block. The one "exception" to this rule is if the code throws an exception, as shown in the previous example.

Watch Semicolons in *switch* Expressions

When writing a case expression, a semicolon is required, but when writing a case block, it is prohibited.

```
int fish = 1;
var name = switch (fish) {
   case 1  -> "Goldfish"         // DOES NOT COMPILE (missing semicolon)
   case 2  -> { yield "Trout"; }; // DOES NOT COMPILE (extra semicolon)
   default -> "Shark";
} // DOES NOT COMPILE (missing semicolon)
```

A bit confusing, right? It's just one of those things you have to train yourself to spot on the exam.

Using Pattern Matching with *switch*

One of the biggest new features of Java 21 is that pattern matching has been extended to switch. There's a number of rules to cover, so let's start with the basics. To use pattern matching with a switch, first start with an object reference variable. *Any object reference type is permitted*, provided the switch makes use of pattern matching. Next, in each case clause, define a type and pattern matching variable.

```
void printDetails(Number height) {
   String message = switch (height) {
      case Integer i -> "Rounded: " + i;
      case Double d  -> "Precise: " + d;
      case Number n  -> "Unknown: " + n;
   };
   System.out.print(message);
}
```

In this example, we output different values depending on the type of the switch variable. The same rules about local variables and flow scoping that we learned about earlier with pattern matching apply. For instance, the pattern matching variable exists only within the case branch for which it is defined. This allows us to reuse the same name for two case branches.

Figure 3.7 shows the structure of pattern matching with a switch expression. It can also be used with a switch statement that does not return a value.

Easy so far, right? From Figure 3.7, you might have noticed it includes a *guard clause*, which is an optional conditional clause that can be added to a case branch. This is similar to what we saw in Figure 3.3 with a pattern matching if statement. The only difference is that with switch, the when keyword is required between the variable and the expression.

Let's try an example. Suppose our zoo has different trainers that can handle different size animals depending on the measurement type.

```
String getTrainer(Number height) {
   return switch (height) {
```

```
      case Integer i when i > 10 -> "Joseph";
      case Integer i -> "Daniel";
      case Double num when num <= 15.5 -> "Peter";
      case Double num -> "Kelly";
      case Number num -> "Ralph";
   };
}
```

In this example, Joseph works with the animal if the height is an Integer greater than 10. Daniel is then selected for all other Integer values. Likewise, Peter handles all Double measurements less than or equal to 15.5, while Kelly handles the remaining Double values. Finally, Ralph handles all animals that don't meet one of the previous requirements, such as if Short was used.

FIGURE 3.7   Pattern matching with switch

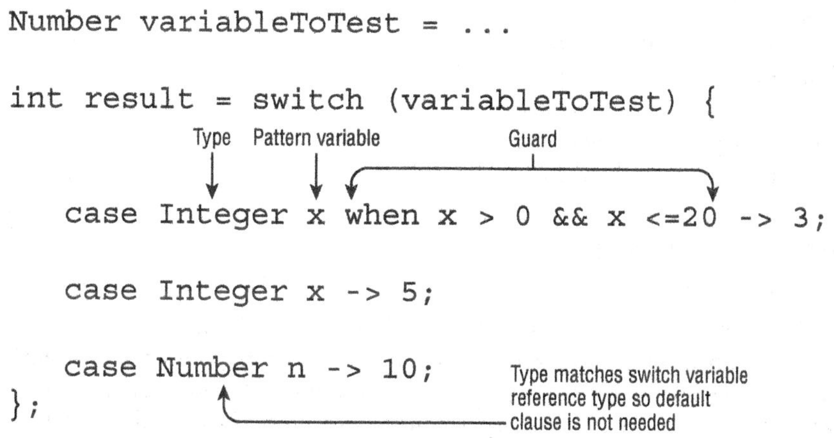

```
Number variableToTest = ...

int result = switch (variableToTest) {
                  Type  Pattern variable        Guard

      case Integer x when x > 0 && x <=20 -> 3;

      case Integer x -> 5;

      case Number n -> 10;        Type matches switch variable
   };                             reference type so default
                                  clause is not needed
```

One advantage of guards is that now switch can do something it's never done before: *it can handle ranges.* Previously, if you wanted to support a range of values with a switch, you had to list all the possible case values. With the when clause, you can support range matches. Quite convenient!

Applying Acceptable Types

One of the simplest rules when working with switch and pattern matching is that the type can't be unrelated. It must be the same type as the switch variable or a subtype.

```
Number fish = 10;
String name = switch (fish) {
   case Integer freshWater -> "Bass";
```

```
    case Number saltWater   -> "ClownFish";
    case String s           -> "Shark";  // DOES NOT COMPILE
};
```

The compiler is smart enough to know a Number can't be cast as a String, resulting in this code not compiling. This wasn't allowed in the previous pattern matching section using instanceof either!

Ordering *switch* Branches

As we mentioned earlier in the chapter, the order of case and default clauses for switch statement matters, because more than one branch might be reached during execution. For switch expressions that don't use pattern matching, ordering isn't important, as only one branch can be reached.

Well, when working with pattern matching, the order matters regardless of the type of switch! For example, consider this new version of printDetails() in which the order has been changed:

```
void printDetails(Number height) {
    String message = switch (height) {
        case Number n  -> "Unknown: " + n;
        case Integer i -> "Rounded: " + i;
        case Double d  -> "Precise: " + d;
    };
    System.out.print(message);
}
```

The code no longer compiles as the second and third case clauses are considered *dominated* by the preceding case Number statement. To put it another way, it is impossible for any process to reach these two case clauses. This is also referred to as *unreachable code*, which we cover more later in this chapter. In most cases, when the compiler detects unreachable code, it results in a compiler error.

Ordering branches is also important if a when clause is used. For example, what if we reordered the first two branches of our getTrainer() method?

```
String getTrainer(Number animal) {
    return switch (animal) {
        case Integer i             -> "Daniel";
        case Integer i when i > 10 -> "Joseph"; // DOES NOT COMPILE

        ...
    };
}
```

In the event that animal is an Integer, Daniel will always be selected. Poor Joseph! Likewise, the compiler does not allow this code to compile.

Exhaustive *switch* Statements

Up until now, only `switch` expressions were required to be exhaustive. When using pattern matching, `switch` statements must be exhaustive too. As before, you can address this with a `default` clause, as this will handle all values that don't match a `case` clause. There is another option, though, that applies only when working with pattern matching.

You may have noticed that we didn't use any `default` clauses in any of our previous pattern matching examples. That's because we defined our last `case` clause with a pattern matching variable type that is *the same as the switch variable reference type.*

That might sound complicated, but it's simpler than it seems. For example, if the variable reference type of the `switch` expression is type `Integer` or `String`, then you just need to make sure the last `case` clause is of type `Integer` or `String`, respectively.

Let's try an illustrative example. What do you expect the output of the following to be?

```
Number zooPatrons = Integer.valueOf(1_000);
switch (zooPatrons) {
    case Integer count -> System.out.print("Welcome: " + count);
}
```

It doesn't compile! Despite the `zooPatrons` object actually being of type `Integer`, the `switch` reference variable is of type `Number`. There are a few ways that we can fix this. First, we can change the reference type of `zooPatrons` to be `Integer`, which results in all possible values of `Integer` being covered.

```
Integer zooPatrons = Integer.valueOf(1_000);
switch (zooPatrons) {
    case Integer count -> System.out.print("Welcome: " + count);
}
```

Alternatively, we can also add a `case` clause at the end for `Number`.

```
Number zooPatrons = Integer.valueOf(1_000);
switch (zooPatrons) {
    case Integer count -> System.out.print("Welcome: " + count);
    case Number count  -> System.out.print("Too many people at the zoo!");
}
```

There is a third option, too! Don't forget, we can always add a `default` clause to a `switch` that covers everything.

That brings us to an interesting question: what if you combine different solutions?

```
Number zooPatrons = Integer.valueOf(1_000);
switch (zooPatrons) {
    case Integer count -> System.out.print("Welcome: " + count);
    case Number count  -> System.out.print("Too many people at the zoo!");
    default            -> System.out.print("The zoo is closed");
}
```

In this case, the code does not compile, regardless of how you order the branches. The compiler is smart enough to realize the last two statements are redundant, as one always dominates the other.

Handling a *null* Case

What if the switch variable is null at runtime? We can try using a default clause but you might be surprised at the result.

```
String fish = null;
System.out.print(switch (fish) {
    case "ClownFish" -> "Hello!";
    case "BlueTang"  -> "Hello again!";
    default          -> "Goodbye";
});
```

This code compiles (it technically is exhaustive) but throws a NullPointerException! One "quick fix" would be to add an if/else statement around the switch, but that would add a lot of extra boilerplate code.

```
String fish = null;
if (fish == null) {
    System.out.print("What type of fish are you?");
} else {
    System.out.print(switch (fish) {
        case "ClownFish" -> "Hello!";
        case "BlueTang"  -> "Hello again!";
        default          -> "Goodbye";
    });
}
```

New to Java 21, switch now supports case null clause when working with object types, allowing us to rewrite our previous example as the following:

```
String fish = null;
System.out.print(switch (fish) {
    case "ClownFish" -> "Hello!";
    case "BlueTang"  -> "Hello again!";
    case null        -> "What type of fish are you?";
    default          -> "Goodbye";
});
```

That's a lot less boilerplate code, now that we don't have to handle null separately.

Case *null* Is Considered Pattern Matching

Any guess as to why the following code snippet does not compile?

```
String fish = null;
switch (fish) {  // DOES NOT COMPILE
   case "ClownFish": System.out.print("Hello!");
   case "BlueTang":  System.out.print("Hello again!");
   case null:        System.out.print("What type of fish are you?");
}
```

Anytime case null is used within a switch, then the switch statement is considered to use pattern matching. As you should remember from the previous section, that means the switch statement *must be exhaustive*. Adding a default branch allows the code to compile.

Since using case null implies pattern matching, the ordering of branches matters anytime case null is used. While case null can appear almost anywhere in switch, it cannot be used after a default statement. For instance, only the first of the following two switch statements compile.

```
System.out.print(switch (fish) {
   case String s when "ClownFish".equals(s) -> "Hello!";
   case null -> "No good";
   case String s when "BlueTang".equals(s) -> "Hello again!";
   default -> "Goodbye";
});
System.out.print(switch (fish) {
   case String s when "ClownFish".equals(s) -> "Hello!";
   case String s when "BlueTang".equals(s) -> "Hello again!";
   default -> "Goodbye";
   case null -> "No good";  // DOES NOT COMPILE
});
```

In the second example, the default clause dominates the case null clause. For the exam, make sure you can identify where default and case null can be used within a switch.

Writing *while* Loops

A common practice when writing software is doing the same task some number of times. You could use the decision structures we have presented so far to accomplish this, but that's going to be a pretty long chain of `if` or `else` statements, especially if you have to execute the same thing 100 times or more.

Enter loops! A *loop* is a repetitive control structure that can execute a statement or block of code multiple times in succession. By using variables that can be assigned new values, each repetition of the statement may be different. The following loop executes exactly 10 times:

```java
int counter = 0;
while (counter < 10) {
    double price = counter * 10;
    System.out.println(price);
    counter++;
}
```

If you don't follow this code, don't panic—we cover it shortly. In this section, we're going to discuss the `while` loop and its two forms. In the next section, we move on to `for` loops, which have their roots in `while` loops.

The *while* Statement

The simplest repetitive control structure in Java is the `while` statement, described in Figure 3.8. Like all repetition control structures, it has a *termination condition*, implemented as a `boolean` expression. A loop will continue as long as this expression evaluates to `true`.

FIGURE 3.8   The structure of a `while` statement

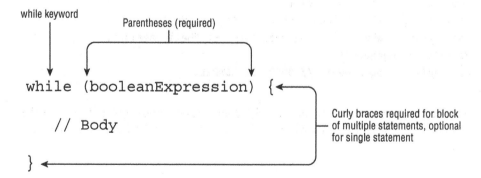

As shown in Figure 3.8, a `while` loop is similar to an `if` statement in that it is composed of a `boolean` expression and a statement, or a block of statements. During execution, the `boolean` expression is evaluated before each iteration of the loop and exits if the evaluation returns `false`.

Let's see how a loop can be used to model a mouse eating a meal:

```
int roomInBelly = 5;
void eatCheese(int bitesOfCheese) {
    while (bitesOfCheese > 0 && roomInBelly > 0) {
        bitesOfCheese--;
        roomInBelly--;
    }
    System.out.println(bitesOfCheese+" pieces of cheese left");
}
```

This method takes an amount of food—in this case, cheese—and continues until the mouse has no room in its belly or there is no food left to eat. With each iteration of the loop, the mouse "eats" one bite of food and loses one spot in its belly. By using a compound `boolean` statement, you ensure that the `while` loop can end for either of the conditions.

One thing to remember is that a `while` loop may terminate after its first evaluation of the `boolean` expression. For example, how many times is `Not full!` printed in the following example?

```
int full = 5;
while (full < 5) {
    System.out.println("Not full!");
    full++;
}
```

The answer? Zero! On the first iteration of the loop, the condition is reached, and the loop exits. This is why `while` loops are often used in places where you expect zero or more executions of the loop. Simply put, the body of the loop may not execute at all.

The *do/while* Statement

The second form a `while` loop can take is called a *do/while* loop, which, like a `while` loop, is a repetition control structure with a termination condition and statement, or a block of statements, as shown in Figure 3.9.

FIGURE 3.9   The structure of a do/while statement

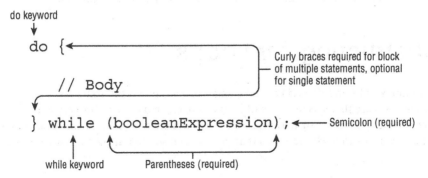

Unlike a `while` loop, though, a do/while loop guarantees that the statement or block will be executed *at least once*. For example, what is the output of the following statements?

```java
int lizard = 0;
do {
   lizard++;
} while (false);
System.out.println(lizard);
```

Java will execute the statement block first and then check the loop condition. Even though the loop exits right away, the statement block is still executed once, and the program prints 1.

Infinite Loops

The single most important thing you should be aware of when you are using any repetition control structures is to make sure they always terminate! Failure to terminate a loop can lead to numerous problems in practice, including overflow exceptions, memory leaks, slow performance, and even bad data. Let's take a look at an example:

```java
int pen = 2;
int pigs = 5;
while (pen < 10)
   pigs++;
```

You may notice one glaring problem with this statement: it will never end. The variable pen is never modified, so the expression (`pen < 10`) will always evaluate to `true`. The result is that the loop will never end, creating what is commonly referred to as an infinite loop. An *infinite loop* is a loop whose termination condition is never reached during runtime.

Anytime you write a loop, you should examine it to determine whether the termination condition is always eventually met under some condition. For example, a loop in which no variables are changing between two executions suggests that the termination condition may not be met. The loop variables should always be moving in a particular direction.

In other words, make sure the loop condition, or the variables the condition is dependent on, are changing between executions. Then, ensure that the termination condition will be eventually reached in all circumstances. As you learn in the last section of this chapter, a loop may also exit under other conditions, such as a `break` or `return` statement.

Constructing *for* Loops

Even though `while` and do/while statements are quite powerful, some tasks are so common in writing software that special types of loops were created—for example, iterating over a statement exactly 10 times or iterating over a list of names. You could easily accomplish these tasks with various `while` loops that you've seen so far, but they usually require a lot of boilerplate code. Wouldn't it be great if there was a looping structure that could do the same thing in a single line of code?

With that, we present the most convenient repetition control structure, for loops. There are two types of for loops, although both use the same for keyword. The first is referred to as the *basic* for loop, and the second is often called the *enhanced* for loop. For clarity, we refer to them as the for loop and the for-each loop, respectively, throughout the book.

The *for* Loop

A basic *for* loop has the same termination condition expression as the while loops, as well as two new sections: an *initialization block* and an *update* statement. Figure 3.10 shows how these components are laid out.

FIGURE 3.10   The structure of a basic for loop

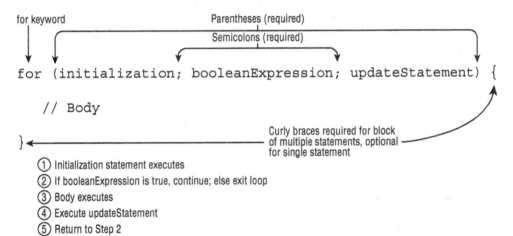

Although Figure 3.10 might seem a little confusing and almost arbitrary at first, the organization of the components and flow allow us to create extremely powerful statements in a single line that otherwise would take multiple lines with a while loop. Each of the three sections is separated by a semicolon. In addition, the initialization and update sections may contain multiple statements, separated by commas.

Variables declared in the initialization block of a for loop have limited scope and are accessible only within the for loop. Be wary of any exam questions in which a variable is declared within the initialization block of a for loop and then read outside the loop. For example, this code does not compile because the loop variable i is referenced outside the loop:

```
for (int i = 0; i < 10; i++)
    System.out.println("Value is: "+i);
System.out.println(i);  // DOES NOT COMPILE
```

Alternatively, variables declared before the `for` loop and assigned a value in the initialization block may be used outside the `for` loop because their scope precedes the creation of the `for` loop.

```
int i;
for (i = 0; i < 10; i++)
   System.out.println("Value is: "+i);
System.out.println(i);
```

Let's take a look at an example that prints the first five numbers, starting with zero:

```
for (int i = 0; i < 5; i++) {
   System.out.print(i + " ");
}
```

The local variable `i` is initialized first to `0`. The variable `i` is only in scope for the duration of the loop and is not available outside the loop once the loop has completed. Like a `while` loop, the `boolean` condition is evaluated on every iteration of the loop *before* the loop executes. Since it returns `true`, the loop executes and outputs `0` followed by a space. Next, the loop executes the update section, which in this case increases the value of `i` to `1`. The loop then evaluates the `boolean` expression a second time, and the process repeats multiple times, printing the following:

```
0 1 2 3 4
```

On the fifth iteration of the loop, the value of `i` reaches 4 and is incremented by 1 to reach 5. On the sixth iteration of the loop, the `boolean` expression is evaluated, and since (`5 < 5`) returns `false`, the loop terminates without executing the statement loop body.

 Real World Scenario

Why *i* in *for* Loops?

You may notice it is common practice to name a `for` loop variable `i`. Long before Java existed, programmers started using `i` as short for increment variable, and the practice exists today, even though many of those programming languages no longer do! For double or triple loops, where `i` is already used, the next letters in the alphabet, `j` and `k`, are often used.

Printing Elements in Reverse

Let's say you wanted to print the same first five numbers from zero as we did in the previous section, but this time in reverse order. The goal then is to print 4 3 2 1 0.

How would you do that? An initial implementation might look like the following:

```
for (var counter = 5; counter > 0; counter--) {
    System.out.print(counter + " ");
}
```

While this snippet does output five distinct values, and it resembles our first `for` loop example, it does not output the same five values. Instead, this is the output:

```
5 4 3 2 1
```

Wait, that's not what we wanted! We wanted 4 3 2 1 0. It starts with 5, because that is the first value assigned to it. Let's fix that by starting with 4 instead:

```
for (var counter = 4; counter > 0; counter--) {
    System.out.print(counter + " ");
}
```

What does this print now? It prints the following:

```
4 3 2 1
```

So close! The problem is that it ends with 1, not 0, because we told it to exit as soon as the value was not strictly greater than 0. If we want to print the same 0 through 4 as our first example, we need to update the termination condition, like this:

```
for (var counter = 4; counter >= 0; counter--) {
    System.out.print(counter + " ");
}
```

Finally! We have code that now prints 4 3 2 1 0 and matches the reverse of our `for` loop example in the previous section. We could have instead used `counter > -1` as the loop termination condition in this example, although `counter >= 0` tends to be more readable.

For the exam, you are going to have to know how to read forward and backward `for` loops. When you see a `for` loop on the exam, pay close attention to the loop variable and operations if the decrement operator, `--`, is used. While incrementing from 0 in a `for` loop is often straightforward, decrementing tends to be less intuitive. In fact, if you do see a `for` loop with a decrement operator on the exam, you should assume they are trying to test your knowledge of loop operations.

Working with *for* Loops

Although most `for` loops you are likely to encounter in your professional development experience will be well defined and similar to the previous examples, there are a number of variations and edge cases you could see on the exam. You should familiarize yourself with the following five examples; variations of these are likely to be seen on the exam.

1. Creating an Infinite Loop

```
for ( ; ; )
   System.out.println("Hello World");
```

Although this `for` loop may look like it does not compile, it will in fact compile and run without issue. It is actually an infinite loop that will print the same statement repeatedly. This example reinforces the fact that the components of the `for` loop are each optional. Note that the semicolons separating the three sections are required, as `for()` without any semicolons will not compile.

2. Adding Multiple Terms to the *for* Statement

```
int x = 0;
for (long y = 0, z = 4; x < 5 && y < 10; x++, y++) {
   System.out.print(y + " "); }
System.out.print(x + " ");
```

This code demonstrates three variations of the `for` loop you may not have seen. First, you can declare a variable, such as x in this example, before the loop begins and use it after it completes. Second, your initialization block, `boolean` expression, and update statements can include extra variables that may or may not reference each other. For example, z is defined in the initialization block and is never used. Finally, the update statement can modify multiple variables. This code will print the following when executed:

```
0 1 2 3 4 5
```

3. Redeclaring a Variable in the Initialization Block

```
int x = 0;
for (int x = 4; x < 5; x++)    // DOES NOT COMPILE
   System.out.print(x + " ");
```

This example looks similar to the previous one, but it does not compile because of the initialization block. The difference is that the declaration of x is repeated in the initialization block after already being declared before the loop, resulting in the compiler stopping because of a duplicate variable declaration. We can fix this loop by removing the declaration of x from the `for` loop as follows:

```
int x = 0;
for ( ; x < 5; x++)
   System.out.print(x + " ");
```

4. Using Incompatible Data Types in the Initialization Block

```
int x = 0;
for (long y = 0, int z = 4; x < 5; x++)  // DOES NOT COMPILE
   System.out.print(y + " ");
```

Like the third example, this code will not compile, although this time for a different reason. The variables in the initialization block must all be of the same type. In the multiple-terms example, y and z were both long, so the code compiled without issue; but in this example, they have different types, so the code will not compile.

5. Using Loop Variables Outside the Loop

```java
for (long y = 0, x = 4; x < 5 && y < 10; x++, y++)
   System.out.print(y + " ");
System.out.print(x);  // DOES NOT COMPILE
```

We covered this already at the start of this section, but it is so important for passing the exam that we discuss it again here. If you notice, x is defined in the initialization block of the loop and then used after the loop terminates. Since x was scoped only for the loop, using it outside the loop will cause a compiler error.

Modifying Loop Variables

As a general rule, it is considered a poor coding practice to modify loop variables as it can lead to an unexpected result, such as in the following examples:

```java
for (int i = 0; i < 10; i++)  // Infinite Loop
   i = 0;

for (int j = 1; j < 10; j++)  // Iterates 5 times
   j++;
```

It also tends to make code difficult for other people to follow.

The for-each Loop

The *for-each* loop is a specialized structure designed to iterate over arrays and various Collections Framework classes, as presented in Figure 3.11.

FIGURE 3.11 The structure of an enhanced for-each loop

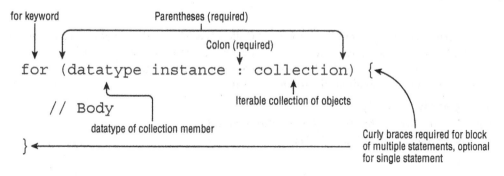

The for-each loop declaration is composed of an initialization section and an object to be iterated over. The right side of the for-each loop must be one of the following:

- A built-in Java array
- An object whose type implements `java.lang.Iterable`

We cover what *implements* means in Chapter 7, but for now you just need to know that the right side must be an array or collection of items, such as a `List` or a `Set`. For the exam, you should know that this does not include all of the Collections Framework classes or interfaces, but only those that implement or extend that `Collection` interface. For example, `Map` is not supported in a for-each loop, although `Map` does include methods that return `Collection` instances.

The left side of the for-each loop must include a declaration for an instance of a variable whose type is compatible with the type of the array or collection on the right side of the statement. On each iteration of the loop, the named variable on the left side of the statement is assigned a new value from the array or collection on the right side of the statement.

Compare these two methods that both print the values of an array, one using a traditional `for` loop and the other using a for-each loop:

```java
void printNames(String[] names) {
    for (int counter = 0; counter < names.length; counter++)
        System.out.println(names[counter]);
}


void printNames(String[] names) {
    for (var name : names)
        System.out.println(name);
}
```

The for-each loop is a lot shorter, isn't it? We no longer have a `counter` loop variable that we need to create, increment, and monitor. Like using a `for` loop in place of a `while` loop, for-each loops are meant to reduce boilerplate code, making code easier to read/write, and freeing you to focus on the parts of your code that really matter.

We can also use a for-each loop on a `List`, since it implements `Iterable`.

```java
void printNames(List<String> names) {
    for (var name : names)
        System.out.println(name);
}
```

We cover generics in detail in Chapter 9, "Collections and Generics." For this chapter, you just need to know that on each iteration, a for-each loop assigns a variable with the same type as the generic argument. In this case, `name` is of type `String`.

So far, so good. What about the following examples?

```java
String birds = "Jay";
for (String bird : birds) // DOES NOT COMPILE
    System.out.print(bird + " ");
```

```java
String[] sloths = new String[3];
for (int sloth : sloths)    // DOES NOT COMPILE
    System.out.print(sloth + " ");
```

The first for-each loop does not compile because the `String birds` cannot be used on the right side of the statement. While a `String` may represent a list of characters, it has to actually be an array or implement `Iterable`. The second example does not compile because the loop variable type on the left side of the statement is `int` and doesn't match the expected type of `String`.

Controlling Flow with Branching

The final types of control flow structures we cover in this chapter are branching statements. Up to now, we have been dealing with single loops that ended only when their `boolean` expression evaluated to `false`. We now show you other ways loops could end, or branch, and you see that the path taken during runtime may not be as straightforward as in the previous examples.

Nested Loops

Before we move into branching statements, we need to introduce the concept of nested loops. A *nested loop* is a loop that contains another loop, including `while`, `do/while`, `for`, and for-each loops. For example, consider the following code that iterates over a two-dimensional array, which is an array that contains other arrays as its members. We cover arrays in detail in Chapter 4, "Core APIs," but for now, assume the following is how you would declare an array of arrays:

```java
int[][] myComplexArray = {{5,2,1,3}, {3,9,8,9}, {5,7,12,7}};
```

```java
for (int[] mySimpleArray : myComplexArray) {
    for (int i = 0; i < mySimpleArray.length; i++) {
        System.out.print(mySimpleArray[i]+"\t");
    }
    System.out.println();
}
```

Notice that we intentionally mix a `for` loop and a for-each loop in this example. The outer loop will execute a total of three times. Each time the outer loop executes, the inner loop is executed four times. When we execute this code, we see the following output:

```
5       2       1       3
3       9       8       9
5       7       12      7
```

Nested loops can include `while` and `do/while`, as shown in this example. See whether you can determine what this code will output:

```
int hungryHippopotamus = 8;
while (hungryHippopotamus > 0) {
   do {
      hungryHippopotamus -= 2;
   } while (hungryHippopotamus>5);
   hungryHippopotamus--;
   System.out.print(hungryHippopotamus+", ");
}
```

The first time this loop executes, the inner loop repeats until the value of `hungry Hippopotamus` is 4. The value will then be decremented to 3, and that will be the output at the end of the first iteration of the outer loop.

On the second iteration of the outer loop, the inner `do/while` will be executed once, even though `hungryHippopotamus` is already not greater than 5. As you may recall, `do/while` statements always execute the body at least once. This will reduce the value to 1, which will be further lowered by the decrement operator in the outer loop to 0. Once the value reaches 0, the outer loop will terminate. The result is that the code will output the following:

```
3, 0,
```

The examples in the rest of this section include many nested loops. You will also encounter nested loops on the exam, so the more practice you have with them, the more prepared you will be.

Adding Optional Labels

One thing we intentionally skipped when we presented `if` statements, `switch` statements, and loops is that they can all have optional labels. A *label* is an optional pointer to the head of a statement that allows the application flow to jump to it or break from it. It is a single identifier that is followed by a colon (`:`). For example, we can add optional labels to one of the previous examples:

```
int[][] myComplexArray = {{5,2,1,3}, {3,9,8,9}, {5,7,12,7}};

OUTER_LOOP: for (int[] mySimpleArray : myComplexArray) {
   INNER_LOOP: for (int i = 0; i < mySimpleArray.length; i++) {
      System.out.print(mySimpleArray[i]+"\t");
   }
   System.out.println();
}
```

Labels follow the same rules for formatting as identifiers. For readability, we show them in *snake_case*, with uppercase letters and underscores between words. When dealing with only one loop, labels do not add any value, but as you learn in the next section, they are extremely useful in nested structures.

While this topic is not on the exam, it is possible to add optional labels to control and block statements. For example, the following is permitted by the compiler, albeit extremely uncommon:

```
int frog = 15;
BAD_IDEA: if (frog > 10)
EVEN_WORSE_IDEA: {
    frog++;
}
```

The *break* Statement

As you saw when working with switch statements, a *break* statement transfers the flow of control out to the enclosing statement. The same holds true for a break statement that appears inside of a while, do/while, or for loop, as it will end the loop early, as shown in Figure 3.12.

FIGURE 3.12   The structure of a break statement

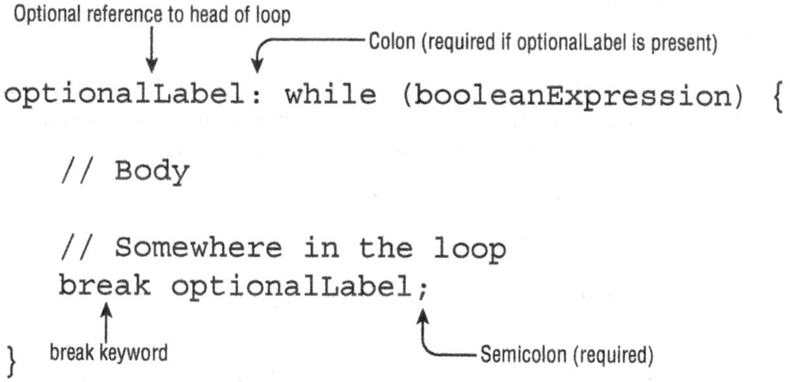

Optional reference to head of loop

Colon (required if optionalLabel is present)

```
optionalLabel: while (booleanExpression) {

    // Body

    // Somewhere in the loop
    break optionalLabel;

}
```

break keyword

Semicolon (required)

Notice in Figure 3.12 that the break statement can take an optional *label* parameter. Without a label parameter, the break statement will terminate the nearest inner loop it is currently in the process of executing. The optional label parameter allows us to break out of a higher-level outer loop. In the following example, we search for the first (x, y) array index position of a number within an unsorted two-dimensional array:

```
10: public class FindInMatrix {
11:    public static void main(String[] args) {
12:        int[][] list = {{1,13}, {5,2}, {2,2}};
13:        int searchValue = 2;
14:        int positionX = -1;
```

```
15:        int positionY = -1;
16:
17:        PARENT_LOOP: for (int i = 0; i < list.length; i++) {
18:           for (int j = 0; j < list[i].length; j++) {
19:              if (list[i][j] == searchValue) {
20:                 positionX = i;
21:                 positionY = j;
22:                 break PARENT_LOOP;
23:              }
24:           }
25:        }
26:        if (positionX == -1 || positionY == -1) {
27:           System.out.print("Value "+searchValue+" not found");
28:        } else {
29:           System.out.print("Value "+searchValue+" found at: " +
30:              "("+positionX+","+positionY+")");
31:        }
32:     } }
```

When executed, this code will output the following:

```
Value 2 found at: (1,1)
```

In particular, take a look at the statement break PARENT_LOOP. This statement will break out of the entire loop structure as soon as the first matching value is found. Now, imagine what would happen if we replaced the body of the inner loop with the following:

```
19:              if (list[i][j]==searchValue) {
20:                 positionX = i;
21:                 positionY = j;
22:                 break;
23:              }
```

How would this change our flow, and would the output change? Instead of exiting when the first matching value is found, the program would now only exit the inner loop when the condition was met. In other words, the structure would find the first matching value of the last inner loop to contain the value, resulting in the following output:

```
Value 2 found at: (2,0)
```

Finally, what if we removed the break altogether?

```
19:              if (list[i][j]==searchValue) {
20:                 positionX = i;
21:                 positionY = j;
22:
23:              }
```

In this case, the code would search for the last value in the entire structure that had the matching value. The output would look like this:

```
Value 2 found at: (2,1)
```

You can see from this example that using a label on a break statement in a nested loop, or not using the break statement at all, can cause the loop structure to behave quite differently.

The *continue* Statement

Let's now extend our discussion of advanced loop control with the *continue* statement, a statement that causes flow to finish the execution of the current loop iteration, as shown in Figure 3.13.

FIGURE 3.13   The structure of a continue statement

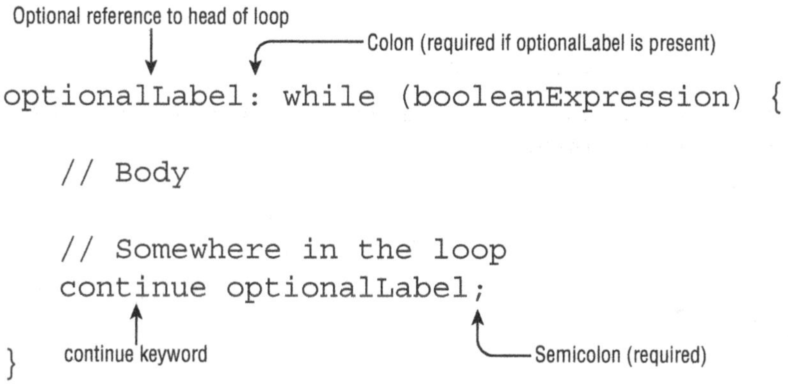

You may notice that the syntax of the continue statement mirrors that of the break statement. In fact, the statements are identical in how they are used, but with different results. While the break statement transfers control to the enclosing statement, the continue statement transfers control to the boolean expression that determines if the loop should continue. In other words, it ends the current iteration of the loop. Also, like the break statement, the continue statement is applied to the nearest inner loop under execution, using optional label statements to override this behavior.

Let's take a look at an example. Imagine we have a zookeeper who is supposed to clean the first leopard in each of four stables but skip stable b entirely.

```
1: public class CleaningSchedule {
2:     public static void main(String[] args) {
3:         CLEANING: for (char stables = 'a'; stables<='d'; stables++) {
4:             for (int leopard = 1; leopard <= 3; leopard++) {
```

```
5:                 if (stables=='b' || leopard==2) {
6:                     continue CLEANING;
7:                 }
8:                 System.out.println("Cleaning: "+stables+","+leopard);
9: } } } }
```

With the structure as defined, the loop will return control to the parent loop any time the first value is b or the second value is 2. On the first, third, and fourth executions of the outer loop, the inner loop prints a statement exactly once and then exits on the next inner loop when leopard is 2. On the second execution of the outer loop, the inner loop immediately exits without printing anything since b is encountered right away. The following is printed:

```
Cleaning: a,1
Cleaning: c,1
Cleaning: d,1
```

Now, imagine we remove the CLEANING label in the continue statement so that control is returned to the inner loop instead of the outer. Line 6 becomes the following:

```
6:                     continue;
```

This corresponds to the zookeeper cleaning all leopards except those labeled 2 or in stable b. The output is then the following:

```
Cleaning: a,1
Cleaning: a,3
Cleaning: c,1
Cleaning: c,3
Cleaning: d,1
Cleaning: d,3
```

Finally, if we remove the continue statement and the associated if statement altogether by removing lines 5–7, we arrive at a structure that outputs all the values, such as this:

```
Cleaning: a,1
Cleaning: a,2
Cleaning: a,3
Cleaning: b,1
Cleaning: b,2
Cleaning: b,3
Cleaning: c,1
Cleaning: c,2
Cleaning: c,3
Cleaning: d,1
Cleaning: d,2
Cleaning: d,3
```

The *return* Statement

Given that this book shouldn't be your first foray into programming, we hope you've come across methods that contain `return` statements. Regardless, we cover how to design and create methods that use them in detail in Chapter 5.

For now, though, you should be familiar with the idea that creating methods and using `return` statements can be used as an alternative to using labels and `break` statements. For example, take a look at this rewrite of our earlier `FindInMatrix` class:

```java
public class FindInMatrixUsingReturn {
    private static int[] searchForValue(int[][] list, int v) {
        for (int i = 0; i < list.length; i++) {
            for (int j = 0; j < list[i].length; j++) {
                if (list[i][j] == v) {
                    return new int[] {i, j};
                }
            }
        }
        return null;
    }

    public static void main(String[] args) {
        int[][] list = { { 1, 13 }, { 5, 2 }, { 2, 2 } };
        int searchValue = 2;
        int[] results = searchForValue(list, searchValue);

        if (results == null) {
            System.out.print("Value " + searchValue + " not found");
        } else {
            System.out.print("Value " + searchValue + " found at: " +
                "(" + results[0] + "," + results[1] + ")");
        }
    }
}
```

This class is functionally the same as the first `FindInMatrix` class we saw earlier using `break`. If you need finer-grained control of the loop with multiple `break` and `continue` statements, the first class is probably better. That said, we find code without labels and `break` statements a lot easier to read and debug. Also, making the search logic an independent function makes the code more reusable and the calling `main()` method a lot easier to read.

For the exam, you will need to know both forms. Just remember that `return` statements can be used to exit loops quickly and can lead to more readable code in practice, especially when used with nested loops.

Unreachable Code

One facet of `break`, `continue`, and `return` that you should be aware of is that any code placed immediately after them in the same block is considered unreachable and will not compile. For example, the following code snippet does not compile:

```
int checkDate = 0;
while (checkDate<10) {
   checkDate++;
   if (checkDate>100) {
      break;
      checkDate++;  // DOES NOT COMPILE
   }
}
```

Even though it is not logically possible for the `if` statement to evaluate to `true` in this code sample, the compiler notices that you have statements immediately following the `break` and will fail to compile with "unreachable code" as the reason. The same is true for `continue` and `return` statements, as shown in the following two examples:

```
int minute = 1;
WATCH: while (minute>2) {
   if (minute++>2) {
      continue WATCH;
      System.out.print(minute);  // DOES NOT COMPILE
   }
}

int hour = 2;
switch (hour) {
   case 1: return; hour++;  // DOES NOT COMPILE
   case 2:
}
```

One thing to remember is that it does not matter if the loop or decision structure actually visits the line of code. For example, the loop could execute zero or infinite times at runtime. Regardless of execution, the compiler will report an error if it finds any code it deems unreachable, in this case any statements immediately following a `break`, `continue`, or `return` statement.

Reviewing Branching

We conclude this section with Table 3.1, which will help remind you when labels and other various statements are permitted in Java. For illustrative purposes our examples used these statements in nested loops, although they can be used inside single loops as well.

TABLE 3.1 Supported control statement features

	Labels	break	continue	yield	when
while	Yes	Yes	Yes	No	No
do/while	Yes	Yes	Yes	No	No
for	Yes	Yes	Yes	No	No
switch	Yes	Yes	No	Yes	Yes

Some of the most time-consuming questions on the exam could involve nested loops with lots of branching. Unless you can spot a compiler error right away, you might consider skipping these questions and coming back to them at the end. Remember, all questions on the exam are weighted evenly!

Summary

This chapter presented how to make intelligent decisions in Java. We covered basic decision-making constructs such as if, else, and switch and showed how to use them to change the path of the process at runtime. We also covered switch expressions and showed how they often lead to more concise code.

In both the if and switch sections, we showed how to apply pattern matching to reduce boilerplate code. Pattern matching, especially with switch, is one of the newer features of Java 21, so expect to see at least one question on the exam on it.

We then moved our discussion to repetition control structures, otherwise known as loops. We showed how to use while and do/while loops to create processes that execute multiple times and also showed how it is important to make sure they eventually terminate. Remember that most of these structures require the evaluation of the termination condition, represented as a boolean expression, to complete.

Next, we covered the extremely convenient repetition control structures: the for and for-each loops. While their syntax is more complex than the traditional while or do/while loops, they are extremely useful in everyday coding and allow you to create complex expressions in a single line of code. With a for-each loop, you don't need to explicitly write a `boolean` expression, since the compiler builds one for you.

We concluded this chapter by discussing advanced control options and how flow can be enhanced through nested loops coupled with `break`, `continue`, and `return` statements. Be wary of questions on the exam that use nested loops, especially ones with labels, and verify that they are being used correctly.

This chapter is especially important because at least one component of this chapter will likely appear in every exam question with sample code. Many of the questions on the exam focus on proper syntactic use of the structures, as they will be a large source of questions that end in "Does not compile." You should be able to answer all of the review questions correctly or fully understand those that you answered incorrectly before moving on to later chapters.

Exam Essentials

Understand *if* and *else* decision control statements.   The `if` and `else` statements come up frequently throughout the exam in questions unrelated to decision control, so make sure you fully understand these basic building blocks of Java.

Apply pattern matching and flow scoping to *if*.   Pattern matching can be used to reduce boilerplate code of some `if` statements, by applying the `instanceof` operator and a variable type/name. It can also include a guard, which is an optional conditional clause, after the pattern variable declaration. Pattern matching uses flow scoping in which the pattern variable is in scope as long as the compiler can definitively determine its type.

Understand *switch* statements and their proper usage.   You should be able to spot a poorly formed `switch` statement on the exam. The `switch` value and data type should be compatible with the `case` clauses, and the values for the `case` clauses must evaluate to compile time constants. Finally, at runtime, a `switch` statement branches to the first matching `case`, or `default` if there is no match, or exits entirely if there is no match and no `default` branch. The process then continues into any proceeding `case` or `default` clause until a `break` or `return` statement is reached.

Use *switch* expressions correctly.   Discern the differences between `switch` statements and `switch` expressions. Understand how to write `switch` expressions correctly, including proper use of semicolons, writing `case` expressions and blocks that yield a consistent value, and making sure all possible values of the `switch` variable are handled by the `switch` expression.

Apply pattern matching to *switch*.   Understand how `switch` statements and expressions support pattern matching and allow any object to be used as the `switch` variable. It also supports a `case` branch with a guard, via the `when` keyword. Pattern matching alters two common rules with switch: a switch statement now must be exhaustive when pattern matching is used, and the ordering of switch expression branches is now important.

Write *while* loops.   Know the syntactical structure of all while and do/while loops. In particular, know when to use one versus the other.

Be able to use *for* loops.   You should be familiar with for and for-each loops and know how to write and evaluate them. Each loop has its own special properties and structures. You should know how to use for-each loops to iterate over lists and arrays.

Understand how *break*, *continue*, and *return* can change flow control.   Know how to change the flow control within a statement by applying a break, continue, or return statement. Also know which control statements can accept break statements and which can accept continue statements. Finally, you should understand how these statements work inside embedded loops or switch statements.

Review Questions

The answers to the chapter review questions can be found in the Appendix.

1. What is the output of the following code snippet?

```
32: Object skips = 10;
33: switch (skips) {
34:     case a when a < 10  -> System.out.print(2);
35:     case b when b >= 10 -> System.out.print(4);
36:     case null -> System.out.print(6);
37:     default    -> System.out.print(8);
38: }
```

   A. 2

   B. 4

   C. 6

   D. 8

   E. Exactly one line does not compile.

   F. Exactly two lines do not compile.

   G. None of the above.

2. Which of the following data types can be used in a `switch` expression? (Choose all that apply.)

   A. enum

   B. int

   C. Byte

   D. long

   E. boolean

   F. double

3. What is the output of the following code snippet?

```
3: int temperature = 4;
4: long humidity = -temperature + temperature * 3;
5: if (temperature>=4)
6: if (humidity < 6) System.out.println("Too Low");
7: else System.out.println("Just Right");
8: else System.out.println("Too High");
```

   A. Too Low

   B. Just Right

   C. Too High

   D. A NullPointerException is thrown at runtime.

   E. The code will not compile because of line 7.

   F. The code will not compile because of line 8.

4. Which of the following data types are permitted on the right side of a for-each expression? (Choose all that apply.)

   A. Double[][]

   B. Object

   C. Map

   D. List

   E. String

   F. char[]

   G. Exception

5. What is the output of calling printReptile(6)?

```
void printReptile(int category) {
    var type = switch (category) {
        case 1,2 -> "Snake";
        case 3,4 -> "Lizard";
        case 5,6 -> "Turtle";
        case 7,8 -> "Alligator";
    };
    System.out.print(type);
}
```

   A. Snake

   B. Lizard

   C. Turtle

   D. Alligator

   E. TurtleAlligator

   F. None of the above

6. What is the output of the following code snippet?

```
List<Integer> myFavoriteNumbers = new ArrayList<>();
myFavoriteNumbers.add(10);
myFavoriteNumbers.add(14);
for (var a : myFavoriteNumbers) {
    System.out.print(a + ", ");
    break;
}
```

```
for (int b : myFavoriteNumbers) {
   continue;
   System.out.print(b + ", ");
}
```

```
for (Object c : myFavoriteNumbers)
   System.out.print(c + ", ");
```

A. It compiles and runs without issue but does not produce any output.

B. 10, 14,

C. 10, 10, 14,

D. 10, 10, 14, 10, 14,

E. Exactly one line of code does not compile.

F. Exactly two lines of code do not compile.

G. Three or more lines of code do not compile.

H. The code contains an infinite loop and does not terminate.

7. Assuming weather is a well-formed nonempty array, which code snippet, when inserted independently into the blank in the following code, prints all of the elements of weather? (Choose all that apply.)

```
private void print(int[] weather) {
   for (_____) {
      System.out.println(weather[i]);
   }
}
```

A. int i=weather.length; i>0; i--

B. int i=0; i<=weather.length-1; ++i

C. var w : weather

D. int i=weather.length-1; i>=0; i--

E. int i=0, int j=3; i<weather.length; ++i

F. int i=0; ++i<10 && i<weather.length;

G. None of the above

8. What is the output of calling printType(11)?

```
31: void printType(Object o) {
32:    if (o instanceof Integer bat) {
33:       System.out.print("int");
34:    } else if (o instanceof Integer bat && bat < 10) {
35:       System.out.print("small int");
36:    } else if (o instanceof Long bat || bat <= 20) {
```

```
37:        System.out.print("long");
38:    } default {
39:        System.out.print("unknown");
40:    }
41: }
```

A. `int`

B. `small int`

C. `long`

D. `unknown`

E. Nothing is printed.

F. The code contains one line that does not compile.

G. The code contains two lines that do not compile.

H. None of the above.

9. Which statements, when inserted independently into the following blank, will cause the code to print 2 at runtime? (Choose all that apply.)

```
int count = 0;
BUNNY: for (int row = 1; row <=3; row++)
    RABBIT: for (int col = 0; col <3 ; col++) {
        if ((col + row) % 2 == 0)
            _____;
        count++;
    }
System.out.println(count);
```

A. `break BUNNY`

B. `break RABBIT`

C. `continue BUNNY`

D. `continue RABBIT`

E. `break`

F. `continue`

G. None of the above, as the code contains a compiler error

10. Given the following method, how many lines contain compilation errors?

```
8:  enum DayOfWeek {
9:      SUNDAY, MONDAY, TUESDAY, WEDNESDAY, THURSDAY, FRIDAY, SATURDAY;
10:     private DayOfWeek getWeekDay(int day, final int thursday) {
11:         int otherDay = day;
12:         int Sunday = 0;
```

```
13:        switch (otherDay) {
14:            default:
15:            case 1: continue;
16:            case thursday: return DayOfWeek.THURSDAY;
17:            case 2,10: break;
18:            case Sunday: return DayOfWeek.SUNDAY;
19:            case DayOfWeek.MONDAY: return DayOfWeek.MONDAY;
20:        }
21:        return DayOfWeek.FRIDAY;
22:    } }
```

A. None, the code compiles and runs without issue.

B. 1.

C. 2.

D. 3.

E. 4.

F. 5.

G. 6.

H. The code compiles but may produce an error at runtime.

11. What is the output of calling `printLocation(Animal.MAMMAL)`?

```
10: class Zoo {
11:    enum Animal {BIRD, FISH, MAMMAL}
12:    void printLocation(Animal a) {
13:        long type = switch (a) {
14:            case BIRD -> 1;
15:            case FISH -> 2;
16:            case MAMMAL -> 3;
17:            default -> 4;
18:        };
19:        System.out.print(type);
20:    } }
```

A. 3

B. 4

C. 34

D. The code does not compile because of line 13.

E. The code does not compile because of line 17.

F. None of the above.

12. What is the result of the following code snippet?

```
3: int sing = 8, squawk = 2, notes = 0;
4: while (sing > squawk) {
5:    sing--;
6:    squawk += 2;
7:    notes += sing + squawk;
8: }
9: System.out.println(notes);
```

A. 11

B. 13

C. 23

D. 33

E. 50

F. The code will not compile because of line 7.

13. What is the result of calling `getHatSize(9f)` on the following code snippet?

```
10: int getHatSize(Number measurement) {
11:    return switch (measurement) {
12:        case Double d -> 1 + d.intValue();
13:        case null     -> 11;
14:        case !(Number n) -> 3 + n.intValue();
15:        case Float f when f < 10 -> 4 + f.intValue();
16:    };
17: }
```

A. 10

B. 11

C. 12

D. 13

E. The code does not compile because it is missing a `default` clause.

F. The code does not compile for a different reason.

14. What is the output of the following code snippet?

```
2: boolean keepGoing = true;
3: int result = 15, meters = 10;
4: do {
5:    meters--;
6:    if (meters==8) keepGoing = false;
7:    result -= 2;
8: } while keepGoing;
9: System.out.println(result);
```

A. 7

B. 9

C. 10

D. 11

E. 15

F. The code will not compile because of line 6.

G. The code does not compile for a different reason.

15. Which statements about the following code snippet are correct? (Choose all that apply.)

```java
for (var penguin : new int[2])
    System.out.println(penguin);

var ostrich = new Character[3];
for (var emu : ostrich)
    System.out.println(emu);

List<Integer> parrots = new ArrayList<Integer>();
for (var macaw  : parrots)
    System.out.println(macaw);
```

A. The data type of penguin is Integer.

B. The data type of penguin is int.

C. The data type of emu is undefined.

D. The data type of emu is Character.

E. The data type of macaw is List.

F. The data type of macaw is Integer.

G. None of the above, as the code does not compile.

16. What is the result of the following code snippet?

```java
final char a = 'A', e = 'E';
char grade = 'B';
switch (grade) {
   default:
   case a:
   case 'B': 'C': System.out.print("great ");
   case 'D':      System.out.print("good "); break;
   case e:
   case 'F':      System.out.print("not good ");
}
```

A. great

B. great good

C. good

D. not good

E. The code does not compile because the data type of one or more `case` clauses does not match the data type of the `switch` variable.

F. None of the above.

17. Given the following array, which code snippets print the elements in reverse order from how they are declared? (Choose all that apply.)

```
char[] wolf = {'W', 'e', 'b', 'b', 'y'};
```

A.
```
int q = wolf.length;
for ( ; ; ) {
    System.out.print(wolf[--q]);
    if (q==0) break;
}
```

B.
```
for (int m=wolf.length-1; m>=0; --m)
    System.out.print(wolf[m]);
```

C.
```
for (int z=0; z<wolf.length; z++)
    System.out.print(wolf[wolf.length-z]);
```

D.
```
int x = wolf.length-1;
for (int j=0; x>=0 && j==0; x--)
    System.out.print(wolf[x]);
```

E.
```
final int r = wolf.length;
for (int w = r-1; r>-1; w = r-1)
    System.out.print(wolf[w]);
```

F.
```
for (int i=wolf.length; i>0; --i)
    System.out.print(wolf[i]);
```

G. None of the above

18. What distinct numbers are printed when the following method is executed? (Choose all that apply.)

```
private void countAttendees() {
    int participants = 4, animals = 2, performers = -1;

    while ((participants = participants + 1) < 10) {}
    do {} while (animals++ <= 1);
    for ( ; performers < 2; performers += 2) {}

    System.out.println(participants);
    System.out.println(animals);
    System.out.println(performers);
}
```

A. 6

B. 3

C. 4

D. 5

E. 10

F. 9

G. The code does not compile.

H. None of the above.

19. What is the output of the following code snippet?

```
2: double iguana = 0;
3: do {
4:     int snake = 1;
5:     System.out.print(snake++ + " ");
6:     iguana--;
7: } while (snake <= 5);
8: System.out.println(iguana);
```

A. 1 2 3 4 -4.0

B. 1 2 3 4 -5.0

C. 1 2 3 4 5 -4.0

D. 0 1 2 3 4 5 -5.0

E. The code does not compile.

F. The code compiles but produces an infinite loop at runtime.

G. None of the above.

20. Which statements, when inserted into the following blanks, allow the code to compile and run without entering an infinite loop? (Choose all that apply.)

```
4:  int height = 1;
5:  L1: while (height++ <10) {
6:      long humidity = 12;
7:      L2: do {
8:          if (humidity-- % 12 == 0) _____;
9:          int temperature = 30;
10:         L3: for ( ; ; ) {
11:             temperature++;
12:             if (temperature>50) _____;
13:         }
14:     } while (humidity > 4);
15: }
```

A. break L2 on line 8; continue L2 on line 12

B. continue on line 8; continue on line 12

C. break L3 on line 8; break L1 on line 12

D. continue L2 on line 8; continue L3 on line 12

E. continue L2 on line 8; continue L2 on line 12

F. None of the above, as the code contains a compiler error

21. A minimum of how many lines need to be corrected before the following method will compile?

```
21: void findZookeeper(Integer id) {
22:     System.out.print(switch (id) {
23:         case 10 -> {"Jane";}
24:         case 20 -> {yield "Lisa";};
25:         case 30 -> "Kelly";
26:         case 30 -> "Sarah";
27:         default -> "Unassigned";
28:     });
29: }
```

A. Zero

B. One

C. Two

D. Three

E. Four

F. Five

22. What is the output of the following code snippet?

```
2: var tailFeathers = 3;
3: final var one = 1;
4: switch (tailFeathers) {
5:    case one: System.out.print(3 + " ");
6:    default: case 3: System.out.print(5 + " ");
7: }
8: while (tailFeathers > 1) {
9:    System.out.print(--tailFeathers + " "); }
```

A. 3

B. 5 1

C. 5 2

D. 3 5 1

E. 5 2 1

F. The code will not compile because of lines 3–5.

G. The code will not compile because of line 6.

23. What is the output of the following code snippet?

```
15: int penguin = 50, turtle = 75;
16: boolean older = penguin >= turtle;
17: if (older = true) System.out.println("Success");
18: else System.out.println("Failure");
19: else if (penguin != 50) System.out.println("Other");
```

A. Success

B. Failure

C. Other

D. The code will not compile because of line 17.

E. The code compiles but throws an exception at runtime.

F. None of the above.

24. What is the output of the following code snippet?

```
22: String zooStatus = "Closed";
23: int visitors = switch (zooStatus) {
24:    case String s when s.equals("Open") -> 10;
25:    case Object s when s != null && !s.equals("") -> 20;
26:    case null -> {yield 30;}
27:    default -> 40;
28: };
29: System.out.print(visitors);
```

A. 10

B. 20

C. 30

D. 40

E. Exactly one line does not compile.

F. Exactly two lines do not compile.

G. Three or more lines do not compile.

25. What is the output of the following code snippet?

```
6:  String instrument = "violin";
7:  final String CELLO = "cello";
8:  String viola = "viola";
9:  int p = -1;
10: switch (instrument) {
11:    case "bass" : break;
12:    case CELLO : p++;
13:    default: p++;
14:    case "VIOLIN": p++;
15:    case "viola" : ++p; break;
16: }
17: System.out.print(p);
```

A. -1

B. 0

C. 1

D. 2

E. 3

F. The code does not compile.

26. What is the output of the following code snippet?

```
9:  int w = 0, r = 1;
10: String name = "";
11: while (w < 2) {
12:    name += "A";
13:    do {
14:       name += "B";
15:       if (name.length()>0) name += "C";
16:       else break;
17:    } while (r <=1);
18:    r++; w++; }
19: System.out.println(name);
```

A. ABC

B. ABCABC

C. ABCABCABC

D. Line 15 contains a compilation error.

E. Line 18 contains a compilation error.

F. The code compiles but never terminates at runtime.

G. The code compiles but throws a `NullPointerException` at runtime.

27. What is printed by the following code snippet?

```
23: byte amphibian = 2;
24: String name = "Salamander";
25: String color = switch (amphibian) {
26:     case 1 -> { yield "Red"; }
27:     case 2 -> { if (name.equals("Frog")) yield "Green";
28:                 yield "Blue"; }
29:     case 3 -> { yield "Purple"; }
30:     default -> throw new RuntimeException();
31: };
32: System.out.print(color);
```

A. Red

B. Green

C. Purple

D. Blue

E. The code does not compile.

F. An exception is thrown at runtime.

28. What is the output of calling `getFish("goldie")`?

```
40: void getFish(Object fish) {
41:     if (!(fish instanceof String guppy))
42:         System.out.print("Eat!");
43:     else if (!(fish instanceof String guppy)) {
44:         throw new RuntimeException();
45:     }
46:     System.out.print("Swim!");
47: }
```

A. `Eat!`

B. `Swim!`

C. `Eat!` followed by an exception

D. Eat!Swim!

E. An exception is printed

F. None of the above

29. What is the result of the following code?

```
1: public class PrintIntegers {
2:    public static void main(String[] args) {
3:        int y = -2;
4:        do System.out.print(++y + " ");
5:        while (y <= 5);
6: } }
```

A. -2 -1 0 1 2 3 4 5

B. -2 -1 0 1 2 3 4

C. -1 0 1 2 3 4 5 6

D. -1 0 1 2 3 4 5

E. The code will not compile because of line 5.

F. The code contains an infinite loop and does not terminate.

30. What is the minimum number of lines that would need to be changed or removed for the following code to compile and return a value when called with dance(10)?

```
41: double dance(Object speed) {
42:    return switch (speed) {
43:        case 5 -> {yield 4};
44:        case 10 -> 8;
45:        case 15,20 -> 12;
46:        default -> 20;
47:        case null -> 16;
48:    }
49: }
```

A. Zero, the code compiles and runs without issue

B. One

C. Two

D. Three

E. Four

F. Five

G. Six

Chapter

4

Core APIs

OCP EXAM OBJECTIVES COVERED IN THIS CHAPTER:

✓ **Handling Date, Time, Text, Numeric and Boolean Values**

- Use primitives and wrapper classes. Evaluate arithmetic and boolean expressions, using the Math API and by applying precedence rules, type conversions, and casting.

- Manipulate text, including text blocks, using String and StringBuilder classes.

- Manipulate date, time, duration, period, instant and time-zone objects including daylight saving time using Date-Time API.

✓ **Working with Arrays and Collections**

- Create arrays, List, Set, Map and Deque collections, and add, remove, update, retrieve and sort their elements.

In the context of an application programming interface (API), an *interface* refers to a group of classes or Java interface definitions giving you access to functionality.

In this chapter, you learn about many core data structures in Java, along with the most common APIs to access them. For example, String and StringBuilder, along with their associated APIs, are used to create and manipulate text data. Then we cover arrays. Finally, we explore math and date/time APIs.

Creating and Manipulating Strings

The String class is such a fundamental class that you'd be hard-pressed to write code without it. After all, you can't even write a main() method without using the String class. A *string* is basically a sequence of characters; here's an example:

```
String name = "Fluffy";
```

As you learned in Chapter 1, "Building Blocks," this is an example of a reference type. You also learned that objects are created using the new keyword. Wait a minute. Something is missing from the previous example: it doesn't have new in it! In Java, these two snippets both create a String:

```
String name = "Fluffy";
String name = new String("Fluffy");
```

Both give you a reference variable named name pointing to the String object "Fluffy". They are subtly different, as you see later in this chapter. For now, just remember that the String class is special and doesn't need to be instantiated with new.

Further, text blocks are another way of creating a String. To review, this text block is the same as the previous variables:

```
String name = """
              Fluffy""";
```

Since a String is a sequence of characters, you probably won't be surprised to hear that it implements the interface CharSequence. This interface is a general way of representing several classes, including String and StringBuilder. You learn more about interfaces in Chapter 7, "Beyond Classes."

In this section, we look at concatenation, common methods, and method chaining.

Concatenating

In Chapter 2, "Operators," you learned how to add numbers. 1 + 2 is clearly 3. But what is "1" + "2"? It's "12" because Java combines the two String objects. Placing one String before the other String and combining them is called string *concatenation*. The exam creators like string concatenation because the + operator can be used in two ways within the same line of code. There aren't lots of rules to know for this, but you have to know them well.

1. If both operands are numeric, + means numeric addition.

2. If either operand is a String, + means concatenation.

3. The expression is evaluated left to right.

Now let's look at some examples:

```
System.out.println(1 + 2);           // 3
System.out.println("a" + "b");       // ab
System.out.println("a" + "b" + 3);   // ab3
System.out.println(1 + 2 + "c");     // 3c
System.out.println("c" + 1 + 2);     // c12
System.out.println("c" + null);      // cnull
```

The first example uses the first rule. Both operands are numbers, so we use normal addition. The second example is simple string concatenation, described in the second rule. The quotes for the String are used only in code; they don't get output.

The third example combines the second and third rules. Since we start on the left, Java figures out what "a" + "b" evaluates to. You already know that one: it's "ab". Then Java looks at the remaining expression of "ab" + 3. The second rule tells us to concatenate since one of the operands is a String.

In the fourth example, we start with the third rule, which tells us to consider 1 + 2. Both operands are numeric, so the first rule tells us the answer is 3. Then we have 3 + "c", which uses the second rule to give us "3c". Notice all three rules are used in one line?

The fifth example shows the importance of the third rule. First we have "c" + 1, which uses the second rule to give us "c1". Then we have "c1" + 2, which uses the second rule again to give us "c12".

Finally, the last example shows how null is represented as a string when concatenated or printed, giving us "cnull".

The exam takes trickery a step further and will try to fool you with something like this:

```
int three = 3;
String four = "4";
System.out.println(1 + 2 + three + four);
```

When you see this, just take it slow, remember the three rules, and be sure to check the variable types. In this example, we start with the third rule, which tells us to consider 1 + 2. The first rule gives us 3. Next, we have 3 + three. Since three is of type int, we still use the first rule, giving us 6. Then, we have 6 + four. Since four is of type String, we switch to the second rule and get a final answer of "64". When you see questions like this, just take your time and check the types. Being methodical pays off.

There is one more thing to know about concatenation, but it is easy. In this example, you just have to remember what += does. Keep in mind, s += "2" means the same thing as s = s + "2".

```
4: var s = "1";              // s currently holds "1"
5: s += "2";                 // s currently holds "12"
6: s += 3;                   // s currently holds "123"
7: System.out.println(s);    // 123
```

On line 5, we are "adding" two strings, which means we concatenate them. Line 6 tries to trick you by adding a number, but it's just like we wrote s = s + 3. We know that a string "plus" anything else means to use concatenation.

To review the rules one more time: use numeric addition if two numbers are involved, use concatenation otherwise, and evaluate from left to right. Have you memorized these three rules yet? Be sure to do so before the exam!

Important *String* Methods

The String class has dozens of methods. Luckily, you need to know only a handful for the exam. The exam creators pick most of the methods developers use in the real world.

For all these methods, you need to remember that a string is a sequence of characters and Java counts from 0 when indexed. Figure 4.1 shows how each character in the string "animals" is indexed.

FIGURE 4.1   Indexing for a string

0	1	2	3	4	5	6
a	n	i	m	a	l	s

You also need to know that a String is immutable, or unchangeable. This means calling a method on a String will return a different String object rather than changing the value of the reference. In this chapter, you use immutable objects. In Chapter 6, "Class Design," you learn how to create immutable objects of your own.

Let's look at a number of methods from the String class. Many of them are straightforward, so we won't discuss them at length. You need to know how to use these methods.

Determining the Length

The method length() returns the number of characters in the String. The method signature is as follows:

```
public int length()
```

The following code shows how to use length():

```
var name = "animals";
System.out.println(name.length());  // 7
```

Wait. It outputs 7? Didn't we just tell you that Java counts from zero? The difference is that zero counting happens only when you're using indexes or positions within a list. When determining the total size or length, Java uses normal counting again.

Getting a Single Character

The method charAt() lets you query the string to find out what character is at a specific index. The method signature is as follows:

```
public char charAt(int index)
```

The following code shows how to use charAt():

```
var name = "animals";
System.out.println(name.charAt(0));  // a
System.out.println(name.charAt(6));  // s
System.out.println(name.charAt(7));  // exception
```

Since indexes start counting with zero, charAt(0) returns the "first" character in the sequence. Similarly, charAt(6) returns the "seventh" character in the sequence. However, charAt(7) is a problem. It asks for the "eighth" character in the sequence, but there are only seven characters present. When something goes wrong that Java doesn't know how to deal with, it throws an exception, as shown here. You learn more about exceptions in Chapter 11, "Exceptions and Localization."

```
java.lang.StringIndexOutOfBoundsException: String index out of range: 7
```

Working with Code Points

In this book and on the exam, we often use the ASCII data encoding format. Around the world some characters use a longer encoding called Unicode which has a wider range and doesn't fit in a char, such as a stylized quote ('). A code point is bigger than a character, so it is expressed as a number. The relevant method signatures are as follows:

```
public int codePointAt(int index)
public int codePointBefore(int index)
public int codePointCount(int beginIndex, int endIndex)
```

The codePointAt() returns the numeric value of the code point at the specified index. The codePointBefore() method does the same, but looks at the value before the index. Finally, the codePointCount() method returns the number of code points between two indexes.

```
var s = "We're done feeding the animals";
System.out.println(s.charAt(0) + " " + s.codePointAt(0));  // W 87
System.out.println(s.charAt(2) + " " + s.codePointAt(2));  // ' 8217
System.out.println(s.codePointBefore(3));                  // 8217
System.out.println(s.codePointCount(0,4));                 // 4
```

Don't worry! You do not need to memorize the ASCII or Unicode values. You just need to know that if you see codePointAt() on the exam that it functions similarly to charAt() for ASCII characters, returning the numeric value of the character at the location.

Getting a Substring

The method substring() is similar to charAt() except it returns a group of characters from the string. The first parameter is the index to start with for the returned string. As usual, this is a zero-based index. There is an optional second parameter, which is the end index you want to stop at.

Notice we said "stop at" rather than "include." This means the endIndex parameter is allowed to be one past the end of the sequence if you want to stop at the end of the sequence. That would be redundant, though, since you could omit the second parameter entirely in that case. In your own code, you want to avoid this redundancy. Don't be surprised if the exam uses it, though. The method signatures are as follows:

```
public String substring(int beginIndex)
public String substring(int beginIndex, int endIndex)
```

It helps to think of indexes a bit differently for the substring methods. Pretend the indexes are right before the character they would point to. Figure 4.2 helps visualize this. Notice how the arrow with the 0 points to the character that would have index 0. The arrow with the 1 points between characters with indexes 0 and 1. There are seven characters in the String. Since Java uses zero-based indexes, this means the last character has an index of 6. The arrow with the 7 points immediately after this last character. This will help you remember that endIndex doesn't give an out-of-bounds exception when it is one past the end of the String.

FIGURE 4.2 Indexes for a substring

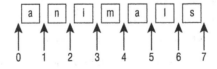

The following code shows how to use substring():

```
var name = "animals";
System.out.println(name.substring(3));                 // mals
System.out.println(name.substring(name.indexOf('m'))); // mals
```

```
System.out.println(name.substring(3, 4));                    // m
System.out.println(name.substring(3, 7));                    // mals
```

The substring() method is the trickiest String method on the exam. The first example says to take the characters starting with index 3 through the end, which gives us "mals". The second example does the same thing, but it calls indexOf() to get the index rather than hard-coding it. This is a common practice when coding because you may not know the index in advance.

The third example says to take the characters starting with index 3 until, but not including, the character at index 4. This is a complicated way of saying we want a String with one character: the one at index 3. This results in "m". The final example says to take the characters starting with index 3 until we get to index 7. Since index 7 is the same as the end of the string, it is equivalent to the first example.

We hope that wasn't too confusing. The next examples are less obvious:

```
System.out.println(name.substring(3, 3));   // empty string
System.out.println(name.substring(3, 2));   // exception
System.out.println(name.substring(3, 8));   // exception
```

The first example in this set prints an empty string. The request is for the characters starting with index 3 until we get to index 3. Since we start and end with the same index, there are *no* characters in between. The second example in this set throws an exception because the indexes can't be backward. Java knows perfectly well that it will never get to index 2 if it starts with index 3. The third example says to continue until the eighth character. There is no eighth position, so Java throws an exception. Granted, there is no seventh character either, but at least there is the "end of string" invisible position.

Let's review this one more time since substring() is so tricky. The method returns the string starting from the requested index. If an end index is requested, it stops right before that index. Otherwise, it goes to the end of the string.

Finding an Index

The method indexOf() looks at the characters in the string and finds the first index that matches the desired value. The indexOf method can work with an individual character or a whole String as input. It can also start and end the search from specific positions. Note, the starting index is inclusive, and the ending index is exclusive. Remember that a char can be passed to an int parameter type. On the exam, you'll only see a char passed to the parameters named ch. The method signatures are as follows:

```
public int indexOf(int ch)
public int indexOf(int ch, int fromIndex)
public int indexOf(int ch, int fromIndex, int endIndex)
public int indexOf(String str)
public int indexOf(String str, int fromIndex)
public int indexOf(String str, int fromIndex, int endIndex)
```

The following code shows you how to use indexOf():

```
10: var name = "animals";
11: System.out.println(name.indexOf('a'));        // 0
12: System.out.println(name.indexOf("al"));        // 4
13: System.out.println(name.indexOf('a', 4));       // 4
14: System.out.println(name.indexOf("al", 5));      // -1
15: System.out.println(name.indexOf('a', 2, 4));    // -1
16: System.out.println(name.indexOf("al", 2, 6));   // 4
```

Since indexes begin with 0, the first 'a' matches at that position. Therefore, line 11 outputs 0. On line 12, Java looks for a more specific string, so it matches later. On line 13, Java shouldn't even look at the characters until it gets to index 4. Line 14 doesn't find anything because it starts looking after the match occurred. Unlike charAt(), the indexOf() method doesn't throw an exception if it can't find a match, instead returning -1. Because indexes start with 0, the caller knows that -1 couldn't be a valid index. This makes it a common value for a method to signify to the caller that no match is found.

Line 15 looks for a match starting at index 2 and earlier than index 4. This means indices 2 or 3. Since neither of those matches, the method returns -1. Finally, line 16 looks for a match starting at index 2 since starting indexes are inclusive. It ends before at index 6 since the end index is exclusive. This means indices 2, 3, 4, and 5. The characters at index 4 and 5 match the target. The first one of those is 4, which is returned.

Adjusting Case

Whew. After that mental exercise, it is nice to have methods that act exactly as they sound! These methods make it easy to convert your data. The method signatures are as follows:

```
public String toLowerCase()
public String toUpperCase()
```

The following code shows how to use these methods:

```
var name = "animals";
System.out.println(name.toUpperCase());      // ANIMALS
System.out.println("Abc123".toLowerCase());   // abc123
```

These methods do what they say. The toUpperCase() method converts any lowercase characters to uppercase in the returned string. The toLowerCase() method converts any uppercase characters to lowercase in the returned string. These methods leave alone any characters other than letters. Also, remember that strings are immutable, so the original string stays the same.

Checking for Equality

The equals() method checks whether two String objects contain exactly the same characters in the same order. The equalsIgnoreCase() method checks whether two String objects contain the same characters, with the exception that it ignores the characters' case. The method signatures are as follows:

```
public boolean equals(Object obj)
public boolean equalsIgnoreCase(String str)
```

You might have noticed that equals() takes an Object rather than a String. This is because the method is the same for all objects. If you pass in something that isn't a String, it will just return false. By contrast, the equalsIgnoreCase() method applies only to String objects, so it can take the more specific type as the parameter.

In Java, String values are case-sensitive. That means "abc" and "ABC" are considered different values. With that in mind, the following code shows how to use these methods:

```
System.out.println("abc".equals("ABC"));              // false
System.out.println("ABC".equals("ABC"));              // true
System.out.println("ABC".equals(6));                  // false
System.out.println("abc".equalsIgnoreCase("ABC"));  // true
```

This example should be fairly intuitive. In the first example, the values aren't exactly the same. In the second, they are exactly the same. The third example shows what happens if you pass a different type. In the last example, the values differ only by case, but it is OK because we called the method that ignores differences in case.

 Real World Scenario

Overriding *toString()*, *equals(Object)*, and *hashCode()*

Knowing how to properly override toString(), equals(Object), and hashCode() was part of Java certification exams in the past. As a professional Java developer, it is still important for you to know at least the basic rules for overriding each of these methods.

- toString(): The toString() method is called when you try to print an object or concatenate the object with a String. It is commonly overridden with a version that prints a unique description of the instance using its instance fields.

- equals(Object): The equals(Object) method is used to compare objects, with the default implementation just using the == operator. You should override the equals(Object) method any time you want to conveniently compare elements for equality, especially if this requires checking numerous fields.

- hashCode(): Any time you override equals(Object), you must override hash Code() to be consistent. This means that for any two objects, if a.equals(b) is true, then a.hashCode()==b.hashCode() must also be true. If they are not consistent, this could lead to invalid data and side effects in hash-based collections such as HashMap and HashSet.

All of these methods provide a default implementation in Object, but if you want to make intelligent use of them, you should override them.

Searching for Substrings

Often, you need to search a larger string to determine if a substring is contained within it. The startsWith() and endsWith() methods look at whether the provided value matches part of the String. There is also an overloaded startsWith() that specifies where in the String to start looking. The contains() method isn't as particular; it looks for matches anywhere in the String. The method signatures are as follows:

```java
public boolean startsWith(String prefix)
public boolean startsWith(String prefix, int fromIndex)
public boolean endsWith(String suffix)
public boolean contains(CharSequence charSeq)
```

The following code shows how to use these methods:

```java
System.out.println("abc".startsWith("a")); // true
System.out.println("abc".startsWith("A")); // false

System.out.println("abc".startsWith("b", 1)); // true
System.out.println("abc".startsWith("b", 2)); // false

System.out.println("abc".endsWith("c"));    // true
System.out.println("abc".endsWith("a"));    // false

System.out.println("abc".contains("b"));    // true
System.out.println("abc".contains("B"));    // false
```

Again, nothing surprising here. Java is doing a case-sensitive check on the values provided. Note that the contains() method is a convenience method so you don't have to write str.indexOf(otherString) != -1.

Replacing Values

The replace() method does a simple search and replace on the string. There's a version that takes char parameters as well as a version that takes CharSequence parameters. The method signatures are as follows:

```java
public String replace(char oldChar, char newChar)
public String replace(CharSequence target, CharSequence replacement)
```

The following code shows how to use these methods:

```java
System.out.println("abcabc".replace('a', 'A')); // AbcAbc
System.out.println("abcabc".replace("a", "A")); // AbcAbc
```

The first example uses the first method signature, passing in char parameters. The second example uses the second method signature, passing in String parameters.

Removing Whitespace

These methods remove blank space from the beginning and/or end of a String. The strip() and trim() methods remove whitespace from the beginning and end of a String. In terms of the exam, whitespace consists of spaces along with the \t (tab) and \n (newline) characters. Other characters, such as \r (carriage return), are also included in what gets trimmed. The strip() method does everything that trim() does, but it supports Unicode.

 You don't need to know about Unicode for the exam. But if you want to test the difference, one of the Unicode whitespace characters is as follows:

```
char ch = '\u2000';
```

Additionally, the stripLeading() method removes whitespace from the beginning of the String and leaves it at the end. The stripTrailing() method does the opposite. It removes whitespace from the end of the String and leaves it at the beginning. The method signatures are as follows:

```
public String strip()
public String stripLeading()
public String stripTrailing()
public String trim()
```

The following code shows how to use these methods:

```
System.out.println("abc".strip());               // abc
System.out.println("\t   a b c\n".strip());      // a b c

String text = " abc\t ";
System.out.println(text.trim().length());          // 3
System.out.println(text.strip().length());         // 3
System.out.println(text.stripLeading().length());  // 5
System.out.println(text.stripTrailing().length()); // 4
```

First, remember that \t is a single character. The backslash escapes the t to represent a tab. The first example prints the original string because there are no whitespace characters at the beginning or end. The second example gets rid of the leading tab, subsequent spaces, and the trailing newline. It leaves the spaces that are in the middle of the string.

The remaining examples just print the number of characters remaining. You can see that trim() and strip() leave the same three characters "abc" because they remove both the leading and trailing whitespace. The stripLeading() method only removes the one whitespace character at the beginning of the String. It leaves the tab and space at the end. The stripTrailing() method removes these two characters at the end but leaves the character at the beginning of the String.

Working with Indentation

Now that Java supports text blocks, it is helpful to have methods that deal with indentation. Both of these are a little tricky, so read carefully!

```
public String indent(int numberSpaces)
public String stripIndent()
```

The indent() method adds the same number of blank spaces to the beginning of each line if you pass a positive number. If you pass a negative number, it tries to remove that number of whitespace characters from the beginning of the line. If you pass zero, the indentation will not change.

 If you call indent() with a negative number and try to remove more whitespace characters than are present at the beginning of the line, Java will remove all that it can find.

This seems straightforward enough. However, indent() also normalizes whitespace characters. What does *normalizing* whitespace mean, you ask? First, a line break is added to the end of the string if not already there. Second, any line breaks are converted to the \n format. Regardless of whether your operating system uses \r\n (Windows) or \n (Mac/Unix), Java will standardize on \n for you.

The stripIndent() method is useful when a String was built with concatenation rather than using a text block. It gets rid of all incidental whitespace. This means that all nonblank lines are shifted left so the same number of whitespace characters are removed from each line and the first character that remains is not blank. Like indent(), \r\n is turned into \n. However, the stripIndent() method does not add a trailing line break if it is missing.

Well, that was a lot of rules. Table 4.1 provides a reference to make them easier to remember.

TABLE 4.1 Rules for indent() and stripIndent()

Method	Indent change	Normalizes existing line breaks	Adds line break at end if missing
indent(n) where n > 0	Adds n spaces to beginning of each line	Yes	Yes
indent(n) where n == 0	No change	Yes	Yes
indent(n) where n < 0	Removes up to n spaces from each line where the same number of characters is removed from each nonblank line	Yes	Yes
stripIndent()	Removes all leading incidental whitespace	Yes	No

The following code shows how to use these methods. Don't worry if the results aren't what you expect. We explain each one.

```
10: var block = """
11:             a
12:              b
13:             c""";
14: var concat = " a\n"
15:            + "  b\n"
16:            + " c";
17: System.out.println(block.length());              // 6
18: System.out.println(concat.length());             // 9
19: System.out.println(block.indent(1).length());    // 10
20: System.out.println(concat.indent(-1).length());  // 7
21: System.out.println(concat.indent(-4).length());  // 6
22: System.out.println(concat.stripIndent().length()); // 6
```

Lines 10–16 create similar strings using a text block and a regular String, respectively. We say "similar" because concat has a whitespace character at the beginning of each line while block does not.

Line 17 counts the six characters in block, which are the three letters, the blank space before b, and the \n after a and b. Line 18 counts the nine characters in concat, which are the three letters, one blank space before a, two blank spaces before b, one blank space before c, and the \n after a and b. Count them up yourself. If you don't understand which characters are counted, it will only get more confusing.

On line 19, we ask Java to add a single blank space to each of the three lines in block. However, the output says we added 4 characters rather than 3 since the length went from 6 to 10. This mysterious additional character is thanks to the line termination normalization. Since the text block doesn't have a line break at the end, indent() adds one!

On line 20, we remove one whitespace character from each of the three lines of concat. This gives a length of seven. We started with nine, got rid of three characters, and added a trailing normalized new line.

On line 21, we ask Java to remove four whitespace characters from the same three lines. Since there are not four whitespace characters, Java does its best. The single space is removed before a and c. Both spaces are removed before b. The length of six should make sense here; we removed one more character here than on line 20.

Finally, line 22 uses the stripIndent() method. All of the lines have at least one whitespace character. Since they do not all have two whitespace characters, the method gets rid of only one character per line. Since no new line is added by stripIndent(), the length is six, which is three less than the original nine.

Checking for Empty or Blank *String*s

Java provides convenience methods for whether a String has a length of zero or contains only whitespace characters. The method signatures are as follows:

```
public boolean isEmpty()
public boolean isBlank()
```

The following code shows how to use these methods:

```
System.out.println(" ".isEmpty());   // false
System.out.println("".isEmpty());    // true
System.out.println(" ".isBlank());   // true
System.out.println("".isBlank());    // true
```

The first line prints false because the String is not empty; it has a blank space in it. The second line prints true because this time, there are no characters in the String. The final two lines print true because there are no characters other than whitespace present.

Formatting Values

There are methods to format String values using formatting flags. Two of the methods take the format string as a parameter, and the other uses an instance for that value. One method takes a Locale, which you learn about in Chapter 11.

The method parameters are used to construct a formatted String in a single method call, rather than via a lot of format and concatenation operations. They return a reference to the instance they are called on so that operations can be chained together. The method signatures are as follows:

```
public static String format(String format, Object... args)
public static String format(Locale loc, String format, Object... args)
public String formatted(Object... args)
```

The following code shows how to use these methods:

```
var name = "Kate";
var orderId = 5;

// All print: Hello Kate, order 5 is ready
System.out.println("Hello "+name+", order "+orderId+" is ready");
System.out.println(String.format("Hello %s, order %d is ready",
   name, orderId));
System.out.println("Hello %s, order %d is ready"
   .formatted(name, orderId));
```

In the format() and formatted() operations, the parameters are inserted and formatted via symbols in the order that they are provided in the vararg. Table 4.2 lists the ones you should know for the exam.

TABLE 4.2   Common formatting symbols

Symbol	Description
%s	Applies to any type, commonly String values
%d	Applies to integer values like int and long

Symbol	Description
%f	Applies to floating-point values like `float` and `double`
%n	Inserts a line break using the system-dependent line separator

The following example uses all four symbols from Table 4.2:

```
var name = "James";
var score = 90.25;
var total = 100;
System.out.println("%s:%n    Score: %f out of %d"
    .formatted(name, score, total));
```

This prints the following:

```
James:
  Score: 90.250000 out of 100
```

Mixing data types may cause exceptions at runtime. For example, the following throws an exception because a floating-point number is used when an integer value is expected:

```
var str = "Food: %d tons".formatted(2.0); // IllegalFormatConversionException
```

Using *format()* with Flags

Besides supporting symbols, Java also supports optional flags between the % and the symbol character. In the previous example, the floating-point number was printed as 90.250000. By default, %f displays exactly six digits past the decimal. If you want to display only one digit after the decimal, you can use %.1f instead of %f. The format() method relies on rounding rather than truncating when shortening numbers. For example, 90.250000 will be displayed as 90.3 (not 90.2) when passed to format() with %.1f.

The format() method also supports two additional features. You can specify the total length of output by using a number before the decimal symbol. By default, the method will fill the empty space with blank spaces. You can also fill the empty space with zeros by placing a single zero before the decimal symbol. The following examples use brackets, [ ], to show the start/end of the formatted value:

```
var pi = 3.14159265359;
System.out.format("[%f]",pi);        // [3.141593]
System.out.format("[%12.8f]",pi);    // [  3.14159265]
System.out.format("[%012f]",pi);     // [00003.141593]
System.out.format("[%12.2f]",pi);    // [        3.14]
System.out.format("[%.3f]",pi);      // [3.142]
```

The format() method supports a lot of other symbols and flags. You don't need to know any of them for the exam beyond what we've discussed already.

Method Chaining

Ready to put together everything you just learned about? It is common to call multiple methods, as shown here:

```
var start = "AniMaL    ";
var trimmed = start.trim();              // "AniMaL"
var lowercase = trimmed.toLowerCase();   // "animal"
var result = lowercase.replace('a', 'A'); // "AnimAl"
System.out.println(result);
```

This is just a series of `String` methods. Each time one is called, the returned value is put in a new variable. There are four `String` values along the way, and `AnimAl` is output.

However, on the exam, there is a tendency to cram as much code as possible into a small space. You'll see code using a technique called *method chaining*. Here's an example:

```
String result = "AniMaL    ".trim().toLowerCase().replace('a', 'A');
System.out.println(result);
```

This code is equivalent to the previous example. It also creates four `String` objects and outputs `AnimAl`. To read code that uses method chaining, start at the left and evaluate the first method. Then call the next method on the returned value of the first method. Keep going until you get to the semicolon.

What do you think the result of this code is?

```
5: String a = "abc";
6: String b = a.toUpperCase();
7: b = b.replace("B", "2").replace('C', '3');
8: System.out.println("a=" + a);
9: System.out.println("b=" + b);
```

On line 5, we set a to point to "abc" and never pointed a to anything else. Since none of the code on lines 6 and 7 changes a, the value remains "abc".

However, b is a little trickier. Line 6 has b pointing to "ABC", which is straightforward. On line 7, we have method chaining. First, "ABC".replace("B", "2") is called. This returns "A2C". Next, "A2C".replace('C', '3') is called. This returns "A23". Finally, b changes to point to this returned `String`. When line 9 executes, b is "A23".

Using the *StringBuilder* Class

A small program can create a lot of `String` objects very quickly. For example, how many objects do you think this piece of code creates?

```
10: String alpha = "";
11: for(char current = 'a'; current <= 'z'; current++)
12:     alpha += current;
13: System.out.println(alpha);
```

The empty String on line 10 is instantiated, and then line 12 appends an "a". However, because the String object is immutable, a new String object is assigned to alpha, and the "" object becomes eligible for garbage collection. The next time through the loop, alpha is assigned a new String object, "ab", and the "a" object becomes eligible for garbage collection. The next iteration assigns alpha to "abc", and the "ab" object becomes eligible for garbage collection, and so on.

This sequence of events continues, and after 26 iterations through the loop, *a total of 27 objects are instantiated*, most of which are immediately eligible for garbage collection.

This is very inefficient. Luckily, Java has a solution. The StringBuilder class creates a String without storing all those interim String values. Unlike the String class, StringBuilder is not immutable.

```
15: StringBuilder alpha = new StringBuilder();
16: for(char current = 'a'; current <= 'z'; current++)
17:     alpha.append(current);
18: System.out.println(alpha);
```

On line 15, a new StringBuilder object is instantiated. The call to append() on line 17 adds a character to the StringBuilder object each time through the for loop, appending the value of current to the end of alpha. This code reuses the same StringBuilder without creating an interim String each time.

In old code, you might see references to StringBuffer. It works the same way, except it supports threads, which you learn about in Chapter 13, "Concurrency." StringBuffer is not on the exam. It performs slower than StringBuilder, so just use StringBuilder.

In this section, we look at creating a StringBuilder and using its common methods.

Mutability and Chaining

We're sure you noticed this from the previous example, but StringBuilder is not immutable. In fact, we gave it 27 different values in the example (a blank plus adding each letter in the alphabet). The exam will likely try to trick you with respect to StringBuilder being mutable and String being immutable.

Chaining makes this even more interesting. When we chained String method calls, the result was a new String with the answer. Chaining StringBuilder methods doesn't work this way. Instead, the StringBuilder changes its own state and returns a reference to itself. Let's look at an example to make this clearer:

```
4: StringBuilder sb = new StringBuilder("start");
5: sb.append("+middle");                    // sb = "start+middle"
6: StringBuilder same = sb.append("+end");   // "start+middle+end"
```

Line 5 adds text to the end of sb. It also returns a reference to sb, which is ignored. Line 6 also adds text to the end of sb and returns a reference to sb. This time the reference is stored in same. This means sb and same point to the same object and would print out the same value.

The exam won't always make the code easy to read by having only one method per line. What do you think this example prints?

```
4: StringBuilder a = new StringBuilder("abc");
5: StringBuilder b = a.append("de");
6: b = b.append("f").append("g");
7: System.out.println("a=" + a);
8: System.out.println("b=" + b);
```

Did you say both print "abcdefg"? Good. There's only one StringBuilder object here. We know that because new StringBuilder() is called only once. On line 5, there are two variables referring to that object, which has a value of "abcde". On line 6, those two variables are still referring to that same object, which now has a value of "abcdefg". Incidentally, the assignment back to b does absolutely nothing. b is already pointing to that StringBuilder.

Creating a *StringBuilder*

There are three ways to construct a StringBuilder:

```
StringBuilder sb1 = new StringBuilder();
StringBuilder sb2 = new StringBuilder("animal");
StringBuilder sb3 = new StringBuilder(10);
```

The first says to create a StringBuilder containing an empty sequence of characters and assign sb1 to point to it. The second says to create a StringBuilder containing a specific value and assign sb2 to point to it. The first two examples tell Java to manage the implementation details. The final example tells Java that we have some idea of how big the eventual value will be and would like the StringBuilder to reserve a certain capacity, or number of slots, for characters.

Important *StringBuilder* Methods

As with String, we aren't going to cover every single method in the StringBuilder class. These are the ones you might see on the exam.

Using Common Methods

These four methods work exactly the same as in the String class. Be sure you can identify the output of this example:

```
var sb = new StringBuilder("animals");
String sub = sb.substring(sb.indexOf("a"), sb.indexOf("al"));
int len = sb.length();
char ch = sb.charAt(6);
System.out.println(sub + " " + len + " " + ch);
```

The correct answer is anim 7 s. The indexOf() method calls return 0 and 4, respectively. The substring() method returns the String starting with index 0 and ending right before index 4.

The length() method returns 7 because it is the number of characters in the StringBuilder rather than an index. Finally, charAt() returns the character at index 6. Here, we do start with 0 because we are referring to indexes. If this doesn't sound familiar, go back and read the section on String again.

Notice that substring() returns a String rather than a StringBuilder. That is why sb is not changed. The substring() method is really just a method that inquires about the state of the StringBuilder.

Appending Values

The append() method is by far the most frequently used method in StringBuilder. In fact, it is so frequently used that we just started using it without comment. Luckily, this method does just what it sounds like: it adds the parameter to the StringBuilder and returns a reference to the current StringBuilder. One of the method signatures is as follows:

```
public StringBuilder append(String str)
```

Notice that we said *one* of the method signatures. There are more than 10 method signatures that look similar but take different data types as parameters, such as int, char, etc. All those methods are provided so you can write code like this:

```
var sb = new StringBuilder().append(1).append('c');
sb.append("-").append(true);
System.out.println(sb);       // 1c-true
```

Nice method chaining, isn't it? The append() method is called directly after the constructor. By having all these method signatures, you can just call append() without having to convert your parameter to a String first.

Applying Code Points

The codePointAt(), codePointBefore(), and codePointCount() methods from String are also available on StringBuilder. There's one more method you need to know for code points that is only on StringBuilder:

```
public StringBuilder appendCodePoint(int codePoint)
```

It works like the append() method in the previous section except it takes an integer representing the Unicode value, converts it to a character, and appends it to the StringBuilder.

```
var sb = new StringBuilder()
   .appendCodePoint(87).append(',')
   .append((char)87).append(',')
```

```
  .append(87).append(',')
  .appendCodePoint(8217);
System.out.println(sb);  // W,W,87,'
```

Like we saw with String, it also handles non-ASCII characters like a stylized quote (').
Again, you do not need to know the numeric values for characters for the exam, but you
should understand how the text in this example is generated.

Inserting Data

The insert() method adds characters to the StringBuilder at the requested index and
returns a reference to the current StringBuilder. Just like append(), there are lots of
method signatures for different types. Here's one:

```
public StringBuilder insert(int offset, String str)
```

Pay attention to the offset in these examples. It is the index where we want to insert the
requested parameter.

```
3: var sb = new StringBuilder("animals");
4: sb.insert(7, "-");                 // sb = animals-
5: sb.insert(0, "-");                 // sb = -animals-
6: sb.insert(4, "-");                 // sb = -ani-mals-
7: System.out.println(sb);
```

Line 4 says to insert a dash at index 7, which happens to be the end of the sequence of
characters. Line 5 says to insert a dash at index 0, which happens to be the very beginning.
Finally, line 6 says to insert a dash right before index 4. The exam creators will try to trip
you up on this. As we add and remove characters, their indexes change. When you see a
question dealing with such operations, draw what is going on using available writing
materials so you won't be confused.

Deleting Contents

The delete() method is the opposite of the insert() method. It removes characters from
the sequence and returns a reference to the current StringBuilder. The deleteCharAt()
method is convenient when you want to delete only one character. The method signatures
are as follows:

```
public StringBuilder delete(int startIndex, int endIndex)
public StringBuilder deleteCharAt(int index)
```

The following code shows how to use these methods:

```
var sb = new StringBuilder("abcdef");
sb.delete(1, 3);                      // sb = adef
sb.deleteCharAt(5);                   // exception
```

First, we delete the characters starting with index 1 and ending right before index 3. This gives us adef. Next, we ask Java to delete the character at position 5. However, the remaining value is only four characters long, so it throws a StringIndexOutOfBoundsException.

The delete() method is more flexible than some others when it comes to array indexes. If you specify a second parameter that is past the end of the StringBuilder, Java will just assume you meant the end. That means this code is legal:

```
var sb = new StringBuilder("abcdef");
sb.delete(1, 100);                    // sb = a
```

Replacing Portions

The replace() method works differently for StringBuilder than it did for String. The method signature is as follows:

```
public StringBuilder replace(int startIndex, int endIndex, String newString)
```

The following code shows how to use this method:

```
var builder = new StringBuilder("pigeon dirty");
builder.replace(3, 6, "sty");
System.out.println(builder);  // pigsty dirty
```

First, Java deletes the characters starting with index 3 and ending right before index 6. This gives us pig dirty. Then Java inserts the value "sty" in that position.

In this example, the number of characters removed and inserted are the same. However, there is no reason they have to be. What do you think this does?

```
var builder = new StringBuilder("pigeon dirty");
builder.replace(3, 100, "");
System.out.println(builder);
```

It prints "pig". Remember, the method is first doing a logical delete. The replace() method allows specifying a second parameter that is past the end of the StringBuilder. That means only the first three characters remain.

Reversing

After all that, it's time for a nice, easy method. The reverse() method does just what it sounds like: it reverses the characters in the sequences and returns a reference to the current StringBuilder. The method signature is as follows:

```
public StringBuilder reverse()
```

The following code shows how to use this method:

```
var sb = new StringBuilder("ABC");
sb.reverse();
System.out.println(sb);
```

As expected, this prints CBA. This method isn't that interesting. Maybe the exam creators like to include it to encourage you to write down the value rather than relying on memory for indexes.

Working with *toString()*

The `Object` class contains a `toString()` method that many classes provide custom implementations of. The `StringBuilder` class is one of these.

The following code shows how to use this method:

```
var sb = new StringBuilder("ABC");
String s = sb.toString();
```

Often `StringBuilder` is used internally for performance purposes, but the end result needs to be a `String`. For example, maybe it needs to be passed to another method that is expecting a `String`.

Understanding Equality

In Chapter 2, you learned how to use == to compare numbers and that object references refer to the same object. Earlier in this chapter, we saw the `equals()` method on `String`. In this section, we look at what it means for two objects to be equivalent or the same. We also look at the impact of the `String` pool on equality.

Comparing *equals()* and ==

Consider the following code that uses == with objects:

```
var one = new StringBuilder();
var two = new StringBuilder();
var three = one.append("a");
System.out.println(one == two);   // false
System.out.println(one == three); // true
```

Since this example isn't dealing with primitives, we know to look for whether the references are referring to the same object. The one and two variables are both completely separate `StringBuilder` objects, giving us two objects. Therefore, the first print statement gives us `false`. The `three` variable is more interesting. Remember how `StringBuilder` methods like to return the current reference for chaining? This means one and `three` both point to the same object, and the second print statement gives us `true`.

You saw earlier that `equals()` uses logical equality rather than object equality for `String` objects.

```
var x = "Hello World";
var z = " Hello World".trim();
System.out.println(x.equals(z)); // true
```

This works because the authors of the `String` class implemented a standard method called `equals()` to check the values inside the `String` rather than the string reference itself. If a class doesn't have an `equals()` method, Java determines whether the references point to the same object, which is exactly what == does.

In case you are wondering, the authors of `StringBuilder` did not implement `equals()`. If you call `equals()` on two `StringBuilder` instances, it will check reference equality. You can call `toString()` on `StringBuilder` to get a `String` to check for equality instead.

Finally, the exam might try to trick you with a question like this. Can you guess why the code doesn't compile?

```
var name = "a";
var builder = new StringBuilder("a");

System.out.println(name == builder);        // DOES NOT COMPILE
```

Remember that == is checking for object reference equality. The compiler is smart enough to know that two references can't possibly point to the same object when they are completely different types.

The String Pool

Since strings are everywhere in Java, they use up a lot of memory. In some production applications, they can use a large amount of memory in the entire program. Java realizes that many strings repeat in the program and solves this issue by reusing common ones. The *string pool*, also known as the intern pool, is a location in the Java Virtual Machine (JVM) that collects all these strings.

The string pool contains literal values and constants that appear in your program. For example, `"name"` is a literal and therefore goes into the string pool. The `myObject.toString()` method returns a string but not a literal, so it does not go into the string pool.

Let's now visit the more complex and confusing scenario, `String` equality, made so in part because of the way the JVM reuses `String` literals.

```
var x = "Hello World";
var y = "Hello World";
System.out.println(x == y);    // true
```

Remember that a `String` is immutable and literals are pooled. The JVM created only one literal in memory. The x and y variables both point to the same location in memory; therefore, the statement outputs `true`. It gets even trickier. Consider this code:

```
var x = "Hello World";
var z = " Hello World".trim();
System.out.println(x == z); // false
```

In this example, we don't have two of the same `String` literal. Although x and z happen to evaluate to the same string, one is computed at runtime. Since it isn't the same at compile time, a new `String` object is created. Let's try another one. What do you think is output here?

```
var singleString = "hello world";
var concat = "hello ";
concat += "world";
System.out.println(singleString == concat); // false
```

This prints `false`. Calling += is just like calling a method and results in a new `String`. You can even force the issue by creating a new `String`:

```
var x = "Hello World";
var y = new String("Hello World");
System.out.println(x == y); // false
```

The first says to use the string pool normally. The second says, "No, JVM, I really don't want you to use the string pool. Please create a new object for me even though it is less efficient."

You can also do the opposite and tell Java to use the string pool. The `intern()` method will use an object in the string pool if one is present.

public String intern()

If the literal is not yet in the string pool, Java will add it at this time.

```
var name = "Hello World";
var name2 = new String("Hello World").intern();
System.out.println(name == name2);     // true
```

First we tell Java to use the string pool normally for name. Then, for name2, we tell Java to create a new object using the constructor but to intern it and use the string pool anyway. Since both variables point to the same reference in the string pool, we can use the == operator.

Let's try another one. What do you think this prints out? Be careful. It is tricky.

```
15: var first = "rat" + 1;
16: var second = "r" + "a" + "t" + "1";
17: var third = "r" + "a" + "t" + new String("1");
18: System.out.println(first == second);
```

```
19: System.out.println(first == second.intern());
20: System.out.println(first == third);
21: System.out.println(first == third.intern());
```

On line 15, we have a compile-time constant that automatically gets placed in the string pool as "rat1". On line 16, we have a more complicated expression that is also a compile-time constant. Therefore, first and second share the same string pool reference. This makes lines 18 and 19 print true.

On line 17, we have a String constructor. This means we no longer have a compile-time constant, and third does not point to a reference in the string pool. Therefore, line 20 prints false. On line 21, the intern() call looks in the string pool. Java notices that first points to the same String and prints true.

Remember to never use intern() or == to compare String objects in your code. You should use the equals() method instead. The only time you should have to deal with these is on the exam.

Understanding Arrays

Up to now, we've been referring to the String and StringBuilder classes as a "sequence of characters." This is true. They are implemented using an *array* of characters. An array is an area of memory on the heap with space for a designated number of elements. A String is implemented as an array with some methods that you might want to use when dealing with characters specifically. A StringBuilder is implemented as an array where the array object is replaced with a new, bigger array object when it runs out of space to store all the characters. A big difference is that an array can be of any other Java type. If we didn't want to use a String for some reason, we could use an array of char primitives directly:

```
char[] letters;
```

This wouldn't be very convenient because we'd lose all the special properties String gives us, such as writing "Java". Keep in mind that letters is a reference variable and not a primitive. The char type is a primitive. But char is what goes into the array and not the type of the array itself. The array itself is of type char[]. You can mentally read the brackets ([]) as "array."

In other words, an array is an ordered list. It can contain duplicates. In this section, we look at creating an array of primitives and objects, sorting, searching, and varargs.

Creating an Array of Primitives

Figure 4.3 shows the most common way to create an array. It specifies the type of the array (int) and the size (3). The brackets tell you this is an array.

FIGURE 4.3   The basic structure of an array

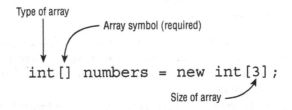

When you use this form to instantiate an array, all elements are set to the default value for that type. As you learned in Chapter 1, the default value of an `int` is 0. Since `numbers` is a reference variable, it points to the array object, as shown in Figure 4.4. As you can see, the default value for all the elements is 0. Also, the indexes start with 0 and count up, just as they did for a `String`.

FIGURE 4.4   An empty array

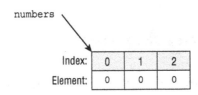

Another way to create an array is to specify all the elements it should start out with.

```
int[] moreNumbers = new int[] {42, 55, 99};
```

In this example, we also create an `int` array of size 3. This time, we specify the initial values of those three elements instead of using the defaults. Figure 4.5 shows what this array looks like.

FIGURE 4.5   An initialized array

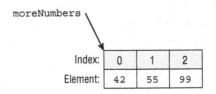

Java recognizes that this expression is redundant. Since you are specifying the type of the array on the left side of the equals sign, Java already knows the type. And since you are specifying the initial values, it already knows the size. As a shortcut, Java lets you write this:

```
int[] moreNumbers = {42, 55, 99};
```

This approach is called an *anonymous array*. It is anonymous because you don't specify the type and size.

Finally, you can type the [] before or after the name, and adding a space is optional. This means that all five of these statements do the exact same thing:

```java
int[] numAnimals;
int [] numAnimals2;
int []numAnimals3;
int numAnimals4[];
int numAnimals5 [];
```

Most people use the first one. You could see any of these on the exam, though, so get used to seeing the brackets in odd places.

Multiple "Arrays" in Declarations

What types of reference variables do you think the following code creates?

```java
int[] ids, types;
```

The correct answer is two variables of type int[]. This seems logical enough. After all, int a, b; created two int variables. What about this example?

```java
int ids[], types;
```

All we did was move the brackets, but it changed the behavior. This time we get one variable of type int[] and one variable of type int. Java sees this line of code and thinks something like this: "They want two variables of type int. The first one is called ids[]. This one is an int[] called ids. The second one is just called types. No brackets, so it is a regular integer."

Needless to say, you shouldn't write code that looks like this. But you do need to understand it for the exam.

Creating an Array with Reference Variables

You can choose any Java type to be the type of the array. This includes classes you create yourself. Let's take a look at a built-in type with String:

```java
String[] bugs = { "cricket", "beetle", "ladybug" };
String[] alias = bugs;
String[] anotherArray = { "cricket", "beetle", "ladybug" };
```

```
System.out.println(bugs.equals(alias));        // true
System.out.println(bugs.equals(anotherArray)); // false
System.out.println(bugs.toString());           // [Ljava.lang.String;@160bc7c0
```

We can call equals() because an array is an object. The first test with alias returns true because of reference equality. Why does the second equality test return false? The equals() method on arrays does not look at the elements of the array.

The second print statement is even more interesting. What on Earth is [Ljava.lang.String;@160bc7c0? You don't have to know this for the exam, but [L means it is an array, java.lang.String is the reference type, and 160bc7c0 is the hash code. You'll get different numbers and letters each time you run it since this is a reference.

 Java provides a method that prints an array nicely:
Arrays.toString(bugs) would print [cricket, beetle, ladybug].

We can see our bugs array represented in memory in Figure 4.6. Make sure you understand this figure. The array does not allocate space for the String objects. Instead, it allocates space for a reference to where the objects are really stored.

FIGURE 4.6   An array pointing to strings

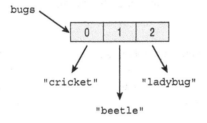

As a quick review, what do you think this array points to?

```
public class Names {
   String names[];
}
```

You got us. It was a review of Chapter 1 and not our discussion on arrays. The answer is null. The code never instantiated the array, so it is just a reference variable to null. Let's try that again: what do you think this array points to?

```
public class Names {
   String names[] = new String[2];
}
```

It is an array because it has brackets. It is an array of type `String` since that is the type mentioned in the declaration. It has two elements because the length is 2. Each of those two slots currently is `null` but has the potential to point to a `String` object.

Remember casting from the previous chapter when you wanted to force a bigger type into a smaller type? You can do that with arrays too:

```
3: String[] strings = { "stringValue" };
4: Object[] objects = strings;
5: String[] againStrings = (String[]) objects;
6: againStrings[0] = new StringBuilder();   // DOES NOT COMPILE
7: objects[0] = new StringBuilder();        // Careful!
```

Line 3 creates an array of type `String`. Line 4 doesn't require a cast because `Object` is a broader type than `String`. On line 5, a cast is needed because we are moving to a more specific type. Line 6 doesn't compile because a `String[]`allows only `String` objects, and `StringBuilder` is not a `String`.

Line 7 is where this gets interesting. From the point of view of the compiler, this is just fine. A `StringBuilder` object can clearly go in an `Object[]`. The problem is that we don't actually have an `Object[]`. We have a `String[]` referred to from an `Object[]` variable. At runtime, the code throws an `ArrayStoreException`. You don't need to memorize the name of this exception, but you do need to know that this line will compile and throw an exception.

Using an Array

Now that you know how to create an array, let's try accessing one:

```
4: String[] mammals = {"monkey", "chimp", "donkey"};
5: System.out.println(mammals.length);       // 3
6: System.out.println(mammals[0]);           // monkey
7: System.out.println(mammals[1]);           // chimp
8: System.out.println(mammals[2]);           // donkey
```

Line 4 declares and initializes the array. Line 5 tells us how many elements the array can hold. The rest of the code prints the array. Notice that elements are indexed starting with 0. This should be familiar from `String` and `StringBuilder`, which also start counting with 0. Those classes also counted `length` as the number of elements. Note that there are no parentheses after `length` since it is not a method. Watch out for compiler errors like the following on the exam!

```
4: String[] mammals = {"monkey", "chimp", "donkey"};
5: System.out.println(mammals.length());        // DOES NOT COMPILE
```

To make sure you understand how `length` works, what do you think this prints?

```
4: var birds = new String[6];
5: System.out.println(birds.length);
```

The answer is 6. Even though all six elements of the array are null, there are still six of them. The length attribute does not consider what is in the array; it considers only how many slots have been allocated.

It is very common to use a loop when reading from or writing to an array. This loop sets each element of numbers to five higher than the current index:

```
5: var numbers = new int[10];
6: for (int i = 0; i < numbers.length; i++)
7:     numbers[i] = i + 5;
8: for(int n : numbers)
9:     System.out.println(n);
```

Line 5 simply instantiates an array with 10 slots. Line 6 is a for loop that uses an extremely common pattern. It starts at index 0, which is where an array begins as well. It keeps going, one at a time, until it hits the end of the array. Line 7 sets the current element of numbers to the index of the element plus 5. Lines 8 and 9 print the numbers in the array, using the for-each loop that you learned about in Chapter 3, "Making Decisions."

The exam will test whether you are being observant by trying to access elements that are not in the array. Can you tell why each of these throws an ArrayIndexOutOfBoundsException for our array of size 10?

```
3: var numbers = new int[10];
4: numbers[10] = 3;
5:
6: numbers[numbers.length] = 5;
7:
8: for (int i = 0; i <= numbers.length; i++)
9:     numbers[i] = i + 5;
```

The first one is trying to see whether you know that indexes start with 0. Since we have 10 elements in our array, this means only numbers[0] through numbers[9] are valid. The second example assumes you are clever enough to know that 10 is invalid and disguises it by using the length field. However, the length is always one more than the maximum valid index. Finally, the for loop incorrectly uses <= instead of <, which is also a way of referring to that tenth index.

Sorting

Java makes it easy to sort an array by providing a sort method—or rather, a bunch of sort methods. Just like StringBuilder allowed you to pass almost anything to append(), you can pass almost any array to Arrays.sort().

Arrays requires an import. To use it, you must have either of the following two statements in your class:

```
import java.util.*;        // import whole package including Arrays
import java.util.Arrays;   // import just Arrays
```

There is one exception, although it doesn't come up often on the exam. You can write `java.util.Arrays` every time it is used in the class instead of specifying it as an import.

Remember that if you are shown a code snippet, you can assume the necessary imports are there. This simple example sorts three numbers:

```
int[] numbers = { 6, 9, 1 };
Arrays.sort(numbers);
for (int i = 0; i < numbers.length; i++)
    System.out.print(numbers[i] +  " ");
```

The result is 1 6 9, as you should expect it to be. Notice that we looped through the output to print the values in the array. Just printing the array variable directly would give the annoying hash of [I@2bd9c3e7. Alternatively, we could have printed `Arrays.toString(numbers)` instead of using the loop. That would have output [1, 6, 9].

Try this again with `String` types:

```
String[] strings = { "10", "9", "100" };
Arrays.sort(strings);
for (String s : strings)
    System.out.print(s + " ");
```

This time the result might not be what you expect. This code outputs 10 100 9. The problem is that `String` sorts in alphabetic order, and 1 sorts before 9. (Numbers sort before letters, and uppercase sorts before lowercase.) In Chapter 9, "Collections and Generics," you learn how to create custom sort orders using something called a *comparator*.

You can use 7Up, the soda, to help remember the order. Numbers (7) sort first, followed by uppercase (U), and then lowercase (p).

Searching

Java also provides a convenient way to search, but only if the array is already sorted. Table 4.3 covers the rules for binary search.

TABLE 4.3   Binary search rules

Scenario	Result
Target element found in sorted array	Index of match
Target element not found in sorted array	Negative value showing one smaller than the negative of the index, where a match needs to be inserted to preserve sorted order
Unsorted array	A surprise; this result is undefined

Let's try these rules with an example:

```
3: int[] numbers = {2,4,6,8};
4: System.out.println(Arrays.binarySearch(numbers, 2)); // 0
5: System.out.println(Arrays.binarySearch(numbers, 4)); // 1
6: System.out.println(Arrays.binarySearch(numbers, 1)); // -1
7: System.out.println(Arrays.binarySearch(numbers, 3)); // -2
8: System.out.println(Arrays.binarySearch(numbers, 9)); // -5
```

Take note of the fact that line 3 is a sorted array. If it wasn't, we couldn't apply either of the other rules. Line 4 searches for the index of 2. The answer is index 0. Line 5 searches for the index of 4, which is 1.

Line 6 searches for the index of 1. Although 1 isn't in the list, the search can determine that it should be inserted at element 0 to preserve the sorted order. Since 0 already means something for array indexes, Java needs to subtract 1 to give us the answer of -1. Line 7 is similar. Although 3 isn't in the list, it would need to be inserted at element 1 to preserve the sorted order. We negate and subtract 1 for consistency, getting -1 -1, also known as -2. Finally, line 8 wants to tell us that 9 should be inserted at index 4. We again negate and subtract 1, getting -4 -1, also known as -5.

What do you think happens in this example?

```
5: int[] numbers = new int[] {3,2,1};
6: System.out.println(Arrays.binarySearch(numbers, 2));
7: System.out.println(Arrays.binarySearch(numbers, 3));
```

Note that on line 5, the array isn't sorted. This means the output will not be defined. When testing this example, line 6 correctly gave 1 as the output. However, line 7 gave the wrong answer. The exam creators will not expect you to know what incorrect values come out. As soon as you see the array isn't sorted, look for an answer choice about unpredictable output.

On the exam, you need to know what a binary search returns in various scenarios. Oddly, you don't need to know why "binary" is in the name. In case you are curious, a binary search splits the array into two equal pieces (remember, 2 is binary) and determines which half the target is in. It repeats this process until only one element is left.

Comparing

Java also provides methods to compare two arrays to determine which is "smaller." First we cover the equals() and compare() methods, and then we go on to mismatch(). These methods are overloaded to take a variety of parameters.

Using *equals()*

While == compares object references, Arrays includes overloaded versions of equals() that lets you check if the arrays are the same size and contain the same elements, in the same order. For example:

```
System.out.println(new int[] {1} == new int[] {1});                    // false
```

```
System.out.println(Arrays.equals(new int[] {1}, new int[] {1}));    // true
System.out.println(Arrays.equals(new int[] {1}, new int[] {2}));    // false
System.out.println(Arrays.equals(new int[] {1}, new int[] {1, 2})); // false
```

When comparing elements, it uses == for primitive values and equals() for object values.

Using *compare()*

There are a bunch of rules you need to know before calling compare(). Luckily, these are the same rules you need to know in Chapter 9 when writing a Comparator.

First you need to learn what the return value means. You do not need to know the exact return values, but you do need to know the following:

- A **negative** number means the first array is smaller than the second.
- A **zero** means the arrays are equal.
- A **positive** number means the first array is larger than the second.

Here's an example:

```
System.out.println(Arrays.compare(new int[] {1}, new int[] {2}));
```

This code prints a negative number. It should be pretty intuitive that 1 is smaller than 2, making the first array smaller.

Now that you know how to compare a single value, let's look at how to compare arrays of different lengths:

- If both arrays are the same length and have the same values in each spot in the same order, return zero.
- If all the elements are the same but the second array has extra elements at the end, return a negative number.
- If all the elements are the same, but the first array has extra elements at the end, return a positive number.
- If the first element that differs is smaller in the first array, return a negative number.
- If the first element that differs is larger in the first array, return a positive number.

Finally, what does smaller mean? Here are some more rules that apply here and to compareTo(), which you see in Chapter 8, "Lambdas and Functional Interfaces":

- null is smaller than any other value.
- For numbers, normal numeric order applies.
- For strings, one is smaller if it is a prefix of another.
- For strings/characters, numbers are smaller than letters.
- For strings/characters, uppercase is smaller than lowercase.

Table 4.4 shows examples of these rules in action.

TABLE 4.4 Arrays.compare() examples

First array	Second array	Result	Reason
new int[] {1, 2}	new int[] {1}	Positive number	The first element is the same, but the first array is longer.
new int[] {1, 2}	new int[] {1, 2}	Zero	Exact match.
new String[] {"a"}	new String[] {"aa"}	Negative number	The first element is a substring of the second.
new String[] {"a"}	new String[] {"A"}	Positive number	Uppercase is smaller than lowercase.
new String[] {"a"}	new String[] {null}	Positive number	null is smaller than a letter.

Finally, this code does not compile because the types are different. When comparing two arrays, they must be the same array type.

```
System.out.println(Arrays.compare(
   new int[] {1}, new String[] {"a"})); // DOES NOT COMPILE
```

Using *mismatch()*

Now that you are familiar with compare(), it is time to learn about mismatch(). If the arrays are equal, mismatch() returns −1. Otherwise, it returns the first index where they differ. Can you figure out what these print?

```
System.out.println(Arrays.mismatch(new int[] {1}, new int[] {1}));
System.out.println(Arrays.mismatch(new String[] {"a"},
   new String[] {"A"}));
System.out.println(Arrays.mismatch(new int[] {1, 2}, new int[] {1}));
```

In the first example, the arrays are the same, so the result is −1. In the second example, the entries at element 0 are not equal, so the result is 0. In the third example, the entries at element 0 are equal, so we keep looking. The element at index 1 is not equal. Or, more specifically, one array has an element at index 1, and the other does not. Therefore, the result is 1.

To make sure you understand the compare() and mismatch() methods, study Table 4.5. If you don't understand why all of the values are there, please go back and study this section again.

TABLE 4.5   Equality vs. comparison vs. mismatch

Method	When arrays contain the same data	When arrays are different
Arrays.equals()	true	false
Arrays.compare()	0	Positive or negative number
Arrays.mismatch()	-1	Zero or positive index

Using Methods with Varargs

When you're creating an array yourself, it looks like what we've seen thus far. When one is passed to your method, there is another way it can look. Here are three examples with a main() method:

```
public static void main(String[] args)
public static void main(String args[])
public static void main(String... args) // varargs
```

The third example uses a syntax called *varargs* (variable arguments), which you saw in Chapter 1. You learn how to call a method using varargs in Chapter 5, "Methods." For now, all you need to know is that you can use a variable defined using varargs as if it were a normal array. For example, args.length and args[0] are legal.

Working with Arrays of Arrays

Arrays are objects, and of course, array components can be objects. It doesn't take much time, rubbing those two facts together, to wonder whether arrays can hold other arrays, and of course, they can.

Creating an Array of Arrays

Multiple array separators are all it takes to declare arrays of arrays. While they aren't really multidimensional, it helps to think of them as such. You can locate them with the type or variable name in the declaration, just as before:

```
int[][] vars1;               // 2D array
int vars2 [][];              // 2D array
int[] vars3[];               // 2D array
int[] vars4 [], space [][];  // 2D and 3D arrays
```

The first two examples are nothing surprising and declare a two-dimensional (2D) array. The third example also declares a 2D array. There's no good reason to use this style other than to confuse readers with your code. The final example declares two arrays on the same line. Adding up the brackets, we see that the vars4 is a 2D array and space is a 3D array. Again, there's no reason to use this style other than to confuse readers of your code. The exam creators like to try to confuse you, though. Luckily, you are on to them and won't let this happen to you!

You can specify the size of your array and the array it contains in the declaration if you like:

```
String [][] rectangle = new String[3][2];
```

The result of this statement is an array rectangle with three elements, each of which refers to an array of two elements. You can think of the addressable range as [0][0] through [2][1], but don't think of it as a structure of addresses like [0,0] or [2,1].

Now suppose we set one of these values:

```
rectangle[0][1] = "set";
```

You can visualize the result as shown in Figure 4.7. This array is sparsely populated because it has a lot of null values. You can see that rectangle still points to an array of three elements and that we have three arrays of two elements. You can also follow the trail from reference to the one value pointing to a String. You start at index 0 in the top array. Then you go to index 1 in the next array.

FIGURE 4.7   A sparsely populated array of arrays

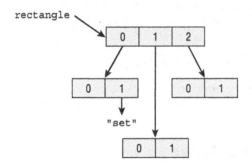

While that array happens to be rectangular in shape, an array doesn't need to be. Consider this one:

```
int[][] differentSizes = {{1, 4}, {3}, {9,8,7}};
```

We still start with an array of three elements. However, this time the elements in the next level are all different sizes. One is of length 2, the next length 1, and the last length 3. See Figure 4.8. This time the array is of primitives, so they are shown as if they are in the array themselves.

FIGURE 4.8 An asymmetric array of arrays

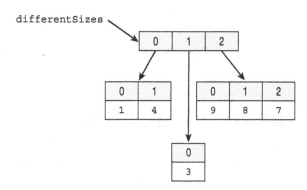

Another way to create an asymmetric array is to initialize just an array's first dimension and define the size of each array component in a separate statement.

```
int [][] args = new int[2][];
args[0] = new int[5];
args[1] = new int[3];
```

This technique reveals what you really get with Java: arrays of arrays that, properly managed, could look like a matrix.

Using an Array of Arrays

The most common operation on an array of arrays is to loop through it. This example prints out a 2D array:

```
var twoD = new int[3][2];
for(int i = 0; i < twoD.length; i++) {
   for(int j = 0; j < twoD[i].length; j++)
      System.out.print(twoD[i][j] + " "); // print element
   System.out.println();                  // time for a new row
}
```

We have two loops here. The first uses index i and goes through the top-level array for twoD. The second uses a different loop variable, j. It is important that these be different variable names so the loops don't get mixed up. The inner loop looks at how many elements are in the second-level array. The inner loop prints the element and leaves a space for readability. When the inner loop completes, the outer loop goes to a new line and repeats the process for the next element.

This entire exercise would be easier to read with the enhanced for loop.

```
for(int[] inner : twoD) {
   for(int num : inner)
```

```
        System.out.print(num + " ");
    System.out.println();
}
```

We'll grant you that it isn't fewer lines, but each line is less complex, and there aren't any loop variables or terminating conditions to mix up.

Calculating with Math APIs

It should come as no surprise that computers are good at computing numbers. Java comes with a powerful Math class with many methods to make your life easier. We just cover a few common ones here that are most likely to appear on the exam. When doing your own projects, look at the Math Javadoc to see what other methods can help you. Additionally, we cover the BigInteger and BigDecimal classes in this section.

Pay special attention to return types in math questions. They are an excellent opportunity for trickery!

Finding the Minimum and Maximum

The Math.min() and Math.max() methods compare two values and return one of them.

The method signatures for Math.min() are as follows:

```
public static double min(double a, double b)
public static float min(float a, float b)
public static int min(int a, int b)
public static long min(long a, long b)
```

There are four overloaded methods, so you always have an API available with the same type. Each method returns whichever of a or b is smaller. The max() method works the same way, except it returns the larger value.

The following shows how to use these methods:

```
int first = Math.max(3, 7);     // 7
int second = Math.min(7, -9);   // -9
```

The first line returns 7 because it is larger. The second line returns −9 because it is smaller. Remember from school that negative values are smaller than positive ones.

Rounding Numbers

The Math.round() method gets rid of the decimal portion of the value, choosing the next higher number if appropriate. If the fractional part is .5 or higher, we round up.

The method signatures for `Math.round()` are as follows:

```
public static long round(double num)
public static int round(float num)
```

There are two overloaded methods to ensure that there is enough room to store a rounded `double` if needed. The following shows how to use this method:

```
long low = Math.round(123.45);        // 123
long high = Math.round(123.50);       // 124
int fromFloat = Math.round(123.45f); // 123
```

The first line returns 123 because .45 is smaller than a half. The second line returns 124 because the fractional part is just barely a half. The final line shows that an explicit `float` triggers the method signature that returns an `int`.

Determining the Ceiling and Floor

The `Math.ceil()` method takes a `double` value. If it is a whole number, it returns the same value. If it has any fractional value, it rounds up to the next whole number. By contrast, the `Math.floor()` method discards any values after the decimal.

The method signatures are as follows:

```
public static double ceil(double num)
public static double floor(double num)
```

The following shows how to use these methods:

```
double c = Math.ceil(3.14);  // 4.0
double f = Math.floor(3.14); // 3.0
```

The first line returns `4.0` because four is the integer, just larger. The second line returns `3.0` because it is the integer, just smaller.

Calculating Exponents

The `Math.pow()` method handles exponents. As you may recall from your elementary school math class, 3^2 means three squared. This is 3 * 3 or 9. Fractional exponents are allowed as well. Sixteen to the 0.5 power means the square root of 16, which is 4. (Don't worry, you won't have to do square roots on the exam.)

The method signature is as follows:

```
public static double pow(double number, double exponent)
```

The following shows how to use this method:

```
double squared = Math.pow(5, 2); // 25.0
```

Notice that the result is 25.0 rather than 25 since it is a `double`. Again, don't worry; the exam won't ask you to do any complicated math.

Generating Random Numbers

The Math.random() method returns a value greater than or equal to 0 and less than 1. The method signature is as follows:

```
public static double random()
```

The following shows how to use this method:

```
double num = Math.random();
```

Since it is a random number, we can't know the result in advance. However, we can rule out certain numbers. For example, it can't be negative because that's less than 0. It can't be 1.0 because that's not less than 1.

While not on the exam, it is common to use the Random class for generating pseudo-random numbers. It allows generating numbers of different types.

Using BigInteger and BigDecimal

All of the Math APIs in the previous section used java primitive types. However, these are not always precise enough. Especially when dealing with money or large numbers. Luckily, Java has built in classes called BigInteger and BigDecimal that can handle values that don't fit into the primitive numeric types. Like String, these classes are immutable so you chain methods to perform multiple operations.

While there are constructors, it is recommended to use the valueOf() method where possible. Note that you can pass a long to either type, but a double only to BigDecimal.

```
var bigInt = BigInteger.valueOf(5_000L);
var bigDecimal = BigDecimal.valueOf(5_000L);
bigDecimal = BigDecimal.valueOf(5_000.00);
```

Both classes provide constants for the most common values like BigInteger.ZERO and BigDecimal.ONE.

There are methods to perform math operations with these types, such as:

```
var bigInt = BigInteger.valueOf(199)
    .add(BigInteger.valueOf(1))
    .divide(BigInteger.TEN)
    .max(BigInteger.valueOf(6));
System.out.println(bigInt);  // 20
```

This example starts by adding 199 and 1 which gives 200. It then divides by 10 resulting in 20. Finally, max() sees that 20 is larger than 6 and we have the result.

Real World Scenario

When to use BigInteger and BigDecimal

In the real world, you would use `BigInteger` to handle integer values that don't fit within `int` or `long`, such as in the following example.

```
System.out.println(new BigInteger("12345123451234512345"));
System.out.println(12345123451234512345L);  // DOES NOT COMPILE
```

Likewise, `BigDecimal` is for larger values that don't fit within `float` or `double`. It is often used for small values that involve money. Why? Well, sometimes floating point numbers are stored in memory in unexpected ways. Consider the following example.

```
double amountInCents1 = 64.1 * 100;
System.out.println(amountInCents1);  // 6409.999999999999
```

The difference between the expected value and actual value is referred to as the floating-point error. Oftentimes, these errors don't significantly change the result of an operation, but it would be bad to do so when working with money! We can fix this by using `BigDecimal` instead.

```
BigDecimal amountInCents2 = BigDecimal.valueOf(64.1)
   .multiply(BigDecimal.valueOf(100));
System.out.println(amountInCents2);  // 6410.0
```

Working with Dates and Times

Java provides a number of APIs for working with dates and times. There's also an old `java.util.Date` class, but it is not on the exam. You need an import statement to work with the modern date and time classes. To use it, add this `import` to your program:

```
import java.time.*;     // import time classes
```

Day vs. Date

In American English, the word *date* is used to represent two different concepts. Sometimes, it is the month/day/year combination when something happened, such as January 1, 2025. Sometimes, it is the day of the month, such as "Today's date is the 6th."

That's right—the words *day* and *date* are often used as synonyms. Be alert to this on the exam, especially if you live someplace where people are more precise about this distinction.

In the following sections, we look at creating and manipulating dates and times, including time zones and daylight saving time.

Creating Dates and Times

In the real world, we usually talk about dates and time zones as if the other person is located near us. For example, if you say to me, "I'll call you at 11 on Tuesday morning," we assume that 11 means the same thing to both of us. But if I live in New York and you live in California, we need to be more specific. California is three hours earlier than New York because the states are in different time zones. You would instead say, "I'll call you at 11 EST (Eastern Standard Time) on Tuesday morning."

When working with dates and times, the first thing to do is to decide how much information you need. The exam gives you four choices.

LocalDate Contains just a date—no time and no time zone. A good example of LocalDate is your birthday this year. It is your birthday for a full day, regardless of what time it is.

LocalTime Contains just a time—no date and no time zone. A good example of LocalTime is midnight. It is midnight at the same time every day.

LocalDateTime Contains both a date and time but no time zone. A good example of LocalDateTime is "the stroke of midnight on New Year's Eve."

ZonedDateTime Contains a date, time, and time zone. A good example of ZonedDateTime is "a conference call at 9 a.m. EST." If you live in California, you'll have to get up really early since the call is at 6 a.m. local time!

You obtain date and time instances using a `static` method.

```
System.out.println(LocalDate.now());
System.out.println(LocalTime.now());
System.out.println(LocalDateTime.now());
System.out.println(ZonedDateTime.now());
```

Each of the four classes has a `static` method called now(), which gives the current date and time. Your output is going to depend on the date/time when you run it and where you live. The authors live in the United States, making the output look like the following when run on July 25 at 9:13 a.m.:

```
2025-07-25
09:13:07.768
2025-07-25T09:13:07.768
2025-07-25T09:13:07.769-04:00[America/New_York]
```

The key is the type of information in the output. The first line contains only a date and no time. The second contains only a time and no date. The time displays hours, minutes, seconds, and fractional seconds. The third contains both a date and a time. The output uses T to separate the date and time when converting LocalDateTime to a String. Finally, the fourth adds the time zone offset and time zone. New York is four time zones away from Greenwich Mean Time (GMT).

Greenwich Mean Time is a time zone in Europe that is used as time zone zero when discussing offsets. You might have also heard of *Coordinated Universal Time*, which is a time zone standard. It is abbreviated as UTC, as a compromise between the English and French names. (That's not a typo. UTC isn't actually the proper acronym in either language!) UTC uses the same time zone zero as GMT.

First, let's try to figure out how far apart the following moments are in time. Notice how India has a half-hour offset, not a full hour. To approach a problem like this, you subtract the time zone from the time. This gives you the GMT equivalent of the time:

```
2025-06-20T06:50+05:30[Asia/Kolkata]    // GMT 2025-06-20 01:20
2025-06-20T07:50-04:00[US/Eastern]      // GMT 2025-06-20 11:50
```

Remember that you need to add when subtracting a negative number. After converting to GMT, you can see that the U.S. Eastern time occurs 10 and a half hours after the Kolkata time.

> The time zone offset can be listed in different ways: +02:00, GMT+2, and UTC+2 all mean the same thing. You might see any of them on the exam.

If you have trouble remembering this, try to memorize one example where the time zones are a few zones apart, and remember the direction. In the United States, most people know that the East Coast is three hours ahead of the West Coast. And most people know that Asia is ahead of Europe. Just don't cross time zone zero in the example that you choose to remember. The calculation works the same way, but it isn't as great a memory aid.

Wait, I Don't Live in the United States

The exam recognizes that exam takers live all over the world, and it will not ask you about the details of U.S. date and time formats. That said, our examples do use U.S. date and time formats, as will the questions on the exam. Just remember that the month comes before the date. Also, Java tends to use a 24-hour clock even though the United States uses a 12-hour clock with a.m./p.m.

Now that you know how to create the current date and time, let's look at other specific dates and times. To begin, let's create just a date with no time. Both of these examples create the same date:

```
var date1 = LocalDate.of(2025, Month.JANUARY, 20);
var date2 = LocalDate.of(2025, 1, 20);
```

Both pass in the year, month, and date. Although it is good to use the Month constants (to make the code easier to read), you can pass the int number of the month directly. Just use the number of the month the same way you would if you were writing the date in real life.

The method signatures are as follows:

```
public static LocalDate of(int year, int month, int dayOfMonth)
public static LocalDate of(int year, Month month, int dayOfMonth)
```

 Up to now, we've been continually telling you that Java counts starting with 0. Well, months are an exception. For months in the new date and time methods, Java counts starting from 1, just as we humans do.

When creating a time, you can choose how detailed you want to be. You can specify just the hour and minute, or you can include the number of seconds. You can even include nanoseconds if you want to be very precise. (A nanosecond is a billionth of a second, although you probably won't need to be that specific.)

```
var time1 = LocalTime.of(6, 15);          // hour and minute
var time2 = LocalTime.of(6, 15, 30);      // + seconds
var time3 = LocalTime.of(6, 15, 30, 200); // + nanoseconds
```

These three times are all different but within a minute of each other. The method signatures are as follows:

```
public static LocalTime of(int hour, int minute)
public static LocalTime of(int hour, int minute, int second)
public static LocalTime of(int hour, int minute, int second, int nanos)
```

You can combine dates and times into one object.

```
var dateTime1 = LocalDateTime.of(2025, Month.JANUARY, 20, 6, 15, 30);
var dateTime2 = LocalDateTime.of(date1, time2);
```

The first line of code shows how you can specify all of the information about the LocalDateTime right in the same line. The second line of code shows how you can create LocalDate and LocalTime objects separately first and then combine them to create a LocalDateTime object.

There are a lot of method signatures since there are more combinations. The following method signatures use integer values:

```
public static LocalDateTime of(int year, int month,
```

```
        int dayOfMonth, int hour, int minute)
public static LocalDateTime of(int year, int month,
        int dayOfMonth, int hour, int minute, int second)
public static LocalDateTime of(int year, int month,
        int dayOfMonth, int hour, int minute, int second, int nanos)
```

Others take a Month reference:

```
public static LocalDateTime of(int year, Month month,
        int dayOfMonth, int hour, int minute)
public static LocalDateTime of(int year, Month month,
        int dayOfMonth, int hour, int minute, int second)
public static LocalDateTime of(int year, Month month,
        int dayOfMonth, int hour, int minute, int second, int nanos)
```

Finally, one takes an existing LocalDate and LocalTime:

```
public static LocalDateTime of(LocalDate date, LocalTime time)
```

To create a ZonedDateTime, we first need to get the desired time zone. We will use US/Eastern in our examples:

```
var zone = ZoneId.of("US/Eastern");
var zoned1 = ZonedDateTime.of(2025, 1, 20,
        6, 15, 30, 200, zone);
var zoned2 = ZonedDateTime.of(date1, time1, zone);
var zoned3 = ZonedDateTime.of(dateTime1, zone);
```

We start by getting the time zone object. Then we use one of three approaches to create the ZonedDateTime. The first passes all of the fields individually. We don't recommend this approach—there are too many numbers, and it is hard to read. A better approach is to pass a LocalDate object and a LocalTime object, or a LocalDateTime object.

Although there are other ways of creating a ZonedDateTime, you only need to know three for the exam:

```
public static ZonedDateTime of(int year, int month,
    int dayOfMonth, int hour, int minute, int second,
    int nanos, ZoneId zone)
public static ZonedDateTime of(LocalDate date, LocalTime time,
    ZoneId zone)
public static ZonedDateTime of(LocalDateTime dateTime, ZoneId zone)
```

Notice that there isn't an option to pass in the Month enum. Also, we did not use a constructor in any of the examples. The date and time classes have private constructors along with static methods that return instances. This is known as the *factory pattern*. The exam creators may throw something like this at you:

```
var d = new LocalDate(); // DOES NOT COMPILE
```

Don't fall for this. You are not allowed to construct a date or time object directly. Another trick is what happens when you pass invalid numbers to of(), for example:

```
var d = LocalDate.of(2025, Month.JANUARY, 32); // DateTimeException
```

You don't need to know the exact exception that's thrown, but it's a clear one:

```
java.time.DateTimeException: Invalid value for DayOfMonth
        (valid values 1-28/31): 32
```

Manipulating Dates and Times

Adding to a date is easy. The date and time classes are immutable. Remember to assign the results of these methods to a reference variable so they are not lost.

```
12: var date = LocalDate.of(2025, Month.JANUARY, 20);
13: System.out.println(date);      // 2025-01-20
14: date = date.plusDays(2);
15: System.out.println(date);      // 2025-01-22
16: date = date.plusWeeks(1);
17: System.out.println(date);      // 2025-01-29
18: date = date.plusMonths(1);
19: System.out.println(date);      // 2025-02-28
20: date = date.plusYears(5);
21: System.out.println(date);      // 2030-02-28
```

This code is nice because it does just what it looks like. We start out with January 20, 2025. On line 14, we add two days to it and reassign it to our reference variable. On line 16, we add a week. This method allows us to write clearer code than plusDays(7). Now date is January 29, 2025. On line 18, we add a month. This would bring us to February 29, 2025. However, 2025 is not a leap year (2020 and 2024 are leap years). Java is smart enough to realize that February 29, 2025, does not exist, and it gives us February 28, 2025, instead. Finally, line 20 adds five years.

February 29 exists only in a leap year. Leap years are years that are a multiple of 4 or 400, but not other multiples of 100. For example, 2000 and 2028 are leap years, but 2100 is not.

There are also nice, easy methods to go backward in time. This time, let's work with LocalDateTime:

```
22: var date = LocalDate.of(2025, Month.JANUARY, 20);
23: var time = LocalTime.of(5, 15);
```

```
24: var dateTime = LocalDateTime.of(date, time);
25: System.out.println(dateTime);        // 2025-01-20T05:15
26: dateTime = dateTime.minusDays(1);
27: System.out.println(dateTime);        // 2025-01-19T05:15
28: dateTime = dateTime.minusHours(10);
29: System.out.println(dateTime);        // 2025-01-18T19:15
30: dateTime = dateTime.minusSeconds(30);
31: System.out.println(dateTime);        // 2025-01-18T19:14:30
```

Line 25 prints the original date of January 20, 2025, at 5:15 a.m. Line 26 subtracts a full day, bringing us to January 19, 2025, at 5:15 a.m. Line 28 subtracts 10 hours, showing that the date will change if the hours cause it to adjust, and it brings us to January 18, 2025, at 19:15 (7:15 p.m.). Finally, line 30 subtracts 30 seconds. You can see that all of a sudden, the display value starts showing seconds. Java is smart enough to hide the seconds and nanoseconds when we aren't using them.

It is common for date and time methods to be chained. For example, without the print statements, the previous example could be rewritten as follows:

```
var date = LocalDate.of(2025, Month.JANUARY, 20);
var time = LocalTime.of(5, 15);
var dateTime = LocalDateTime.of(date, time)
        .minusDays(1).minusHours(10).minusSeconds(30);
```

When you have a lot of manipulations to make, this chaining comes in handy. There are two ways that the exam creators can try to trick you. What do you think this prints?

```
var date = LocalDate.of(2025, Month.JANUARY, 20);
date.plusDays(10);
System.out.println(date);
```

It prints 2025-01-20. Adding 10 days was useless because the program ignored the result. Whenever you see immutable types, pay attention to make sure that the return value of a method call isn't ignored. The exam also may test to see if you remember what each of the date and time objects includes. Do you see what is wrong here?

```
var date = LocalDate.of(2025, Month.JANUARY, 20);
date = date.plusMinutes(1);        // DOES NOT COMPILE
```

LocalDate does not contain time. This means you cannot add minutes to it. This can be tricky in a chained sequence of addition/subtraction operations, so make sure you know which methods in Table 4.6 can be called on which types.

TABLE 4.6   Methods in `LocalDate`, `LocalTime`, `LocalDateTime`, and `ZonedDateTime`

	Can call on LocalDate?	Can call on LocalTime?	Can call on LocalDateTime or ZonedDateTime?

`plusYears()`
`minusYears()`
`withYear()`
`withDayOfYear()`
	Yes	No	Yes

`plusMonths()`
`minusMonths()`
`withMonth()`
	Yes	No	Yes

`plusWeeks()` `minusWeeks()`	Yes	No	Yes

`plusDays()`
`minusDays()`
`withDayOfMonth()`
	Yes	No	Yes

`plusHours()`
`minusHours()`
`withHour()`
	No	Yes	Yes

`plusMinutes()`
`minusMinutes()`
`withMinute()`
	No	Yes	Yes

`plusSeconds()`
`minusSeconds()`
`withSecond()`
	No	Yes	Yes

`plusNanos()`
`minusNanos()`
`withNano()`
	No	Yes	Yes

Table 4.6 also includes methods that you can use to create a copy of an object with specific field(s) altered to the specified value. For example:

```java
var date = LocalDate.of(2025, Month.FEBRUARY, 20);   // 2025-02-20
var differentDay = date.withDayOfMonth(15);          // 2025-02-15
```

```
var differentMonth = date.withDayOfYear(3);          // 2025-01-03
var allChanged = date.withYear(2026)
  .withMonth(4)
  .withDayOfMonth(10);                                // 2026-04-10
```

Finally, there are methods to convert from one type to another. For example:

```
var date = LocalDate.of(2025, Month.MARCH, 3);
var withTime = date.atTime(5, 30);   // 2025-03-03T05:30
var start = date.atStartOfDay();     // 2025-03-03T00:00
```

The at_____() methods combine the instance variable and the parameter into one new object. They are listed in Table 4.7.

TABLE 4.7 Conversion methods in LocalDate, LocalTime, and LocalDateTime

LocalDate **to** LocalDateTime	atStartOfDay() atTime(int hour, int minute) atTime(int hour, int minute, int second) atTime(int hour, int minute, int second, int nanos) atTime(LocalTime time)
LocalTime **to** LocalDate	atDate(LocalDate date)
LocalDateTime **to** ZonedDateTime	atZone(ZoneId zoneId)

Working with Periods

Now you know enough to do something fun with dates! Our zoo performs animal enrichment activities to give the animals something enjoyable to do. The head zookeeper has decided to switch the toys every month. This system will continue for three months to see how it works out.

```
public static void main(String[] args) {
    var start = LocalDate.of(2025, Month.JANUARY, 1);
    var end = LocalDate.of(2025, Month.MARCH, 30);
    performAnimalEnrichment(start, end);
}
private static void performAnimalEnrichment(LocalDate start, LocalDate end) {
    var upTo = start;
    while (upTo.isBefore(end)) {  // check if still before end
```

```
    System.out.println("give new toy: " + upTo);
    upTo = upTo.plusMonths(1); // add a month
} }
```

This code works fine. It adds a month to the date until it hits the end date. The problem is that this method can't be reused. Our zookeeper wants to try different schedules to see which works best.

 NOTE   LocalDate and LocalDateTime have a method to convert themselves into long values, equivalent to the number of milliseconds that have passed since January 1, 1970, referred to as the *epoch*. What's special about this date? That's what Unix started using for date standards, so Java reused it.

Luckily, Java has a Period class that we can pass in. This code does the same thing as the previous example:

```
public static void main(String[] args) {
    var start = LocalDate.of(2025, Month.JANUARY, 1);
    var end = LocalDate.of(2025, Month.MARCH, 30);
    var period = Period.ofMonths(1);    // create a period
    performAnimalEnrichment(start, end, period);
}
private static void performAnimalEnrichment(LocalDate start, LocalDate end,
    Period period) {                    // uses the generic period

    var upTo = start;
    while (upTo.isBefore(end)) {
        System.out.println("give new toy: " + upTo);
        upTo = upTo.plus(period); // adds the period
} }
```

The method can add an arbitrary period of time that is passed in. This allows us to reuse the same method for different periods of time as our zookeeper changes their mind.

A Period can be positive (forward in time) or negative (backwards in time.) There are five ways to create a Period class.

```
var annually = Period.ofYears(1);          // every 1 year
var quarterly = Period.ofMonths(3);        // every 3 months
var everyThreeWeeks = Period.ofWeeks(-3);  // every 3 weeks going backwards
var everyOtherDay = Period.ofDays(2);      // every 2 days
var everyYearAndAWeek = Period.of(1, 0, 7); // every year plus 1 week
```

There's one catch. You cannot chain methods when creating a `Period`. The following code looks like it is equivalent to the `everyYearAndAWeek` example, but it's not. Only the last method is used because the methods are `static` methods.

```
var wrong = Period.ofYears(1).ofWeeks(1); // every week
```

This tricky code is really like writing the following:

```
var wrong = Period.ofYears(1);
wrong = Period.ofWeeks(1);
```

This is clearly not what you intended! That's why the `of()` method allows you to pass in the number of years, months, and days. They are all included in the same period. You will get a compiler warning about this. Compiler warnings tell you that something is wrong or suspicious without failing compilation.

The `of()` method takes only years, months, and days. The ability to use another factory method to pass weeks is merely a convenience. As you might imagine, the actual period is stored in terms of years, months, and days. When you print out the value, Java displays any nonzero parts using the format shown in Figure 4.9.

FIGURE 4.9   Period format

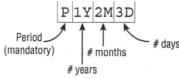

```
System.out.println(Period.of(1,2,3));
```

As you can see, the P always starts out the `String` to show it is a period measure. Then come the number of years, number of months, and number of days. If any of these are zero, they are omitted.

Can you figure out what this outputs?

```
System.out.println(Period.ofMonths(3));
```

The output is P3M. Remember that Java omits any measures that are zero. You can also create a period by getting the amount of time between two `LocalDate` objects:

```
var xmas = LocalDate.of(2025, Month.DECEMBER, 25);
var newYears = LocalDate.of(2026, Month.JANUARY, 1);

System.out.println(Period.between(xmas, newYears));   // P7D
System.out.println(Period.between(newYears, xmas));   // P-7D
```

Notice how order matters. The first time `Period.between()` returns a period representing seven days, but the second time it returns a period of negative seven days.

The last thing to know about `Period` is what objects it can be used with. Let's look at some code:

```
3:  var date = LocalDate.of(2025, 3, 20);
4:  var time = LocalTime.of(6, 15);
5:  var dateTime = LocalDateTime.of(date, time);
6:  var period = Period.ofMonths(-1);
7:  System.out.println(date.plus(period));      // 2025-02-20
8:  System.out.println(dateTime.plus(period));  // 2025-02-20T06:15
9:  System.out.println(time.plus(period));      // Exception
```

Lines 7 and 8 work as expected. They subtract a month from March 20, 2025, giving us February 20, 2025. The first has only the date, and the second has both the date and time.

Line 9 attempts to add a month to an object that has only a time. This won't work. Java throws an `UnsupportedTemporalTypeException` and complains that we attempted to use an `Unsupported unit: Months`.

As you can see, you have to pay attention to the type of date and time objects every place you see them.

Working with Durations

You've probably noticed by now that a `Period` is a day or more of time. There is also `Duration`, which is intended for smaller units of time. For `Duration`, you can specify the number of days, hours, minutes, seconds, or nanoseconds. And yes, you could pass 365 days to make a year, but you really shouldn't—that's what `Period` is for.

Conveniently, `Duration` works roughly the same way as `Period`, except it is used with objects that have time. `Duration` is output beginning with PT, which you can think of as a period of time. A `Duration` is stored in hours, minutes, and seconds. The number of seconds includes fractional seconds.

We can create a `Duration` using a number of different granularities:

```
var daily = Duration.ofDays(1);             // PT24H
var hourly = Duration.ofHours(1);           // PT1H
var everyMinute = Duration.ofMinutes(1);    // PT1M
var everyTenSeconds = Duration.ofSeconds(10); // PT10S
var everyMilli = Duration.ofMillis(1);      // PT0.001S
var everyNano = Duration.ofNanos(1);        // PT0.000000001S
```

`Duration` doesn't have a factory method that takes multiple units like `Period` does. If you want something to happen every hour and a half, you specify 90 minutes.

`Duration` includes another more generic factory method. It takes a number and a `TemporalUnit`. The idea is, say, something like "5 seconds." However, `TemporalUnit` is an interface. At the moment, there is only one implementation named `ChronoUnit`.

The previous example could be rewritten like this:

```
var daily = Duration.of(1, ChronoUnit.DAYS);
var hourly = Duration.of(1, ChronoUnit.HOURS);
var everyMinute = Duration.of(1, ChronoUnit.MINUTES);
var everyTenSeconds = Duration.of(10, ChronoUnit.SECONDS);
var everyMilli = Duration.of(1, ChronoUnit.MILLIS);
var everyNano = Duration.of(1, ChronoUnit.NANOS);
```

ChronoUnit also includes some convenient units such as ChronoUnit.HALF_DAYS to represent 12 hours.

ChronoUnit for Differences

ChronoUnit is a great way to determine how far apart two Temporal values are. Temporal includes LocalDate, LocalTime, and so on. ChronoUnit is in the java.time.temporal package.

```
var one = LocalTime.of(5, 15);
var two = LocalTime.of(6, 55);
var date = LocalDate.of(2025, 1, 20);
System.out.println(ChronoUnit.HOURS.between(one, two));    // 1
System.out.println(ChronoUnit.MINUTES.between(one, two));  // 100
System.out.println(ChronoUnit.MINUTES.between(one, date)); // DateTimeException
```

The first print statement shows that between truncates rather than rounds. The second shows how easy it is to count in different units. Just change the ChronoUnit type. The last reminds us that Java will throw an exception if we mix up what can be done on date versus time objects.

Alternatively, you can truncate any object with a time element. For example:

```
LocalTime time = LocalTime.of(3,12,45);
System.out.println(time);        // 03:12:45
LocalTime truncated = time.truncatedTo(ChronoUnit.MINUTES);
System.out.println(truncated); // 03:12
```

This example zeroes out any fields smaller than minutes. In our case, it gets rid of the seconds.

Using a Duration works the same way as using a Period. For example:

```
7:  var date = LocalDate.of(2025, 1, 20);
8:  var time = LocalTime.of(6, 15);
```

```
9:  var dateTime = LocalDateTime.of(date, time);
10: var duration = Duration.ofHours(6);

11: System.out.println(dateTime.plus(duration));  // 2025-01-20T12:15
12: System.out.println(time.plus(duration));      // 12:15
13: System.out.println(
14:    date.plus(duration));  // UnsupportedTemporalTypeException
```

Line 11 shows that we can add hours to a LocalDateTime, since it contains a time. Line 12 also works, since all we have is a time. Line 13 fails because we cannot add hours to an object that does not contain a time.

Let's try that again, but add 23 hours this time.

```
7:  var date = LocalDate.of(2025, 1, 20);
8:  var time = LocalTime.of(6, 15);
9:  var dateTime = LocalDateTime.of(date, time);
10: var duration = Duration.ofHours(23);
11: System.out.println(dateTime.plus(duration));  // 2025-01-21T05:15
12: System.out.println(time.plus(duration));      // 05:15
13: System.out.println(
14:    date.plus(duration));  // UnsupportedTemporalTypeException
```

This time we see that Java moves forward past the end of the day. Line 11 goes to the next day since we pass midnight. Line 12 doesn't have a day, so the time just wraps around—just like on a real clock.

Period vs. Duration

Remember that Period and Duration are not equivalent. This example shows a Period and Duration of the same length:

```
var date = LocalDate.of(2025, 5, 25);
var period = Period.ofDays(1);
var days = Duration.ofDays(1);

System.out.println(date.plus(period));  // 2025-05-26
System.out.println(date.plus(days));    // Unsupported unit: Seconds
```

Since we are working with a LocalDate, we are required to use Period. Duration has time units in it, even if we don't see them, and they are meant only for objects with time. Make sure you can fill in Table 4.8 to identify which objects can use Period and Duration.

TABLE 4.8 Where to use `Duration` and `Period`

	Can use with Period?	Can use with Duration?
LocalDate	Yes	No
LocalDateTime	Yes	Yes
LocalTime	No	Yes
ZonedDateTime	Yes	Yes

Working with Instants

The `Instant` class represents a specific moment in time in the GMT time zone. Suppose that you want to run a timer.

```
var now = Instant.now();
// Do something time consuming
var later = Instant.now();

var duration = Duration.between(now, later);
System.out.println(duration.toMillis());  // Returns number milliseconds
```

In our case, the "something time consuming" was just over a second, and the program printed out 1025.

If you have a `ZonedDateTime`, you can turn it into an `Instant`:

```
var date = LocalDate.of(2025, 5, 25);
var time = LocalTime.of(11, 55, 00);
var zone = ZoneId.of("US/Eastern");
var zonedDateTime = ZonedDateTime.of(date, time, zone);

var instant = zonedDateTime.toInstant(); // 2025-05-25T15:55:00Z
System.out.println(zonedDateTime); // 2025-05-25T11:55-04:00[US/Eastern]
System.out.println(instant);       // 2025-05-25T15:55:00Z
```

The last two lines represent the same moment in time. The `ZonedDateTime` includes a time zone. The `Instant` gets rid of the time zone and turns it into an `Instant` of time in GMT.

You cannot convert a `LocalDateTime` to an `Instant`. Remember that an `Instant` is a point in time. A `LocalDateTime` does not contain a time zone, and it is therefore not universally recognized around the world as the same moment in time.

Accounting for Daylight Saving Time

Some countries observe *daylight saving time*. This is where the clocks are adjusted by an hour twice a year to make better use of the sunlight. Not all countries participate, and those that do use different weekends for the change. You only have to work with U.S. daylight saving time on the exam, and that's what we describe here.

The exam question will let you know if a date/time mentioned falls on a weekend when the clocks are scheduled to be changed. If it is not mentioned in a question, you can assume that it is a normal weekend. The act of moving the clock forward or back occurs at 2:00 a.m., which falls very early Sunday morning.

Figure 4.10 shows what happens with the clocks. When we change our clocks in March, time springs forward from 1:59 a.m. to 3:00 a.m. When we change our clocks in November, time falls back, and we experience the hour from 1:00 a.m. to 1:59 a.m. twice. Children learn this as "Spring forward in the spring, and fall back in the fall."

FIGURE 4.10   How daylight saving time works

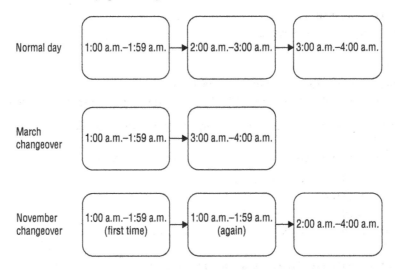

For example, on March 9, 2025, we move our clocks forward an hour and jump from 2:00 a.m. to 3:00 a.m. This means that there is no 2:30 a.m. that day. If we wanted to know the time an hour later than 1:30, it would be 3:30.

```
var date = LocalDate.of(2025, Month.MARCH, 9);
var time = LocalTime.of(1, 30);
var zone = ZoneId.of("US/Eastern");
var dateTime = ZonedDateTime.of(date, time, zone);

System.out.println(dateTime);  // 2025-03-09T01:30-05:00[US/Eastern]
```

```
System.out.println(dateTime.getHour());    // 1
System.out.println(dateTime.getOffset()); // -05:00

dateTime = dateTime.plusHours(1);
System.out.println(dateTime);    // 2025-03-09T03:30-04:00[US/Eastern]
System.out.println(dateTime.getHour());    // 3
System.out.println(dateTime.getOffset()); // -04:00
```

Notice that two things change in this example. The time jumps from 1:30 to 3:30. The UTC offset also changes. Remember when we calculated GMT time by subtracting the time zone from the time? You can see that we went from 6:30 GMT (1:30 minus –5:00) to 7:30 GMT (3:30 minus –4:00). This shows that the time really did change by one hour from GMT's point of view. We printed the hour and offset fields separately for emphasis.

Similarly, in November, an hour after the initial 1:30 a.m. is also 1:30 a.m. because at 2:00 a.m. we repeat the hour. This time, try to calculate the GMT time yourself for all three times to confirm that we really do move only one hour at a time.

```
var date = LocalDate.of(2025, Month.NOVEMBER, 2);
var time = LocalTime.of(1, 30);
var zone = ZoneId.of("US/Eastern");
var dateTime = ZonedDateTime.of(date, time, zone);
System.out.println(dateTime); // 2025-11-02T01:30-04:00[US/Eastern]

dateTime = dateTime.plusHours(1);
System.out.println(dateTime); // 2025-11-02T01:30-05:00[US/Eastern]

dateTime = dateTime.plusHours(1);
System.out.println(dateTime); // 2025-11-02T02:30-05:00[US/Eastern]
```

Did you get it? We went from 5:30 GMT to 6:30 GMT, to 7:30 GMT.

Finally, trying to create a time that doesn't exist just rolls forward:

```
var date = LocalDate.of(2025, Month.MARCH, 9);
var time = LocalTime.of(2, 30);
var zone = ZoneId.of("US/Eastern");
var dateTime = ZonedDateTime.of(date, time, zone);
System.out.println(dateTime);    // 2025-03-09T03:30-04:00[US/Eastern]
```

Java is smart enough to know that there is no 2:30 a.m. that night and switches over to the appropriate GMT offset.

Yes, it is annoying that Oracle expects you to know this even if you aren't in the United States—or for that matter, in a part of the United States that doesn't follow daylight saving time. The exam creators are in the United States, and they decided that everyone needs to know how U.S. time zones work.

Summary

In this chapter, you learned that a `String` is an immutable sequence of characters. Calling the constructor explicitly is optional. The concatenation operator (+) creates a new `String` with the content of the first `String` followed by the content of the second `String`. If either operand involved in the + expression is a `String`, concatenation is used; otherwise, addition is used. `String` literals are stored in the string pool. The `String` class has many methods.

By contrast, a `StringBuilder` is a mutable sequence of characters. Most of the methods return a reference to the current object to allow method chaining. The `StringBuilder` class has many methods.

Calling == on `String` objects will check whether they point to the same object in the pool. Calling == on `StringBuilder` references will check whether they are pointing to the same `StringBuilder` object. Calling `equals()` on `String` objects will check whether the sequence of characters is the same. Calling `equals()` on `StringBuilder` objects will check whether they are pointing to the same object rather than looking at the values inside.

An array is a fixed-size area of memory on the heap that has space for primitives or pointers to objects. You specify the size when creating it. For example, `int[] a = new int[6];`. Indexes begin with 0, and elements are referred to using a [0]. The `Arrays.sort()` method sorts an array. `Arrays.binarySearch()` searches a sorted array and returns the index of a match. If no match is found, it negates the position where the element would need to be inserted and subtracts 1. `Arrays.compare()` and `Arrays.mismatch()` check whether two arrays are the equivalent. Methods that are passed varargs (`...`) can be used as if a normal array was passed in. In an array of arrays, the second-level arrays and beyond can be different sizes.

The `Math` class provides a number of `static` methods for performing mathematical operations. For example, you can get minimums or maximums. You can round or even generate random numbers. Some methods work on any numeric primitive, and others only work on `double`.

A `LocalDate` contains just a date, a `LocalTime` contains just a time, and a `LocalDateTime` contains both a date and a time. All three have private constructors and are created using `LocalDate.now()` or `LocalDate.of()` (or the equivalents for that class). Dates and times can be manipulated using plus_____(), minus_____(), at_____(), or with_____() methods. The `Period` class represents a number of days, months, or years to add to or subtract from a `LocalDate` or `LocalDateTime`. The date and time classes are all immutable, which means the return value must be used.

Exam Essentials

Be able to determine the output of code using *String*.   Know the rules for concatenating with `String` and how to use common `String` methods. Know that a `String` is immutable. Pay special attention to the fact that indexes are zero-based and that the `substring()` method gets the string up until right before the index of the second parameter.

Be able to determine the output of code using *StringBuilder*.   Know that a `StringBuilder` is mutable and how to use common `StringBuilder` methods. Know that `substring()` does not change the value of a `StringBuilder`, whereas `append()`, `delete()`, and `insert()` do change it. Also note that most `StringBuilder` methods return a reference to the current instance of `StringBuilder`.

Understand the difference between == and *equals()*.   `==` checks object equality. `equals()` depends on the implementation of the object it is being called on. For the `String` class, `equals()` checks the characters inside of it.

Be able to determine the output of code using arrays.   Know how to declare and instantiate arrays. Be able to access each element and know when an index is out of bounds. Recognize correct and incorrect output when searching and sorting.

Identify the return types of *Math* methods.   Depending on the primitive passed in, the `Math` methods may return different primitive results.

Recognize invalid uses of dates and times.   `LocalDate` does not contain time fields, and `LocalTime` does not contain date fields. Watch for operations being performed on the wrong type. Also watch for adding or subtracting time and ignoring the result. Be comfortable with date math, including time zones and daylight saving time.

Review Questions

The answers to the chapter review questions can be found in the Appendix.

1. What is output by the following code?

```
1: public class Fish {
2:    public static void main(String[] args) {
3:       int numFish = 4;
4:       String fishType = "tuna";
5:       String anotherFish = numFish + 1;
6:       System.out.println(anotherFish + " " + fishType);
7:       System.out.println(numFish + " " + 1);
8: } }
```

   A. 4 1

   B. 5

   C. 5 tuna

   D. 5tuna

   E. 51tuna

   F. The code does not compile.

2. Which of these array declarations are not legal? (Choose all that apply.)

   A. `int[][] scores = new int[5][];`

   B. `Object[][][] cubbies = new Object[3][0][5];`

   C. `String beans[] = new beans[6];`

   D. `java.util.Date[] dates[] = new java.util.Date[2][];`

   E. `int[][] types = new int[];`

   F. `int[][] java = new int[][];`

3. Note that March 12, 2028, is the weekend when we spring forward, and November 5, 2028, is when we fall back for daylight saving time. Which of the following can fill in the blank without the code throwing an exception? (Choose all that apply.)

```
var zone = ZoneId.of("US/Eastern");
var date = _____;
var time = LocalTime.of(2, 15);
var z = ZonedDateTime.of(date, time, zone);
```

   A. `LocalDate.of(2028, 3, 12)`

   B. `LocalDate.of(2028, 3, 40)`

   C. `LocalDate.of(2028, 11, 5)`

   D. `LocalDate.of(2028, 11, 6)`

    E. LocalDate.of(2029, 2, 29)

    F. LocalDate.of(2028, MonthEnum.MARCH, 12);

4. Which of the following are output by this code? (Choose all that apply.)

```
3: var s = "Hello";
4: var t = new String(s);
5: if ("Hello".equals(s)) System.out.println("one");
6: if (t == s) System.out.println("two");
7: if (t.intern() == s) System.out.println("three");
8: if ("Hello" == s) System.out.println("four");
9: if ("Hello".intern() == t) System.out.println("five");
```

    A. one

    B. two

    C. three

    D. four

    E. five

    F. The code does not compile.

    G. None of the above.

5. What is the result of the following code?

```
7: var sb = new StringBuilder();
8: sb.append("aaa").insert(1, "bb").insert(4, "ccc");
9: System.out.println(sb);
```

    A. abbaaccc

    B. abbaccca

    C. bbaaaccc

    D. bbaaccca

    E. An empty line.

    F. The code does not compile.

6. How many of these lines contain a compiler error?

```
23: double one = Math.pow(1, 2);
24: int two = Math.round(1.0);
25: float three = Math.random();
26: var doubles = new double[] {one, two, three};
```

    A. 0

    B. 1

    C. 2

    D. 3

    E. 4

7. Which of these statements is true of the two values? (Choose all that apply.)

```
2025-08-28T05:00 GMT-04:00
2025-08-28T09:00 GMT-06:00
```

  A. The first date/time is earlier.

  B. The second date/time is earlier.

  C. Both date/times are the same.

  D. The date/times are two hours apart.

  E. The date/times are six hours apart.

  F. The date/times are 10 hours apart.

8. Which of the following return 5 when run independently? (Choose all that apply.)

```
var string = "12345";
var builder = new StringBuilder("12345");
```

  A. `builder.charAt(4)`

  B. `builder.replace(2, 4, "6").charAt(3)`

  C. `builder.replace(2, 5, "6").charAt(2)`

  D. `string.charAt(5)`

  E. `string.length`

  F. `string.replace("123", "1").charAt(2)`

  G. None of the above

9. Which of the following are true about arrays? (Choose all that apply.)

  A. The first element is index 0.

  B. The first element is index 1.

  C. Arrays are fixed size.

  D. Arrays are immutable.

  E. Calling `equals()` on two different arrays containing the same primitive values always returns `true`.

  F. Calling `equals()` on two different arrays containing the same primitive values always returns `false`.

  G. Calling `equals()` on two different arrays containing the same primitive values can return `true` or `false`.

10. How many of these lines contain a compiler error?

```
23: int one = Math.min(5, 3);
24: long two = Math.round(5.5);
25: double three = Math.floor(6.6);
26: var doubles = new double[] {one, two, three};
```

A. 0
B. 1
C. 2
D. 3
E. 4

11. What is the output of the following code?

```
var date = LocalDate.of(2025, 4, 3);
date.plusDays(2);
date.plusHours(3);
System.out.println(date.getYear() + " " + date.getMonth()
    + " " + date.getDayOfMonth());
```

A. 2025 MARCH 4
B. 2025 MARCH 6
C. 2025 APRIL 3
D. 2025 APRIL 5
E. The code does not compile.
F. A runtime exception is thrown.

12. What is output by the following code ignoring any new lines in the ouput? (Choose all that apply.)

```
var numbers = "012345678".indent(1);
numbers = numbers.stripLeading();
System.out.println(numbers.substring(1, 3));
System.out.println(numbers.substring(7, 7));
System.out.println(numbers.substring(7));
```

A. 12
B. 123
C. 7
D. 78
E. A blank line.
F. An exception is thrown.

13. What is the result of the following code?

```
public class Lion {
    public void roar(String roar1, StringBuilder roar2) {
        roar1.concat("!!!");
        roar2.append("!!!");
    }
    public static void main(String[] args) {
```

```
        var roar1 = "roar";
        var roar2 = new StringBuilder("roar");
        new Lion().roar(roar1, roar2);
        System.out.println(roar1 + " " + roar2);
} }
```

A. roar roar

B. roar roar!!!

C. roar!!! Roar

D. roar!!! Roar!!!

E. An exception is thrown.

F. The code does not compile.

14. Given the following, which can correctly fill in the blank allowing the code to compile? (Choose all that apply.)

```
var date = LocalDate.now();
var time = LocalTime.now();
var dateTime = date._____(time);
var zoneId = ZoneId.systemDefault();
var zonedDateTime = ZonedDateTime.of(dateTime, zoneId);
Instant instant = _____;
```

A. asTime()

B. atTime()

C. withTime()

D. dateTime.toInstant()

E. new Instant()

F. zonedDateTime.toInstant()

15. What is the output of the following? (Choose all that apply.)

```
var arr = new String[] { "PIG", "pig", "123"};
Arrays.sort(arr);
System.out.println(Arrays.toString(arr));
System.out.println(Arrays.binarySearch(arr, "Pippa"));
```

A. [pig, PIG, 123]

B. [PIG, pig, 123]

C. [123, PIG, pig]

D. [123, pig, PIG]

E. -3

F. -2

G. The results of binarySearch() are undefined in this example.

16. Which of these statements are true? (Choose all that apply.)

```
var letters = new StringBuilder("abcdefg");
```

A. `letters.substring(1, 2)` returns a single-character `String`.
B. `letters.substring(2, 2)` returns a single-character `String`.
C. `letters.substring(6, 5)` returns a single-character `String`.
D. `letters.substring(6, 6)` returns a single-character `String`.
E. `letters.substring(1, 2)` throws an exception.
F. `letters.substring(2, 2)` throws an exception.
G. `letters.substring(6, 5)` throws an exception.
H. `letters.substring(6, 6)` throws an exception.

17. What is the result of the following code? (Choose all that apply.)

```
13: String s1 = """
14:     purr""";
15: String s2 = "";
16:
17: s1.toUpperCase();
18: s1.trim();
19: s1.substring(1, 3);
20: s1 += "two";
21:
22: s2 += 2;
23: s2 += 'c';
24: s2 += false;
25:
26: if ( s2 == "2cfalse") System.out.println("==");
27: if ( s2.equals("2cfalse")) System.out.println("equals");
28: System.out.println(s1.length());
```

A. 2
B. 4
C. 7
D. 10
E. ==
F. equals
G. An exception is thrown.
H. The code does not compile.

18. Which of the following fill in the blank to print a positive integer? (Choose all that apply.)

```
String[] s1 = { "Camel", "Peacock", "Llama"};
String[] s2 = { "Camel", "Llama", "Peacock"};
String[] s3 = { "Camel"};
String[] s4 = { "Camel", null};
System.out.println(Arrays._____);
```

A. compare(s1, s2)

B. mismatch(s1, s2)

C. compare(s3, s4)

D. mismatch (s3, s4)

E. compare(s4, s4)

F. mismatch (s4, s4)

19. Note that March 12, 2028 is the weekend that clocks spring ahead for daylight saving time. What is the output of the following? (Choose all that apply.)

```
var date = LocalDate.of(2028, Month.MARCH, 12);
var time = LocalTime.of(1, 30);
var zone = ZoneId.of("US/Eastern");
var dateTime1 = ZonedDateTime.of(date, time, zone);
var dateTime2 = dateTime1.plus(1, ChronoUnit.HOURS);

long diff = ChronoUnit.HOURS.between(dateTime1, dateTime2);
int hour = dateTime2.getHour();
boolean offset = dateTime1.getOffset()
   == dateTime2.getOffset();
System.out.println("diff = " + diff);
System.out.println("hour = " + hour);
System.out.println("offset = " + offset);
```

A. diff = 1

B. diff = 2

C. hour = 2

D. hour = 3

E. offset = true

F. The code does not compile.

G. A runtime exception is thrown.

20. Which of the following can fill in the blank to print avaJ? (Choose all that apply.)

```
3: var puzzle = new StringBuilder("Java");
4: puzzle._____;
5: System.out.println(puzzle);
```

A. `reverse()`

B. `append("vaJ$").substring(0, 4)`

C. `append("vaJ$").delete(0, 3).deleteCharAt(puzzle.length() - 1)`

D. `append("vaJ$").delete(0, 3).deleteCharAt(puzzle.length())`

E. None of the above

21. What is the output of the following code?

```java
var date = LocalDate.of(2025, Month.APRIL, 30);
date.plusDays(2);
date.plusYears(3);
System.out.println(date.getYear() + " " + date.getMonth()
    + " " + date.getDayOfMonth());
```

A. `2025 APRIL 30`

B. `2025 MAY 2`

C. `2028 APRIL 2`

D. `2028 APRIL 30`

E. `2028 MAY 2`

F. The code does not compile.

G. A runtime exception is thrown.

22. What is the output of the following?

```java
var result = LocalDate.of(2025, Month.OCTOBER, 31)
    .plusYears(1)
    .plusMonths(-5)
    .plusMonths(1)
    .withYear(2026)
    .atTime(LocalTime.of(13, 4));
System.out.println(result);
```

A. `2025-06-30T13:04`

B. `2026-04-304`

C. `2026-04-30T13:04`

D. `2026-06-30T`

E. `2026-06-30T13:04`

F. The code does not compile.

G. A runtime exception is thrown.

Chapter

5

Methods

✓ **Using Object-Oriented Concepts in Java**

- Create classes and records, and define and use instance and static fields and methods, constructors, and instance and static initializers.

- Implement overloaded methods, including var-arg methods.

In previous chapters, you learned how to write snippets of code without much thought about the methods that contained the code. In this chapter, you explore methods in depth including modifiers, arguments, varargs, overloading, and autoboxing. Many of these fundamentals, such as access and `static` modifiers, are applicable to classes and other types throughout the rest of the book. If you're having difficulty, you might want to read this chapter twice!

Designing Methods

Every interesting Java program we've seen has had a `main()` method. You can write other methods too. For example, you can write a basic method to take a nap, as shown in Figure 5.1.

FIGURE 5.1   Method declaration

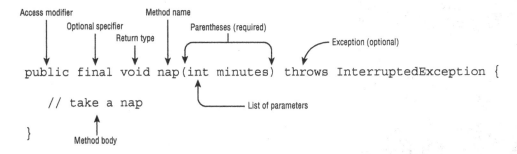

This is called a *method declaration*, which specifies all the information needed to call the method. There are a lot of parts, and we cover each one in more detail. Two of the parts—the method name and parameter list—are called the *method signature*. The method signature provides instructions for *how* callers can reference this method. The method signature does not include the return type and access modifiers, which control *where* the method can be referenced.

Table 5.1 is a brief reference to the elements of a method declaration. Don't worry if it seems like a lot of information—by the time you finish this chapter, it will all fit together.

TABLE 5.1   Parts of a method declaration in Figure 5.1

Element	Value in nap() example	Required?
Access modifier	`public`	No
Optional specifier	`final`	No
Return type	`void`	Yes
Method name	`nap`	Yes
Parameter list	`(int minutes)`	Yes, but can be empty parentheses
Method signature	`nap(int minutes)`	Yes
Exception list	`throws InterruptedException`	No

Method body	`{`
	`  // take a nap`
	`}`
		Yes, except for `abstract` methods

To call this method, just use the method signature and provide an `int` value in parentheses:

`nap(10);`

Let's start by taking a look at each of these parts of a basic method.

Access Modifiers

An access modifier determines what classes a method can be accessed from. Think of it like a security guard. Some classes are good friends, some are distant relatives, and some are complete strangers. Access modifiers help to enforce when these components are allowed to talk to each other. Java offers four choices of access:

private   The `private` modifier means the method can be called only from within the same class.

Package Access   With package access, the method can be called only from a class in the same package. This one is tricky because there is no keyword. You simply omit the access modifier. Package access is sometimes referred to as package-private or default access (even within this book!).

protected   The protected modifier means the method can be called only from a class in the same package or a subclass.

public   The public modifier means the method can be called from anywhere.

 For simplicity, we're primarily concerned with access modifiers applied to methods and fields in this chapter. Rules for access modifiers are also applicable to classes and other types you learn about in Chapter 7, "Beyond Classes," such as interfaces, enums, and records.

We explore the impact of the various access modifiers later in this chapter. For now, just master identifying valid syntax of methods. The exam creators like to trick you by putting method elements in the wrong order or using incorrect values.

We'll see practice examples as we go through each of the method elements in this chapter. Make sure you understand why each of these is a valid or invalid method declaration. Pay attention to the access modifiers as you figure out what is wrong with the ones that don't compile when inserted into a class:

```
public class ParkTrip {
    public void skip1() {}
    default void skip2() {} // DOES NOT COMPILE
    void public skip3() {}  // DOES NOT COMPILE
    void skip4() {}
}
```

The skip1() method is a valid declaration with public access. The skip4() method is a valid declaration with package access. The skip2() method doesn't compile because default is not a valid access modifier. There is a default keyword, which is used in switch statements and interfaces, but default is never used as an access modifier. The skip3() method doesn't compile because the access modifier is specified after the return type.

Optional Specifiers

There are a number of optional specifiers for methods, shown in Table 5.2. Unlike with access modifiers, you can have multiple specifiers in the same method (although not all combinations are legal). When this happens, you can specify them in any order. And since these specifiers are optional, you are allowed to not have any of them at all. This means you can have zero or more specifiers in a method declaration.

As you can see in Table 5.2, four of the method modifiers are covered in later chapters, and the last two aren't even in scope for the exam (and are seldom used in real life). In this chapter, we focus on introducing you to these modifiers. Using them often requires a lot more rules.

TABLE 5.2   Optional specifiers for methods

Modifier	Description	Chapter covered
static	Indicates the method is a member of the shared class object	Chapter 5
abstract	Used in an abstract class or interface when the method body is excluded	Chapter 6
final	Specifies that the method may not be overridden in a subclass	Chapter 6
default	Used in an interface to provide a default implementation of a method for classes that implement the interface	Chapter 7
synchronized	Used with multithreaded code	Chapter 13
native	Used when interacting with code written in another language, such as C++	Out of scope
strictfp	Used for making floating-point calculations portable	Out of scope

While access modifiers and optional specifiers can appear in any order, *they must all appear before the return type*. In practice, it is common to list the access modifier first. As you'll also learn in upcoming chapters, some specifiers are not compatible with one another. For example, you can't declare a method (or class) both final and abstract.

 Remember, access modifiers and optional specifiers can be listed in any order, but once the return type is specified, the rest of the parts of the method are written in a specific order: name, parameter list, exception list, body.

Again, just focus on syntax for now. Do you see why these compile or don't compile?

```
public class Exercise {
    public void bike1() {}
    public final void bike2() {}
    public static final void bike3() {}
    public final static void bike4() {}
    public modifier void bike5() {}       // DOES NOT COMPILE
    public void final bike6() {}          // DOES NOT COMPILE
    final public void bike7() {}
}
```

The `bike1()` method is a valid declaration with no optional specifier. This is OK—it is optional, after all. The `bike2()` method is a valid declaration, with `final` as the optional specifier. The `bike3()` and `bike4()` methods are valid declarations with both `final` and `static` as optional specifiers. The order of these two keywords doesn't matter. The `bike5()` method doesn't compile because `modifier` is not a valid optional specifier. The `bike6()` method doesn't compile because the optional specifier is after the return type.

The `bike7()` method does compile. Java allows the optional specifiers to appear before the access modifier. This is a weird case and not one you need to know for the exam. We are mentioning it so you don't get confused when practicing.

Return Type

The next item in a method declaration is the return type. It must appear after any access modifiers or optional specifiers and before the method name. The return type might be an actual Java type such as `String` or `int`. If there is no return type, the `void` keyword is used. This special return type comes from the English language: *void* means "without contents."

NOTE   Remember that a method must have a return type. If no value is returned, the `void` keyword must be used. You cannot omit the return type.

When checking return types, you also have to look inside the method body. Methods with a return type other than `void` are required to have a `return` statement inside the method body. This `return` statement must include the primitive or object to be returned. Methods that have a return type of `void` are permitted to have a `return` statement with no value returned or omit the `return` statement entirely. Think of a `return` statement in a `void` method as the method saying, "I'm done!" and quitting early, such as the following:

```java
public void swim(int distance) {
    if(distance <= 0) {
        // Exit early, nothing to do!
        return;
    }
    System.out.print("Fish is swimming " + distance + " meters");
}
```

Ready for some examples? Can you explain why these methods compile or don't?

```java
public class Hike {
    public void hike1() {}
    public void hike2() { return; }
    public String hike3() { return ""; }
    public String hike4() {}              // DOES NOT COMPILE
    public hike5() {}                     // DOES NOT COMPILE
    public String int hike6() { }         // DOES NOT COMPILE
}
```

```
String hike7(int a) {                  // DOES NOT COMPILE
    if (1 < 2) return "orange";
  }
}
```

Since the return type of the `hike1()` method is `void`, the `return` statement is optional. The `hike2()` method shows the optional `return` statement that correctly doesn't return anything. The `hike3()` method is a valid declaration with a `String` return type and a `return` statement that returns a `String`. The `hike4()` method doesn't compile because the `return` statement is missing. The `hike5()` method doesn't compile because the return type is missing. The `hike6()` method doesn't compile because it attempts to use two return types. You get only one return type.

The `hike7()` method is a little tricky. There is a `return` statement, but it doesn't always get run. Even though 1 is always less than 2, the compiler won't fully evaluate the `if` statement and requires a `return` statement if this condition is `false`. What about this modified version?

```
String hike8(int a) {
    if (1 < 2) return "orange";
    return "apple";                    // COMPILER WARNING
  }
```

The code compiles, although the compiler will produce a warning about *unreachable code* (or *dead code*). This means the compiler was smart enough to realize you wrote code that cannot possibly be reached.

When returning a value, it needs to be assignable to the return type. Can you spot what's wrong with two of these examples?

```
public class Measurement {
    int getHeight1() {
        int temp = 9;
        return temp;
    }
    int getHeight2() {
        int temp = 9L;  // DOES NOT COMPILE
        return temp;
    }
    int getHeight3() {
        long temp = 9L;
        return temp;    // DOES NOT COMPILE
    }
}
```

The `getHeight2()` method doesn't compile because you can't assign a `long` to an `int`. The `getHeight3()` method doesn't compile because you can't return a `long` value as an int. If this wasn't clear to you, you should go back to Chapter 2, "Operators," and reread the sections about numeric types and casting.

Method Name

Method names follow the same rules we practiced with variable names in Chapter 1, "Building Blocks." To review, an identifier may only contain letters, numbers, currency symbols, or _. Also, the first character is not allowed to be a number, and reserved words are not allowed. Finally, the single underscore character is not allowed.

By convention, methods begin with a lowercase letter, but they are not required to. Since this is a review of Chapter 1, we can jump right into practicing with some examples:

```
public class BeachTrip {
    public void jog1() {}
    public void 2jog() {}      // DOES NOT COMPILE
    public jog3 void() {}      // DOES NOT COMPILE
    public void Jog_$() {}
    public _() {}              // DOES NOT COMPILE
    public void() {}           // DOES NOT COMPILE
}
```

The jog1() method is a valid declaration with a traditional name. The 2jog() method doesn't compile because identifiers are not allowed to begin with numbers. The jog3() method doesn't compile because the method name is before the return type. The Jog_$() method is a valid declaration. While it certainly isn't good practice to start a method name with a capital letter and end with punctuation, it is legal. The _ method is not allowed since it consists of a single underscore. The final line of code doesn't compile because the method name is missing.

Parameter List

Although the parameter list is required, it doesn't have to contain any parameters. This means you can just have an empty pair of parentheses after the method name, as follows:

```
public class Sleep {
    void nap() {}
}
```

If you do have multiple parameters, you separate them with a comma. There are a couple more rules for the parameter list that you'll see when we cover varargs shortly. For now, let's practice looking at method declarations with "regular" parameters:

```
public class PhysicalEducation {
    public void run1() {}
    public void run2 {}                    // DOES NOT COMPILE
```

```
    public void run3(int a) {}
    public void run4(int a; int b) {}   // DOES NOT COMPILE
    public void run5(int a, int b) {}
}
```

The run1() method is a valid declaration without any parameters. The run2() method doesn't compile because it is missing the parentheses around the parameter list. The run3() method is a valid declaration with one parameter. The run4() method doesn't compile because the parameters are separated by a semicolon rather than a comma. Semicolons are for separating statements, not for parameter lists. The run5() method is a valid declaration with two parameters.

Method Signature

A method signature, composed of the method name and parameter list, is what Java uses to uniquely determine exactly which method you are attempting to call. Once it determines *which* method you are trying to call, it then determines *if* the call is allowed. For example, attempting to access a private method outside the class or assigning the return value of a void method to an int variable results in compiler errors. Neither of these compiler errors is related to the method signature, though.

It's important to note that the names of the parameters in the method signature are not used as part of a method signature. The parameter list is about the *types* of parameters and their *order*. For example, the following two methods have the exact same signature:

```
// DOES NOT COMPILE
public class Trip {
    public void visitZoo(String name, int waitTime) {}
    public void visitZoo(String attraction, int rainFall) {}
}
```

Despite having different parameter names, these two methods have the same signature and cannot be declared within the same class. Changing the order of parameter types does allow the method to compile, though:

```
public class Trip {
    public void visitZoo(String name, int waitTime) {}
    public void visitZoo(int rainFall, String attraction) {}
}
```

We cover these rules in more detail when we get to method overloading later in this chapter.

Exception List

In Java, code can indicate that something went wrong by throwing an exception. We cover this in Chapter 11, "Exceptions and Localization." For now, you just need to know that it is

optional and where in the method declaration it goes if present. For example,
`InterruptedException` is a type of `Exception`. You can list as many types of exceptions
as you want in this clause, separated by commas. Here's an example:

```
public class ZooMonorail {
    public void zeroExceptions() {}

    public void oneException() throws IllegalArgumentException {}

    public void twoExceptions() throws
        IllegalArgumentException, InterruptedException {}
}
```

While the list of exceptions is optional, it may be required by the compiler, depending on
what appears inside the method body. You learn more about this, as well as how methods
calling them may be required to handle these exception declarations, in Chapter 11.

Method Body

The final part of a method declaration is the method body. A method body is simply a code
block. It has braces that contain zero or more Java statements. We've spent several chapters
looking at Java statements by now, so you should find it easy to figure out why the following
compile or don't:

```
public class Bird {
    public void fly1() {}
    public void fly2()          // DOES NOT COMPILE
    public void fly3(int a) { int name = 5; }
}
```

The `fly1()` method is a valid declaration with an empty method body. The `fly2()`
method doesn't compile because it is missing the braces around the empty method body.
Methods are required to have a body unless they are declared `abstract`. We cover
`abstract` methods in Chapter 6, "Class Design." The `fly3()` method is a valid declaration
with one statement in the method body.

Congratulations! You've made it through the basics of identifying correct and incorrect
method declarations. Now you can delve into more detail.

Declaring Local and Instance Variables

Now that we have methods, we need to talk a little bit about the variables that they can
create or use. As you might recall from Chapter 1, local variables are those defined within a

method or block, while instance variables are those that are defined as a member of a class. Let's take a look at an example:

```java
public class Lion {
    int hunger = 4;

    public int feedZooAnimals() {
        int snack = 10;   // Local variable
        if(snack > 4) {
            long dinnerTime = snack++;
            hunger--;
        }
        return snack;
    }
}
```

In the Lion class, snack and dinnertime are local variables accessible only within their respective code blocks, while hunger is an instance variable and created in every object of the Lion class.

The object or value returned by a method may be available outside the method, but the variable reference snack is gone. Keep this in mind while reading this chapter: all local variable references are destroyed after the block is executed, but the objects they point to may still be accessible.

Local Variable Modifiers

There's only one modifier that can be applied to a local variable: final. Easy to remember, right? When writing methods, developers may want to create a variable that does not change during the course of the method. In this code sample, trying to change the value or object these variables reference results in a compiler error:

```java
public void zooAnimalCheckup(boolean isWeekend) {
    final int rest;
    if(isWeekend) rest = 5; else rest = 20;
    System.out.print(rest);

    final var giraffe = new Animal();
    final int[] friends = new int[5];

    rest = 10;              // DOES NOT COMPILE
    giraffe = new Animal(); // DOES NOT COMPILE
    friends = null;         // DOES NOT COMPILE
}
```

As shown with the `rest` variable, we don't need to assign a value when a `final` variable is declared. The rule is only that it must be assigned a value before it can be used. We can even use `var` and `final` together. Contrast this with the following example:

```
public void zooAnimalCheckup(boolean isWeekend) {
    final int rest;
    if(isWeekend) rest = 5;
    System.out.print(rest);   // DOES NOT COMPILE
}
```

The `rest` variable might not have been assigned a value, such as if `isWeekend` is `false`. Since the compiler does not allow the use of local variables that may not have been assigned a value, the code does not compile.

Does using the `final` modifier mean we can't modify the data? Nope. The `final` attribute refers only to the variable reference; the contents can be freely modified (assuming the object isn't immutable).

```
public void zooAnimalCheckup() {
    final int rest = 5;
    final Animal giraffe = new Animal();
    final int[] friends = new int[5];

    giraffe.setName("George");
    friends[2] = 2;
}
```

The `rest` variable is a primitive, so it's just a value that can't be modified. On the other hand, the contents of the `giraffe` and `friends` variables can be freely modified, provided the variables aren't reassigned.

> While it might not seem obvious, marking a local variable `final` is often a good practice. For example, you may have a complex method in which a variable is referenced dozens of times. It would be really bad if someone came in and reassigned the variable in the middle of the method. Using the `final` attribute is like sending a message to other developers to leave the variable alone!

Effectively Final Variables

An *effectively final* local variable is one that is not modified after it is assigned. This means that the value of a variable doesn't change after it is set, regardless of whether it is explicitly marked as `final`. If you aren't sure whether a local variable is effectively final, just add the `final` keyword. If the code still compiles, the variable is effectively final.

Given this definition, which of the following variables are effectively final?

```
11: public String zooFriends() {
12:     String name = "Harry the Hippo";
```

```
13:     var size = 10;
14:     boolean wet;
15:     if(size > 100) size++;
16:     name.substring(0);
17:     wet = true;
18:     return name;
19: }
```

Remember, a quick test of effectively final is to just add `final` to the variable declaration and see if it still compiles. In this example, name and wet are effectively final and can be updated with the `final` modifier, but not `size`. The name variable is assigned a value on line 12 and not reassigned. Line 16 creates a value that is never used. Remember from Chapter 4, "Core APIs," that strings are immutable. The `size` variable is not effectively final because it could be incremented on line 15. The wet variable is assigned a value only once and not modified afterward.

Effectively Final Parameters

Recall from Chapter 1 that *method and constructor parameters are local variables that have been pre-initialized*. In the context of local variables, the same rules around `final` and effectively final apply. This is especially important in Chapter 7 and Chapter 8, "Lambdas and Functional Interfaces," since local classes and lambda expressions declared within a method can only reference local variables that are `final` or effectively final.

Instance Variable Modifiers

Like methods, instance variables can have different access levels, such as `private`, package, `protected`, and `public`. Remember, package access is indicated by the lack of any modifiers. We cover each of the different access modifiers shortly in this chapter. Instance variables can also use optional specifiers, described in Table 5.3.

TABLE 5.3   Optional specifiers for instance variables

Modifier	Description	Chapter Covered
final	Specifies that the instance variable must be initialized with each instance of the class exactly once	Chapter 5
volatile	Instructs the JVM that the value in this variable may be modified by other threads	Chapter 13
transient	Used to indicate that an instance variable should not be serialized with the class	Chapter 14

Looks like we only need to discuss final in this chapter! If an instance variable is marked final, then it must be assigned a value when it is declared or when the object is instantiated. Like a local final variable, it cannot be assigned a value more than once, though. The following PolarBear class demonstrates these properties:

```
public class PolarBear {
    final int age = 10;
    final int fishEaten;
    final String name;

    { fishEaten = 10; }

    public PolarBear() {
        name = "Robert";
    }
}
```

The age variable is given a value when it is declared, while the fishEaten variable is assigned a value in an instance initializer. The name variable is given a value in the no-argument constructor. Failing to initialize an instance variable (or assigning a value more than once) will lead to a compiler error. We talk about final variable initialization in more detail when we cover constructors in the next chapter.

In Chapter 1, we show that instance variables receive default values based on their type when not set. For example, int receives a default value of 0, while an object reference receives a default value of null. The compiler does not apply a default value to final variables, though. A final instance or final static variable must receive a value when it is declared or as part of initialization.

Working with Varargs

As mentioned in Chapter 4, a method may use a varargs parameter (variable argument) as if it is an array. Creating a method with a varargs parameter is a bit more complicated. In fact, calling such a method may not use an array at all.

Creating Methods with Varargs

There are a number of important rules for creating a method with a varargs parameter.

Rules for Creating a Method with a Varargs Parameter

1. A method can have at most one varargs parameter.

2. If a method contains a varargs parameter, it must be the last parameter in the list.

Given these rules, can you identify why each of these does or doesn't compile? (Yes, there is a lot of practice in this chapter. You have to be really good at identifying valid and invalid methods for the exam.)

```
public class VisitAttractions {
    public void walk1(int... steps) {}
    public void walk2(int start, int... steps) {}
    public void walk3(int... steps, int start) {}     // DOES NOT COMPILE
    public void walk4(int... start, int... steps) {}  // DOES NOT COMPILE
}
```

The walk1() method is a valid declaration with one varargs parameter. The walk2() method is a valid declaration with one int parameter and one varargs parameter. The walk3() and walk4() methods do not compile because they have a varargs parameter in a position that is not the last one.

Calling Methods with Varargs

When calling a method with a varargs parameter, you have a choice. You can pass in an array, or you can list the elements of the array and let Java create it for you. Given our previous walk1() method, which takes a varargs parameter, we can call it one of two ways:

```
// Pass an array
int[] data = new int[] {1, 2, 3};
walk1(data);
```

```
// Pass a list of values
walk1(1,2,3);
```

Regardless of which one you use to call the method, the method will receive an array containing the elements. We can reinforce this with the following example:

```
public void walk1(int... steps) {
    int[] step2 = steps;     // Not necessary, but shows steps is of type int[]
    System.out.print(step2.length);
}
```

You can even omit the varargs values in the method call, and Java will create an array of length zero for you.

```
walk1();
```

Accessing Elements of a Vararg

Accessing a varargs parameter is just like accessing an array. It uses array indexing. Here's an example:

```
16: public static void run(int... steps) {
17:    System.out.print(steps[1]);
18: }
19: public static void main(String[] args) {
20:    run(11, 77);     // 77
21: }
```

Line 20 calls a varargs method with two parameters. When the method is called, it sees an array of size 2. Since indexes are zero-based, 77 is printed.

Using Varargs with Other Method Parameters

Finally! You get to do something other than identify whether method declarations are valid. Instead, you get to look at method calls. Can you figure out why each method call outputs what it does? For now, feel free to ignore the static modifier in the walkDog() method declaration; we cover that later in the chapter.

```
1:  public class DogWalker {
2:     public static void walkDog(int start, int... steps) {
3:        System.out.println(steps.length);
4:     }
5:     public static void main(String[] args) {
6:        walkDog(1);                    // 0
7:        walkDog(1, 2);                 // 1
8:        walkDog(1, 2, 3);              // 2
9:        walkDog(1, new int[] {4, 5});  // 2
10:    } }
```

Line 6 passes 1 as start but nothing else. This means Java creates an array of length 0 for steps. Line 7 passes 1 as start and one more value. Java converts this one value to an array of length 1. Line 8 passes 1 as start and two more values. Java converts these two values to an array of length 2. Line 9 passes 1 as start and an array of length 2 directly as steps.

You've seen that Java will create an empty array if no parameters are passed for a vararg. However, it is still possible to pass null explicitly. The following snippet does compile:

```
walkDog(1, null);     // Triggers NullPointerException in walkDog()
```

Since null isn't an int, Java treats it as an array reference that happens to be null. It just passes on the null array object to walkDog(). Then the walkDog() method throws an exception because it tries to determine the length of null.

Applying Access Modifiers

You already saw that there are four access levels: `private`, package, `protected`, and `public` access. We are going to discuss them in order from most restrictive to least restrictive:

- `private`: Only accessible within the same class.
- Package access: `private` plus other members of the same package. Sometimes referred to as package-private or default access.
- `protected`: Package access plus access within subclasses.
- `public`: `protected` plus classes in the other packages.

We will explore the impact of these four levels of access on members of a class.

Private Access

Let's start with `private` access, which is the simplest. Only code in the same class can call `private` methods or access `private` fields.

First, take a look at Figure 5.2. It shows the classes you'll use to explore private and package access. The big boxes are the names of the packages. The smaller boxes inside them are the classes in each package. You can refer back to this figure if you want to quickly see how the classes relate.

FIGURE 5.2   Classes used to show `private` and package access

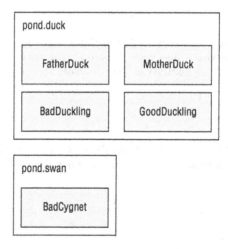

This is perfectly legal code because everything is one class:

```
1: package pond.duck;
2: public class FatherDuck {
```

```
3:     private String noise = "quack";
4:     private void quack() {
5:        System.out.print(noise);            // private access is ok
6:     }
7: }
```

So far, so good. FatherDuck declares a private method quack() and uses private instance variable noise on line 5.

Now we add another class:

```
1: package pond.duck;
2: public class BadDuckling {
3:     public void makeNoise() {
4:        var duck = new FatherDuck();
5:        duck.quack();                      // DOES NOT COMPILE
6:        System.out.print(duck.noise);      // DOES NOT COMPILE
7:     }
8: }
```

BadDuckling is trying to access an instance variable and a method it has no business touching. On line 5, it tries to access a private method in another class. On line 6, it tries to access a private instance variable in another class. Both generate compiler errors. Bad duckling!

Our bad duckling is only a few days old and doesn't know better yet. Luckily, you know that accessing private members of other classes is not allowed, and you need to use a different type of access.

 In the previous example, FatherDuck and BadDuckling are in separate files, but what if they were declared in the same file? Even then, the code would still not compile as Java prevents access outside the class.

Package Access

Luckily, MotherDuck is more accommodating about what her ducklings can do. She allows classes in the same package to access her members. When there is no access modifier, Java assumes package access.

```
package pond.duck;
public class MotherDuck {
   String noise = "quack";
   void quack() {
      System.out.print(noise);              // package access is ok
   }
}
```

MotherDuck can refer to noise and call quack(). After all, members in the same class are certainly in the same package. The big difference is that MotherDuck lets other classes in the same package access members, whereas FatherDuck doesn't (due to being private). GoodDuckling has a much better experience than BadDuckling:

```
package pond.duck;
public class GoodDuckling {
   public void makeNoise() {
      var duck = new MotherDuck();
      duck.quack();                     // package access is ok
      System.out.print(duck.noise);     // package access is ok
   }
}
```

GoodDuckling succeeds in learning to quack() and make noise by copying its mother. Notice that all the classes covered so far are in the same package, pond.duck. This allows package access to work.

In this same pond, a swan just gave birth to a baby swan. A baby swan is called a *cygnet*. The cygnet sees the ducklings learning to quack and decides to learn from MotherDuck as well.

```
package pond.swan;
import pond.duck.MotherDuck;              // import another package
public class BadCygnet {
   public void makeNoise() {
      var duck = new MotherDuck();
      duck.quack();                     // DOES NOT COMPILE
      System.out.print(duck.noise);     // DOES NOT COMPILE
   }
}
```

Oh, no! MotherDuck only allows lessons to other ducks by restricting access to the pond.duck package. Poor little BadCygnet is in the pond.swan package, and the code doesn't compile. Remember that when there is no access modifier on a member, only classes in the same package can access the member.

Protected Access

Protected access allows everything that package access does, and more. The protected access modifier adds the ability to access members of a parent class. We cover creating subclasses in depth in Chapter 6. For now, we cover the simplest possible use of a subclass. In the following example, the "child" ClownFish class is a subclass of the "parent" Fish class, using the extends keyword to connect them:

```
public class Fish {}
```

```
public class ClownFish extends Fish {}
```

By extending a class, the subclass gains access to all `protected` and `public` members of the parent class, as if they were declared in the subclass. If the two classes are in the same package, then the subclass also gains access to all package members.

Figure 5.3 shows the many classes we create in this section. There are a number of classes and packages, so don't worry about keeping them all in your head. Just check back with this figure as you go.

FIGURE 5.3   Classes used to show protected access

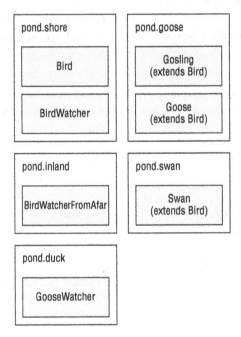

First, create a `Bird` class and give `protected` access to its members:

```
package pond.shore;
public class Bird {
   protected String text = "floating";
   protected void floatInWater() {
      System.out.print(text);          // protected access is ok
   }
}
```

Next, we create a subclass:

```
package pond.goose;                    // Different package than Bird
import pond.shore.Bird;
public class Gosling extends Bird {    // Gosling is a subclass of Bird
```

```
    public void swim() {
        floatInWater();              // protected access is ok
        System.out.print(text);      // protected access is ok
    }
    public static void main(String[] args) {
        new Gosling().swim();
    }
}
```

This is a simple subclass. It *extends* the Bird class. Extending means creating a subclass that has access to any protected or public members of the parent class. Running this program prints floating twice: once from calling floatInWater(), and once from the print statement in swim(). Since Gosling is a subclass of Bird, it can access these members even though it is in a different package.

Remember that protected also gives us access to everything that package access does. This means a class in the same package as Bird can access its protected members.

```
package pond.shore;                  // Same package as Bird
public class BirdWatcher {
    public void watchBird() {
        Bird bird = new Bird();
        bird.floatInWater();         // protected access is ok
        System.out.print(bird.text); // protected access is ok
    }
}
```

Since Bird and BirdWatcher are in the same package, BirdWatcher can access package members of the bird variable. The definition of protected allows access to subclasses and classes in the same package. This example uses the same package part of that definition.

Now let's try the same thing from a different package:

```
package pond.inland;                 // Different package than Bird
import pond.shore.Bird;
public class BirdWatcherFromAfar {   // Not a subclass of Bird
    public void watchBird() {
        Bird bird = new Bird();
        bird.floatInWater();         // DOES NOT COMPILE
        System.out.print(bird.text); // DOES NOT COMPILE
    }
}
```

BirdWatcherFromAfar is not in the same package as Bird, and it doesn't inherit from Bird. This means it is not allowed to access protected members of Bird.

Got that? Subclasses and classes in the same package are the only ones allowed to access `protected` members.

There is one gotcha for `protected` access. Consider this class:

```
1:  package pond.swan;                    // Different package than Bird
2:  import pond.shore.Bird;
3:  public class Swan extends Bird {      // Swan is a subclass of Bird
4:      public void swim() {
5:          floatInWater();               // protected access is ok
6:          System.out.print(text);       // protected access is ok
7:      }
8:      public void helpOtherSwanSwim() {
9:          Swan other = new Swan();
10:         other.floatInWater();         // subclass access to superclass
11:         System.out.print(other.text); // subclass access to superclass
12:     }
13:     public void helpOtherBirdSwim() {
14:         Bird other = new Bird();
15:         other.floatInWater();         // DOES NOT COMPILE
16:         System.out.print(other.text); // DOES NOT COMPILE
17:     }
18: }
```

Take a deep breath. This is interesting. Swan is not in the same package as Bird but does extend it—which implies it has access to the `protected` members of Bird since it is a subclass. And it does. Lines 5 and 6 refer to `protected` members via inheriting them.

Lines 10 and 11 also successfully use `protected` members of Bird. This is allowed because these lines refer to a Swan object. Swan inherits from Bird, so this is OK. It is sort of a two-phase check. The Swan class is allowed to use `protected` members of Bird, and we are referring to a Swan object. Granted, it is a Swan object created on line 9 rather than an inherited one, but it is still a Swan object.

Lines 15 and 16 do *not* compile. Wait a minute. They are almost exactly the same as lines 10 and 11! There's one key difference. This time a Bird reference is used rather than inheritance. It is created on line 14. Bird is in a different package, and this code isn't inheriting from Bird, so it doesn't get to use `protected` members. Say what, now? We just got through saying repeatedly that Swan inherits from Bird. And it does. However, the variable reference isn't a Swan. The code just happens to be in the Swan class.

It's OK to be confused. This is arguably one of the most confusing points on the exam. Looking at it a different way, the `protected` rules apply under two scenarios:

- A member is used without referring to a variable. This is the case on lines 5 and 6. In this case, we are taking advantage of inheritance, and `protected` access is allowed.

- A member is used through a variable. This is the case on lines 10, 11, 15, and 16. In this case, the rules for the reference type of the variable are what matter. If it is a subclass, `protected` access is allowed. This works for references to the same class or a subclass.

We're going to try this again to make sure you understand what is going on. Can you figure out why these examples don't compile?

```
package pond.goose;
import pond.shore.Bird;
public class Goose extends Bird {
    public void helpGooseSwim() {
        Goose other = new Goose();
        other.floatInWater();
        System.out.print(other.text);
    }
    public void helpOtherGooseSwim() {
        Bird other = new Goose();
        other.floatInWater();          // DOES NOT COMPILE
        System.out.print(other.text);  // DOES NOT COMPILE
    }
}
```

The first method is fine. In fact, it is equivalent to the Swan example. Goose extends Bird. Since we are in the Goose subclass and referring to a Goose reference, it can access protected members. The second method is a problem. Although the object happens to be a Goose, it is stored in a Bird reference. We are not allowed to refer to members of the Bird class since we are not in the same package and the reference type of other is not a subclass of Goose.

What about this one?

```
package pond.duck;
import pond.goose.Goose;
public class GooseWatcher {
    public void watch() {
        Goose goose = new Goose();
        goose.floatInWater();      // DOES NOT COMPILE
    }
}
```

This code doesn't compile because we are not in the Goose class. The floatInWater() method is declared in Bird. GooseWatcher is not in the same package as Bird, nor does it extend Bird. Goose extends Bird. That only lets Goose refer to floatInWater(), not callers of Goose.

If this is still puzzling, try it. Type in the code and try to make it compile. Then reread this section. Don't worry—it wasn't obvious to us the first time either!

Public Access

Protected access was a tough concept. Luckily, the last type of access modifier is easy: public means anyone can access the member from anywhere.

The Java module system redefines "anywhere," and it becomes possible to restrict access to public code outside a module. We cover this in more detail in Chapter 12, "Modules." When given code samples, you can assume they are in the same module unless explicitly stated otherwise.

Let's create a class that has public members:

```java
package pond.duck;
public class DuckTeacher {
   public String name = "helpful";
   public void swim() {
      System.out.print(name);                // public access is ok
   }
}
```

DuckTeacher allows access to any class that wants it. Now we can try it:

```java
package pond.goose;
import pond.duck.DuckTeacher;
public class LostDuckling {
   public void swim() {
      var teacher = new DuckTeacher();
      teacher.swim();                         // allowed
      System.out.print("Thanks " + teacher.name);   // allowed
   }
}
```

LostDuckling is able to refer to swim() and name on DuckTeacher because they are public. The story has a happy ending. LostDuckling has learned to swim and can find its parents—all because DuckTeacher made members public.

Reviewing Access Modifiers

Make sure you know why everything in Table 5.4 is true. Use the first column for the first blank and the first row for the second blank. Also, remember that a member is a method or field.

TABLE 5.4   A method in _____ can access a _____ member.

	private	**package**	protected	public
the same class	Yes	Yes	Yes	Yes
another class in the same package	No	Yes	Yes	Yes
a subclass in a different package	No	No	Yes	Yes
an unrelated class in a different package	No	No	No	Yes

Accessing Static Data

When the static keyword is applied to a variable, method, or class, it belongs to the class rather than a specific instance of the class. In this section, you see that the static keyword can also be applied to import statements.

Designing Static Methods and Variables

Except for the main() method, we've been looking at instance methods. Methods and variables declared static don't require an instance of the class. They are shared among all users of the class. For instance, take a look at the following Penguin class:

```java
public class Penguin {
    String name;
    static String nameOfTallestPenguin;
}
```

In this class, every Penguin instance has its own name like Willy or Lilly, but only one Penguin among all the instances is the tallest. You can think of a static variable as being a member of the single class object that exists independently of any instances of that class. Consider the following example:

```java
public static void main(String[] unused) {
    var p1 = new Penguin();
    p1.name = "Lilly";
    p1.nameOfTallestPenguin = "Lilly";
    var p2 = new Penguin();
    p2.name = "Willy";
    p2.nameOfTallestPenguin = "Willy";

    System.out.println(p1.name);                   // Lilly
    System.out.println(p1.nameOfTallestPenguin);   // Willy
    System.out.println(p2.name);                   // Willy
    System.out.println(p2.nameOfTallestPenguin);   // Willy
}
```

We see that each penguin instance is updated with its own unique name. The nameOfTallestPenguin field is static and therefore shared, though, so anytime it is updated, it impacts all instances of the class.

You have seen one static method since Chapter 1. The main() method is a static method. That means you can call it using the class name:

```java
public class Koala {
    public static int count = 0;              // static variable
```

```
   public static void main(String[] args) {    // static method
      System.out.print(count);
   }
}
```

Here the JVM basically calls `Koala.main()` to get the program started. You can do this too. We can have a `KoalaTester` that does nothing but call the `main()` method:

```
public class KoalaTester {
   public static void main(String[] args) {
      Koala.main(new String[0]);              // call static method
   }
}
```

Quite a complicated way to print 0, isn't it? When we run `KoalaTester`, it makes a call to the `main()` method of `Koala`, which prints the value of `count`. The purpose of all these examples is to show that `main()` can be called just like any other `static` method.

In addition to `main()` methods, `static` methods have two main purposes:

- For utility or helper methods that don't require any object state. Since there is no need to access instance variables, having `static` methods eliminates the need for the caller to instantiate an object just to call the method.

- For state that is shared by all instances of a class, like a counter. All instances must share the same state. Methods that merely use that state should be `static` as well.

In the following sections, we look at some examples covering other `static` concepts.

Accessing a Static Variable or Method

Usually, accessing a `static` member is easy.

```
public class Snake {
   public static long hiss = 2;
}
```

You just put the class name before the method or variable, and you are done. Here's an example:

```
System.out.println(Snake.hiss);
```

Nice and easy. There is one rule that is trickier. You can use an instance of the object to call a `static` method. The compiler checks for the type of the reference and uses that instead of the object—which is sneaky of Java. This code is perfectly legal:

```
5: Snake s = new Snake();
6: System.out.println(s.hiss);  // s is a Snake
7: s = null;
8: System.out.println(s.hiss);  // s is still a Snake
```

Believe it or not, this code outputs 2 twice. Line 6 sees that s is a Snake and hiss is a static variable, so it reads that static variable. Line 8 does the same thing. Java doesn't care that s happens to be null. Since we are looking for a static variable, it doesn't matter.

> Remember to look at the reference type for a variable when you see a static method or variable. The exam creators will try to trick you into thinking a NullPointerException is thrown because the variable happens to be null. Don't be fooled!

One more time, because this is really important: what does the following output?

```
Snake.hiss = 4;
Snake snake1 = new Snake();
Snake snake2 = new Snake();
snake1.hiss = 6;
snake2.hiss = 5;
System.out.println(Snake.hiss);
```

We hope you answered 5. There is only one hiss variable since it is static. It is set to 4 and then 6 and finally winds up as 5. All the Snake variables are just distractions.

Class vs. Instance Membership

There's another way the exam creators will try to trick you regarding static and instance members. A static member cannot call an instance member without referencing an instance of the class. This shouldn't be a surprise since static doesn't require any instances of the class to even exist.

The following is a common mistake for rookie programmers to make:

```
public class MantaRay {
    private String name = "Sammy";
    public static void first() {  }
    public static void second() {  }
    public void third() {  System.out.print(name); }
    public static void main(String args[]) {
        first();
        second();
        third();            // DOES NOT COMPILE
    }
}
```

The compiler will give you an error about making a static reference to an instance method. If we fix this by adding static to third(), we create a new problem. Can you figure out what it is?

```
public static void third() {  System.out.print(name); }   // DOES NOT COMPILE
```

All this does is move the problem. Now, third() is referring to an instance variable name. There are two ways we could fix this. The first is to add static to the name variable as well.

```
public class MantaRay {
    private static String name = "Sammy";
    ...
    public static void third() {  System.out.print(name); }
    ...
}
```

The second solution would have been to call third() as an instance method and not use static for the method or the variable.

```
public class MantaRay {
    private String name = "Sammy";
    ...
    public void third() {  System.out.print(name); }
    public static void main(String args[]) {
        ...
        var ray = new MantaRay();
        ray.third();
    }
}
```

The exam creators like this topic—a lot. A static method or instance method can call a static method because static methods don't require an object to use. Only an instance method can call another instance method on the same class without using a reference variable, because instance methods do require an object. Similar logic applies for instance and static variables.

Suppose we have a Giraffe class:

```
public class Giraffe {
    public void eat(Giraffe g) {}
    public void drink() {};
    public static void allGiraffeGoHome(Giraffe g) {}
    public static void allGiraffeComeOut() {}
}
```

Make sure you understand Table 5.5 before continuing.

TABLE 5.5   Static vs. instance calls

Method	Calling	Legal?
allGiraffeGoHome()	allGiraffeComeOut()	Yes
allGiraffeGoHome()	drink()	No
allGiraffeGoHome()	g.eat()	Yes
eat()	allGiraffeComeOut()	Yes
eat()	drink()	Yes
eat()	g.eat()	Yes

Let's try one more example so you have more practice at recognizing this scenario. Do you understand why the following lines fail to compile?

```
1:  public class Gorilla {
2:     public static int count;
3:     public static void addGorilla() { count++; }
4:     public void babyGorilla() { count++; }
5:     public void announceBabies() {
6:        addGorilla();
7:        babyGorilla();
8:     }
9:     public static void announceBabiesToEveryone() {
10:       addGorilla();
11:       babyGorilla();      // DOES NOT COMPILE
12:    }
13:    public int total;
14:    public static double average
15:       = total / count;  // DOES NOT COMPILE
16: }
```

Lines 3 and 4 are fine because both static and instance methods can refer to a static variable. Lines 5–8 are fine because an instance method can call a static method. Line 11 doesn't compile because a static method cannot call an instance method. Similarly, line 15 doesn't compile because a static variable is trying to use an instance variable.

A common use for static variables is counting the number of instances:

```
public class Counter {
   private static int count;
```

```
    public Counter() { count++; }
    public static void main(String[] args) {
        Counter c1 = new Counter();
        Counter c2 = new Counter();
        Counter c3 = new Counter();
        System.out.println(count);      // 3
    }
}
```

Each time the constructor is called, it increments count by one. This example relies on the fact that static (and instance) variables are automatically initialized to the default value for that type, which is 0 for int. See Chapter 1 to review the default values.

Also notice that we didn't write Counter.count. We could have. It isn't necessary because we are already in that class, so the compiler can infer it.

> Make sure you understand this section really well. It comes up throughout this book. You even see a similar topic when we discuss interfaces in Chapter 7. For example, a static interface method cannot call a default interface method without a reference, much the same way that within a class, a static method cannot call an instance method without a reference.

Static Variable Modifiers

Referring back to Table 5.3, static variables can be declared with the same modifiers as instance variables, such as final, transient, and volatile. While some static variables are meant to change as the program runs, like our count example, others are meant to never change. This type of static variable is known as a *constant*. It uses the final modifier to ensure the variable never changes.

Constants use the modifier static final and a different naming convention than other variables. They use all uppercase letters with underscores between "words." Here's an example:

```
public class ZooPen {
    private static final int NUM_BUCKETS = 45;
    public static void main(String[] args) {
        NUM_BUCKETS = 5;  // DOES NOT COMPILE
    }
}
```

The compiler will make sure that you do not accidentally try to update a final variable. This can get interesting. Do you think the following compiles?

```
import java.util.*;
public class ZooInventoryManager {
```

```
    private static final String[] treats = new String[10];
    public static void main(String[] args) {
        treats[0] = "popcorn";
    }
}
```

It actually does compile since `treats` is a reference variable. We are allowed to modify the referenced object or array's contents. All the compiler can do is check that we don't try to reassign `treats` to point to a different object.

The rules for `static final` variables are similar to instance `final` variables, except they do not use `static` constructors (there is no such thing!) and use `static` initializers instead of instance initializers.

```
public class Panda {
    final static String name = "Ronda";
    static final int bamboo;
    static final double height; // DOES NOT COMPILE
    static { bamboo = 5;}
}
```

The `name` variable is assigned a value when it is declared, while the `bamboo` variable is assigned a value in a `static` initializer. The `height` variable is not assigned a value anywhere in the class definition, so that line does not compile. Remember, `final` variables must be initialized with a value. Next, we cover `static` initializers.

Static Initializers

In Chapter 1, we covered instance initializers that looked like unnamed methods—just code inside braces. Now we introduce `static` initializers, which look similar. We just add the `static` keyword to specify that they should be run when the class is first loaded. Here's an example:

```
private static final int NUM_SECONDS_PER_MINUTE;
private static final int NUM_MINUTES_PER_HOUR;
private static final int NUM_SECONDS_PER_HOUR;
static {
    NUM_SECONDS_PER_MINUTE = 60;
    NUM_MINUTES_PER_HOUR = 60;
}
static {
    NUM_SECONDS_PER_HOUR
        = NUM_SECONDS_PER_MINUTE * NUM_MINUTES_PER_HOUR;
}
```

All `static` initializers run when the class is first used, in the order they are defined. The statements in them run and assign any `static` variables as needed. There is something interesting about this example. We just got through saying that `final` variables aren't allowed to be reassigned. The key here is that the `static` initializer is the first assignment. And since it occurs up front, it is OK.

Let's try another example to make sure you understand the distinction:

```
14: private static int one;
15: private static final int two;
16: private static final int three = 3;
17: private static final int four;      // DOES NOT COMPILE
18: static {
19:     one = 1;
20:     two = 2;
21:     three = 3;                       // DOES NOT COMPILE
22:     two = 4;                         // DOES NOT COMPILE
23: }
```

Line 14 declares a `static` variable that is not `final`. It can be assigned as many times as we like. Line 15 declares a `final` variable without initializing it. This means we can initialize it exactly once in a `static` block. Line 22 doesn't compile because this is the second attempt. Line 16 declares a `final` variable and initializes it at the same time. We are not allowed to assign it again, so line 21 doesn't compile. Line 17 declares a `final` variable that never gets initialized. The compiler gives a compiler error because it knows that the `static` blocks are the only place the variable could possibly be initialized. Since the programmer forgot, this is clearly an error.

 Real World Scenario

Try to Avoid *static* and Instance Initializers

Using `static` and instance initializers can make your code much harder to read. Everything that could be done in an instance initializer could be done in a constructor instead. Many people find the constructor approach easier to read.

There is a common case to use a `static` initializer: when you need to initialize a `static` field and the code to do so requires more than one line. This often occurs when you want to initialize a collection like an `ArrayList` or a `HashMap`. When you do need to use a `static` initializer, put all the `static` initialization in the same block. That way, the order is obvious.

Static Imports

In Chapter 1, you saw that you can import a specific class or all the classes in a package. If you haven't seen ArrayList or List before, don't worry, because we cover them in detail in Chapter 9, "Collections and Generics."

```
import java.util.ArrayList;
import java.util.*;
```

We could use this technique to import two classes:

```
import java.util.List;
import java.util.Arrays;
public class Imports {
   public static void main(String[] args) {
      List<String> list = Arrays.asList("one", "two");
   }
}
```

Imports are convenient because you don't need to specify where each class comes from each time you use it. There is another type of import called a *static import*. Regular imports are for importing classes, while static imports are for importing static members of classes like variables and methods.

Just like regular imports, you can use a wildcard or import a specific member. The idea is that you shouldn't have to specify where each static method or variable comes from each time you use it. An example of when static imports shine is when you are referring to a lot of constants in another class.

We can rewrite our previous example to use a static import. Doing so yields the following:

```
import java.util.List;
import static java.util.Arrays.asList;          // static import
public class ZooParking {
   public static void main(String[] args) {
      List<String> list = asList("one", "two"); // No Arrays. prefix
   }
}
```

In this example, we are specifically importing the asList method. This means that any time we refer to asList in the class, it will call Arrays.asList().

An interesting case is what would happen if we created an asList method in our ZooParking class. Java would give it preference over the imported one, and the method we coded would be used.

The exam will try to trick you by misusing `static` imports. This example shows almost everything you can do wrong. Can you figure out what is wrong with each one?

```
1: import static java.util.Arrays;        // DOES NOT COMPILE
2: import static java.util.Arrays.asList;
3: static import java.util.Arrays.*;      // DOES NOT COMPILE
4: public class BadZooParking {
5:     public static void main(String[] args) {
6:         Arrays.asList("one");          // DOES NOT COMPILE
7:     }
8: }
```

Line 1 tries to use a `static` import to import a class. Remember that `static` imports are only for importing `static` members like a method or variable. Regular imports are for importing a class. Line 3 tries to see whether you are paying attention to the order of keywords. The syntax is `import static` and not vice versa. Line 6 is sneaky. The `asList` method is imported on line 2. However, the `Arrays` class is not imported anywhere. This makes it OK to write `asList("one")` but not `Arrays.asList("one")`.

There's only one more scenario with `static` imports. In Chapter 1, you learned that importing two classes with the same name gives a compiler error. This is true of `static` imports as well. The compiler will complain if you try to explicitly do a `static` import of two methods with the same name or two `static` variables with the same name. Here's an example:

```
import static zoo.A.TYPE;
import static zoo.B.TYPE;      // DOES NOT COMPILE
```

Luckily, when this happens, we can just refer to the `static` members via their class name in the code instead of trying to use a `static` import.

In a large program, `static` imports can be overused. When importing from too many places, it can be hard to remember where each `static` member comes from. Use them sparingly!

Passing Data among Methods

Java is a "pass-by-value" language. This means that a copy of the variable is made and the method receives that copy. Assignments made in the method do not affect the caller. Let's look at an example:

```
2: public static void main(String[] args) {
3:     int num = 4;
4:     newNumber(num);
```

```
5:      System.out.print(num);       // 4
6: }
7: public static void newNumber(int num) {
8:      num = 8;
9: }
```

On line 3, num is assigned the value of 4. On line 4, we call a method. On line 8, the num parameter in the method is set to 8. Although this parameter has the same name as the variable on line 3, this is a coincidence. The name could be anything. The exam will often use the same name to try to confuse you. The variable on line 3 never changes because no assignments are made to it.

Passing Objects

Now that you've seen primitives, let's try an example with a reference type. What do you think is output by the following code?

```
public class Dog {
    public static void main(String[] args) {
        String name = "Webby";
        speak(name);
        System.out.print(name);
    }
    public static void speak(String name) {
        name = "Georgette";
    }
}
```

The correct answer is Webby. Just as in the primitive example, the variable assignment is only to the method parameter and doesn't affect the caller.

Notice how we keep talking about variable assignments. This is because we can call methods on the parameters. As an example, here is code that calls a method on the StringBuilder passed into the method:

```
public class Dog {
    public static void main(String[] args) {
        var name = new StringBuilder("Webby");
        speak(name);
        System.out.print(name);    // WebbyGeorgette
    }
    public static void speak(StringBuilder s) {
        s.append("Georgette");
    }
}
```

In this case, speak() calls a method on the parameter. It doesn't reassign s to a different object. In Figure 5.4, you can see how pass-by-value is still used. The variable s is a copy of the variable name. Both point to the same StringBuilder, which means that changes made to the StringBuilder are available to both references.

FIGURE 5.4 Copying a reference with pass-by-value

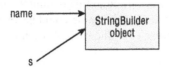

```
name  ─────────►  ┌─────────────┐
                  │ StringBuilder│
                  │   object    │
              s ─►└─────────────┘
```

 Real World Scenario

Pass-by-Value vs. Pass-by-Reference

Different languages handle parameters in different ways. Pass-by-value is used by many languages, including Java. In this example, the swap() method does not change the original values. It only changes a and b within the method.

```java
public static void main(String[] args) {
    int original1 = 1;
    int original2 = 2;
    swap(original1, original2);
    System.out.println(original1);    // 1
    System.out.println(original2);    // 2
}

public static void swap(int a, int b) {
    int temp = a;
    a = b;
    b = temp;
}
```

The other approach is pass-by-reference. It is used by default in a few languages, such as Perl. We aren't going to show you Perl code here because you are studying for the Java exam, and we don't want to confuse you. In a pass-by-reference language, the variables would be swapped and the output would be reversed.

To review, Java uses pass-by-value to get data into a method. Assigning a new primitive or reference to a parameter doesn't change the caller. Calling methods on a reference to an object can affect the caller.

Returning Objects

Getting data back from a method is easier. A copy is made of the primitive or reference and returned from the method. Most of the time, this returned value is used. For example, it might be stored in a variable. If the returned value is not used, the result is ignored. Watch for this on the exam. Ignored returned values are tricky.

Let's try an example. Pay attention to the return types.

```
1:  public class ZooTickets {
2:     public static void main(String[] args) {
3:        int tickets = 2;                            // tickets = 2
4:        String guests = "abc";                      // guests  = abc
5:        addTickets(tickets);                        // tickets = 2
6:        guests = addGuests(guests);                 // guests  = abcd
7:        System.out.println(tickets + guests);       // 2abcd
8:     }
9:     public static int addTickets(int tickets) {
10:       tickets++;
11:       return tickets;
12:    }
13:    public static String addGuests(String guests) {
14:       guests += "d";
15:       return guests;
16:    }
17: }
```

This is a tricky one because there is a lot to keep track of. When you see such questions on the exam, write down the values of each variable. Lines 3 and 4 are straightforward assignments. Line 5 calls a method. Line 10 increments the method parameter to 3 but leaves the tickets variable in the main() method as 2. While line 11 returns the value, the caller ignores it. The method call on line 6 doesn't ignore the result, so guests becomes "abcd". Remember that this is happening because of the returned value and not the method parameter.

Autoboxing and Unboxing Variables

Java supports some helpful features around passing primitive and wrapper data types, such as int and Integer. Remember from Chapter 1 that we can explicitly convert between primitives and wrapper classes using built-in methods.

```
5: int quack = 5;
6: Integer quackquack = Integer.valueOf(quack);     // Convert int to Integer
7: int quackquackquack = quackquack.intValue();     // Convert Integer to int
```

Useful, but a bit verbose. Luckily, Java has handlers built into the Java language that automatically convert between primitives and wrapper classes and back again. *Autoboxing* is the process of converting a primitive into its equivalent wrapper class, while *unboxing* is the process of converting a wrapper class into its equivalent primitive.

```
5: int quack = 5;
6: Integer quackquack = quack;          // Autoboxing
7: int quackquackquack = quackquack;    // Unboxing
```

The new code is equivalent to the previous code, as the compiler is "doing the work" of converting the types automatically for you. Autoboxing applies to all primitives and their associated wrapper types, such as the following:

```
Short tail = 8;                         // Autoboxing
Character p = Character.valueOf('p');
char paw = p;                           // Unboxing
Boolean nose = true;                    // Autoboxing
Integer e = Integer.valueOf(9);
long ears = e;                          // Unboxing, then implicit casting
```

Each of these examples compiles without issue. In the last line, e is unboxed to an int value. Since an int value can be stored in a long variable via implicit casting, the compiler allows the assignment.

Limits of Autoboxing and Numeric Promotion

While Java will implicitly cast a smaller primitive to a larger type, as well as autobox, it will not do both at the same time. Do you see why the following does not compile?

```
Long badGorilla = 8;  // DOES NOT COMPILE
```

The compiler will automatically cast or autobox the int value to long or Integer, respectively. Neither of these types can be assigned to a Long reference variable, though, so the code does not compile. Compare this behavior to the previous example with ears, where the unboxed primitive value could be implicitly cast to a larger primitive type.

What do you think happens if you try to unbox a null?

```
10: Character elephant = null;
11: char badElephant = elephant;    // NullPointerException
```

On line 10, we store null in a Character reference. This is legal because a null reference can be assigned to any reference variable. On line 11, we try to unbox that null to a char primitive. This is a problem. Java tries to get the char value of null. Since calling any method on null gives a NullPointerException, that is just what we get. Be careful when you see null in relation to autoboxing and unboxing.

Where autoboxing and unboxing really shine is when we apply them to method calls.

```java
public class Chimpanzee {
    public void climb(long t) {}
    public void swing(Integer u) {}
    public void jump(int v) {}
    public static void main(String[] args) {
        var c = new Chimpanzee();
        c.climb(123);
        c.swing(123);
        c.jump(123L);  // DOES NOT COMPILE
    }
}
```

In this example, the call to climb() compiles because the int value can be implicitly cast to a long. The call to swing() also is permitted, because the int value is autoboxed to an Integer. On the other hand, the call to jump() results in a compiler error because a long must be explicitly cast to an int. In other words, Java will not automatically convert to a narrower type.

As before, the same limitation around autoboxing and numeric promotion applies to method calls. For example, the following does not compile:

```java
public class Gorilla {
    public void rest(Long x) {
        System.out.print("long");
    }
    public static void main(String[] args) {
        var g = new Gorilla();
        g.rest(8);  // DOES NOT COMPILE
    }
}
```

Java will cast or autobox the value automatically, but not both at the same time. Finally, autoboxing can be used when initializing an array. The following creates two arrays with Integer and Double values, respectively.

```java
Integer[] openingHours    = { 9, 12 };
Double[] temperaturesAtZoo = { 74.1, 93.2 };
```

The types have to be compatible, though, as shown in the following examples.

```java
Integer[] winterHours = { 10.5, 17.0 };  // DOES NOT COMPILE
Double[] summerHours  = { 9, 21 };       // DOES NOT COMPILE
```

Overloading Methods

Now that you are familiar with the rules for declaring and using methods, it is time to look at creating methods with the same name in the same class. *Method overloading* occurs when methods in the same class have the same name but different method signatures, which means they use different parameter lists. (Overloading differs from overriding, which you learn about in Chapter 6.)

We've been showing how to call overloaded methods for a while. `System.out.println()` and `StringBuilder`'s `append()` methods provide many overloaded versions, so you can pass just about anything to them without having to think about it. In both of these examples, the only change was the type of the parameter. Overloading also allows different numbers of parameters.

Everything other than the method name can vary for overloading methods. This means there can be different access modifiers, optional specifiers (like `static`), return types, and exception lists.

The following shows five overloaded versions of the `fly()` method:

```
public class Falcon {
    public void fly(int numMiles) {}
    public void fly(short numFeet) {}
    public boolean fly() { return false; }
    void fly(int numMiles, short numFeet) {}
    public void fly(short numFeet, int numMiles) throws Exception {}
}
```

As you can see, we can overload by changing anything in the parameter list. We can have a different type, more types, or the same types in a different order. Also notice that the return type, access modifier, and exception list are irrelevant to overloading. Only the method name and parameter list matter.

Now let's look at an example that is not valid overloading:

```
public class Eagle {
    public void fly(int numMiles) {}
    public int fly(int numMiles) { return 1; }      // DOES NOT COMPILE
}
```

This method doesn't compile because it differs from the original only by return type. The method signatures are the same, so they are duplicate methods as far as Java is concerned.

What about these; why do they not compile?

```
public class Hawk {
    public void fly(int numMiles) {}
    public static void fly(int numMiles) {}         // DOES NOT COMPILE
    public void fly(int numKilometers) {}           // DOES NOT COMPILE
}
```

Again, the method signatures of these three methods are the same. You cannot declare methods in the same class where the only difference is that one is an instance method and one is a `static` method. You also cannot have two methods that have parameter lists with the same variable types and in the same order. As we mentioned earlier, the names of the parameters in the list do not matter when determining the method signature.

Calling overloaded methods is easy. You just write code, and Java calls the right one. For example, look at these two methods:

```java
public class Dove {
   public void fly(int numMiles) {
      System.out.println("int");
   }
   public void fly(short numFeet) {
      System.out.println("short");
   }
}
```

The call `fly((short) 1)` prints `short`. It looks for matching types and calls the appropriate method. Of course, it can be more complicated than this.

Now that you know the basics of overloading, let's look at some more complex scenarios that you may encounter on the exam.

Reference Types

Java picks the most specific version of a method that it can. What do you think this code outputs?

```java
public class Pelican {
   public void fly(String s) {
      System.out.print("string");
   }

   public void fly(Object o) {
      System.out.print("object");
   }
   public static void main(String[] args) {
      var p = new Pelican();
      p.fly("test");
      System.out.print("-");
      p.fly(56);
   }
}
```

The answer is `string-object`. The first call passes a `String` and finds a direct match. There's no reason to use the `Object` version when there is a nice `String` parameter list just waiting to be called. The second call looks for an `int` parameter list. When it doesn't find one, it autoboxes to `Integer`. Since it still doesn't find a match, it goes to the `Object` one.

Let's try another. What does this print?

```java
import java.time.*;
import java.util.*;
public class Parrot {
    public static void print(List<Integer> i) {
        System.out.print("I");
    }
    public static void print(CharSequence c) {
        System.out.print("C");
    }
    public static void print(Object o) {
        System.out.print("O");
    }
    public static void main(String[] args){
        print("abc");
        print(Arrays.asList(3));
        print(LocalDate.of(2019, Month.JULY, 4));
    }
}
```

The answer is `CIO`. The code is due for a promotion! The first call to `print()` passes a `String`. As you learned in Chapter 4, `String` and `StringBuilder` implement the `CharSequence` interface. You also learned that `Arrays.asList()` can be used to create a `List<Integer>` object, which explains the second output. The final call to `print()` passes a `LocalDate`. This is a class you might not know, but that's OK. It clearly isn't a sequence of characters or a list. That means the `Object` method signature is used.

Primitives

Primitives work in a way that's similar to reference variables. Java tries to find the most specific matching overloaded method. What do you think happens here?

```java
public class Ostrich {
    public void fly(int i) {
        System.out.print("int");
    }
    public void fly(long l) {
        System.out.print("long");
    }
```

```
    public static void main(String[] args) {
        var p = new Ostrich();
        p.fly(123);
        System.out.print("-");
        p.fly(123L);
    }
}
```

The answer is int-long. The first call passes an int and sees an exact match. The second call passes a long and also sees an exact match. If we comment out the overloaded method with the int parameter list, the output becomes long-long. Java has no problem calling a larger primitive. However, it will not do so unless a better match is not found.

Autoboxing

As we saw earlier, autoboxing applies to method calls, but what happens if you have both a primitive and an integer version?

```
public class Kiwi {
    public void fly(int numMiles) {}
    public void fly(Integer numMiles) {}
}
```

These method overloads are valid. *Java tries to use the most specific parameter list it can find.* This is true for autoboxing as well as other matching types we talk about in this section.

This means calling fly(3) will call the first method. When the primitive int version isn't present, Java will autobox. However, when the primitive int version is provided, there is no reason for Java to do the extra work of autoboxing.

Arrays

Unlike the previous example, this code does not result in autoboxing:

```
public static void walk(int[] ints) {}
public static void walk(Integer[] integers) {}
```

Arrays have been around since the beginning of Java. They specify their actual types. What about generic types, such as List<Integer>? We cover this topic in Chapter 9.

Varargs

Which method do you think is called if we pass an int[]?

```
public class Toucan {
    public void fly(int[] lengths) {}
```

```
    public void fly(int... lengths) {}      // DOES NOT COMPILE
}
```

Trick question! Remember that Java treats varargs as if they were an array. This means the method signature is the same for both methods. Since we are not allowed to overload methods with the same parameter list, this code doesn't compile. Even though the code doesn't look the same, it compiles to the same parameter list.

Now that we've just gotten through explaining that the two methods are similar, it is time to mention how they are different. It shouldn't be a surprise that you can call either method by passing an array:

```
fly(new int[] { 1, 2, 3 });  // Allowed to call either fly() method
```

However, you can only call the varargs version with stand-alone parameters:

```
fly(1, 2, 3);  // Allowed to call only the fly() method using varargs
```

Obviously, this means they don't compile *exactly* the same. The parameter list is the same, though, and that is what you need to know with respect to overloading for the exam.

Putting It All Together

So far, all the rules for when an overloaded method is called should be logical. Java calls the most specific method it can. When some of the types interact, the Java rules focus on backward compatibility. A long time ago, autoboxing and varargs didn't exist. Since old code still needs to work, this means autoboxing and varargs come last when Java looks at overloaded methods. Ready for the official order? Table 5.6 lays it out for you.

TABLE 5.6   The order that Java uses to choose the right overloaded method

Rule	Example of what will be chosen for glide(1,2)
Exact match by type	String glide(int i, int j)
Larger primitive type	String glide(long i, long j)
Autoboxed type	String glide(Integer i, Integer j)
Varargs	String glide(int... nums)

Let's give this a practice run using the rules in Table 5.6. What do you think this outputs?

```
public class Glider {
    public static String glide(String s) {
        return "1";
```

```
    }
    public static String glide(String... s) {
        return "2";
    }
    public static String glide(Object o) {
        return "3";
    }
    public static String glide(String s, String t) {
        return "4";
    }
    public static void main(String[] args) {
        System.out.print(glide("a"));
        System.out.print(glide("a", "b"));
        System.out.print(glide("a", "b", "c"));
    }
}
```

It prints out 142. The first call matches the signature taking a single String because that is the most specific match. The second call matches the signature taking two String parameters since that is an exact match. It isn't until the third call that the varargs version is used since there are no better matches.

Summary

In this chapter, we presented a lot of rules for declaring methods and variables. Methods start with access modifiers and optional specifiers in any order (although commonly with access modifiers first). The access modifiers we discussed in this chapter are private, package (omitted), protected, and public. The optional specifier for methods we covered in this chapter is static. We cover additional method modifiers in future chapters.

Next comes the method return type, which is void if there is no return value. The method name and parameter list are provided next, which compose the unique method signature. The method name uses standard Java identifier rules, while the parameter list is composed of zero or more types with names. An optional list of exceptions may also be added following the parameter list. Finally, a block defines the method body (which is omitted for abstract methods).

Access modifiers are used for a lot more than just methods, so make sure you understand them well. Using the private keyword means the code is only available from within the same class. Package access means the code is available only from within the same package. Using the protected keyword means the code is available from the same package or subclasses. Using the public keyword means the code is available from anywhere.

Both static methods and static variables are shared by all instances of the class. When referenced from outside the class, they are called using the class name—for example, Pigeon.fly(). Instance members are allowed to call static members, but static members are not allowed to call instance members. In addition, static imports are used to import static members.

We also presented the final modifier and showed how it can be applied to local, instance, and static variables. Remember, a local variable is effectively final if it is not modified after it is assigned. One quick test for this is to add the final modifier and see if the code still compiles.

Java uses pass-by-value, which means that calls to methods create a copy of the parameters. Assigning new values to those parameters in the method doesn't affect the caller's variables. Calling methods on objects that are method parameters changes the state of those objects and is reflected in the caller. Java supports autoboxing and unboxing of primitives and wrappers automatically within a method and through method calls.

Overloaded methods are methods with the same name but a different parameter list. Java calls the most specific method it can find. Exact matches are preferred, followed by wider primitives. After that comes autoboxing and finally varargs.

Make sure you understand everything in this chapter. It sets the foundation of what you learn in the next chapters.

Exam Essentials

Be able to identify correct and incorrect method declarations.   Be able to view a method signature and know if it is correct, contains invalid or conflicting elements, or contains elements in the wrong order.

Identify when a method or field is accessible.   Recognize when a method or field is accessible when the access modifier is: private, package (omitted), protected, or public.

Understand how to declare and use final variables.   Local, instance, and static variables may be declared final. Be able to understand how to declare them and how they can (or cannot) be used.

Be able to spot effectively final variables.   Effectively final variables are local variables that are not modified after being assigned. Given a local variable, be able to determine if it is effectively final.

Recognize valid and invalid uses of static imports.   Static imports import static members. They are written as import static, not *static import*. Make sure they are importing static methods or variables rather than class names.

Apply autoboxing and unboxing.   The process of automatically converting from a primitive value to a wrapper class is called autoboxing, while the reciprocal process is called unboxing. Watch for a `NullPointerException` when performing unboxing.

State the output of code involving methods.   Identify when to call `static` rather than instance methods based on whether the class name or object comes before the method. Recognize that instance methods can call `static` methods and that `static` methods need an instance of the object in order to call an instance method.

Recognize the correct overloaded method.   Exact matches are used first, followed by wider primitives, followed by autoboxing, followed by varargs. Assigning new values to method parameters does not change the caller, but calling methods on them can.

Review Questions

The answers to the chapter review questions can be found in the Appendix.

1. Which statements about the `final` modifier are correct? (Choose all that apply.)

    A. Instance and `static` variables can be marked `final`.

    B. A variable is effectively final only if it is marked `final`.

    C. An object that is marked `final` cannot be modified.

    D. Local variables cannot be declared with type `var` and the `final` modifier.

    E. A primitive that is marked `final` cannot be modified.

2. Which of the following can fill in the blank in this code to make it compile? (Choose all that apply.)
    ```
    public class Ant {
        _____ void method() {}
    }
    ```

    A. `default`

    B. `final`

    C. `private`

    D. `Public`

    E. `String`

    F. `zzz:`

3. Which of the following methods compile? (Choose all that apply.)

    A. `final static void rain() {}`

    B. `public final int void snow() {}`

    C. `private void int hail() {}`

    D. `static final void sleet() {}`

    E. `void final ice() {}`

    F. `void public slush() {}`

4. Which of the following can fill in the blank and allow the code to compile? (Choose all that apply.)

    `final _____ song = 6;`

    A. `int`

    B. `Integer`

    C. `long`

    D. `Long`

    E. `double`

    F. `Double`

5. Which of the following methods compile? (Choose all that apply.)

   A. `public void january() { return; }`

   B. `public int february() { return null;}`

   C. `public void march() {}`

   D. `public int april() { return 9;}`

   E. `public int may() { return 9.0;}`

   F. `public int june() { return;}`

6. Which of the following methods compile? (Choose all that apply.)

   A. `public void violin(int... nums) {}`

   B. `public void viola(String values, int... nums) {}`

   C. `public void cello(int... nums, String values) {}`

   D. `public void bass(String... values, int... nums) {}`

   E. `public void flute(String[] values, ...int nums) {}`

   F. `public void oboe(String[] values, int[] nums) {}`

7. Given the following method, which of the method calls return 2? (Choose all that apply.)

   ```
   public int juggle(boolean b, boolean... b2) {
       return b2.length;
   }
   ```

   A. `juggle();`

   B. `juggle(true);`

   C. `juggle(true, true);`

   D. `juggle(true, true, true);`

   E. `juggle(true, {true, true});`

   F. `juggle(true, new boolean[2]);`

8. Which of the following statements is correct?

   A. Package access is more lenient than `protected` access.

   B. A `public` class that has private fields and package methods is not visible to classes outside the package.

   C. You can use access modifiers so only some of the classes in a package see a particular package class.

   D. You can use access modifiers to allow access to all methods and not any instance variables.

   E. You can use access modifiers to restrict access to all classes that begin with the word `Test`.

9. Given the following class definitions, which lines in the `main()` method generate a compiler error? (Choose all that apply.)

```
// Classroom.java
package my.school;
public class Classroom {
    private int roomNumber;
    protected static String teacherName;
    static int globalKey = 54321;
    public static int floor = 3;
    Classroom(int r, String t) {
        roomNumber = r;
        teacherName = t; } }
```

```
// School.java
1: package my.city;
2: import my.school.*;
3: public class School {
4:     public static void main(String[] args) {
5:         System.out.println(Classroom.globalKey);
6:         Classroom room = new Classroom(101, "Mrs. Anderson");
7:         System.out.println(room.roomNumber);
8:         System.out.println(Classroom.floor);
9:         System.out.println(Classroom.teacherName); } }
```

A. None: the code compiles fine.

B. Line 5.

C. Line 6.

D. Line 7.

E. Line 8.

F. Line 9.

10. What is the output of executing the `Chimp` program?

```
// Rope.java
1: package rope;
2: public class Rope {
3:     public static int LENGTH = 5;
4:     static {
5:         LENGTH = 10;
6:     }
7:     public static void swing() {
```

```
8:        System.out.print("swing ");
9:    } }
```

// Chimp.java

```
1: import rope.*;
2: import static rope.Rope.*;
3: public class Chimp {
4:    public static void main(String[] args) {
5:        Rope.swing();
6:        new Rope().swing();
7:        System.out.println(LENGTH);
8:    } }
```

A. swing swing 5

B. swing swing 10

C. Compiler error on line 2 of Chimp

D. Compiler error on line 5 of Chimp

E. Compiler error on line 6 of Chimp

F. Compiler error on line 7 of Chimp

11. Which statements are true of the following code? (Choose all that apply.)

```
1:  public class Rope {
2:     public static void swing() {
3:         System.out.print("swing");
4:     }
5:     public void climb() {
6:         System.out.println("climb");
7:     }
8:     public static void play() {
9:         swing();
10:        climb();
11:    }
12:    public static void main(String[] args) {
13:        Rope rope = new Rope();
14:        rope.play();
15:        Rope rope2 = null;
16:        System.out.print("-");
17:        rope2.play();
18:    } }
```

A. The code compiles as is.

B. There is exactly one compiler error in the code.

C. There are exactly two compiler errors in the code.

D. If the line(s) with compiler errors are removed, the output is `swing-climb`.

E. If the line(s) with compiler errors are removed, the output is `swing-swing`.

F. If the line(s) with compile errors are removed, the code throws a `NullPointerException`.

12. How many variables in the following method are effectively final?

```
10: public void feed() {
11:    int monkey = 0;
12:    if(monkey > 0) {
13:       var giraffe = monkey++;
14:       String name;
15:       name = "geoffrey";
16:    }
17:    String name = "milly";
18:    var food = 10;
19:    while(monkey <= 10) {
20:       food = 0;
21:    }
22:    name = null;
23: }
```

A. 1.

B. 2.

C. 3.

D. 4.

E. 5.

F. None of the above. The code does not compile.

13. What is the output of the following code?

```
// RopeSwing.java
import rope.*;
import static rope.Rope.*;
public class RopeSwing {
   private static Rope rope1 = new Rope();
   private static Rope rope2 = new Rope();
   {
      System.out.println(rope1.length);
```

```
      }
      public static void main(String[] args) {
         rope1.length = 2;
         rope2.length = 8;
         System.out.println(rope1.length);
      }
   }
```

```
// Rope.java
package rope;
public class Rope {
   public static int length = 0;
}
```

A. 02

B. 08

C. 2

D. 8

E. The code does not compile.

F. An exception is thrown.

14. How many lines in the following code have compiler errors?

```
1:  public class RopeSwing {
2:     private static final String leftRope;
3:     private static final String rightRope;
4:     private static final String bench;
5:     private static final String name = "name";
6:     static {
7:        leftRope = "left";
8:        rightRope = "right";
9:     }
10:    static {
11:       name = "name";
12:       rightRope = "right";
13:    }
14:    public static void main(String[] args) {
15:       bench = "bench";
16:    }
17: }
```

A. 0
B. 1
C. 2
D. 3
E. 4
F. 5

15. Which of the following can replace line 2 to make this code compile?

```
1: import java.util.*;
2: // INSERT CODE HERE
3: public class Imports {
4:     public void method(ArrayList<String> list) {
5:         sort(list);
6:     }
7: }
```

A. import static java.util.Collections;
B. import static java.util.Collections.*;
C. import static java.util.Collections.sort(ArrayList<String>);
D. static import java.util.Collections;
E. static import java.util.Collections.*;
F. static import java.util.Collections.sort(ArrayList<String>);

16. What is the result of the following statements?

```
1:  public class Test {
2:      public void print(byte x) {
3:          System.out.print("byte-");
4:      }
5:      public void print(int x) {
6:          System.out.print("int-");
7:      }
8:      public void print(float x) {
9:          System.out.print("float-");
10:     }
11:     public void print(Object x) {
12:         System.out.print("Object-");
13:     }
14:     public static void main(String[] args) {
15:         Test t = new Test();
16:         short s = 123;
```

```
17:        t.print(s);
18:        t.print(true);
19:        t.print(6.789);
20:    }
21: }
```

A. byte-float-Object-

B. int-float-Object-

C. byte-Object-float-

D. int-Object-float-

E. int-Object-Object-

F. byte-Object-Object-

17. What is the result of the following program?

```
1:  public class Squares {
2:     public static long square(int x) {
3:        var y = x * (long) x;
4:        x = -1;
5:        return y;
6:     }
7:     public static void main(String[] args) {
8:        var value = 9;
9:        var result = square(value);
10:       System.out.println(value);
11:    } }
```

A. -1

B. 9

C. 81

D. Compiler error on line 9

E. Compiler error on a different line

18. Which of the following are output by the following code? (Choose all that apply.)

```
public class StringBuilders {
   public static StringBuilder work(StringBuilder a,
      StringBuilder b) {
      a = new StringBuilder("a");
      b.append("b");
      return a;
   }
   public static void main(String[] args) {
```

```
        var s1 = new StringBuilder("s1");
        var s2 = new StringBuilder("s2");
        var s3 = work(s1, s2);
        System.out.println("s1 = " + s1);
        System.out.println("s2 = " + s2);
        System.out.println("s3 = " + s3);
    }
}
```

A. s1 = a

B. s1 = s1

C. s2 = s2

D. s2 = s2b

E. s3 = a

F. The code does not compile.

19. Which of the following will compile when independently inserted in the following code? (Choose all that apply.)

```
1:  public class Order3 {
2:      final String value1 = "red";
3:      static String value2 = "blue";
4:      String value3 = "yellow";
5:      {
6:          // CODE SNIPPET 1
7:      }
8:      static {
9:          // CODE SNIPPET 2
10:     } }
```

A. Insert at line 6: value1 = "green";

B. Insert at line 6: value2 = "purple";

C. Insert at line 6: value3 = "orange";

D. Insert at line 9: value1 = "magenta";

E. Insert at line 9: value2 = "cyan";

F. Insert at line 9: value3 = "turquoise";

20. Which of the following are true about the following code? (Choose all that apply.)

```
public class Run {
    static void execute() {
        System.out.print("1-");
    }
```

```
   static void execute(int num) {
      System.out.print("2-");
   }
   static void execute(Integer num) {
      System.out.print("3-");
   }
   static void execute(Object num) {
      System.out.print("4-");
   }
   static void execute(int... nums) {
      System.out.print("5-");
   }
   public static void main(String[] args) {
      Run.execute(100);
      Run.execute(100L);
   }
}
```

A. The code prints out 2-4-.

B. The code prints out 3-4-.

C. The code prints out 4-2-.

D. The code prints out 4-4-.

E. The code prints 3-4- if you remove the method `static void execute(int num)`.

F. The code prints 4-4- if you remove the method `static void execute(int num)`.

21. Which method signatures are valid overloads of the following method signature? (Choose all that apply.)

```
public void moo(int m, int... n)
```

A. `public void moo(int a, int... b)`

B. `public int moo(char ch)`

C. `public void moooo(int... z)`

D. `private void moo(int... x)`

E. `public void moooo(int y)`

F. `public void moo(int... c, int d)`

G. `public void moo(int... i, int j...)`

Chapter

6

Class Design

OCP EXAM OBJECTIVES COVERED IN THIS CHAPTER:

✓ **Using Object-Oriented Concepts in Java**

- Create classes and records, and define and use instance and static fields and methods, constructors, and instance and static initializers.

- Understand variable scopes, apply encapsulation, and create immutable objects. Use local variable type inference.

- Implement inheritance, including abstract and sealed types as well as record classes. Override methods, including that of the Object class. Implement polymorphism and differentiate between object type and reference type. Perform reference type casting, identify object types using the instanceof operator, and pattern matching with the instanceof operator and the switch construct.

In Chapter 1, "Building Blocks," we introduced the basic definition of a class in Java. In Chapter 5, "Methods," we delved into methods and modifiers and showed how you can use them to build more structured classes. In this chapter, we take things a step further and show how class structure and inheritance is one of the most powerful features in the Java language.

At its core, proper Java class design is about code reusability, increased functionality, and standardization. For example, by creating a new class that extends an existing class, you may gain access to a slew of inherited primitives, objects, and methods, which increases code reuse.

This chapter is the culmination of some of the most important topics in Java including inheritance, class design, constructors, order of initialization, overriding methods, abstract classes, and immutable objects. Read this chapter carefully and make sure you understand all of the topics well. This chapter forms the basis of Chapter 7, "Beyond Classes," in which we expand our discussion of types to include other top-level and nested types.

Understanding Inheritance

When creating a new class in Java, you can define the class as inheriting from an existing class. *Inheritance* is the process by which a subclass automatically includes certain members of the class, including primitives, objects, or methods, defined in the parent class.

For illustrative purposes, we refer to any class that inherits from another class as a *subclass* or *child class*, as it is considered a descendant of that class. Alternatively, we refer to the class that the child inherits from as the *superclass* or *parent class*, as it is considered an ancestor of the class.

When working with other types, like interfaces, we tend to use the general terms *subtype* and *supertype*. You see this more in the next chapter.

Declaring a Subclass

Let's begin with the declaration of a class and its subclass. Figure 6.1 shows an example of a superclass, `Mammal`, and subclass `Rhinoceros`.

FIGURE 6.1 Subclass and superclass declarations

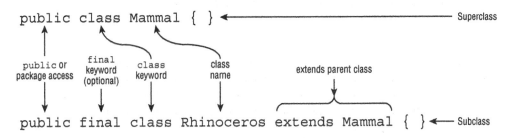

We indicate a class is a subclass by declaring it with the `extends` keyword. We don't need to declare anything in the superclass other than making sure it is not marked `final`. More on that shortly.

One key aspect of inheritance is that it is transitive. Given three classes [X, Y, Z], if X extends Y, and Y extends Z, then X is considered a subclass or descendant of Z. Likewise, Z is a superclass or ancestor of X. We sometimes use the term *direct* subclass or descendant to indicate the class directly extends the parent class. For example, X is a direct descendant only of class Y, not Z.

In the previous chapter, you learned that there are four access levels: `public`, `protected`, package, and `private`. When one class inherits from a parent class, all `public` and `protected` members are automatically available as part of the child class. If the two classes are in the same package, then package members are available to the child class. Last but not least, `private` members are restricted to the class they are defined in and are never available via inheritance. This doesn't mean the parent class can't have `private` members that can hold data or modify an object; it just means the subclass doesn't have direct access to them.

Let's take a look at a simple example:

```
public class BigCat {
    protected double size;
}

public class Jaguar extends BigCat {
    public Jaguar() {
        size = 10.2;
    }
    public void printDetails() {
        System.out.print(size);
    }
}

public class Spider {
```

```
   public void printDetails() {
      System.out.println(size);  // DOES NOT COMPILE
   }
}
```

Jaguar is a subclass or child of BigCat, making BigCat a superclass or parent of Jaguar. In the Jaguar class, size is accessible because it is marked protected. Via inheritance, the Jaguar subclass can read or write size as if it were its own member. Contrast this with the Spider class, which has no access to size since it is not inherited.

Class Modifiers

Like methods and variables, a class declaration can have various modifiers. Table 6.1 lists the modifiers you should know for the exam.

TABLE 6.1   Class modifiers

Modifier	Description	Chapter covered
final	The class may not be extended.	Chapter 6
abstract	The class is abstract, may contain abstract methods, and requires a concrete subclass to instantiate.	Chapter 6
sealed	The class may only be extended by a specific list of classes.	Chapter 7
non-sealed	A subclass of a sealed class permits potentially unnamed subclasses.	Chapter 7
static	Used for static nested classes defined within a class.	Chapter 7

We cover abstract classes later in this chapter. In the next chapter, we cover sealed and non-sealed classes, as well as static nested classes.

For now, let's talk about marking a class final. The final modifier prevents a class from being extended any further. For example, the following does not compile:

```
public class Mammal {}

public final class Rhinoceros extends Mammal {}

public class Clara extends Rhinoceros {}  // DOES NOT COMPILE
```

On the exam, pay attention to any class marked `final`. If you see another class extending it, you know immediately the code does not compile.

Single vs. Multiple Inheritance

Java supports *single inheritance*, by which a class may inherit from only one direct parent class. Java also supports multiple levels of inheritance, by which one class may extend another class, which in turn extends another class. You can have any number of levels of inheritance, allowing each descendant to gain access to its ancestor's members.

To truly understand single inheritance, it may be helpful to contrast it with *multiple inheritance*, by which a class may have multiple direct parents. By design, Java doesn't support multiple inheritance in the language because multiple inheritance can lead to complex, often difficult-to-maintain data models. Java does allow one exception to the single inheritance rule, which you see in Chapter 7—a class may implement multiple interfaces.

Figure 6.2 illustrates the various types of inheritance models. The items on the left are considered single inheritance because each child has exactly one parent. You may notice that single inheritance doesn't preclude parents from having multiple children. The right side shows items that have multiple inheritance. As you can see, a `Dog` object has multiple parent designations.

FIGURE 6.2   Types of inheritance

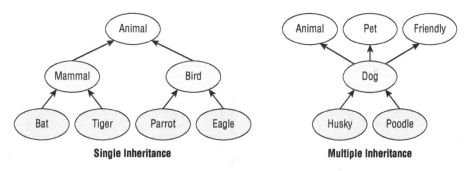

Part of what makes multiple inheritance complicated is determining which parent to inherit values from in case of a conflict. For example, if you have an object or method defined in all of the parents, which one does the child inherit? There is no natural ordering for parents in this example, which is why *Java avoids these issues by disallowing multiple inheritance altogether.*

Inheriting *Object*

Throughout our discussion of Java in this book, we have thrown around the word *object* numerous times—and with good reason. In Java, all classes inherit from a single class:

java.lang.Object, or Object for short. Furthermore, Object is the only class that doesn't have a parent class.

You might be wondering, *"None of the classes I've written so far extend Object, so how do all classes inherit from it?"* The answer is that the compiler has been automatically inserting code into any class you write that doesn't extend a specific class. For example, the following two are equivalent:

```
public class Zoo { }
```

```
public class Zoo extends java.lang.Object { }
```

The key is that when Java sees you define a class that doesn't extend another class, the compiler automatically adds the syntax extends java.lang.Object to the class definition. The result is that every class gains access to any accessible methods in the Object class. For example, the toString() and equals() methods are available in Object; therefore, they are accessible in all classes. Without being overridden in a subclass, though, they may not be particularly useful. We cover overriding methods later in this chapter.

On the other hand, when you define a new class that extends an existing class, Java *does not* automatically extend the Object class. Since all classes inherit from Object, extending an existing class means the child already inherits from Object by definition. If you look at the inheritance structure of any class, it will always end with Object on the top of the tree, as shown in Figure 6.3.

FIGURE 6.3   Java object inheritance

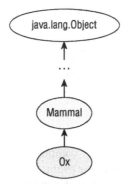

All objects inherit java.lang.Object

Primitive types such as int and boolean do not inherit from Object, since they are not classes. As you learned in Chapter 5, through autoboxing they can be assigned or passed as an instance of an associated wrapper class, which does inherit Object.

Creating Classes

Now that we've established how inheritance works in Java, we can use it to define and create complex class relationships. In this section, we review the basics for creating and working with classes.

Extending a Class

Let's create two files in the same package, `Animal.java` and `Lion.java`.

```java
// Animal.java
public class Animal {
    private int age;
    protected String name;
    public int getAge() {
        return age;
    }
    public void setAge(int newAge) {
        age = newAge;
    }
}
```

```java
// Lion.java
public class Lion extends Animal {
    protected void setProperties(int age, String n) {
        setAge(age);
        name = n;
    }
    public void roar() {
        System.out.print(name + ", age " + getAge() + ", says: Roar!");
    }
    public static void main(String[] args) {
        var lion = new Lion();
        lion.setProperties(3, "kion");
        lion.roar();
    }
}
```

There's a lot going on here, we know! The `age` variable exists in the parent `Animal` class and is not directly accessible in the `Lion` child class. It is indirectly accessible via the `setAge()` method. The `name` variable is `protected`, so it is inherited in the `Lion` class and directly accessible. We create the Lion instance in the main() method and use setProperties() to set instance variables. Finally, we call the roar() method, which prints the following:

```
kion, age 3, says: Roar!
```

Let's take a look at the members of the Lion class. The instance variable age is marked private and is not directly accessible from the subclass Lion. Therefore, the following would not compile:

```java
public class Lion extends Animal {
    public void roar() {
        System.out.print("Lion's age: " + age);  // DOES NOT COMPILE
    }
}
```

Remember when working with subclasses that private members are never inherited, and package members are only inherited if the two classes are in the same package. If you need a refresher on access modifiers, it may help to read Chapter 5 again.

Applying Class Access Modifiers

Like variables and methods, you can apply access modifiers to classes. As you might remember from Chapter 1, a top-level class is one not defined inside another class. Also remember that a .java file can have at most one public top-level class.

While you can only have one public top-level class, you can have as many classes (in any order) with package access as you want. In fact, you don't even need to declare a public class! The following declares three classes, each with package access:

```java
// Bear.java
class Bird {}
class Bear {}
class Fish {}
```

Trying to declare a top-level class with protected or private class will lead to a compiler error, though.

```java
// ClownFish.java
protected class ClownFish{} // DOES NOT COMPILE
```

```java
// BlueTang.java
private class BlueTang {} // DOES NOT COMPILE
```

Does that mean a class can never be declared protected or private? Not exactly. In Chapter 7, we present nested types and show that when you define a class inside another, it can use any access modifier.

Accessing the *this* Reference

What happens when a method parameter has the same name as an existing instance variable? Let's take a look at an example. What do you think the following program prints?

```java
public class Flamingo {
    private String color = null;
    public void setColor(String color) {
        color = color;
    }
    public static void main(String... unused) {
        var f = new Flamingo();
        f.setColor("PINK");
        System.out.print(f.color);
    }
}
```

If you said null, then you'd be correct. Java uses the most granular scope, so when it sees color = color, it thinks you are assigning the method parameter value to itself (not the instance variable). The assignment completes successfully within the method, but the value of the instance variable color is never modified and is null when printed in the main() method.

The fix when you have a local variable with the same name as an instance variable is to use the this reference or keyword. The this reference refers to the current instance of the class and can be used to access any member of the class, including inherited members. It can be used in any instance method, constructor, or instance initializer block. It cannot be used when there is no implicit instance of the class, such as in a static method or static initializer block. We apply this to our previous method implementation as follows:

```java
public void setColor(String color) {
    this.color = color;  // Sets the instance variable with method parameter
}
```

The corrected code will now print PINK as expected. In many cases, the this reference is optional. If Java encounters a variable or method it cannot find, it will check the class hierarchy to see if it is available.

Now let's look at some examples that aren't common but that you might see on the exam:

```java
1:  public class Duck {
2:      private String color;
3:      private int height;
4:      private int length;
5:
6:      public void setData(int length, int theHeight) {
7:          length = this.length;  // Backwards -- no good!
```

```
 8:          height = theHeight;    // Fine, because a different name
 9:          this.color = "white";  // Fine, but this. reference not necessary
10:      }
11:
12:      public static void main(String[] args) {
13:          Duck b = new Duck();
14:          b.setData(1,2);
15:          System.out.print(b.length + " " + b.height + " " + b.color);
16:      } }
```

This code compiles and prints the following:

```
0 2 white
```

This might not be what you expected, though. Line 7 is incorrect, and you should watch for it on the exam. The instance variable length starts out with a 0 value. That 0 is assigned to the method parameter length. The instance variable stays at 0. Line 8 is more straightforward. The parameter theHeight and instance variable height have different names. Since there is no naming collision, this is not required. Finally, line 9 shows that a variable assignment is allowed to use the this reference even when there is no duplication of variable names.

Calling the *super* Reference

In Java, a variable or method can be defined in both a parent class and a child class. This means the object instance actually holds two copies of the same variable with the same underlying name. When this happens, how do we reference the version in the parent class instead of the current class? Let's take a look at this example:

```
// Reptile.java
1: public class Reptile {
2:     protected int speed = 10;
3: }
```

```
// Crocodile.java
1: public class Crocodile extends Reptile {
2:     protected int speed = 20;
3:     public int getSpeed() {
4:         return speed;
5:     }
6:     public static void main(String[] data) {
7:         var croc = new Crocodile();
8:         System.out.println(croc.getSpeed());  // 20
9:     } }
```

One of the most important things to remember about this code is that an instance of Crocodile stores two separate values for speed: one at the Reptile level and one at the Crocodile level. On line 4, Java first checks to see if there is a local variable or method parameter named speed. Since there is not, it then checks this.speed; and since it exists, the program prints 20.

 Declaring a variable with the same name as an inherited variable is referred to as *hiding* a variable and is discussed later in this chapter.

But what if we want the program to print the value in the Reptile class? Within the Crocodile class, we can access the parent value of speed instead, by using the super reference or keyword. The super reference is similar to the this reference, except that it excludes any members found in the current class. In other words, the member must be accessible via inheritance.

```
3:    public int getSpeed() {
4:        return super.speed;  // Causes the program to now print 10
5:    }
```

Let's see if you've gotten the hang of this and super. What does the following program output?

```
1:  class Insect {
2:      protected int numberOfLegs = 4;
3:      String label = "buggy";
4:  }
5:
6:  public class Beetle extends Insect {
7:      protected int numberOfLegs = 6;
8:      short age = 3;
9:      public void printData() {
10:         System.out.println(this.label);
11:         System.out.println(super.label);
12:         System.out.println(this.age);
13:         System.out.println(super.age);
14:         System.out.println(numberOfLegs);
15:     }
16:     public static void main(String []n) {
17:         new Beetle().printData();
18:     }
19: }
```

That was a trick question—this program code would not compile! Let's review each line of the printData() method. Since label is defined in the parent class, it is accessible via both this and super references. For this reason, lines 10 and 11 compile and would both print buggy if the class compiled. On the other hand, the variable age is defined only in the current class, making it accessible via this but not super. For this reason, line 12 compiles (and would print 3), but line 13 does not. Remember, while this includes current and inherited members, super only includes inherited members.

Last but not least, what would line 14 print if line 13 was commented out? Even though both numberOfLegs variables are accessible in Beetle, Java checks outward, starting with the narrowest scope. For this reason, the value of numberOfLegs in the Beetle class is used, and 6 is printed. In this example, this.numberOfLegs and super.numberOfLegs refer to different variables with distinct values.

Since this includes inherited members, you often only use super when you have a naming conflict via inheritance. For example, you have a method or variable defined in the current class that matches a method or variable in a parent class. This commonly comes up in method overriding and variable hiding, which are discussed later in this chapter.

Phew, that was a lot! Using this and super can take a little getting used to. Since we use them often in upcoming sections, make sure you understand the last example really well before moving forward.

Declaring Constructors

As you learned in Chapter 1, a constructor is a special method that matches the name of the class and has no return type. It is called when a new instance of the class is created. For the exam, *you'll need to know a lot of rules about constructors*. In this section, we show how to create and call constructors.

Creating a Constructor

Let's start with a simple constructor:

```java
public class Bunny {
   public Bunny() {
      System.out.print("hop");
   }
}
```

The name of the constructor, Bunny, matches the name of the class, Bunny, and there is no return type, not even void. That makes this a constructor. Can you tell why these two are not valid constructors for the Bunny class?

```java
public class Bunny {
   public bunny() {}        // DOES NOT COMPILE
   public void Bunny() {}
}
```

The first one doesn't match the class name because Java is case-sensitive. Since it doesn't match, Java knows it can't be a constructor and is supposed to be a regular method. However, it is missing the return type and doesn't compile. The second method is a perfectly good method but is not a constructor because it has a return type.

Like method parameters, constructor parameters can be any valid class, array, or primitive type, including generics, but may not include var. For example, the following does not compile:

```java
public class Bonobo {
   public Bonobo(var food) {  // DOES NOT COMPILE
   }
}
```

A class can have multiple constructors, as long as each constructor has a unique constructor signature. In this case, that means the constructor parameters must be distinct. Like methods with the same name but different signatures, declaring multiple constructors with different signatures is referred to as *constructor overloading*. The following Turtle class has four distinct overloaded constructors:

```java
public class Turtle {
   private String name;
   public Turtle() {
      name = "John Doe";
   }
   public Turtle(int age) {}
   public Turtle(long age) {}
   public Turtle(String newName, String... favoriteFoods) {
      name = newName;
   }
}
```

Constructors are used when creating a new object. This process is called *instantiation* because it creates a new instance of the class. A constructor is called when we write new followed by the name of the class we want to instantiate. Here's an example:

```java
new Turtle(15)
```

When Java sees the new keyword, it allocates memory for the new object. It then looks for a constructor with a matching signature and calls it.

The Default Constructor

Every class in Java has a constructor, whether you code one or not. If you don't include any constructors in the class, Java will create one for you without any parameters. This Java-created constructor is called the *default constructor* and is added any time a class is declared without any constructors. We often refer to it as the default no-argument constructor, for clarity. Here's an example:

```java
public class Rabbit {
   public static void main(String[] args) {
      new Rabbit();      // Calls the default constructor
   }
}
```

In the `Rabbit` class, Java sees that no constructor was coded and creates one. The previous class is equivalent to the following, in which the default constructor is provided and therefore not inserted by the compiler:

```java
public class Rabbit {
   public Rabbit() {}
   public static void main(String[] args) {
      new Rabbit();      // Calls the user-defined constructor
   }
}
```

The default constructor has an empty parameter list and an empty body. It is fine for you to type this in yourself. However, since it doesn't do anything, Java is happy to generate it for you and save you some typing.

We keep saying *generated*. This happens during the compile step. If you look at the file with the `.java` extension, the constructor will still be missing. It only makes an appearance in the compiled file with the `.class` extension.

For the exam, one of the most important rules you need to know is that the compiler *only inserts the default constructor when no constructors are defined*. Which of these classes do you think has a default constructor?

```java
public class Rabbit1 {}
```

```java
public class Rabbit2 {
   public Rabbit2() {}
}
```

```java
public class Rabbit3 {
   public Rabbit3(boolean b) {}
}
```

```java
public class Rabbit4 {
   private Rabbit4() {}
}
```

Only `Rabbit1` gets a default no-argument constructor. It doesn't have a constructor coded, so Java generates a default no-argument constructor. `Rabbit2` and `Rabbit3` both have `public` constructors already. `Rabbit4` has a `private` constructor. Since these three classes have a constructor defined, the default no-argument constructor is not inserted for you.

Let's take a quick look at how to call these constructors:

```
1: public class RabbitsMultiply {
2:    public static void main(String[] args) {
3:       var r1 = new Rabbit1();
4:       var r2 = new Rabbit2();
5:       var r3 = new Rabbit3(true);
6:       var r4 = new Rabbit4();  // DOES NOT COMPILE
7:    } }
```

Line 3 calls the generated default no-argument constructor. Lines 4 and 5 call the user-provided constructors. Line 6 does not compile. Rabbit4 made the constructor private so that other classes could not call it.

> Having only private constructors in a class tells the compiler not to provide a default no-argument constructor. It also prevents other classes from instantiating the class. This is useful when a class has only static methods or the developer wants to have full control of all calls to create new instances of the class.

Calling Overloaded Constructors with *this()*

Have the basics about creating and referencing constructors? Good, because things are about to get a bit more complicated. Since a class can contain multiple overloaded constructors, these constructors can actually call one another. Let's start with a simple class containing two overloaded constructors:

```
public class Hamster {
   private String color;
   private int weight;
   public Hamster(int weight, String color) {  // First constructor
      this.weight = weight;
      this.color = color;
   }
   public Hamster(int weight) {                 // Second constructor
      this.weight = weight;
      color = "brown";
   }
}
```

One of the constructors takes a single int parameter. The other takes an int and a String. These parameter lists are different, so the constructors are successfully overloaded.

There is a bit of duplication, as this.weight is assigned the same way in both constructors. In programming, even a bit of duplication tends to turn into a lot of duplication as we keep adding "just one more thing." For example, imagine that we have five variables being set like this.weight, rather than just one. What we really want is for the first constructor to call the second constructor with two parameters. So, how can you have a constructor call another constructor? You might be tempted to rewrite the first constructor as the following:

```java
public Hamster(int weight) {  // Second constructor
   Hamster(weight, "brown");  // DOES NOT COMPILE
}
```

This will not work. Constructors can be called only by writing new before the name of the constructor. They are not like normal methods that you can just call. What happens if we stick new before the constructor name?

```java
public Hamster(int weight) {      // Second constructor
   new Hamster(weight, "brown");  // Compiles, but creates an extra object
}
```

This attempt does compile. It doesn't do what we want, though. When this constructor is called, it creates a new object with the default weight and color. It then constructs a different object with the desired weight and color. In this manner, we end up with two objects, one of which is discarded after it is created. That's not what we want. We want weight and color set on the object we are trying to instantiate in the first place.

Java provides a solution: this()—yes, the same keyword we used to refer to instance members, but with parentheses. When this() is used with parentheses, Java calls another constructor on the same instance of the class.

```java
public Hamster(int weight) {  // Second constructor
   this(weight, "brown");
}
```

Success! Now Java calls the constructor that takes two parameters, with weight and color set as expected.

---

this vs. this()

Despite using the same keyword, this and this() are very different. The first, this, refers to an instance of the class, while the second, this(), refers to a constructor call within the class. The exam may try to trick you by using both together, so make sure you know which one to use and why.

Calling this() has one special rule you need to know. If you choose to call it, the this() call must be the first statement in the constructor. The side effect of this is that there can be only one call to this() in any constructor.

```
3:    public Hamster(int weight) {
4:        System.out.println("chew");
5:        // Set weight and default color
6:        this(weight, "brown");      // DOES NOT COMPILE
7:    }
```

Even though a print statement on line 4 doesn't change any variables, it is still a Java statement and is not allowed to be inserted before the call to this(). The comment on line 5 is just fine. Comments aren't considered statements and are allowed anywhere.

There's one last rule for overloaded constructors that you should be aware of. Consider the following definition of the Gopher class:

```
public class Gopher {
    public Gopher(int dugHoles) {
        this(5);  // DOES NOT COMPILE
    }
}
```

The compiler is capable of detecting that this constructor is calling itself infinitely. This is often referred to as a *cycle* and is similar to the infinite loops that we discussed in Chapter 3, "Making Decisions." Since the code can never terminate, the compiler stops and reports this as an error. Likewise, this also does not compile.

```
public class Gopher {
    public Gopher() {
        this(5);  // DOES NOT COMPILE
    }
    public Gopher(int dugHoles) {
        this();   // DOES NOT COMPILE
    }
}
```

In this example, the constructors call each other, and the process continues infinitely. Since the compiler can detect this, it reports an error.

Here we summarize the rules you should know about constructors that we covered in this section. Study them well!

- A class can contain many overloaded constructors, provided the signature for each is distinct.
- The compiler inserts a default no-argument constructor if no constructors are declared.
- If a constructor calls this(), then it must be the first line of the constructor.
- Java does not allow cyclic constructor calls.

Calling Parent Constructors with *super()*

Congratulations, you're well on your way to becoming an expert in using constructors! There's one more set of rules we need to cover, though, for calling constructors in the parent class. After all, how do instance members of the parent class get initialized?

The first statement of *every* constructor is a call to a parent constructor using super() or another constructor in the class using this(). Read the previous sentence twice to make sure you remember it. It's really important!

> For simplicity in this section, we often refer to super() and this() to refer to any parent or overloaded constructor call, even those that take arguments.

Let's take a look at the Animal class and its subclass Zebra and see how their constructors can be properly written to call one another:

```
public class Animal {
    private int age;
    public Animal(int age) {
        super();      // Refers to constructor in java.lang.Object
        this.age = age;
    }
}


public class Zebra extends Animal {
    public Zebra(int age) {
        super(age);  // Refers to constructor in Animal
    }
    public Zebra() {
        this(4);     // Refers to constructor in Zebra with int argument
    }
}
```

In the Animal class, the first statement of the constructor is a call to the parent constructor defined in java.lang.Object, which takes no arguments. In the second class, Zebra, the first statement of the first constructor is a call to Animal's constructor, which takes a single argument. The Zebra class also includes a second no-argument constructor that doesn't call super() but instead calls the other constructor within the Zebra class using this(4).

---

super vs. super()

Like this and this(), super and super() are unrelated in Java. The first, super, is used to reference members of the parent class, while the second, super(), calls a parent constructor. Anytime you see the keyword super on the exam, make sure it is being used properly.

Like calling this(), calling super() can only be used as the first statement of the constructor. For example, the following two class definitions will not compile:

```
public class Zoo {
    public Zoo() {
        System.out.println("Zoo created");
        super();     // DOES NOT COMPILE
    }
}
```

```
public class Zoo {
    public Zoo() {
        super();
        System.out.println("Zoo created");
        super();     // DOES NOT COMPILE
    }
}
```

The first class will not compile because the call to the parent constructor must be the first statement of the constructor. In the second code snippet, super() is the first statement of the constructor, but it is also used as the third statement. Since super() can only be called once as the first statement of the constructor, the code will not compile.

If the parent class has more than one constructor, the child class may use any valid and accessible parent constructor in its definition, as shown in the following example:

```
public class Animal {
    private int age;
    private String name;
    public Animal(int age, String name) {
        super();
        this.age = age;
        this.name = name;
    }
    public Animal(int age) {
        super();
        this.age = age;
        this.name = null;
    }
}
```

```
public class Gorilla extends Animal {
    public Gorilla(int age) {
        super(age, "Gorilla");  // Calls the first Animal constructor
```

```
  }
  public Gorilla() {
     super(5);                 // Calls the second Animal constructor
  }
}
```

In this example, the first child constructor takes one argument, age, and calls the parent constructor, which takes two arguments, age and name. The second child constructor takes no arguments, and it calls the parent constructor, which takes one argument, age. In this example, notice that the child constructors are not required to call matching parent constructors. Any valid parent constructor is acceptable as long as it is accessible and the appropriate input parameters to the parent constructor are provided.

Understanding Compiler Enhancements

Wait a second: we said the first line of every constructor is a call to either this() or super(), but we've been creating classes and constructors throughout this book, and we've rarely done either. How did these classes compile?

The answer is that the Java compiler automatically inserts a call to the no-argument constructor super() if you do not explicitly call this() or super() as the first line of a constructor. For example, the following three class and constructor definitions are equivalent, because the compiler will automatically convert them all to the last example:

```
public class Donkey {}
```

```
public class Donkey {
   public Donkey() {}
}
```

```
public class Donkey {
   public Donkey() {
      super();
   }
}
```

Make sure you understand the differences between these three Donkey class definitions and why Java will automatically convert them all to the last definition. While reading the next section, keep in mind the process the Java compiler performs.

Default Constructor Tips and Tricks

We've presented a lot of rules so far, and you might have noticed something. Let's say we have a class that doesn't include a no-argument constructor. What happens if we define a subclass with no constructors, or a subclass with a constructor that doesn't include a super() reference?

```
public class Mammal {
   public Mammal(int age) {}
}

public class Seal extends Mammal {}  // DOES NOT COMPILE

public class Elephant extends Mammal {
   public Elephant() {}              // DOES NOT COMPILE
}
```

The answer is that neither subclass compiles. Since Mammal defines a constructor, the compiler does not insert a no-argument constructor. The compiler will insert a default no-argument constructor into Seal, though, but it will be a simple implementation that just calls a nonexistent parent default constructor.

```
public class Seal extends Mammal {
   public Seal() {
      super();  // DOES NOT COMPILE
   }
}
```

Likewise, Elephant will not compile for similar reasons. The compiler doesn't see a call to super() or this() as the first line of the constructor so it inserts a call to a nonexistent no-argument super() automatically.

```
public class Elephant extends Mammal {
   public Elephant() {
      super();  // DOES NOT COMPILE
   }
}
```

In these cases, the compiler will not help, and you *must* create at least one constructor in your child class that explicitly calls a parent constructor via the super() command.

```
public class Seal extends Mammal {
   public Seal() {
      super(6);  // Explicit call to parent constructor
   }
}

public class Elephant extends Mammal {
   public Elephant() {
      super(4);  // Explicit call to parent constructor
   }
}
```

Subclasses may include no-argument constructors even if their parent classes do not. For example, the following compiles because `Elephant` includes a no-argument constructor:

```
public class AfricanElephant extends Elephant {}
```

It's a lot to take in, we know. For the exam, you should be able to spot right away why classes such as our first `Seal` and `Elephant` implementations did not compile.

---

super() Always Refers to the Most Direct Parent

A class may have multiple ancestors via inheritance. In our previous example, `AfricanElephant` is a subclass of `Elephant`, which in turn is a subclass of `Mammal`. For constructors, though, `super()` always refers to the most direct parent. In this example, calling `super()` inside the `AfricanElephant` class always refers to the `Elephant` class and never to the `Mammal` class.

We conclude this section by adding two constructor rules to your skill set.

- If a constructor calls `super()` or `this()`, then it must be the first line of the constructor.
- If the constructor does not contain a `this()` or `super()` reference, then the compiler automatically inserts `super()` with no arguments as the first line of the constructor.

Congratulations, you've learned everything we can teach you about declaring constructors. Next, we move on to initialization and discuss how to use constructors.

Initializing Objects

In Chapter 1, we covered order of initialization, albeit in a very simplistic manner. *Order of initialization* refers to how members of a class are assigned values. They can be given default values, like 0 for an `int`, or require explicit values, such as for `final` variables. In this section, we go into much more detail about how order of initialization works and how to spot errors on the exam.

Initializing Classes

We begin our discussion of order of initialization with class initialization. First, we initialize the class, which involves invoking all `static` members in the class hierarchy, starting with the highest superclass and working downward. This is sometimes referred to as *loading* the class. The Java Virtual Machine (JVM) controls when the class is initialized, although you can assume the class is loaded before it is used. The class may be initialized when the program first starts, when a `static` member of the class is referenced, or shortly before an instance of the class is created.

One of the most important rules with class initialization is that it happens at most once for each class. The class may also never be loaded if it is not used in the program. We summarize the order of initialization for a class as follows:

Initialize Class X

1. Initialize the superclass of X.

2. Process all `static` variable declarations in the order in which they appear in the class.

3. Process all `static` initializers in the order in which they appear in the class.

Taking a look at an example, what does the following program print?

```java
public class Animal {
    static { System.out.print("A"); }
}

public class Hippo extends Animal {
    public static void main(String[] grass) {
        System.out.print("C");
        new Hippo();
        new Hippo();
        new Hippo();
    }
    static { System.out.print("B"); }
}
```

It prints ABC exactly once. Since the `main()` method is inside the `Hippo` class, the class will be initialized first, starting with the superclass and printing AB. Afterward, the `main()` method is executed, printing C. Even though the `main()` method creates three instances, the class is loaded only once.

Why the *Hippo* Program Printed *C* After *AB*

In the previous example, the `Hippo` class was initialized before the `main()` method was executed. This happened because our `main()` method was inside the class being executed, so it had to be loaded on startup. What if you instead called `Hippo` inside another program?

```java
public class HippoFriend {
    public static void main(String[] grass) {
        System.out.print("C");
        new Hippo();
    }
}
```

Assuming the class isn't referenced anywhere else, this program will likely print CAB, with the Hippo class not being loaded until it is needed inside the main() method. We say *likely* because the rules for when classes are loaded are determined by the JVM at runtime. For the exam, you just need to know that a class must be initialized before it is referenced or used. Also, the class containing the program entry point, aka the main() method, is loaded before the main() method is executed.

Initializing *final* Fields

Before we delve into order of initialization for instance members, we need to talk about final fields (instance variables) for a minute. When we presented instance and class variables in Chapter 1, we told you they are assigned a default value based on their type if no value is specified. For example, a double is initialized with 0.0, while an object reference is initialized to null. A default value is only applied to a non-final field, though.

As you saw in Chapter 5, final static variables must be explicitly assigned a value exactly once. Fields marked final follow similar rules. They can be assigned values in the line in which they are declared or in an instance initializer.

```
public class MouseHouse {
    private final int volume;
    private final String name = "The Mouse House";  // Declaration assignment
    {
        volume = 10;  // Instance initializer assignment
    }
}
```

Unlike static class members, though, final instance fields can also be set in a constructor. The constructor is part of the initialization process, so it is allowed to assign final instance variables. For the exam, you need to know one important rule: *by the time the constructor completes, all final instance variables must be assigned a value exactly once.*

Let's try this in an example:

```
public class MouseHouse {
    private final int volume;
    private final String name;
    public MouseHouse() {
        this.name = "Empty House";   // Constructor assignment
    }
    {
        volume = 10;  // Instance initializer assignment
    }
}
```

Unlike local `final` variables, which are not required to have a value unless they are actually used, `final` instance variables *must* be assigned a value. If they are not assigned a value when they are declared or in an instance initializer, then they must be assigned a value in the constructor declaration. Failure to do so will result in a compiler error.

```java
public class MouseHouse {
   private final int volume;
   private final String type;
   {
      this.volume = 10;
   }
   public MouseHouse(String type) {
      this.type = type;
   }
   public MouseHouse() {  // DOES NOT COMPILE
      this.volume = 2;    // DOES NOT COMPILE
   }
}
```

In this example, the first constructor that takes a `String` argument compiles. In terms of assigning values, each constructor is reviewed individually, which is why the second constructor does not compile. First, the constructor fails to set a value for the `type` variable. The compiler detects that a value is never set for `type` and reports an error. Second, the constructor sets a value for the `volume` variable, even though it was already assigned a value by the instance initializer.

> On the exam, be wary of any instance variables marked `final`. Make sure they are assigned a value in the line where they are declared, in an instance initializer, or in a constructor. They should be assigned a value only once, and failure to assign a value is considered a compiler error.

What about `final` instance variables when a constructor calls another constructor in the same class? In that case, you have to follow the flow carefully, making sure every `final` instance variable is assigned a value exactly once. We can replace our previous bad constructor with the following one that does compile:

```java
public MouseHouse() {
   this(null);
}
```

This constructor does not perform any assignments to any `final` instance variables, but it calls the `MouseHouse(String)` constructor, which we observed compiles without issue. We use `null` here to demonstrate that the variable does not need to be an object value. We can assign a `null` value to `final` instance variables as long as they are explicitly set.

Initializing Instances

We've covered class initialization and final fields, so now it's time to move on to order of initialization for objects. We'll warn you that this can be a bit cumbersome at first, but the exam isn't likely to ask questions more complicated than the examples in this section. We promise to take it slowly, though.

First, start at the lowest-level constructor where the new keyword is used. Remember, the first line of every constructor is a call to this() or super(), and if omitted, the compiler will automatically insert a call to the parent no-argument constructor super(). Then, progress upward and note the order of constructors. Finally, initialize each class starting with the superclass, processing the instance initializers and constructors within each class, in the reverse order in which each class was instantiated. We summarize the order of initialization for an instance as follows:

Initialize Instance of X

1. Initialize *Class* X if it has not been previously initialized.

2. Initialize the superclass instance of X.

3. Process all instance variable declarations in the order in which they appear in the class.

4. Process all instance initializers in the order in which they appear in the class.

5. Initialize the constructor, including any overloaded constructors referenced with this().

Let's try an example with no inheritance. See if you can figure out what the following application outputs:

```
1:   public class ZooTickets {
2:       private String name = "BestZoo";
3:       { System.out.print(name + "-"); }
4:       private static int COUNT = 0;
5:       static { System.out.print(COUNT + "-"); }
6:       static { COUNT += 10; System.out.print(COUNT + "-"); }
7:
8:       public ZooTickets() {
9:           System.out.print("z-");
10:      }
11:
12:      public static void main(String... patrons) {
13:          new ZooTickets();
14:      } }
```

The output is as follows:

```
0-10-BestZoo-z-
```

First, we have to initialize the class. Since there is no superclass declared, which means the superclass is Object, we can start with the static components of ZooTickets.

In this case, lines 4, 5, and 6 are executed, printing `0-` and `10-`. Next, we initialize the instance created on line 13. Again, since no superclass is declared, we start with the instance components. Lines 2 and 3 are executed, which prints `BestZoo-`. Finally, we run the constructor on lines 8–10, which outputs `z-`.

Next, let's try a simple example with inheritance:

```
class Primate {
   public Primate() {
      System.out.print("Primate-");
   } }
```

```
class Ape extends Primate {
   public Ape(int fur) {
      System.out.print("Ape1-");
   }
   public Ape() {
      System.out.print("Ape2-");
   } }
```

```
public class Chimpanzee extends Ape {
   public Chimpanzee() {
      super(2);
      System.out.print("Chimpanzee-");
   }
   public static void main(String[] args) {
      new Chimpanzee();
   } }
```

The compiler inserts the `super()` command as the first statement of both the `Primate` and `Ape` constructors. The code will execute with the parent constructors called first and yield the following output:

`Primate-Ape1-Chimpanzee-`

Notice that only one of the two `Ape()` constructors is called. You need to start with the call to `new Chimpanzee()` to determine which constructors will be executed. Remember, constructors are executed from the bottom up, but since the first line of every constructor is a call to another constructor, the flow ends up with the parent constructor executed before the child constructor.

The next example is a little harder. What do you think happens here?

```
1:  public class Cuttlefish {
2:     private String name = "swimmy";
3:     { System.out.println(name); }
```

```
4:      private static int COUNT = 0;
5:      static { System.out.println(COUNT); }
6:      { COUNT++; System.out.println(COUNT); }
7:
8:      public Cuttlefish() {
9:          System.out.println("Constructor");
10:     }
11:
12:     public static void main(String[] args) {
13:         System.out.println("Ready");
14:         new Cuttlefish();
15:     } }
```

The output looks like this:

```
0
Ready
swimmy
1
Constructor
```

No superclass is declared, so we can skip any steps that relate to inheritance. We first process the `static` variables and `static` initializers—lines 4 and 5, with line 5 printing 0. Now that the `static` initializers are out of the way, the `main()` method can run, which prints Ready. Next we create an instance declared on line 14. Lines 2, 3, and 6 are processed, with line 3 printing swimmy and line 6 printing 1. Finally, the constructor is run on lines 8–10, which prints Constructor.

Ready for a more difficult example, the kind you might see on the exam? What does the following output?

```
1:   class GiraffeFamily {
2:      static { System.out.print("A"); }
3:      { System.out.print("B"); }
4:
5:      public GiraffeFamily(String name) {
6:          this(1);
7:          System.out.print("C");
8:      }
9:
10:     public GiraffeFamily() {
11:         System.out.print("D");
12:     }
13:
```

```
14:     public GiraffeFamily(int stripes) {
15:         System.out.print("E");
16:     }
17: }
18: public class Okapi extends GiraffeFamily {
19:     static { System.out.print("F"); }
20:
21:     public Okapi(int stripes) {
22:         super("sugar");
23:         System.out.print("G");
24:     }
25:     { System.out.print("H"); }
26:
27:     public static void main(String[] grass) {
28:         new Okapi(1);
29:         System.out.println();
30:         new Okapi(2);
31:     }
32: }
```

The program prints the following:

```
AFBECHG
BECHG
```

Let's walk through it. Start with initializing the Okapi class. Since it has a superclass GiraffeFamily, initialize it first, printing A on line 2. Next, initialize the Okapi class, printing F on line 19.

After the classes are initialized, execute the main() method on line 27. The first line of the main() method creates a new Okapi object, triggering the instance initialization process. Per the second rule, the superclass instance of GiraffeFamily is initialized first. Per our fourth rule, the instance initializer in the superclass GiraffeFamily is called, and B is printed on line 3. Per the fifth rule, we initialize the constructors. In this case, this involves calling the constructor on line 5, which in turn calls the overloaded constructor on line 14. The result is that EC is printed, as the constructor bodies are unwound in the reverse order that they were called.

The process then continues with the initialization of the Okapi instance itself. Per the fourth and fifth rules, H is printed on line 25, and G is printed on line 23, respectively. The process is a lot simpler when you don't have to call any overloaded constructors. Line 29 then inserts a line break in the output. Finally, line 30 initializes a new Okapi object. The order and initialization are the same as line 28, sans the class initialization, so BECHG is printed again. Notice that D is never printed, as only two of the three constructors in the superclass GiraffeFamily are called.

This example is tricky for a few reasons. There are multiple overloaded constructors, lots of initializers, and a complex constructor pathway to keep track of. Luckily, questions like this are uncommon on the exam. If you see one, just write down what is going on as you read the code.

We conclude this section by listing important rules you should know for the exam:

- A class is initialized at most once by the JVM before it is referenced or used.
- All static final variables must be assigned a value exactly once, either when they are declared or in a static initializer.
- All final fields must be assigned a value exactly once, either when they are declared, in an instance initializer, or in a constructor.
- Non-final static and instance variables defined without a value are assigned a default value based on their type.
- The order of initialization is as follows: variable declarations, then initializers, and finally constructors.

Inheriting Members

Now that we've created a class, what can we do with it? One of Java's biggest strengths is leveraging its inheritance model to simplify code. For example, let's say you have five classes, each of which extends from the Animal class. Furthermore, each class defines an eat() method with an identical implementation. In this scenario, it's a lot better to define eat() once in the Animal class than to have to maintain the same method in five separate classes.

Inheriting a class not only grants access to inherited methods in the parent class but also sets the stage for collisions between methods defined in both the parent class and the subclass. In this section, we review the rules for method inheritance and how Java handles such scenarios.

We refer to the ability of an object to take on many different forms as *polymorphism*. We cover this more in the next chapter, but for now you just need to know that an object can be used in a variety of ways, in part based on the reference variable used to call the object.

Overriding a Method

What if a method with the same signature is defined in both the parent and child classes? For example, you may want to define a new version of the method and have it behave differently for that subclass. The solution is to override the method in the child class. In Java, *overriding* a method occurs when a subclass declares a new implementation for an inherited method with the same signature and compatible return type.

NOTE   Remember that a method signature is composed of the name of the method and method parameters. It does not include the return type, access modifiers, optional specifiers, or any declared exceptions.

When you override a method, you may still reference the parent version of the method using the super keyword. In this manner, the keywords this and super allow you to select between the current and parent versions of a method, respectively. We illustrate this with the following example:

```
public class Marsupial {
    public double getAverageWeight() {
        return 50;
    }
}
public class Kangaroo extends Marsupial {
    public double getAverageWeight() {
        return super.getAverageWeight()+20;
    }
    public static void main(String[] args) {
        System.out.println(new Marsupial().getAverageWeight());  // 50.0
        System.out.println(new Kangaroo().getAverageWeight());   // 70.0
    }
}
```

In this example, the Kangaroo class overrides the getAverageWeight() method but in the process calls the parent version using the super reference.

Method Overriding Infinite Calls

You might be wondering whether the use of super in the previous example was required. For example, what would the following code output if we removed the super keyword?

```
public double getAverageWeight() {
    return getAverageWeight()+20;  // StackOverflowError
}
```

In this example, the compiler would not call the parent Marsupial method; it would call the current Kangaroo method. The application will attempt to call itself infinitely and produce a StackOverflowError at runtime.

To override a method, you must follow a number of rules. The compiler performs the following checks when you override a method:

1. The method in the child class must have the same signature as the method in the parent class.

2. The method in the child class must be at least as accessible as the method in the parent class.

3. The method in the child class may not declare a checked exception that is new or broader than the class of any exception declared in the parent class method.

4. If the method returns a value, it must be the same or a subtype of the method in the parent class, known as *covariant return types*.

While these rules may seem confusing or arbitrary at first, they are needed for consistency. Without these rules in place, it is possible to create contradictions within the Java language.

Rule #1: Method Signatures

The first rule of overriding a method is somewhat self-explanatory. If two methods have the same name but different signatures, the methods are overloaded, not overridden. Overloaded methods are considered independent and do not share the same polymorphic properties as overridden methods.

We covered overloading a method in Chapter 5, and it is similar to over-riding a method, as both involve defining a method using the same name. Overloading differs from overriding in that overloaded methods use a different parameter list. For the exam, it is important that you understand this distinction and that overridden methods have the same signature and a lot more rules than overloaded methods.

Rule #2: Access Modifiers

What's the purpose of the second rule about access modifiers? Let's try an illustrative example:

```
public class Camel {
    public int getNumberOfHumps() {
        return 1;
    } }
```

```
public class BactrianCamel extends Camel {
    private int getNumberOfHumps() {  // DOES NOT COMPILE
        return 2;
    } }
```

In this example, BactrianCamel attempts to override the getNumberOfHumps() method defined in the parent class but fails because the access modifier private is more restrictive than the one defined in the parent version of the method. Let's say BactrianCamel was allowed to compile, though. What would this program print?

```
public class Rider {
    public static void main(String[] args) {
        Camel c = new BactrianCamel();
        System.out.print(c.getNumberOfHumps());  // ???
    } }
```

The answer is, we don't know. The reference type for the object is `Camel`, where the method is declared `public`, but the object is actually an instance of type `BactrianCamel`, where the method is declared `private`. Java avoids these types of ambiguity problems by limiting overriding a method to access modifiers that are as accessible or more accessible than the version in the inherited method.

Rule #3: Checked Exceptions

The third rule says that overriding a method cannot declare new checked exceptions or checked exceptions broader than the inherited method. This is done for polymorphic reasons similar to limiting access modifiers. In other words, you could end up with an object that is more restrictive than the reference type it is assigned to, resulting in a checked exception that is not handled or declared. One implication of this rule is that overridden methods are free to declare any number of new unchecked exceptions.

> If you don't know what a checked or unchecked exception is, don't worry. We cover this in Chapter 11, "Exceptions and Localization." For now, you just need to know that the rule applies only to checked exceptions. It's also helpful to know that both IOException and FileNotFoundException are checked exceptions, and that FileNotFoundException is a subclass of IOException.

Let's try an example:

```java
public class Reptile {
    protected void sleep() throws IOException {}

    protected void hide() {}

    protected void exitShell() throws FileNotFoundException {}
}

public class GalapagosTortoise extends Reptile {
    public void sleep() throws FileNotFoundException {}

    public void hide() throws FileNotFoundException {} // DOES NOT COMPILE

    public void exitShell() throws IOException {}       // DOES NOT COMPILE
}
```

In this example, we have three overridden methods. These overridden methods use the more accessible `public` modifier, which is allowed per our second rule for overridden methods. The first overridden method `sleep()` in `GalapagosTortoise` compiles without issue because the declared exception is narrower than the exception declared in the parent class.

The overridden `hide()` method does not compile because it declares a new checked exception not present in the parent declaration. The overridden `exitShell()` also does not compile, since `IOException` is a broader checked exception than `FileNotFoundException`. We revisit these exception classes, including memorizing which ones are subclasses of each other, in Chapter 11.

Rule #4: Covariant Return Types

The fourth and final rule around overriding a method is probably the most complicated, as it requires knowing the relationships between the return types. The overriding method must use a return type that is covariant with the return type of the inherited method.

Let's try an example for illustrative purposes:

```java
public class Rhino {
    protected CharSequence getName() {
        return "rhino";
    }
    protected String getColor() {
        return "grey, black, or white";
} }

public class JavanRhino extends Rhino {
    public String getName() {
        return "javan rhino";
    }
    public CharSequence getColor() {  // DOES NOT COMPILE
        return "grey";
} }
```

The subclass `JavanRhino` attempts to override two methods from `Rhino`: `getName()` and `getColor()`. Both overridden methods have the same name and signature as the inherited methods. The overridden methods also have a broader access modifier, `public`, than the inherited methods. Remember, a broader access modifier is acceptable in an overridden method.

From Chapter 4, "Core APIs," we learned that `String` implements the `CharSequence` interface, making `String` a subtype of `CharSequence`. Therefore, the return type of `getName()` in `JavanRhino` is covariant with the return type of `getName()` in `Rhino`.

On the other hand, the overridden `getColor()` method does not compile because `CharSequence` is not a subtype of `String`. To put it another way, all `String` values are `CharSequence` values, but not all `CharSequence` values are `String` values. For instance, a `StringBuilder` is a `CharSequence` but not a `String`. For the exam, you need to know if the return type of the overriding method is the same as or a subtype of the return type of the inherited method.

A simple test for covariance is the following: given an inherited return type A and an overriding return type B, can you assign an instance of B to a reference variable for A without a cast? If so, then they are covariant. This rule applies to primitive types and object types alike. If one of the return types is void, then they both must be void, as nothing is covariant with void except itself.

That's everything you need to know about overriding methods for this chapter. In Chapter 9, "Collections and Generics," we revisit overriding methods involving generics. There's always more to learn!

 Real World Scenario

Marking Methods with the @*Override* Annotation

An annotation is a metadata tag that provides additional information about your code. You can use the @Override annotation to tell the compiler that you are attempting to override a method.

```
public class Fish {
    public void swim() {};
}
public class Shark extends Fish {
    @Override
    public void swim() {};
}
```

When the method is correctly overridden, adding the annotation doesn't impact the code. On the other hand, when the method is incorrectly overridden, this annotation can prevent you from making a mistake. The following does not compile because of the presence of the @Override annotation:

```
public class Fish {
    public void swim() {};
}
public class Shark extends Fish {
    @Override
    public void swim(int speed) {};  // DOES NOT COMPILE
}
```

The compiler sees that you are attempting a method override and looks for an inherited version of swim() that takes an int value. Since the compiler doesn't find one, it reports an error. While knowing advanced topics (such as how to create annotations) is not required for the exam, knowing how to use them properly is.

Redeclaring *private* Methods

What happens if you try to override a `private` method? In Java, you can't override `private` methods since they are not inherited. Just because a child class doesn't have access to the parent method doesn't mean the child class can't define its own version of the method. It just means, strictly speaking, that the new method is *not an overridden version* of the parent class's method.

Java permits you to redeclare a new method in the child class with the same or modified signature as the method in the parent class. This method in the child class is a separate and independent method, unrelated to the parent version's method, so none of the rules for overriding methods is invoked. For example, these two declarations compile:

```
public class Beetle {
   private String getSize() {
      return "Undefined";
} }
```

```
public class RhinocerosBeetle extends Beetle {
   private int getSize() {
      return 5;
} }
```

Notice that the return type differs in the child method from `String` to `int`. In this example, the method `getSize()` in the parent class is not inherited, so the method in the child class is a new method and not an override of the method in the parent class.

What if the `getSize()` method was declared `public` in `Beetle`? In this case, the method in `RhinocerosBeetle` would be an invalid override. The access modifier in `RhinocerosBeetle` is more restrictive, and the return types are not covariant.

Hiding Static Methods

A `static` method cannot be overridden because class objects do not inherit from each other in the same way as instance objects. On the other hand, they can be hidden. A *hidden method* occurs when a child class defines a `static` method with the same name and signature as an inherited `static` method defined in a parent class. Method hiding is similar to but not exactly the same as method overriding. The previous four rules for overriding a method must be followed when a method is hidden. In addition, a new fifth rule is added for hiding a method:

5. The method defined in the child class must be marked as `static` if it is marked as `static` in a parent class.

Put simply, it is method hiding if the two methods are marked `static` and method overriding if they are not marked `static`. If one is marked `static` and the other is not, the class will not compile.

Let's review some examples of the new rule:

```java
public class Bear {
   public static void eat() {
      System.out.println("Bear is eating");
   } }
```

```java
public class Panda extends Bear {
   public static void eat() {
      System.out.println("Panda is chewing");
   }
   public static void main(String[] args) {
      eat();
   } }
```

In this example, the code compiles and runs. The eat() method in the Panda class hides the eat() method in the Bear class, printing "Panda is chewing" at runtime. Because they are both marked as static, this is not considered an overridden method. That said, there is still some inheritance going on. If you remove the eat() declaration in the Panda class, then the program prints "Bear is eating" instead.

See if you can figure out why each of the method declarations in the SunBear class does not compile:

```java
public class Bear {
   public static void sneeze() {
      System.out.println("Bear is sneezing");
   }
   public void hibernate() {
      System.out.println("Bear is hibernating");
   }
   public static void laugh() {
      System.out.println("Bear is laughing");
   }
}
```

```java
public class SunBear extends Bear {
   public void sneeze() {            // DOES NOT COMPILE
      System.out.println("Sun Bear sneezes quietly");
   }
   public static void hibernate() { // DOES NOT COMPILE
      System.out.println("Sun Bear is going to sleep");
   }
```

```
    protected static void laugh() {  // DOES NOT COMPILE
       System.out.println("Sun Bear is laughing");
    }
}
```

In this example, sneeze() is marked static in the parent class but not in the child class. The compiler detects that you're trying to override using an instance method. However, sneeze() is a static method that should be hidden, causing the compiler to generate an error. The second method, hibernate(), does not compile for the opposite reason. The method is marked static in the child class but not in the parent class.

Finally, the laugh() method does not compile. Even though both versions of the method are marked static, the version in SunBear has a more restrictive access modifier than the one it inherits, and it breaks the second rule for overriding methods. Remember, the four rules for overriding methods must be followed when hiding static methods.

Hiding Variables

As you saw with method overriding, there are lots of rules when two methods have the same signature and are defined in both the parent and child classes. Luckily, the rules for variables with the same name in the parent and child classes are much simpler. In fact, Java doesn't allow variables to be overridden. Variables can be hidden, though.

A *hidden variable* occurs when a child class defines a variable with the same name as an inherited variable defined in the parent class. This creates two distinct copies of the variable within an instance of the child class: one instance defined in the parent class and one defined in the child class.

As when hiding a static method, you can't override a variable; you can only hide it. Let's take a look at a hidden variable. What do you think the following application prints?

```
class Carnivore {
    protected boolean hasFur = false;
}

public class Meerkat extends Carnivore {
    protected boolean hasFur = true;

    public static void main(String[] args) {
       Meerkat m = new Meerkat();
       Carnivore c = m;
       System.out.println(m.hasFur);  // true
       System.out.println(c.hasFur);  // false
    }
}
```

Confused about the output? Both of these classes define a hasFur variable, but with different values. Even though only one object is created by the main() method, both variables exist independently of each other. The output changes depending on the reference variable used.

If you didn't understand the last example, don't worry. We cover polymorphism in more detail in the next chapter. For now, you just need to know that overriding a method replaces the parent method on all reference variables (other than super), whereas hiding a method or variable replaces the member only if a child reference type is used.

Writing *final* Methods

We conclude our discussion of method inheritance with a somewhat self-explanatory rule: final methods cannot be overridden. By marking a method final, you forbid a child class from replacing this method. This rule is in place both when you override a method and when you hide a method. In other words, you cannot hide a static method in a child class if it is marked final in the parent class.

Let's take a look at an example:

```java
public class Bird {
    public final boolean hasFeathers() {
        return true;
    }
    public final static void flyAway() {}
}

public class Penguin extends Bird {
    public final boolean hasFeathers() {  // DOES NOT COMPILE
        return false;
    }
    public final static void flyAway() {}  // DOES NOT COMPILE
}
```

In this example, the instance method hasFeathers() is marked as final in the parent class Bird, so the child class Penguin cannot override the parent method, resulting in a compiler error. The static method flyAway() is also marked final, so it cannot be hidden in the subclass. In this example, whether or not the child method uses the final keyword is irrelevant—the code will not compile either way.

This rule applies only to inherited methods. For example, if the two methods were marked private in the parent Bird class, then the Penguin class, as defined, would compile. In that case, the private methods would be redeclared, not overridden or hidden.

Creating Abstract Classes

When designing a model, we sometimes want to create an entity that cannot be instantiated directly. For example, imagine that we have a Canine class with subclasses Wolf, Fox, and Coyote. We want other developers to be able to create instances of the subclasses, but perhaps we don't want them to be able to create a Canine instance. In other words, we want to force all objects of Canine to have a particular type at runtime.

Introducing Abstract Classes

Enter abstract classes. An *abstract class* is a class declared with the abstract modifier that cannot be instantiated directly and may contain abstract methods. Let's take a look at an example based on the Canine data model:

```
public abstract class Canine {}

public class Wolf extends Canine {}
public class Fox extends Canine {}
public class Coyote extends Canine {}
```

In this example, other developers can create instances of Wolf, Fox, or Coyote, but not Canine. Sure, they can pass a variable reference as a Canine, but the underlying object must be a subclass of Canine at runtime.

But wait, there's more! An abstract class can contain abstract methods. An *abstract method* is a method declared with the abstract modifier that does not define a body. Put another way, an abstract method forces subclasses to override the method.

Why would we want this? Polymorphism, of course! By declaring a method abstract, we can guarantee that some version will be available on an instance without having to specify what that version is in the abstract parent class.

```
public abstract class Canine {
   public abstract String getSound();
   public void bark() { System.out.println(getSound()); }
}

public class Wolf extends Canine {
   public String getSound() {
      return "Wooooooof!";
   } }

public class Fox extends Canine {
   public String getSound() {
      return "Squeak!";
   } }

public class Coyote extends Canine {
   public String getSound() {
      return "Roar!";
   } }
```

We can then create an instance of `Fox` and assign it to the parent type `Canine`. The overridden method will be used at runtime.

```
public static void main(String[] p) {
    Canine w = new Fox();
    w.bark();  // Squeak!
}
```

Easy so far. But there are some rules you need to be aware of:

- Only instance methods can be marked `abstract` within a class, not variables, constructors, or `static` methods.
- An abstract class can include zero or more abstract methods, while a non-abstract class cannot contain any.
- A non-abstract class that extends an abstract class must implement all inherited abstract methods.
- Overriding an abstract method follows the existing rules for overriding methods that you learned about earlier in the chapter.

Let's see if you can spot why each of these class declarations does not compile:

```
public class FennecFox extends Canine {
    public int getSound() {
        return 10;
    } }
```

```
public class ArcticFox extends Canine {}
```

```
public class Direwolf extends Canine {
    public abstract rest();
    public String getSound() {
        return "Roof!";
    } }
```

```
public class Jackal extends Canine {
    public abstract String name;
    public String getSound() {
        return "Laugh";
    } }
```

First off, the `FennecFox` class does not compile because it is an invalid method override. In particular, the return types are not covariant. The `ArcticFox` class does not compile because it does not override the abstract `getSound()` method. The `Direwolf` class does not compile because it is not abstract but declares an abstract method `rest()`. Finally, the `Jackal` class does not compile because variables cannot be marked abstract.

An abstract class is most commonly used when you want another class to inherit properties of a particular class, but you want the subclass to fill in some of the implementation details.

Earlier, we said that an abstract class is one that cannot be instantiated. This means that if you attempt to instantiate it, the compiler will report an exception, as in this example:

```
abstract class Alligator {
   public static void main(String... food) {
      var a = new Alligator();  // DOES NOT COMPILE
   }
}
```

An abstract class can be initialized, but only as part of the instantiation of a non-abstract subclass.

Declaring Abstract Methods

An abstract method is always declared without a body. It also includes a semicolon (;) after the method declaration. As you saw in the previous example, an abstract class may include non-abstract methods, in this case with the `bark()` method. In fact, an abstract class can include all of the same members as a non-abstract class, including variables, `static` and instance methods, constructors, etc.

It might surprise you to know that an abstract class is not required to include any abstract methods. For example, the following code compiles even though it doesn't define any abstract methods:

```
public abstract class Llama {
   public void chew() {}
}
```

Even without abstract methods, the class cannot be directly instantiated. For the exam, keep an eye out for abstract methods declared outside abstract classes, such as the following:

```
public class Egret {  // DOES NOT COMPILE
   public abstract void peck();
}
```

The exam creators like to include invalid class declarations, mixing non-abstract classes with abstract methods.

Like the `final` modifier, the `abstract` modifier can be placed before or after the access modifier in class and method declarations, as shown in this `Tiger` class:

```
abstract public class Tiger {
   abstract public int claw();
}
```

The `abstract` modifier cannot be placed after the `class` keyword in a class declaration or after the return type in a method declaration. The following `Bear` and `howl()` declarations do not compile for these reasons:

```
public class abstract Bear {     // DOES NOT COMPILE
    public int abstract howl();  // DOES NOT COMPILE
}
```

It is not possible to define an abstract method that has a body or default implementation. You can still define a default method with a body—you just can't mark it as `abstract`. As long as you do not mark the method as `final`, the subclass has the option to override the inherited method.

Creating a Concrete Class

An abstract class becomes usable when it is extended by a concrete subclass. A *concrete class* is a non-abstract class. The first concrete subclass that extends an abstract class is required to implement all inherited abstract methods. This includes implementing any inherited abstract methods from inherited interfaces, as you see in the next chapter.

When you see a concrete class extending an abstract class on the exam, check to make sure that it implements all of the required abstract methods. Can you see why the following `Walrus` class does not compile?

```
public abstract class Animal {
    public abstract String getName();
}
```

```
public class Walrus extends Animal {} // DOES NOT COMPILE
```

In this example, we see that `Animal` is marked as `abstract` and `Walrus` is not, making `Walrus` a concrete subclass of `Animal`. Since `Walrus` is the first concrete subclass, it must implement all inherited abstract methods—`getName()` in this example. Because it doesn't, the compiler reports an error with the declaration of `Walrus`.

We highlight the *first* concrete subclass for a reason. An abstract class can extend a non-abstract class and vice versa. Anytime a concrete class is extending an abstract class, it must implement all of the methods that are inherited as abstract. Let's illustrate this with a set of inherited classes:

```
public abstract class Mammal {
    abstract void showHorn();
    abstract void eatLeaf();
}
```

```
public abstract class Rhino extends Mammal {
   void showHorn() {}  // Inherited from Mammal
}
```

```
public class BlackRhino extends Rhino {
   void eatLeaf() {}   // Inherited from Mammal
}
```

In this example, the BlackRhino class is the first concrete subclass, while the Mammal and Rhino classes are abstract. The BlackRhino class inherits the eatLeaf() method as abstract and is therefore required to provide an implementation, which it does.

What about the showHorn() method? Since the parent class, Rhino, provides an implementation of showHorn(), the method is inherited in the BlackRhino as a non-abstract method. For this reason, the BlackRhino class is permitted but not required to override the showHorn() method. The three classes in this example are correctly defined and compile.

What if we changed the Rhino declaration to remove the abstract modifier?

```
public class Rhino extends Mammal {  // DOES NOT COMPILE
   void showHorn() {}
}
```

By changing Rhino to a concrete class, it becomes the first non-abstract class to extend the abstract Mammal class. Therefore, it must provide an implementation of both the showHorn() and eatLeaf() methods. Since it only provides one of these methods, the modified Rhino declaration does not compile.

Let's try one more example. The following concrete class Lion inherits two abstract methods, getName() and roar():

```
public abstract class Animal {
   abstract String getName();
}
```

```
public abstract class BigCat extends Animal {
   protected abstract void roar();
}
```

```
public class Lion extends BigCat {
   public String getName() {
      return "Lion";
   }
   public void roar() {
      System.out.println("The Lion lets out a loud ROAR!");
   }
}
```

In this sample code, BigCat extends Animal but is marked as abstract; therefore, it is not required to provide an implementation for the getName() method. The class Lion is not marked as abstract, and as the first concrete subclass, it must implement all of the inherited abstract methods not defined in a parent class. All three of these classes compile successfully.

Creating Constructors in Abstract Classes

Even though abstract classes cannot be instantiated, they are still initialized through constructors by their subclasses. For example, consider the following program:

```java
abstract class Mammal {
    abstract CharSequence chew();
    public Mammal() {
        System.out.println(chew());  // Does this line compile?
    }
}

public class Platypus extends Mammal {
    String chew() { return "yummy!"; }
    public static void main(String[] args) {
        new Platypus();
    }
}
```

Using the constructor rules you learned about earlier in this chapter, the compiler inserts a default no-argument constructor into the Platypus class, which first calls super() in the Mammal class. The Mammal constructor is only called when the abstract class is being initialized through a subclass; therefore, there is an implementation of chew() at the time the constructor is called. This code compiles and prints yummy! at runtime.

For the exam, remember that abstract classes are initialized with constructors in the same way as non-abstract classes. For example, if an abstract class does not provide a constructor, the compiler will automatically insert a default no-argument constructor.

The primary difference between a constructor in an abstract class and a non-abstract class is that a constructor in an abstract class can be called only when it is being initialized by a non-abstract subclass. This makes sense, as abstract classes cannot be instantiated.

Spotting Invalid Declarations

We conclude our discussion of abstract classes with a review of potential issues you're more likely to encounter on the exam than in real life. The exam writers are fond of questions with methods marked as abstract for which an implementation is also defined. For example, can you see why each of the following methods does not compile?

```
public abstract class Turtle {
   public abstract long eat()         // DOES NOT COMPILE
   public abstract void swim() {}; // DOES NOT COMPILE
   public abstract int getAge() {  // DOES NOT COMPILE
       return 10;
   }
   public abstract void sleep;        // DOES NOT COMPILE
   public void goInShell();        // DOES NOT COMPILE
}
```

The first method, eat(), does not compile because it is marked abstract but does not end with a semicolon (;). The next two methods, swim() and getAge(), do not compile because they are marked abstract, but they provide an implementation block enclosed in braces ({}). For the exam, remember that an abstract method declaration must end in a semicolon without any braces. The next method, sleep, does not compile because it is missing parentheses, (), for method arguments. The last method, goInShell(), does not compile because it is not marked abstract and therefore must provide a body enclosed in braces.

Make sure you understand why each of the previous methods does not compile and that you can spot errors like these on the exam. If you come across a question on the exam in which a class or method is marked abstract, make sure the class is properly implemented before attempting to solve the problem.

abstract and *final* Modifiers

What would happen if you marked a class or method both abstract and final? If you mark something abstract, you intend for someone else to extend or implement it. But if you mark something final, you are preventing anyone from extending or implementing it. These concepts are in direct conflict with each other.

Due to this incompatibility, Java does not permit a class or method to be marked both abstract and final. For example, the following code snippet will not compile:

```
public abstract final class Tortoise {  // DOES NOT COMPILE
   public abstract final void walk();   // DOES NOT COMPILE
}
```

In this example, neither the class nor the method declarations will compile because they are marked both abstract and final. The exam doesn't tend to use final modifiers on classes or methods often, so if you see them, make sure they aren't used with the abstract modifier.

abstract and *private* Modifiers

A method cannot be marked as both abstract and private. This rule makes sense if you think about it. How would you define a subclass that implements a required method if the method is not inherited by the subclass? The answer is that you can't, which is why the compiler will complain if you try to do the following:

```java
public abstract class Whale {
    private abstract void sing();  // DOES NOT COMPILE
}

public class HumpbackWhale extends Whale {
    private void sing() {
        System.out.println("Humpback whale is singing");
    } }
```

In this example, the abstract method sing() defined in the parent class Whale is not visible to the subclass HumpbackWhale. Even though HumpbackWhale does provide an implementation, it is not considered an override of the abstract method since the abstract method is not inherited. The compiler recognizes this in the parent class and reports an error as soon as private and abstract are applied to the same method.

 While it is not possible to declare a method abstract and private, it is possible (albeit redundant) to declare a method final and private.

If we changed the access modifier from private to protected in the parent class Whale, would the code compile?

```java
public abstract class Whale {
    protected abstract void sing();
}

public class HumpbackWhale extends Whale {
    private void sing() {  // DOES NOT COMPILE
        System.out.println("Humpback whale is singing");
    }
}
```

In this modified example, the code will still not compile, but for a completely different reason. If you remember the rules for overriding a method, the subclass cannot reduce the visibility of the parent method, sing(). Because the method is declared protected in the parent class, it must be marked as protected or public in the child class. Even with abstract methods, the rules for overriding methods must be followed.

abstract and static Modifiers

As we discussed earlier in the chapter, a static method can only be hidden, not overridden. It is defined as belonging to the class, not an instance of the class. If a static method cannot be overridden, then it follows that it also cannot be marked `abstract` since it can never be implemented. For example, the following class does not compile:

```
abstract class Hippopotamus {
   abstract static void swim();  // DOES NOT COMPILE
}
```

For the exam, make sure you know which modifiers can and cannot be used with one another, especially for abstract classes and interfaces.

Creating Immutable Objects

As you might remember from Chapter 4, an immutable object is one that cannot change state after it is created. The *immutable objects pattern* is an object-oriented design pattern in which an object cannot be modified after it is created.

Immutable objects are helpful when writing secure code because you don't have to worry about the values changing. They also simplify code when dealing with concurrency since immutable objects can be easily shared between multiple threads.

Declaring an Immutable Class

Although there are a variety of techniques for writing an immutable class, you should be familiar with a common strategy for making a class immutable:

1. Mark the class as `final` or make all of the constructors `private`.
2. Mark all the instance variables `private` and `final`.
3. Don't define any setter methods.
4. Don't allow referenced mutable objects to be modified.
5. Use a constructor to set all properties of the object, making a copy if needed.

The first rule prevents anyone from creating a mutable subclass. The second and third rules ensure that callers don't make changes to instance variables and are the hallmarks of good encapsulation, a topic we discuss along with records in Chapter 7.

The fourth rule for creating immutable objects is subtle. Basically, it means you shouldn't expose an accessor (or getter) method for mutable instance fields. Can you see why the following creates a mutable object?

```
import java.util.*;
public final class Animal {  // Not an immutable object declaration
   private final ArrayList<String> favoriteFoods;

   public Animal() {
      this.favoriteFoods = new ArrayList<String>();
      this.favoriteFoods.add("Apples");
   }
```

```
public List<String> getFavoriteFoods() {
   return favoriteFoods;
} }
```

We carefully followed the first three rules, but unfortunately, a malicious caller could still modify our data.

```
var zebra = new Animal();
System.out.println(zebra.getFavoriteFoods());  // [Apples]

zebra.getFavoriteFoods().clear();
zebra.getFavoriteFoods().add("Chocolate Chip Cookies");
System.out.println(zebra.getFavoriteFoods());  // [Chocolate Chip Cookies]
```

Oh no! Zebras should not eat Chocolate Chip Cookies! It's not an immutable object if we can change its contents! If we don't have a getter for the favoriteFoods object, how do callers access it? Simple: by using delegate or wrapper methods to read the data.

```
import java.util.*;
public final class Animal {  // An immutable object declaration
   private final List<String> favoriteFoods;

   public Animal() {
      this.favoriteFoods = new ArrayList<String>();
      this.favoriteFoods.add("Apples");
   }

   public int getFavoriteFoodsCount() {
      return favoriteFoods.size();
   }

   public String getFavoriteFoodsItem(int index) {
      return favoriteFoods.get(index);
   } }
```

In this improved version, the data is still available. However, it is a true immutable object because the mutable variable cannot be modified by the caller.

Copy on Read Accessor Methods

Besides delegating access to any private mutable objects, another approach is to make a copy of the mutable object any time it is requested.

```
public ArrayList<String> getFavoriteFoods() {
   return new ArrayList<String>(this.favoriteFoods);
}
```

> Of course, changes in the copy won't be reflected in the original, but at least the original is protected from external changes. This can be an expensive operation if called frequently by the caller.

Performing a Defensive Copy

So, what's this about the fifth and final rule for creating immutable objects? In designing our class, let's say we want a rule that the data for favoriteFoods is provided by the caller and that it always contains at least one element. This rule is often called an invariant; it is true any time we have an instance of the object.

```java
import java.util.*;
public final class Animal {  // Not an immutable object declaration
   private final ArrayList<String> favoriteFoods;

   public Animal(ArrayList<String> favoriteFoods) {
      if (favoriteFoods == null || favoriteFoods.size() == 0)
         throw new RuntimeException("favoriteFoods is required");
      this.favoriteFoods = favoriteFoods;
   }

   public int getFavoriteFoodsCount() {
      return favoriteFoods.size();
   }

   public String getFavoriteFoodsItem(int index) {
      return favoriteFoods.get(index);
   } }
```

To ensure that favoriteFoods is provided, we validate it in the constructor and throw an exception if it is not provided. So is this immutable? Not quite! A malicious caller might be tricky and keep their own secret reference to our favoriteFoods object, which they can modify directly.

```java
var favorites = new ArrayList<String>();
favorites.add("Apples");

var zebra = new Animal(favorites);  // Caller still has access to favorites
System.out.println(zebra.getFavoriteFoodsItem(0));  // [Apples]

favorites.clear();
```

```
favorites.add("Chocolate Chip Cookies");
System.out.println(zebra.getFavoriteFoodsItem(0));   // [Chocolate Chip Cookies]
```

Whoops! It seems like `Animal` is not immutable anymore, since its contents can change after it is created. The solution is to make a copy of the list object containing the same elements.

```
public Animal(List<String> favoriteFoods) {
    if (favoriteFoods == null || favoriteFoods.size() == 0)
        throw new RuntimeException("favoriteFoods is required");
    this.favoriteFoods = new ArrayList<String>(favoriteFoods);
}
```

The copy operation is called a *defensive copy* because the copy is being made in case other code does something unexpected. It's the same idea as defensive driving: prevent a problem before it exists. With this approach, our `Animal` class is once again immutable.

Summary

This chapter took the basic class structures we've presented throughout the book and expanded them by introducing the notion of inheritance. Java classes follow a single-inheritance pattern in which every class has exactly one direct parent class, with all classes eventually inheriting from `java.lang.Object`.

Inheriting a class gives you access to all of the `public` and `protected` members of the class. It also gives you access to package members of the class if the classes are in the same package. All instance methods, constructors, and instance initializers have access to two special reference variables: `this` and `super`. Both `this` and `super` provide access to all inherited members, with only `this` providing access to all members in the current class declaration.

Constructors are special methods that use the class name and do not have a return type. They are used to instantiate new objects. Declaring constructors requires following a number of important rules. If no constructor is provided, the compiler will automatically insert a default no-argument constructor in the class. The first line of every constructor is a call to an overloaded constructor, `this()`, or a parent constructor, `super()`; otherwise, the compiler will insert a call to `super()` as the first line of the constructor. In some cases, such as if the parent class does not define a no-argument constructor, this can lead to compilation errors. Pay close attention on the exam to any class that defines a constructor with arguments and doesn't define a no-argument constructor.

Classes are initialized in a predetermined order: superclass initialization; `static` variables and `static` initializers in the order that they appear; instance variables and instance initializers in the order they appear; and finally, the constructor. All `final` instance variables must be assigned a value exactly once.

We reviewed overloaded, overridden, hidden, and redeclared methods and showed how they differ. A method is overloaded if it has the same name but a different signature as another accessible method. A method is overridden if it has the same signature as an inherited method, with access modifiers, exceptions, and a return type that are compatible. A static method is hidden if it has the same signature as an inherited static method. Finally, a method is redeclared if it has the same name and possibly the same signature as an uninherited method.

We then moved on to abstract classes, which are just like regular classes except that they cannot be instantiated and may contain abstract methods. An abstract class can extend a non-abstract class, and vice versa. Abstract classes can be used to define a framework that other developers write subclasses against. An abstract method is one that does not include a body when it is declared. An abstract method can be placed only inside an abstract class or interface. Next, an abstract method can be overridden with another abstract declaration or a concrete implementation, provided the rules for overriding methods are followed. The first concrete class must implement all of the inherited abstract methods, whether they are inherited from an abstract class or an interface.

Finally, this chapter showed you how to create immutable objects in Java. Although there are a number of different techniques to do so, we included the most common one you should know for the exam. Immutable objects are extremely useful in practice, especially in multi-threaded applications, since they do not change.

Exam Essentials

Be able to write code that extends other classes.   A Java class that extends another class inherits all of its public and protected methods and variables. If the class is in the same package, it also inherits all package members of the class. Classes that are marked final cannot be extended. Finally, all classes in Java extend java.lang.Object either directly or from a superclass.

Be able to distinguish and use this, this(), super, and super().   To access a current or inherited member of a class, the this reference can be used. To access an inherited member, the super reference can be used. The super reference is often used to reduce ambiguity, such as when a class reuses the name of an inherited method or variable. The calls to this() and super() are used to access constructors in the same class and parent class, respectively.

Evaluate code involving constructors.   The first line of every constructor is a call to another constructor within the class using this() or a call to a constructor of the parent class using the super() call. The compiler will insert a call to super() if no constructor call is declared. If the parent class doesn't contain a no-argument constructor, an explicit call to the parent constructor must be provided. Be able to recognize when the default constructor is provided. Remember that the order of initialization is to initialize all classes in the class hierarchy, starting with the superclass. Then the instances are initialized, again starting with the superclass. All `final` variables must be assigned a value exactly once by the time the constructor is finished.

Understand the rules for method overriding.   Java allows methods to be overridden, or replaced, by a subclass if certain rules are followed: a method must have the same signature, be at least as accessible as the parent method, must not declare any new or broader exceptions and must use covariant return types. Methods marked `final` may not be overridden or hidden.

Recognize the difference between method overriding and method overloading.   Both method overloading and overriding involve creating a new method with the same name as an existing method. When the method signature is the same, it is referred to as method overriding and must follow a specific set of override rules to compile. When the method signature is different, with the method taking different inputs, it is referred to as method overloading, and none of the override rules is required. Method overriding is important to polymorphism because it replaces all calls to the method, even those made in a superclass.

Understand the rules for hiding methods and variables.   When a `static` method is overridden in a subclass, it is referred to as method hiding. Likewise, variable hiding is when an inherited variable name is reused in a subclass. In both situations, the original method or variable still exists and is accessible depending on where it is accessed and the reference type used. For method hiding, the use of `static` in the method declaration must be the same between the parent and child class. Finally, variable and method hiding should generally be avoided since it leads to confusing and difficult-to-follow code.

Be able to write code that creates and extends abstract classes.   In Java, classes and methods can be declared as `abstract`. An abstract class cannot be instantiated. An instance of an abstract class can be obtained only through a concrete subclass. Abstract classes can include any number of abstract and non-abstract methods, including zero. Abstract methods follow all the method override rules and may be defined only within abstract classes. The first concrete subclass of an abstract class must implement all the inherited methods. Abstract classes and methods may not be marked as `final`.

Create immutable objects.   An immutable object is one that cannot be modified after it is declared. An immutable class is commonly implemented with a `private` constructor, no setter methods, and no ability to modify mutable objects contained within the class.

Review Questions

The answers to the chapter review questions can be found in the Appendix.

1. Which code can be inserted to have the code print 2?

```java
public class BirdSeed {
    private int numberBags;
    boolean call;

    public BirdSeed() {
        // LINE 1
        call = false;
        // LINE 2
    }

    public BirdSeed(int numberBags) {
        this.numberBags = numberBags;
    }

    public static void main(String[] args) {
        var seed = new BirdSeed();
        System.out.print(seed.numberBags);
    } }
```

   A. Replace line 1 with `BirdSeed(2);`
   B. Replace line 2 with `BirdSeed(2);`
   C. Replace line 1 with `new BirdSeed(2);`
   D. Replace line 2 with `new BirdSeed(2);`
   E. Replace line 1 with `this(2);`
   F. Replace line 2 with `this(2);`
   G. The code prints 2 without any changes.

2. Which modifier pairs can be used together in a method declaration? (Choose all that apply.)
   A. `static` and `final`
   B. `private` and `static`
   C. `static` and `abstract`
   D. `private` and `abstract`
   E. `abstract` and `final`
   F. `private` and `final`

3. Which of the following statements about methods are true? (Choose all that apply.)

    A. Overloaded methods must have the same signature.

    B. Overridden methods must have the same signature.

    C. Hidden methods must have the same signature.

    D. Overloaded methods must have the same return type.

    E. Overridden methods must have the same return type.

    F. Hidden methods must have the same return type.

4. What is the output of the following program?

```
1:  class Mammal {
2:      private void sneeze() {}
3:      public Mammal(int age) {
4:          System.out.print("Mammal");
5:      } }
6:  public class Platypus extends Mammal {
7:      int sneeze() { return 1; }
8:      public Platypus() {
9:          System.out.print("Platypus");
10:     }
11:     public static void main(String[] args) {
12:         new Mammal(5);
13:     } }
```

    A. Platypus

    B. Mammal

    C. PlatypusMammal

    D. MammalPlatypus

    E. The code will compile if line 7 is changed.

    F. The code will compile if line 9 is changed.

5. Which of the following completes the constructor so that this code prints out 50?

```
class Speedster {
    int numSpots;
}
public class Cheetah extends Speedster {
    int numSpots;

    public Cheetah(int numSpots) {
        // INSERT CODE HERE
    }
```

```
    public static void main(String[] args) {
        Speedster s = new Cheetah(50);
        System.out.print(s.numSpots);
    }
}
```

A. `numSpots = numSpots;`

B. `numSpots = this.numSpots;`

C. `this.numSpots = numSpots;`

D. `numSpots = super.numSpots;`

E. `super.numSpots = numSpots;`

F. The code does not compile regardless of the code inserted into the constructor.

G. None of the above.

6. Which of the following declare immutable classes? (Choose all that apply.)

```
public final class Moose {
    private final int antlers;
}

public class Caribou {
    private int antlers = 10;
}

public class Reindeer {
    private final int antlers = 5;
}

public final class Elk {}

public final class Deer {
    private final Object o = new Object();
}
```

A. Moose

B. Caribou

C. Reindeer

D. Elk

E. Deer

F. None of the above

7. What is the output of the following code?

```
1:  class Arthropod {
2:     protected void printName(long input) {
3:         System.out.print("Arthropod");
4:     }
5:     void printName(int input) {
6:         System.out.print("Spooky");
7:     } }
8:  public class Spider extends Arthropod {
9:     protected void printName(int input) {
10:        System.out.print("Spider");
11:    }
12:    public static void main(String[] args) {
13:        Arthropod a = new Spider();
14:        a.printName((short)4);
15:        a.printName(4);
16:        a.printName(5L);
17:    } }
```

A. SpiderSpiderArthropod

B. SpiderSpiderSpider

C. SpiderSpookyArthropod

D. SpookySpiderArthropod

E. The code will not compile because of line 5.

F. The code will not compile because of line 9.

G. None of the above.

8. What is the result of the following code?

```
1:  abstract class Bird {
2:     private final void fly() { System.out.println("Bird"); }
3:     protected Bird() { System.out.print("Wow-"); }
4:  }
5:  public class Pelican extends Bird {
6:     public Pelican() { System.out.print("Oh-"); }
7:     protected void fly() { System.out.println("Pelican"); }
8:     public static void main(String[] args) {
9:         var chirp = new Pelican();
10:        chirp.fly();
11: } }
```

A. Oh-Bird

B. Oh-Pelican

C. Wow-Oh-Bird

D. Wow-Oh-Pelican

E. The code contains a compilation error.

F. None of the above.

9. Which of the following statements about overridden methods are true? (Choose all that apply.)

A. An overridden method must contain method parameters that are the same or covariant with the method parameters in the inherited method.

B. An overridden method may declare a new exception, provided it is not checked.

C. An overridden method must be more accessible than the method in the parent class.

D. An overridden method may declare a broader checked exception than the method in the parent class.

E. If an inherited method returns `void`, then the overridden version of the method must return `void`.

F. None of the above.

10. Which of the following pairs, when inserted into the blanks, allow the code to compile? (Choose all that apply.)

```
1:  public class Howler {
2:      public Howler(long shadow) {
3:          _____;
4:      }
5:      private Howler(int moon) {
6:          super();
7:      }
8:  }
9:  class Wolf extends Howler {
10:     protected Wolf(String stars) {
11:         super(2L);
12:     }
13:     public Wolf() {
14:         _____;
15:     }
16: }
```

A. `this(3)` at line 3, `this("")` at line 14.

B. `this()` at line 3, `super(1)` at line 14.

C. `this((short)1)` at line 3, `this(null)` at line 14.

D. `super()` at line 3, `super()` at line 14.

E. `this(2L)` at line 3, `super((short)2)` at line 14.

F. `this(5)` at line 3, `super(null)` at line 14.

G. Remove lines 3 and 14.

11. What is the result of the following?

```
1:  public class PolarBear {
2:     StringBuilder value = new StringBuilder("t");
3:     { value.append("a"); }
4:     { value.append("c"); }
5:     private PolarBear() {
6:        value.append("b");
7:     }
8:     public PolarBear(String s) {
9:        this();
10:       value.append(s);
11:    }
12:    public PolarBear(CharSequence p) {
13:       value.append(p);
14:    }
15:    public static void main(String[] args) {
16:       Object bear = new PolarBear();
17:       bear = new PolarBear("f");
18:       System.out.println(((PolarBear)bear).value);
19:    } }
```

A. `tacb`

B. `tacf`

C. `tacbf`

D. `tcafb`

E. `taftacb`

F. The code does not compile.

G. An exception is thrown.

12. How many lines of the following program contain a compilation error?

```
1:  public class Rodent {
2:     public Rodent(Integer x) {}
3:     protected static Integer chew() throws Exception {
4:        System.out.println("Rodent is chewing");
5:        return 1;
6:     }
```

```
7:   }
8:   class Beaver extends Rodent {
9:      public Number chew() throws RuntimeException {
10:        System.out.println("Beaver is chewing on wood");
11:        return 2;
12:   } }
```

A. None

B. 1

C. 2

D. 3

E. 4

F. 5

13. Which of these classes compile and will include a default constructor created by the compiler? (Choose all that apply.)

A.
```
public class Bird {}
```

B.
```
public class Bird {
   public bird() {}
}
```

C.
```
public class Bird {
   public bird(String name) {}
}
```

D.
```
public class Bird {
   public Bird() {}
}
```

E.
```
public class Bird {
   Bird(String name) {}
}
```

F.
```
public class Bird {
   private Bird(int age) {}
}
```

G.
```
public class Bird {
   public Bird bird() { return null; }
}
```

14. Which of the following statements about inheritance are correct? (Choose all that apply.)

A. A class can directly extend any number of classes.

B. A class can implement any number of interfaces.

C. All variables inherit `java.lang.Object`.

D. If class A is extended by B, then B is a superclass of A.

E. If class C implements interface D, then C is a subtype of D.

F. Multiple inheritance is the property of a class to have multiple direct superclasses.

15. Which statement about the following program is correct?

```
1: abstract class Nocturnal {
2:    boolean isBlind();
3: }
4: public class Owl extends Nocturnal {
5:    public boolean isBlind() { return false; }
6:    public static void main(String[] args) {
7:        var nocturnal = (Nocturnal)new Owl();
8:        System.out.println(nocturnal.isBlind());
9: } }
```

A. It compiles and prints `true`.

B. It compiles and prints `false`.

C. The code will not compile because of line 2.

D. The code will not compile because of line 5.

E. The code will not compile because of line 7.

F. The code will not compile because of line 8.

G. None of the above.

16. What is the result of the following?

```
1:  class Arachnid {
2:     static StringBuilder sb = new StringBuilder();
3:     { sb.append("c"); }
4:     static
5:     { sb.append("u"); }
6:     { sb.append("r"); }
7:  }
8:  public class Scorpion extends Arachnid {
9:     static
10:    { sb.append("q"); }
11:    { sb.append("m"); }
12:    public static void main(String[] args) {
```

```
13:       System.out.print(Scorpion.sb + " ");
14:       System.out.print(Scorpion.sb + " ");
15:       new Arachnid();
16:       new Scorpion();
17:       System.out.print(Scorpion.sb);
18:    } }
```

A. qu qu qumrcrc

B. u u ucrcrm

C. uq uq uqmcrcr

D. uq uq uqcrcrm

E. qu qu qumcrcr

F. qu qu qucrcrm

G. The code does not compile.

17. Which of the following are true? (Choose all that apply.)

A. this() can be called from anywhere in a constructor.

B. this() can be called from anywhere in an instance method.

C. this.variableName can be called from any instance method in the class.

D. this.variableName can be called from any static method in the class.

E. You can call the default constructor written by the compiler using this().

F. You can access a private constructor with the main() method in the same class.

18. Which statements about the following classes are correct? (Choose all that apply.)

```
1:  public class Mammal {
2:     private void eat() {}
3:     protected static void drink() {}
4:     public Integer dance(String p) { return null; }
5:  }
6:  class Primate extends Mammal {
7:     public void eat(String p) {}
8:  }
9:  class Monkey extends Primate {
10:    public static void drink() throws RuntimeException {}
11:    public Number dance(CharSequence p) { return null; }
12:    public int eat(String p) {}
13: }
```

A. The eat() method in Mammal is correctly overridden on line 7.

B. The eat() method in Mammal is correctly overloaded on line 7.

C. The drink() method in Mammal is correctly overridden on line 10.

D. The `drink()` method in `Mammal` is correctly hidden on line 10.

E. The `dance()` method in `Mammal` is correctly overridden on line 11.

F. The `dance()` method in `Mammal` is correctly overloaded on line 11.

G. The `eat()` method in `Primate` is correctly hidden on line 12.

H. The `eat()` method in `Primate` is correctly overloaded on line 12.

19. What is the output of the following code?

```
1:  class Reptile {
2:      {System.out.print("A");}
3:      public Reptile(int hatch) {}
4:      void layEggs() {
5:         System.out.print("Reptile");
6:      } }
7:  public class Lizard extends Reptile {
8:      static {System.out.print("B");}
9:      public Lizard(int hatch) {}
10:     public final void layEggs() {
11:        System.out.print("Lizard");
12:     }
13:     public static void main(String[] args) {
14:         var reptile = new Lizard(1);
15:         reptile.layEggs();
16:     } }
```

A. AALizard

B. BALizard

C. BLizardA

D. ALizard

E. The code will not compile because of line 3.

F. None of the above.

20. Which statement about the following program is correct?

```
1:  class Bird {
2:      int feathers = 0;
3:      Bird(int x) { this.feathers = x; }
4:      Bird fly() {
5:         return new Bird(1);
6:      } }
7:  class Parrot extends Bird {
8:      protected Parrot(int y) { super(y); }
```

```
9:       protected Parrot fly() {
10:          return new Parrot(2);
11:      } }
12: public class Macaw extends Parrot {
13:      public Macaw(int z) { super(z); }
14:      public Macaw fly() {
15:          return new Macaw(3);
16:      }
17:      public static void main(String... sing) {
18:          Bird p = new Macaw(4);
19:          System.out.print(((Parrot)p.fly()).feathers);
20:      } }
```

A. One line contains a compiler error.

B. Two lines contain compiler errors.

C. Three lines contain compiler errors.

D. The code compiles but throws a `ClassCastException` at runtime.

E. The program compiles and prints 3.

F. The program compiles and prints 0.

21. Which of the following are properties of immutable classes? (Choose all that apply.)

A. The class can contain setter methods, provided they are marked `final`.

B. The class must not be able to be extended outside the class declaration.

C. The class may not contain any instance variables.

D. The class must be marked `static`.

E. The class may not contain any `static` variables.

F. The class may only contain `private` constructors.

G. The data for mutable instance variables may be read, provided they cannot be modified by the caller.

22. What does the following program print?

```
1:  class Person {
2:      static String name;
3:      void setName(String q) { name = q; } }
4:  public class Child extends Person {
5:      static String name;
6:      void setName(String w) { name = w; }
7:      public static void main(String[] p) {
8:          final Child m = new Child();
9:          final Person t = m;
```

```
10:        m.name = "Elysia";
11:        t.name = "Sophia";
12:        m.setName("Webby");
13:        t.setName("Olivia");
14:        System.out.println(m.name + " " + t.name);
15:    } }
```

A. Elysia Sophia

B. Webby Olivia

C. Olivia Olivia

D. Olivia Sophia

E. The code does not compile.

F. None of the above.

23. What is the output of the following program?

```
1: class Canine {
2:     public Canine(boolean t) { logger.append("a"); }
3:     public Canine() { logger.append("q"); }
4:
5:     private StringBuilder logger = new StringBuilder();
6:     protected void print(String v) { logger.append(v); }
7:     protected String view() { return logger.toString(); }
8: }
9:
10: class Fox extends Canine {
11:     public Fox(long x) { print("p"); }
12:     public Fox(String name) {
13:         this(2);
14:         print("z");
15:     }
16: }
17:
18: public class Fennec extends Fox {
19:     public Fennec(int e) {
20:         super("tails");
21:         print("j");
22:     }
23:     public Fennec(short f) {
24:         super("eevee");
25:         print("m");
26:     }
```

```
27:
28:     public static void main(String... unused) {
29:         System.out.println(new Fennec(1).view());
30:     } }
```

A. qpz

B. qpzj

C. jzpa

D. apj

E. apjm

F. The code does not compile.

G. None of the above.

24. What is printed by the following program?

```
1:  class Antelope {
2:     public Antelope(int p) {
3:         System.out.print("4");
4:     }
5:     { System.out.print("2"); }
6:     static { System.out.print("1"); }
7:  }
8:  public class Gazelle extends Antelope {
9:     public Gazelle(int p) {
10:         super(6);
11:         System.out.print("3");
12:     }
13:     public static void main(String hopping[]) {
14:         new Gazelle(0);
15:     }
16:     static { System.out.print("8"); }
17:     { System.out.print("9"); }
18: }
```

A. 182640

B. 182943

C. 182493

D. 421389

E. The code does not compile.

F. The output cannot be determined until runtime.

25. Which of the following are true about a concrete class? (Choose all that apply.)

A. A concrete class can be declared as `abstract`.

B. A concrete class must implement all inherited abstract methods.

C. A concrete class can be marked as `final`.

D. A concrete class must be immutable.

E. A concrete method that implements an abstract method must match the method declaration of the abstract method exactly.

26. What is the output of the following code?

```
4:  public abstract class Whale {
5:     public abstract void dive();
6:     public static void main(String[] args) {
7:        Whale whale = new Orca();
8:        whale.dive(3);
9:     }
10: }
11: class Orca extends Whale {
12:    static public int MAX = 3;
13:    public void dive() {
14:       System.out.println("Orca diving");
15:    }
16:    public void dive(int... depth) {
17:       System.out.println("Orca diving deeper "+MAX);
18: } }
```

A. `Orca diving`

B. `Orca diving deeper 3`

C. The code will not compile because of line 4.

D. The code will not compile because of line 8.

E. The code will not compile because of line 11.

F. The code will not compile because of line 12.

G. The code will not compile because of line 17.

H. None of the above.

Chapter

7

Beyond Classes

OCP EXAM OBJECTIVES COVERED IN THIS CHAPTER:

✓ **Using Object-Oriented Concepts in Java**

- Declare and instantiate Java objects including nested class objects, and explain the object life-cycle including creation, reassigning references, and garbage collection.

- Create classes and records, and define and use instance and static fields and methods, constructors, and instance and static initializers.

- Understand variable scopes, apply encapsulation, and create immutable objects. Use local variable type inference.

- Implement inheritance, including abstract and sealed types as well as record classes. Override methods, including that of the Object class. Implement polymorphism and differentiate between object type and reference type. Perform reference type casting, identify object types using the instanceof operator, and pattern matching with the instanceof operator and the switch construct.

- Create and use interfaces, identify functional interfaces, and utilize private, static, and default interface methods.

- Create and use enum types with fields, methods, and constructors.

In Chapter 6, "Class Design," we showed you how to create, initialize, and extend both abstract and concrete classes. In this chapter, we move beyond classes to other types available in Java, including interfaces, enums, sealed classes, and records. Many of the same basic rules you learned about in Chapter 5, "Methods," still apply, such as access modifiers and static members, although there are additional rules for each type. We also cover encapsulation and how to properly protect instance members. Finally, we conclude this chapter by discussing nested types and polymorphic inheritance.

For this chapter, remember that a Java file may have at most one public top-level type, and it must match the name of the file. This applies to classes, enums, records, and so on. Also, remember that a top-level type can only be declared with public or package access.

Annotations to Know for the Exam

Another top-level type available in Java is annotations, which are metadata "tags" that can be applied to classes, types, methods, and even variables. Besides the @Override and @FunctionalInterface annotations, which we cover in other chapters, the exam expects you to be aware of the following three annotations:

- @Deprecated lets other developers know that a feature is no longer supported and may be removed in future releases. If your code makes use of a @Deprecated class or method, it can trigger a compiler warning.

- @SuppressWarnings instructs the compiler to ignore notifying the user of any warnings generated within a section of code.

- @SafeVarargs lets other developers know that a method does not perform any potential unsafe operations on its vararg parameters.

In practice, creating your own annotations is also a useful skill, although this knowledge is not required for the exam.

Implementing Interfaces

In Chapter 6, you learned about abstract classes, specifically how to create and extend one. Since classes can only extend one class, they had limited use for inheritance. On the other hand, a class may implement any number of interfaces. An *interface* is an abstract data type that declares a list of abstract methods that any class implementing the interface must provide.

Over time, the precise definition of an interface has changed, as additional method types are now supported. In this chapter, we start with a basic definition of an interface and expand it to cover all of the supported members.

Declaring and Using an Interface

In Java, an interface is defined with the `interface` keyword, analogous to the `class` keyword used when defining a class. Refer to Figure 7.1 for a proper interface declaration.

FIGURE 7.1   Defining an interface

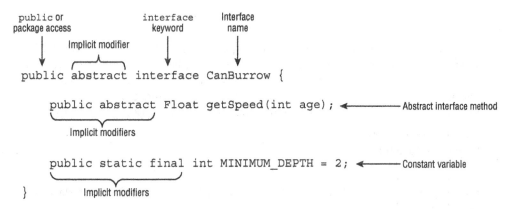

In Figure 7.1, our interface declaration includes a single abstract method and a constant variable. Interface variables are referred to as constants because they are assumed to be `public`, `static`, and `final`. They are initialized with a constant value when they are declared. Since they are `public` and `static`, they can be used outside the interface declaration without requiring an instance of the interface. Figure 7.1 also includes an abstract method that, like an interface variable, is assumed to be `public`.

 For brevity, we often say "an instance of an interface" in this chapter to mean an instance of a class that implements the interface.

What does it mean for a variable or method to be assumed to be something? One aspect of an interface declaration that differs from an abstract class is that it contains implicit modifiers. An *implicit modifier* is a modifier that the compiler automatically inserts into the code. For example, an interface is always considered to be `abstract`, *even if it is not marked so!* We cover rules and examples for implicit modifiers in more detail shortly.

Let's start with a simple example. Imagine that we have an interface WalksOnTwoLegs, defined as follows:

```
public abstract interface WalksOnTwoLegs {}
```

It compiles because interfaces are not required to define any methods. The abstract modifier in this example is optional for interfaces, with the compiler inserting it if it is not provided. Now, consider the following two examples:

```
final interface WalksOnEightLegs {}  // DOES NOT COMPILE

public class Biped {
   public static void main(String[] args) {
      var e = new WalksOnTwoLegs();          // DOES NOT COMPILE
   }
}
```

The WalksOnEightLegs interface doesn't compile because interfaces cannot be marked as final for the same reason that abstract classes cannot be marked as final. Marking an interface final implies no class could ever implement it. The Biped class also doesn't compile, as WalksOnTwoLegs is an interface and cannot be instantiated.

How do you use an interface? Let's say we have an interface Climb, defined as follows:

```
public interface Climb {
   Number getSpeed(int age);
}
```

Next, we have a concrete class FieldMouse that implements the Climb interface, as shown in Figure 7.2.

FIGURE 7.2 Implementing an interface

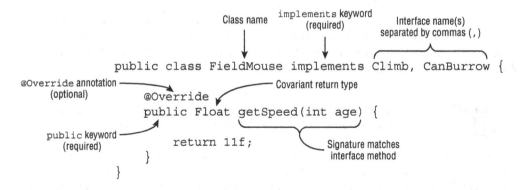

The FieldMouse class declares that it implements the Climb interface and includes an overridden version of getSpeed() inherited from the Climb interface. The @Override annotation is optional. It serves to let other developers know that the method is inherited.

The method signature of `getSpeed()` matches exactly, and the return type is covariant, since a `Float` can be implicitly cast to a `Number`. The access modifier of the interface method is implicitly `public` in `Climb`, although the concrete class `FieldMouse` must explicitly declare it.

As shown in Figure 7.2, a class can implement multiple interfaces, each separated by a comma (,). If any of the interfaces define abstract methods, then the concrete class is required to override them. In this case, `FieldMouse` implements the `CanBurrow` interface that we saw in Figure 7.1. In this manner, the class overrides two abstract methods at the same time with one method declaration. You learn more about duplicate and compatible interface methods in this chapter.

Extending an Interface

Like a class, an interface can extend another interface using the `extends` keyword.

```
public interface Nocturnal {}
```

```
public interface HasBigEyes extends Nocturnal {}
```

Unlike a class, which can extend only one class, an interface can extend multiple interfaces.

```
public interface Nocturnal {
   public int hunt();
}
```

```
public interface CanFly {
   public void flap();
}
```

```
public interface HasBigEyes extends Nocturnal, CanFly {}
```

```
public class Owl implements HasBigEyes {
   public int hunt() { return 5; }
   public void flap() { System.out.println("Flap!"); }
}
```

In this example, the `Owl` class implements the `HasBigEyes` interface and must implement the `hunt()` and `flap()` methods. Extending two interfaces is permitted because interfaces are not initialized as part of a class hierarchy. Unlike abstract classes, they do not contain constructors and are not part of instance initialization. Interfaces simply define a set of rules and methods that a class implementing them must follow.

Inheriting an Interface

Like an abstract class, when a concrete class inherits an interface, all of the inherited abstract methods must be implemented. We illustrate this principle in Figure 7.3. How many abstract methods does the concrete Swan class inherit?

FIGURE 7.3   Interface Inheritance

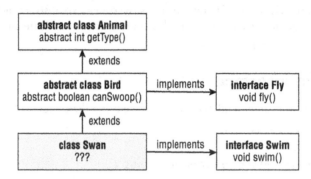

Give up? The concrete Swan class inherits four abstract methods that it must override: getType(), canSwoop(), fly(), and swim().

Let's take a look at another example involving an abstract class that implements an interface:

```
public interface HasTail {
    public int getTailLength();
}

public interface HasWhiskers {
    public int getNumberOfWhiskers();
}

public abstract class HarborSeal implements HasTail, HasWhiskers {}

public class CommonSeal extends HarborSeal {}  // DOES NOT COMPILE
```

The HarborSeal class compiles because it is abstract and not required to implement any of the abstract methods it inherits. The concrete CommonSeal class, though, must override all inherited abstract methods.

Mixing Class and Interface Keywords

The exam creators are fond of questions that mix class and interface terminology. Although a class can implement an interface, a class cannot extend an interface. Likewise, while an interface can extend another interface, an interface cannot implement another interface. The following examples illustrate these principles:

```
public interface CanRun {}
public class Cheetah extends CanRun {}    // DOES NOT COMPILE

public class Hyena {}
public interface HasFur extends Hyena {} // DOES NOT COMPILE
```

Be wary of exam questions that mix class and interface declarations.

Inheriting Duplicate Abstract Methods

Java supports inheriting two abstract methods that have compatible method declarations.

```
public interface Herbivore { public int eatPlants(int plantsLeft); }

public interface Omnivore { public int eatPlants(int foodRemaining); }

public class Bear implements Herbivore, Omnivore {
  public int eatPlants(int plants) {
    System.out.print("Eating plants");
    return plants - 1;
  } }
```

By *compatible*, we mean a method can be written that properly overrides both inherited methods: for example, by using covariant return types that you learned about in Chapter 6. Notice that the method parameter names don't need to match, just the type.

The following is an example of an incompatible declaration:

```
public interface Herbivore { public void eatPlants(int plantsLeft); }

public interface Omnivore  { public int eatPlants(int foodRemaining); }

public class Tiger implements Herbivore, Omnivore { // DOES NOT COMPILE
  // Doesn't matter!
}
```

The implementation of Tiger doesn't matter in this case since it's impossible to write a version of Tiger that satisfies both inherited abstract methods. The code does not compile, regardless of what is declared inside the Tiger class.

Inserting Implicit Modifiers

As mentioned earlier, an implicit modifier is one that the compiler will automatically insert. It's reminiscent of the compiler inserting a default no-argument constructor if you do not define a constructor, which you learned about in Chapter 6. You can choose to insert these implicit modifiers yourself or let the compiler insert them for you.

The following list includes the implicit modifiers for interfaces that you need to know for the exam:

- Interfaces are *implicitly* abstract.
- Interface variables are *implicitly* public, static, and final.
- Interface methods without a body are *implicitly* abstract.
- Interface methods without the private modifier are *implicitly* public.

The last rule applies to abstract, default, and static interface methods, which we cover in the next section.

Let's take a look at an example. The following two interface definitions are equivalent, as the compiler will convert them both to the second declaration:

```
public interface Soar {
    int MAX_HEIGHT = 10;
    final static boolean UNDERWATER = true;
    void fly(int speed);
    abstract void takeoff();
    public abstract double dive();
}
```

```
public abstract interface Soar {
    public static final int MAX_HEIGHT = 10;
    public final static boolean UNDERWATER = true;
    public abstract void fly(int speed);
    public abstract void takeoff();
    public abstract double dive();
}
```

In this example, we've marked in bold the implicit modifiers that the compiler automatically inserts.

Conflicting Modifiers

What happens if a developer marks a method or variable with a modifier that conflicts with an implicit modifier? For example, if an abstract method is implicitly public, can it be explicitly marked protected or private?

```
public interface Dance {
    private int count = 4;    // DOES NOT COMPILE
    protected void step();    // DOES NOT COMPILE
}
```

Neither of these interface member declarations compiles, as the compiler will apply the `public` modifier to both, resulting in a conflict.

Differences between Interfaces and Abstract Classes

Even though abstract classes and interfaces are both considered abstract types, only interfaces make use of implicit modifiers. How do the `play()` methods differ in the following two definitions?

```
abstract class Husky {      // abstract modifier required
   abstract void play();   // abstract modifier required
}


interface Poodle {          // abstract modifier optional
   void play();            // abstract modifier optional
}
```

Both of these method definitions are considered abstract. That said, the Husky class will not compile if the `play()` method is not marked `abstract`, whereas the method in the `Poodle` interface will compile with or without the `abstract` modifier.

What about the access level of the `play()` method? Can you spot anything wrong with the following class definitions that use our abstract types?

```
public class Webby extends Husky {
   void play() {}        // play() is declared with package access in Husky
}


public class Georgette implements Poodle {
   void play() {}        // DOES NOT COMPILE - play() is public in Poodle
}
```

The `Webby` class compiles, but the `Georgette` class does not. Even though the two method implementations are identical, the method in the `Georgette` class reduces the access modifier on the method from `public` to package access.

Declaring Concrete Interface Methods

Table 7.1 lists the six interface member types that you need to know for the exam. We've already covered abstract methods and constants, so we focus on the remaining four concrete methods in this section.

In Table 7.1, the membership type determines how it is able to be accessed. A method with a membership type of *class* is shared among all instances of the interface, whereas a method with a membership type of *instance* is associated with a particular instance of the interface.

TABLE 7.1   Interface member types

	Membership type	Required modifiers	Implicit modifiers	Has value or body?
Constant variable	Class	—	`public` `static` `final`	Yes
`abstract` method	Instance	—	`public` `abstract`	No
`default` method	Instance	`default`	`public`	Yes
`static` method	Class	`static`	`public`	Yes
`private` method	Instance	`private`	—	Yes
`private static` method	Class	`private` `static`	—	Yes

What About *protected* or Package Interface Members?

Interfaces do not support `protected` members, as a class cannot extend an interface. They also do not support package access members, although more likely for syntax reasons and backward compatibility. Since interface methods without an access modifier have been considered implicitly `public`, changing this behavior to package access would break many existing programs!

Writing a *default* Interface Method

The first type of concrete method you should be familiar with for the exam is a default method. A *default method* is a method defined in an interface with the `default` keyword and includes a method body. It may be optionally overridden by a class implementing the interface.

One use of `default` methods is for backward compatibility. You can add a new `default` method to an interface without the need to modify all of the existing classes that implement the interface. The older classes will just use the *default* implementation of the method defined in the interface. This is where the name `default` method comes from!

The following is an example of a `default` method defined in an interface:

```
public interface IsColdBlooded {
    boolean hasScales();
    default double getTemperature() {
        return 10.0;
    }
}
```

This example defines two interface methods, one `abstract` and one `default`. The following Snake class, which implements `IsColdBlooded`, must implement `hasScales()`. It may rely on the default implementation of `getTemperature()` or override the method with its own version:

```
public class Snake implements IsColdBlooded {
    public boolean hasScales() {         // Required override
        return true;
    }
    public double getTemperature() {     // Optional override
        return 12.2;
    } }
```

Note that the `default` interface method modifier is not the same as the `default` label used in a `switch`. Likewise, even though package access is sometimes referred to as *default* access, that feature is implemented by omitting an access modifier. Sorry if this is confusing! We agree Java has overused the word *default* over the years!

For the exam, you should be familiar with various rules for declaring `default` methods.

Default Interface Method Definition Rules

1. A `default` method may be declared only within an interface.
2. A `default` method must be marked with the `default` keyword and include a method body.
3. A `default` method is implicitly `public`.
4. A `default` method cannot be marked `abstract`, `final`, or `static`.
5. A `default` method may be overridden by a class that implements the interface.
6. If a class inherits two or more `default` methods with the same method signature, then the class must override the method.

The first rule should give you some comfort in that you'll only see `default` methods in interfaces. If you see them in a class or enum on the exam, something is wrong. The second rule just denotes syntax, as `default` methods must use the `default` keyword. For example, the following code snippets will not compile because they mix up concrete and abstract interface methods:

```
public interface Carnivore {
    public default void eatMeat();         // DOES NOT COMPILE
    public int getRequiredFoodAmount() {  // DOES NOT COMPILE
        return 13;
    } }
```

The next three rules for default methods follow from the relationship with abstract interface methods. Like abstract interface methods, default methods are implicitly public. Unlike abstract methods, though, default interface methods cannot be marked abstract since they provide a body. They also cannot be marked as final, because they are designed so that they can be overridden in classes implementing the interface, just like abstract methods. Finally, they cannot be marked static since they are associated with the instance of the class implementing the interface.

Inheriting Duplicate *default* Methods

The last rule for creating a default interface method requires some explanation. For example, what value would the following code output?

```
public interface Walk {
    public default int getSpeed() { return 5; }
}
```

```
public interface Run {
    public default int getSpeed() { return 10; }
}
```

```
public class Cat implements Walk, Run {}  // DOES NOT COMPILE
```

In this example, Cat inherits the two default methods for getSpeed(), so which does it use? Since Walk and Run are considered siblings in terms of how they are used in the Cat class, it is not clear whether the code should output 5 or 10. In this case, the compiler throws up its hands and says, "Too hard, I give up!" and fails.

All is not lost, though. If the class implementing the interfaces *overrides* the duplicate default method, the code will compile without issue. By overriding the conflicting method, the ambiguity about which version of the method to call has been removed. For example, the following modified implementation of Cat will compile:

```
public class Cat implements Walk, Run {
    public int getSpeed() { return 1; }
}
```

Calling a *default* Method

A `default` method exists on any object inheriting the interface, not on the interface itself. In other words, you should treat it like an inherited method that can be optionally overridden, rather than as a `static` method. Consider the following:

```
public interface Dance {
    default int getRhythm() { return 33; }
}


public class Snake implements Dance {
    static void move() {
        var snake = new Snake();
        System.out.print(snake.getRhythm());
        System.out.print(Dance.getRhythm()); // DOES NOT COMPILE
    } }
```

The first call to getRhythm() compiles because it is called on an instance of the Snake class. The second does not compile because it is not a `static` method and requires an instance of Dance.

In the previous section, we showed how our Cat class could override a pair of conflicting `default` methods, but what if the Cat class wanted to access the "hidden" version of getSpeed() in Walk or Run? Is it still accessible?

Yes, but it requires some special syntax.

```
public class Cat implements Walk, Run {
    public int getSpeed() {
        return 1;
    }

    public int getWalkSpeed() {
        return Walk.super.getSpeed();
    } }
```

This is an area where a `default` method getSpeed() exhibits properties of both an instance and `static` method. We use the interface name to indicate which method we want to call, but we use the super keyword to show that we are following instance inheritance, not class inheritance. Note that calling Walk.this.getSpeed() would not have worked. A bit confusing, we know, *but you need to be familiar with this syntax for the exam.*

Declaring *static* Interface Methods

Interfaces can also include `static` methods. These methods are defined explicitly with the `static` keyword and, for the most part, behave just like `static` methods defined in classes.

Static Interface Method Definition Rules

1. A `static` method must be marked with the `static` keyword and include a method body.
2. A `static` method without an access modifier is implicitly `public`.
3. A `static` method cannot be marked `abstract` or `final`.
4. A `static` method is not inherited and cannot be accessed in a class implementing the interface without a reference to the interface name.

These rules should follow from what you know so far of classes, interfaces, and `static` methods. For example, you can't declare `static` methods without a body in classes, either. Like `default` and abstract interface methods, `static` interface methods are implicitly `public` if they are declared without an access modifier. As you see shortly, you can use the `private` access modifier with `static` methods.

Let's take a look at a `static` interface method:

```
public interface Hop {
    static int getJumpHeight() {
        return 8;
} }
```

Since the method is defined without an access modifier, the compiler will automatically insert the `public` access modifier. The method `getJumpHeight()` works just like a `static` method as defined in a class. In other words, it can be accessed without an instance of a class.

```
public class Skip implements Hop {
    public int skip() {
        return Hop.getJumpHeight();
} }
```

The last rule about inheritance might be a little confusing, so let's look at an example. The following is an example of a class Bunny that implements Hop and does not compile:

```
public class Bunny implements Hop {
    public void printDetails() {
        System.out.println(getJumpHeight());  // DOES NOT COMPILE
} }
```

Without an explicit reference to the name of the interface, the code will not compile, even though Bunny implements Hop. This can be easily fixed by using the interface name:

```
public class Bunny implements Hop {
    public void printDetails() {
        System.out.println(Hop.getJumpHeight());
} }
```

Notice we don't have the same problem we did when we inherited two `default` interface methods with the same signature. Java "solved" the multiple inheritance problem of `static` interface methods by not allowing them to be inherited!

Reusing Code with *private* Interface Methods

The last two types of concrete methods that can be added to interfaces are `private` and `private static` interface methods. Because both types of methods are `private`, they can only be used in the interface declaration in which they are declared. For this reason, they were added primarily to reduce code duplication. For example, consider the following code sample:

```java
public interface Schedule {
    default void wakeUp()       { checkTime(7);  }
    private void haveBreakfast() { checkTime(9);  }
    static void workOut()       { checkTime(18); }
    private static void checkTime(int hour) {
        if (hour > 17) {
            System.out.println("You're late!");
        } else {
            System.out.println("You have "+(17-hour)+" hours left "
                + "to make the appointment");
        }
    }
}
```

You could write this interface without using a `private` method by copying the contents of the `checkTime()` method into the places it is used. It's a lot shorter and easier to read if you don't! Since the authors of Java were nice enough to add this feature for our convenience, we might as well use it!

We could have also declared `checkTime()` as public in the previous example, but this would expose the method to use outside the interface. One important tenet of encapsulation is to not expose the internal workings of a class or interface when not required. We cover encapsulation later in this chapter.

The difference between a non-`static` `private` method and a `static` one is analogous to the difference between an instance and `static` method declared within a class. In particular, it's all about what methods each can be called from.

Private Interface Method Definition Rules

1. A `private` interface method must be marked with the `private` modifier and include a method body.

2. A `private static` interface method may be called by any method within the interface definition.

3. A `private` interface method may only be called by `default` and other `private` non-`static` methods within the interface definition.

Another way to think of it is that a `private` interface method is only accessible to non-`static` methods defined within the interface. A `private static` interface method, on the other hand, can be accessed by any method in the interface. For both types of `private` methods, a class inheriting the interface cannot directly invoke them.

Reviewing Interface Members

We conclude our discussion of interface members with Table 7.2, which shows the access rules for members within and outside an interface.

TABLE 7.2   Interface member access

	Accessible from `default` and `private` methods within the interface?	Accessible from `static` methods within the interface?	Accessible from methods in classes inheriting the interface?	Accessible without an instance of the interface?
Constant variable	Yes	Yes	Yes	Yes
`abstract` method	Yes	No	Yes	No
`default` method	Yes	No	Yes	No
`static` method	Yes	Yes	Yes (interface name required)	Yes (interface name required)
`private` method	Yes	No	No	No
`private static` method	Yes	Yes	No	No

While Table 7.2 might seem like a lot to remember, here are some quick tips for the exam:

- Treat `abstract`, `default`, and non-`static` `private` methods as belonging to an instance of the interface.
- Treat `static` methods and variables as belonging to the interface class object.
- All `private` interface method types are only accessible within the interface declaration.

Using these rules, which of the following methods do not compile?

```
public interface ZooTrainTour {
    abstract int getTrainName();
    private static void ride() {}
    default void playHorn() { getTrainName(); ride(); }
    public static void slowDown() { playHorn(); }
    static void speedUp() { ride(); }
}
```

The `ride()` method is `private` and `static`, so it can be accessed by any `default` or `static` method within the interface declaration. The `getTrainName()` is abstract, so it can be accessed by a `default` method associated with the instance. The `slowDown()` method is `static`, though, and cannot call a `default` or `private` method, such as `playHorn()`, without an explicit reference object. Therefore, the `slowDown()` method does not compile.

Give yourself a pat on the back! You just learned a lot about interfaces, probably more than you thought possible. Now take a deep breath. Ready? The next type we are going to cover is enums.

Working with Enums

In programming, it is common to have a type that can only have a finite set of values, such as days of the week, seasons of the year, primary colors, and so on. An *enumeration*, or *enum* for short, is like a fixed set of constants.

Using an enum is much better than using a bunch of constants because it provides type-safe checking. With numeric or `String` constants, you can pass an invalid value and not find out until runtime. With enums, it is impossible to create an invalid enum value without introducing a compiler error.

Enumerations show up whenever you have a set of items whose types are known at compile time. Common examples include the compass directions, the months of the year, the planets in the solar system, and the cards in a deck (well, maybe not the planets in a solar system, given that Pluto had its planetary status revoked).

Creating Simple Enums

To create an enum, declare a type with the `enum` keyword, a name, and a list of values, as shown in Figure 7.4.

We refer to an enum that only contains a list of values as a *simple enum*. When working with simple enums, the semicolon at the end of the list is optional. Keep the `Season` enum handy, as we use it throughout this section.

FIGURE 7.4   Defining a simple enum

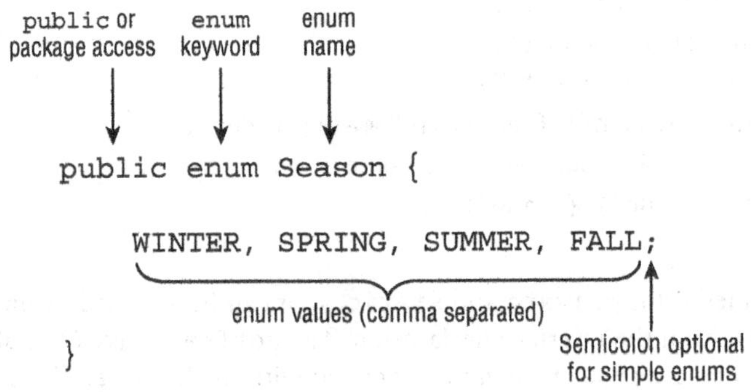

```
public or      enum      enum
package access keyword   name

      ↓          ↓        ↓

   public enum Season {

      WINTER, SPRING, SUMMER, FALL;

         enum values (comma separated)
                                        Semicolon optional
   }                                    for simple enums
```

Enum values are considered constants and are commonly written using snake_case. For example, an enum declaring a list of ice cream flavors might include values like VANILLA, ROCKY_ROAD, MINT_CHOCOLATE_CHIP, and so on.

Using an enum is super easy.

```
var s = Season.SUMMER;
System.out.println(Season.SUMMER);        // SUMMER
System.out.println(s == Season.SUMMER);   // true
```

As you can see, enums print the name of the enum when toString() is called. They can be compared using == because they are like static final constants. In other words, you can use equals() or == to compare enums, since each enum value is initialized only once in the Java Virtual Machine (JVM).

One thing that you can't do is extend an enum.

```
public enum ExtendedSeason extends Season {} // DOES NOT COMPILE
```

The values in an enum are fixed. You cannot add more by extending the enum nor can you mark an enum final. On the other hand, an enum can implement an interface, which we will cover shortly.

Calling Common Enum Methods

An enum provides a values() method to get an array of all of the values. You can use this like any normal array, including in a for-each loop. In addition, each enum value includes two methods, name() and ordinal(). The following shows all three methods:

```
for(var season: Season.values()) {
   System.out.println(season.name() + " " + season.ordinal());
}
```

The ordinal() method returns an int value, which denotes the order in which the value is declared in the enum:

```
WINTER 0
SPRING 1
SUMMER 2
FALL 3
```

In general, code is easier to read if you stick to the human-readable enum value, rather than the ordinal() value. You also can't compare an int and an enum value directly anyway since an enum value is an object.

```
if (Season.SUMMER == 2) {} // DOES NOT COMPILE
```

An enum provides a useful valueOf() method for converting from a String to an enum value. This is helpful when working with older code or parsing user input. The String passed in must match the enum value exactly, though.

```
Season s = Season.valueOf("SUMMER"); // SUMMER
Season t = Season.valueOf("summer"); // IllegalArgumentException
```

The first statement works and assigns the proper enum value to s. Note that this line is not creating an enum value, at least not directly. Each enum value is created once when the enum is first loaded. Once the enum has been loaded, it retrieves the single enum value with the matching name.

The second statement encounters a problem. There is no enum value with the lowercase name summer. Java throws up its hands in defeat and throws an IllegalArgumentException.

Using Enums in *switch* Statements

As we saw in Chapter 3, "Making Decisions," enums can be used in switch statements and expressions. Enums have the unique property that they do not require a default branch for an exhaustive switch if all enum values are handled.

```
String getWeather(Season value) {
    return switch (value) {
        case SUMMER        -> "Too hot";
        case Season.WINTER -> "Too cold";
        case SPRING, FALL  -> "Just right";
    };
}
```

A default branch can also be added but is not required, so long as all values are handled. Also notice that within each case clause, the name of the enum, Season, is now optional. In previous versions of Java, the name of the enum was disallowed.

While each enum value has an accompanying ordinal value, it cannot be used directly within a `case` clause. For example, this does not compile:

```
String getWeather(Season value) {
   return switch (value) {
      case SUMMER -> "Too hot";
      case 0       -> "Too cold";  // DOES NOT COMPILE
      default      -> "Just right";
   };
}
```

Working with Complex Enums

While a simple enum is composed of just a list of values, we can define a *complex enum* with additional elements. Let's say our zoo wants to keep track of traffic patterns to determine which seasons get the most visitors.

```
21: interface Visitors { void printVisitors(); }
22: enum SeasonWithVisitors implements Visitors {
23:    WINTER("Low"), SPRING("Medium"), SUMMER("High"), FALL("Medium");
24:
25:    private final String visitors;
26:    public static final String DESCRIPTION = "Weather enum";
27:    private SeasonWithVisitors(String visitors) {
28:       System.out.print("constructing,");
29:       this.visitors = visitors;
30:    }
31:    @Override public void printVisitors() {
32:       System.out.println(visitors);
33:    } }
```

There are a few things to notice here. On line 23, the list of enum values ends with a semicolon (`;`). While this is optional for a simple enum, it is required if there is anything in the enum besides the values. Lines 25–33 are regular Java code. We have instance and `static` variables (lines 25–26), a constructor (lines 27–30), and a method (lines 31–33).

 You might have noticed that in our enum example, the list of values comes first. This was not an accident. For complex enums (and trivially simple enums), the list of values always comes first.

Creating Enum Variables

An enum declaration can include both `static` and instance variables. In our `SeasonWithVisitors` implementation (lines 25–26), we mark the variables `final`, so that our enum properties cannot be modified.

Although it is possible to create an enum with instance variables that can be modified, it is a very poor practice to do so since they are shared within the JVM. When designing enum values, they should be immutable.

Declaring Enum Constructors

All enum constructors are implicitly `private`, with the modifier being optional. This is reasonable since you can't extend an enum and the constructors can be called only within the enum itself. In fact, an enum constructor will not compile if it contains a `public` or `protected` modifier.

```
27:     public SeasonWithVisitors(String visitors) {  // DOES NOT COMPILE
```

What about all of the parentheses on line 23 of our `SeasonWithVisitors` enum? Those are constructor calls, but without the new keyword normally used for objects. The first time we ask for any of the enum values, Java constructs all of the enum values. After that, Java just returns the already constructed enum values.

Given this explanation, you can see why this code snippet calls each constructor only once:

```
System.out.print("begin,");
var firstCall = SeasonWithVisitors.SUMMER;    // Prints 4 times
System.out.print("middle,");
var secondCall = SeasonWithVisitors.SUMMER;   // Doesn't print anything
System.out.print("end");
```

This program prints the following:

begin,constructing,constructing,constructing,constructing,**middle**,**end**

If the `SeasonWithVisitors` enum was used earlier in the program (and therefore initialized sooner), then the line that declares the `firstCall` variable would not print anything.

Writing Enum Methods

Like a class, an enum can contain `static` and instance methods. An enum can even implement an interface as we saw on lines 21–22 of our `SeasonWithVisitors` enum. We include the `@Override` annotation on line 31 to make it clear it is an inherited method.

How do we call an enum instance method? That's easy, too: we just use the enum value followed by the method call.

```
SeasonWithVisitors.SUMMER.printVisitors();
```

Sometimes you want to define different methods for each enum. For example, our zoo has different seasonal hours. It is cold and gets dark early in the winter. We can keep track of the hours through instance variables, or we can let each enum value manage hours itself.

```
public enum SeasonWithTimes {
    WINTER {
        public String getHours() { return "10am-3pm"; }
    },
```

```
   SPRING {
      public String getHours() { return "9am-5pm"; }
   },
   SUMMER {
      public String getHours() { return "9am-7pm"; }
   },
   FALL {
      public String getHours() { return "9am-5pm"; }
   };
   public abstract String getHours();
}
```

What's going on here? It looks like we created an abstract class and a bunch of tiny subclasses. In a way, we are. The enum itself has an abstract method. This means that each and every enum value is required to implement this method. If we forget to implement the method for one of the values, we get a compiler error:

```
The enum constant WINTER must implement the abstract method getHours()
```

But what if we don't want each and every enum value to have a method? No problem. We can create an implementation for all values and override it only for the special cases.

```
public enum SeasonWithTimes {
   WINTER {
      public String getHours() { return "10am-3pm"; }
   },
   SUMMER {
      public String getHours() { return "9am-7pm"; }
   },
   SPRING, FALL;
   public String getHours() { return "9am-5pm"; }
}
```

This looks better. We only code the special cases and let the others use the enum-provided implementation.

> Just because an enum can have lots of methods doesn't mean that it should. Try to keep your enums simple. If your enum is more than a screen length or two, it is probably too long. When enums get too long or too complex, they are difficult to read.

Sealing Classes

An enum with many constructors, fields, and methods may start to resemble a full-featured class. What if we could create a class but limit the direct subclasses to a fixed set of classes? Enter sealed classes! A *sealed class* is a class that restricts which other classes may extend it.

Declaring a Sealed Class

Let's start with a simple example. A sealed class declares a list of classes that can extend it, while the subclasses declare that they extend the sealed class. Figure 7.5 declares a sealed class with two subclasses.

Figure 7.5 includes three keywords that you should be familiar with for the exam.

FIGURE 7.5   Defining a sealed class

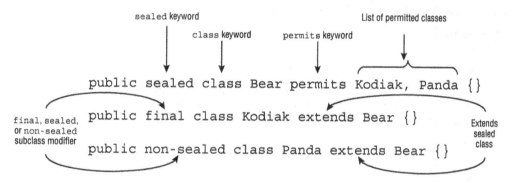

Sealed Class Keywords

- **sealed**: Indicates that a class or interface may only be extended/implemented by named classes or interfaces

- **permits**: Used with the `sealed` keyword to list the classes and interfaces allowed

- **non-sealed**: Applied to a class or interface that extends a sealed class, indicating that it can be extended by unspecified classes

Pretty easy so far, right? The exam is just as likely to test you on what sealed classes cannot be used for. For example, can you see why each of these two sets of declarations do not compile?

```
public class sealed Frog permits GlassFrog {}  // DOES NOT COMPILE
public final class GlassFrog extends Frog {}
```

```
public abstract sealed class Mammal permits Wolf {}
public final class Wolf extends Mammal {}
public final class Tiger extends Mammal {}  // DOES NOT COMPILE
```

The first example does not compile because the `class` and `sealed` modifiers are in the wrong order. The modifier has to be before the `class` type. The second example does not compile because `Tiger` isn't listed in the declaration of `Mammal`.

 NOTE   Sealed classes are commonly declared with the `abstract` modifier, although this is certainly not required.

Declaring a sealed class with the `sealed` modifier is the easy part. Most of the time, if you see a question on the exam about sealed classes, they are testing your knowledge of whether the subclass extends the sealed class properly. There are a number of important rules you need to know for the exam, so read the next sections carefully.

Compiling Sealed Classes

Let's say we create a `Penguin` class and compile it in a new package without any other source code. With that in mind, does the following compile?

```
// Penguin.java
package zoo;
public sealed class Penguin permits Emperor {}
```

No, it does not! Why? The answer is that a sealed class needs to be declared (and compiled) in the same package as its direct subclasses. But what about the subclasses themselves? They must each extend the sealed class. For example, the following two declarations do not compile:

```
// Penguin.java
package zoo;
public sealed class Penguin permits Emperor {}   // DOES NOT COMPILE
```

```
// Emperor.java
package zoo;
public final class Emperor {}
```

Even though the `Emperor` class is declared, it does not extend the `Penguin` class.

> **NOTE**   But wait, there's more! In Chapter 12, "Modules," you learn about *named modules*, which allow sealed classes and their direct subclasses in different packages, provided they are in the same named module.

Specifying the Subclass Modifier

While some types, like interfaces, have a certain number of implicit modifiers, sealed classes do not. *Every class that directly extends a sealed class must specify exactly one of the following three modifiers*: `final`, `sealed`, or `non-sealed`. Remember this rule for the exam!

Creating *final* Subclasses

The first modifier we're going to look at that can be applied to a direct subclass of a sealed class is the `final` modifier. A sealed class with only `final` subclasses has a fixed set of types, which is similar to an enum with a fixed set of values.

```
public sealed class Antelope permits Gazelle {}

public final class Gazelle extends Antelope {}

public class DamaGazelle extends Gazelle {}  // DOES NOT COMPILE
```

Just as with a regular class, the `final` modifier prevents the subclass `Gazelle` from being extended further.

Creating *sealed* Subclasses

Next, let's look at an example using the `sealed` modifier:

```
public sealed class Fish permits ClownFish {}

public sealed class ClownFish extends Fish permits OrangeClownFish {}

public final class OrangeClownFish extends ClownFish {}
```

The `sealed` modifier applied to the subclass `ClownFish` means the same kind of rules that we applied to the parent class `Fish` must be present. Namely, `ClownFish` defines its own list of permitted subclasses. Notice in this example that `OrangeClownFish` is an indirect subclass of `Fish` but is not named in the `Fish` class.

Despite allowing indirect subclasses not named in `Fish`, the list of classes that can inherit `Fish` is still fixed at compile time. If you have a reference to a `Fish` object, it must be a `Fish`, `ClownFish`, or `OrangeClownFish`.

Creating *non-sealed* Subclasses

The non-`sealed` modifier is used to open a sealed parent class to potentially unknown subclasses.

```
abstract sealed class Mammal permits Feline {}
non-sealed class Feline extends Mammal {}
class Tiger extends Feline {}
```

In this example, we are able to create an indirect subclass of `Mammal`, called `Tiger`, not named in the declaration of `Mammal`. Also notice that `Tiger` is not `final`, so it may be extended by any subclass, such as `BengalTiger`.

```
class BengalTiger extends Tiger {}
```

At first glance, this might seem a bit counterintuitive. After all, we were able to create subclasses of `Mammal` that were not declared in `Mammal`. So is `Mammal` still sealed? Yes, but that's thanks to polymorphism. Any instance of `Tiger` or `BengalTiger` is also an instance of `Feline`, which is named in the `Mammal` declaration. We discuss polymorphism more toward the end of this chapter. For now, you just need to understand that `Mammal` is sealed to `Feline` and its subclasses.

If you're still worried about opening a sealed class too much with a non-sealed subclass, remember that the person writing the sealed class can see the declaration of all direct subclasses at compile time. They can decide whether to allow the non-sealed subclass to be supported.

Omitting the *permits* Clause

Up until now, all of the examples you've seen have required a permits clause when declaring a sealed class, but this is not always the case. Imagine that you have a Snake.java file with two top-level classes defined inside it:

```
// Snake.java
public sealed class Snake permits Cobra {}
final class Cobra extends Snake {}
```

In this case, the permits clause is optional and can be omitted. The extends keyword is still required in the subclass, though:

```
// Snake.java
public sealed class Snake {}
final class Cobra extends Snake {}
```

If these classes were in separate files, this code would not compile! To omit the permits clause, the declarations must be in the same file.

The permits clause can also be omitted if the subclasses are nested.

```
public sealed class Snake {
    final class Cobra extends Snake {}
}
```

We cover nested classes shortly. For now, you just need to know that a nested class is a class defined inside another class and that the omit rule also applies to nested classes. Table 7.3 is a handy reference to these cases.

TABLE 7.3 Usage of the permits clause in sealed classes

Location of direct subclasses	permits clause
In a different file from the sealed class	Required
In the same file as the sealed class	Permitted, but not required
Nested inside of the sealed class	Permitted, but not required

---

Referencing Nested Subclasses

While it makes the code easier to read if you omit the `permits` clause for nested sub-classes, you are welcome to name them. However, the syntax might be different than you expect.

```
public sealed class Snake permits Cobra {  // DOES NOT COMPILE
    final class Cobra extends Snake {}
}
```

This code does not compile because Cobra requires a reference to the Snake namespace. The following fixes this issue:

```
public sealed class Snake permits Snake.Cobra {
    final class Cobra extends Snake {}
}
```

When all of your subclasses are nested, we strongly recommend omitting the `permits` class.

Sealing Interfaces

Besides classes, interfaces can also be sealed. The idea is analogous to classes, and many of the same rules apply. For example, the sealed interface must appear in the same package or named module as the classes or interfaces that directly extend or implement it.

One distinct feature of a sealed interface is that the `permits` list can apply to *a class that implements the interface* or *an interface that extends the interface*.

```
// Sealed interface
public sealed interface Swims permits Duck, Swan, Floats {}

// Classes permitted to implement sealed interface
public final class Duck implements Swims {}
public final class Swan implements Swims {}

// Interface permitted to extend sealed interface
public non-sealed interface Floats extends Swims {}
```

What modifiers are permitted for interfaces that extend a sealed interface? Well, remember that interfaces are implicitly `abstract` and cannot be marked `final`. For this reason, interfaces that extend a sealed interface can only be marked `sealed` or `non-sealed`. They cannot be marked `final`.

Applying Pattern Matching to a Sealed Class

Remember from Chapter 3, switch now supports pattern matching. Imagine if we could treat a sealed class like an enum in a switch by applying pattern matching. Well, we can! Given a sealed class Fish with two direct subclasses:

```
abstract sealed class Fish permits Trout, Bass {}
final class Trout extends Fish {}
final class Bass extends Fish {}
```

We can define a switch expression that does not require a default clause:

```
public String getType(Fish fish) {
   return switch (fish) {
      case Trout t -> "Trout!";
      case Bass b -> "Bass!";
   };
}
```

This only works because Fish is abstract and sealed, and all possible subclasses are handled. If we remove the abstract modifier in the Fish declaration, then the switch expression would not compile. As an exercise to the reader, see if you can figure out how many different ways there are to change the switch expression that would allow it to compile again.

Like enums, make sure that if a switch uses a sealed class with pattern matching that all possible types are covered or a default clause is included.

Reviewing Sealed Class Rules

Any time you see a sealed class on the exam, pay close attention to the subclass declaration and modifiers.

Sealed Class Rules

- Sealed classes are declared with the sealed and permits modifiers.
- Sealed classes must be declared in the same package or named module as their direct subclasses.
- Direct subclasses of sealed classes must be marked final, sealed, or non-sealed. For interfaces that extend a sealed interface, only sealed and non-sealed modifiers are permitted.
- The permits clause is optional if the sealed class and its direct subclasses are declared within the same file or the subclasses are nested within the sealed class.
- Interfaces can be sealed to limit the classes that implement them or the interfaces that extend them.

Encapsulating Data with Records

Records are incredibly useful tools for creating data-oriented classes that remove a ton of boilerplate code. Before we get into records, it helps to have some context of why they were added to the language, so we start with encapsulation.

Understanding Encapsulation

A *POJO*, which stands for Plain Old Java Object, is a class used to model and pass data around, often with few or no complex methods (hence the "plain" part of the definition). You might have also heard of a JavaBean, which is POJO that has some additional rules applied.

Let's create a simple POJO with two fields:

```
public class Crane {
    int numberEggs;
    String name;
    public Crane(int numberEggs, String name) {
        this.numberEggs = numberEggs;
        this.name = name;
    }
}
```

Uh oh, the fields are package access. Why do we care? That means someone outside the class in the same package could change these values and create invalid data such as this:

```
public class Poacher {
    public void badActor() {
        var mother = new Crane(5, "Cathy");
        mother.numberEggs = -100;
    }
}
```

This is clearly no good. We do not want the mother `Crane` to have a negative number of eggs! Encapsulation to the rescue. *Encapsulation* is a way to protect class members by restricting access to them. In Java, it is commonly implemented by declaring all instance variables `private`. Callers are required to use methods to retrieve or modify instance variables.

Encapsulation is about protecting a class from unexpected use. It also allows us to modify the methods and behavior of the class later without someone already having direct access to an instance variable within the class. For example, we can change the data type of an instance variable but maintain the same method signatures. In this manner, we maintain full control over the internal workings of a class.

Let's take a look at the newly encapsulated (and immutable) Crane class:

```
1:  public final class Crane {
2:      private final int numberEggs;
3:      private final String name;
4:      public Crane(int numberEggs, String name) {
5:          if (numberEggs >= 0) this.numberEggs = numberEggs;  // guard
6:          else throw new IllegalArgumentException();
7:          this.name = name;
8:      }
9:      public int getNumberEggs() {              // getter
10:         return numberEggs;
11:     }
12:     public String getName() {                 // getter
13:         return name;
14:     }
15: }
```

Note that the instance variables are now private on lines 2 and 3. This means only code within the class can read or write their values. Since we wrote the class, we know better than to set a negative number of eggs. We added a method on lines 9–11 to read the value, which is called an *accessor method* or a getter.

You might have noticed that we marked the class and its instance variables final, and we don't have any *mutator methods*, or setters, to modify the value of the instance variables. That's because we want our class to be immutable in addition to being well encapsulated. As you saw in Chapter 6, the immutable objects pattern is an object-oriented design pattern in which an object cannot be modified after it is created. Instead of modifying an immutable object, you create a new object that contains any properties from the original object you want copied over.

To review, remember that data is private and getters/setters are public. You don't even have to provide getters and setters. As long as the instance variables are private, you are good. For example, the following class is well encapsulated, although it is not terribly useful since it doesn't declare any non-private methods:

```
public class Vet {
    private String name = "Dr Rogers";
    private int yearsExperience = 25;
}
```

You must omit the setters for a class to be immutable. Review Chapter 6 for the additional rules on creating immutable objects.

Applying Records

Our Crane class was 15 lines long. We can write that much more succinctly, as shown in Figure 7.6. Putting aside the guard clause on numberEggs in the constructor for a moment, this record is equivalent and immutable!

FIGURE 7.6   Defining a record

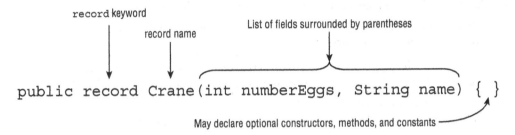

Wow! It's only one line long! A *record* is a special type of data-oriented class in which the compiler inserts boilerplate code for you.

In fact, the compiler inserts *much more* than the 14 lines we wrote earlier. As a bonus, the compiler inserts *useful* implementations of the Object methods equals(), hashCode(), and toString(). We've covered a lot in one line of code!

Now imagine that we had 10 data fields instead of 2. That's a lot of methods we are saved from writing. And we haven't even talked about constructors! Worse yet, any time someone changes a field, dozens of lines of related code may need to be updated. For example, name may be used in the constructor, toString(), equals() method, and so on. If we have an application with hundreds of POJOs, a record can save us valuable time.

Creating an instance of a Crane and printing some fields is easy:

```
var mommy = new Crane(4, "Cammy");
System.out.println(mommy.numberEggs());  // 4
System.out.println(mommy.name());        // Cammy
```

A few things should stand out here. First, we never defined any constructors or methods in our Crane declaration. How does the compiler know what to do? Behind the scenes, it creates a constructor for you with the parameters in the same order in which they appear in the record declaration. Omitting or changing the type order will lead to compiler errors:

```
var mommy1 = new Crane("Cammy", 4);  // DOES NOT COMPILE
var mommy2 = new Crane("Cammy");     // DOES NOT COMPILE
```

For each field, it also creates an accessor as the field name, plus a set of parentheses. Unlike traditional POJOs or JavaBeans, the methods don't have the prefix get or is. Just a few more characters that records save you from having to type! Finally, records override a number of methods in Object for you.

Members Automatically Added to Records

- **Constructor**: A constructor with the parameters in the same order as the record declaration
- **Accessor method**: One accessor for each field
- **equals()**: A method to compare two elements that returns `true` if each field is equal in terms of `equals()`
- **hashCode()**: A consistent `hashCode()` method using all of the fields
- **toString()**: A `toString()` implementation that prints each field of the record in a convenient, easy-to-read format

The following shows examples of the new methods. Remember that the `println()` method will call the `toString()` method automatically on any object passed to it.

```
var father = new Crane(0, "Craig");
System.out.println(father);              // Crane[numberEggs=0, name=Craig]

var copy = new Crane(0, "Craig");
System.out.println(copy);                // Crane[numberEggs=0, name=Craig]
System.out.println(father.equals(copy)); // true
System.out.println(father.hashCode() + ", " + copy.hashCode()); // 1007, 1007
```

That's the basics of records. We say "basics" because there's a lot more you can do with them, as you see in the next sections.

Given our one-line declaration of Crane, imagine how much code and work would be required to write an equivalent class. It could easily take 40+ lines! It might be a fun exercise to try to write all the methods that records supply.

Fun fact: it is legal to have a record without any fields. It is simply declared with the `record` keyword and parentheses:

```
public record Crane() {}
```

This is not the kind of thing you'd use in your own code, but it could come up on the exam.

Declaring Constructors

What if you need to declare a record with some guards as we did earlier? In this section, we cover two ways we can accomplish this with records.

The Long Constructor

First, we can just declare the constructor the compiler normally inserts automatically, which we refer to as the *long constructor*.

```
public record Crane(int numberEggs, String name) {
   public Crane(int numberEggs, String name) {
      if (numberEggs < 0) throw new IllegalArgumentException();
      this.numberEggs = numberEggs;
      this.name = name;
   }
}
```

The compiler will not insert a constructor if you define one with the same list of parameters in the same order. Since each field is final, the constructor must set every field. For example, this record does not compile:

```
public record Crane(int numberEggs, String name) {
   public Crane(int numberEggs, String name) {}  // DOES NOT COMPILE
}
```

While being able to declare a constructor is a nice feature of records, it's also problematic. If we have 20 fields, we'll need to declare assignments for every one, introducing the boilerplate we sought to remove. Oh, bother!

Compact Constructors

Luckily, the authors of Java added the ability to define a compact constructor for records. A *compact constructor* is a special type of constructor used for records to process validation and transformations succinctly. It takes no parameters and implicitly sets all fields. Figure 7.7 shows an example of a compact constructor.

FIGURE 7.7 Declaring a compact constructor

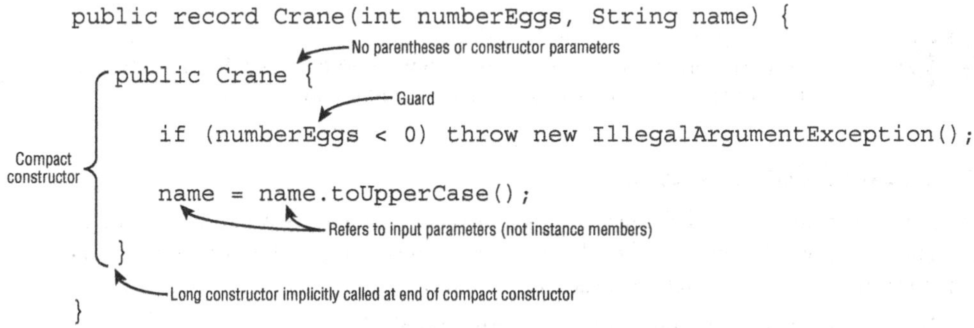

Great! Now we can check the values we want, and we don't have to list all the constructor parameters and trivial assignments. Java will execute the full constructor after the compact constructor. You should also remember that a compact constructor is declared without parentheses, as the exam might try to trick you on this. As shown in Figure 7.7, we can even transform constructor parameters as we discuss more in the next section.

Transforming Parameters

Compact constructors give you the opportunity to apply transformations to any of the input values. See if you can figure out what the following compact constructor does:

```java
public record Crane(int numberEggs, String name) {
   public Crane {
      if (name == null || name.length() < 1)
         throw new IllegalArgumentException();
      name = name.substring(0, 1).toUpperCase()
         + name.substring(1).toLowerCase();
   }
}
```

Give up? It validates the string, then formats it such that only the first letter is capitalized. As before, Java calls the full constructor after the compact constructor but with the modified constructor parameters.

While compact constructors can modify the constructor parameters, *they cannot modify the fields of the record*. For example, this does not compile:

```java
public record Crane(int numberEggs, String name) {
   public Crane {
      this.numberEggs = 10;   // DOES NOT COMPILE
   }
}
```

Removing the this reference allows the code to compile, as the constructor parameter is modified instead.

> Although we covered both the long and compact forms of record constructors in this section, it is highly recommended that you stick with the compact form unless you have a good reason not to.

Overloaded Constructors

You can also create overloaded constructors that take a completely different list of parameters. They are more closely related to the long-form constructor and don't use any of the syntactical features of compact constructors.

```java
public record Crane(int numberEggs, String name) {
   public Crane(String firstName, String lastName) {
      this(0, firstName + " " + lastName);
   }
}
```

The first line of an overloaded constructor must be an explicit call to another constructor via this(). If there are no other constructors, the long constructor must be called. Contrast this with what you learned about in Chapter 6, where calling super() or this() was often optional in constructor declarations. Also, unlike compact constructors, you can only transform the data on the first line. After the first line, all of the fields will already be assigned, and the object is immutable.

```
public record Crane(int numberEggs, String name) {
    public Crane(int numberEggs, String firstName, String lastName) {
        this(numberEggs + 1, firstName + " " + lastName);
        numberEggs = 10; // NO EFFECT (applies to parameter, not instance field)
        this.numberEggs = 20; // DOES NOT COMPILE
    }
}
```

 Only the long constructor, with fields that match the record declaration, supports setting field values with a this reference. Compact and overloaded constructors do not.

As you saw in Chapter 6, you also can't declare two record constructors that call each other infinitely or as a cycle.

```
public record Crane(int numberEggs, String name) {
    public Crane(String name) {
        this(1);   // DOES NOT COMPILE
    }
    public Crane(int numberEggs) {
        this("");   // DOES NOT COMPILE
    }
}
```

Understanding Record Immutability

As you saw, records don't have setters. Every field is inherently final and cannot be modified after it has been written in the constructor. To "modify" a record, you have to make a new object and copy all of the data you want to preserve.

```
var cousin = new Crane(3, "Jenny");
var friend = new Crane(cousin.numberEggs(), "Janeice");
```

Just as interfaces are implicitly abstract, records are also *implicitly* final. The final modifier is optional but assumed.

```
public final record Crane(int numberEggs, String name) {}
```

Like enums, that means you can't extend or inherit a record.

```
public record BlueCrane() extends Crane {}   // DOES NOT COMPILE
```

Also like enums, a record can implement a regular or sealed interface, provided it implements all of the abstract methods.

```
public interface Bird {}
public record Crane(int numberEggs, String name) implements Bird {}
```

While instance members of a record are final, the static members are not required to be. For example, the following defines an immutable record in which a static value is updated every time a record is created.

```
public record WhoopingCrane(String name, int position) {
   private static int counter = 0;
   public WhoopingCrane(String name) {
      this(name, counter++);
   }
}
```

Although well beyond the scope of this book, there are some good reasons to make data-oriented classes immutable. Doing so can lead to less error-prone code, as a new object is established any time the data is modified. It also makes them inherently thread-safe and usable in concurrent frameworks.

Using Pattern Matching with Records

New to Java 21, records have been updated to support pattern matching. Initially, you might think this is not actually something new. After all, we could use records with pattern matching in Java 17. The new feature is really about the *members of the record*, rather than the record itself. Let's try an example:

```
1:   record Monkey(String name, int age) {}
2:
3:   public class Zoo {
4:      public static void main(String[] args) {
5:
6:         Object animal = new Monkey("George", 3);
7:
8:         if(animal instanceof Monkey(String name, int myAge)) {
9:            System.out.println("Hello " + name);
10:           System.out.println("Your age is " + myAge);
11:        } } }
```

Wait, what's going on in line 8? It looks like we redeclared the declaration of the record. Don't worry, we didn't! What we did do, though, is define a pattern that is compatible with the Monkey record. We also named two elements, name and myAge. Like the pattern matching you saw in Chapter 3, this allows us to use them as local variables on line 9 and 10, without a reference variable.

For the exam, you should be aware of the following rules when working with pattern matching and records:

- If any field declared in the record is included, then all fields must be included.

- The order of fields must be the same as in the record.

- The names of the fields do not have to match.

- At compile time, the type of the field must be compatible with the type declared in the record.

- The pattern may not match at runtime if the record supports elements of various types.

Working with records and pattern matching has some similarities to casting. For example, the compiler will disallow things that it knows to be invalid. There are some differences, though, that we will get to shortly.

Quiz time! Given our previous Monkey record, which of the following lines of code do not compile?

```
11: if(animal instanceof Monkey myMonkey) {}
12: if(animal instanceof Monkey(String n, int a) myMonkey) {}
13: if(animal instanceof Monkey(String n, long a)) {}
14: if(animal instanceof Monkey(Object n, int a)) {}
```

The first example compiles, as this is just simple pattern matching that we saw in Chapter 3. Line 12 does not compile, though. You can name the record or its fields, but not both. Line 13 also does not compile, as numeric promotion is not supported. The last line does compile, as String is compatible with Object.

Matching Records

The last two rules for record matching warrant a bit more discussion. Pattern matching for records include matching both the type of the record *and the type of each field*. Given the five pattern matching statements, what does the following code print?

```
1:  record Fish(Object type) {}
2:  public class Veterinarian {
3:      public static void main(String[] args) {
4:          Fish f1 = new Fish("Nemo");
5:          Fish f2 = new Fish(Integer.valueOf(1));
6:
7:          if(f1 instanceof Fish(Object t)) {
8:              System.out.print("Match1-");
```

```
9:         }
10:        if(f1 instanceof Fish(String t)) {
11:            System.out.print("Match2-");
12:        }
13:        if(f1 instanceof Fish(Integer t)) {
14:            System.out.print("Match3-");
15:        }
16:        if(f2 instanceof Fish(String t)) {
17:            System.out.print("Match4-");
18:        }
19:        if(f2 instanceof Fish(Integer x)) {
20:            System.out.print("Match5");
21:    } } }
```

The first and second pattern matching statements match because "Nemo" can be implicitly cast to Object and String, respectively. The third statement compiles but does not match, as "Nemo" cannot be cast to Integer. Likewise, the fourth statement compiles but does not match, as the numeric value cannot be cast to String. Finally, the last statement matches as the type of both is Integer. The code compiles and prints the following at runtime:

```
Match1-Match2-Match5
```

What happens if we change the declaration of Fish to the following?

```
1:  record Fish(Integer type) {}
```

First off, our f1 variable declared on line 4 would no longer compile! Assuming we fix the variable declaration, though, lines 10 and 16 would not compile. The compiler is smart enough to know that no instance of Fish is capable of matching an Integer to a String.

Nesting Record Patterns

If a record includes other record values as members, then you can *optionally* pattern match the fields within the record. Ready to see how this works? Let's start with two records.

```
record Bear(String name, List<String> favoriteThings) {}
record Couple(Bear a, Bear b) {}
```

Now, let's say we define a Couple instance within a method.

```
var c = new Couple(new Bear("Yogi", List.of("PicnicBaskets")),
    new Bear("Fozzie", List.of("BadJokes")));
```

Which of the following pattern matching statements compile?

```
if(c instanceof Couple(Bear a, Bear b)) {
    System.out.print(a.name() + " " + b.name());
}
if(c instanceof Couple(Bear(String firstName, List<String> f),
```

```java
        Bear b)) {
     System.out.print(firstName + " " + b.name());
}
if(c instanceof Couple(Bear(String name, List<String> f1),
        Bear(String name, List<String> f2))) {
     System.out.print(name + " " + name);
}
```

The first pattern matching statement compiles and uses `Couple` without expanding the nested `Bear` records. The second example expands the first `Bear` record, making `firstName` and `b` local variables within the pattern matching statement. The third pattern matching statement does not compile. Although you can expand both records, you have to give them distinct names. We can fix this, though, by expanding the nested types to have unique names.

```java
if(c instanceof Couple(Bear(String name1, List<String> f1),
        Bear(String name2, List<String> f2))) {
     System.out.print(name1 + " " + name2);
}
```

Matching Records with *var* and Generics

You can also use var in a pattern matching record. Let's apply this to our previous examples.

```java
var c = new Couple(new Bear("Yogi", List.of("PicnicBaskets")),
     new Bear("Fozzie", List.of("BadJokes")));

if (c instanceof Couple(var a, var b)) {
     System.out.print(a.name() + " " + b.name());
}
if (c instanceof Couple(Bear(var firstName, List<String> f), var b)) {
     System.out.print(firstName + " " + b.name());
}
```

As you can see, you can replace any element reference type with var. When var is used for one of the elements of the record, the compiler assumes the type to be the exact match for the type in the record.

Pattern matching generics within records follow the similar rules for overloading generic methods. Don't worry if you haven't seen overloading generics before, we'll be covering it in Chapter 9, "Collections and Generics." Let's try a few examples, though, to see the kinds of things that exam might throw at you. Each of the following compiles without issue:

```java
if(c instanceof Couple(Bear(var n, Object f),                 var b)) {}
if(c instanceof Couple(Bear(var n, List f),                   var b)) {}
if(c instanceof Couple(Bear(var n, List<?> f),                var b)) {}
if(c instanceof Couple(Bear(var n, List<? extends Object> f), var b)) {}
if(c instanceof Couple(Bear(var n, ArrayList<String> f),      var b)) {}
```

There are limits, though. For example, the following two examples do not compile:

```
if(c instanceof Couple(Bear(var n, List<> f),        var b)) {}
if(c instanceof Couple(Bear(var n, List<Object> f), var b)) {}
```

The first example does not compile because the diamond operator (<>) cannot be used for pattern matching (nor overloading generics). The second example does not compile because List<Object> is not compatible with List<String>. This would also not compile if these types were applied to method parameters of inherited methods, due to type erasure. Again, we'll be covering generics and type erasure in much more detail in Chapter 9.

In these examples, remember that f is the pattern type, not the original List<String>. Given this, can you deduce why this code does not compile?

```
if(c instanceof Couple(Bear(var n, List f), var b)
      && f.getFirst().toLowerCase().contains("p")) {  // DOES NOT COMPILE
   System.out.print("Yummy");
}
```

The reference type of f is List, not List<String>, therefore f.getFirst() returns an Object reference, not a String reference. Since toLowerCase() is not defined on Object, the code does not compile. To compile you would either have to explicitly cast it to a String or use a different pattern matching type.

Applying Pattern Matching Records to Switch

It might not be a surprise that you can use switch with pattern matching and records. The rules are the same as you've already learned, we're just combing the switch pattern matching rules you learned about in Chapter 3 with what we covered in this chapter.

Let's say we have a Snake record as follows:

```
record Snake(Object data) {}
```

Next, let's construct a method that operates on an instance of Snake.

```
long showData(Snake snake) {
   return switch(snake) {
      case Snake(Long hiss)      -> hiss + 1;
      case Snake(Integer nagina) -> nagina + 10;
      case Snake(Number crowley) -> crowley.intValue() + 100;
      case Snake(Object kaa)     -> -1;
   };
}
```

As you might recall from Chapter 3, a default clause is not required if all types are covered in the pattern matching expression. Given this code, see if you can follow the output generated by each of these examples:

```
System.out.println(showData(new Snake(1)));     // 11
System.out.println(showData(new Snake(2L)));    // 3
System.out.println(showData(new Snake(3.0)));   // 103
```

Remember, the type matters for any associated when clauses. For example, the following does not compile since kaa is of type Object, which does not have a doubleValue() method:

```
long showData(Snake snake) {
   return switch(snake) {
      case Snake(Object kaa) when kaa.doubleValue() > 0 -> -1;
      default -> 1_000;
   };
}
```

Congrats, you've learned everything you need to know about pattern matching with records for the exam. Since it's a new feature, expect to see at least one question on it!

Customizing Records

Since records are data-oriented, we've focused on the features of records you are likely to use. Records actually support many of the same features as a class. Here are some of the members that records can include and that you should be familiar with for the exam:

- Overloaded and compact constructors
- Instance methods including overriding any provided methods (accessors, equals(), hashCode(), toString())
- Nested classes, interfaces, annotations, enums, and records

As an illustrative example, the following overrides two instance methods using the optional @Override annotation:

```
public record Crane(int numberEggs, String name) {
   @Override public int numberEggs() { return 10; }
   @Override public String toString() { return name; }
}
```

While you can add methods, static fields, and other data types, *you cannot add instance fields outside the record declaration*, even if they are private and final. Doing so defeats the purpose of using a record and could break immutability!

```
public record Crane(int numberEggs, String name) {
   private static int TYPE = 10;
   public int size;                            // DOES NOT COMPILE
   private final boolean friendly = true;  // DOES NOT COMPILE
}
```

Records also do not support instance initializers. All initialization for the fields of a record must happen in a constructor. They do support static initializers, though.

```
public record Crane(int numberEggs, String name) {
   static { System.out.print("Hello Bird!"); }
```

```
    { System.out.print("Goodbye Bird!"); }    // DOES NOT COMPILE
    { this.name = "Big"; }                     // DOES NOT COMPILE
}
```

In this example, the first initializer compiles because it is `static`, while the second and third do not because they are instance initializers.

While it's a useful feature that records support many of the same members as a class, try to keep them simple. Like the POJOs and JavaBeans they were born out of, the more complicated they get, the less usable they become.

This is the second time we've mentioned nested types, the first being with sealed classes and now records. Don't worry; we're covering them soon!

Creating Nested Classes

A *nested class* is a class that is defined within another class. A nested class can come in one of four flavors, with all supporting instance and `static` variables as members.

- *Inner class*: A non-`static` type defined at the member level of a class
- *Static nested class*: A `static` type defined at the member level of a class
- *Local class*: A class defined within a method body
- *Anonymous class*: A special case of a local class that does not have a name

There are many benefits of using nested classes. They can define helper classes and restrict them to the containing class, thereby improving encapsulation. They can make it easy to create a class that will be used in only one place. They can even make the code cleaner and easier to read.

When used improperly, though, nested classes can sometimes make the code harder to read. They also tend to tightly couple the enclosing and inner class, but there may be cases where you want to use the inner class by itself. In this case, you should move the inner class out into a separate top-level class.

Unfortunately, the exam tests edge cases where programmers wouldn't typically use a nested class. This tends to create code that is difficult to read, so please never do this in practice!

By convention and throughout this chapter, we often use the term *nested class* to refer to all nested *types*, including nested interfaces, enums, records, and annotations. You might even come across literature that refers to all of them as inner classes. We agree that this can be confusing!

Declaring an Inner Class

An *inner class*, also called a *member inner class*, is a non-`static` type defined at the member level of a class (the same level as the methods, instance variables, and constructors). Because they are not top-level types, they can use any of the four access levels, not just `public` and package access.

Inner classes have the following properties:

- Can be declared `public`, `protected`, package, or `private`
- Can extend a class and implement interfaces
- Can be marked `abstract` or `final`
- Can access members of the outer class, including `private` members

The last property is pretty cool. It means that the inner class can access variables in the outer class without doing anything special. Ready for a complicated way to print `Hi` three times?

```
1:  public class Home {
2:      private String greeting = "Hi";  // Outer class instance variable
3:
4:      protected class Room {           // Inner class declaration
5:          public int repeat = 3;
6:          public void enter() {
7:              for (int i = 0; i < repeat; i++) greet(greeting);
8:          }
9:          private static void greet(String message) {
10:             System.out.println(message);
11:         }
12:     }
13:
14:     public void enterRoom() {        // Instance method in outer class
15:         var room = new Room();       // Create the inner class instance
16:         room.enter();
17:     }
18:     public static void main(String[] args) {
19:         var home = new Home();       // Create the outer class instance
20:         home.enterRoom();
21: } }
```

An inner class declaration looks just like a stand-alone class declaration except that it happens to be located inside another class. Line 7 shows that the inner class just refers to `greeting` as if it were available in the Room class. This works because it is, in fact, available. Even though the variable is `private`, it is accessed within that same class.

Since an inner class is not `static`, it has to be called using an instance of the outer class. That means you have to create two objects. Line 19 creates the outer Home object, while line 15 creates the inner Room object. It's important to notice that line 15 doesn't require an explicit instance of Home because it is an instance method within Home. This works because `enterRoom()` is an instance method within the Home class. Both Room and `enterRoom()` are members of Home.

Instantiating an Instance of an Inner Class

There is another way to instantiate Room that looks odd at first. OK, well, maybe not just at first. This syntax isn't used often enough to get used to it:

```
20:    public static void main(String[] args) {
21:        var home = new Home();
22:        Room room = home.new Room();   // Create the inner class instance
23:        room.enter();
24:    }
```

Let's take a closer look at lines 21 and 22. We need an instance of Home to create a Room. We can't just call new Room() inside the `static main()` method, because Java won't know which instance of Home it is associated with. Java solves this by calling new as if it were a method on the home variable. We can shorten lines 21–23 to a single line:

```
21:        new Home().new Room().enter();   // Sorry, it looks ugly to us too!
```

Creating .*class* Files for Inner Classes

Compiling the Home.java class with which we have been working creates two class files. You should be expecting the Home.class file. For the inner class, the compiler creates Home$Room.class. You don't need to know this syntax for the exam. We mention it so that you aren't surprised to see files with $ appearing in your directories. You do need to understand that multiple class files are created from a single .java file.

Referencing Members of an Inner Class

Inner classes can have the same variable names as outer classes, making scope a little tricky. There is a special way of calling this to say which variable you want to access. This is something you might see on the exam but, ideally, not in the real world.

In fact, you aren't limited to just one inner class. While the following is common on the exam, please never do this in code you write. Here is how to nest multiple classes and access a variable with the same name in each:

```
1:  public class A {
2:      private int x = 10;
```

```
3:     class B {
4:        private int x = 20;
5:        class C {
6:           private int x = 30;
7:           public void allTheX() {
8:              System.out.println(x);        // 30
9:              System.out.println(this.x);    // 30
10:             System.out.println(B.this.x); // 20
11:             System.out.println(A.this.x); // 10
12:     } } }
13:     public static void main(String[] args) {
14:        A a = new A();
15:        A.B b = a.new B();
16:        A.B.C c = b.new C();
17:        c.allTheX();
18: }}
```

Yes, this code makes us cringe too. It has two nested classes. Line 14 instantiates the outermost one. Line 15 uses the awkward syntax to instantiate a B. Notice that the type is A.B. We could have written B as the type because that is available at the member level of A. Java knows where to look for it. On line 16, we instantiate a C. This time, the A.B.C type is necessary to specify. C is too deep for Java to know where to look. Then line 17 calls a method on the instance variable c.

Lines 8 and 9 are the type of code that we are used to seeing. They refer to the instance variable on the current class—the one declared on line 6, to be precise. Line 10 uses this in a special way. We still want an instance variable. But this time, we want the one on the B class, which is the variable on line 4. Line 11 does the same thing for class A, getting the variable from line 2.

Inner Classes Require an Instance

Take a look at the following and see whether you can figure out why two of the three constructor calls do not compile:

```
public class Fox {
   private class Den {}
   public void goHome() {
      new Den();
   }
   public static void visitFriend() {
      new Den(); // DOES NOT COMPILE
```

```
      }
   }

   public class Squirrel {
      public void visitFox() {
         new Den();  // DOES NOT COMPILE
      }
   }
```

The first constructor call compiles because goHome() is an instance method, and therefore the call is associated with the this instance. The second call does not compile because it is called inside a static method. You can still call the constructor, but you have to explicitly give it a reference to a Fox instance.

The last constructor call does not compile for two reasons. Even though it is an instance method, it is not an instance method inside the Fox class. Adding a Fox reference would not fix the problem entirely, though. Den is private and not accessible in the Squirrel class.

Creating a *static* Nested Class

A *static nested class* is a static type defined at the member level. Unlike an inner class, a static nested class can be instantiated without an instance of the enclosing class. The trade-off, though, is that it can't access instance variables or methods declared in the outer class.

In other words, it is like a top-level class except for the following:

- The nesting creates a namespace because the enclosing class name must be used to refer to it.

- It can additionally be marked private or protected.

- The enclosing class can refer to the fields and methods of the static nested class.

Let's take a look at an example:

```
1: public class Park {
2:    static class Ride {
3:       private int price = 6;
4:    }
5:    public static void main(String[] args) {
6:       var ride = new Ride();
7:       System.out.println(ride.price);
8: } }
```

Line 6 instantiates the nested class. Since the class is static, you do not need an instance of Park to use it. You are allowed to access private instance variables, as shown on line 7.

Nested Records are Implicitly *static*

If you see a nested record, it is implicitly static. This means it can be used without a reference to the outer class. It also means it cannot access member variables of the outer class. We can compare and contrast this with two implementations of Emu, one that uses a record and the other that uses a class.

```
11: class Emu1 {
12:     String name = "Emmy";
13:     static Feathers createFeathers() {
14:         return new Feathers("grey");
15:     }
16:     record Feathers(String color) {
17:         void fly() {
18:             System.out.print(name + "  is flying");  // DOES NOT COMPILE
19:         } } }
20:
21: class Emu2 {
22:     String name = "Emmy";
23:     static Feathers createFeathers() {
24:         return new Feathers("grey");  // DOES NOT COMPILE
25:     }
26:     class Feathers {
27:         void fly() {
28:             System.out.print(name + "  is flying");
29:         } } }
```

Line 14 compiles without issue because the record is implicitly static. Line 24 does not compile, though, as the class version of Feathers is not static and would require an instance of Emu2 to create. Likewise, the outer variable, name, is only visible to the nested class if it is not static, as shown by line 28 compiling and line 18 not compiling.

Writing a Local Class

A *local class* is a nested class defined within a method. Like local variables, a local class declaration does not exist until the method is invoked, and it goes out of scope when the method returns. This means you can create instances only from within the method. Those instances can still be returned from the method. This is just how local variables work.

Local classes are not limited to being declared only inside methods. For example, they can be declared inside constructors and initializers. For simplicity, we limit our discussion to methods in this chapter.

Local classes have the following properties:

- Do not have an access modifier.
- Can be declared `final` or `abstract`.
- Can include instance and `static` members.
- Have access to all fields and methods of the enclosing class (when defined in an instance method).
- Can access `final` and effectively final local variables.

Remember when we presented effectively final in Chapter 5? Well, we said it would come in handy later, and it's later! If you need a refresher on `final` and effectively final, turn back to Chapter 5 now. Don't worry; we'll wait!

Ready for an example? Here's a complicated way to multiply two numbers:

```
1:   public class PrintNumbers {
2:       private int length = 5;
3:       public void calculate() {
4:           final int width = 20;
5:           class Calculator {
6:               public void multiply() {
7:                   System.out.print(length * width);
8:               }
9:           }
10:          var calculator = new Calculator();
11:          calculator.multiply();
12:      }
13:      public static void main(String[] args) {
14:          var printer = new PrintNumbers();
15:          printer.calculate();  // 100
16:      }
17: }
```

Lines 5–9 are the local class. That class's scope ends on line 12, where the method ends. Line 7 refers to an instance variable and a `final` local variable, so both variable references are allowed from within the local class.

Earlier, we made the statement that local variable references are allowed if they are `final` or effectively final. As an illustrative example, consider the following:

```
public void processData() {
   final int length = 5;
   int width = 10;
   int height = 2;
   class VolumeCalculator {
      public int multiply() {
         return length * width * height; // DOES NOT COMPILE
      }
   }
   width = 2;
}
```

The `length` and `height` variables are `final` and effectively final, respectively, so neither causes a compilation issue. On the other hand, the `width` variable is reassigned during the method, so it cannot be effectively final. For this reason, the local class declaration does not compile.

Defining an Anonymous Class

An *anonymous class* is a specialized form of a local class that does not have a name. It is declared and instantiated all in one statement using the new keyword, a type name with parentheses, and a set of braces {}. Anonymous classes must extend an existing class or implement an existing interface. They are useful when you have a short implementation that will not be used anywhere else. Here's an example:

```
1:  public class ZooGiftShop {
2:     abstract class SaleTodayOnly {
3:        abstract int dollarsOff();
4:     }
5:     public int admission(int basePrice) {
6:        SaleTodayOnly sale = new SaleTodayOnly() {
7:           int dollarsOff() { return 3; }
8:        };  // Don't forget the semicolon!
9:        return basePrice - sale.dollarsOff();
10: } }
```

Lines 2–4 define an `abstract` class. Lines 6–8 define the anonymous class. Notice how this anonymous class does not have a name. The code says to instantiate a new `SaleTodayOnly` object. But wait: `SaleTodayOnly` is `abstract`. This is OK because we provide the class body right there—anonymously. In this example, writing an anonymous class is equivalent to writing a local class with an unspecified name that extends `SaleTodayOnly` and immediately uses it.

Pay special attention to the semicolon on line 8. We are declaring a local variable on these lines. Local variable declarations are required to end with semicolons, just like other Java statements—even if they are long and happen to contain an anonymous class.

Now we convert this same example to implement an `interface` instead of extending an `abstract` class:

```
1:   public class ZooGiftShop {
2:       interface SaleTodayOnly {
3:           int dollarsOff();
4:       }
5:       public int admission(int basePrice) {
6:           SaleTodayOnly sale = new SaleTodayOnly() {
7:               public int dollarsOff() { return 3; }
8:           };
9:           return basePrice - sale.dollarsOff();
10: } }
```

The most interesting thing here is how little has changed. Lines 2–4 declare an `interface` instead of an `abstract` class. Line 7 is `public` instead of using default access since interfaces require `abstract` methods to be `public`. And that is it. The anonymous class is the same whether you implement an interface or extend a class! Java figures out which one you want automatically. Just remember that in this second example, an instance of a class is created on line 6, not an interface.

But what if we want to both implement an `interface` and extend a class? You can't do so with an anonymous class unless the class to extend is `java.lang.Object`. The `Object` class doesn't count in the rule. Remember that an anonymous class is just an unnamed local class. You can write a local class and give it a name if you have this problem. Then you can extend a class and implement as many interfaces as you like. If your code is this complex, a local class probably isn't the most readable option anyway.

You can even define anonymous classes outside a method body. The following may look like we are instantiating an interface as an instance variable, but the `{}` after the interface name indicates that this is an anonymous class implementing the interface:

```
public class Gorilla {
    interface Climb {}
    Climb climbing = new Climb() {};
}
```

 Real World Scenario

Anonymous Classes and Lambda Expressions

Prior to Java 8, anonymous classes were frequently used for asynchronous tasks and event handlers. For example, the following shows an anonymous class used as an event handler in a JavaFX application:

```
    var redButton = new Button();
    redButton.setOnAction(new EventHandler<ActionEvent>() {
        public void handle(ActionEvent e) {
            System.out.println("Red button pressed!");
        }
    });
```

Since the introduction of lambda expressions, anonymous classes are now often replaced with much shorter implementations:

```
    Button redButton = new Button();
    redButton.setOnAction(e -> System.out.println("Red button pressed!"));
```

We cover lambda expressions in detail in the next chapter.

Reviewing Nested Classes

For the exam, make sure you know the information in Table 7.4 about which syntax rules are permitted in Java.

TABLE 7.4   Modifiers in nested classes

Permitted modifiers	Inner class	static nested class	Local class	Anonymous class
Access modifiers	All	All	None	None
abstract	Yes	Yes	Yes	No
final	Yes	Yes	Yes	No

You should also know the information in Table 7.5 about types of access. For example, the exam might try to trick you by having a static class access an outer class instance variable without a reference to the outer class.

TABLE 7.5   Nested class access rules

	Inner class	static nested class	Local class	Anonymous class
Can include instance and static members?	Yes	Yes	Yes	Yes

TABLE 7.5   Nested class access rules *(continued)*

	Inner class	static nested class	Local class	Anonymous class
Can extend a class or implement any number of interfaces?	Yes	Yes	Yes	No—must have exactly one superclass or one interface
Can access instance members of enclosing class?	Yes	No	Yes (if declared in an instance method)	Yes (if declared in an instance method)
Can access local variables of enclosing method?	N/A	N/A	Yes (if `final` or effectively final)	Yes (if `final` or effectively final)

Understanding Polymorphism

We conclude this chapter with a discussion of polymorphism, the property of an object to take on many different forms. To put this more precisely, a Java object may be accessed using the following:

- A reference with the same type as the object
- A reference that is a superclass of the object
- A reference of an interface the object implements or inherits

Furthermore, a cast is not required if the object is being reassigned to a supertype or interface of the object. Phew, that's a lot! Don't worry; it'll make sense shortly.

Let's illustrate this polymorphism property with the following example:

```java
public class Primate {
   public boolean hasHair() {
      return true;
   }
}

public interface HasTail {
   public abstract boolean isTailStriped();
}

public class Lemur extends Primate implements HasTail {
   public boolean isTailStriped() {
```

```
        return false;
    }
    public int age = 10;
    public static void main(String[] args) {
        Lemur lemur = new Lemur();
        System.out.println(lemur.age);

        HasTail hasTail = lemur;
        System.out.println(hasTail.isTailStriped());

        Primate primate = lemur;
        System.out.println(primate.hasHair());
    } }
```

This code compiles and prints the following output:

```
10
false
true
```

The most important thing to note about this example is that only one object, Lemur, is created. Polymorphism enables an instance of Lemur to be reassigned or passed to a method using one of its supertypes, such as Primate or HasTail.

Once the object has been assigned to a new reference type, only the methods and variables available to that reference type are callable on the object without an explicit cast. For example, the following snippets of code will not compile:

```
HasTail hasTail = new Lemur();
System.out.println(hasTail.age);               // DOES NOT COMPILE

Primate primate = new Lemur();
System.out.println(primate.isTailStriped()); // DOES NOT COMPILE
```

In this example, the reference hasTail has direct access only to methods defined with the HasTail interface; therefore, it doesn't know that the variable age is part of the object. Likewise, the reference primate has access only to methods defined in the Primate class, and it doesn't have direct access to the isTailStriped() method.

Object vs. Reference

In Java, all objects are accessed by reference, so as a developer you never have direct access to the object itself. Conceptually, though, you should consider the object as the entity that exists in memory, allocated by the Java. Regardless of the type of the reference you have for the object in memory, the object itself doesn't change. For example, since all objects inherit java.lang.Object, they can all be reassigned to java.lang.Object, as shown in the following example:

```
Lemur lemur = new Lemur();
Object lemurAsObject = lemur;
```

Even though the Lemur object has been assigned to a reference with a different type, the object itself has not changed and still exists as a Lemur object in memory. What has changed, then, is our ability to access methods within the Lemur class with the lemurAsObject reference. Without an explicit cast back to Lemur, as you see in the next section, we no longer have access to the Lemur properties of the object.

We can summarize this principle with the following two rules:

1. The type of the object determines which properties exist within the object in memory.

2. The type of the reference to the object determines which methods and variables are accessible to the Java program.

It therefore follows that successfully changing a reference of an object to a new reference type may give you access to new properties of the object; but remember, those properties existed before the reference change occurred.

Using the Lemur example, we illustrate this property in Figure 7.8.

FIGURE 7.8   Object versus reference

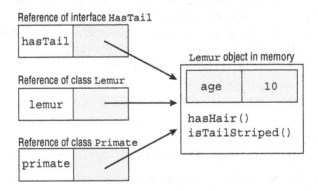

As you can see in the figure, the same object exists in memory regardless of which reference is pointing to it. Depending on the type of the reference, we may only have access to certain methods. For example, the hasTail reference has access to the method isTailStriped() but doesn't have access to the variable age defined in the Lemur class. As you learn in the next section, it is possible to reclaim access to the variable age by explicitly casting the hasTail reference to a reference of type Lemur.

Real World Scenario

Using Interface References

When working with a group of objects that implement a common interface, it is considered a good coding practice to use an interface as the reference type. This is especially common with collections that you learn about in Chapter 9. Consider the following method:

```
public void sortAndPrintZooAnimals(List<String> animals) {
   Collections.sort(animals);
   for(String a : animals) System.out.println(a);
}
```

This method sorts and prints animals in alphabetical order. At no point is this class interested in what the actual underlying object for animals is. It might be an ArrayList or another type. The point is, our code works on any of these types because we used the interface reference type rather than a class type.

Casting Objects

In the previous example, we created a single instance of a Lemur object and accessed it via superclass and interface references. Once we changed the reference type, though, we lost access to more specific members defined in the subclass that still exist within the object. We can reclaim those references by casting the object back to the specific subclass it came from:

```
Lemur lemur = new Lemur();

Primate primate = lemur;        // Implicit Cast to supertype

Lemur lemur2 = (Lemur)primate;  // Explicit Cast to subtype

Lemur lemur3 = primate;         // DOES NOT COMPILE (missing cast)
```

In this example, we first create a Lemur object and implicitly cast it to a Primate reference. Since Lemur is a subtype of Primate, this can be done without a cast operator. We then cast it back to a Lemur object using an explicit cast, gaining access to all of the methods and fields in the Lemur class. The last line does not compile because an explicit cast is required. Even though the object is stored in memory as a Lemur object, we need an explicit cast to assign it to Lemur.

Casting objects is similar to casting primitives, as you saw in Chapter 2, "Operators." When casting objects, you do not need a cast operator if casting to an inherited supertype. This is referred to as an *implicit cast* and applies to classes or interfaces the object inherits.

Alternatively, if you want to access a subtype of the current reference, you need to perform an explicit cast with a compatible type. If the underlying object is not compatible with the type, then a `ClassCastException` will be thrown at runtime.

When reviewing a question on the exam that involves casting and polymorphism, be sure to remember what the instance of the object actually is. Then, focus on whether the compiler will allow the object to be referenced with or without explicit casts.

We summarize these concepts into a set of rules for you to memorize for the exam:

1. Casting a reference from a subtype to a supertype doesn't require an explicit cast.

2. Casting a reference from a supertype to a subtype requires an explicit cast.

3. At runtime, an invalid cast of a reference to an incompatible type results in a `ClassCastException` being thrown.

4. The compiler disallows casts to unrelated types.

Disallowed Casts

The first three rules are just a review of what we've said so far. The last rule is a bit more complicated. The exam may try to trick you with a cast that the compiler knows is not permitted (aka impossible). In the previous example, we were able to cast a `Primate` reference to a `Lemur` reference because `Lemur` is a subclass of `Primate` and therefore related. Consider this example instead:

```
public class Bird {}

public class Fish {
    public static void main(String[] args) {
        Fish fish = new Fish();
        Bird bird = (Bird)fish;  // DOES NOT COMPILE
    }
}
```

In this example, the classes `Fish` and `Bird` are not related through any class hierarchy that the compiler is aware of; therefore, the code will not compile. While they both extend `Object` implicitly, they are considered unrelated types since one cannot be a subtype of the other.

Casting Interfaces

While the compiler can enforce rules about casting to unrelated types for classes, it cannot always do the same for interfaces. Remember, interfaces support multiple inheritance, which limits what the compiler can reason about them. While a given class may not implement an interface, it's possible that some subclass may implement the interface. When holding a reference to a particular class, the compiler doesn't know which specific subtype it is holding.

Let's try an example. Do you think the following program compiles?

```
1: interface Canine {}
2: interface Dog {}
```

```
3: class Wolf implements Canine {}
4:
5: public class BadCasts {
6:    public static void main(String[] args) {
7:       Wolf wolfy = new Wolf();
8:       Dog badWolf = (Dog)wolfy;
9:    } }
```

In this program, a Wolf object is created and then assigned to a Wolf reference type on line 7. With interfaces, the compiler has limited ability to enforce many rules because even though a reference type may not implement an interface, one of its subclasses could. Therefore, it allows the invalid cast to the Dog reference type on line 8, even though Dog and Wolf are not related. Fear not, even though the code compiles, it still throws a ClassCastException at runtime.

This limitation aside, the compiler can enforce one rule around interface casting. The compiler does not allow a cast from an interface reference to an object reference if the object type cannot possibly implement the interface, such as if the class is marked final. For example, what if we changed line 3 of our previous code?

```
3: final class Wolf implements Canine {}
```

Line 8 no longer compiles. The compiler recognizes that there are no possible subclasses of Wolf capable of implementing the Dog interface.

The *instanceof* Operator

The instanceof operator can be used to check whether an object belongs to a particular class or interface and to prevent a ClassCastException at runtime. As we saw in Chapter 3, it can also be used with pattern matching. Consider the following example:

```
1: class Rodent {}
2:
3: public class Capybara extends Rodent {
4:    public static void main(String[] args) {
5:       Rodent rodent = new Rodent();
6:       var capybara = (Capybara)rodent;  // ClassCastException
7:    }
8: }
```

This program throws an exception on line 6. We can replace line 6 with the following:

```
6:       if(rodent instanceof Capybara c) {
7:          // Do stuff
8:       }
```

Now the code snippet doesn't throw an exception at runtime and performs the cast only if the instanceof operator is successful.

Just as the compiler does not allow casting an object to unrelated types, it also does not allow `instanceof` to be used with unrelated types. We can demonstrate this with our unrelated `Bird` and `Fish` classes:

```java
public class Bird {}
```

```java
public class Fish {
    public static void main(String[] args) {
        Fish fish = new Fish();
        if (fish instanceof Bird b) {  // DOES NOT COMPILE
            // Do stuff
        } } }
```

Polymorphism and Method Overriding

In Java, polymorphism states that when you override a method, you replace all calls to it, even those defined in the parent class. As an example, what do you think the following code snippet outputs?

```java
class Penguin {
    public int getHeight() { return 3; }
    public void printInfo() {
        System.out.print(this.getHeight());
    } }
```

```java
public class EmperorPenguin extends Penguin {
    public int getHeight() { return 8; }
    public static void main(String []fish) {
        new EmperorPenguin().printInfo();
    } }
```

If you said 8, then you are well on your way to understanding polymorphism. In this example, the object being operated on in memory is an `EmperorPenguin`. The `getHeight()` method is overridden in the subclass, meaning all calls to it are replaced at runtime. Despite `printInfo()` being defined in the `Penguin` class, calling `getHeight()` on the object calls the method associated with the precise object in memory, not the current reference type where it is called. Even using the `this` reference, which is optional in this example, does not call the parent version because the method has been replaced.

Polymorphism's ability to replace methods at runtime via overriding is one of the most important properties of Java. It allows you to create complex inheritance models with subclasses that have their own custom implementation of overridden methods. It also means the parent class does not need to be updated to use the custom or overridden method. If the method is properly overridden, then the overridden version will be used in all places that it is called.

Remember, you can choose to limit polymorphic behavior by marking methods `final`, which prevents them from being overridden by a subclass.

Calling the Parent Version of an Overridden Method

Just because a method is overridden doesn't mean the parent method is completely inaccessible. We can use the super reference that you learned about in Chapter 6 to access it. How can you modify our previous example to print 3 instead of 8? You could try calling `super.getHeight()` in the parent Penguin class:

```
class Penguin {
   public int getHeight() { return 3; }
   public void printInfo() {
      System.out.print(super.getHeight());  // DOES NOT COMPILE
   }
}
```

Unfortunately, this does not compile, as super refers to the superclass of Penguin; in this case, Object. The solution is to override `printInfo()` in the child EmperorPenguin class and use super there.

```
public class EmperorPenguin extends Penguin {
   public int getHeight() { return 8; }
   public void printInfo() {
      System.out.print(super.getHeight());
   }
   public static void main(String []fish) {
      new EmperorPenguin().printInfo();  // 3
   }
}
```

Overriding vs. Hiding Members

While method overriding replaces the method everywhere it is called, `static` method and variable hiding do not. Strictly speaking, hiding members is not a form of polymorphism since the methods and variables maintain their individual properties. Unlike method overriding, hiding members is very sensitive to the reference type and location where the member is being used.

Let's take a look at an example:

```
class Penguin {
   public static int getHeight() { return 3; }
```

```
   public void printInfo() {
      System.out.println(this.getHeight());
} }

public class CrestedPenguin extends Penguin {
   public static int getHeight() { return 8; }
   public static void main(String... fish) {
      new CrestedPenguin().printInfo();
} }
```

The CrestedPenguin example is nearly identical to our previous EmperorPenguin example, although as you probably already guessed, it prints 3 instead of 8. The getHeight() method is static and is therefore hidden, not overridden. The result is that calling getHeight() in CrestedPenguin returns a different value than calling it in Penguin, even if the underlying object is the same. Contrast this with overriding a method, where it returns the same value for an object regardless of which class it is called in.

What about the fact that we used this to access a static method in this.getHeight()? As discussed in Chapter 5, while you are permitted to use an instance reference to access a static variable or method, doing so is often discouraged. The compiler will warn you when you access static members in a non-static way. In this case, the this reference had no impact on the program output.

Besides the location, the reference type can also determine the value you get when you are working with hidden members. Ready? Let's try a more complex example:

```
class Marsupial {
   protected int age = 2;
   public static boolean isBiped() {
      return false;
} }

public class Kangaroo extends Marsupial {
   protected int age = 6;
   public static boolean isBiped() {
      return true;
   }

   public static void main(String[] args) {
      Kangaroo joey = new Kangaroo();
      Marsupial moey = joey;
      System.out.println(joey.isBiped());
      System.out.println(moey.isBiped());
      System.out.println(joey.age);
      System.out.println(moey.age);
} }
```

The program prints the following:

```
true
false
6
2
```

In this example, only *one object* (of type Kangaroo) is created and stored in memory! Since static methods can only be hidden, not overridden, Java uses the reference type to determine which version of isBiped() should be called, resulting in joey.isBiped() printing true and moey.isBiped() printing false.

Likewise, the age variable is hidden, not overridden, so the reference type is used to determine which value to output. This results in joey.age returning 6 and moey.age returning 2.

For the exam, make sure you understand these examples, as they show how hidden and overridden methods are fundamentally different. In practice, overriding methods is the cornerstone of polymorphism and an extremely powerful feature.

 Real World Scenario

Don't Hide Members in Practice

Although Java allows you to hide variables and static methods, it is considered an extremely poor coding practice. As you saw in the previous example, the value of the variable or method can change depending on what reference is used, making your code very confusing, difficult to follow, and challenging for others to maintain. This is further compounded when you start modifying the value of the variable in both the parent and child methods, since it may not be clear which variable you're updating.

When you're defining a new variable or static method in a child class, it is considered good coding practice to select a name that is not already used by an inherited member. Redeclaring private methods and variables is considered less problematic, though, because the child class does not have access to the variable in the parent class to begin with.

Summary

In this chapter, we presented numerous topics in advanced object-oriented design, covering many top-level types beyond classes. We started with interfaces and described how they can support multiple inheritance. Remember, interfaces and their members can include a number of implicit modifiers inserted by the compiler automatically. We then covered all six types of interface members you need to know for the exam: abstract methods, static constants, default methods, static methods, private methods, and private static methods.

We next moved on to enums, which are compile time constant properties. Simple enums are composed of a list of values, while complex enums can include constructors, methods, and fields. Enums can also be used in switch statements and expressions. When an enum method is marked abstract, each enum value must provide an implementation.

We covered sealed classes and how they allow classes to function like enumerated types in which only certain subclasses are permitted. For the exam, it's important to remember that the subclasses of a sealed class must be marked final, sealed, or non-sealed. If the subclasses of the sealed class are defined in the same file, then the permits clause may be omitted in the sealed class declaration. Finally, sealed interfaces may be used to limit which classes can implement an interface, which interfaces may extend an interface, or both.

Records are a compact way of declaring an immutable and encapsulated POJO in which the compiler adds a lot of the boilerplate code for you. Remember, encapsulation is the practice of preventing external callers from accessing the internal components of an object. Records include automatic creation of the accessor methods, a long constructor, and useful implementations of equals(), hashCode(), and toString(). Records can include overloaded and compact constructors to support data validation and transformation. Records do not permit instance variables outside the record declaration, since this could break immutability, but they do allow methods, static members, and nested types. They can also be used with pattern matching.

We then moved on to nested types. For simplicity, we focused on nested classes and covered each of the four types. An inner class requires an instance of the outer class to use, while a static nested class does not. A local class is commonly defined within a method or block. Local classes can only access local variables that are final and effectively final. Anonymous classes are a special type of local class that does not have a name. Anonymous classes are required to extend exactly one class or implement one interface. Inner, local, and anonymous classes can access private members of the class in which they are defined, provided the latter two are used inside an instance method.

We concluded this chapter with a discussion of polymorphism, which is central to the Java language, and showed how objects can be accessed in a variety of forms. Make sure you understand when casts are needed for accessing objects and are able to spot the difference between compile time and runtime cast problems.

Exam Essentials

Be able to write code that creates, extends, and implements interfaces. Interfaces are specialized abstract types that focus on abstract methods and constant variables. An interface may extend any number of interfaces and, in doing so, inherits their abstract methods. An interface cannot extend a class, nor can a class extend an interface. A class may implement any number of interfaces.

Know which interface methods an interface method can reference. Non-static private, default, and abstract interface methods are associated with an instance of an interface. Non-static private and default interface methods may reference any method within the interface declaration. Alternatively, static interface methods are associated with class membership and can only reference other static members. Finally, private methods can only be referenced within the interface declaration.

Be able to create and use enum types. An enum is a data structure that defines a list of values. If the enum does not contain any other elements, the semicolon (;) after the values is optional. An enum can be used in switch statements and contain instance variables, constructors, and methods. Enum constructors are implicitly private. Enums can include methods, both as members or within individual enum values. If the enum declares an abstract method, each enum value must implement it.

Be able to recognize when sealed classes are being correctly used. A sealed class is one that defines a list of permitted subclasses that extend it. Be able to use the correct modifier (final, sealed, or non-sealed) when working with sealed classes. Understand when the permits clause may be omitted.

Identify properly encapsulated classes. Instance variables in encapsulated classes are private. All code that retrieves the value or updates it uses methods. Encapsulated classes may include accessor (getter) or mutator (setter) methods, although this is not required.

Understand records and know which members the compiler is adding automatically. Records are encapsulated and immutable types in which the compiler inserts a long constructor, accessor methods, and useful implementations of equals(), hashCode(), and toString(). Each of these elements may be overridden. Be able to recognize compact constructors and know that they are used only for validation and transformation of constructor parameters, not for accessing fields. Recognize that when a record is declared with an instance member, it does not compile. Be able to use records with pattern matching.

Be able to declare and use nested classes. There are four types of nested types: inner classes, static classes, local classes, and anonymous classes. Instantiating an inner class requires an instance of the outer class. On the other hand, static nested classes can be created without a reference to the outer class. Local and anonymous classes cannot be declared with an access modifier. Anonymous classes are limited to extending a single class or implementing one interface.

Understand polymorphism. An object may take on a variety of forms, referred to as polymorphism. The object is viewed as existing in memory in one concrete form but is accessible in many forms through reference variables. Changing the reference type of an object may grant access to new members, but the members always exist in memory.

Review Questions

The answers to the chapter review questions can be found in the Appendix.

1. Which of the following are valid record declarations? (Choose all that apply.)

    ```java
    public record Iguana(int age) {
       private static final int age = 10; }
    ```

    ```java
    public final record Gecko() {}
    ```

    ```java
    public abstract record Chameleon()  {
       private static String name; }
    ```

    ```java
    public record BeardedDragon(boolean fun) {
       @Override public boolean fun() { return false; } }
    ```

    ```java
    public record Reptile(long size) {
       public Reptile {
          if(size == 1) throw new IllegalArgumentException();
       } }
    ```

    ```java
    public record Newt(double age) extends Reptile {
       public Newt(double age) {
          age = this.age % 2 == 0 ? 5 : 10;
       } }
    ```

    A. Iguana
    B. Gecko
    C. Chameleon
    D. BeardedDragon
    E. Reptile
    F. Newt
    G. None of the above

2. Which of the following statements can be inserted in the blank line so that the code will compile successfully? (Choose all that apply.)

    ```java
    interface CanHop {}
    public class Frog implements CanHop {
       public static void main(String[] args) {
          _____ frog = new TurtleFrog();
       }
    }
    ```

```
class BrazilianHornedFrog extends Frog {}
class TurtleFrog extends Frog {}
```

A. Frog

B. TurtleFrog

C. BrazilianHornedFrog

D. CanHop

E. var

F. Long

G. None of the above; the code contains a compilation error.

3. What is the result of the following program?

```
11: public class Favorites {
12:     enum Flavors {
13:         VANILLA, CHOCOLATE, STRAWBERRY
14:         public Flavors() {}
15:     }
16:     public static void main(String[] args) {
17:         for(final var e : Flavors.values())
18:             System.out.print((e.ordinal() % 2) + " ");
19:     } }
```

A. 0 1 0

B. 1 0 1

C. Exactly one line of code does not compile.

D. More than one line of code does not compile.

E. The code compiles but produces an exception at runtime.

F. None of the above.

4. What is the output of the following program?

```
public sealed class ArmoredAnimal permits Armadillo {
    public ArmoredAnimal(int size) {}
    @Override public String toString() { return "Strong"; }
    public static void main(String[] a) {
        var c = new Armadillo(10, null);
        System.out.println(c);
    }
}
class Armadillo extends ArmoredAnimal {
    @Override public String toString() { return "Cute"; }
    public Armadillo(int size, String name) {
        super(size);
    }
}
```

    A. Strong

    B. Cute

    C. The program does not compile.

    D. The code compiles but produces an exception at runtime.

    E. None of the above.

5. Which statement about the following program is correct?

```
1: interface HasExoskeleton {
2:     double size = 2.0f;
3:     abstract int getNumberOfSections();
4: }
5: abstract class Insect implements HasExoskeleton {
6:     abstract int getNumberOfLegs();
7: }
8: public class Beetle extends Insect {
9:     int getNumberOfLegs() { return 6; }
10:     int getNumberOfSections(int count) { return 1; }
11: }
```

    A. It compiles without issue.

    B. The code will produce a `ClassCastException` if called at runtime.

    C. The code will not compile because of line 2.

    D. The code will not compile because of line 5.

    E. The code will not compile because of line 8.

    F. The code will not compile because of line 10.

6. Which statements about the following program are correct? (Choose all that apply.)

```
1: public abstract interface Herbivore {
2:     int amount = 10;
3:     public void eatGrass();
4:     public abstract int chew() { return 13; }
5: }
6:
7: abstract class IsAPlant extends Herbivore {
8:     Object eatGrass(int season) { return null; }
9: }
```

    A. It compiles and runs without issue.

    B. The code will not compile because of line 1.

    C. The code will not compile because of line 2.

    D. The code will not compile because of line 4.

E.   The code will not compile because of line 7.

F.   The code will not compile because line 8 contains an invalid method override.

7.   What is the output of the following program?

```
1: interface Aquatic {
2:    int getNumOfGills(int p);
3: }
4: public class ClownFish implements Aquatic {
5:    String getNumOfGills() { return "14"; }
6:    int getNumOfGills(int input) { return 15; }
7:    public static void main(String[] args) {
8:        System.out.println(new ClownFish().getNumOfGills(-1));
9: } }
```

A.   14

B.   15

C.   The code will not compile because of line 4.

D.   The code will not compile because of line 5.

E.   The code will not compile because of line 6.

F.   None of the above.

8.   Given the following, select the statements that can be inserted into the blank line so that the code will compile and print true at runtime? (Choose all that apply.)

```
record Walrus(List<String> diet) {}
record Exhibit(Walrus animal, String location) {}

var e = new Exhibit(new Walrus(List.of("Wally")), "Artic");
System.out.print(e instanceof _____);
```

A.   `Exhibit(Walrus(List<Integer> z), Object a)`

B.   `Exhibit(Walrus(List m), Object n)`

C.   `Object w && w.animal().diet().size() == 0`

D.   `Exhibit(Walrus(var i), var i)`

E.   `Exhibit(var p, var q)`

F.   `Exhibit(List<?> g, var h)`

G.   `Exhibit(var x, CharSequence y)`

H.   `Exhibit(Walrus(null), var v)`

I.   None of the above

9.   Which of the following statements can be inserted in the blank so that the code will compile successfully? (Choose all that apply.)

```
abstract class Snake {}
class Cobra extends Snake {}
```

```
class GardenSnake extends Cobra {}
public class SnakeHandler {
    private Snake snakey;
    public void setSnake(Snake mySnake) { this.snakey = mySnake; }
    public static void main(String[] args) {
        new SnakeHandler().setSnake(_____);
    } }
```

A. `new Cobra()`

B. `new Snake()`

C. `new Object()`

D. `new String("Snake")`

E. `new GardenSnake()`

F. `null`

G. None of the above. The class does not compile, regardless of the value inserted in the blank.

10. What types can be inserted in the blanks on the lines marked X and Z that allow the code to compile? (Choose all that apply.)

```
interface Walk { private static List move() { return null; } }
interface Run extends Walk { public ArrayList move(); }
class Leopard implements Walk {
    public _____ move() {  // X
        return null;
    }
}
class Panther implements Run {
    public _____ move() {  // Z
        return null;
    }
}
```

A. `Integer` on the line marked X

B. `ArrayList` on the line marked X

C. `List` on the line marked X

D. `List` on the line marked Z

E. `ArrayList` on the line marked Z

F. None of the above, since the Run interface does not compile.

G. Does not compile for a different reason.

11. What is the result of compiling and executing the following code?

```
1:  public class Movie {
2:     private int butter = 5;
3:     private Movie() {}
4:     protected class Popcorn {
5:        private Popcorn() {}
6:        public static int butter = 10;
7:        public void startMovie() {
8:           System.out.println(butter);
9:        }
10:    }
11:    public static void main(String[] args) {
12:       var movie = new Movie();
13:       Movie.Popcorn in = new Movie().new Popcorn();
14:       in.startMovie();
15:    } }
```

A. The output is 5.

B. The output is 10.

C. Line 6 generates a compiler error.

D. Line 12 generates a compiler error.

E. Line 13 generates a compiler error.

F. The code compiles but produces an exception at runtime.

12. Which variables or members are accessible from within the hiss() method? (Choose all that apply.)

```
13: public class BoaConstrictor {
14:    private Body body;
15:    BoaConstrictor(Body b) { this.body = b; }
16:    private long tail = 10;
17:    record Body(int stripes) {
18:       private static int counter = 0;
19:       int counter() { return counter; }
20:       Body {
21:          stripes = stripes + counter++;
22:       }
23:       private void hiss() {} } }
```

A. counter()

B. tail

C. body

D. `stripes()`

E. `stripes`

F. `counter`

G. Line 15 does not compile.

H. Line 17 does not compile.

I. Lines 20–22 do not compile.

13. What is the result of the following program?

```
public class Weather {
    enum Seasons {
        WINTER, SPRING, SUMMER, FALL
    }

    public static void main(String[] args) {
        Seasons v = null;
        switch (v) {
            case Seasons.SPRING -> System.out.print("s");
            case Seasons.WINTER -> System.out.print("w");
            case Seasons.SUMMER -> System.out.print("m");
            default -> System.out.println("missing data"); }
    } }
```

A. `s`

B. `w`

C. `m`

D. `missing data`

E. Exactly one line of code does not compile.

F. More than one line of code does not compile.

G. The code compiles but produces an exception at runtime.

14. Which statements about sealed classes are correct? (Choose all that apply.)

A. A sealed interface restricts which subinterfaces may extend it.

B. A sealed class cannot be indirectly extended by a class that is not listed in its `permits` clause.

C. A sealed class can be extended by an `abstract` class.

D. A sealed class can be extended by a subclass that uses the `nonsealed` modifier.

E. A sealed interface restricts which subclasses may implement it.

F. A sealed class cannot contain any nested subclasses.

G. None of the above.

15. Which line allows the code to print Not scared at runtime?

```
public class Ghost {
   public static void boo() {
      System.out.println("Not scared");
   }
   protected final class Spirit {
      public void boo() {
         System.out.println("Booo!!!");
      }
   }
   public static void main(String... haunt) {
      var g = new Ghost().new Spirit() {};
      _____;
} }
```

- **A.** g.boo()
- **B.** g.super.boo()
- **C.** new Ghost().boo()
- **D.** g.Ghost.boo()
- **E.** new Spirit().boo()
- **F.** None of the above

16. The following code appears in a file named Ostrich.java. What is the result of compiling the source file?

```
1: public class Ostrich {
2:    private int count;
3:    static class OstrichWrangler {
4:       public int stampede() {
5:          return count;
6:       } } }
```

- **A.** The code compiles successfully, and one bytecode file is generated: Ostrich.class.
- **B.** The code compiles successfully, and two bytecode files are generated: Ostrich.class and OstrichWrangler.class.
- **C.** The code compiles successfully, and two bytecode files are generated: Ostrich.class and Ostrich$OstrichWrangler.class.
- **D.** A compiler error occurs on line 3.
- **E.** A compiler error occurs on line 5.

17. Which lines of the following interface declarations do not compile? (Choose all that apply.)

```
1: public interface Omnivore {
2:    int amount = 10;
```

```
3:     static boolean gather = true;
4:     static void eatGrass() {}
5:     int findMore() { return 2; }
6:     default float rest() { return 2; }
7:     protected int chew() { return 13; }
8:     private static void eatLeaves() {}
9: }
```

A. All of the lines compile without issue.

B. Line 2.

C. Line 3.

D. Line 4.

E. Line 5.

F. Line 6.

G. Line 7.

H. Line 8.

18. What is printed by the following program?

```
public class Deer {
    enum Food {APPLES, BERRIES, GRASS}
    protected class Diet {
        private Food getFavorite() {
            return Food.BERRIES;
        }
    }
    public static void main(String[] seasons) {
        System.out.print(switch(new Diet().getFavorite()) {
            case APPLES -> "a";
            case BERRIES -> "b";
            default -> "c";
        });
    } }
```

A. a

B. b

C. c

D. The code declaration of the `Diet` class does not compile.

E. The `main()` method does not compile.

F. The code compiles but produces an exception at runtime.

G. None of the above.

19. Which of the following is printed by the Bear program?

```java
public class Bear {
   enum FOOD {
      BERRIES, INSECTS {
         public boolean isHealthy() { return true; }},
      FISH, ROOTS, COOKIES, HONEY;
      public abstract boolean isHealthy();
   }
   public static void main(String[] args) {
      System.out.print(FOOD.INSECTS);
      System.out.print(FOOD.INSECTS.ordinal());
      System.out.print(FOOD.INSECTS.isHealthy());
      System.out.print(FOOD.COOKIES.isHealthy());
   } }
```

A. insects

B. Insects

C. 0

D. 1

E. false

F. The code does not compile.

20. What is the output of this code?

```java
13: record Gorilla(int x, Double y) {
14:    Gorilla {}
15:    Gorilla() { this(1,2.0); }
16: }
17: record Family(Gorilla parent1, Gorilla parent2) {}
18:
19: var family = new Family(
20:    new Gorilla(1, null), new Gorilla(0, 1.2));
21: System.out.print(switch (family) {
22:    case Family(var a, var b) -> "1";
23:    case Family(Gorilla c, Gorilla (int d, double e)) -> "2";
24:    case Family(Gorilla (int f, Double g), var h) -> "3";
25:    case Family(Gorilla i, Gorilla (int j, Double k)) -> "4";
26:    case Family(Object m, Object n) -> "5";
27:    case null -> "6";
28:    default -> "7";
29: });
```

A. 1
B. 2
C. 3
D. 4
E. 5
F. 6
G. 7
H. None of the above

21. Given the following record declaration, which line of code can fill in the blank and allow the code to compile?

```
public record RabbitFood(int size, String brand, LocalDate expires) {
    public static int MAX_STORAGE = 100;
    public RabbitFood() {

        _____;

    }
}
```

A. `size = MAX_STORAGE`
B. `this.size = 10`
C. `if(expires.isAfter(LocalDate.now())) throw new`
    `RuntimeException()`
D. `if(brand==null) super.brand = "Unknown"`
E. `throw new RuntimeException()`
F. None of the above

22. Which of the following can be inserted in the `rest()` method? (Choose all that apply.)

```
public class Lion {
    class Cub {}
    static class Den {}
    static void rest() {

        _____;

    } }
```

A. `Cub a = Lion.new Cub()`
B. `Lion.Cub b = new Lion().Cub()`
C. `Lion.Cub c = new Lion().new Cub()`
D. `var d = new Den()`
E. `var e = Lion.new Cub()`
F. `Lion.Den f = Lion.new Den()`

G. `Lion.Den g = new Lion.Den()`

H. `var h = new Cub()`

23. Given the following program, what can be inserted into the blank line that would allow it to print Swim! at runtime?

```
interface Swim {
   default void perform() { System.out.print("Swim!"); }
}
interface Dance {
   default void perform() { System.out.print("Dance!"); }
}
public class Penguin implements Swim, Dance {
   public void perform() { System.out.print("Smile!"); }
   private void doShow() {
      _____;
   }
   public static void main(String[] eggs) {
      new Penguin().doShow();
   } }
```

A. `super.perform()`

B. `Swim.perform()`

C. `super.Swim.perform()`

D. `Swim.super.perform()`

E. The code does not compile regardless of what is inserted into the blank.

F. The code compiles, but due to polymorphism, it is not possible to produce the requested output without creating a new object.

24. Which lines of the following interface do not compile? (Choose all that apply.)

```
1: public interface BigCat {
2:    abstract String getName();
3:    static int hunt() { getName(); return 5; }
4:    default void climb() { rest(); }
5:    private void roar() { getName();  climb(); hunt(); }
6:    private static boolean sneak() { roar(); return true; }
7:    private int rest() { return 2; };
8: }
```

A. Line 2

B. Line 3

C. Line 4

D. Line 5

E. Line 6

F. Line 7

G. None of the above

25. What does the following program print?

```
1:  public class Zebra {
2:      private int x = 24;
3:      public int hunt() {
4:          String message = "x is ";
5:          abstract class Stripes {
6:              private int x = 0;
7:              public void print() {
8:                  System.out.print(message + Zebra.this.x);
9:              }
10:         }
11:         var s = new Stripes() {};
12:         s.print();
13:         return x;
14:     }
15:     public static void main(String[] args) {
16:         new Zebra().hunt();
17:     } }
```

A. x is 0

B. x is 24

C. Line 6 generates a compiler error.

D. Line 8 generates a compiler error.

E. Line 11 generates a compiler error.

F. None of the above.

26. What is the output of the following program?

```
20: public enum Animals {
21:     MAMMAL(List.of(2,4)),
22:     INVERTEBRATE(List.of(2, 4, 6, 8, 100)),
23:     BIRD(null) {
24:         public int stand() {
25:             return legs.get(0) + 4;
26:         }
27:     };
28:     List<Integer> legs;
29:     Animals(List<Integer> legs) {
```

```
30:        this.legs = legs;
31:    }
32:    public int stand() { return legs.get(0); }
33:    public static void main(String[] a) {
34:        Animals.BIRD.legs = List.of(-1);
35:        System.out.println(Animals.BIRD.stand());
36:    } }
```

A. null

B. -1

C. 3

D. 4

E. Compiler error on lines 23.

F. Compiler error on lines 24.

G. Compiler error on line 34.

H. The code compiles but produces a NullPointerException at runtime.

I. None of the above.

27. Assuming a record is defined with at least one field, which components does the compiler always insert, each of which may be overridden or redeclared? (Choose all that apply.)

A. A no-argument constructor

B. An accessor method for each field

C. The toString() method

D. The equals() method

E. A mutator method for each field

F. A sort method for each field

G. The hashCode() method

28. Which of the following classes and interfaces do not compile? (Choose all that apply.)

```
public abstract class Camel { void travel(); }

public interface EatsGrass { private abstract int chew(); }

public abstract class Elephant {
    abstract private class SleepsAlot {
        abstract int sleep();
    } }

public class Eagle { abstract soar(); }

public interface Spider { default void crawl() {} }
```

A. Camel

B. EatsGrass

C. Elephant

D. Eagle

E. Spider

29. How many lines of the following program contain a compilation error?

```
1:  class Primate {
2:      protected int age = 2;
3:      { age = 1; }
4:      public Primate() {
5:          this().age = 3;
6:      }
7:  }
8:  public class Orangutan {
9:      protected int age = 4;
10:     { age = 5; }
11:     public Orangutan() {
12:         this().age = 6;
13:     }
14:     public static void main(String[] bananas) {
15:         final Primate x = (Primate)new Orangutan();
16:         System.out.println(x.age);
17:     }
18: }
```

A. None, and the program prints 1 at runtime.

B. None, and the program prints 3 at runtime.

C. None, but it causes a `ClassCastException` at runtime.

D. 1

E. 2

F. 3

G. 4

30. Assuming the following classes are declared as top-level types in the same file, which classes contain compiler errors? (Choose all that apply.)

```
sealed class Bird {
    public final class Flamingo extends Bird {}
}
```

```
sealed class Monkey {}

class EmperorTamarin extends Monkey {}

non-sealed class Mandrill extends Monkey {}

sealed class Friendly extends Mandrill permits Silly {}

final class Silly {}
```

A. Bird
B. Monkey
C. EmperorTamarin
D. Mandrill
E. Friendly
F. Silly
G. All of the classes compile without issue.

Chapter

8

Lambdas and Functional Interfaces

✓ **Using Object-Oriented Concepts in Java**

- Understand variable scopes, apply encapsulation, and create immutable objects. Use local variable type inference.

- Create and use interfaces, identify functional interfaces, and utilize private, static, and default interface methods.

In this chapter, we start by introducing lambdas, a new piece of syntax. Lambdas allow you to specify code that will be run later in the program.

Next, we introduce the concept of functional interfaces, showing how to write your own and identify whether an interface is a functional interface. After that, we introduce another new piece of syntax: method references. These are like a shorter form of lambdas.

Then we introduce the functional interfaces you need to know for the exam. Finally, we emphasize how variables fit into lambdas.

Lambdas, method references, and functional interfaces are used quite a bit in Chapter 9, "Collections and Generics," and Chapter 10, "Streams."

Writing Simple Lambdas

Java is an object-oriented language at heart. You've seen plenty of objects by now. *Functional programming* is a way of writing code more declaratively. You specify what you want to do rather than dealing with the state of objects. You focus more on expressions than loops.

Functional programming uses lambda expressions to write code. A *lambda expression* is a block of code that gets passed around. You can think of a lambda expression as an unnamed method existing inside an anonymous class like the ones you saw in Chapter 7, "Beyond Classes." It has parameters and a body just like full-fledged methods do, but it doesn't have a name like a real method. Lambda expressions are often referred to as *lambdas* for short. You might also know them as *closures* if Java isn't your first language. If you had a bad experience with closures in the past, don't worry. They are far simpler in Java.

Lambdas allow you to write powerful code in Java. In this section, we cover an example of why lambdas are helpful and the syntax of lambdas.

Looking at a Lambda Example

Our goal is to print out all the animals in a list according to some criteria. We show you how to do this without lambdas to illustrate how lambdas are useful. We start with the `Animal` record.

```
public record Animal(String species, boolean canHop, boolean canSwim) { }
```

The `Animal` record has three fields. Let's say we have a list of animals, and we want to process the data based on a particular attribute. For example, we want to print all animals that can hop. We can define an interface to generalize this concept and support a large variety of checks.

```java
public interface CheckTrait {
    boolean test(Animal a);
}
```

The first thing we want to check is whether the Animal can hop. We provide a class that implements our interface.

```java
public class CheckIfHopper implements CheckTrait {
    public boolean test(Animal a) {
        return a.canHop();
    }
}
```

This class may seem simple—and it is. This is part of the problem that lambdas solve. Just bear with us for a bit. Now we have everything we need to write our code to find out if an Animal can hop.

```java
1:  import java.util.*;
2:  public class TraditionalSearch {
3:      public static void main(String[] args) {
4:
5:          // list of animals
6:          var animals = new ArrayList<Animal>();
7:          animals.add(new Animal("fish", false, true));
8:          animals.add(new Animal("kangaroo", true, false));
9:          animals.add(new Animal("rabbit", true, false));
10:         animals.add(new Animal("turtle", false, true));
11:
12:         // pass class that does check
13:         print(animals, new CheckIfHopper());
14:     }
15:     private static void print(List<Animal> animals, CheckTrait checker) {
16:         for (Animal animal : animals) {
17:
18:             // General check
19:             if (checker.test(animal))
20:                 System.out.print(animal + " ");
21:         }
22:         System.out.println();
23:     }
24: }
```

Line 6 shows configuring an `ArrayList` with a specific type of `Animal`. The `print()` method on line 15 is very general—it can check for any trait. This is good design. It shouldn't need to know what specifically we are searching for in order to print a list of animals.

What happens if we want to print the `Animals` that swim? Sigh. We need to write another class, `CheckIfSwims`. Granted, it is only a few lines, but it is a whole new file. Then we need to add a new line under line 13 that instantiates that class. That's two things just to do another check.

Why can't we specify the logic we care about right here? It turns out that we can, with lambda expressions. We could repeat the whole class here and make you find the one line that changed. Instead, we just show you that we can keep our `print()` method declaration unchanged. Let's replace line 13 with the following, which uses a lambda:

```
13:        print(animals, a -> a.canHop());
```

Don't worry that the syntax looks a little funky. You'll get used to it, and we describe it in the next section. We also explain the bits that look like magic. For now, just focus on how easy it is to read. We are telling Java that we only care if an `Animal` can hop.

It doesn't take much imagination to figure out how we would add logic to get the `Animals` that can swim. We only have to add one line of code—no need for an extra class to do something simple. Here's that other line:

```
13:        print(animals, a -> a.canSwim());
```

How about `Animals` that cannot swim?

```
13:        print(animals, a -> !a.canSwim());
```

The point is that it is really easy to write code that uses lambdas once you get the basics in place. This code uses a concept called *deferred execution*, which means that code is specified now but will run later. In this case, "later" is inside the `print()` method body, as opposed to when it is passed to the method.

Learning Lambda Syntax

One of the simplest lambda expressions you can write is the one you just saw.

`a -> a.canHop()`

Lambdas work with interfaces that have exactly one abstract method. In this case, Java looks at the `CheckTrait` interface, which has one method. The lambda in our example suggests that Java should call a method with an `Animal` parameter that returns a `boolean` value that's the result of `a.canHop()`. We know all this because we wrote the code. But how does Java know?

Java relies on *context* when figuring out what lambda expressions mean. Context refers to where and how the lambda is interpreted. For example, if we see someone in line to enter the zoo and they have their wallet out, it is fair to assume they want to buy zoo tickets. Alternatively, if they are in the concession line with their wallet out, they are probably hungry.

Referring to our earlier example, we passed the lambda as the second parameter of the print method().

```
print(animals, a -> a.canHop());
```

The print() method expects a CheckTrait as the second parameter.

```
private static void print(List<Animal> animals, CheckTrait checker) { ... }
```

Since we are passing a lambda instead, Java tries to map our lambda to the abstract method declaration in the CheckTrait interface.

```
boolean test(Animal a);
```

Since that interface's method takes an Animal, the lambda parameter has to be an Animal. And since that interface's method returns a boolean, we know the lambda returns a boolean.

The syntax of lambdas is tricky because many parts are optional. These two lines do the exact same thing:

```
a -> a.canHop()
```

```
(Animal a) -> { return a.canHop(); }
```

Let's look at what is going on here. The first example, shown in Figure 8.1, has three parts.

- A single parameter specified with the name a
- The arrow operator (->) to separate the parameter and body
- A body that calls a single method and returns the result of that method

FIGURE 8.1 Lambda syntax omitting optional parts

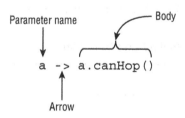

The second example shows the most verbose form of a lambda that returns a boolean (see Figure 8.2).

- A single parameter specified with the name a and stating that the type is Animal
- The arrow operator (->) to separate the parameter and body
- A body that has one or more lines of code, including a semicolon and a return statement

FIGURE 8.2 Lambda syntax including optional parts

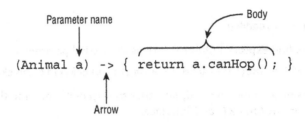

The parentheses around the lambda parameters can be omitted only if there is a single parameter and its type is not explicitly stated. Java does this because developers commonly use lambda expressions this way and can do as little typing as possible.

It shouldn't be news to you that we can omit braces when we have only a single statement. We did this with if statements and loops already. Java allows you to omit a return statement and semicolon (;) when no braces are used. This special shortcut doesn't work when you have two or more statements. At least this is consistent with using {} to create blocks of code elsewhere.

The syntax in Figure 8.1 and Figure 8.2 can be mixed and matched. For example, the following are valid:

```
a -> { return a.canHop(); }
(Animal a) -> a.canHop()
```

Here's a fun fact: s -> {} is a valid lambda. If there is no code on the right side of the expression, you don't need the semicolon or return statement.

Table 8.1 shows examples of valid lambdas that return a boolean.

TABLE 8.1 Valid lambdas that return a boolean

Lambda	# of parameters
() -> true	0
x -> x.startsWith("test")	1
(String x) -> x.startsWith("test")	1
(x, y) -> { return x.startsWith("test"); }	2
(String x, String y) -> x.startsWith("test")	2

The first row takes zero parameters and always returns the boolean value true. The second row takes one parameter and calls a method on it, returning the result. The third row does the same, except that it explicitly defines the type of the variable. The final two rows take two parameters and ignore one of them—there isn't a rule that says you must use all defined parameters.

Now let's make sure you can identify invalid syntax for each row in Table 8.2, where each lambda is supposed to return a boolean. Make sure you understand what's wrong with these.

TABLE 8.2 Invalid lambdas that should return a boolean

Invalid lambda	Reason
x, y -> x.startsWith("fish")	Missing parentheses on left
x -> { x.startsWith("camel"); }	Missing return on right
x -> { return x.startsWith("giraffe") }	Missing semicolon inside braces
String x -> x.endsWith("eagle")	Missing parentheses on left

Remember that the parentheses are optional *only* when there is one parameter and it doesn't have a type declared. Those are the basics of writing a lambda. At the end of the chapter, we cover additional rules about using variables in a lambda.

Assigning Lambdas to *var*

Why do you think this line of code doesn't compile?

```
var invalid = (Animal a) -> a.canHop();  // DOES NOT COMPILE
```

Remember when we talked about Java inferring information about the lambda from the context? Well, var assumes the type based on the context as well. There's not enough context here! Neither the lambda nor var have enough information to determine what type of functional interface should be used.

Coding Functional Interfaces

Earlier in the chapter, we declared the CheckTrait interface, which has exactly one method for implementers to write. Lambdas have a special relationship with such interfaces. In fact, these interfaces have a name. A *functional interface* is an interface that contains a single abstract method. Your friend Sam can help you remember this because it is officially known as a *single abstract method (SAM)* rule.

Defining a Functional Interface

Let's take a look at an example of a functional interface and a class that implements it:

```
@FunctionalInterface
public interface Sprint {
    public void sprint(int speed);
}

public class Tiger implements Sprint {
    public void sprint(int speed) {
        System.out.println("Animal is sprinting fast! " + speed);
    }
}
```

In this example, the Sprint interface is a functional interface because it contains exactly one abstract method, and the Tiger class is a valid class that implements the interface.

The *@FunctionalInterface* Annotation

The @FunctionalInterface annotation tells the compiler that you intend for the code to be a functional interface. If the interface does not follow the rules for a functional interface, the compiler will give you an error.

```
@FunctionalInterface  // DOES NOT COMPILE
public interface Dance {
    void move();
    void rest();
}
```

Java includes @FunctionalInterface on some, but not all, functional interfaces. This annotation means the authors of the interface promise it will be safe to use in a lambda in the future. However, just because you don't see the annotation doesn't mean it's not a functional interface. Remember that having exactly one abstract method is what makes it a functional interface, not the annotation.

Consider the following four interfaces. Given our previous Sprint functional interface, which of the following are functional interfaces?

```
public interface Dash extends Sprint {}

public interface Skip extends Sprint {
```

```java
    void skip();
}

public interface Sleep {
    private void snore() {}
    default int getZzz() { return 1; }
}

public interface Climb {
    void reach();
    default void fall() {}
    static int getBackUp() { return 100; }
    private static boolean checkHeight() { return true; }
}
```

All four of these are valid interfaces, but not all of them are functional interfaces. The `Dash` interface is a functional interface because it extends the `Sprint` interface and inherits the single abstract method `sprint()`. The `Skip` interface is not a valid functional interface because it has two abstract methods: the inherited `sprint()` method and the declared `skip()` method.

The `Sleep` interface is also not a valid functional interface. Neither `snore()` nor `getZzz()` meets the criteria of a single abstract method. Even though `default` methods function like abstract methods, in that they can be overridden in a class implementing the interface, they are insufficient for satisfying the single abstract method requirement.

Finally, the `Climb` interface is a functional interface. Despite defining a slew of `static`, `private`, and `default` methods, it contains only one abstract method: `reach()`.

Adding Object Methods

All classes inherit certain methods from `Object`. For the exam, you should know the following `Object` method signatures:

- `public String toString()`
- `public boolean equals(Object)`
- `public int hashCode()`

We bring this up now because there is one exception to the single abstract method rule that you should be familiar with. If a functional interface includes an abstract method with the same signature as a `public` method found in `Object`, *those methods do not count toward the single abstract method test.* The motivation behind this rule is that any class that implements the interface will inherit from `Object`, as all classes do, and therefore always implement these methods.

 Since Java assumes all classes extend from `Object`, you also cannot declare an interface method that is incompatible with `Object`. For example, declaring an abstract method int toString() in an interface would not compile since Object's version of the method returns a String.

Let's take a look at an example. Is the Soar class a functional interface?

```
public interface Soar {
   abstract String toString();
}
```

It is not. Since toString() is a public method implemented in Object, it does not count toward the single abstract method test. On the other hand, the following implementation of Dive is a functional interface:

```
public interface Dive {
   String toString();
   public boolean equals(Object o);
   public abstract int hashCode();
   public void dive();
}
```

The dive() method is the single abstract method, while the others are not counted since they are public methods defined in the Object class.

Be wary of examples that resemble methods in the Object class but are not actually defined in the Object class. Do you see why the following is not a valid functional interface?

```
public interface Hibernate {
   String toString();
   public boolean equals(Hibernate o);
   public abstract int hashCode();
   public void rest();
}
```

Despite looking a lot like our Dive interface, the Hibernate interface uses equals(Hibernate) instead of equals(Object). Because this does not match the method signature of the equals(Object) method defined in the Object class, this interface is counted as containing two abstract methods: equals(Hibernate) and rest().

Using Method References

Method references are another way to make the code easier to read, such as simply mentioning the name of the method. Like lambdas, it takes time to get used to the new syntax. In this section, we show the syntax along with the four types of method references. We also mix in lambdas with method references.

Suppose we are coding a duckling that is trying to learn how to quack. First we have a functional interface:

```
public interface LearnToSpeak {
    void speak(String sound);
}
```

Next, we discover that our duckling is lucky. There is a helper class that the duckling can work with. We've omitted the details of teaching the duckling how to quack and left the part that calls the functional interface:

```
public class DuckHelper {
    public static void teacher(String name, LearnToSpeak learner) {
        // Exercise patience (omitted)
        learner.speak(name);
    }
}
```

Finally, it is time to put it all together and meet our little Duckling. This code implements the functional interface using a lambda:

```
public class Duckling {
    public static void makeSound(String sound) {
        LearnToSpeak learner = s -> System.out.println(s);
        DuckHelper.teacher(sound, learner);
    }
}
```

Not bad. There's a bit of redundancy, though. The lambda declares one parameter named s. However, it does nothing other than pass that parameter to another method. A method reference lets us remove that redundancy and instead write this:

```
LearnToSpeak learner = System.out::println;
```

The :: operator tells Java to call the println() method later. It will take a little while to get used to the syntax. Once you do, you may find your code is shorter and less distracting without writing as many lambdas.

Remember that :: is like a lambda, and it is used for deferred execution with a functional interface. You can even imagine the method reference as a lambda if it helps you.

A method reference and a lambda behave the same way at runtime. You can pretend the compiler turns your method references into lambdas for you.

There are four formats for method references.

- static methods
- Instance methods on a particular object

- Instance methods on a parameter to be determined at runtime
- Constructors

Let's take a brief look at each of these in turn. In each example, we show the method reference and its lambda equivalent. For now, we create a separate functional interface for each example. In the next section, we introduce built-in functional interfaces so you don't have to keep writing your own.

Calling *static* Methods

For this first example, we use a functional interface that converts a double to a long:

```
interface Converter {
    long round(double num);
}
```

We can implement this interface with the round() method in Math. Here we assign a method reference and a lambda to this functional interface:

```
14: Converter methodRef = Math::round;
15: Converter lambda = x -> Math.round(x);
16:
17: System.out.println(methodRef.round(100.1));  // 100
```

On line 14, we reference a method with one parameter, and Java knows that it's like a lambda with one parameter. Additionally, Java knows to pass that parameter to the method.

Wait a minute. You might be aware that the round() method is overloaded—it can take a double or a float. How does Java know that we want to call the version with a double? With both lambdas and method references, Java infers information from the *context*. In this case, we said that we were declaring a Converter, which has a method taking a double parameter. Java looks for a method that matches that description. If it can't find it or finds multiple matches, then the compiler will report an error. The latter is sometimes called an *ambiguous* type error.

Calling Instance Methods on a Particular Object

For this example, our functional interface checks if a String starts with a specified value.

```
interface StringStart {
    boolean beginningCheck(String prefix);
}
```

Conveniently, the String class has a startsWith() method that takes one parameter and returns a boolean. Let's look at how to use method references with this code:

```
18: var str = "Zoo";
19: StringStart methodRef = str::startsWith;
```

```
20: StringStart lambda = s -> str.startsWith(s);
21:
22: System.out.println(methodRef.beginningCheck("A"));  // false
```

Line 19 shows that we want to call str.startsWith() and pass a single parameter to be supplied at runtime. This would be a nice way of filtering the data in a list.

A method reference doesn't have to take any parameters. In this example, we create a functional interface with a method that doesn't take any parameters but returns a value:

```
interface StringChecker {
    boolean check();
}
```

We implement it by checking if the String is empty.

```
18: var str = "";
19: StringChecker methodRef = str::isEmpty;
20: StringChecker lambda = () -> str.isEmpty();
21:
22: System.out.print(methodRef.check());  // true
```

Since the method on String is an instance method, we call the method reference on an instance of the String class.

While all method references can be turned into lambdas, the opposite is not always true. For example, consider this code:

```
var str = "";
StringChecker lambda = () -> str.startsWith("Zoo");
```

How might we write this as a method reference? You might try one of the following:

```
StringChecker methodReference = str::startsWith;           // DOES NOT COMPILE

StringChecker methodReference = str::startsWith("Zoo");  // DOES NOT COMPILE
```

Neither of these works! While we can pass the str as part of the method reference, there's no way to pass the "Zoo" parameter with it. Therefore, it is not possible to write this lambda as a method reference.

Calling Instance Methods on a Parameter

This time, we are going to call the same instance method that doesn't take any parameters. The trick is that we will do so without knowing the instance in advance. We need a different functional interface this time since it needs to know about the String.

```
interface StringParameterChecker {
    boolean check(String text);
}
```

We can implement this functional interface as follows:

```
23: StringParameterChecker methodRef = String::isEmpty;
24: StringParameterChecker lambda = s -> s.isEmpty();
25:
26: System.out.println(methodRef.check("Zoo"));  // false
```

Line 23 says the method that we want to call is declared in `String`. It looks like a `static` method, but it isn't. Instead, Java knows that `isEmpty()` is an instance method that does not take any parameters. Java uses the parameter supplied at runtime as the instance on which the method is called.

Compare lines 23 and 24 with lines 19 and 20 of our instance example. They look similar, although one references a local variable named `str`, while the other only references the functional interface parameters.

You can even combine the two types of instance method references. Again, we need a new functional interface that takes two parameters.

```
interface StringTwoParameterChecker {
    boolean check(String text, String prefix);
}
```

Pay attention to the parameter order when reading the implementation.

```
26: StringTwoParameterChecker methodRef = String::startsWith;
27: StringTwoParameterChecker lambda = (s, p) -> s.startsWith(p);
28:
29: System.out.println(methodRef.check("Zoo", "A"));  // false
```

Since the functional interface takes two parameters, Java has to figure out what they represent. The first one will always be the instance of the object for instance methods. Any others are to be method parameters.

Remember that line 26 may look like a `static` method, but it is really a method reference declaring that the instance of the object will be specified later. Line 27 shows some of the power of a method reference. We were able to replace two lambda parameters this time.

Calling Constructors

A *constructor reference* is a special type of method reference that uses new instead of a method and instantiates an object. For this example, our functional interface will not take any parameters but will return a `String`.

```
interface EmptyStringCreator {
    String create();
}
```

To call this, we use new as if it were a method name.

```
30: EmptyStringCreator methodRef = String::new;
31: EmptyStringCreator lambda = () -> new String();
```

```
32:
33: var myString = methodRef.create();
34: System.out.println(myString.equals("Snake"));   // false
```

It expands like the method references you have seen so far. In the previous example, the lambda doesn't have any parameters.

Method references can be tricky. This time we create a functional interface that takes one parameter and returns a result:

```
interface StringCopier {
    String copy(String value);
}
```

In the implementation, notice that line 32 in the following example has the same method reference as line 30 in the previous example:

```
32: StringCopier methodRef = String::new;
33: StringCopier lambda = x -> new String(x);
34:
35: var myString = methodRef.copy("Zebra");
36: System.out.println(myString.equals("Zebra"));   // true
```

This means you can't always determine which method can be called by looking at the method reference. Instead, you have to look at the context to see what parameters are used and if there is a return type. In this example, Java sees that we are passing a String parameter and calls the constructor of String that takes such a parameter.

Reviewing Method References

Reading method references is helpful in understanding the code. Table 8.3 shows the four types of method references. If this table doesn't make sense, please reread the previous section. It can take a few tries before method references start to add up.

TABLE 8.3   Method references

Type	Before colon	After colon	Example
static methods	Class name	Method name	Math::random
Instance methods on a particular object	Instance variable name	Method name	str::startsWith
Instance methods on a parameter	Class name	Method name	String::isEmpty
Constructor	Class name	New	String::new

Working with Built-in Functional Interfaces

It would be inconvenient to write your own functional interface any time you want to write a lambda. Luckily, a large number of general-purpose functional interfaces are provided for you. We cover them in this section.

The core functional interfaces in Table 8.4 are provided in the `java.util.function` package. We cover generics in the next chapter, but for now, you just need to know that <T> allows the interface to take an object of a specified type. If a second type parameter is needed, we use the next letter, U. If a distinct return type is needed, we choose R for *return* as the generic type.

TABLE 8.4   Common functional interfaces

Functional interface	Return type	Method name	# of parameters
Supplier<T>	T	get()	0
Consumer<T>	void	accept(T)	1 (T)
BiConsumer<T, U>	void	accept(T,U)	2 (T, U)
Predicate<T>	boolean	test(T)	1 (T)
BiPredicate<T, U>	boolean	test(T,U)	2 (T, U)
Function<T, R>	R	apply(T)	1 (T)
BiFunction<T, U, R>	R	apply(T,U)	2 (T, U)
UnaryOperator<T>	T	apply(T)	1 (T)
BinaryOperator<T>	T	apply(T,T)	2 (T, T)

For the exam, you need to memorize Table 8.4. We will give you lots of practice in this section to help make it memorable. Before you ask, most of the time we don't assign the implementation of the interface to a variable. The interface name is implied, and it is passed directly to the method that needs it. We are introducing the names so that you can better understand and remember what is going on. By the next chapter, we will assume that you have this down and stop creating the intermediate variable.

You learn about a few more functional interfaces later in the book. In the next chapter, we cover Comparator. In Chapter 13, "Concurrency," we discuss Runnable and Callable. These may show up on the exam when you are asked to recognize functional interfaces.

Let's look at how to implement each of these interfaces. Since both lambdas and method references appear all over the exam, we show an implementation using both where possible. After introducing the interfaces, we also cover some convenience methods available on these interfaces.

Implementing *Supplier*

A Supplier is used when you want to generate or supply values without taking any input. The Supplier interface is defined as follows:

```
@FunctionalInterface
public interface Supplier<T> {
    T get();
}
```

You can create a LocalDate object using the factory method now(). This example shows how to use a Supplier to call this factory:

```
Supplier<LocalDate> s1 = LocalDate::now;
Supplier<LocalDate> s2 = () -> LocalDate.now();

LocalDate d1 = s1.get();
LocalDate d2 = s2.get();

System.out.println(d1);   // 2025-02-20
System.out.println(d2);   // 2025-02-20
```

This example prints a date twice. It's also a good opportunity to review static method references. The LocalDate::now method reference is used to create a Supplier to assign to an intermediate variable s1. A Supplier is often used when constructing new objects. For example, we can print two empty StringBuilder objects.

```
Supplier<StringBuilder> s1 = StringBuilder::new;
Supplier<StringBuilder> s2 = () -> new StringBuilder();

System.out.println(s1.get());   // Empty string
System.out.println(s2.get());   // Empty string
```

This time, we used a constructor reference to create the object. We've been using generics to declare what type of Supplier we are using. This can be a little long to read. Can you figure out what the following does? Just take it one step at a time.

```
Supplier<ArrayList<String>> s3 = ArrayList::new;
```

```
ArrayList<String> a1 = s3.get();
System.out.println(a1);  // []
```

We have a Supplier of a certain type. That type happens to be ArrayList<String>. Then calling get() creates a new instance of ArrayList<String>, which is the generic type of the Supplier—in other words, a generic that contains another generic. Be sure to look at the code carefully when this type of thing comes up.

Notice how we called get() on the functional interface. What would happen if we tried to print out s3 itself?

```
System.out.println(s3);
```

The code prints something like this:

```
functionalinterface.BuiltIns$$Lambda$1/0x0000000800066840@4909b8da
```

That's the result of calling toString() on a lambda. Yuck. This actually does mean something. Our test class is named BuiltIns, and it is in a package that we created named functionalinterface. Then comes $$, which means the class doesn't exist in a class file on the file system. It exists only in memory. You don't need to worry about the rest.

Implementing *Consumer* and *BiConsumer*

You use a Consumer when you want to do something with a parameter but not return anything. BiConsumer does the same thing, except that it takes two parameters. The interfaces are defined as follows:

```
@FunctionalInterface
public interface Consumer<T> {
    void accept(T t);
    // omitted default method
}
```

```
@FunctionalInterface
public interface BiConsumer<T, U> {
    void accept(T t, U u);
    // omitted default method
}
```

You'll notice this pattern. *Bi* means two. It comes from Latin, but you can remember it from English words like *binary* (0 or 1) or *bicycle* (two wheels). The interface method will always take two inputs when you see *Bi*.

Printing is a common use of the Consumer interface.

```
Consumer<String> c1 = System.out::println;
Consumer<String> c2 = x -> System.out.println(x);
```

```
c1.accept("Annie");   // Annie
c2.accept("Annie");   // Annie
```

BiConsumer is called with two parameters. They don't have to be the same type. For example, we can put a key and a value in a map using this interface:

```
var map = new HashMap<String, Integer>();
BiConsumer<String, Integer> b1 = map::put;
BiConsumer<String, Integer> b2 = (k, v) -> map.put(k, v);

b1.accept("chicken", 7);
b2.accept("chick", 1);

System.out.println(map);   // {chicken=7, chick=1}
```

The output is {chicken=7, chick=1}, which shows that both BiConsumer implementations were called. When declaring b1, we used an instance method reference on an object since we want to call a method on the local variable map. The code to instantiate b1 is a good bit shorter than the code for b2. This is probably why the exam is so fond of method references.

As another example, we use the same type for both generic parameters:

```
var map = new HashMap<String, String>();
BiConsumer<String, String> b1 = map::put;
BiConsumer<String, String> b2 = (k, v) -> map.put(k, v);

b1.accept("chicken", "Cluck");
b2.accept("chick", "Tweep");

System.out.println(map);   // {chicken=Cluck, chick=Tweep}
```

This shows that a BiConsumer can use the same type for both the T and U generic parameters.

Implementing *Predicate* and *BiPredicate*

Predicate is often used when filtering or matching. Both are common operations. A BiPredicate is just like a Predicate, except that it takes two parameters instead of one. The interfaces are defined as follows:

```
@FunctionalInterface
public interface Predicate<T> {
   boolean test(T t);
   // omitted default and static methods
}
```

```
@FunctionalInterface
public interface BiPredicate<T, U> {
    boolean test(T t, U u);
    // omitted default methods
}
```

You can use a Predicate to test a condition.

```
Predicate<String> p1 = String::isEmpty;
Predicate<String> p2 = x -> x.isEmpty();

System.out.println(p1.test(""));  // true
System.out.println(p2.test(""));  // true
```

This prints true twice. More interesting is a BiPredicate. This example also prints true twice:

```
BiPredicate<String, String> b1 = String::startsWith;
BiPredicate<String, String> b2 =
    (string, prefix) -> string.startsWith(prefix);

System.out.println(b1.test("chicken", "chick"));  // true
System.out.println(b2.test("chicken", "chick"));  // true
```

The method reference includes both the instance variable and parameter for startsWith(). This is a good example of how method references save quite a lot of typing. The downside is that they are less explicit, and you really have to understand what is going on!

Implementing *Function* and *BiFunction*

A Function is responsible for turning one parameter into a value of a potentially different type and returning it. Similarly, a BiFunction is responsible for turning two parameters into a value and returning it. The interfaces are defined as follows:

```
@FunctionalInterface
public interface Function<T, R> {
    R apply(T t);
    // omitted default and static methods
}
```

```
@FunctionalInterface
public interface BiFunction<T, U, R> {
    R apply(T t, U u);
    // omitted default method
}
```

For example, this function converts a String to the length of the String:

```
Function<String, Integer> f1 = String::length;
Function<String, Integer> f2 = x -> x.length();

System.out.println(f1.apply("cluck"));   // 5
System.out.println(f2.apply("cluck"));   // 5
```

This function turns a String into an Integer. Well, technically, it turns the String into an int, which is autoboxed into an Integer. The types don't have to be different. The following combines two String objects and produces another String:

```
BiFunction<String, String, String> b1 = String::concat;
BiFunction<String, String, String> b2 =
    (string, toAdd) -> string.concat(toAdd);

System.out.println(b1.apply("baby ", "chick"));   // baby chick
System.out.println(b2.apply("baby ", "chick"));   // baby chick
```

The first two types in the BiFunction are the input types. The third is the result type. For the method reference, the first parameter is the instance that concat() is called on, and the second is passed to concat().

Implementing *UnaryOperator* and *BinaryOperator*

UnaryOperator and BinaryOperator are special cases of a Function. They require all type parameters to be the same type. A UnaryOperator transforms its value into one of the same type. For example, incrementing by one is a unary operation. In fact, UnaryOperator extends Function. A BinaryOperator merges two values into one of the same type. Adding two numbers is a binary operation. Similarly, BinaryOperator extends BiFunction. The interfaces are defined as follows:

```
@FunctionalInterface
public interface UnaryOperator<T> extends Function<T, T> {
    // omitted static method
}


@FunctionalInterface
public interface BinaryOperator<T> extends BiFunction<T, T, T> {
    // omitted static methods
}
```

This means the method signatures look like this:

```
T apply(T t);          // UnaryOperator


T apply(T t1, T t2);   // BinaryOperator
```

In the Javadoc, you'll notice that these methods are inherited from the Function/BiFunction superclass. The generic declarations on the subclass are what force the type to be the same. For the unary example, notice how the return type is the same type as the parameter.

```
UnaryOperator<String> u1 = String::toUpperCase;
UnaryOperator<String> u2 = x -> x.toUpperCase();

System.out.println(u1.apply("chirp"));  // CHIRP
System.out.println(u2.apply("chirp"));  // CHIRP
```

This prints CHIRP twice. We don't need to specify the return type in the generics because UnaryOperator requires it to be the same as the parameter. And now here's the binary example:

```
BinaryOperator<String> b1 = String::concat;
BinaryOperator<String> b2 = (string, toAdd) -> string.concat(toAdd);

System.out.println(b1.apply("baby ", "chick"));  // baby chick
System.out.println(b2.apply("baby ", "chick"));  // baby chick
```

Notice that this does the same thing as the BiFunction example. The code is more succinct, which shows the importance of using the best functional interface. It's nice to have one generic type specified instead of three.

Checking Functional Interfaces

It's really important to know the number of parameters, types, return value, and method name for each of the functional interfaces. Now would be a good time to memorize Table 8.4 if you haven't done so already. Let's do some examples to practice.

What functional interface would you use in these three situations?

- Returns a String without taking any parameters
- Returns a Boolean and takes a String
- Returns an Integer and takes two Integers

Ready? Think about what your answers are before continuing. Really. You have to know this cold. OK, the first one is a Supplier<String> because it generates an object and takes zero parameters. The second one is a Function<String,Boolean> because it takes one parameter and returns another type. It's a little tricky. You might think it is a Predicate<String>. Note that a Predicate returns a boolean primitive and not a Boolean object.

Finally, the third one is either a BinaryOperator<Integer> or a BiFunction <Integer,Integer,Integer>. Since BinaryOperator is a special case of BiFunction, either is a correct answer. BinaryOperator<Integer> is the better answer of the two since it is more specific.

Let's try this exercise again but with code. It's harder with code. The first thing you do is look at how many parameters the lambda takes and whether there is a return value. What functional interface would you use to fill in the blanks for these?

```
6: _____ <List> ex1 = x -> "".equals(x.get(0));
7: _____ <Long> ex2 = (Long l) -> System.out.println(l);
8: _____ <String, String> ex3 = (s1, s2) -> false;
```

Again, think about the answers before continuing. Ready? Line 6 passes one List parameter to the lambda and returns a boolean. This tells us that it is a Predicate or Function. Since the generic declaration has only one parameter, it is a Predicate.

Line 7 passes one Long parameter to the lambda and doesn't return anything. This tells us that it is a Consumer. Line 8 takes two parameters and returns a boolean. When you see a boolean returned, think Predicate unless the generics specify a Boolean return type. In this case, there are two parameters, so it is a BiPredicate.

Are you finding these easy? If not, review Table 8.4 again. We aren't kidding. You need to know the table really well. Now that you are fresh from studying the table, we are going to play "identify the error." These are meant to be tricky.

```
6: Function<List<String>> ex1 = x -> x.get(0); // DOES NOT COMPILE
7: UnaryOperator<Long> ex2 = (Long l) -> 3.14; // DOES NOT COMPILE
```

Line 6 claims to be a Function. A Function needs to specify two generic types: the input parameter type and the return value type. The return value type is missing from line 6, causing the code not to compile. Line 7 is a UnaryOperator, which returns the same type as it is passed in. The example returns a double rather than a Long, causing the code not to compile.

Using Convenience Methods on Functional Interfaces

By definition, all functional interfaces have a single abstract method. This doesn't mean they can have only one method, though. Several of the common functional interfaces provide a number of helpful default interface methods.

Table 8.5 shows the convenience methods on the built-in functional interfaces that you need to know for the exam. All of these facilitate modifying or combining functional interfaces of the same type. Note that Table 8.5 shows only the main interfaces. The BiConsumer, BiFunction, and BiPredicate interfaces have similar methods available.

TABLE 8.5 Convenience methods

Interface instance	Method return type	Method name	Method parameters
Consumer	Consumer	andThen()	Consumer
Function	Function	andThen()	Function
Function	Function	compose()	Function

TABLE 8.5   Convenience methods *(continued)*

Interface instance	Method return type	Method name	Method parameters
Predicate	Predicate	and()	Predicate
Predicate	Predicate	negate()	—
Predicate	Predicate	or()	Predicate

Let's start with these two `Predicate` variables:

```
Predicate<String> egg = s -> s.contains("egg");
Predicate<String> brown = s -> s.contains("brown");
```

Now we want a `Predicate` for brown eggs and another for all other colors of eggs. We could write this by hand, as shown here:

```
Predicate<String> brownEggs = s -> s.contains("egg") && s.contains("brown");
Predicate<String> otherEggs = s -> s.contains("egg") && !s.contains("brown");
```

This works, but it's not great. It's a bit long to read, and it contains duplication. What if we decide the letter *e* should be capitalized in *egg*? We'd have to change it in three variables: egg, brownEggs, and otherEggs. A better way to deal with this situation is to use two of the `default` methods on `Predicate`.

```
Predicate<String> brownEggs = egg.and(brown);
Predicate<String> otherEggs = egg.and(brown.negate());
```

Neat! Now we are reusing the logic in the original `Predicate` variables to build two new ones. It's shorter and clearer what the relationship is between variables. We can also change the spelling of *egg* in one place, and the other two objects will have new logic because they reference it.

Moving on to `Consumer`, let's take a look at the `andThen()` method, which runs two functional interfaces in sequence.

```
Consumer<String> c1 = x -> System.out.print("1: " + x);
Consumer<String> c2 = x -> System.out.print(",2: " + x);

Consumer<String> combined = c1.andThen(c2);
combined.accept("Annie");   // 1: Annie,2: Annie
```

Notice how the same parameter is passed to both c1 and c2. This shows that the `Consumer` instances are run in sequence and are independent of each other. By contrast, the `compose()` method on `Function` chains functional interfaces. However, it passes along the output of one to the input of another.

```
Function<Integer, Integer> before = x -> x + 1;
Function<Integer, Integer> after = x -> x * 2;

Function<Integer, Integer> combined = after.compose(before);
System.out.println(combined.apply(3));    // 8
```

This time, the before runs first, turning the 3 into 4. Then the after runs, doubling the 4 to 8. All of the methods in this section are helpful for simplifying your code as you work with functional interfaces.

Learning the Functional Interfaces for Primitives

Remember when we told you to memorize Table 8.4 with the common functional interfaces? Did you? If you didn't, go do it now. We'll wait. We are about to make it more involved. There are also a large number of special functional interfaces for primitives. These are useful in Chapter 10 when we cover streams and optionals.

Most of them are for the double, int, and long types. There is one exception, which is BooleanSupplier. We cover that before introducing the functional interfaces for double, int, and long.

Functional Interfaces for *boolean*

BooleanSupplier is a separate type. It has one method to implement.

```
@FunctionalInterface
public interface BooleanSupplier {
    boolean getAsBoolean();
}
```

It works just as you've come to expect from functional interfaces. Here's an example:

```
12: BooleanSupplier b1 = () -> true;
13: BooleanSupplier b2 = () -> Math.random()> .5;
14: System.out.println(b1.getAsBoolean());    // true
15: System.out.println(b2.getAsBoolean());    // false
```

Lines 12 and 13 each create a BooleanSupplier, which is the only functional interface for boolean. Line 14 prints true, since it is the result of b1. Line 15 prints true or false, depending on the random value generated.

Functional Interfaces for *double, int,* and *long*

Most of the functional interfaces are for double, int, and long. Table 8.6 shows the equivalent of Table 8.4 for these primitives. You probably won't be surprised that you have to memorize it. Luckily, you've memorized Table 8.4 by now and can apply what you've learned to Table 8.6.

TABLE 8.6   Common functional interfaces for primitives

Functional interfaces	Return type	Single abstract method	# of parameters
DoubleSupplier IntSupplier LongSupplier	double int long	getAsDouble getAsInt getAsLong	0
DoubleConsumer IntConsumer LongConsumer	void	accept	1 (double) 1 (int) 1 (long)
DoublePredicate IntPredicate LongPredicate	boolean	test	1 (double) 1 (int) 1 (long)
DoubleFunction<R> IntFunction<R> LongFunction<R>	R	apply	1 (double) 1 (int) 1 (long)
DoubleUnaryOperator IntUnaryOperator LongUnaryOperator	double int long	applyAsDouble applyAsInt applyAsLong	1 (double) 1 (int) 1 (long)
DoubleBinaryOperator IntBinaryOperator LongBinaryOperator	double int long	applyAsDouble applyAsInt applyAsLong	2 (double, double) 2 (int, int) 2 (long, long)

There are a few things to notice that are different between Table 8.4 and Table 8.6.

- Generics are gone from some of the interfaces, and instead the type name tells us what primitive type is involved. In other cases, such as IntFunction, only the return type generic is needed because we're converting a primitive int into an object.

- The single abstract method is often renamed when a primitive type is returned.

In addition to Table 8.4 equivalents, some interfaces are specific to primitives. Table 8.7 lists these.

TABLE 8.7   Primitive-specific functional interfaces

Functional interfaces	Return type	Single abstract method	# of parameters
ToDoubleFunction<T> ToIntFunction<T> ToLongFunction<T>	double int long	applyAsDouble applyAsInt applyAsLong	1 (T)

Functional interfaces	Return type	Single abstract method	# of parameters
ToDoubleBiFunction<T, U>	double	applyAsDouble	2 (T, U)
ToIntBiFunction<T, U>	int	applyAsInt	
ToLongBiFunction<T, U>	long	applyAsLong	
DoubleToIntFunction	int	applyAsInt	1 (double)
DoubleToLongFunction	long	applyAsLong	1 (double)
IntToDoubleFunction	double	applyAsDouble	1 (int)
IntToLongFunction	long	applyAsLong	1 (int)
LongToDoubleFunction	double	applyAsDouble	1 (long)
LongToIntFunction	int	applyAsInt	1 (long)
ObjDoubleConsumer<T>	void	accept	2 (T, double)
ObjIntConsumer<T>			2 (T, int)
ObjLongConsumer<T>			2 (T, long)

We've been using functional interfaces for a while now, so you should have a good grasp of how to read the table. Let's do one example just to be sure. Which functional interface would you use to fill in the blank to make the following code compile?

```
var d = 1.0;
_____ f1 = x -> 1;
f1.applyAsInt(d);
```

When you see a question like this, look for clues. You can see that the functional interface in question takes a double parameter and returns an int. You can also see that it has a single abstract method named applyAsInt. The DoubleToIntFunction and ToIntFunction functional interfaces meet all three of those criteria.

Working with Variables in Lambdas

Now that we've learned about functional interfaces, we will use them to show different approaches for variables. They can appear in three places with respect to lambdas: the parameter list, local variables declared inside the lambda body, and variables referenced from the lambda body. All three of these are opportunities for the exam to trick you. We explore each one so you'll be alert when tricks show up!

Listing Parameters

Earlier in this chapter, you learned that specifying the type of parameters is optional. Additionally, var can be used in place of the specific type. That means all three of these statements are interchangeable:

```
Predicate<String> p = x -> true;
Predicate<String> p = (var x) -> true;
Predicate<String> p = (String x) -> true;
```

The exam might ask you to identify the type of the lambda parameter. In our example, the answer is String. How did we figure that out? A lambda infers the types from the surrounding context. That means you get to do the same.

In this case, the lambda is being assigned to a Predicate that takes a String. Another place to look for the type is in a method signature. Let's try another example. Can you figure out the type of x?

```
public void whatAmI() {
    consume((var x) -> System.out.print(x), 123);
}
public void consume(Consumer<Integer> c, int num) {
    c.accept(num);
}
```

If you guessed Integer, you were right. The whatAmI() method creates a lambda to be passed to the consume() method. Since the consume() method expects an Integer as the generic, we know that is what the inferred type of x will be.

But wait; there's more. In some cases, you can determine the type without even seeing the method signature. What do you think the type of x is here?

```
public void counts(List<Integer> list) {
    list.sort((var x, var y) -> x.compareTo(y));
}
```

The answer is again Integer. Since we are sorting a list, we can use the type of the list to determine the type of the lambda parameter.

Since lambda parameters are just like method parameters, you can add modifiers to them. Specifically, you can add the final modifier or an annotation, as shown in this example:

```
public void counts(List<Integer> list) {
    list.sort((final var x, @Deprecated var y) -> x.compareTo(y));
}
```

While this tends to be uncommon in real life, modifiers such as these have been known to appear in passing on the exam.

Parameter List Formats

You have three formats for specifying parameter types within a lambda: without types, with types, and with `var`. The compiler requires all parameters in the lambda to use the same format. Can you see why the following are not valid?

```
5: (var x, y) -> "Hello"                 // DOES NOT COMPILE
6: (var x, Integer y) -> true            // DOES NOT COMPILE
7: (String x, var y, Integer z) -> true  // DOES NOT COMPILE
8: (Integer x, y) -> "goodbye"           // DOES NOT COMPILE
```

Lines 5 needs to remove `var` from x or add it to y. Next, lines 6 and 7 need to use the type or `var` consistently. Finally, line 8 needs to remove `Integer` from x or add a type to y.

Using Local Variables Inside a Lambda Body

While it is most common for a lambda body to be a single expression, it is legal to define a block. That block can have anything that is valid in a normal Java block, including local variable declarations.

The following code does just that. It creates a local variable named c that is scoped to the lambda block:

```
(a, b) -> { int c = 0; return 5; }
```

Now let's try another one. Do you see what's wrong here?

```
(a, b) -> { int a = 0; return 5; }     // DOES NOT COMPILE
```

We tried to redeclare a, which is not allowed. Java doesn't let you create a local variable with the same name as one already declared in that scope. While this kind of error is less likely to come up in real life, it has been known to appear on the exam!

Now let's try a hard one. How many syntax errors do you see in this method?

```
11: public void variables(int a) {
12:     int b = 1;
13:     Predicate<Integer> p1 = a -> {
14:         int b = 0;
15:         int c = 0;
16:         return b == c; }
17: }
```

There are three syntax errors. The first is on line 13. The variable a was already used in this scope as a method parameter, so it cannot be reused. The next syntax error comes on line 14, where the code attempts to redeclare local variable b. The third syntax error is quite subtle and on line 16. See it? Look really closely.

The variable p1 is missing a semicolon at the end. There is a semicolon before the },
but that is inside the block. While you don't normally have to look for missing semicolons,
lambdas are tricky in this space, so beware!

 Real World Scenario

Keep Your Lambdas Short

Having a lambda with multiple lines and a return statement is often a clue that you
should refactor and put that code in a method. For example, the previous example could be
rewritten as follows:

```
Predicate<Integer> p1 = a -> returnSame(a);
```

This simpler form can be further refactored to use a method reference:

```
Predicate<Integer> p1 = this::returnSame;
```

You might be wondering why this is so important. In Chapter 10, lambdas and method
references are used in chained method calls. The shorter the lambda, the easier it is to
read the code.

Referencing Variables from the Lambda Body

Lambda bodies are allowed to reference some variables from the surrounding code. The
following code is legal:

```
public class Crow {
    private String color;
    public void caw(String name) {
        String volume = "loudly";
        Consumer<String> consumer = s ->
            System.out.println(name + " says "
                + volume + " that she is " + color);
    }
}
```

This shows that a lambda can access an instance variable, method parameter, or local variable under certain conditions. Instance variables (and class variables) are always allowed.

The only thing lambdas cannot access are variables that are not final or effectively final.
If you need a refresher on effectively final, see Chapter 5, "Methods."

It gets even more interesting when you look at where the compiler errors occur when the
variables are not effectively final.

```
2:  public class Crow {
3:      private String color;
```

```
4:      public void caw(String name) {
5:          String volume = "loudly";
6:          name = "Caty";
7:          color = "black";
8:
9:          Consumer<String> consumer = s ->
10:            System.out.println(name + " says "        // DOES NOT COMPILE
11:                + volume + " that she is " + color);   // DOES NOT COMPILE
12:         volume = "softly";
13:     }
14: }
```

In this example, the method parameter name is not effectively final because it is set on line 6. However, the compiler error occurs on line 10. It's not a problem to assign a value to a non-final variable. However, once the lambda tries to use it, we do have a problem. The variable is no longer effectively final, so the lambda is not allowed to use the variable.

The variable volume is not effectively final either since it is updated on line 12. In this case, the compiler error is on line 11. That's before the reassignment! Again, the act of assigning a value is only a problem from the point of view of the lambda. Therefore, the lambda has to be the one to generate the compiler error.

To review, make sure you've memorized Table 8.8.

TABLE 8.8 Rules for accessing a variable from a lambda body inside a method

Variable type	Rule
Instance variable	Allowed
Static variable	Allowed
Local variable	Allowed if final or effectively final
Method parameter	Allowed if final or effectively final
Lambda parameter	Allowed

Summary

We spent a lot of time in this chapter teaching you how to use lambda expressions, and with good reason. The next two chapters depend heavily on your ability to create and use lambda expressions. We recommend you understand this chapter well before moving on.

Lambda expressions, or lambdas, allow passing around blocks of code. The full syntax looks like this:

```
(String a, String b) -> { return a.equals(b); }
```

The parameter types can be omitted. When only one parameter is specified without a type, the parentheses can also be omitted. The braces, semicolon, and `return` statement can be omitted for a single statement, making the short form as follows:

```
a -> a.equals(b)
```

Lambdas can be passed to a method expecting an instance of a functional interface. A lambda can define parameters or variables in the body as long as their names are different from existing local variables. The body of a lambda is allowed to use any instance or class variables. Additionally, it can use any local variables or method parameters that are `final` or effectively final.

A method reference is a compact syntax for writing lambdas that refer to methods. There are four types: `static` methods, instance methods on a particular object, instance methods on a parameter, and constructor references.

A functional interface has a single abstract method. Any functional interface can be implemented with a lambda expression. You must know the built-in functional interfaces.

You should review the tables in the chapter. While there are many tables, some share common patterns, making it easier to remember them. You absolutely must memorize Table 8.4, which lists the common functional interfaces.

Exam Essentials

Write simple lambda expressions. Look for the presence or absence of optional elements in lambda code. Parameter types are optional. Braces, a semicolon, and the `return` keyword are optional when the body is a single statement. Parentheses are optional when only one parameter is specified and the type is implicit.

Determine whether a variable can be used in a lambda body. Local variables and method parameters must be `final` or effectively final to be referenced. This means the code must compile if you were to add the `final` keyword to these variables. Instance and class variables are always allowed.

Translate method references to the "long-form" lambda. Be able to convert method references into regular lambda expressions, and vice versa. For example, `System.out::print` and `x -> System.out.print(x)` are equivalent. Remember that the order of method parameters is inferred for method references.

Determine whether an interface is a functional interface. Use the single abstract method (SAM) rule to determine whether an interface is a functional interface. Other interface method types (`default`, `private`, `static`, and `private static`) do not count toward the single abstract method count, nor do any `public` methods with signatures found in `Object`.

Identify the correct functional interface given the number of parameters, return type, and method name—and vice versa. The most common functional interfaces are `Supplier`, `Consumer`, `Function`, and `Predicate`. There are also binary versions and primitive versions of many of these methods. You can use the number of parameters and return type to tell them apart.

Review Questions

The answers to the chapter review questions can be found in the Appendix.

1. What is the result of the following class?

```
1:  import java.util.function.*;
2:
3:  public class Panda {
4:      int age;
5:      public static void main(String[] args) {
6:          Panda p1 = new Panda();
7:          p1.age = 1;
8:          check(p1, p -> p.age < 5);
9:      }
10:     private static void check(Panda panda,
11:         Predicate<Panda> pred) {
12:         String result =
13:             pred.test(panda) ? "match" : "not match";
14:         System.out.print(result);
15: } }
```

A. match

B. not match

C. Compiler error on line 8

D. Compiler error on lines 10 and 11

E. Compiler error on lines 12 and 13

F. A runtime exception

2. What is the result of the following code?

```
1:  interface Climb {
2:      boolean isTooHigh(int height, int limit);
3:  }
4:
5:  public class Climber {
6:      public static void main(String[] args) {
7:          check((h, m) -> h.append(m).isEmpty(), 5);
8:      }
9:      private static void check(Climb climb, int height) {
10:         if (climb.isTooHigh(height, 10))
11:             System.out.println("too high");
12:         else
```

```
13:            System.out.println("ok");
14:    }
15: }
```

A. ok

B. too high

C. Compiler error on line 7.

D. Compiler error on line 10.

E. Compiler error on a different line.

F. A runtime exception is thrown.

3. Which statements about functional interfaces are true? (Choose all that apply.)

    A. A functional interface can contain `default` and `private` methods.

    B. A functional interface can be defined as a class or an interface.

    C. Abstract methods with signatures that are contained in `public` methods of `java.lang.Object` do not count toward the abstract method count for a functional interface.

    D. A functional interface cannot contain `static` or `private static` methods.

    E. A functional interface must be marked with the `@FunctionalInterface` annotation.

4. Which lambda can replace the `MySecret` class to return the same value? (Choose all that apply.)

```
interface Secret {
    String magic(double d);
}

class MySecret implements Secret {
    public String magic(double d) {
        return "Poof";
    } }
```

    A. `(e) -> "Poof"`

    B. `(e) -> {"Poof"}`

    C. `(e) -> { String e = ""; "Poof" }`

    D. `(e) -> { String e = ""; return "Poof"; }`

    E. `(e) -> { String e = ""; return "Poof" }`

    F. `(e) -> { String f = ""; return "Poof"; }`

5. Which of the following functional interfaces contain an abstract method that returns a primitive value? (Choose all that apply.)

    A. `BooleanSupplier`

    B. `CharSupplier`

    C. `DoubleSupplier`

    D. `FloatSupplier`

    E. `IntSupplier`

    F. `StringSupplier`

6. Which of the following lambda expressions can be passed to a function of `Predicate<String>` type? (Choose all that apply.)

    A. `s -> s.isEmpty()`

    B. `s --> s.isEmpty()`

    C. `(String s) -> s.isEmpty()`

    D. `(String s) --> s.isEmpty()`

    E. `(StringBuilder s) -> s.isEmpty()`

    F. `(StringBuilder s) --> s.isEmpty()`

7. Which of these statements is true about the following code?

```
public void method() {
    x((var x) -> {}, (var x, var y) -> false);
}
public void x(Consumer<String> x, BinaryOperator<Boolean> y) {}
```

    A. The code does not compile because of one of the variables named x.

    B. The code does not compile because of one of the variables named y.

    C. The code does not compile for another reason.

    D. The code compiles, and the x in each lambda refers to the same type.

    E. The code compiles, and the x in each lambda refers to a different type.

8. Which of the following is equivalent to this code?

```
UnaryOperator<Integer> u = x -> x * x;
```

    A. `BiFunction<Integer> f = x -> x*x;`

    B. `BiFunction<Integer, Integer> f = x -> x*x;`

    C. `BinaryOperator<Integer, Integer> f = x -> x*x;`

    D. `Function<Integer> f = x -> x*x;`

    E. `Function<Integer, Integer> f = x -> x*x;`

    F. None of the above

9. Which statements are true? (Choose all that apply.)

    A. The `Consumer` interface is good for printing out an existing value.

    B. The `Supplier` interface is good for printing out an existing value.

    C. The `IntegerSupplier` interface returns an `int`.

    D. The `Predicate` interface returns an `int`.

    E. The `Function` interface has a method named `test()`.

    F. The `Predicate` interface has a method named `test()`.

10. Which of the following can be inserted without causing a compilation error? (Choose all that apply.)

```
public void remove(List<Character> chars) {
    char end = 'z';
    Predicate<Character> predicate = c -> {
        char start = 'a'; return start <= c && c <= end; };

    // INSERT LINE HERE
}
```

A. `char start = 'a';`

B. `char c = 'x';`

C. `chars = null;`

D. `end = '1';`

E. None of the above

11. How many times is `true` printed out by this code?

```
import java.util.function.Predicate;
public class Fantasy {
    public static void scary(String animal) {
        var dino = s -> "dino".equals(animal);
        var dragon = s -> "dragon".equals(animal);
        var combined = dino.or(dragon);
        System.out.println(combined.test(animal));
    }
    public static void main(String[] args) {
        scary("dino");
        scary("dragon");
        scary("unicorn");
    }
}
```

A. One.

B. Two.

C. Three.

D. The code does not compile.

E. A runtime exception is thrown.

12. What does the following code output?

```
Function<Integer, Integer> s = a -> a + 4;
Function<Integer, Integer> t = a -> a * 3;
Function<Integer, Integer> c = s.compose(t);
System.out.print(c.apply(1));
```

A. 7

B. 15

C. The code does not compile because of the data types in the lambda expressions.

D. The code does not compile because of the `compose()` call.

E. The code does not compile for another reason.

13. Which is true of the following code?

```
int length = 3;

for (int i = 0; i<3; i++) {
    if (i%2 == 0) {
        Supplier<Integer> supplier = () -> length; // A
        System.out.println(supplier.get());        // B
    } else {
        int j = i;
        Supplier<Integer> supplier = () -> j;      // C
        System.out.println(supplier.get());        // D
    }
}
```

A. The first compiler error is on line A.

B. The first compiler error is on line B.

C. The first compiler error is on line C.

D. The first compiler error is on line D.

E. The code compiles successfully.

14. Which of the following are valid lambda expressions? (Choose all that apply.)

A. `(Wolf w, var c) -> 39`

B. `(final Camel c) -> {}`

C. `(a,b,c) -> {int b = 3; return 2;}`

D. `(x,y) -> new RuntimeException()`

E. `(var y) -> return 0;`

F. `() -> {float r}`

G. `(Cat a, b) -> {}`

15. Which lambda expression, when entered into the blank line in the following code, causes the program to print hahaha? (Choose all that apply.)

```
import java.util.function.Predicate;
public class Hyena {
    private int age = 1;
```

```
public static void main(String[] args) {
    var p = new Hyena();
    double height = 10;
    int age = 1;
    testLaugh(p, ——————————————— );
    age = 2;
}
static void testLaugh(Hyena panda, Predicate<Hyena> joke) {
    var r = joke.test(panda) ? "hahaha" : "silence";
    System.out.print(r);
}
}
```

A. `var -> p.age <= 10`

B. `shenzi -> age==1`

C. `p -> true`

D. `age==1`

E. `shenzi -> age==2`

F. `h -> h.age < 5`

G. None of the above, as the code does not compile

16. Which of the following can be inserted without causing a compilation error?

```
public void remove(List<Character> chars) {
    char end = 'z';

    // INSERT LINE HERE

    Predicate<Character> predicate = c -> {
        char start = 'a'; return start <= c && c <= end; };
}
```

A. `char start = 'a';`

B. `char c = 'x';`

C. `chars = null;`

D. `end = '1';`

E. None of the above

17. What is the result of running the following class?

```
1:  import java.util.function.*;
2:
3:  public class Panda {
```

```
4:      int age;
5:      public static void main(String[] args) {
6:          Panda p1 = new Panda();
7:          p1.age = 1;
8:          check(p1, p -> {p.age < 5});
9:      }
10:     private static void check(Panda panda,
11:         Predicate<Panda> pred) {
12:         String result = pred.test(panda)
13:             ? "match" : "not match";
14:         System.out.print(result);
15: } }
```

A. match

B. not match

C. Compiler error on line 8.

D. Compiler error on line 10.

E. Compiler error on line 12.

F. A runtime exception is thrown.

18. Which functional interfaces complete the following code? For line 7, assume m and n are instances of functional interfaces that exist and have the same type as y. (Choose three.)

```
6:  _____ x = String::new;
7:  _____ y = m.andThen(n);
8:  _____ z = a -> a + a;
```

A. BinaryConsumer<String, String>

B. BiConsumer<String, String>

C. BinaryFunction<String, String>

D. BiFunction<String, String>

E. Predicate<String>

F. Supplier<String>

G. UnaryOperator<String>

H. UnaryOperator<String, String>

19. Which of the following compiles and prints out the entire set?

```
Set<?> set = Set.of("lion", "tiger", "bear");
var s = Set.copyOf(set);
Consumer<Object> consumer = _____;
s.forEach(consumer);
```

A. `() -> System.out.println(s)`

B. `s -> System.out.println(s)`

C. `(s) -> System.out.println(s)`

D. `System.out.println(s)`

E. `System::out::println`

F. `System.out::println`

20. Which lambda can replace the new `Sloth()` call in the `main()` method and produce the same output at runtime?

```
import java.util.List;
interface Yawn {
    String yawn(double d, List<Integer> time);
}
class Sloth implements Yawn {
    public String yawn(double zzz, List<Integer> time) {
        return "Sleep: " + zzz;
    } }
public class Vet {
    public static String takeNap(Yawn y) {
        return y.yawn(10, null);
    }
    public static void main(String... unused) {
        System.out.print(takeNap(new Sloth()));
    } }
```

A. `(z,f) -> { String x = ""; return "Sleep: " + x }`

B. `(t,s) -> { String t = ""; return "Sleep: " + t; }`

C. `(w,q) -> {"Sleep: " + w}`

D. `(e,u) -> { String g = ""; "Sleep: " + e }`

E. `(a,b) -> "Sleep: " + (double)(b==null ? a : a)`

F. `(r,k) -> { String g = ""; return "Sleep:"; }`

G. None of the above, as the program does not compile

21. Which of the following are valid functional interfaces? (Choose all that apply.)

```
public interface Transport {
    public int go();
    public boolean equals(Object o);
}


public abstract class Car {
```

```
    public abstract Object swim(double speed, int duration);
}

public interface Locomotive extends Train {
    public int getSpeed();
}

public interface Train extends Transport {}

abstract interface Spaceship extends Transport {
    default int blastOff();
}

public interface Boat {
    int hashCode();
    int hashCode(String input);
}
```

A. Boat
B. Car
C. Locomotive
D. Spaceship
E. Transport
F. Train
G. None of these is a valid functional interface.

Chapter

9

Collections and Generics

OCP EXAM OBJECTIVES COVERED IN THIS CHAPTER:

✓ **Working with Arrays and Collections**

- Create arrays, List, Set, Map and Deque collections, and add, remove, update, retrieve and sort their elements.

In this chapter, we introduce the Java Collections Framework classes and interfaces you need to know for the exam. The thread-safe collections are discussed in Chapter 13, "Concurrency."

As you may remember from Chapter 8, "Lambdas and Functional Interfaces," we covered lambdas, method references, and built-in functional interfaces. Many of these are used throughout this chapter.

Next, we cover details about `Comparator`, `Comparable`, and sorting. We also introduce the new sequenced collections interfaces. Finally, we discuss how to create your own classes and methods that use generics so that the same class can be used with many types.

Using Common Collection APIs

A *collection* is a group of objects contained in a single object. The *Java Collections Framework* is a set of classes in `java.util` for storing collections. There are four main interfaces in the Java Collections Framework.

- **List:** A *list* is an ordered collection of elements that allows duplicate entries. Elements in a list can be accessed by an `int` index.

- **Set:** A *set* is a collection that does not allow duplicate entries.

- **Queue:** A *queue* is a collection that orders its elements in a specific order for processing. A Deque is a subinterface of `Queue` that allows access at both ends.

- **Map:** A *map* is a collection that maps keys to values, with no duplicate keys allowed. The elements in a map are key/value pairs.

Figure 9.1 shows the `Collection` interface, its subinterfaces, and some classes that implement the interfaces that you should know for the exam. The interfaces are shown in rectangles, with the classes in rounded boxes.

Notice that Map doesn't implement the `Collection` interface. It is considered part of the Java Collections Framework even though it isn't technically a `Collection`. It is a collection (note the lowercase), though, in that it contains a group of objects. The reason maps are treated differently is that they need different methods due to being key/value pairs.

FIGURE 9.1   Java Collections Framework

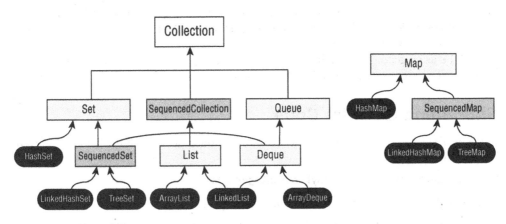

Notice anything new in Figure 9.1? Brand new to Java 21 are sequenced collections! We'll discuss SequencedSet, SequencedCollection, and SequencedMap later in this chapter.

In this section, we discuss the common methods that the Collections API provides to the implementing classes. Many of these methods are *convenience methods* that could be implemented in other ways but make your code easier to write and read. This is why they are convenient.

In this section, we use ArrayList and HashSet as our implementation classes, but they can apply to any class that inherits the Collection interface. We cover the specific properties of each Collection class in the next section.

Understanding Generic Types

In the previous chapter, we showed you numerous functional interfaces that use generics. But what are generics? In Java, *generics* is just a way of saying parameterized type. For example, a List<Integer> is a list of numbers, while Set<String> is a set of strings.

Without generics, we'd have to write a lot of code like the following:

```
List numbers = new ArrayList(List.of(1,2,3));
Integer element = (Integer)numbers.get(0);   // Required cast to compile
numbers.add("Welcome to the zoo!");          // Unrelated types allowed
```

With generics we can do better. The following change not only does away with the required cast from the previous code but also helps prevent unrelated objects from being added to the collection:

```
List<Integer> numbers = new ArrayList<Integer>(List.of(1,2,3));
Integer element = numbers.get(0);      // No cast required
numbers.add("Welcome to the zoo!");    // DOES NOT COMPILE
```

Getting a compiler error is good. You'll know right away that something is wrong rather than hoping to discover it later. Generics are convenient because the code for List, Set, and other collections does not change based on the generic type. You can even use your own class as the type, such as List<Visitor>.

We'll be using generics throughout this chapter, and even show you how to define your own generic classes toward the end of this chapter.

Shortening Generics Code

In the previous section, you saw generics that declare the type on both the left and right sides like the following:

```
List<Integer> list = new ArrayList<Integer>();
```

You might even have generics that contain other generics, such as this:

```
Map<Long,List<Integer>> mapOfLists = new HashMap<Long,List<Integer>>();
```

That's a lot of duplicate code to write! In this section, we offer two ways of shortening this code.

Applying the Diamond Operator

The *diamond operator* (<>) is a shorthand notation that allows you to omit the generic type from the right side of a statement when the type can be inferred. It is called the diamond operator because <> looks like a diamond. Compare the previous declarations with these new, much shorter versions:

```
List<Integer> list = new ArrayList<>();
Map<Long,List<Integer>> mapOfLists = new HashMap<>();
```

To the compiler, both these declarations and our previous ones are equivalent. Note the diamond operator cannot be used as the type in a variable declaration. It can be used only on the right side of an assignment operation. For example, neither of the following compiles:

```
List<> list = new ArrayList<Integer>();        // DOES NOT COMPILE

class InvalidUse {
   void use(List<> data) {}                     // DOES NOT COMPILE
}
```

Applying *var*

As you've seen earlier in this book, you can also use var to shorten expressions with generics.

```
var list = new ArrayList<Integer>();
var mapOfLists = new HashMap<Long,List<Integer>>();
```

Notice how the generic type is back on the right side. That's because var infers the type from the right side of the declaration, whereas the diamond operator infers it from the left side.

Which style you use, var or diamond operator, is up to you. Just don't specify the generic type on both sides of the =, because that's redundant!

Using Both Shorteners

What happens if you use both var and the diamond operator?

```
var map = new HashMap<>();
```

Believe it or not, this does compile! If you try to have them both infer, there isn't enough information and you get Object as the generic type. This is equivalent to the following:

```
HashMap<Object, Object> map = new HashMap<Object, Object>();
```

Adding Data

The add() method inserts a new element into the Collection and returns whether it was successful. The method signature is as follows:

```
public boolean add(E element)
```

Remember that the Collections Framework uses generics. You will see E appear frequently. It means the generic type that was used to create the collection. For some Collection types, add() always returns true. For other types, there is logic as to whether the add() call was successful. The following shows how to use this method:

```
3: Collection<String> list = new ArrayList<>();
4: System.out.println(list.add("Sparrow")); // true
5: System.out.println(list.add("Sparrow")); // true
6:
7: Collection<String> set = new HashSet<>();
8: System.out.println(set.add("Sparrow")); // true
9: System.out.println(set.add("Sparrow")); // false
```

A List allows duplicates, making the return value true each time. A Set does not allow duplicates. On line 9, we tried to add a duplicate so that Java returns false from the add() method.

Removing Data

The remove() method removes a single matching value in the Collection and returns whether it was successful. The method signature is as follows:

```
public boolean remove(Object object)
```

This time, the boolean return value tells us whether a match was removed. The following shows how to use this method:

```
3: Collection<String> birds = new ArrayList<>();
4: birds.add("hawk");                             // [hawk]
5: birds.add("hawk");                             // [hawk, hawk]
6: System.out.println(birds.remove("cardinal")); // false
7: System.out.println(birds.remove("hawk"));      // true
8: System.out.println(birds);                     // [hawk]
```

Line 6 tries to remove an element that is not in birds. It returns false because no such element is found. Line 7 tries to remove an element that is in birds, so it returns true. Notice that it removes only one match.

Counting Elements

The isEmpty() and size() methods look at how many elements are in the Collection. The method signatures are as follows:

```
public boolean isEmpty()
public int size()
```

The following shows how to use these methods:

```
Collection<String> birds = new ArrayList<>();
System.out.println(birds.isEmpty()); // true
System.out.println(birds.size());    // 0
birds.add("hawk");                    // [hawk]
birds.add("hawk");                    // [hawk, hawk]
System.out.println(birds.isEmpty()); // false
System.out.println(birds.size());    // 2
```

At the beginning, birds has a size of 0 and is empty. It has a capacity that is greater than 0. After we add elements, the size becomes positive, and it is no longer empty.

Clearing the Collection

The clear() method provides an easy way to discard all elements of the Collection. The method signature is as follows:

```
public void clear()
```

The following shows how to use this method:

```
Collection<String> birds = new ArrayList<>();
birds.add("hawk");                      // [hawk]
birds.add("hawk");                      // [hawk, hawk]
System.out.println(birds.isEmpty()); // false
System.out.println(birds.size());    // 2
birds.clear();                          // []
System.out.println(birds.isEmpty()); // true
System.out.println(birds.size());    // 0
```

After calling `clear()`, `birds` is back to being an empty `ArrayList` of size 0.

Checking Contents

The `contains()` method checks whether a certain value is in the `Collection`. The method signature is as follows:

```
public boolean contains(Object object)
```

The following shows how to use this method:

```
Collection<String> birds = new ArrayList<>();
birds.add("hawk");                              // [hawk]
System.out.println(birds.contains("hawk"));  // true
System.out.println(birds.contains("robin")); // false
```

The `contains()` method calls `equals()` on elements of the `ArrayList` to see whether there are any matches.

Removing with Conditions

The `removeIf()` method removes all elements that match a condition. We can specify what should be deleted using a block of code or even a method reference.

The method signature looks like the following. (We explain what the `?  super` means in the "Working with Generics" section later in this chapter.)

```
public boolean removeIf(Predicate<? super E> filter)
```

It uses a `Predicate`, which takes one parameter and returns a `boolean`. Let's take a look at an example:

```
4: Collection<String> list = new ArrayList<>();
5: list.add("Magician");
6: list.add("Assistant");
7: System.out.println(list);      // [Magician, Assistant]
8: list.removeIf(s -> s.startsWith("A"));
9: System.out.println(list);      // [Magician]
```

Line 8 shows how to remove all of the String values that begin with the letter A. This allows us to make the Assistant disappear. Let's try an example with a method reference:

```
11: Collection<String> set = new HashSet<>();
12: set.add("Wand");
13: set.add("");
14: set.removeIf(String::isEmpty); // s -> s.isEmpty()
15: System.out.println(set);       // [Wand]
```

On line 14, we remove any empty String objects from set. The comment on that line shows the lambda equivalent of the method reference. Line 15 shows that the removeIf() method successfully removed one element from list.

Iterating on a Collection

There's a forEach() method that you can call on a Collection instead of writing a loop. It uses a Consumer that takes a single parameter and doesn't return anything. The method signature is as follows:

```
public void forEach(Consumer<? super T> action)
```

Cats like to explore, so let's print out two of them using both method references and lambdas:

```
Collection<String> cats = List.of("Annie", "Ripley");
cats.forEach(System.out::println);
cats.forEach(c -> System.out.println(c));
```

The cats have discovered how to print their names. Now they have more time to play (as do we)!

Other Iteration Approaches

There are other ways to iterate through a Collection. For example, in Chapter 3, "Making Decisions," you saw how to loop through a list using an enhanced for loop.

```
for (String element: coll)
   System.out.println(element);
```

You may see another older approach used.

```
Iterator<String> iter = coll.iterator();
while(iter.hasNext()) {
   String name = iter.next();
   System.out.println(name);
}
```

Pay attention to the difference between these techniques. The hasNext() method checks whether there is a next value. In other words, it tells you whether next() will execute without throwing an exception. The next() method actually moves the Iterator to the next element.

Determining Equality

There is a custom implementation of equals() so you can compare two Collections to compare the type and contents. The implementation will vary. For example, ArrayList checks order, while HashSet does not.

```
boolean equals(Object object)
```

The following shows an example:

```
23: var list1 = List.of(1, 2);
24: var list2 = List.of(2, 1);
25: var set1 = Set.of(1, 2);
26: var set2 = Set.of(2, 1);
27:
28: System.out.println(list1.equals(list2));   // false
29: System.out.println(set1.equals(set2));     // true
30: System.out.println(list1.equals(set1));    // false
```

Line 28 prints false because the elements are in a different order, and a List cares about order. By contrast, line 29 prints true because a Set is not sensitive to order. Finally, line 30 prints false because the types are different.

Unboxing *nulls*

Java protects us from many problems with Collections. However, it is still possible to write a NullPointerException.

```
3: var heights = new ArrayList<Integer>();
4: heights.add(null);
5: int h = heights.get(0);   // NullPointerException
```

On line 4, we add a null to the list. This is legal because a null reference can be assigned to any reference variable. On line 5, we try to unbox that null to an int primitive. This is a problem. Java tries to get the int value of null. Since calling any method on null gives a NullPointerException, that is just what we get. Be careful when you see null in relation to autoboxing.

Using the *List* Interface

Now that you're familiar with some common `Collection` interface methods, let's move on to specific interfaces. You use a list when you want an ordered collection that can contain duplicate entries. For example, a list of names may contain duplicates, as two animals can have the same name. Items can be retrieved and inserted at specific positions in the list based on an `int` index, much like an array. Unlike an array, though, many `List` implementations can change in size after they are declared.

Lists are commonly used because there are many situations in programming where you need to keep track of a list of objects. For example, you might make a list of what you want to see at the zoo: first, see the lions, because they go to sleep early; second, see the pandas, because there is a long line later in the day; and so forth.

Figure 9.2 shows how you can envision a `List`. Each element of the `List` has an index, and the indexes begin with zero.

FIGURE 9.2   Example of a `List`

List

Ordered Index	Data
0	lions
1	pandas
2	zebras
...	...

Sometimes you don't care about the order of elements in a list. `List` is like the "go to" data type. When we make a shopping list before going to the store, the order of the list happens to be the order in which we thought of the items. We probably aren't attached to that particular order, but it isn't hurting anything.

While the classes implementing the `List` interface have many methods, you need to know only the most common ones. Conveniently, these methods are the same for all of the implementations that might show up on the exam.

The main thing all `List` implementations have in common is that they are ordered and allow duplicates. Beyond that, they each offer different functionality. We look at the implementations that you need to know and the available methods.

Pay special attention to which names are classes and which are interfaces. The exam may ask you which is the best class or which is the best interface for a scenario.

Comparing List Implementations

Reviewing Figure 9.1, you need to know about two classes that implement the `List` interface: `ArrayList` and `LinkedList`. An `ArrayList` is like a resizable array. When elements are added, the `ArrayList` automatically grows. When you aren't sure which collection to use, use an `ArrayList`.

The main benefit of an `ArrayList` is that you can look up any element in constant time. Adding or removing an element is slower than accessing an element. This makes an `ArrayList` a good choice when you are reading more often than (or the same amount as) writing to the `ArrayList`.

A `LinkedList` is special because it implements both `List` and `Deque`. It has all the methods of a `List`. It also has additional methods to facilitate adding or removing from the beginning and/or end of the list.

The main benefits of a `LinkedList` are that you can access, add to, and remove from the beginning and end of the list in constant time. The trade-off is that dealing with an arbitrary index takes linear time. This makes a `LinkedList` a good choice when you'll be using it as `Deque`.

Creating a *List* with a Factory

When you create a `List` of type `ArrayList` or `LinkedList`, you know the type. There are a few special methods where you get a `List` back but don't know the type. These methods let you create a `List` including data in one line using a factory method. This is convenient, especially when testing. Some of these methods return an immutable object. As we saw in Chapter 6, "Class Design," an immutable object cannot be changed or modified. Table 9.1 summarizes these three methods to create a list.

TABLE 9.1 Factory methods to create a `List`

Method	Description	Can add elements?	Can replace elements?	Can delete elements?
`Arrays.asList(varargs)`	Returns fixed size list backed by an array	No	Yes	No
`List.of(varargs)`	Returns immutable list	No	No	No
`List.copyOf (collection)`	Returns immutable list with copy of original collection's values	No	No	No

Let's take a look at an example of these three methods:

```
16: String[] array = new String[] {"a", "b", "c"};
17: List<String> asList = Arrays.asList(array); // [a, b, c]
```

```
18: List<String> of = List.of(array);        // [a, b, c]
19: List<String> copy = List.copyOf(asList);  // [a, b, c]
20:
21: array[0] = "z";
22:
23: System.out.println(asList);               // [z, b, c]
24: System.out.println(of);                   // [a, b, c]
25: System.out.println(copy);                 // [a, b, c]
26:
27: asList.set(0, "x");
28: System.out.println(Arrays.toString(array)); // [x, b, c]
```

Line 17 creates a List that is backed by an array. Line 21 changes the array, and line 23 reflects that change. Lines 27 and 28 show the other direction where changing the List updates the underlying array. Lines 18 and 19 each create an immutable List.

When run independently, the following shows both types are immutable by throwing an exception when trying to set a value.

```
of.set(0, "y");    // UnsupportedOperationException
copy.set(0, "y");  // UnsupportedOperationException
```

Similarly, each of the following lines throws an exception when adding or removing a value:

```
asList.add("z");  // UnsupportedOperationException
of.remove(0);     // UnsupportedOperationException
copy.remove(0);   // UnsupportedOperationException
```

Creating a *List* with a Constructor

Most Collections have two constructors that you need to know for the exam. The following shows them for LinkedList:

```
var linked1 = new LinkedList<String>();
var linked2 = new LinkedList<String>(linked1);
```

The first says to create an empty LinkedList containing all the defaults. The second tells Java that we want to make a copy of another LinkedList. Granted, linked1 is empty in this example, so it isn't particularly interesting.

ArrayList has an extra constructor you need to know. We now show the three constructors.

```
var list1 = new ArrayList<String>();
var list2 = new ArrayList<String>(list1);
var list3 = new ArrayList<String>(10);
```

The first two are the common constructors you need to know for all `Collections`. The final example says to create an `ArrayList` containing a specific number of slots, but again not to assign any. You can think of this as the size of the underlying array.

Working with *List* Methods

The methods in the `List` interface are for working with indexes. In addition to the inherited `Collection` methods, you should also know the methods in Table 9.2 for the exam.

TABLE 9.2   List methods

Method	Description
`boolean add(E element)`	Adds element to end (available on all `Collection` APIs).
`void add(int index, E element)`	Adds element at index and moves the rest toward the end.
`E get(int index)`	Returns element at index.
`int indexOf(Object o)`	Returns the index of the first matching element or -1 if not found.
`int lastIndexOf(Object o)`	Returns the index of the last matching element or -1 if not found.
`E remove(int index)`	Removes element at index and moves the rest toward the front.
`default void replaceAll( UnaryOperator<E> op)`	Replaces each element in list with the result of operator.
`E set(int index, E e)`	Replaces element at index and returns original. Throws `IndexOutOfBoundsException` if index is invalid.
`default void sort( Comparator<? super E> c)`	Sorts list. We cover this later in the chapter in the "Sorting Data" section.

The following statements demonstrate most of these methods for working with a `List`:

```
3:  List<String> list = new ArrayList<>();
4:  list.add("SD");              // [SD]
5:  list.add(0, "NY");           // [NY,SD]
6:  list.set(1, "FL");           // [NY,FL]
```

```
7:  System.out.println(list.get(0));  // NY
8:  list.remove("NY");                // [FL]
9:  list.remove(0);                   // []
10: list.set(0, "?");                 // IndexOutOfBoundsException
```

On line 3, list starts out empty. Line 4 adds an element to the end of the list. Line 5 adds an element at index 0 that bumps the original index 0 to index 1. Notice how the ArrayList is now automatically one larger. Line 6 replaces the element at index 1 with a new value.

Line 7 uses the get() method to print the element at a specific index. Line 8 removes the element matching NY. Finally, line 9 removes the element at index 0, and list is empty again.

Line 10 throws an IndexOutOfBoundsException because there are no elements in the List. Since there are no elements to replace, even index 0 isn't allowed. If line 10 were moved up between lines 4 and 5, the call would succeed.

The output would be the same if you tried these examples with LinkedList. Although the code would be less efficient, it wouldn't be noticeable until you had very large lists.

Now let's take a look at the replaceAll() method. It uses a UnaryOperator that takes one parameter and returns a value of the same type.

```
var numbers = Arrays.asList(1, 2, 3);
numbers.replaceAll(x -> x*2);
System.out.println(numbers);    // [2, 4, 6]
```

This lambda doubles the value of each element in the list. The replaceAll() method calls the lambda on each element of the list and replaces the value at that index.

Overloaded *remove()* Methods

We've now seen two overloaded remove() methods. The one from Collection removes an object that matches the parameter. By contrast, the one from List removes an element at a specified index.

This gets tricky when you have an Integer type. What do you think the following prints?

```
31: var list = new LinkedList<Integer>();
32: list.add(3);
33: list.add(2);
34: list.add(1);
35: list.remove(2);
36: list.remove(Integer.valueOf(2));
37: System.out.println(list);
```

The correct answer is [3]. Let's look at how we got there. At the end of line 34, we have [3, 2, 1]. Line 35 passes a primitive, which means we are requesting deletion of the element at index 2. This leaves us with [3, 2]. Then line 36 passes an Integer object, which means we are deleting the value 2. That brings us to [3].

The remove() method that takes an element will return false if the element is not found. Contrast this with the remove() method that takes an int, which throws an exception if the element is not found:

```
var list = new LinkedList<Integer>();
list.remove(Integer.valueOf(100));  // Returns false
list.remove(100);                   // IndexOutOfBoundsException
```

Searching a List

From Table 9.2, the List interface includes two methods for searching for elements, indexOf() and lastIndexOf(). They work similarly to the methods of the same name in the String class:

```
var list = List.of("peacock", "chicken", "peacock", "turkey");

System.out.println(list.indexOf("peacock"));       // 0
System.out.println(list.lastIndexOf("peacock"));   // 2
System.out.println(list.indexOf("penguin"));       // -1
```

Later in this chapter, we'll show you how to perform a more efficient search by first sorting the list and then using the Collections.binarySearch() method.

Converting from *List* to an Array

Since an array can be passed as a vararg, Table 9.1 covered how to convert an array to a List. You should also know how to do the reverse. Let's start with turning a List into an array.

```
13: List<String> list = new ArrayList<>();
14: list.add("hawk");
15: list.add("robin");
16: Object[] objectArray = list.toArray();
17: String[] stringArray = list.toArray(new String[0]);
18: list.clear();
19: System.out.println(objectArray.length);     // 2
20: System.out.println(stringArray.length);     // 2
```

Line 16 shows that a List knows how to convert itself to an array. The only problem is that it defaults to an array of class Object. This isn't usually what you want. Line 17 specifies the type of the array and does what we want. The advantage of specifying a size of 0 for the parameter is that Java will create a new array of the proper size for the return value. If you like, you can suggest a larger array to be used instead. If the List fits in that array, it will be returned. Otherwise, a new array will be created.

Also, notice that line 18 clears the original List. This does not affect either array. The array is a newly created object with no relationship to the original List. It is simply a copy.

Using the *Set* Interface

You use a Set when you don't want to allow duplicate entries. For example, you might want to keep track of the unique animals that you want to see at the zoo. You aren't concerned with the order in which you see these animals, but there isn't time to see them more than once. You just want to make sure you see the ones that are important to you and remove them from the set of outstanding animals to see after you see them.

Figure 9.3 shows how you can envision a Set. The main thing that all Set implementations have in common is that they do not allow duplicates. We look at each implementation that you need to know for the exam and how to write code using Set.

FIGURE 9.3   Example of a Set

Set

pandas

lions

zebras

Comparing *Set* Implementations

Reviewing Figure 9.1 again, you need to know about three classes that implement the Set interface: HashSet, LinkedHashSet, TreeSet. A HashSet stores its elements in a *hash table*, which means the keys are a hash and the values are an Object. This means the HashSet uses the hashCode() method of the objects to retrieve them more efficiently. Remember that a valid hashCode() doesn't mean every object will get a unique value, but the method is often written so that hash values are spread out over a large range to reduce collisions.

A LinkedHashSet is basically a HashSet with an imaginary LinkedList running across its elements. This allows you to iterate over the set in a well-defined encounter order, which is often the order the elements were inserted. That said, LinkedHashSet also includes methods to add/remove elements from the front or back of the set, allowing you to change the ordering as needed.

Finally, a `TreeSet` stores its elements in a sorted tree structure. The main benefit is that the set is always in sorted order. The trade-off is that adding or removing an element could take longer than with a `HashSet`, especially as the tree grows larger.

Figure 9.4 shows how you can envision these three classes being stored. `HashSet` is more complicated in reality, but this is fine for the purpose of the exam.

FIGURE 9.4   Examples of Sets

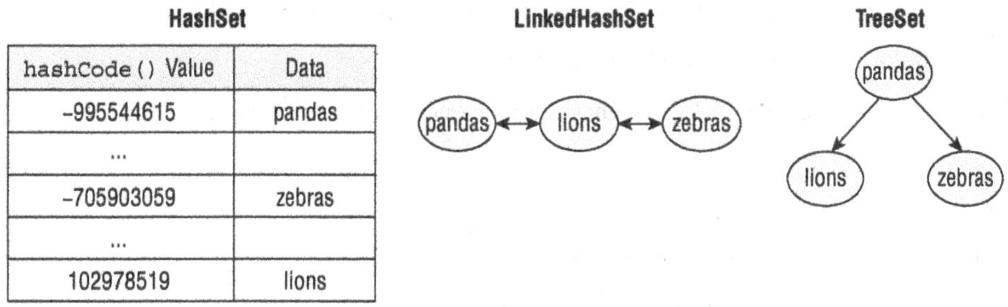

For the exam, you don't need to know how to create a hash or tree set class (the implementation can be complex). Phew! You just need to know how to use them!

Working with *Set* Methods

Like a `List`, you can create an immutable `Set` in one line or make a copy of an existing one.

```
Set<Character> letters = Set.of('c', 'a', 't');
Set<Character> copy = Set.copyOf(letters);
```

Those are the only extra methods you need to know for the `Set` interface for the exam! You do have to know how sets behave with respect to the traditional `Collection` methods. You also have to know the differences between the types of sets. Let's start with `HashSet`.

```
3: Set<Integer> set = new HashSet<>();
4: boolean b1 = set.add(66);  // true
5: boolean b2 = set.add(10);  // true
6: boolean b3 = set.add(66);  // false
7: boolean b4 = set.add(8);   // true
8: for (Integer value: set)
9:    System.out.print(value + ","); // 66,8,10,
```

The `add()` methods should be straightforward. They return `true` unless the `Integer` is already in the set. Line 6 returns `false`, because we already have 66 in the set, and a set must preserve uniqueness. Line 8 prints the elements of the set in an *arbitrary* order. In this case, it happens not to be sorted order or the order in which we added the elements.

Remember that the equals() method is used to determine equality. The hashCode() method is used to know which bucket to look in so that Java doesn't have to look through the whole set to find out whether an object is there. The best case is that hash codes are unique and Java has to call equals() on only one object. The worst case is that all implementations return the same hashCode() and Java has to call equals() on every element of the set anyway.

Let's replace line 3 with a LinkedHashSet and see how the output changes.

```
3: Set<Integer> set = new LinkedHashSet<>();
```

This time, the code prints the elements in the order they were inserted.

```
66,10,8,
```

Finally, we can use a TreeSet on line 3.

```
3: Set<Integer> set = new TreeSet<>();
```

The elements are now printed out in their natural sorted order.

```
8,10,66,
```

Number wrapper types implement the Comparable interface in Java, which is used for sorting. Later in the chapter, you learn how to create your own Comparable objects.

Using the *Queue* and *Deque* Interfaces

You use a Queue when elements are added and removed in a specific order. You can think of a queue as a line. For example, when you want to enter a stadium and someone is waiting in line, you get in line behind that person. And if you are British, you get in the queue behind that person, making this really easy to remember! This is a *FIFO* (first-in, first-out) queue.

A Deque (double-ended queue), often pronounced "deck" extends Queue but is different from a regular queue in that you can insert and remove elements from both the front (head) and back (tail). Think, "Dr. Woodie Flowers, come right to the front! You are the only one who gets this special treatment. Everyone else will have to start at the back of the line."

You can envision a double-ended queue as shown in Figure 9.5.

FIGURE 9.5   Example of a Deque

Supposing we are using this as a FIFO queue. Rover is first, which means he was first to arrive. Bella is last, which means she was last to arrive and has the longest wait remaining.

All queues have specific requirements for adding and removing the next element. Beyond that, they each offer different functionality. We look at the implementations you need to know and the available methods.

Comparing *Deque* Implementations

Reviewing Figure 9.1 one more time (you should know it well by now!), LinkedList and ArrayDeque both implement the Deque interface, which inherits Queue. You saw LinkedList earlier in the List section. The main benefit of a LinkedList is that it implements both the List and Deque interfaces. The trade-off is that it isn't as efficient as a "pure" queue. You can use the ArrayDeque class if you don't need the List methods.

Working with *Queue* and *Deque* Methods

The Queue interface contains six methods, shown in Table 9.3. There are three capabilities, each with two versions of the methods: one that throws an exception, and one that uses the return type to convey the same information. We've bolded the ones that throw an exception when something goes wrong, like trying to read from an empty Queue.

TABLE 9.3   Queue methods

Functionality	Methods
Add to back	**boolean add(E e)** boolean offer(E e)
Read from front	**E element()** E peek()
Get and remove from front	**E remove()** E poll()

Let's look at the following simple queue example:

```
4: Queue<Integer> queue = new LinkedList<>();
5: queue.add(10);
6: queue.add(4);
7: System.out.println(queue.remove());    // 10
8: System.out.println(queue.peek());      // 4
```

Lines 5 and 6 add elements to the queue. Line 7 asks the first element waiting the longest to come off the queue. Line 8 checks for the next entry in the queue while leaving it in place.

Next, we move on to the Deque interface. Since the Deque interface supports double-ended queues, it inherits all Queue methods and adds more so that it is clear if we are working with the front or back of the queue. Table 9.4 shows the methods when using it as a double-ended queue.

TABLE 9.4 Deque methods

Functionality	Methods
Add to front	**void addFirst(E e)** boolean offerFirst(E e)
Add to back	**void addLast(E e)** public boolean offerLast(E e)
Read from front	**E getFirst()** E peekFirst()
Read from back	**E getLast()** E peekLast()
Get and remove from front	**E removeFirst()** E pollFirst()
Get and remove from back	**E removeLast()** E pollLast()

Let's try an example that works with both ends of the queue:

```
Deque<Integer> deque = new LinkedList<>();
```

This is more complicated, so we use Figure 9.6 to show what the queue looks like at each step of the code.

Lines 13 and 14 successfully add an element to the front and back of the queue, respectively. Some queues are limited in size, which would cause offering an element to the queue to fail. You won't encounter a scenario like that on the exam. Line 15 looks at the first element in the queue, but it does not remove it. Lines 16 and 17 remove the elements from the queue, one from each end. This results in an empty queue. Lines 18 and 19 try to look at the first element of the queue, which results in null.

In addition to FIFO queues, there are *LIFO* (last-in, first-out) queues, which are commonly referred to as *stacks*. Picture a stack of plates. You always add to or remove from the top of the stack to avoid a mess. Luckily, we can use the same double-ended queue implementations. Different methods are used for clarity, as shown in Table 9.5.

FIGURE 9.6   Working with a Deque

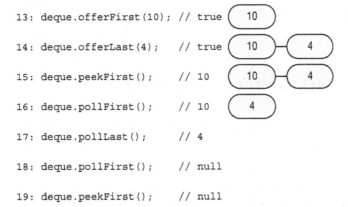

```
13: deque.offerFirst(10); // true
14: deque.offerLast(4);   // true
15: deque.peekFirst();    // 10
16: deque.pollFirst();    // 10
17: deque.pollLast();     // 4
18: deque.pollFirst();    // null
19: deque.peekFirst();    // null
```

TABLE 9.5   Using a Deque as a stack

Functionality	Methods
Add to the front/top	**void push(E e)**
Remove from the front/top	**E pop()**
Get first element	**E peek()**

Let's try another one using the Deque as a stack:

```
Deque<Integer> stack = new ArrayDeque<>();
```

This time, Figure 9.7 shows what the stack looks like at each step of the code. Lines 13 and 14 successfully put an element on the front/top of the stack. The remaining code looks at the front as well.

FIGURE 9.7   Working with a stack

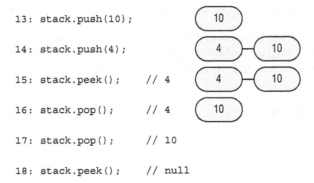

```
13: stack.push(10);
14: stack.push(4);
15: stack.peek();   // 4
16: stack.pop();    // 4
17: stack.pop();    // 10
18: stack.peek();   // null
```

When using a Deque, it is really important to determine if it is being used as a FIFO queue, a LIFO stack, or a double-ended queue. To review, a FIFO queue is like a line of people. You get on in the back and off in the front. A LIFO stack is like a stack of plates. You put the plate on the top and take it off the top. A double-ended queue uses both ends.

Using the *Map* Interface

You use a Map when you want to identify values by a key. For example, when you use the contact list in your phone, you look up "George" rather than looking through each phone number in turn.

You can envision a Map as shown in Figure 9.8. You don't need to know the names of the specific interfaces that the different maps implement, but you do need to know that LinkedHashMap is ordered and TreeMap is sorted.

FIGURE 9.8   Example of a Map

Map

Key	Value
George	555-555-5555
May	777-777-7777

The main thing that all Map classes have in common is that they have keys and values. Beyond that, they each offer different functionality. We look at the implementations you need to know and the available methods.

Map.of() and Map.copyOf()

Just like List and Set, there is a factory method to create a Map. You pass up to 10 pairs of keys and values.

```
Map.of("key1", "value1", "key2", "value2");
```

Unlike List and Set, this is less than ideal. Passing keys and values is harder to read because you have to keep track of which parameter is which. Luckily, there is a better way. Map also provides a method that lets you supply key/value pairs.

```
Map.ofEntries(
    Map.entry("key1", "value1"),
    Map.entry("key2", "value2"));
```

Now we can't forget to pass a value. If we leave out a parameter, the entry() method won't compile. Conveniently, Map.copyOf(map) works just like the List and Set interface copyOf() methods.

Comparing *Map* Implementations

From Figure 9.1, HashMap, LinkedHashMap, and TreeMap are the three classes that implement the Map interface. A HashMap stores the keys in a hash table. This means that it uses the hashCode() method of the keys to retrieve their values more efficiently.

Like LinkedHashSet, the LinkedHashMap supports iterating over the elements in a well-defined order. This is generally the insertion order, although it also includes methods to add/remove elements at the front or back of the map.

Finally, a TreeMap stores the keys in a sorted tree structure. The main benefit is that the keys are always in sorted order. Like a TreeSet, the trade-off is that adding and checking whether a key is present takes longer as the tree grows larger.

Working with *Map* Methods

Given that Map doesn't extend Collection, more methods are specified on the Map interface. Since there are both keys and values, we need generic type parameters for both. The class uses K for key and V for value. The methods you need to know for the exam are in Table 9.6. Some of the method signatures are simplified to make them easier to understand.

TABLE 9.6 Map methods

Method	Description
void **clear()**	Removes all keys and values from map.
boolean **containsKey(** Object key)	Returns whether key is in map.
boolean **containsValue(** Object value)	Returns whether value is in map.
Set<Map.Entry<K,V>> **entrySet()**	Returns Set of key/value pairs.
void **forEach(** BiConsumer<K, V> action)	Loops through each key/value pair.
V **get**(Object key)	Returns value mapped by key or null if none is mapped.

TABLE 9.6 Map methods *(continued)*

Method	Description
V **getOrDefault**(Object key, V defaultValue)	Returns value mapped by key or default value if none is mapped.
boolean **isEmpty**()	Returns whether map is empty.
Set<K> **keySet**()	Returns set of all keys.
V **merge**(K key, V value, BiFunction<V, V, V> func)	Sets value if key not set. Runs function if key is set, to determine new value. Removes if value is null.
V **put**(K key, V value)	Adds or replaces key/value pair. Returns previous value or null.
V **putIfAbsent**(K key, V value)	Adds value if key not present and returns null. Otherwise, returns existing value.
V **remove**(Object key)	Removes and returns value mapped to key. Returns null if none.
V **replace**(K key, V value)	Replaces value for given key if key is set. Returns original value or null if none.
void **replaceAll**(BiFunction<K, V, V> func)	Replaces each value with results of function.
int **size**()	Returns number of entries (key/value pairs) in map.
Collection<V> **values**()	Returns Collection of all values.

While Table 9.6 is a pretty long list of methods, don't worry; many of the names are straightforward. Also, many exist as a convenience. For example, containsKey() can be replaced with a get() call that checks if the result is null. Which one you use is up to you.

Calling Basic Methods

Let's start by comparing the behavior of each of the Map classes. Consider the following method:

```
void addElementsAndPrint(Map<String, String> map) {
    map.put("koala", "bamboo");
```

```
map.put("lion", "meat");
map.put("giraffe", "leaf");
String food = map.get("koala"); // bamboo
for (String key: map.keySet())
    System.out.print(key + ",");
}
```

Here we use the put() method to add key/value pairs to the map and get() to get a value given a key. We also use the keySet() method to get all the keys. We can then apply this method to each of our three Map classes.

```
addElementsAndPrint(new HashMap<>());        // koala,giraffe,lion,
addElementsAndPrint(new LinkedHashMap<>());  // koala,lion,giraffe,
addElementsAndPrint(new TreeMap<>());        // giraffe,koala,lion,
```

Like we saw with the Set classes, HashMap prints the elements in an arbitrary ordering using the hashCode() of the key. LinkedHashMap prints the elements in the order in which they were inserted. Finally, TreeMap prints the elements based on the order of the keys.

Using our HashMap instance, we can try some boolean checks.

```
System.out.println(map.containsKey("lion"));    // true
System.out.println(map.containsValue("lion"));  // false
System.out.println(map.size());      // 3
map.clear();
System.out.println(map.size());       // 0
System.out.println(map.isEmpty());   // true
```

The first two lines show that keys and values are checked separately. We can see that there are three key/value pairs in our map. Then we clear out the contents of the map and see that there are zero elements and it is empty.

Do you see why this doesn't compile?

```
System.out.println(map.contains("lion"));        // DOES NOT COMPILE
```

It doesn't compile because the contains() method is on the Collection interface but not the Map interface.

In the following sections, we show Map methods you might not be as familiar with.

Iterating through a *Map*

You saw the forEach() method earlier in the chapter. Note that it works a little differently on a Map. This time, the lambda used by the forEach() method has two parameters: the key and the value. Let's look at an example, shown here:

```
Map<Integer, Character> map = new HashMap<>();
map.put(1, 'a');
map.put(2, 'b');
map.put(3, 'c');
map.forEach((k, v) -> System.out.println(v));
```

The lambda has both the key and value as the parameters. It happens to print out the value but could do anything with the key and/or value. Interestingly, since we don't care about the key, this particular code could have been written with the `values()` method and a method reference instead.

```
map.values().forEach(System.out::println);
```

Another way of iterating over the data in a map is using `entrySet()`, which returns a set of `Map.Entry<K, V>` objects. If this type seems a little strange, don't worry! This is just a fancy way of storing the key/value pair in an object. It provides methods to retrieve the key and value of each pair.

```
map.entrySet().forEach(e ->
   System.out.println(e.getKey() + " " + e.getValue()));
```

In this case, each element e is of type `Map.Entry<Integer, Character>`.

Getting Values Safely

The `get()` method returns `null` if the requested key is not in the map. Sometimes you prefer to have a different value returned. Luckily, the `getOrDefault()` method makes this easy. Let's compare the two methods.

```
3: Map<Character, String> map = new HashMap<>();
4: map.put('x', "spot");
5: System.out.println("X marks the " + map.get('x'));
6: System.out.println("X marks the " + map.getOrDefault('x', ""));
7: System.out.println("Y marks the " + map.get('y'));
8: System.out.println("Y marks the " + map.getOrDefault('y', ""));
```

This code prints the following:

```
X marks the spot
X marks the spot
Y marks the null
Y marks the
```

As you can see, lines 5 and 6 have the same output because `get()` and `getOrDefault()` behave the same way when the key is present. They return the value mapped by that key. Lines 7 and 8 give different output, showing that `get()` returns `null` when the key is not present. By contrast, `getOrDefault()` returns the empty string we passed as a parameter.

Replacing Values

These methods are similar to the `List` version, except a key is involved:

```
21: Map<Integer, Integer> map = new HashMap<>();
22: map.put(1, 2);
23: map.put(2, 4);
```

```
24: Integer original = map.replace(2, 10); // 4
25: System.out.println(map);     // {1=2, 2=10}
26: map.replaceAll((k, v) -> k + v);
27: System.out.println(map);     // {1=3, 2=12}
```

Line 24 replaces the value for key 2 and returns the original value. Line 26 calls a function and sets the value of each element of the map to the result of that function. In our case, we added the key and value together.

Note that replace() and replaceAll() do not modify the Map if it does not contain the key. Contrast this with put(), which will always attempt to set a value.

Putting If Absent

The putIfAbsent() method sets a value in the map but skips it if the value is already set to a non-null value.

```
Map<String, String> favorites = new HashMap<>();
favorites.put("Jenny", "Bus Tour");
favorites.put("Tom", null);
favorites.putIfAbsent("Jenny", "Tram");
favorites.putIfAbsent("Sam", "Tram");
favorites.putIfAbsent("Tom", "Tram");
System.out.println(favorites); // {Tom=Tram, Jenny=Bus Tour, Sam=Tram}
```

As you can see, Jenny's value is not updated because one was already present. Sam wasn't there at all, so he was added. Tom was present as a key but had a null value. Therefore, he was updated as well.

Merging Data

The merge() method adds logic of what to choose. Suppose we want to choose the ride with the longest name. We can write code to express this by passing a mapping function to the merge() method.

```
11: BiFunction<String, String, String> mapper = (v1, v2)
12:    -> v1.length()> v2.length() ? v1: v2;
13:
14: Map<String, String> favorites = new HashMap<>();
15: favorites.put("Jenny", "Bus Tour");
16: favorites.put("Tom", "Tram");
17:
18: String jenny = favorites.merge("Jenny", "Skyride", mapper);
19: String tom = favorites.merge("Tom", "Skyride", mapper);
20:
```

```
21: System.out.println(favorites); // {Tom=Skyride, Jenny=Bus Tour}
22: System.out.println(jenny);      // Bus Tour
23: System.out.println(tom);        // Skyride
```

The code on lines 11 and 12 takes two parameters and returns a value. Our implementation returns the one with the longest name. Line 18 calls this mapping function, and it sees that Bus Tour is longer than Skyride, so it leaves the value as Bus Tour. Line 19 calls this mapping function again. This time, Tram is shorter than Skyride, so the map is updated. Line 21 prints out the new map contents. Lines 22 and 23 show that the result is returned from merge().

The merge() method also has logic for what happens if null values or missing keys are involved. In this case, it doesn't call the BiFunction at all, and it simply uses the new value.

```
BiFunction<String, String, String> mapper =
  (v1, v2) -> v1.length()> v2.length() ? v1 : v2;
Map<String, String> favorites = new HashMap<>();
favorites.put("Sam", null);
favorites.merge("Tom", "Skyride", mapper);
favorites.merge("Sam", "Skyride", mapper);
System.out.println(favorites);   // {Tom=Skyride, Sam=Skyride}
```

Notice that the mapping function isn't called. If it were, we'd have a NullPointerException. The mapping function is used only when there are two actual values to decide between.

The final thing to know about merge() is what happens when the mapping function is called and returns null. The key is removed from the map when this happens.

```
BiFunction<String, String, String> mapper = (v1, v2) -> null;
Map<String, String> favorites = new HashMap<>();
favorites.put("Jenny", "Bus Tour");
favorites.put("Tom", "Bus Tour");

favorites.merge("Jenny", "Skyride", mapper);
favorites.merge("Sam", "Skyride", mapper);
System.out.println(favorites);   // {Tom=Bus Tour, Sam=Skyride}
```

Tom was left alone since there was no merge() call for that key. Sam was added since that key was not in the original list. Jenny was removed because the mapping function returned null.

Table 9.7 shows all of these scenarios as a reference.

TABLE 9.7 Behavior of the merge() method

If the requested key _____	And mapping function returns _____	Then:
Has a null value in map	N/A (mapping function not called)	Update key's value in map with value parameter.

If the requested key	And mapping function returns _____	Then:
Has a non-null value in map	null	Remove key from map.
Has a non-null value in map	A non-null value	Set value to mapping function result.
Is not in map	N/A (mapping function not called)	Add key with value parameter to map directly without calling mapping function.

Sorting Data

We discussed "order" for the TreeSet and TreeMap classes. For numbers, order is obvious—it is numerical order. For String objects, order is defined according to the Unicode character mapping.

 Remember 7Up from Chapter 4, "Core APIs"? When working with a String, numbers sort before letters, and uppercase letters sort before lowercase letters.

We use Collections.sort() in many of these examples. It returns void because the method parameter is what gets sorted.

You can also sort objects that you create yourself. Java provides an interface called Comparable. If your class implements Comparable, it can be used in data structures that require comparison. In fact, you've seen many Comparable classes in this book include String, StringBuilder, BigDecimal, BigInteger and the primitive wrapper classes. There is also a class called Comparator, which is used to specify that you want to use a different order than the object itself provides.

Comparable and Comparator are similar enough to be tricky. The exam likes to see if it can trick you into mixing up the two. Don't be confused! In this section, we discuss Comparable first. Then, as we go through Comparator, we point out all of the differences.

Creating a *Comparable* Class

The Comparable interface has only one method. In fact, this is the entire interface:

```java
public interface Comparable<T> {
    int compareTo(T o);
}
```

The generic T lets you implement this method and specify the type of your object. This lets you avoid a cast when implementing compareTo(). Any object can be Comparable.

For example, we have a bunch of ducks and want to sort them by name. First, we create a record that inherits Comparable<Duck>, and then we implement the compareTo() method.

```
public record Duck(String name) implements Comparable<Duck> {
    public int compareTo(Duck d) {
        return name.compareTo(d.name);  // Sorts ascendingly by name
    }
}
```

Next, we can sort the ducks as follows:

```
11: var ducks = new ArrayList<Duck>();
12: ducks.add(new Duck("Quack"));
13: ducks.add(new Duck("Puddles"));
14: Collections.sort(ducks);  // sort by name
15: System.out.print(ducks);  // [Duck[name=Puddles], Duck[name=Quack]]
```

If we didn't implement the Comparable interface, all we have is a method named compareTo(), and line 14 would not compile. We could also implement Comparable<Object> or some other class for T, but this wouldn't be as useful for sorting a group of Duck objects.

Finally, the Duck class implements compareTo(). Since Duck is comparing objects of type String and the String class already has a compareTo() method, it can just delegate.

> You might have noticed we use a record here. From Chapter 7, "Beyond Classes," a record provides a lot of useful boilerplate code like construc-tors and meaningful implementations of toString(). Just remember, both records and classes can implement Comparable.

Designing a *compareTo()* method

In the previous example, we relied on the built-in String compareTo() method, but often you need to create your own. When writing a compareTo() method, the most important part is the return value. The following rules should apply to the return type of your compareTo() method:

- The number 0 is returned when the current object is equivalent to the argument to compareTo().

- A negative number (less than 0) is returned when the current object is smaller than the argument to compareTo().

- A positive number (greater than 0) is returned when the current object is larger than the argument to compareTo().

Let's look at an implementation of compareTo() that compares numbers instead of String objects:

```
2: public record ZooDuck(int id, String name) implements Comparable<ZooDuck> {
3:    public int compareTo(ZooDuck d) {
4:       return id - d.id;  // Sorts ascendingly by id
5:    }
6: }
```

Line 4 shows one way to compare two int values. We could have used Integer.compare(id, d.id), but we wanted to show you how to create your own. Be sure you can recognize both approaches. Remember that id - d.id sorts in ascending order, and d.id - id sorts in descending order.

Let's try this new method out in some code:

```
21: var d1 = new ZooDuck (5, "Daffy");
22: var d2 = new ZooDuck(7, "Donald");
23: System.out.println(d1.compareTo(d2));    // -2
24: System.out.println(d1.compareTo(d1));    // 0
25: System.out.println(d2.compareTo(d1));    // 2
```

Line 23 compares a smaller id to a larger one, and therefore it prints a negative number. Line 24 compares animals with the same id, and therefore it prints 0. Line 25 compares a larger id to a smaller one, and therefore it returns a positive number.

Casting the *compareTo()* Argument

When dealing with legacy code or code that does not use generics, the compareTo() method requires a cast since it is passed an Object. We can accomplish this using pattern-matching that you saw in Chapter 3.

```
public record LegacyDuck(String name) implements Comparable {
   public int compareTo(Object obj) {
      if(obj instanceof LegacyDuck d)
         return name.compareTo(d.name);
      throw new UnsupportedOperationException("Not a duck");
} }
```

Since we don't specify a generic type for Comparable, Java assumes that we want an Object.

Checking for *null*

When working with Comparable and Comparator in this chapter, we tend to assume the data has values, but this is not always the case. When writing your own compare methods, you should check the data before comparing it if it is not validated ahead of time.

```
public record MissingDuck(String name) implements Comparable<MissingDuck> {
   public int compareTo(MissingDuck quack) {
      if (quack == null)
```

```
        throw new IllegalArgumentException("Poorly formed duck!");
    if (this.name == null && quack.name == null)
        return 0;
    else if (this.name == null) return -1;
    else if (quack.name == null) return 1;
    else return name.compareTo(quack.name);
} }
```

This method throws an exception if it is passed a `null` `MissingDuck` object. What about the ordering? If the `name` of a duck is `null`, it's sorted first.

Keeping *compareTo()* and *equals()* Consistent

If you write a class that implements `Comparable`, you introduce new business logic for determining equality. The `compareTo()` method returns `0` if two objects are equal, while your `equals()` method returns `true` if two objects are equal. A *natural ordering* that uses `compareTo()` is said to be *consistent with equals* if, and only if, `x.equals(y)` is `true` whenever `x.compareTo(y)` equals `0`.

Similarly, `x.equals(y)` must be `false` whenever `x.compareTo(y)` is not `0`. You are strongly encouraged to make your `Comparable` classes consistent with equals because not all collection classes behave predictably if the `compareTo()` and `equals()` methods are not consistent.

For example, the following `Product` class defines a `compareTo()` method that is not consistent with equals:

```java
public class Product implements Comparable<Product> {
    private int id;
    private String name;

    public int hashCode() { return id; }

    public boolean equals(Object obj) {
        if (obj instanceof Product other)
            return this.id == other.id;
        return false;
    }

    public int compareTo(Product obj) {
        return this.name.compareTo(obj.name);
    } }
```

This class checks equality with `id`, but orders by `name`. Assuming names are not unique, this means we could have many pairs of elements in which `compareTo()` returns `0`, but `equals()` returns `false`.

One way to fix this is to update the methods to rely on the same attributes. If you still need to sort things by name, you can use a Comparator defined outside the class, as shown in the next section.

Comparing Data with a *Comparator*

Sometimes you want to sort an object that did not implement Comparable, or you want to sort objects in different ways at different times. Suppose that we add weight to our Duck class.

```
public record Duck(String name, int weight) implements Comparable<Duck> {
    public int compareTo(Duck d) {
        return name.compareTo(d.name);
    }
    public String toString() { return name; }
}
```

We also override toString() so our next set of output is shorter. We now have the following:

```
11: Comparator<Duck> byWeight = new Comparator<>() {
12:     public int compare(Duck d1, Duck d2) {
13:         return d1.weight() - d2.weight();
14:     }
15: };
16: var ducks = new ArrayList<Duck>();
17: ducks.add(new Duck("Quack", 7));
18: ducks.add(new Duck("Puddles", 10));
19: Collections.sort(ducks);
20: System.out.println(ducks);   // [Puddles, Quack]
21: Collections.sort(ducks, byWeight);
22: System.out.println(ducks);   // [Quack, Puddles]
```

The Duck class itself can define only one compareTo() method. In this case, name was chosen. If we want to sort by something else, we have to define that sort order outside the compareTo() method using a separate class or lambda expression.

Lines 11–15 show how to define a Comparator using an anonymous class. On lines 19–22, we sort with the class's internal Comparator and then with the separate Comparator to see the difference in output.

Comparator is a functional interface since there is only one abstract method to implement. This means that we can rewrite the Comparator on lines 11–15 using a lambda expression, as shown here:

```
Comparator<Duck> byWeight = (d1, d2) -> d1.weight()-d2.weight();
```

Alternatively, we can use a method reference and a helper method to specify that we want to sort by weight.

```
Comparator<Duck> byWeight = Comparator.comparing(Duck::weight);
```

In this example, `Comparator.comparing()` is a `static` interface method that creates a `Comparator` given a lambda expression or method reference. Convenient, isn't it?

Is *Comparable* a Functional Interface?

We said that `Comparator` is a functional interface because it has a single abstract method. `Comparable` is also a functional interface since it also has a single abstract method. However, using a lambda for `Comparable` would be silly. The point of `Comparable` is to implement it inside the object being compared.

Comparing *Comparable* and *Comparator*

There are several differences between `Comparable` and `Comparator`. We've listed them for you in Table 9.8.

TABLE 9.8   Comparison of Comparable and Comparator

Difference	Comparable	Comparator
Package name	`java.lang`	`java.util`
Interface must be implemented by class comparing?	Yes	No
Method name in interface	`compareTo()`	`compare()`
Number of parameters	1	2
Common to declare using a lambda	No	Yes

Memorize this table—really. The exam will try to trick you by mixing up the two and seeing if you can catch it. Do you see why this doesn't compile?

```
var byWeight = new Comparator<Duck>() { // DOES NOT COMPILE
   public int compareTo(Duck d1, Duck d2) {
      return d1.getWeight()-d2.getWeight();
   }
};
```

The method name is wrong. A `Comparator` must implement a method named `compare()`. Pay special attention to method names and the number of parameters when you see `Comparator` and `Comparable` in questions.

Comparing Multiple Fields

When writing a `Comparator` that compares multiple instance variables, the code gets a little messy. Suppose that we have a `Squirrel` record, as shown here:

```
public record Squirrel(int weight, String species) {}
```

We want to write a `Comparator` to sort by species name. If two squirrels are from the same species, we want to sort the one that weighs the least first. We could do this with code that looks like this:

```
public class MultiFieldComparator implements Comparator<Squirrel> {
   public int compare(Squirrel s1, Squirrel s2) {
      int result = s1.species().compareTo(s2.species());
      if (result != 0) return result;
      else return s1.weight() - s2.weight();
} }
```

This works assuming no species' names are `null`. It checks one field. If they don't match, we are finished sorting. If they do match, it looks at the next field. This isn't easy to read, though. It is also easy to get wrong. Changing `!=` to `==` breaks the sort completely.

Alternatively, we can use method references and build the `Comparator`. This code represents logic for the same comparison:

```
Comparator<Squirrel> c = Comparator.comparing(Squirrel::species)
   .thenComparingInt(Squirrel::weight);
```

This time, we chain the methods. First, we create a `Comparator` on species ascending. Then, if there is a tie, we sort by weight. We can also sort in descending order. Some methods on `Comparator`, like `thenComparingInt()`, are `default` methods.

Suppose we want to sort in descending order by species.

```
var c = Comparator.comparing(Squirrel::species).reversed();
```

Table 9.9 shows the helper methods you should know for building a `Comparator`. We've omitted the parameter types to keep you focused on the methods. They use many of the functional interfaces you learned about in the previous chapter.

TABLE 9.9 Helper static methods for building a Comparator

Method	Description
comparing(function)	Compare by results of function that returns any `Object` (or primitive autoboxed into `Object`).
comparingDouble(function)	Compare by results of function that returns `double`.

TABLE 9.9　Helper static methods for building a Comparator *(continued)*

Method	Description
comparingInt(function)	Compare by results of function that returns int.
comparingLong(function)	Compare by results of function that returns long.
naturalOrder()	Sort using order specified by the Comparable implementation on the object itself.
reverseOrder()	Sort using reverse of order specified by Comparable implementation on the object itself.

Table 9.10 shows the methods that you can chain to a Comparator to further specify its behavior.

TABLE 9.10　Helper default methods for building a Comparator

Method	Description
reversed()	Reverse order of chained Comparator.
thenComparing(function)	If previous Comparator returns 0, use this comparator function that returns Object or can be autoboxed into one. Otherwise, return result from previous Comparator.
thenComparingDouble(function)	If previous Comparator returns 0, use this comparator function that returns double. Otherwise, return result from previous Comparator.
thenComparingInt(function)	If previous Comparator returns 0, use this comparator function that returns int. Otherwise, return result from previous Comparator.
thenComparingLong(function)	If previous Comparator returns 0, use this comparator function that returns long. Otherwise, return result from previous Comparator.

You've probably noticed by now that we often ignore null values in checking equality and comparing objects. This works fine for the exam. In the real world, though, things aren't so neat. You will have to decide how to handle null values or prevent them from being in your object.

Sorting and Searching

Now that you've learned all about `Comparable` and `Comparator`, we can finally do something useful with them, like sorting. The `Collections.sort()` method uses the `compareTo()` method to sort. It expects the objects to be sorted to be `Comparable`.

```
2:  public class SortRabbits {
3:      static record Rabbit(int id) {}
4:      public static void main(String[] args) {
5:          List<Rabbit> rabbits = new ArrayList<>();
6:          rabbits.add(new Rabbit(3));
7:          rabbits.add(new Rabbit(1));
8:          Collections.sort(rabbits);  // DOES NOT COMPILE
9:      }
10: }
```

Java knows that the `Rabbit` record is not `Comparable`. It knows sorting will fail, so it doesn't even let the code compile. You can fix this by passing a `Comparator` to `sort()`. Remember that a `Comparator` is useful when you want to specify sort order without using a `compareTo()` method.

```
8:          Comparator<Rabbit> c = (r1, r2) -> r1.id - r2.id;
9:          Collections.sort(rabbits, c);
10:         System.out.println(rabbits);  // [Rabbit[id=1], Rabbit[id=3]]
```

Suppose you want to sort the rabbits in descending order. You could change the `Comparator` to `r2.id - r1.id`. Alternatively, you could reverse the contents of the list afterward:

```
8:          Comparator<Rabbit> c = (r1, r2) -> r1.id - r2.id;
9:          Collections.sort(rabbits, c);
10:         Collections.reverse(rabbits);
11:         System.out.println(rabbits);  // [Rabbit[id=3], Rabbit[id=1]]
```

The `sort()` and `binarySearch()` methods allow you to pass in a `Comparator` object when you don't want to use the natural order.

Reviewing *binarySearch()*

The `binarySearch()` method requires a sorted `List`.

```
11: List<Integer> list = Arrays.asList(6,9,1,8);
12: Collections.sort(list); // [1, 6, 8, 9]
13: System.out.println(Collections.binarySearch(list, 6)); // 1
14: System.out.println(Collections.binarySearch(list, 3)); // -2
```

Line 12 sorts the List so we can call binary search properly. Line 13 prints the index at which a match is found. Line 14 prints one less than the negated index of where the requested value would need to be inserted. The number 3 would need to be inserted at index 1 (after the number 1 but before the number 6). Negating that gives us −1, and subtracting 1 gives us −2.

There is a trick in working with binarySearch(). What do you think the following outputs?

```
3: var names = Arrays.asList("Fluffy", "Hoppy");
4: Comparator<String> c = Comparator.reverseOrder();
5: var index = Collections.binarySearch(names, "Hoppy", c);
6: System.out.println(index);
```

The answer happens to be −1. Before you panic, you don't need to know that the answer is −1. You do need to know that the answer is not defined. Line 3 creates a list, [Fluffy, Hoppy]. This list happens to be sorted in ascending order. Line 4 creates a Comparator that reverses the natural order. Line 5 requests a binary search in descending order. Since the list is not in that order, we don't meet the precondition for doing a search.

While the result of calling binarySearch() on an improperly sorted list is undefined, sometimes you can get lucky. For example, search starts in the middle of an odd-numbered list. If you happen to ask for the middle element, the index returned will be what you expect.

Earlier in the chapter, we talked about collections that require classes to implement Comparable. Unlike sorting, they don't check that you have implemented Comparable at compile time.

Going back to our Rabbit that does not implement Comparable, we try to add it to a TreeSet:

```
2:  public class UseTreeSet {
3:      record Rabbit(int id) {}
4:      public static void main(String[] args) {
5:          Set<Duck> ducks = new TreeSet<>();
6:          ducks.add(new Duck("Puddles"));
7:
8:          Set<Rabbit> rabbits = new TreeSet<>();
9:          rabbits.add(new Rabbit(1));  // ClassCastException
10: } }
```

Line 6 is fine. Duck does implement Comparable. TreeSet is able to sort it into the proper position in the set. Line 9 is a problem. When TreeSet tries to sort it, Java discovers the fact that Rabbit does not implement Comparable. Java throws an exception that looks like this:

```
Exception in thread "main" java.lang.ClassCastException:
   class UseTreeSet$Rabbit cannot be cast to class java.lang.Comparable
```

It may seem weird for this exception to be thrown when the first object is added to the set. After all, there is nothing to compare yet. Java works this way for consistency.

Just like searching and sorting, you can tell collections that require sorting that you want to use a specific `Comparator`. For example:

```
8: Set<Rabbit> rabbits = new TreeSet<>((r1, r2) -> r1.id - r2.id);
9: rabbits.add(new Rabbit(1));
```

Now Java knows that you want to sort by `id`, and all is well. A `Comparator` is a helpful object. It lets you separate sort order from the object to be sorted. Notice that line 9 in both of the previous examples is the same. It's the declaration of the `TreeSet` that has changed.

Sorting a *List*

While you can call `Collections.sort(list)`, you can also sort directly on the list object.

```
3: List<String> bunnies = new ArrayList<>();
4: bunnies.add("long ear");
5: bunnies.add("floppy");
6: bunnies.add("hoppy");
7: System.out.println(bunnies);    // [long ear, floppy, hoppy]
8: bunnies.sort((b1, b2) -> b1.compareTo(b2));
9: System.out.println(bunnies);    // [floppy, hoppy, long ear]
```

On line 8, we sort the list alphabetically. The `sort()` method takes a `Comparator` that provides the sort order. Remember that `Comparator` takes two parameters and returns an `int`. If you need a review of what the return value of a `compare()` operation means, check the `Comparator` section in this chapter or the "Comparing" section in Chapter 4. This is really important to memorize!

Introducing Sequenced Collections

New to Java 21 are *sequenced collections*, which includes the three interfaces from Figure 9.1.

- `SequencedCollection`
- `SequencedSet`
- `SequencedMap`

A sequenced collection is a collection in which the encounter order is well-defined. By *encounter order*, it means all of the elements can be read in a repeatable way. While the elements of the collection may be sorted, it is not required.

Working with *SequencedCollection*

Let's start with the simplest example of a sequenced collection, one you've been working with throughout this book. An ArrayList is a SequencedCollection, as its first and last elements are well-defined, as is the ordering of all elements in between.

Table 9.11 includes various methods available on a SequencedCollection.

TABLE 9.11   SequencedCollection Methods

Method	Description
addFirst(E e)	Adds element as the first element in the collection
addLast(E e)	Adds element as the last element in the collection
getFirst()	Retrieves the first element in the collection
getLast()	Retrieves the last element in the collection
removeFirst()	Removes the first element in the collection
removeLast()	Removes the last element in the collection
reversed()	Returns a reverse-ordered view of the collection

For ArrayList, it should be pretty obvious how most of these methods are implemented. For example, to add or retrieve the first element in the list, you could call the add(0,e) and get(0), respectively. The purpose of the SequencedCollection interface isn't necessarily to add new functionality, but to make it easier to work with related types. For example, let's say we have the following method that welcomes the next visitor to the zoo:

```
public void welcomeNext(SequencedCollection<String> visitors) {
   System.out.println("Welcome to the Zoo! " + visitors.getFirst());
   visitors.removeFirst();
}
```

We can now apply various sequenced collections to this method:

```
var visitArrayList = new ArrayList<String>(List.of("Huey", "Dewey", "Louie"));
var visitLinkedList = new LinkedList<String>(List.of("Moe", "Larry", "Shemp"));
var visitTreeSet = new TreeSet<String>(Set.of("Alvin", "Simon", "Theodore"));

welcomeNext(visitArrayList);  // Welcome to the Zoo! Huey
```

```
welcomeNext(visitLinkedList); // Welcome to the Zoo! Moe
welcomeNext(visitTreeSet);    // Welcome to the Zoo! Alvin
```

Sequenced collections grant us the ability to work with lots of different types that all have a well-defined encounter order. Using some of the other methods from Table 9.11, we can even rearrange the elements.

```
public void moveToEnd(SequencedCollection<String> visitors) {
   visitors.addLast(visitors.removeFirst());
}
```

What happens if we call this new method on another group of collections?

```
var visitArrayList = new ArrayList<String>(
   List.of("Bluey", "Bingo", "Socks"));
var visitLinkedList = new LinkedList<String>(List.of("Garfield", "Odie"));
var visitTreeSet = new TreeSet<String>(Set.of("Tom", "Jerry"));

moveToEnd(visitArrayList);
welcomeNext(visitArrayList);  // Welcome to the Zoo! Bingo

moveToEnd(visitLinkedList);
welcomeNext(visitLinkedList); // Welcome to the Zoo! Odie

moveToEnd(visitTreeSet);      // java.lang.UnsupportedOperationException
welcomeNext(visitTreeSet);
```

Uh-oh, why didn't the last example work? Just because a method implements SequencedCollection doesn't mean the class supports all of the methods in Table 9.11. In this example, the addLast() call fails at runtime because you can't insert an item at the end of a sorted structure. Doing so could violate the comparator within the TreeSet.

 For the exam, you don't need to know which collections support which methods found in Table 9.11, but you should know the difference between a sequenced collection and a sorted collection.

A SequencedSet is a subtype of SequencedCollection; therefore, it inherits all its methods. It only applies to SequencedCollection classes that also implement Set, such as LinkedHashSet and TreeSet.

Working with *SequencedMap*

As you can probably guess, a SequencedMap is a Map with a defined encounter order. We define common methods in Table 9.12.

TABLE 9.12   Common SequencedMap Methods

Method	Description
firstEntry()	Retrieves the first key/value pair in the map
lastEntry()	Retrieves the last key/value pair in the map
pollFirstEntry()	Removes and retrieves the first key/value pair in the map
pollLastEntry()	Removes and retrieves the last key/value pair in the map
putFirst(K k, V v)	Adds the key/value pair as the first element in the map
putLast(K k, V v)	Adds the key/value pair as the last element in the map
reversed()	Returns a reverse-ordered view of the map

Let's define a method for working with SequencedMap.

```
public void welcomeNext(SequencedMap<String, String> visitors) {
   System.out.println("Welcome to the Zoo! " + visitors.pollFirstEntry());
}
```

What do you think the following snippet prints?

```
var visitHashMap = new HashMap<String,String>(
   Map.of("1", "Yakko", "2", "Wakko", "3", "Dot"));
welcomeNext(visitHashMap);
```

Trick question! It actually doesn't compile. Like we explained with HashSet earlier, a HashMap does not have an ordering, so it cannot be used as a SequencedMap. What about this example?

```
var visitTreeMap = new TreeMap<String,String>(
   Map.of("Pink", "Blossom", "Green", "Buttercup", "Blue", "Bubbles"));
welcomeNext(visitTreeMap);
```

If you guessed Welcome to the Zoo! Blue=Bubbles, then you were paying attention when we covered TreeMap. A TreeMap sorts things by the natural order of its keys, not the order in which they were added to the map. Since Blue is the first key in sorted order, it is the first pair printed.

Most of the collections that you have worked with throughout this book are sequenced. Two notable exceptions are HashSet and HashMap.

Reviewing Collection Types

We conclude this part of the chapter by reviewing rules that apply to various collection types, as well as an overview of all the types covered in this chapter.

Using Unmodifiable Wrapper Views

An *unmodifiable view* is a wrapper object around a collection that cannot be modified through the view itself. While the view object cannot be modified, the underlying data can still be modified.

There are four methods you should be familiar with for the exam that create unmodifiable views of a collection:

```
Collection<String> coll = Collections.unmodifiableCollection(List.of("brown"));
List<String> list       = Collections.unmodifiableList(List.of("orange"));
Set<String> set         = Collections.unmodifiableSet(Set.of("green"));
Map<String,Integer> map = Collections.unmodifiableMap(Map.of("red", 1));
```

Let's consider some code that uses them:

```
10: Map<String, Integer> map = new TreeMap<>();
11: map.put("blue", 41);
12: map.put("red", 90);
13: List<String> list = Arrays.asList("green", "yellow");
14: Set<String> set = new HashSet<>(list);
15:
16: Map<String, Integer> mapView = Collections.unmodifiableMap(map);
18: Collection<String> collView = Collections.unmodifiableCollection(list);
19: List<String> listView       = Collections.unmodifiableList(list);
20: Set<String> setView         = Collections.unmodifiableSet(set);
```

As you might expect, trying to modify an unmodifiable view throws an exception. When run independently, each of the following compiles and throws an UnsupportedOperationException at runtime.

```
collView.add("pink");
setView.remove("green");
mapView.put("blue", 42);
```

However, since it is a view, nothing prevents you from changing the original values. For example:

```
24: System.out.println(mapView);   // {blue=41, red=90}
25: System.out.println(collView);  // [green, yellow]
26: System.out.println(listView);  // [green, yellow]
```

```
27: System.out.println(setView);    // [green, yellow]
28:
29: map.put("blue", 105);
30: list.set(1, "purple");
31:
32: System.out.println(mapView);    // {blue=105, red=90}
33: System.out.println(collView);   // [green, purple]
34: System.out.println(listView);   // [green, purple]
35: System.out.println(setView);    // [green, yellow]
```

On line 29, notice that the value of blue is changed to 105 in the original TreeMap and it shows up as changed in mapView on line 32. The list variable created on line 13 refers to a fixed sized backed array. Which means both collView and listView represent a view of a List that refers to a backed array. Since the value is set on line 30, it remains the same size, and the change properly shows up in our views.

However, setView has not changed value. The constructor on line 14 makes a new set that is disconnected from the original data structure. This means line 30 has no effect on set.

What happens if we try adding elements to these collections?

```
36: set.add("orange");
37: System.out.println(setView);    // [green, yellow, orange]
38:
39: list.add("orange");                 // UnsupportedOperationException
```

Line 36 successfully modifies the underlying HashSet, with the changes reflected in the view on line 37. Line 39 throws an exception at runtime. Remember, the list was created with Arrays.asList(). As we saw earlier in the chapter, you can replace elements in such objects but you cannot add/remove elements. For the exam, remember to check the type of the underlying object to determine if things can be added, removed, or modified.

Comparing Collection Types

Make sure that you can fill in Table 9.13 to compare the four collection types from memory.

TABLE 9.13   Java Collections Framework types

Type	Can contain duplicate elements?	Elements always ordered?	Has keys and values?	Must add/remove in specific order?
List	Yes	Yes (by index)	No	No
Queue	Yes	Yes (retrieved in defined order)	No	Yes
Set	No	No	No	No
Map	Yes (for values)	No	Yes	No

Additionally, make sure you can fill in Table 9.14 to describe the types on the exam.

TABLE 9.14   Collection classes

Type	Java Collections Framework interfaces	Ordered?	Sorted?	Calls hashCode?	Calls compareTo?
ArrayDeque	Deque SequencedCollection	Yes	No	No	No
ArrayList	List SequencedCollection	Yes	No	No	No
HashMap	Map	No	No	Yes	No
HashSet	Set	No	No	Yes	No
LinkedList	Deque List SequencedCollection	Yes	No	No	No
LinkedHashSet	Set SequencedSet	Yes	No	No	No
LinkedHashMap	Map SequencedMap	Yes	No	No	No
TreeMap	Map SequencedMap	Yes	Yes	No	Yes
TreeSet	Set SequencedCollection SequencedSet	Yes	Yes	No	Yes

The exam expects you to know that data structures that involve sorting require you to tread carefully with null. For sorted sets, that means null is not permitted; and for sorted maps, this means null keys are not permitted.

Finally, the exam expects you to be able to choose the right collection type given a description of a problem. We recommend first identifying which type of collection the question is asking about. Figure out whether you are looking for a list, map, queue, or set. This lets you eliminate a number of answers. Then you can figure out which of the remaining choices is the best answer.

Real World Scenario

Older Collections

There are a few collections that are no longer on the exam but that you might come across in older code. All three were early Java data structures you could use with threads.

- Vector: Implements List
- Hashtable: Implements Map
- Stack: Implements List

These classes are rarely used anymore, as there are much better concurrent alternatives that we cover in Chapter 13.

Working with Generics

We conclude this chapter with one of the most useful, and at times most confusing, features in the Java language: generics. In this section, we present more advanced topics including creating generic classes and methods.

Creating Generic Classes

You can introduce generics into your own classes. The syntax for introducing a generic is to declare a *formal type parameter* in angle brackets. For example, the following class named Crate has a generic type variable declared after the name of the class:

```
public class Crate<T> {
    private T contents;
    public T lookInCrate() {
        return contents;
    }
    public void packCrate(T contents) {
        this.contents = contents;
    }
}
```

The generic type T is available anywhere within the Crate class. When you instantiate the class, you tell the compiler what T should be for that particular instance.

Naming Conventions for Generics

A type parameter can be named anything you want. The convention is to use single upper-case letters to make it obvious that they aren't real class names. The following are common letters to use:

- E for an element

- K for a map key

- V for a map value

- N for a number

- T for a generic data type

- S, U, V, and so forth for multiple generic types

For example, suppose an `Elephant` class exists, and we are moving our elephant to a new and larger enclosure in our zoo. (The San Diego Zoo did this in 2009. It was interesting seeing the large metal crate.)

```
Elephant elephant = new Elephant();
Crate<Elephant> crateForElephant = new Crate<>();
crateForElephant.packCrate(elephant);
Elephant inNewHome = crateForElephant.lookInCrate();
```

To be fair, we didn't pack the crate so much as the elephant walked into it. However, you can see that the `Crate` class is able to deal with an `Elephant` without knowing anything about it.

This probably doesn't seem particularly impressive. We could have just typed in `Elephant` instead of `T` when coding `Crate`. What if we wanted to create a `Crate` for another animal?

```
Crate<Zebra> crateForZebra = new Crate<>();
```

Now we couldn't have simply hard-coded `Elephant` in the `Crate` class since a `Zebra` is not an `Elephant`. However, we could have created an `Animal` superclass or interface and used that in `Crate`.

Generic classes become useful when the classes used as the type parameter can have absolutely nothing to do with each other. For example, we need to ship our 120-pound robot to another city.

```
Robot joeBot = new Robot();
Crate<Robot> robotCrate = new Crate<>();
robotCrate.packCrate(joeBot);
```

```
// ship to Houston
Robot atDestination = robotCrate.lookInCrate();
```

Now it is starting to get interesting. The Crate class works with any type of class. Before generics, we would have needed Crate to use the Object class for its instance variable, which would have put the burden on the caller to cast the object it receives on emptying the crate.

In addition to Crate not needing to know about the objects that go into it, those objects don't need to know about Crate. We aren't requiring the objects to implement an interface named Crateable or the like. A class can be put in the Crate without any changes at all.

 Don't worry if you can't think of a use for generic classes of your own. Unless you are writing a library for others to reuse, generics hardly show up in the class definitions you write. You've already seen them frequently in the code you call, such as functional interfaces and collections.

Generic classes aren't limited to having a single type parameter. This class shows two generic parameters.

```
public class SizeLimitedCrate<T, U> {
    private T contents;
    private U sizeLimit;
    public SizeLimitedCrate(T contents, U sizeLimit) {
        this.contents = contents;
        this.sizeLimit = sizeLimit;
} }
```

T represents the type that we are putting in the crate. U represents the unit that we are using to measure the maximum size for the crate. To use this generic class, we can write the following:

```
Elephant elephant = new Elephant();
Integer numPounds = 15_000;
SizeLimitedCrate<Elephant, Integer> c1
    = new SizeLimitedCrate<>(elephant, numPounds);
```

Here we specify that the type is Elephant, and the unit is Integer. We also throw in a reminder that numeric literals can contain underscores.

Understanding Type Erasure

Specifying a generic type allows the compiler to enforce proper use of the generic type. For example, specifying the generic type of Crate as Robot is like replacing the T in the Crate class with Robot. However, this is just for compile time.

Behind the scenes, the compiler replaces all references to T in Crate with Object. In other words, after the code compiles, your generics are just Object types. The Crate class looks like the following at runtime:

```
public class Crate {
    private Object contents;
    public Object lookInCrate() {
        return contents;
    }
    public void packCrate(Object contents) {
        this.contents = contents;
    }
}
```

This means there is only one class file. There aren't different copies for different parameterized types. (Some other languages work that way.) This process of removing the generics syntax from your code is referred to as *type erasure*. Type erasure allows your code to be compatible with older versions of Java that do not contain generics.

The compiler adds the relevant casts for your code to work with this type of erased class. For example, you type the following:

```
Robot r = crate.lookInCrate();
```

The compiler turns it into the following:

```
Robot r = (Robot) crate.lookInCrate();
```

In the following sections, we look at the implications of generics and type erasure for method declarations.

Overloading a Generic Method

Only one of these two methods is allowed in a class because type erasure will reduce both sets of arguments to (List input).

```
public class LongTailAnimal {
    protected void chew(List<Object> input) {}
    protected void chew(List<Double> input) {}  // DOES NOT COMPILE
}
```

For the same reason, you also can't overload a generic method from a parent class.

```
public class LongTailAnimal {
    protected void chew(List<Object> input) {}
}

public class Anteater extends LongTailAnimal {
    protected void chew(List<Double> input) {}  // DOES NOT COMPILE
}
```

Both of these examples fail to compile because of type erasure. In the compiled form, the generic type is dropped, and it appears as an invalid overloaded method. Now, let's look at another version of the same subclass:

```java
public class Anteater extends LongTailAnimal {
    protected void chew(List<Object> input) {}
    protected void chew(ArrayList<Double> input) {}
}
```

The first `chew()` method compiles because it uses the same generic type in the overridden method as the one defined in the parent class. The second `chew()` method compiles as well. However, it is an overloaded method because one of the method arguments is a `List` and the other is an `ArrayList`. When working with generic methods, it's important to consider the underlying type.

Returning Generic Types

When you're working with overridden methods that return generics, the return values must be covariant. In terms of generics, this means the return type of the class or interface declared in the overriding method must be a subtype of the class defined in the parent class. The generic parameter type must match its parent's type exactly.

Given the following declaration for the `Mammal` class, which of the two subclasses, `Monkey` and `Goat`, compile?

```java
public class Mammal {
    public List<CharSequence> play() { ... }
    public CharSequence sleep() { ... }
}

public class Monkey extends Mammal {
    public ArrayList<CharSequence> play() { ... }
}

public class Goat extends Mammal {
    public List<String> play() { ... }   // DOES NOT COMPILE
    public String sleep() { ... }
}
```

The `Monkey` class compiles because `ArrayList` is a subtype of `List`. The `play()` method in the `Goat` class does not compile, though. For the return types to be covariant, the generic type parameter must match. Even though `String` is a subtype of `CharSequence`, it does not exactly match the generic type defined in the `Mammal` class. Therefore, this is considered an invalid override.

Notice that the `sleep()` method in the `Goat` class does compile since `String` is a subtype of `CharSequence`. This example shows that covariance applies to the return type, just not the generic parameter type.

For the exam, it might be helpful for you to apply type erasure to questions involving generics to ensure that they compile properly. Once you've determined which methods are overridden and which are being overloaded, work backward, making sure the generic types match for overridden methods. And remember, generic methods cannot be overloaded by changing the generic parameter type only.

Implementing Generic Interfaces

Just like a class, an interface can declare a formal type parameter. For example, the following Shippable interface uses a generic type as the argument to its ship() method:

```
public interface Shippable<T> {
    void ship(T t);
}
```

There are three ways a class can approach implementing this interface. The first is to specify the generic type in the class. The following concrete class says that it deals only with robots. This lets it declare the ship() method with a Robot parameter.

```
class ShippableRobotCrate implements Shippable<Robot> {
    public void ship(Robot t) { }
}
```

The next way is to create a generic class. The following concrete class allows the caller to specify the type of the generic:

```
class ShippableAbstractCrate<U> implements Shippable<U> {
    public void ship(U t) { }
}
```

In this example, the type parameter could have been named anything, including T. We used U in the example to avoid confusion about what T refers to. The exam won't mind trying to confuse you by using the same type parameter name.

The final way is to not use generics at all. This is the old way of writing code. It generates a compiler warning about Shippable being a *raw type*, but it does compile. Here the ship() method has an Object parameter since the generic type is not defined:

```
class ShippableCrate implements Shippable {
    public void ship(Object t) { }
}
```

Real World Scenario

What You Can't Do with Generic Types

There are some limitations on what you can do with a generic type. These aren't on the exam, but it will be helpful to refer to this scenario when you are writing practice programs and run into one of these situations.

Most of the limitations are due to type erasure. Oracle refers to a type whose information is fully available at runtime as a *reifiable type*. Reifiable types can do anything that Java allows. Non-reifiable types have some limitations.

Here are the things that you can't do with generics (and by "can't," we mean without resorting to contortions like passing in a class object):

- **Call a constructor:** Writing new T() is not allowed because at runtime, it would be new Object().

- **Create an array of that generic type:** This one is the most annoying, but it makes sense because you'd be creating an array of Object values.

- **Call instanceof:** This is not allowed because at runtime List<Integer> and List<String> look the same to Java, thanks to type erasure.

- **Use a primitive type as a generic type parameter:** This isn't a big deal because you can use the wrapper class instead. If you want a type of int, just use Integer.

- **Create a static variable as a generic type parameter:** This is not allowed because the type is linked to the instance of the class.

- **Catch an exception of type T**: Even if T extends Exception, it cannot be used in a catch block since the precise type is not known.

Writing Generic Methods

Up until this point, you've seen formal type parameters declared on the class or interface level. It is also possible to declare them on the method level. This is often useful for static methods since they aren't part of an instance that can declare the type. However, it is also allowed on non-static methods.

In this example, both methods use a generic parameter:

```
public class Handler {
    public static <T> void prepare(T t) {
        System.out.println("Preparing " + t);
    }
    public static <T> Crate<T> ship(T t) {
        System.out.println("Shipping " + t);
        return new Crate<T>();
    }
}
```

The method parameter is the generic type T. Before the return type, we declare the formal type parameter of <T>. In the ship() method, we show how you can use the generic parameter in the return type, Crate<T>, for the method.

Unless a method is obtaining the generic formal type parameter from the class/interface, it is specified immediately before the return type of the method. This can lead to some interesting-looking code!

```
2: public class More {
3:    public static <T> void sink(T t) { }
4:    public static <T> T identity(T t) { return t; }
5:    public static T noGood(T t) { return t; } // DOES NOT COMPILE
6: }
```

Line 3 shows the formal parameter type immediately before the return type of void. Line 4 shows the return type being the formal parameter type. It looks weird, but it is correct. Line 5 omits the formal parameter type and therefore does not compile.

 Real World Scenario

Optional Syntax for Invoking a Generic Method

You can call a generic method normally, and the compiler will try to figure out which one you want. Alternatively, you can specify the type explicitly to make it obvious what the type is.

```
Box.<String>ship("package");
Box.<String[]>ship(args);
```

It is up to you whether this makes things clearer. You should at least be aware that this syntax exists.

When you have a method declare a generic parameter type, it is independent of the class generics. Take a look at this class that declares a generic T at both levels:

```
1: public class TrickyCrate<T> {
2:    public <T> T tricky(T t) {
3:        return t;
4:    }
5: }
```

See if you can figure out the type of T on lines 1 and 2 when we call the code as follows:

```
10: public static String crateName() {
11:    TrickyCrate<Robot> crate = new TrickyCrate<>();
12:    return crate.tricky("bot");
13: }
```

Clearly, "T is for tricky." Let's see what is happening. On line 1, T is Robot because that is what gets referenced when constructing a Crate. On line 2, T is String because that is what is passed to the method. When you see code like this, take a deep breath and write down what is happening so you don't get confused.

Creating a Generic Record

Generics can also be used with records. This record takes a single generic type parameter:

```
public record CrateRecord<T>(T contents) {
   @Override
   public T contents() {
      if (contents == null)
         throw new IllegalStateException("missing contents");
      return contents;
   }
}
```

This works the same way as classes. You can create a record of the robot!

```
Robot robot = new Robot();
CrateRecord<Robot> record = new CrateRecord<>(robot);
```

This is convenient. Now we have an immutable, generic record!

Bounding Generic Types

By now, you might have noticed that generics don't seem particularly useful since they are treated as Objects and, therefore, don't have many methods available. Bounded wildcards solve this by restricting what types can be used in a generic. A *bounded parameter type* is a generic type that specifies a bound for the generic. Be warned that this is the hardest section in the chapter, so don't feel bad if you have to read it more than once.

A *wildcard generic type* is an unknown generic type represented with a question mark (?). You can use generic wildcards in three ways, as shown in Table 9.15. This section looks at each of these three wildcard types.

TABLE 9.15   Types of bounds

Type of bound	Syntax	Example
Unbounded wildcard	?	List<?> a = new ArrayList<String>();
Wildcard with upper bound	? extends type	List<? extends Exception> a = new ArrayList<RuntimeException>();
Wildcard with lower bound	? super type	List<? super Exception> a = new ArrayList<Object>();

Creating Unbounded Wildcards

An unbounded wildcard represents any data type. You use ? when you want to specify that any type is OK with you. Let's suppose that we want to write a method that looks through a list of any type.

```java
public static void printList(List<Object> list) {
    for (Object x: list)
        System.out.println(x);
}
public static void main(String[] args) {
    List<String> keywords = new ArrayList<>();
    keywords.add("java");
    printList(keywords); // DOES NOT COMPILE
}
```

Wait. What's wrong? A String is a subclass of an Object. This is true. However, List<String> cannot be assigned to List<Object>. We know, it doesn't sound logical. Java is trying to protect us from ourselves with this one. Imagine if we could write code like this:

```java
4: List<Integer> numbers = new ArrayList<>();
5: numbers.add(Integer.valueOf(42));
6: List<Object> objects = numbers; // DOES NOT COMPILE
7: objects.add("forty two");
8: System.out.println(numbers.get(1));
```

On line 4, the compiler promises us that only Integer objects will appear in numbers. If line 6 compiled, line 7 would break that promise by putting a String in there since numbers and objects are references to the same object. Good thing the compiler prevents this.

Going back to printing a list, we cannot assign a List<String> to a List<Object>. That's fine; we don't need a List<Object>. What we really need is a List of "whatever." That's what List<?> is. The following code does what we expect:

```java
public static void printList(List<?> list) {
    for (Object x: list)
        System.out.println(x);
}
public static void main(String[] args) {
    List<String> keywords = new ArrayList<>();
    keywords.add("java");
    printList(keywords);
}
```

The printList() method takes any type of list as a parameter. The keywords variable is of type List<String>. We have a match! List<String> is a list of anything. "Anything" just happens to be a String here.

Finally, let's look at the impact of var. Do you think these two statements are equivalent?

```
List<?> x1 = new ArrayList<>();
var x2 = new ArrayList<>();
```

They are not. There are two key differences. First, x1 is of type List, while x2 is of type ArrayList. Additionally, we can only assign x2 to a List<Object>. These two variables do have one thing in common. Both return type Object when calling the get() method.

Creating Upper-Bounded Wildcards

Let's try to write a method that adds up the total of a list of numbers. We've established that a generic type can't just use a subclass.

```
ArrayList<Number> list = new ArrayList<Integer>(); // DOES NOT COMPILE
```

Instead, we need to use a wildcard:

```
List<? extends Number> list = new ArrayList<Integer>();
```

The upper-bounded wildcard says that any class that extends Number or Number itself can be used as the formal parameter type:

```
public static long total(List<? extends Number> list) {
   long count = 0;
   for (Number number: list)
      count += number.longValue();
   return count;
}
```

Remember how we kept saying that type erasure makes Java think that a generic type is an Object? That is still happening here. Java converts the previous code to something equivalent to the following:

```
public static long total(List list) {
   long count = 0;
   for (Object obj: list) {
      Number number = (Number) obj;
      count += number.longValue();
   }
   return count;
}
```

Something interesting happens when we work with upper bounds or unbounded wildcards. The list becomes logically immutable and therefore cannot be modified. Technically, you can remove elements from the list, but the exam won't ask about this.

```
2: static class Sparrow extends Bird { }
3: static class Bird { }
4:
```

```
5: public static void main(String[] args) {
6:     List<? extends Bird> birds = new ArrayList<Bird>();
7:     birds.add(new Sparrow()); // DOES NOT COMPILE
8:     birds.add(new Bird());    // DOES NOT COMPILE
9: }
```

The problem stems from the fact that Java doesn't know what type List<? extends Bird> really is. It could be List<Bird> or List<Sparrow> or some other generic type that hasn't even been written yet. Line 7 doesn't compile because we can't add a Sparrow to List<? extends Bird>, and line 8 doesn't compile because we can't add a Bird to List<Sparrow>. From Java's point of view, both scenarios are equally possible, so neither is allowed.

Now let's try an example with an interface. We have an interface and two classes that implement it.

```
interface Flyer { void fly(); }
class HangGlider implements Flyer { public void fly() {} }
class Goose implements Flyer { public void fly() {} }
```

We also have two methods that use it. One just lists the interface, and the other uses an upper bound.

```
private void anyFlyer(List<Flyer> flyer) {}
private void groupOfFlyers(List<? extends Flyer> flyer) {}
```

Note that we used the keyword extends rather than implements. Upper bounds are like anonymous classes in that they use extends regardless of whether we are working with a class or an interface.

You already learned that a variable of type List<Flyer> can be passed to either method. A variable of type List<Goose> can be passed only to the one with the upper bound. This shows a benefit of generics. Random flyers don't fly together. We want our groupOfFlyers() method to be called only with the same type. Geese fly together but don't fly with hang gliders.

Creating Lower-Bounded Wildcards

Let's try to write a method that adds a string "quack" to two lists.

```
List<String> strings = new ArrayList<String>();
strings.add("tweet");

List<Object> objects = new ArrayList<Object>(strings);
addSound(strings);
addSound(objects);
```

The problem is that we want to pass a List<String> and a List<Object> to the same method. First, make sure you understand why the first three examples in Table 9.16 do *not* solve this problem.

TABLE 9.16 Why we need a lower bound

static void addSound(_____ list) { list.add("quack"); }	Method compiles	Can pass a List<String>	Can pass a List<Object>
List<?>	No	Yes	Yes
List<? extends Object>	No	Yes	Yes
List<Object>	Yes	No (with generics, must pass exact match)	Yes
List<? super String>	Yes	Yes	Yes

To solve this problem, we need to use a lower bound.

```
public static void addSound(List<? super String> list) {
    list.add("quack");
}
```

With a lower bound, we are telling Java that the list will be a list of String objects or a list of some objects that are a superclass of String. Either way, it is safe to add a String to that list.

Just like generic classes, you probably won't use this in your code unless you are writing code for others to reuse. Even then, it would be rare. But it's on the exam, so now is the time to learn it!

Understanding Generic Supertypes

When you have subclasses and superclasses, lower bounds can get tricky.

```
3: List<? super IOException> exceptions = new ArrayList<Exception>();
4: exceptions.add(new Exception()); // DOES NOT COMPILE
5: exceptions.add(new IOException());
6: exceptions.add(new FileNotFoundException());
```

Line 3 references a List that could be List<IOException> or List<Exception> or List<Object>. Line 4 does not compile because we could have a List<IOException>, and an Exception object wouldn't fit in there.

Line 5 is fine. IOException can be added to any of those types. Line 6 is also fine. FileNotFoundException can also be added to any of those three types. This is tricky because FileNotFoundException is a subclass of IOException, and the keyword says super. Java says, "Well, FileNotFoundException also happens to be an IOException, so everything is fine."

Putting It All Together

At this point, you know everything that you need to know to ace the exam questions on generics. It is possible to put these concepts together to write some *really* confusing code, which the exam likes to do.

This section is going to be difficult to read. It contains the hardest questions that you could possibly be asked about generics. The exam questions will probably be easier to read than these. We want you to encounter the really tough ones here so that you are ready for the exam. In other words, don't panic. Take it slow, and reread the code a few times. You'll get it.

Combining Generic Declarations

Let's try an example. First, we declare three classes that the example will use:

```
class A {}
class B extends A {}
class C extends B {}
```

Ready? Can you figure out why these do or don't compile? Also, try to figure out what they do.

```
6: List<?> list1 = new ArrayList<A>();
7: List<? extends A> list2 = new ArrayList<A>();
8: List<? super A> list3 = new ArrayList<A>();
```

Line 6 creates an `ArrayList` that can hold instances of class A. It is stored in a variable with an unbounded wildcard. Any generic type can be referenced from an unbounded wildcard, making this OK.

Line 7 tries to store a list in a variable declaration with an upper-bounded wildcard. This is OK. You can have `ArrayList<A>`, `ArrayList<B>`, or `ArrayList<C>` stored in that reference. Line 8 is also OK. This time, you have a lower-bounded wildcard. The lowest type you can reference is A. Since that is what you have, it compiles.

Did you get those right? Let's try a few more.

```
9:  List<? extends B> list4 = new ArrayList<A>(); // DOES NOT COMPILE
10: List<? super B> list5 = new ArrayList<A>();
11: List<?> list6 = new ArrayList<? extends A>(); // DOES NOT COMPILE
```

Line 9 has an upper-bounded wildcard that allows `ArrayList<B>` or `ArrayList<C>` to be referenced. Since you have `ArrayList<A>` that is trying to be referenced, the code does not compile. Line 10 has a lower-bounded wildcard, which allows a reference to `ArrayList<A>`, `ArrayList<B>`, or `ArrayList<Object>`.

Finally, line 11 allows a reference to any generic type since it is an unbounded wildcard. The problem is that you need to know what that type will be when instantiating the `ArrayList`. It wouldn't be useful anyway, because you can't add any elements to that `ArrayList`.

Passing Generic Arguments

Now on to the methods. Same question: try to figure out why they don't compile or what they do. We will present the methods one at a time because there is more to think about.

```
<T> T first(List<? extends T> list) {
    return list.get(0);
}
```

The first method, `first()`, is a perfectly normal use of generics. It uses a method-specific type parameter, T. It takes a parameter of List<T>, or some subclass of T, and it returns a single object of that T type. For example, you could call it with a List<String> parameter and have it return a String. Or you could call it with a List<Number> parameter and have it return a Number. Or—well, you get the idea.

Given that, you should be able to see what is wrong with this one:

```
<T> <? extends T> second(List<? extends T> list) { // DOES NOT COMPILE
    return list.get(0);
}
```

The next method, `second()`, does not compile because the return type isn't actually a type. You are writing the method. You know what type it is supposed to return. You don't get to specify this as a wildcard.

Now be careful—this one is extra tricky:

```
<B extends A> B third(List<B> list) {
    return new B(); // DOES NOT COMPILE
}
```

This method, `third()`, does not compile. <B extends A> says that you want to use B as a type parameter just for this method and that it needs to extend the A class. Coincidentally, B is also the name of a class. Well, it isn't a coincidence. It's an evil trick. Within the scope of the method, B can represent class A, B, or C, because all extend the A class. Since B no longer refers to the B class in the method, you can't instantiate it.

After that, it would be nice to get something straightforward.

```
void fourth(List<? super B> list) {}
```

We finally get a method, `fourth()`, that is a normal use of generics. You can pass the type List<B>, List<A>, or List<Object>.

Finally, can you figure out why this example does not compile?

```
<X> void fifth(List<X super B> list) { } // DOES NOT COMPILE
```

This last method, `fifth()`, does not compile because it tries to mix a method-specific type parameter with a wildcard. A wildcard must have a ? in it.

Phew. You made it through generics. It's the hardest topic in this chapter (and why we covered it last!). Remember that it's OK if you need to go over this material a few times to get your head around it.

Summary

The Java Collections Framework includes four main types of data structures: lists, sets, queues, and maps. The Collection interface is the parent interface of List, Set, and Queue. Additionally, Deque extends Queue. The Map interface does not extend Collection. You need to recognize the following:

- **List:** An ordered collection of elements that allows duplicate entries.
  - **ArrayList:** Standard resizable list.
  - **LinkedList:** Can easily add/remove from beginning or end.
- **Set**: Does not allow duplicates.
  - **HashSet:** Uses hashCode() to find unordered elements.
  - **LinkedHashSet:** Well-defined encounter order.
  - **TreeSet:** Sorted. Does not allow null values.
- **Queue/Deque:** Orders elements for processing.
  - **ArrayDeque:** Double-ended queue.
  - **LinkedList:** Double-ended queue and list.
- **Map:** Maps unique keys to values.
  - **HashMap:** Uses hashCode() to find keys.
  - **LinkedHashMap:** Well-defined encounter order.
  - **TreeMap:** Sorted map. Does not allow null keys.

Java 21 now includes sequenced collections, for types with a defined encounter order.

- **SequencedCollection:** ArrayDeque, ArrayList, LinkedList, LinkedHashSet, and TreeSet.
- **SequencedSet:** LinkedHashSet and TreeSet.
- **SequencedMap:** LinkedHashMap and TreeMap.

The Comparable interface declares the compareTo() method. This method returns a negative number if the object is smaller than its argument, 0 if the two objects are equal, and a positive number otherwise. The compareTo() method is declared on the object that is being compared, and it takes one parameter. The Comparator interface defines the compare() method. A negative number is returned if the first argument is smaller, zero if they are equal, and a positive number otherwise. The compare() method can be declared in any code, and it takes two parameters. A Comparator is often implemented using a lambda.

Generics are type parameters for code. To create a class with a generic parameter, add <T> after the class name. You can use any name you want for the type parameter. Single uppercase letters are common choices. Generics allow you to specify wildcards. <?> is an unbounded wildcard that means any type. <? extends Object> is an upper bound that means any type that is Object or extends it. <? extends MyInterface> means any type that implements MyInterface. <? super Number> is a lower bound that means any type that is Number or a superclass. A compiler error results from code that attempts to add an item in a list with an unbounded or upper-bounded wildcard.

Exam Essentials

Pick the correct type of collection from a description.   A List allows duplicates and orders the elements. A Set does not allow duplicates. A Deque orders its elements to facilitate retrievals from the front or back. A Map maps keys to values. Be familiar with the differences in implementations of these interfaces.

Work with convenience methods.   The Collections Framework contains many methods such as contains(), forEach(), and removeIf() that you need to know for the exam. There are too many to list in this paragraph for review, so please do review the tables in this chapter.

Understand how to use sequenced collections.   Other than HashSet and HashMap, most collection classes now implement a sequenced collection interface (SequencedCollection or SequencedMap or SequencedSet). This includes methods that support iterating over the collection in a predictable encounter order. The methods make it easier to work with related types using a consistent interface.

Differentiate between *Comparable* and *Comparator*.   Classes that implement Comparable are said to have a natural ordering and implement the compareTo() method. A class is allowed to have only one natural ordering. A Comparator takes two objects in the compare() method. Different ones can have different sort orders. A Comparator is often implemented using a lambda such as (a, b) -> a.num - b.num.

Identify valid and invalid uses of generics and wildcards.   <T> represents a type parameter. Any name can be used, but a single uppercase letter is the convention. <?> is an unbounded wildcard. <? extends X> is an upper-bounded wildcard. <? super X> is a lower-bounded wildcard.

Review Questions

The answers to the chapter review questions can be found in the Appendix   .

1. Suppose you need to display a collection of products for sale, which may contain duplicates. Additionally, you have a collection of sales that you need to track, sorted by the natural order of the sale ID, and you need to retrieve the text of each. Which two of the following classes best suit your needs for each of these scenarios? (Choose two.)

   A. ArrayList

   B. HashMap

   C. HashSet

   D. LinkedList

   E. SequencedTreeSet

   F. TreeMap

2. Which of the following are true? (Choose all that apply.)

   ```
   12: List<?> q = List.of("mouse", "parrot");
   13: var v = List.of("mouse", "parrot");
   14:
   15: q.removeIf(String::isEmpty);
   16: q.removeIf(s -> s.length() == 4);
   17: v.removeIf(String::isEmpty);
   18: v.removeIf(s -> s.length() == 4);
   ```

   A. This code compiles and runs without error.

   B. Exactly one of these lines contains a compiler error.

   C. Exactly two of these lines contain a compiler error.

   D. Exactly three of these lines contain a compiler error.

   E. Exactly four of these lines contain a compiler error.

   F. If any lines with compiler errors are removed, this code runs without throwing an exception.

   G. If any lines with compiler errors are removed, this code throws an exception.

3. What is the result of the following statements?

   ```
   3:  var greetings = new ArrayDeque<String>();
   4:  greetings.offerLast("hello");
   5:  greetings.offerLast("hi");
   6:  greetings.offerFirst("ola");
   7:  greetings.pop();
   8:  greetings.peek();
   ```

```
9:   while (greetings.peek() != null)
10:     System.out.print(greetings.pop());
```

A. hello

B. hellohi

C. hellohiola

D. hiola

E. The code does not compile.

F. An exception is thrown.

4. Which of these statements compile? (Choose all that apply.)

A. `HashSet<Number> hs = new HashSet<Integer>();`

B. `HashSet<? super ClassCastException> set = new HashSet<Exception>();`

C. `List<> list = new ArrayList<String>();`

D. `List<Object> values = new HashSet<Object>();`

E. `List<Object> objects = new ArrayList<? extends Object>();`

F. `Map<String, ? extends Number> hm = new HashMap<String, Integer>();`

5. What is the result of the following code?

```
1: public record Hello<T>(T t) {
2:     public Hello(T t) { this.t = t; }
3:     private <T> void println(T message) {
4:         System.out.print(t + "-" + message);
5:     }
6:     public static void main(String[] args) {
7:         new Hello<String>("hi").println(1);
8:         new Hello("hola").println(true);
9:     } }
```

A. hi followed by a runtime exception.

B. hi-1hola-true

C. The first compiler error is on line 1.

D. The first compiler error is on line 3.

E. The first compiler error is on line 8.

F. The first compiler error is on another line.

6. Which of the following can fill in the blank to print [7, 5, 3]? (Choose all that apply.)

```
8: public record Platypus(String name, int beakLength) {
9:     @Override public String toString() {return "" + beakLength;}
```

```
10:
11:     public static void main(String[] args) {
12:         Platypus p1 = new Platypus("Paula", 3);
13:         Platypus p2 = new Platypus("Peter", 5);
14:         Platypus p3 = new Platypus("Peter", 7);
15:
16:         List<Platypus> list = Arrays.asList(p1, p2, p3);
17:
18:         Collections.sort(list, Comparator.comparing_____);
19:
20:         System.out.println(list);
21:     }
22: }
```

A.
```
(Platypus::beakLength)
```

B.
```
(Platypus::beakLength).reversed()
```

C.
```
(Platypus::name)
   .thenComparing(Platypus::beakLength)
```

D.
```
(Platypus::name)
   .thenComparing(
   Comparator.comparing(Platypus::beakLength)
   .reversed())
```

E.
```
(Platypus::name)
   .thenComparingNumber(Platypus::beakLength)
   .reversed()
```

F.
```
(Platypus::name)
   .thenComparingInt(Platypus::beakLength)
   .reversed()
```

7. Which of the following method signatures are valid overrides of the hairy() method in the Alpaca class? (Choose all that apply.)

```
import java.util.*;

public class Alpaca {
    public List<String> hairy(List<String> list) { return null; }
}
```

A. public List<String> hairy(List<CharSequence> list) {
return null; }

B. public List<String> hairy(List<String> list) { return null; }

C. public List<String> hairy(List<Integer> list) { return null; }

D. public List<CharSequence> hairy(List<String> list) {
return null; }

E. public Object hairy(List<String> list) { return null; }

F. public ArrayList<String> hairy(List<String> list) {
return null; }

8. Which of the following fills in the blank, allowing the code to compile and run without issue?

```
11: SequencedCollection<String> animals = new _____<>();
12: animals.addFirst("lions");
13: animals.addLast("tigers");
14: for(var a : animals)
15:     System.out.println(a);
16: System.out.println(animals.get(0));
```

A. HashSet

B. LinkedList

C. TreeSetMap

D. HashMap

E. None of the above

9. What is the result of the following program?

```
3:  public class MyComparator implements Comparator<String> {
4:      public int compare(String a, String b) {
5:          return b.toLowerCase().compareTo(a.toLowerCase());
6:      }
7:      public static void main(String[] args) {
8:          String[] values = { "123", "Abb", "aab" };
9:          Arrays.sort(values, new MyComparator());
10:         for (var s: values)
11:             System.out.print(s + " ");
12:     }
13: }
```

A. Abb aab 123

B. aab Abb 123

C. 123 Abb aab

D. 123 aab Abb

E. The code does not compile.

F. A runtime exception is thrown.

10. Which of these statements can fill in the blank so that the `Helper` class compiles successfully? (Choose all that apply.)

```
2:  public class Helper {
3:      public static <U extends Exception>
4:          void printException(U u) {
5:
6:          System.out.println(u.getMessage());
7:      }
8:      public static void main(String[] args) {
9:          Helper._____;
10:  } }
```

- **A.** `printException(new FileNotFoundException("A"))`
- **B.** `printException(new Exception("B"))`
- **C.** `<Throwable>printException(new Exception("C"))`
- **D.** `<NullPointerException>printException(new NullPointerException ("D"))`
- **E.** `printException(new Throwable("E"))`

11. Which of the following will compile when filling in the blank? (Choose all that apply.)

```
var list = List.of(1, 2, 3);
var set = Set.of(1, 2, 3);
var map = Map.of(1, 2, 3, 4);

_____.forEach(System.out::println);
```

- **A.** `list`
- **B.** `set`
- **C.** `map`
- **D.** `map.keys()`
- **E.** `map.keySet()`
- **F.** `map.values()`
- **G.** `map.valueSet()`

12. Which of these statements can fill in the blank so that the `Wildcard` class compiles successfully? (Choose all that apply.)

```
3:  public class Wildcard {
4:      public void showSize(List<?> list) {
5:          System.out.println(list.size());
6:      }
7:      public static void main(String[] args) {
8:          Wildcard card = new Wildcard();
9:          _____;
10:         card.showSize(list);
11:  } }
```

   A. `List<?> list = new HashSet <String>()`

   B. `ArrayList<? super Date> list = new ArrayList<Date>()`

   C. `List<?> list = new ArrayList<?>()`

   D. `List<Exception> list = new LinkedList<java.io.IOException>()`

   E. `ArrayList <? extends Number> list = new ArrayList <Integer>()`

   F. None of the above

13. What is the result of the following program?

```
3:  public record Sorted(int num, String text)
4:      implements Comparable<Sorted>, Comparator<Sorted> {
5:
6:      public String toString() { return "" + num; }
7:      public int compareTo(Sorted s) {
8:          return text.compareTo(s.text);
9:      }
10:     public int compare(Sorted s1, Sorted s2) {
11:         return s1.num - s2.num;
12:     }
13:     public static void main(String[] args) {
14:         var s1 = new Sorted(88, "a");
15:         var s2 = new Sorted(55, "b");
16:         SequencedSet<Sorted> t1 = new TreeSet<Sorted>();
17:         t1.add(s1); t1.add(s2);
18:         var t2 = new TreeSet<Sorted>(s1);
19:         t2.add(s1); t2.add(s2);
20:         System.out.println(t1 + " " + t2);
21:     } }
```

   A. `[55, 88] [55, 88]`

   B. `[55, 88] [88, 55]`

   C. `[88, 55] [55, 88]`

   D. `[88, 55] [88, 55]`

   E. The code does not compile.

   F. A runtime exception is thrown.

14. What is the result of the following code?

```
Comparator<Integer> c1 = (o1, o2) -> o2 - o1;
Comparator<Integer> c2 = Comparator.naturalOrder();
Comparator<Integer> c3 = Comparator.reverseOrder();

var list = Arrays.asList(5, 4, 7, 2);
```

```
Collections.sort(list,_____);
Collections.reverse(list);
Collections.reverse(list);
System.out.println(Collections.binarySearch(list, 2));
```

A. One or more of the comparators can fill in the blank so that the code prints 0.

B. One or more of the comparators can fill in the blank so that the code prints 1.

C. One or more of the comparators can fill in the blank so that the code prints 2.

D. The result is undefined regardless of which comparator is used.

E. A runtime exception is thrown regardless of which comparator is used.

F. The code does not compile.

15. Which of the following lines can be inserted to make the code compile? (Choose all that apply.)

```
class W {}
class X extends W {}
class Y extends X {}
class Z<Y> {
    // INSERT CODE HERE
}
```

A. W w1 = new W();

B. W w2 = new X();

C. W w3 = new Y();

D. Y y1 = new W();

E. Y y2 = new X();

F. Y y3 = new Y();

16. Which options are true of the following code? (Choose all that apply.)

```
_____ q = new LinkedList<>();
var u = Collections.unmodifiableCollection(q);
q.add(10);
q.add(12);
q.remove(1);
System.out.print(u);
```

A. If we fill in the blank with List<Integer>, the output is [10].

B. If we fill in the blank with Queue<Integer>, the output is [10].

C. If we fill in the blank with var, the output is [10].

D. One or more of the scenarios does not compile.

E. One or more of the scenarios throws a runtime exception.

17. What is the result of the following code?

```
4: Map m = new HashMap();
5: m.put(123, "456");
6: m.put("abc", "def");
7: System.out.println(m.contains("123"));
```

A. false

B. true

C. Compiler error on line 4.

D. Compiler error on line 5.

E. Compiler error on line 7.

F. A runtime exception is thrown.

18. What is the result of the following code? (Choose all that apply.)

```
48: var map = Map.of(1,2, 3, 6);
49: var list = List.copyOf(map.entrySet());
50:
51: List<Integer> one = List.of(8, 16, 2);
52: var copy = List.copyOf(one);
53: var copyOfCopy = List.copyOf(copy);
54: var thirdCopy = new ArrayList<>(copyOfCopy);
55:
56: list.replaceAll(x -> x * 2);
57: one.replaceAll(x -> x * 2);
58: thirdCopy.replaceAll(x -> x * 2);
59:
60: System.out.println(thirdCopy);
```

A. One line fails to compile.

B. Two lines fail to compile.

C. Three lines fail to compile.

D. The code compiles but throws an exception at runtime.

E. If any lines with compiler errors are removed, the code throws an exception at runtime.

F. If any lines with compiler errors are removed, the code prints [16, 32, 4].

G. The code compiles and prints [16, 32, 4] without any changes.

19. What code change is needed to make the method compile, assuming there is no class named T?

```
public static T identity(T t) {
    return t;
}
```

A. Add <T> after the public keyword.

B. Add <T> after the static keyword.

C. Add <T> after T.

D. Add <?> after the public keyword.

E. Add <?> after the static keyword.

F. No change is required. The code already compiles.

20. Assuming keys are printed in order, what is the result of the following?

```
var map = new HashMap<Integer, Integer>();
map.put(1, 10);
map.put(2, 20);
map.put(3, null);
map.merge(1, 3, (a,b) -> a + b);
map.merge(3, 3, (a,b) -> a + b);
System.out.println(map);
```

A. {1=10, 2=20}

B. {1=10, 2=20, 3=null}

C. {1=10, 2=20, 3=3}

D. {1=13, 2=20}

E. {1=13, 2=20, 3=null}

F. {1=13, 2=20, 3=3}

G. The code does not compile.

H. An exception is thrown.

21. Which of the following statements are true? (Choose all that apply.)

A. Comparable is in the java.util package.

B. Comparator is in the java.util package.

C. compare() is in the Comparable interface.

D. compare() is in the Comparator interface.

E. compare() takes one method parameter.

F. compare() takes two method parameters.

22. What is the output of the following code snippet?

```
21: SequencedMap<Integer, String> cats = new TreeMap<>();
22: cats.put(3, "Snowball");
23: cats.put(2, "Sugar");
24: cats.put(1, "Minnie Mouse");
25: cats.pollFirstEntry();
26: var id = cats.lastEntry().getKey();
```

```
27: cats.pollFirstEntry();
28: System.out.print(cats.firstEntry().getValue());
```

A. `Minnie Mouse`

B. `Snowball`

C. `Sugar`

D. The code does not compile.

E. The code compiles, but an exception is thrown at runtime.

23. What is the output of the following code snippet?

```
var fishes = new TreeSet<String>();
fishes.add("Koi");
fishes.addFirst("clown");
fishes.add("carp");
for(var fish : fishes)
    System.out.print(fish + ", ");
```

A. `carp, clown, Koi,`

B. `carp, Koi, clown,`

C. `clown, carp, Koi,`

D. `clown, Koi, carp,`

E. `Koi, carp, clown,`

F. `Koi, clown, carp,`

G. The code does not compile.

H. The code compiles but throws an exception at runtime.

Chapter

10

Streams

OCP EXAM OBJECTIVES COVERED IN THIS CHAPTER:

✓ **Working with Streams and Lambda expressions**

- Use Java object and primitive Streams, including lambda expressions implementing functional interfaces, to create, filter, transform, process, and sort data.

- Perform decomposition, concatenation, and reduction, and grouping and partitioning on sequential and parallel streams.

By now, you should be comfortable with the lambda and method reference syntax. Both are used when implementing functional interfaces. If you need more practice, you may want to go back and review Chapter 8, "Lambdas and Functional Interfaces," and Chapter 9, "Collections and Generics." In this chapter, we add actual functional programming to that, focusing on the Streams API.

Note that the Streams API in this chapter is used for functional programming. By contrast, there are also java.io streams, which we talk about in Chapter 14, "I/O." Despite both using the word *stream*, they are nothing alike.

In this chapter, we introduce Optional. Then we introduce the Stream pipeline and tie it all together. You might want to read this chapter twice before doing the review questions so that you really get it. Functional programming tends to have a steep learning curve but can be very exciting once you get the hang of it.

Returning an *Optional*

Suppose that you are taking an introductory Java class and receive scores of 90 and 100 on the first two exams. Now, we ask you what your average is. An average is calculated by adding the scores and dividing by the number of scores, so you have (90+100)/2. This gives 190/2, so you answer with 95. Great!

Now suppose that you are taking your second class on Java, and it is the first day of class. We ask you what your average is in this class that just started. You haven't taken any exams yet, so you don't have anything to average. It wouldn't be accurate to say that your average is zero. That sounds bad and isn't true. There simply isn't any data, so you don't have an average.

How do we express this "we don't know" or "not applicable" answer in Java? We use the Optional type. An Optional is created using a factory. You can either request an empty Optional or pass a value for the Optional to wrap. Think of an Optional as a box that might have something in it or might instead be empty. Figure 10.1 shows both options.

Creating an *Optional*

Here's how to code our average method:

```
10: public static Optional<Double> average(int... scores) {
11:     if (scores.length == 0) return Optional.empty();
```

```
12:    int sum = 0;
13:    for (int score: scores) sum += score;
14:    return Optional.of((double) sum / scores.length);
15: }
```

FIGURE 10.1 Optional

Optional.empty()

Optional.of(95)

Line 11 returns an empty Optional when we can't calculate an average. Lines 12 and 13 add up the scores. There is a functional programming way of doing this math, but we will get to that later in the chapter. In fact, the entire method could be written in one line, but that wouldn't teach you how Optional works! Line 14 creates an Optional to wrap the average.

Did you notice that we use a static method to create an Optional? That's because Optional relies on a factory pattern and does not expose any public constructors.

Calling the method shows what is in our two boxes:

```
System.out.println(average(90, 100)); // Optional[95.0]
System.out.println(average());         // Optional.empty
```

An Optional can take a generic type, making it easier to retrieve values from it. You can see that one Optional<Double> contains a value and the other is empty. Normally, we want to check whether a value is there and/or get it out of the box. Here's one way to do that:

```
Optional<Double> opt = average(90, 100);
if (opt.isPresent())
   System.out.println(opt.get()); // 95.0
```

First we check whether the Optional contains a value. Then we print it out. What if we didn't do the check and the Optional was empty?

```
Optional<Double> opt = average();
System.out.println(opt.get()); // NoSuchElementException
```

We'd get an exception since there is no value inside the Optional.

```
java.util.NoSuchElementException: No value present
```

When creating an Optional, it is common to want to use empty() when the value is null. You can do this with an if statement or ternary operator. We use the ternary operator (? :) to simplify the code, which you saw in Chapter 2, "Operators."

```
Optional o = (value == null) ? Optional.empty() : Optional.of(value);
```

If value is null, o is assigned the empty Optional. Otherwise, we wrap the value. Since this is such a common pattern, Java provides a factory method to do the same thing.

```
Optional o = Optional.ofNullable(value);
```

That covers the static methods you need to know about Optional. Table 10.1 summarizes most of the instance methods on Optional that you need to know for the exam. There are a few others that involve chaining. We cover those later in the chapter.

TABLE 10.1 Common Optional instance methods

Method	When Optional is empty	When Optional contains value
get()	Throws exception	Returns value
ifPresent(Consumer c)	Does nothing	Calls Consumer with value
isPresent()	Returns false	Returns true
orElse(T other)	Returns other parameter	Returns value
orElseGet(Supplier s)	Returns result of calling Supplier	Returns value
orElseThrow()	Throws NoSuchElementException	Returns value
orElseThrow(Supplier s)	Throws exception created by calling Supplier	Returns value

You've already seen get() and isPresent(). The other methods allow you to write code that uses an Optional in one line without having to use the ternary operator. This makes the code easier to read. Instead of using an if statement, which we used when checking the average earlier, we can specify a Consumer to be run when there is a value inside the Optional. When there isn't, the method simply skips running the Consumer.

```
Optional<Double> opt = average(90, 100);
opt.ifPresent(System.out::println);
```

Using ifPresent() better expresses our intent. We want something done if a value is present. You can think of it as an if statement with no else.

Dealing with an Empty *Optional*

The remaining methods allow you to specify what to do if a value isn't present. There are a few choices. The first two allow you to specify a return value either directly or using a Supplier.

```
30: Optional<Double> opt = average();
31: System.out.println(opt.orElse(Double.NaN));
32: System.out.println(opt.orElseGet(() -> Math.random()));
```

This prints something like the following:

```
NaN
0.49775932295380165
```

Line 31 shows that you can return a specific value or variable. In our case, we print the "not a number" value. Line 32 shows using a Supplier to generate a value at runtime to return instead. I'm glad our professors didn't give us a random average, though!

Alternatively, we can have the code throw an exception if the Optional is empty.

```
30: Optional<Double> opt = average();
31: System.out.println(opt.orElseThrow());
```

This prints something like the following:

```
Exception in thread "main" java.util.NoSuchElementException:
  No value present
  at java.base/java.util.Optional.orElseThrow(Optional.java:382)
```

Without specifying a Supplier for the exception, Java will throw a NoSuchElementException. Alternatively, we can have the code throw a custom exception if the Optional is empty. Remember that the stack trace looks weird because the lambdas are generated rather than named classes.

```
30: Optional<Double> opt = average();
31: System.out.println(opt.orElseThrow(
32:     () -> new IllegalStateException()));
```

This prints something like the following:

```
Exception in thread "main" java.lang.IllegalStateException
  at optionals.Methods.lambda$orElse$1(Methods.java:31)
  at java.base/java.util.Optional.orElseThrow(Optional.java:408)
```

Line 32 shows using a Supplier to create an exception that should be thrown. Notice that we do not write throw new IllegalStateException(). The orElseThrow() method takes care of actually throwing the exception when we run it.

The two methods that take a Supplier have different names. Do you see why this code does not compile?

```
System.out.println(opt.orElseGet(
    () -> new IllegalStateException())); // DOES NOT COMPILE
```

The opt variable is an `Optional<Double>`. This means the `Supplier` must return a `Double`. Since this `Supplier` returns an exception, the type does not match.

The last example with `Optional` is really easy. What do you think this does?

```
Optional<Double> opt = average(90, 100);
System.out.println(opt.orElse(Double.NaN));
System.out.println(opt.orElseGet(() -> Math.random()));
System.out.println(opt.orElseThrow());
```

It prints out `95.0` three times. Since the value does exist, there is no need to use the "or else" logic.

Is *Optional* the Same as *null?*

An alternative to `Optional` is to return `null`. There are a few shortcomings with this approach. One is that there isn't a clear way to express that `null` might be a special value. By contrast, returning an `Optional` is a clear statement in the API that there might not be a value.

Another advantage of `Optional` is that you can use a functional programming style with `ifPresent()` and the other methods rather than needing an `if` statement. Finally, you see toward the end of the chapter that you can chain `Optional` calls.

Using Streams

A *stream* in Java is a sequence of data. A *stream pipeline* consists of the operations that run on a stream to produce a result. Note that people often use stream and stream pipeline interchangeably to mean stream pipeline. First, we look at the flow of pipelines conceptually. After that, we get into the code.

Understanding the Pipeline Flow

Think of a stream pipeline as an assembly line in a factory. Suppose that we are running an assembly line to make signs for the animal exhibits at the zoo. We have a number of jobs. It is one person's job to take the signs out of a box. It is a second person's job to paint the sign. It is a third person's job to stencil the name of the animal on the sign. It's the last person's job to put the completed sign in a box to be carried to the proper exhibit.

Notice that the second person can't do anything until one sign has been taken out of the box by the first person. Similarly, the third person can't do anything until one sign has been painted, and the last person can't do anything until it is stenciled.

The assembly line for making signs is finite. Once we process the contents of our box of signs, we are finished. *Finite* streams have a limit. Other assembly lines essentially run forever, like one for food production. Of course, they do stop at some point when the factory closes down, but pretend that doesn't happen. Or think of a sunrise/sunset cycle as *infinite*, since it doesn't end for an inordinately large period of time.

Another important feature of an assembly line is that each person touches each element to do their operation, and then that piece of data is gone. It doesn't come back. The next person deals with it at that point. This is different than the lists and queues that you saw in the previous chapter. With a list, you can access any element at any time. With a queue, you are limited in which elements you can access, but all of the elements are there. With streams, the data isn't generated up front—it is created when needed. This is an example of *lazy evaluation*, which delays execution until necessary.

Many things can happen in the assembly line stations along the way. In functional programming, these are called *stream operations*. Just like with the assembly line, operations occur in a pipeline. Someone has to start and end the work, and there can be any number of stations in between. After all, a job with one person isn't an assembly line! There are three parts to a stream pipeline, as shown in Figure 10.2.

- **Source:** Where the stream comes from.

- **Intermediate operations:** Transforms the stream into another one. There can be as few or as many intermediate operations as you'd like. Since streams use lazy evaluation, the intermediate operations do not run until the terminal operation runs.

- **Terminal operation:** Produces a result. Since streams can be used only once, the stream is no longer valid after a terminal operation completes.

FIGURE 10.2   Stream pipeline

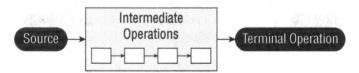

Notice that the operations are unknown to us. When viewing the assembly line from the outside, you care only about what comes in and goes out. What happens in between is an implementation detail.

You will need to know the differences between intermediate and terminal operations well. Make sure you can fill in Table 10.2.

TABLE 10.2   Intermediate vs. terminal operations

Scenario	Intermediate operation	Terminal operation
Required part of useful pipeline?	No	Yes
Can exist multiple times in pipeline?	Yes	No

TABLE 10.2   Intermediate vs. terminal operations *(continued)*

Scenario	Intermediate operation	Terminal operation
Return type is stream type?	Yes	No
Executed upon method call?	No	Yes
Stream valid after call?	Yes	No

A factory typically has a foreperson who oversees the work. Java serves as the foreperson when working with stream pipelines. This is a really important role, especially when dealing with lazy evaluation and infinite streams. Think of declaring the stream as giving instructions to the foreperson. As the foreperson finds out what needs to be done, they set up the stations and tell the workers what their duties will be. However, the workers do not start until the foreperson tells them to begin. The foreperson waits until they see the terminal operation to kick off the work. They also watch the work and stop the line as soon as work is complete.

Let's look at a few examples of this. We aren't using code in these examples because it is really important to understand the stream pipeline concept before starting to write the code. Figure 10.3 shows a stream pipeline with one intermediate operation.

FIGURE 10.3   Steps in running a stream pipeline

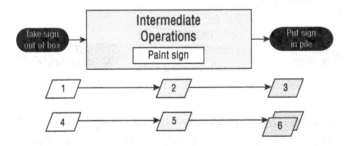

Let's take a look at what happens from the point of view of the foreperson. First, they see that the source is taking signs out of the box. The foreperson sets up a worker at the table to unpack the box and says to await a signal to start. Then the foreperson sees the intermediate operation to paint the sign. They set up a worker with paint and say to await a signal to start. Finally, the foreperson sees the terminal operation to put the signs into a pile. They set up a worker to do this and yell that all three workers should start.

Suppose that there are two signs in the box. Step 1 is the first worker taking one sign out of the box and handing it to the second worker. Step 2 is the second worker painting it and handing it to the third worker. Step 3 is the third worker putting it in the pile. Steps 4–6 are this same process for the other sign. Then the foreperson sees that there are no signs left and shuts down the entire enterprise.

The foreperson is smart and can make decisions about how to best do the work based on what is needed. As an example, let's explore the stream pipeline in Figure 10.4.

FIGURE 10.4   A stream pipeline with a limit

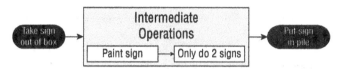

The foreperson still sees a source of taking signs out of the box and assigns a worker to do that on command. They still see an intermediate operation to paint and set up another worker with instructions to wait and then paint. Then they see an intermediate step that we need only two signs. They set up a worker to count the signs that go by and notify the foreperson when the worker has seen two. Finally, they set up a worker for the terminal operation to put the signs in a pile.

This time, suppose that there are 10 signs in the box. We start like last time. The first sign makes its way down the pipeline. The second sign also makes its way down the pipeline. When the worker in charge of counting sees the second sign, they tell the foreperson. The foreperson lets the terminal operation worker finish their task and then yells, "Stop the line." It doesn't matter that there are eight more signs in the box. We don't need them, so it would be unnecessary work to paint them. And we all want to avoid unnecessary work!

Similarly, the foreperson would have stopped the line after the first sign if the terminal operation was to find the first sign that gets created.

In the following sections, we cover the three parts of the pipeline. We also discuss special types of streams for primitives and how to print a stream.

Creating Stream Sources

In Java, the streams we have been talking about are represented by the Stream<T> interface, defined in the java.util.stream package.

Creating Finite Streams

For simplicity, we start with finite streams. There are a few ways to create them.

```
11: Stream<String> empty = Stream.empty();          // count = 0
12: Stream<Integer> singleElement = Stream.of(1);   // count = 1
13: Stream<Integer> fromArray = Stream.of(1, 2, 3); // count = 3
```

Line 11 shows how to create an empty stream. Line 12 shows how to create a stream with a single element. Line 13 shows how to create a stream from a varargs.

Java also provides a convenient way of converting a `Collection` to a stream.

```
14: var list = List.of("a", "b", "c");
15: Stream<String> fromList = list.stream();
```

Line 15 shows that it is a simple method call to create a stream from a list. This is helpful since such conversions are common.

Creating a Parallel Stream

It is just as easy to create a parallel stream from a list.

```
24: var list = List.of("a", "b", "c");
25: Stream<String> fromListParallel = list.parallelStream();
```

This is a great feature because you can write code that uses concurrency before even learning what a thread is. Using parallel streams is like setting up multiple tables of workers who can do the same task. Painting would be a lot faster if we could have five painters painting signs instead of just one. Just keep in mind some tasks cannot be done in parallel, such as putting the signs away in the order that they were created in the stream. Also be aware that there is a cost in coordinating the work, so for smaller streams, it might be faster to do it sequentially. You learn much more about running tasks concurrently in Chapter 13, "Concurrency."

Creating Infinite Streams

So far, this isn't particularly impressive. We could do all this with lists. We can't create an infinite list, though, which makes streams more powerful.

```
17: Stream<Double> randoms = Stream.generate(Math::random);
18: Stream<Integer> oddNumbers = Stream.iterate(1, n -> n + 2);
```

Line 17 generates a stream of random numbers. How many random numbers? However many you need. Remember that the source doesn't actually create the values until you call a terminal operation. Later in the chapter, you learn about operations like `limit()` to turn the infinite stream into a finite stream making it safe to print them out without crashing the program.

Line 18 gives you more control. The `iterate()` method takes a seed or starting value as the first parameter. This is the first element that will be part of the stream. The other parameter is a lambda expression that is passed the previous value and generates the next value. As with the random numbers example, it will keep on producing odd numbers as long as you need them.

Printing a Stream Reference

If you try printing a stream object, you'll get something like the following:

```
System.out.print(stream); // java.util.stream.ReferencePipeline$3@4517d9a3
```

This is different from a `Collection`, where you see the contents. You don't need to know this for the exam. We mention it so that you aren't caught by surprise when writing code for practice.

What if you wanted just odd numbers less than 100? There's an overloaded version of `iterate()` that helps:

```
19: Stream<Integer> oddNumberUnder100 = Stream.iterate(
20:    1,                   // seed
21:    n -> n < 100,        // Predicate to specify when done
22:    n -> n + 2);         // UnaryOperator to get next value
```

This method takes three parameters. Notice how they are separated by commas (,) just like in all other methods. The exam may try to trick you by using semicolons since it is similar to a `for` loop. Additionally, you have to take care that you aren't accidentally creating a stream that will run forever.

Reviewing Stream Creation Methods

To review, make sure you know all the methods in Table 10.3. These are the ways of creating a source for streams, given a `Collection` instance `coll`.

TABLE 10.3   Creating a source

Method	Finite or infinite?	Notes
`Stream.empty()`	Finite	Creates `Stream` with zero elements.
`Stream.of(varargs)`	Finite	Creates `Stream` with elements listed.
`coll.stream()`	Finite	Creates `Stream` from `Collection`.
`coll.parallelStream()`	Finite	Creates `Stream` from `Collection` where the stream can run in parallel.
`Stream.generate(supplier)`	Infinite	Creates `Stream` by calling `Supplier` for each element upon request.
`Stream.iterate(seed, unaryOperator)`	Infinite	Creates `Stream` by using seed for first element and then calling `UnaryOperator` for each subsequent element upon request.
`Stream.iterate(seed, predicate, unaryOperator)`	Finite or infinite	Creates `Stream` by using seed for first element and then calling `UnaryOperator` for each subsequent element upon request. Stops if `Predicate` returns false.

Using Common Terminal Operations

You can perform a terminal operation without any intermediate operations but not the other way around. This is why we talk about terminal operations first. *Reductions* are a special type of terminal operation where all of the contents of the stream are combined into a single primitive or Object. For example, you might end up with an int or a Collection.

Table 10.4 summarizes this section. Feel free to use it as a guide to remember the most important points as we go through each one individually. We explain them from simplest to most complex rather than alphabetically.

TABLE 10.4   Terminal stream operations

Method	What happens for infinite streams	Return value	Reduction
count()	Does not terminate	long	Yes
min() max()	Does not terminate	Optional<T>	Yes
findAny() findFirst()	Terminates	Optional<T>	No
allMatch() anyMatch() noneMatch()	Sometimes terminates	boolean	No
forEach()	Does not terminate	void	No
reduce()	Does not terminate	Varies	Yes
collect()	Does not terminate	Varies	Yes

Counting

The count() method determines the number of elements in a finite stream. For an infinite stream, it never terminates. Why? Count from 1 to infinity, and let us know when you are finished! Or rather, don't do that, because we'd rather you study for the exam than spend the rest of your life counting. The count() method is a reduction because it looks at each element in the stream and returns a single value. The method signature is as follows:

```
public long count()
```

This example shows calling count() on a finite stream:

```
Stream<String> s = Stream.of("monkey", "gorilla", "bonobo");
System.out.println(s.count()); // 3
```

Finding the Minimum and Maximum

The min() and max() methods allow you to pass a custom comparator and find the smallest or largest value in a finite stream according to that sort order. Like the count() method, min() and max() hang on an infinite stream because they cannot be sure that a smaller or larger value isn't coming later in the stream. Both methods are reductions because they return a single value after looking at the entire stream. The method signatures are as follows:

```
public Optional<T> min(Comparator<? super T> comparator)
public Optional<T> max(Comparator<? super T> comparator)
```

This example finds the animal with the fewest letters in its name:

```
Stream<String> s = Stream.of("monkey", "ape", "bonobo");
Optional<String> min = s.min((s1, s2) -> s1.length() - s2.length());
min.ifPresent(System.out::println); // ape
```

Notice that the code returns an Optional rather than the value. This allows the method to specify that no minimum or maximum was found. We use the Optional method ifPresent() and a method reference to print out the minimum only if one is found. As an example of where there isn't a minimum, let's look at an empty stream:

```
Optional<?> minEmpty = Stream.empty().min((s1, s2) -> 0);
System.out.println(minEmpty.isPresent()); // false
```

Since the stream is empty, the comparator is never called, and no value is present in the Optional.

> What if you need both the min() and max() values of the same stream? For now, you can't have both, at least not using these methods. Remember, a stream can have only one terminal operation. Once a terminal operation has been run, the stream cannot be used again. As you see later in this chapter, there are built-in summary methods for some *numeric* streams that will calculate a set of values for you.

Finding a Value

The findAny() and findFirst() methods return an element of the stream unless the stream is empty. If the stream is empty, they return an empty Optional. This is the first method you've seen that can terminate with an infinite stream. Since Java generates only the amount of stream you need, the infinite stream needs to generate only one element.

As its name implies, the findAny() method can return any element of the stream. When called on the streams you've seen up until now, it commonly returns the first element, although this behavior is not guaranteed. As you see in Chapter 13, the findAny() method is more likely to return a random element when working with parallel streams.

These methods are terminal operations but not reductions. The reason is that they sometimes return without processing all of the elements. This means that they return a value based on the stream but do not reduce the entire stream into one value.

The method signatures are as follows:

```
public Optional<T> findAny()
public Optional<T> findFirst()
```

This example finds an animal:

```
Stream<String> s = Stream.of("monkey", "gorilla", "bonobo");
Stream<String> infinite = Stream.generate(() -> "chimp");


s.findAny().ifPresent(System.out::println);            // monkey (usually)
infinite.findAny().ifPresent(System.out::println); // chimp
```

Finding any one match is more useful than it sounds. Sometimes we just want to sample the results and get a representative element, but we don't need to waste the processing generating them all. After all, if we plan to work with only one element, why bother looking at more?

Matching

The allMatch(), anyMatch(), and noneMatch() methods search a stream and return information about how the stream pertains to the predicate. These may or may not terminate for infinite streams. It depends on the data. Like the find methods, they are not reductions because they do not necessarily look at all of the elements.

The method signatures are as follows:

```
public boolean anyMatch(Predicate <? super T> predicate)
public boolean allMatch(Predicate <? super T> predicate)
public boolean noneMatch(Predicate <? super T> predicate)
```

This example checks whether animal names begin with letters:

```
var list = List.of("monkey", "2", "chimp");
Stream<String> infinite = Stream.generate(() -> "chimp");
Predicate<String> pred = x -> Character.isLetter(x.charAt(0));


System.out.println(list.stream().anyMatch(pred));   // true
System.out.println(list.stream().allMatch(pred));   // false
System.out.println(list.stream().noneMatch(pred));  // false
System.out.println(infinite.anyMatch(pred));        // true
```

This shows that we can reuse the same predicate, but we need a different stream each time. The anyMatch() method returns true because two of the three elements match. The allMatch() method returns false because one doesn't match. The noneMatch() method also returns false because at least one matches. Calling anyMatch() on the infinite stream is fine because we match right away and the call terminates. However, consider what happens if you try calling allMatch():

```
Stream<String> infinite = Stream.generate(() -> "chimp");
Predicate<String> pred = x -> Character.isLetter(x.charAt(0));
System.out.println(infinite.allMatch(pred));        // Never terminates
```

Because allMatch() needs to check every element, it will run until we kill the program.

Remember that allMatch(), anyMatch(), and noneMatch() return a boolean. By contrast, the find methods return an Optional because they return an element of the stream.

Iterating

As in the Java Collections Framework, it is common to iterate over the elements of a stream. As expected, calling forEach() on an infinite stream does not terminate. Since there is no return value, it is not a reduction.

Before you use it, consider if another approach would be better. Developers who learned to write loops first tend to use them for everything. For example, a loop with an if statement could be written with a filter. You will learn about filters in the intermediate operations section.

The method signature is as follows:

```
public void forEach(Consumer<? super T> action)
```

Notice that this is the only terminal operation with a return type of void. If you want something to happen, you have to make it happen in the Consumer. Here's one way to print the elements in the stream (there are other ways, which we cover later in the chapter):

```
Stream<String> s = Stream.of("Monkey", "Gorilla", "Bonobo");
s.forEach(System.out::print); // MonkeyGorillaBonobo
```

Remember that you can call forEach() directly on a Collection or on a Stream. Don't get confused on the exam when you see both approaches.

Notice that you can't use a traditional for loop on a stream.

```
Stream<Integer> s = Stream.of(1);
for (Integer i  : s) {} // DOES NOT COMPILE
```

While forEach() sounds like a loop, it is really a terminal operator for streams. Streams cannot be used as the source in a for-each loop because they don't implement the Iterable interface.

Reducing

The reduce() methods combine a stream into a single object. They are (obviously) reductions, which means they process all elements. The three method signatures are these:

```
public T reduce(T identity, BinaryOperator<T> accumulator)

public Optional<T> reduce(BinaryOperator<T> accumulator)
```

```
public <U> U reduce(U identity,
   BiFunction<U,? super T,U> accumulator,
   BinaryOperator<U> combiner)
```

Let's take them one at a time. The most common way of doing a reduction is to start with an initial value and keep merging it with the next value. Think about how you would concatenate an array of `String` objects into a single `String` without functional programming. It might look something like this:

```
var array = new String[] { "w", "o", "l", "f" };
var result = "";
for (var s: array) result = result + s;
System.out.println(result); // wolf
```

The *identity* is the initial value of the reduction, in this case an empty `String`. The *accumulator* combines the current result with the current value in the stream. With lambdas, we can do the same thing with a stream and reduction:

```
Stream<String> stream = Stream.of("w", "o", "l", "f");
String word = stream.reduce("", (s, c) -> s + c);
System.out.println(word); // wolf
```

Notice how we still have the empty `String` as the identity. We also still concatenate the `String` objects to get the next value. We can even rewrite this with a method reference:

```
Stream<String> stream = Stream.of("w", "o", "l", "f");
String word = stream.reduce("", String::concat);
System.out.println(word); // wolf
```

Let's try another one. Can you write a reduction to multiply all of the `Integer` objects in a stream? Try it. Our solution is shown here:

```
Stream<Integer> stream = Stream.of(3, 5, 6);
System.out.println(stream.reduce(1, (a, b) -> a*b)); // 90
```

We set the identity to 1 and the accumulator to multiplication. In many cases, the identity isn't really necessary, so Java lets us omit it. When you don't specify an identity, an `Optional` is returned because there might not be any data. There are three choices for what is in the `Optional`:

- If the stream is empty, an empty `Optional` is returned.
- If the stream has one element, it is returned.
- If the stream has multiple elements, the accumulator is applied to combine them.

The following illustrates each of these scenarios:

```
BinaryOperator<Integer> op = (a, b) -> a * b;
Stream<Integer> empty = Stream.empty();
```

```
Stream<Integer> oneElement = Stream.of(3);
Stream<Integer> threeElements = Stream.of(3, 5, 6);

empty.reduce(op).ifPresent(System.out::println);           // no output
oneElement.reduce(op).ifPresent(System.out::println);      // 3
threeElements.reduce(op).ifPresent(System.out::println);   // 90
```

Why are there two similar methods? Why not just always require the identity? Java could have done that. However, sometimes it is nice to differentiate the case where the stream is empty rather than the case where there is a value that happens to match the identity being returned from the calculation. The signature returning an Optional lets us differentiate these cases. For example, we might return Optional.empty() when the stream is empty and Optional.of(3) when there is a value.

The third method signature is used when we are dealing with different types. It allows Java to create intermediate reductions and then combine them at the end. Let's take a look at an example that counts the number of characters in each String:

```
Stream<String> stream = Stream.of("w", "o", "l", "f!");
int length = stream.reduce(0, (i, s) -> i+s.length(), (a, b) -> a+b);
System.out.println(length); // 5
```

The first parameter (0) is the value for the *initializer*. If we had an empty stream, this would be the answer. The second parameter is the *accumulator*. Unlike the accumulators you saw previously, this one handles mixed data types. In this example, the first argument, i, is an Integer, while the second argument, s, is a String. It adds the length of the current String to our running total. The third parameter is called the *combiner*, which combines any intermediate totals. In this case, a and b are both Integer values.

The three-argument reduce() operation is useful when working with parallel streams because it allows the stream to be decomposed and reassembled by separate threads. For example, if we needed to count the length of four 100-character strings, the first two values and the last two values could be computed independently. The intermediate result (200 + 200) would then be combined into the final value.

Collecting

The collect() method is a special type of reduction called a *mutable reduction*. It is more efficient than a regular reduction because we use the same mutable object while accumulating. Common mutable objects include StringBuilder and ArrayList. This is a really useful method, because it lets us get data out of streams and into another form. The method signatures are as follows:

```
public <R> R collect(Supplier<R> supplier,
    BiConsumer<R, ? super T> accumulator,
    BiConsumer<R, R> combiner)


public <R,A> R collect(Collector<? super T, A,R> collector)
```

Let's start with the first signature, which is used when we want to code specifically how collecting should work. Our wolf example from reduce can be converted to use collect():

```
Stream<String> stream = Stream.of("w", "o", "l", "f");

StringBuilder word = stream.collect(
    StringBuilder::new,
    StringBuilder::append,
    StringBuilder::append);


System.out.println(word); // wolf
```

The first parameter is the *supplier*, which creates the object that will store the results as we collect data. Remember that a Supplier doesn't take any parameters and returns a value. In this case, it constructs a new StringBuilder.

The second parameter is the *accumulator*, which is a BiConsumer that takes two parameters and doesn't return anything. It is responsible for adding one more element to the data collection. In this example, it appends the next String to the StringBuilder.

The final parameter is the *combiner*, which is another BiConsumer. It is responsible for taking two data collections and merging them. This is useful when we are processing in parallel. Two smaller collections are formed and then merged into one. This would work with StringBuilder only if we didn't care about the order of the letters. In this case, the accumulator and combiner have similar logic.

Now let's look at an example where the logic is different in the accumulator and combiner:

```
Stream<String> stream = Stream.of("w", "o", "l", "f");

TreeSet<String> set = stream.collect(
    TreeSet::new,
    TreeSet::add,
    TreeSet::addAll);


System.out.println(set); // [f, l, o, w]
```

The collector has three parts as before. The supplier creates an empty TreeSet. The accumulator adds a single String from the Stream to the TreeSet. The combiner adds all of the elements of one TreeSet to another in case the operations were done in parallel and need to be merged.

We started with the long signature because that's how you implement your own collector. It is important to know how to do this for the exam and understand how collectors work. In practice, many common collectors come up over and over. Rather than making developers keep reimplementing the same ones, Java provides a class with common collectors cleverly named `Collectors`. This approach also makes the code easier to read because it is more expressive. For example, we could rewrite the previous example as follows:

```
Stream<String> stream = Stream.of("w", "o", "l", "f");
TreeSet<String> set =
   stream.collect(Collectors.toCollection(TreeSet::new));
System.out.println(set); // [f, l, o, w]
```

If we didn't need the set to be sorted, we could make the code even shorter:

```
Stream<String> stream = Stream.of("w", "o", "l", "f");
Set<String> set = stream.collect(Collectors.toSet());
System.out.println(set); // [f, w, l, o]
```

You might get different output for this last one since `toSet()` makes no guarantees as to which implementation of `Set` you'll get. It is likely to be a `HashSet`, but you shouldn't expect or rely on that.

> The exam expects you to know about common predefined collectors in addition to being able to write your own by passing a supplier, accumulator, and combiner.

Later in this chapter, we show many `Collectors` that are used for grouping data. It's a big topic, so it's best to master how streams work before adding too many `Collectors` into the mix.

Using Common Intermediate Operations

Unlike a terminal operation, an intermediate operation produces a stream as its result. An intermediate operation can also deal with an infinite stream simply by returning another infinite stream. Since elements are produced only as needed, this works fine. The assembly line worker doesn't need to worry about how many more elements are coming through and instead can focus on the current element.

Filtering

The `filter()` method returns a `Stream` with elements that match a given expression. Here is the method signature:

```
public Stream<T> filter(Predicate<? super T> predicate)
```

This operation is easy to remember and powerful because we can pass any `Predicate` to it. For example, this retains all elements that begin with the letter *m*:

```
Stream<String> s = Stream.of("monkey", "gorilla", "bonobo");
s.filter(x -> x.startsWith("m"))
   .forEach(System.out::print); // monkey
```

Removing Duplicates

The distinct() method returns a stream with duplicate values removed. The duplicates do not need to be adjacent to be removed. As you might imagine, Java calls equals() to determine whether the objects are equivalent. The method signature is as follows:

```
public Stream<T> distinct()
```

Here's an example:

```
Stream<String> s = Stream.of("duck", "duck", "duck", "goose");
s.distinct()
    .forEach(System.out::print); // duckgoose
```

Restricting by Position

The limit() and skip() methods can make a Stream smaller. The limit() method could also make a finite stream out of an infinite stream. The method signatures are shown here:

```
public Stream<T> limit(long maxSize)
public Stream<T> skip(long n)
```

The following code creates an infinite stream of numbers counting from 1. The skip() operation returns an infinite stream starting with the numbers counting from 6, since it skips the first five elements. The limit() call takes the first two of those. Now we have a finite stream with two elements, which we can then print with the forEach() method:

```
Stream<Integer> s = Stream.iterate(1, n -> n + 1);
s.skip(5)
    .limit(2)
    .forEach(System.out::print); // 67
```

Mapping

The map() method creates a one-to-one mapping from the elements in the stream to the elements of the next step in the stream. The method signature is as follows:

```
public <R> Stream<R> map(Function<? super T, ? extends R> mapper)
```

This one looks more complicated than the others you have seen. It uses the lambda expression to figure out the type passed to that function and the one returned.

> The map() method on streams is for transforming data. Don't confuse it with the Map interface, which maps keys to values.

As an example, this code converts a list of String objects to a list of Integer objects representing their lengths:

```
Stream<String> s = Stream.of("monkey", "gorilla", "bonobo");
s.map(String::length)
    .forEach(System.out::print); // 676
```

Remember that `String::length` is shorthand for the lambda `x -> x.length()`, which clearly shows it is a function that turns a `String` into an `Integer`.

Using *flatMap*

The `flatMap()` method takes each element in the stream and makes any elements it contains top-level elements in a single stream. This is helpful when you want to remove empty elements from a stream or combine a stream of lists. We are showing you the method signature for consistency with the other methods so you don't think we are hiding anything. You aren't expected to be able to read this:

```
public <R> Stream<R> flatMap(
    Function<? super T, ? extends Stream<? extends R>> mapper)
```

This gibberish basically says that it returns a `Stream` of the type that the function contains at a lower level. Don't worry about the signature. It's a headache.

What you should understand is the example. This gets all of the animals into the same level and removes the empty list.

```
List<String> zero = List.of();
var one = List.of("Bonobo");
var two = List.of("Mama Gorilla", "Baby Gorilla");
Stream<List<String>> animals = Stream.of(zero, one, two);

animals.flatMap(m -> m.stream())
    .forEach(System.out::println);
```

Here's the output:

```
Bonobo
Mama Gorilla
Baby Gorilla
```

As you can see, it removed the empty list completely and changed all elements of each list to be at the top level of the stream.

Concatenating Streams

While `flatMap()` is good for the general case, there is a more convenient way to concatenate two streams:

```
var one = Stream.of("Bonobo");
var two = Stream.of("Mama Gorilla", "Baby Gorilla");

Stream.concat(one, two)
    .forEach(System.out::println);
```

This produces the same three lines as the previous example. The two streams are concatenated, and the terminal operation, `forEach()`, is called.

Sorting

The sorted() method returns a stream with the elements sorted. Just like sorting arrays, Java uses natural ordering unless we specify a comparator. The method signatures are these:

```
public Stream<T> sorted()
public Stream<T> sorted(Comparator<? super T> comparator)
```

Calling the first signature uses the default sort order.

```
Stream<String> s = Stream.of("brown-", "bear-");
s.sorted()
    .forEach(System.out::print); // bear-brown-
```

We can optionally use a Comparator implementation via a method or a lambda. In this example, we are using a method:

```
Stream<String> s = Stream.of("brown bear-", "grizzly-");
s.sorted(Comparator.reverseOrder())
    .forEach(System.out::print); // grizzly-brown bear-
```

Here we pass a Comparator to specify that we want to sort in the reverse of natural sort order. Ready for a tricky one? Do you see why this doesn't compile?

```
Stream<String> s = Stream.of("brown bear-", "grizzly-");
s.sorted(Comparator::reverseOrder);  // DOES NOT COMPILE
```

Take a look at the second sorted() method signature again. It takes a Comparator, which is a functional interface that takes two parameters and returns an int. However, Comparator::reverseOrder doesn't do that. Because reverseOrder() takes no arguments and returns a value, the method reference is equivalent to () -> Comparator .reverseOrder(), which is really a Supplier<Comparator>. This is not compatible with sorted(). We bring this up to remind you that you really do need to know method references well.

Taking a Peek

The peek() method is our final intermediate operation. It is useful for debugging because it allows us to perform a stream operation without changing the stream. The method signature is as follows:

```
public Stream<T> peek(Consumer<? super T> action)
```

You might notice the intermediate peek() operation takes the same argument as the terminal forEach() operation. Think of peek() as an intermediate version of forEach() that returns the original stream to you.

The most common use for peek() is to output the contents of the stream as it goes by. Suppose that we made a typo and counted bears beginning with the letter g instead of b. We are puzzled why the count is 1 instead of 2. We can add a peek() method to find out why.

```
var stream = Stream.of("black bear", "brown bear", "grizzly");
long count = stream.filter(s -> s.startsWith("g"))
```

```
   .peek(System.out::println).count();                    // grizzly
System.out.println(count);                                 // 1
```

In Chapter 9, you saw that peek() looks only at the first element when working with a Queue. In a stream, peek() looks at each element that goes through that part of the stream pipeline. It's like having a worker take notes on how a particular step of the process is doing.

Danger: Changing State

In general, it is bad practice to have side effects in a stream pipeline. For example, it is better to use a collector to create a new list than to change the elements in an existing one. Similarly, if you are trying to keep track of something, it is better to have the stream return a count than to increment an instance variable counter. However, on the exam, you may see side effects to make the code more concise such as the following.

```
private static int count = 20;
public void incrementCountBadly() {
   Stream.iterate(0, n -> n + 1)
      .limit(10)
      .forEach(p -> count++);
}
```

Similarly, peek() is intended to perform an operation without changing the result. Here's a straightforward stream pipeline that doesn't use peek():

```
   var numbers = new ArrayList<>();
   var letters = new ArrayList<>();
   numbers.add(1);
   letters.add('a');

   Stream<List<?>> stream = Stream.of(numbers, letters);
   stream.map(List::size).forEach(System.out::print); // 11
```

Now we add a peek() call and note that Java doesn't prevent us from writing bad peek code:

```
   Stream<List<?>> bad = Stream.of(numbers, letters);
   bad.peek(x -> x.remove(0))
      .map(List::size)
      .forEach(System.out::print); // 00
```

This example is bad because peek() is modifying the data structure that is used in the stream, which causes the result of the stream pipeline to be different than if the peek wasn't present.

Putting Together the Pipeline

Streams allow you to use chaining and express what you want to accomplish rather than how to do so. Let's say we wanted to get the first two names of our friends alphabetically that are four characters long. Without streams, we'd have to write something like the following:

```
var list = List.of("Toby", "Anna", "Leroy", "Alex");
List<String> filtered = new ArrayList<>();
for (String name: list)
    if (name.length() == 4) filtered.add(name);


Collections.sort(filtered);
var iter = filtered.iterator();
if (iter.hasNext()) System.out.println(iter.next());
if (iter.hasNext()) System.out.println(iter.next());
```

This works. It takes some reading and thinking to figure out what is going on. The problem we are trying to solve gets lost in the implementation. It is also very focused on the how rather than on the what. With streams, the equivalent code is as follows:

```
var list = List.of("Toby", "Anna", "Leroy", "Alex");
list.stream().filter(n -> n.length() == 4).sorted()
    .limit(2).forEach(System.out::println);
```

Before you say that it is harder to read, we can format it.

```
var list = List.of("Toby", "Anna", "Leroy", "Alex");
list.stream()
    .filter(n -> n.length() == 4)
    .sorted()
    .limit(2)
    .forEach(System.out::println);
```

The difference is that we express what is going on. We care about String objects of length 4. Then we want them sorted. Then we want the first two. Then we want to print them out. It maps better to the problem that we are trying to solve, and it is simpler.

Once you start using streams in your code, you may find yourself using them in many places. Having shorter, briefer, and clearer code is definitely a good thing!

In this example, you see all three parts of the pipeline. Figure 10.5 shows how each intermediate operation in the pipeline feeds into the next.

FIGURE 10.5 Stream pipeline with multiple intermediate operations

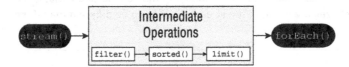

Remember that the assembly line foreperson is figuring out how to best implement the stream pipeline. They set up all of the tables with instructions to wait before starting. They tell the `limit()` worker to inform them when two elements go by. They tell the `sorted()` worker that they should just collect all of the elements as they come in and sort them all at once. After sorting, they should start passing them to the `limit()` worker one at a time. The data flow looks like this:

1. The `stream()` method sends Toby to `filter()`. The `filter()` method sees that the length is good and sends Toby to `sorted()`. The `sorted()` method can't sort yet because it needs all of the data, so it holds Toby.

2. The `stream()` method sends Anna to `filter()`. The `filter()` method sees that the length is good and sends Anna to `sorted()`. The `sorted()` method can't sort yet because it needs all of the data, so it holds Anna.

3. The `stream()` method sends Leroy to `filter()`. The `filter()` method sees that the length is not a match, and it takes Leroy out of the assembly line processing.

4. The `stream()` method sends Alex to `filter()`. The `filter()` method sees that the length is good and sends Alex to `sorted()`. The `sorted()` method can't sort yet because it needs all of the data, so it holds Alex. It turns out `sorted()` does have all of the required data, but it doesn't know it yet.

5. The foreperson lets `sorted()` know that it is time to sort, and the sort occurs.

6. The `sorted()` method sends Alex to `limit()`. The `limit()` method remembers that it has seen one element and sends Alex to `forEach()`, printing `Alex`.

7. The `sorted()` method sends Anna to `limit()`. The `limit()` method remembers that it has seen two elements and sends Anna to `forEach()`, printing `Anna`.

8. The `limit()` method has now seen all of the elements that are needed and tells the foreperson. The foreperson stops the line, and no more processing occurs in the pipeline.

Make sense? Let's try a few more examples to make sure that you understand this well. What do you think the following does?

```
Stream.generate(() -> "Elsa")
    .filter(n -> n.length() == 4)
    .sorted()
    .limit(2)
    .forEach(System.out::println);
```

It hangs until you kill the program, or it throws an exception after running out of memory. The foreperson has instructed `sorted()` to wait until everything to sort is present. That never happens because there is an infinite stream. What about this example?

```
Stream.generate(() -> "Elsa")
    .filter(n -> n.length() == 4)
    .limit(2)
    .sorted()
    .forEach(System.out::println);
```

This one prints Elsa twice. The filter lets elements through, and limit() stops the earlier operations after two elements. Now sorted() can sort because we have a finite list. Finally, what do you think this does?

```
Stream.generate(() -> "Olaf Lazisson")
    .filter(n -> n.length() == 4)
    .limit(2)
    .sorted()
    .forEach(System.out::println);
```

This one hangs as well until we kill the program. The filter doesn't allow anything through, so limit() never sees two elements. This means we have to keep waiting and hope that they show up.

You can even chain two pipelines together. See if you can identify the two sources and two terminal operations in this code.

```
30: long count =  Stream.of("goldfish", "finch")
31:     .filter(s -> s.length()> 5)
32:     .collect(Collectors.toList())
33:     .stream()
34:     .count();
35: System.out.println(count);    // 1
```

Lines 30–32 are one pipeline, and lines 33 and 34 are another. For the first pipeline, line 30 is the source, and line 32 is the terminal operation. For the second pipeline, line 33 is the source, and line 34 is the terminal operation. Now that's a complicated way of outputting the number 1!

On the exam, you might see long or complex pipelines as answer choices. If this happens, focus on the differences between the answers. Those will be your clues to the correct answer. This approach will also save you time by not having to study the whole pipeline on each option.

When you see chained pipelines, note where the source and terminal operations are. This will help you keep track of what is going on. You can even rewrite the code in your head to have a variable in between so it isn't as long and complicated. Our prior example can be written as follows:

```
List<String> helper =  Stream.of("goldfish", "finch")
    .filter(s -> s.length()> 5)
    .collect(Collectors.toList());
long count = helper.stream()
    .count();
System.out.println(count);
```

Which style you use is up to you. However, you need to be able to read both styles before you take the exam.

Working with Primitive Streams

Up until now, all of the streams we've created used the Stream interface with a generic type, like Stream<String>, Stream<Integer>, and so on. For numeric values, we have been using wrapper classes. We did this with the Collections API in Chapter 9, so it should feel natural.

Java actually includes other stream interfaces besides Stream that you can use to work with select primitives: int, double, and long. Let's take a look at why this is needed. Suppose that we want to calculate the sum of numbers in a finite stream:

```
Stream<Integer> stream = Stream.of(1, 2, 3);
System.out.println(stream.reduce(0, (s, n) -> s + n));  // 6
```

Not bad. It wasn't hard to write a reduction. We started the accumulator with zero. We then added each number to that running total as it came up in the stream. There is another way of doing that, shown here:

```
Stream<Integer> stream = Stream.of(1, 2, 3);
System.out.println(stream.mapToInt(x -> x).sum());  // 6
```

This time, we converted our Stream<Integer> to an IntStream and asked the IntStream to calculate the sum for us. An IntStream has many of the same intermediate and terminal methods as a Stream but includes specialized methods for working with numeric data. The primitive streams know how to perform certain common operations automatically.

It's even more useful for operations that are more work to calculate like average:

```
IntStream intStream = IntStream.of(1, 2, 3);
OptionalDouble avg = intStream.average();
System.out.println(avg.getAsDouble());  // 2.0
```

Not only is it possible to calculate the average, but it is also easy to do so. Clearly, primitive streams are important. We look at creating and using such streams, including optionals and functional interfaces.

Creating Primitive Streams

Here are the three types of primitive streams:

- **IntStream:** Used for the primitive types int, short, byte, and char
- **LongStream:** Used for the primitive type long
- **DoubleStream:** Used for the primitive types double and float

Why doesn't each primitive type have its own primitive stream? These three are the most common, so the API designers went with them.

When you see the word *stream* on the exam, pay attention to the case. With a capital *S* or in code, Stream is the name of the interface that contains an Object type. With a lowercase *s*, a stream is a concept that might be a Stream, DoubleStream, IntStream, or LongStream.

Table 10.5 shows some of the methods that are *unique* to primitive streams. Notice that we don't include methods in the table like empty() that you already know from the Stream interface.

TABLE 10.5 Common primitive stream methods

Method	Primitive stream	Description
OptionalDouble average()	IntStream LongStream DoubleStream	Arithmetic mean of elements
Stream<T> boxed()	IntStream LongStream DoubleStream	Stream<T> where T is wrapper class associated with primitive value
OptionalInt max()	IntStream	Maximum element of stream
OptionalLong max()	LongStream	
OptionalDouble max()	DoubleStream	
OptionalInt min()	IntStream	Minimum element of stream
OptionalLong min()	LongStream	
OptionalDouble min()	DoubleStream	
IntStream range(int a, int b)	IntStream	Returns primitive stream from a (inclusive) to b (exclusive)
LongStream range(long a, long b)	LongStream	
IntStream rangeClosed(int a, int b)	IntStream	Returns primitive stream from a (inclusive) to b (inclusive)
LongStream rangeClosed(long a, long b)	LongStream	
int sum()	IntStream	Returns sum of elements in stream
long sum()	LongStream	
double sum()	DoubleStream	

Method	Primitive stream	Description
IntSummaryStatistics summaryStatistics()	IntStream	Returns object containing numerous stream statistics such as average, min, max, etc.
LongSummaryStatistics summaryStatistics()	LongStream	
DoubleSummaryStatistics summaryStatistics()	DoubleStream	

Some of the methods for creating a primitive stream are equivalent to how we created the source for a regular Stream. You can create an empty stream with this:

```
DoubleStream empty = DoubleStream.empty();
```

Another way is to use the of() factory method from a single value or by using the varargs overload.

```
DoubleStream oneValue = DoubleStream.of(3.14);
oneValue.forEach(System.out::println);

DoubleStream varargs = DoubleStream.of(1.0, 1.1, 1.2);
varargs.forEach(System.out::println);
```

This code outputs the following:

```
3.14
1.0
1.1
1.2
```

You can also use the two methods for creating infinite streams, just like we did with Stream.

```
var random = DoubleStream.generate(Math::random);
var fractions = DoubleStream.iterate(.5, d -> d / 2);
random.limit(3).forEach(System.out::println);
fractions.limit(3).forEach(System.out::println);
```

Since the streams are infinite, we added a limit intermediate operation so that the output doesn't print values forever. The first stream calls a static method on Math to get a random double. Since the numbers are random, your output will obviously be different. The second stream keeps creating smaller numbers, dividing the previous value by two each time. The output from when we ran this code was as follows:

```
0.07890654781186413
0.28564363465842346
```

```
0.6311403511266134
0.5
0.25
0.125
```

 You don't need to know this for the exam, but the Random class provides a method to get primitives streams of random numbers directly. Fun fact! For example, ints() generates an infinite IntStream of primitives.

When dealing with int or long primitives, it is common to count. Suppose that we wanted a stream with the numbers from 1 through 5. We could write this using what we've explained so far:

```
IntStream count = IntStream.iterate(1, n -> n + 1).limit(5);
count.forEach(System.out::print); // 12345
```

This code does print out the numbers 1–5. However, it is a lot of code to do something so simple. Java provides a method that can generate a range of numbers.

```
IntStream range = IntStream.range(1, 6);
range.forEach(System.out::print); // 12345
```

This is better. If we wanted numbers 1–5, why did we pass 1–6? The first parameter to the range() method is *inclusive*, which means it includes the number. The second parameter to the range() method is *exclusive*, which means it stops right before that number. However, it still could be clearer. We want the numbers 1–5 inclusive. Luckily, there's another method, rangeClosed(), which is inclusive on both parameters.

```
IntStream rangeClosed = IntStream.rangeClosed(1, 5);
rangeClosed.forEach(System.out::print); // 12345
```

Even better. This time we expressed that we want a closed range or an inclusive range. This method better matches how we express a range of numbers in plain English.

Mapping Streams

Another way to create a primitive stream is by mapping from another stream type. Table 10.6 shows that there is a method for mapping between any stream types.

TABLE 10.6 Mapping methods between types of streams

Source stream	To create Stream	To create DoubleStream	To create IntStream	To create LongStream
Stream<T>	map()	mapToDouble()	mapToInt()	mapToLong()
DoubleStream	mapToObj()	map()	mapToInt()	mapToLong()

Source stream	To create Stream	To create DoubleStream	To create IntStream	To create LongStream
IntStream	mapToObj()	mapToDouble()	map()	mapToLong()
LongStream	mapToObj()	mapToDouble()	mapToInt()	map()

Obviously, they have to be compatible types for this to work. Java requires a mapping function to be provided as a parameter, for example:

```
Stream<String> objStream = Stream.of("penguin", "fish");
IntStream intStream = objStream.mapToInt(s -> s.length());
```

This function takes an Object, which is a String in this case. The function returns an int. The function mappings are intuitive here. They take the source type and return the target type. In this example, the actual function type is ToIntFunction. Table 10.7 shows the mapping function names. As you can see, they do what you might expect.

TABLE 10.7   Function parameters when mapping between types of streams

Source stream	To create Stream	To create DoubleStream	To create IntStream	To create LongStream
Stream<T>	Function<T,R>	ToDouble Function<T>	ToInt Function<T>	ToLong Function<T>
Double Stream	Double Function<R>	DoubleUnary Operator	DoubleToInt Function	DoubleToLong Function
IntStream	IntFunction<R>	IntToDouble Function	IntUnary Operator	IntToLong Function
LongStream	Long Function<R>	LongToDouble Function	LongToInt Function	LongUnary Operator

You do have to memorize Table 10.6 and Table 10.7. It's not as hard as it might seem. There are patterns in the names if you remember a few rules. For Table 10.6, mapping to the same type you started with is just called map(). When returning an object stream, the method is mapToObj(). Beyond that, it's the name of the primitive type in the map method name.

For Table 10.7, you can start by thinking about the source and target types. When the target type is an object, you drop the To from the name. When the mapping is to the same type you started with, you use a unary operator instead of a function for the primitive streams.

Using *flatMap()*

We can use this approach on primitive streams as well. It works the same way as on a regular Stream, except the method name is different. Here's an example:

```
var integerList = new ArrayList<Integer>();
IntStream ints = integerList.stream()
    .flatMapToInt(x -> IntStream.of(x));
DoubleStream doubles = integerList.stream()
    .flatMapToDouble(x -> DoubleStream.of(x));
LongStream longs = integerList.stream()
    .flatMapToLong(x -> LongStream.of(x));
```

Additionally, you can create a Stream from a primitive stream. These methods show two ways of accomplishing this:

```
private static Stream<Integer> mapping(IntStream stream) {
    return stream.mapToObj(x -> x);
}

private static Stream<Integer> boxing(IntStream stream) {
    return stream.boxed();
}
```

The first one uses the mapToObj() method we saw earlier. The second one is more succinct. It does not require a mapping function because all it does is autobox each primitive to the corresponding wrapper object. The boxed() method exists on all three types of primitive streams.

Using *Optional* with Primitive Streams

Earlier in the chapter, we wrote a method to calculate the average of an int[] and promised a better way later. Now that you know about primitive streams, you can calculate the average in one line.

```
var stream = IntStream.rangeClosed(1,10);
OptionalDouble optional = stream.average();
```

The return type is not the Optional you have become accustomed to using. It is a new type called OptionalDouble. Why do we have a separate type, you might wonder? Why not just use Optional<Double>? The difference is that OptionalDouble is for a primitive and Optional<Double> is for the Double wrapper class. Working with the primitive optional class looks similar to working with the Optional class itself.

```
optional.ifPresent(System.out::println);                    // 5.5
System.out.println(optional.getAsDouble());                 // 5.5
System.out.println(optional.orElseGet(() -> Double.NaN));   // 5.5
```

The only noticeable difference is that we called getAsDouble() rather than get(). This makes it clear that we are working with a primitive. Also, orElseGet() takes a DoubleSupplier instead of a Supplier.

As with the primitive streams, there are three type-specific classes for primitives. Table 10.8 shows the minor differences among the three. You probably won't be surprised that you have to memorize this table as well. This is really easy to remember since the primitive name is the only change. As you should remember from the terminal operations section, a number of stream methods return an optional such as min() or findAny(). These each return the corresponding optional type. The primitive stream implementations also add two new methods that you need to know. The sum() method does not return an optional. If you try to add up an empty stream, you simply get zero. The average() method always returns an OptionalDouble since an average can potentially have fractional data for any type.

TABLE 10.8   Optional types for primitives

	OptionalDouble	OptionalInt	OptionalLong
Getting as primitive	getAsDouble()	getAsInt()	getAsLong()
orElseGet() parameter type	DoubleSupplier	IntSupplier	LongSupplier
Return type of max() and min()	OptionalDouble	OptionalInt	OptionalLong
Return type of sum()	double	int	long
Return type of average()	OptionalDouble	OptionalDouble	OptionalDouble

Let's try an example to make sure that you understand this:

```
5: LongStream longs = LongStream.of(5, 10);
6: long sum = longs.sum();
7: System.out.println(sum);     // 15
8: DoubleStream doubles = DoubleStream.generate(() -> Math.PI);
9: OptionalDouble min = doubles.min(); // runs infinitely
```

Line 5 creates a stream of long primitives with two elements. Line 6 shows that we don't use an optional to calculate a sum. Line 8 creates an infinite stream of double primitives. Line 9 is there to remind you that a question about code that runs infinitely can appear with primitive streams as well.

Summarizing Statistics

You've learned enough to be able to get the maximum value from a stream of int primitives. If the stream is empty, we want to throw an exception.

```
private static int max(IntStream ints) {
    OptionalInt optional = ints.max();
    return optional.orElseThrow(RuntimeException::new);
}
```

This should be old hat by now. We got an OptionalInt because we have an IntStream. If the optional contains a value, we return it. Otherwise, we throw a new RuntimeException.

Now we want to change the method to take an IntStream and return a range. The range is the minimum value subtracted from the maximum value. Uh-oh. Both min() and max() are terminal operations, which means that they use up the stream when they are run. We can't run two terminal operations against the same stream. Luckily, this is a common problem, and the primitive streams solve it for us with summary statistics. *Statistic* is just a big word for a number that was calculated from data.

```
private static int range(IntStream ints) {
    IntSummaryStatistics stats = ints.summaryStatistics();
    if (stats.getCount() == 0) throw new RuntimeException();
    return stats.getMax() - stats.getMin();
}
```

Here we asked Java to perform many calculations about the stream. Summary statistics include the following:

- **getCount():** Returns a long representing the number of values.
- **getAverage():** Returns a double representing the average. If the stream is empty, returns 0.0.
- **getSum():** Returns the sum as a double for DoubleSummaryStatistics, and long for IntSummaryStatistics and LongSummaryStastistics.
- **getMin():** Returns the smallest number (minimum) as a double, int, or long, depending on the type of the stream. If the stream is empty, returns the largest numeric value based on the type.
- **getMax():** Returns the largest number (maximum) as a double, int, or long depending on the type of the stream. If the stream is empty, returns the smallest numeric value based on the type.

Working with Advanced Stream Pipeline Concepts

Congrats, you have only a few more topics left! In this last stream section, we learn about the relationship between streams and the underlying data, chaining `Optional`, grouping collectors, and using `Spliterator`. After this, you should be a pro with streams!

Linking Streams to the Underlying Data

What do you think this outputs?

```
25: var cats = new ArrayList<String>();
26: cats.add("Annie");
27: cats.add("Ripley");
28: var stream = cats.stream();
29: cats.add("KC");
30: System.out.println(stream.count());
```

The correct answer is 3. Lines 25–27 create a `List` with two elements. Line 28 requests that a stream be created from that `List`. Remember that streams are lazily evaluated. This means the stream isn't created on line 28. An object is created that knows where to look for the data when it is needed. On line 29, the `List` gets a new element. On line 30, the stream pipeline sees three elements when it runs giving us that count.

Chaining *Optionals*

By now, you are familiar with the benefits of chaining operations in a stream pipeline. A few of the intermediate operations for streams are available for `Optional`, as shown in Table 10.9.

TABLE 10.9   Advanced `Optional` instance methods

Method	When Optional is empty	When Optional contains value
filter(Predicate p)	Returns empty Optional	Returns Optional containing the element if it matches the Predicate, otherwise empty Optional
flatMap(Function f)	Returns empty Optional	Returns Optional with Function applied to the element. Return type of Function must inherit Optional.
map(Function f)	Returns empty Optional	Returns Optional with Function applied to the element

Suppose you are given an Optional<Integer> and asked to print the value, but only if it is a three-digit number. Without functional programming, you could write the following:

```
private static void threeDigit(Optional<Integer> optional) {
    if (optional.isPresent()) {  // outer if
        var num = optional.get();
        var string = "" + num;
        if (string.length() == 3) // inner if
            System.out.println(string);
    }
}
```

This works, but it contains nested if statements. That's extra complexity. Let's try this again with functional programming:

```
private static void threeDigit(Optional<Integer> optional) {
    optional.map(n -> "" + n)          // part 1
        .filter(s -> s.length() == 3)  // part 2
        .ifPresent(System.out::println); // part 3
}
```

This is much shorter and more expressive. With lambdas, the exam is fond of carving up a single statement and identifying the pieces with a comment. We've done that here to show what happens with both the functional programming and nonfunctional programming approaches.

Suppose that we are given an empty Optional. The first approach returns false for the outer if statement. The second approach sees an empty Optional and has both map() and filter() pass it through. Then ifPresent() sees an empty Optional and doesn't call the Consumer parameter.

The next case is where we are given an Optional.of(4). The first approach returns false for the inner if statement. The second approach maps the number 4 to "4". The filter() then returns an empty Optional since the filter doesn't match, and ifPresent() doesn't call the Consumer parameter.

The final case is where we are given an Optional.of(123). The first approach returns true for both if statements. The second approach maps the number 123 to "123". The filter() then returns the same Optional, and ifPresent() now does call the Consumer parameter.

Now suppose that we wanted to get an Optional<Integer> representing the length of the String contained in another Optional. Easy enough:

```
Optional<Integer> result = optional.map(String::length);
```

What if instead we had a helper method that takes a String and did the logic of calculating something for us? It would return Optional<Integer>, such as this:

```
public static Optional<Integer> calculator(String text) {
    // Calculation logic here
}
```

Using map to call it doesn't work:

```
Optional<Integer> result = optional
    .map(ChainingOptionals::calculator); // DOES NOT COMPILE
```

The problem is that calculator returns `Optional<Integer>`. The map() method adds another Optional, giving us `Optional<Optional<Integer>>`. Well, that's no good. The solution is to call flatMap(), instead:

```
Optional<Integer> result = optional
    .flatMap(ChainingOptionals::calculator);
```

This one works because flatMap removes the unnecessary layer. In other words, it flattens the result. Chaining calls to flatMap() is useful when you want to transform one Optional type to another.

 Real World Scenario

Checked Exceptions and Functional Interfaces

You might have noticed by now that most functional interfaces do not declare checked exceptions. This is normally OK. However, it is a problem when working with methods that declare checked exceptions. Suppose that we have a class with a method that throws a checked exception.

```
import java.io.*;
import java.util.*;
public class ExceptionCaseStudy {
    private static List<String> create() throws IOException {
        throw new IOException();
    }
}
```

Now we use it in a stream.

```
public void good() throws IOException {
    ExceptionCaseStudy.create().stream().count();
}
```

Nothing new here. The create() method throws a checked exception. The calling method handles or declares it. Now, what about this one?

```
public void bad() throws IOException {
    Supplier<List<String>> s = ExceptionCaseStudy::create; // DOES NOT COMPILE
}
```

The actual compiler error is as follows:

```
unhandled exception type IOException
```

Say what now? The problem is that the functional interface to which this method reference expands does not declare an exception. The Supplier interface does not allow checked exceptions. There are two approaches to get around this problem. One is to catch the exception and turn it into an unchecked exception.

```
public void ugly() {
    Supplier<List<String>> s = () -> {
        try {
            return ExceptionCaseStudy.create();
        } catch (IOException e) {
            throw new RuntimeException(e);
        }
    };
}
```

This works. But the code is ugly. One of the benefits of functional programming is that the code is supposed to be easy to read and concise. Another alternative is to create a wrapper method with try/catch.

```
private static List<String> createSafe() {
    try {
        return ExceptionCaseStudy.create();
    } catch (IOException e) {
        throw new RuntimeException(e);
    } }
```

Now we can use the safe wrapper in our Supplier without issue.

```
public void wrapped() {
    Supplier<List<String>> s2 = ExceptionCaseStudy::createSafe;
}
```

Collecting Results

You're almost finished learning about streams. The last topic builds on what you've learned so far to group the results. Early in the chapter, you saw the collect() terminal operation. There are many predefined collectors, including those shown in Table 10.10. These collectors are available via static methods on the Collectors class. We look at the different types of collectors in the following sections. We left out the generic types for simplicity.

TABLE 10.10   Examples of grouping/partitioning collectors

Collector	Description	Return value when passed to collect
averagingDouble(ToDoubleFunction f) averagingInt(ToIntFunction f) averagingLong(ToLongFunction f)	Calculates average for three core primitive types	Double
counting()	Counts number of elements	Long
filtering(Predicate p, Collector c)	Applies filter before calling down-stream collector	R
groupingBy(Function f)	Creates map grouping by spec-ified function with optional map type supplier and optional down-stream collector of type D	Map<K, List<T>>
groupingBy(Function f, Collector dc)		Map<K, List<D>>
groupingBy(Function f, Supplier s, Collector dc)		Map<K, List<D>>
joining(CharSequence cs)	Creates single String using cs as delimiter bet-ween elements if one is specified	String
maxBy(Comparator c) minBy(Comparator c)	Finds largest/small-est elements	Optional<T>
mapping(Function f, Collector dc)	Adds another level of collectors	Collector
partitioningBy(Predicate p) partitioningBy(Predicate p, Collector dc)	Creates map grouping by speci-fied predicate with optional further downstream collector	Map<Boolean, List<T>>

TABLE 10.10   Examples of grouping/partitioning collectors *(continued)*

Collector	Description	Return value when passed to collect
summarizingDouble(ToDoubleFunction f) summarizingInt(ToIntFunction f) summarizingLong(ToLongFunction f)	Calculates average, min, max, etc.	DoubleSummaryStatistics IntSummaryStatistics LongSummaryStatistics
summingDouble(ToDoubleFunction f) summingInt(ToIntFunction f) summingLong(ToLongFunction f)	Calculates sum for our three core primitive types	Double Integer Long
teeing(Collector c1, Collector c2, BiFunction f)	Works with results of two collectors to create new type	R
toList() toSet()	Creates arbitrary type of list or set	List Set
toCollection(Supplier s)	Creates Collection of specified type	Collection
toMap(Function k, Function v) toMap(Function k, Function v, BinaryOperator m) toMap(Function k, Function v, BinaryOperator m, Supplier s)	Creates map using functions to map keys, values, optional merge function, and optional map type supplier	Map

There is one more collector called reducing(). You don't need to know it for the exam. It is a general reduction in case all of the previous collectors don't meet your needs.

Using Basic Collectors

Luckily, many of these collectors work the same way. Let's look at an example:

```
var ohMy = Stream.of("lions", "tigers", "bears");
String result = ohMy.collect(Collectors.joining(", "));
System.out.println(result); // lions, tigers, bears
```

Notice how the predefined collectors are in the `Collectors` class rather than the `Collector` interface. This is a common theme, which you saw with `Collection` versus `Collections`. In fact, you see this pattern again in Chapter 14 when working with `Paths` and `Path` and other related types.

We pass the predefined `joining()` collector to the `collect()` method. All elements of the stream are then merged into a `String` with the specified delimiter between each element. It is important to pass the `Collector` to the `collect` method. It exists to help collect elements. A `Collector` doesn't do anything on its own.

Let's try another one. What is the average length of the three animal names?

```
var ohMy = Stream.of("lions", "tigers", "bears");
Double result = ohMy.collect(Collectors.averagingInt(String::length));
System.out.println(result); // 5.333333333333333
```

The pattern is the same. We pass a collector to `collect()`, and it performs the average for us. This time, we needed to pass a function to tell the collector what to average. We used a method reference, which returns an `int` upon execution. With primitive streams, the result of an average was always a `double`, regardless of what type is being averaged. For collectors, it is a `Double` since those need an `Object`.

Often, you'll find yourself interacting with code that was written without streams. This means that it will expect a `Collection` type rather than a `Stream` type. No problem. You can still express yourself using a `Stream` and then convert to a `Collection` at the end. For example:

```
var ohMy = Stream.of("lions", "tigers", "bears");
TreeSet<String> result = ohMy
    .filter(s -> s.startsWith("t"))
    .collect(Collectors.toCollection(TreeSet::new));
System.out.println(result); // [tigers]
```

This time we have all three parts of the stream pipeline. `Stream.of()` is the source for the stream. The intermediate operation is `filter()`. Finally, the terminal operation is `collect()`, which creates a `TreeSet`. If we didn't care which implementation of `Set` we got, we could have written `Collectors.toSet()`, instead.

Using toList()

One of the most common collectors is `Collectors.toList()`, which turns the result back into a `List`. In fact, it is so common that there is a shortcut. Both of these do almost the same thing:

```
Stream<String> ohMy1 = Stream.of("lions", "tigers", "bears");
List<String> mutableList = ohMy1.collect(Collectors.toList());

Stream<String> ohMy2 = Stream.of("lions", "tigers", "bears");
List<String> immutableList = ohMy2.toList();
```

Almost? While both return a List<String>, the contract is different. The
Collectors.toList() gives you a mutable list that you can edit later. The shorter
toList() does not allow changes. We can see the difference in the following additional
lines of code:

```
mutableList.add("zebras");   // No issues
immutableList.add("zebras"); // UnsupportedOperationException
```

At this point, you should be able to use all of the Collectors in Table 10.10 except
groupingBy(), mapping(), partitioningBy(), toMap(), and teeing().

Collecting into Maps

Code using Collectors involving maps can get quite long. We will build it up slowly. Make
sure that you understand each example before going on to the next one. Let's start with a
straightforward example to create a map from a stream:

```
var ohMy = Stream.of("lions", "tigers", "bears");
Map<String, Integer> map = ohMy.collect(
   Collectors.toMap(s -> s, String::length));
System.out.println(map); // {lions=5, bears=5, tigers=6}
```

When creating a map, you need to specify two functions. The first function tells the
collector how to create the key. In our example, we use the provided String as the key. The
second function tells the collector how to create the value. In our example, we use the length
of the String as the value.

Returning the same value passed into a lambda is a common operation,
so Java provides a method for it. You can rewrite s -> s as
Function.identity(). It is not shorter and may or may not be clearer,
so use your judgment about whether to use it.

Now we want to do the reverse and map the length of the animal name to the name itself.
Our first incorrect attempt is shown here:

```
var ohMy = Stream.of("lions", "tigers", "bears");
Map<Integer, String> map = ohMy.collect(Collectors.toMap(
   String::length,
   k -> k)); // BAD
```

Running this gives an exception similar to the following:

```
Exception in thread "main" java.lang.IllegalStateException:
   Duplicate key 5 (attempted merging values lions and bears)
```

What's wrong? Two of the animal names are the same length. We didn't tell Java what to do. Should the collector choose the first one it encounters? The last one it encounters? Concatenate the two? Since the collector has no idea what to do, it "solves" the problem by throwing an exception and making it our problem. How thoughtful. Let's suppose that our requirement is to create a comma-separated String with the animal names. We could write this:

```
var ohMy = Stream.of("lions", "tigers", "bears");
Map<Integer, String> map = ohMy.collect(Collectors.toMap(
   String::length,
   k -> k,
   (s1, s2) -> s1 + "," + s2));
System.out.println(map);                    // {5=lions,bears, 6=tigers}
System.out.println(map.getClass()); // class java.util.HashMap
```

It so happens that the Map returned is a HashMap. This behavior is not guaranteed. Suppose that we want to mandate that the code return a TreeMap instead. No problem. We would just add a constructor reference as a parameter:

```
var ohMy = Stream.of("lions", "tigers", "bears");
TreeMap<Integer, String> map = ohMy.collect(Collectors.toMap(
   String::length,
   k -> k,
   (s1, s2) -> s1 + "," + s2,
   TreeMap::new));
System.out.println(map);                    // {5=lions,bears, 6=tigers}
System.out.println(map.getClass()); // class java.util.TreeMap
```

This time we get the type that we specified. With us so far? This code is long but not particularly complicated. We did promise you that the code would be long!

Grouping, Partitioning, and Mapping

Great job getting this far. The exam creators like asking about groupingBy() and partitioningBy(), so make sure you understand these sections very well. Now suppose that we want to get groups of names by their length. We can do that by saying that we want to group by length.

```
var ohMy = Stream.of("lions", "tigers", "bears");
Map<Integer, List<String>> map = ohMy.collect(
   Collectors.groupingBy(String::length));
System.out.println(map);       // {5=[lions, bears], 6=[tigers]}
```

The groupingBy() collector tells collect() that it should group all of the elements of the stream into a Map. The function determines the keys in the Map. Each value in the Map is a List of all entries that match that key.

 Note that the function you call in groupingBy() cannot return null. It does not allow null keys.

Suppose that we don't want a List as the value in the map and prefer a Set instead. No problem. There's another method signature that lets us pass a *downstream collector*. This is a second collector that does something special with the values.

```
var ohMy = Stream.of("lions", "tigers", "bears");
Map<Integer, Set<String>> map = ohMy.collect(
    Collectors.groupingBy(
        String::length,
        Collectors.toSet()));
System.out.println(map);    // {5=[lions, bears], 6=[tigers]}
```

We can even change the type of Map returned through yet another parameter.

```
var ohMy = Stream.of("lions", "tigers", "bears");
TreeMap<Integer, Set<String>> map = ohMy.collect(
    Collectors.groupingBy(
        String::length,
        TreeMap::new,
        Collectors.toSet()));
System.out.println(map); // {5=[lions, bears], 6=[tigers]}
```

This is very flexible. What if we want to change the type of Map returned but leave the type of values alone as a List? There isn't a method for this specifically because it is easy enough to write with the existing ones.

```
var ohMy = Stream.of("lions", "tigers", "bears");
TreeMap<Integer, List<String>> map = ohMy.collect(
    Collectors.groupingBy(
        String::length,
        TreeMap::new,
        Collectors.toList()));
System.out.println(map);
```

Partitioning is a special case of grouping. With partitioning, there are only two possible groups: true and false. *Partitioning* is like splitting a list into two parts.

Suppose that we are making a sign to put outside each animal's exhibit. We have two sizes of signs. One can accommodate names with five or fewer characters. The other is needed for longer names. We can partition the list according to which sign we need.

```
var ohMy = Stream.of("lions", "tigers", "bears");
Map<Boolean, List<String>> map = ohMy.collect(
```

```
Collectors.partitioningBy(s -> s.length() <= 5));
System.out.println(map);     // {false=[tigers], true=[lions, bears]}
```

Here we pass a `Predicate` with the logic for which group each animal name belongs in. Now suppose that we've figured out how to use a different font, and seven characters can now fit on the smaller sign. No worries. We just change the `Predicate`.

```
var ohMy = Stream.of("lions", "tigers", "bears");
Map<Boolean, List<String>> map = ohMy.collect(
    Collectors.partitioningBy(s -> s.length() <= 7));
System.out.println(map);     // {false=[], true=[lions, tigers, bears]}
```

Notice that there are still two keys in the map—one for each boolean value. It so happens that one of the values is an empty list, but it is still there. As with `groupingBy()`, we can change the type of `List` to something else.

```
var ohMy = Stream.of("lions", "tigers", "bears");
Map<Boolean, Set<String>> map = ohMy.collect(
    Collectors.partitioningBy(
        s -> s.length() <= 7,
        Collectors.toSet()));
System.out.println(map);     // {false=[], true=[lions, tigers, bears]}
```

Unlike `groupingBy()`, we cannot change the type of `Map` that is returned. However, there are only two keys in the map, so does it really matter which `Map` type we use?

Instead of using the downstream collector to specify the type, we can use any of the collectors that we've already shown. For example, we can group by the length of the animal name to see how many of each length we have.

```
var ohMy = Stream.of("lions", "tigers", "bears");
Map<Integer, Long> map = ohMy.collect(
    Collectors.groupingBy(
        String::length,
        Collectors.counting()));
System.out.println(map);     // {5=2, 6=1}
```

Debugging Complicated Generics

When working with `collect()`, there are often many levels of generics, making compiler errors unreadable. Here are three useful techniques for dealing with this situation:

- Start over with a simple statement, and keep adding to it. By making one tiny change at a time, you will know which code introduced the error.

- Extract parts of the statement into separate statements. For example, try writing `Collectors.groupingBy(String::length, Collectors.counting());`. If it compiles, you know that the problem lies elsewhere. If it doesn't compile, you have a much shorter statement to troubleshoot.

▪ Use generic wildcards for the return type of the final statement: for example,
Map<?, ?>. If that change alone allows the code to compile, you'll know that the
problem lies with the return type not being what you expect.

Finally, there is a mapping() collector that lets us go down a level and add another
collector. Suppose that we wanted to get the first letter of the first animal alphabetically of
each length. Why? Perhaps for random sampling. The examples on this part of the exam are
fairly contrived as well. We'd write the following:

```
var ohMy = Stream.of("lions", "tigers", "bears");
Map<Integer, Optional<Character>> map = ohMy.collect(
    Collectors.groupingBy(
        String::length,
        Collectors.mapping(
            s -> s.charAt(0),
            Collectors.minBy((a, b) -> a - b))));
System.out.println(map);    // {5=Optional[b], 6=Optional[t]}
```

We aren't going to tell you that this code is easy to read. We will tell you that it is the
most complicated thing you need to understand for the exam. Comparing it to the previous
example, you can see that we replaced counting() with mapping(). It so happens that
mapping() takes two parameters: the function for the value and how to group it further.

You might see collectors used with a static import to make the code shorter. The exam
might even use var for the return value and less indentation than we used. This means you
might see something like this:

```
var ohMy = Stream.of("lions", "tigers", "bears");
var map = ohMy.collect(groupingBy(String::length,
    mapping(s -> s.charAt(0), minBy((a, b) -> a - b))));
System.out.println(map);    // {5=Optional[b], 6=Optional[t]}
```

The code does the same thing as in the previous example. This means it is important to
recognize the collector names because you might not have the Collectors class name to
call your attention to it.

Teeing Collectors

Suppose you want to return two things. As we've learned, this is problematic with streams
because you only get one pass. The summary statistics are good when you want those
operations. Luckily, you can use teeing() to return multiple values of your own.

First, define the return type. We use a record here:

```
record Separations(String spaceSeparated, String commaSeparated) {}
```

Now we write the stream. As you read, pay attention to the number of `Collectors`:

```
var list = List.of("x", "y", "z");
Separations result = list.stream()
  .collect(Collectors.teeing(
            Collectors.joining(" "),
            Collectors.joining(","),
            (s, c) -> new Separations(s, c)));
System.out.println(result);
```

When executed, the code prints the following:

```
Separations[spaceSeparated=x y z, commaSeparated=x,y,z]
```

There are three `Collectors` in this code. Two of them are for `joining()` and produce the values we want to return. The third is `teeing()`, which combines the results into the single object we want to return. This way, Java is happy because only one object is returned, and we are happy because we don't have to go through the stream twice.

Using a *Spliterator*

Suppose you buy a bag of food so two children can feed the animals at the petting zoo. To avoid arguments, you have come prepared with an extra empty bag. You take roughly half the food out of the main bag and put it into the bag you brought from home. The original bag still exists with the other half of the food.

A `Spliterator` provides this level of control over processing. It starts with a `Collection` or a stream—that is your bag of food. You call `trySplit()` to take some food out of the bag. The rest of the food stays in the original `Spliterator` object.

The characteristics of a `Spliterator` depend on the underlying data source. A `Collection` data source is a basic `Spliterator`. By contrast, when using a `Stream` data source, the `Spliterator` can be parallel or even infinite. The `Stream` itself is executed lazily rather than when the `Spliterator` is created.

Implementing your own `Spliterator` can get complicated and is conveniently not on the exam. You do need to know how to work with some of the common methods declared on this interface. The simplified methods you need to know are in Table 10.11.

TABLE 10.11   Spliterator methods

Method	Description
`Spliterator<T> trySplit()`	Returns `Spliterator` containing ideally half of the data, which is removed from the current `Spliterator`. This method can be called multiple times and will eventually return `null` when data is no longer splittable.

TABLE 10.11   Spliterator methods *(continued)*

Method	Description
`void forEachRemaining(Consumer<T> c)`	Processes remaining elements in Spliterator.
`boolean tryAdvance(Consumer<T> c)`	Processes a single element from Spliterator if any remain. Returns whether element was processed.

Now let's look at an example where we divide the bag into three:

```
12: var stream = List.of("bird-", "bunny-", "cat-", "dog-", "fish-", "lamb-",
13:     "mouse-");
14: Spliterator<String> originalBagOfFood = stream.spliterator();
15: Spliterator<String> emmasBag = originalBagOfFood.trySplit();
16: emmasBag.forEachRemaining(System.out::print);  // bird-bunny-cat-
17:
18: Spliterator<String> jillsBag = originalBagOfFood.trySplit();
19: jillsBag.tryAdvance(System.out::print);          // dog-
20: jillsBag.forEachRemaining(System.out::print);  // fish-
21:
22: originalBagOfFood.forEachRemaining(System.out::print); // lamb-mouse-
```

On lines 12 and 13, we define a List. Lines 14 and 15 create two Spliterator references. The first is the original bag, which contains all seven elements. The second is our split of the original bag, putting roughly half of the elements at the front into Emma's bag. We then print the three contents of Emma's bag on line 16.

Our original bag of food now contains four elements. We create a new Spliterator on line 18 and put the first two elements into Jill's bag. We use tryAdvance() on line 19 to output a single element, and then line 20 prints all remaining elements (just one left!).

We started with seven elements, removed three, and then removed two more. This leaves us with two elements in the original bag created on line 14. These two items are output on line 22.

Now let's try an example with a Stream. This is a complicated way to print out 123:

```
var originalBag = Stream.iterate(1, n -> ++n)
    .spliterator();
```

```
Spliterator<Integer> newBag = originalBag.trySplit();

newBag.tryAdvance(System.out::print); // 1
newBag.tryAdvance(System.out::print); // 2
newBag.tryAdvance(System.out::print); // 3
```

You might have noticed that this is an infinite stream. No problem! The Spliterator recognizes that the stream is infinite and doesn't attempt to give you half. Instead, newBag contains a large number of elements. We get the first three since we call tryAdvance() three times. It would be a bad idea to call forEachRemaining() on an infinite stream!

Note that a Spliterator can have a number of characteristics such as CONCURRENT, ORDERED, SIZED, and SORTED. You will only see a straightforward Spliterator on the exam. For example, our infinite stream was not SIZED.

Summary

An Optional<T> can be empty or store a value. You can check whether it contains a value with isPresent() and get() the value inside. You can return a different value with orElse(T t) or throw an exception with orElseThrow(). There are even three methods that take functional interfaces as parameters: ifPresent(Consumer c), orElseGet(Supplier s), and orElseThrow(Supplier s). There are three optional types for primitives: OptionalDouble, OptionalInt, and OptionalLong. These have the methods getAsDouble(), getAsInt(), and getAsLong(), respectively.

A stream pipeline has three parts. The source is required, and it creates the data in the stream. There can be zero or more intermediate operations, which aren't executed until the terminal operation runs. The first stream interface we covered was Stream<T>, which takes a generic argument T. The Stream<T> interface includes many useful intermediate operations including filter(), map(), flatMap(), and sorted(). Examples of terminal operations include allMatch(), count(), and forEach().

Besides the Stream<T> interface, there are three primitive streams: DoubleStream, IntStream, and LongStream. In addition to the usual Stream<T> methods, IntStream and LongStream have range() and rangeClosed(). The call range(1, 10) on IntStream and LongStream creates a stream of the primitives from 1 to 9. By contrast, rangeClosed(1, 10) creates a stream of the primitives from 1 to 10. The primitive streams have math operations including average(), max(), and sum(). They also have summaryStatistics() to get many statistics in one call.

You can use a Collector to transform a stream into a traditional collection. You can even group fields to create a complex map in one line. Partitioning works the same way as grouping, except that the keys are always true and false. A partitioned map always has two keys, even if the value is empty for the key. A teeing collector allows you to combine the results of two other collectors.

You should memorize Table 10.6 and Table 10.7. At the least, be able to spot incompatibilities, such as type differences. Finally, remember that streams are lazily evaluated. They take lambdas or method references as parameters, which execute later when the method is run.

Exam Essentials

Write code that uses *Optional*. Creating an Optional uses Optional.empty() or Optional.of(). Retrieval frequently uses isPresent() and get(). Alternatively, there are the functional ifPresent() and orElseGet() methods.

Recognize which operations cause a stream pipeline to execute. Intermediate operations do not run until the terminal operation is encountered. If no terminal operation is in the pipeline, a Stream is returned but not executed. Examples of terminal operations include collect(), forEach(), min(), and reduce().

Determine which terminal operations are reductions. Reductions use all elements of the stream in determining the result. The reductions that you need to know are collect(), count(), max(), min(), and reduce(). A mutable reduction collects into the same object as it goes. The collect() method is a mutable reduction.

Write code for common intermediate operations. The filter() method returns a Stream<T> filtering on a Predicate<T>. The map() method returns a Stream, transforming each element of type T to another type R through a Function <T,R>. The flatMap() method flattens nested streams into a single level and removes empty streams.

Compare primitive streams to *Stream<T>*. Primitive streams are useful for performing common operations on numeric types, including statistics like average(), sum(), and so on. There are three primitive stream interfaces: DoubleStream, IntStream, and LongStream. There are also three primitive Optional classes: OptionalDouble, OptionalInt, and OptionalLong. Aside from BooleanSupplier, they all involve the double, int, or long primitives.

Convert primitive stream types to other primitive stream types. Normally, when mapping, you just call the map() method. When changing the interface used for the stream, a different method is needed. To convert to Stream, you use mapToObj(). To convert to DoubleStream, you use mapToDouble(). To convert to IntStream, you use mapToInt(). To convert to LongStream, you use mapToLong().

Use *peek()* to inspect the stream. The peek() method is an intermediate operation often used for debugging purposes. It executes a lambda or method reference on the input and passes that same input through the pipeline to the next operator. It is useful for printing out what passes through a certain point in a stream.

Search a stream. The findFirst() and findAny() methods return a single element from a stream in an Optional. The anyMatch(), allMatch(), and noneMatch() methods return a boolean. Be careful, because these three can hang if called on an infinite stream with some data. All of these methods are terminal operations.

Sort a stream. The sorted() method is an intermediate operation that sorts a stream. There are two versions: the signature with zero parameters that sorts using the natural sort order, and the signature with one parameter that sorts using that Comparator as the sort order.

Compare *groupingBy()* and *partitioningBy()*.   The groupingBy() method is used in a terminal operation that creates a Map. The keys and return types are determined by the parameters you pass. The values in the Map are a Collection for all the entries that map to that key. The partitioningBy() method also returns a Map. This time, the keys are true and false. The values are again a Collection of matches. If there are no matches for that boolean, the Collection is empty.

Review Questions

The answers to the chapter review questions can be found in the Appendix.

1. What could be the output of the following?

    ```
    var stream = Stream.iterate("", (s) -> s + "1");
    System.out.println(stream.limit(2).map(x -> x + "2"));
    ```

    A. 12112

    B. 212

    C. 212112

    D. `java.util.stream.ReferencePipeline$3@4517d9a3`

    E. The code does not compile.

    F. An exception is thrown.

    G. The code hangs.

2. What could be the output of the following?

    ```
    Predicate<String> predicate = s -> s.startsWith("g");
    var stream1 = Stream.generate(() -> "growl!");
    var stream2 = Stream.generate(() -> "growl!");
    var b1 = stream1.anyMatch(predicate);
    var b2 = stream2.allMatch(predicate);
    System.out.println(b1 + " " + b2);
    ```

    A. true false

    B. true true

    C. `java.util.stream.ReferencePipeline$3@4517d9a3`

    D. The code does not compile.

    E. An exception is thrown.

    F. The code hangs.

3. What could be the output of the following?

    ```
    Predicate<String> predicate = s -> s.length()> 3;
    var stream = Stream.iterate("-",
        s -> ! s.isEmpty(), (s) -> s + s);
    var b1 = stream.noneMatch(predicate);
    var b2 = stream.anyMatch(predicate);
    System.out.println(b1 + " " + b2);
    ```

    A. false false

    B. false true

C. `java.util.stream.ReferencePipeline$3@4517d9a3`

D. The code does not compile.

E. An exception is thrown.

F. The code hangs.

4. Which are true statements about terminal operations in a stream that runs successfully? (Choose all that apply.)

A. At most one terminal operation can exist in a stream pipeline.

B. Terminal operations are a required part of the stream pipeline in order to get a result.

C. Terminal operations have `Stream` as the return type.

D. The `peek()` method is an example of a terminal operation.

E. The referenced `Stream` may be used after calling a terminal operation.

5. Which of the following sets `result` to `8.0`? (Choose all that apply.)

A.
```java
double result = LongStream.of(6L, 8L, 10L)
    .mapToInt(x -> (int) x)
    .collect(Collectors.groupingBy(x -> x))
    .keySet()
    .stream()
    .collect(Collectors.averagingInt(x -> x));
```

B.
```java
double result = LongStream.of(6L, 8L, 10L)
    .mapToInt(x -> x)
    .boxed()
    .collect(Collectors.groupingBy(x -> x))
    .keySet()
    .stream()
    .collect(Collectors.averagingInt(x -> x));
```

C.
```java
double result = LongStream.of(6L, 8L, 10L)
    .mapToInt(x -> (int) x)
    .boxed()
    .collect(Collectors.groupingBy(x -> x))
    .keySet()
     .stream()
    .collect(Collectors.averagingInt(x -> x));
```

D.
```java
double result = LongStream.of(6L, 8L, 10L)
    .mapToInt(x -> (int) x)
```

```
    .collect(Collectors.groupingBy(x -> x, Collectors.toSet()))
    .keySet()
    .stream()
    .collect(Collectors.averagingInt(x -> x));
```

E.
```
double result = LongStream.of(6L, 8L, 10L)
    .mapToInt(x -> x)
    .boxed()
    .collect(Collectors.groupingBy(x -> x, Collectors.toSet()))
    .keySet()
    .stream()
    .collect(Collectors.averagingInt(x -> x));
```

F.
```
double result = LongStream.of(6L, 8L, 10L)
    .mapToInt(x -> (int) x)
    .boxed()
    .collect(Collectors.groupingBy(x -> x, Collectors.toSet()))
    .keySet()
    .stream()
    .collect(Collectors.averagingInt(x -> x));
```

6. Which of the following methods can fill in the blank so that the code prints out `false`?

```
var s = Stream.generate(() -> "meow");
var match = s._____(String::isEmpty);
System.out.println(match);
```

   A. Only `allMatch`

   B. Only `anyMatch`

   C. Only `noneMatch`

   D. Both `allMatch` and `anyMatch`

   E. Both `allMatch` and `noneMatch`

   F. None of the above

7. We have a method that returns a sorted list without changing the original. We want to rewrite it. Which of the following pairs can fill in the blanks in `refactored()` to do the same with streams?

```
private static List<String> sort(List<String> list) {
    var copy = new ArrayList<String>(list);
    Collections.sort(copy, (a, b) -> b.compareTo(a));
    return copy;
}
```

```
private static List<String> refactored(List<String> list) {
    return list.stream()
        ._____((a, b) -> b.compareTo(a))
        ._____;
}
```

A. compare and toList()

B. compare and sort()

C. compareTo and toList()

D. compareTo and sort()

E. sorted and collect()

F. sorted and collect(Collectors.toList())

8. Which of the following are true given this declaration? (Choose all that apply.)

```
var is = IntStream.empty();
```

A. is.average() returns the type int.

B. is.average() returns the type OptionalInt.

C. is.findAny() returns the type int.

D. is.findAny() returns the type OptionalInt.

E. is.sum() returns the type int.

F. is.sum() returns the type OptionalInt.

9. Which of the following can we add after line 6 for the code to run without error and not produce any output? (Choose all that apply.)

```
4: var stream = LongStream.of(1, 2, 3);
5: var opt = stream.map(n -> n * 10)
6:     .filter(n -> n < 5).findFirst();
```

A.
```
if (opt.isPresent())
    System.out.println(opt.get());
```

B.
```
if (opt.isPresent())
    System.out.println(opt.getAsLong());
```

C.
```
opt.ifPresent(System.out.println);
```

D.
```
opt.ifPresent(System.out::println);
```

E. None of these; the code does not compile.

F. None of these; line 6 throws an exception at runtime.

10. Given the four statements (L, M, N, O), select the order that would cause the code to output 10 lines.

```
Stream.generate(() -> "1")
   L: .filter(x -> x.length()> 1)
   M: .forEach(System.out::println)
   N: .limit(10)
   O: .peek(System.out::println)
;
```

A. L, N

B. L, N, O

C. L, N, M

D. L, N, M, O

E. L, O, M

F. N, M

G. N, O

11. What changes need to be made together for this code to print the string 12345? (Choose all that apply.)

```
Stream.iterate(1, x -> x++)
   .limit(5).map(x -> x)
   .collect(Collectors.joining());
```

A. Changing `Collectors.joining()` to `Collectors.joining(",")`

B. Changing `map(x -> x)` to `map(x -> "" + x)`

C. Changing `x -> x++` to `x -> ++x`

D. Adding `.forEach(System.out::print)` after the call to `collect()`

E. Wrapping the entire line in a `System.out.print` statement

F. None of the above; the code already prints 12345

12. Which is true of the following code?

```
Set<String> birds = Set.of("oriole", "flamingo");
Stream.concat(birds.stream(), birds.stream(), birds.stream())
   .sorted()         // line X
   .distinct()
   .findAny()
   .ifPresent(System.out::println);
```

A. It is guaranteed to print `flamingo` as is and when line X is removed.

B. It is guaranteed to print `oriole` as is and when line X is removed.

C. It is guaranteed to print `flamingo` as is, but not when line X is removed.

D. It is guaranteed to print `oriole` as is, but not when line X is removed.

E. The output may vary as is.

F. The code does not compile.

G. It throws an exception because the same list is used as the source for multiple streams.

13. Which of the following is true?

```
List<Integer> x1 = List.of(1, 2, 3);
List<Integer> x2 = List.of(4, 5, 6);
List<Integer> x3 = List.of();
Stream.of(x1, x2, x3).map(x -> x + 1)
    .flatMap(x -> x.stream())
    .forEach(System.out::print);
```

A. The code compiles and prints 123456.

B. The code compiles and prints 234567.

C. The code compiles but does not print anything.

D. The code compiles but prints stream references.

E. The code runs infinitely.

F. The code does not compile.

G. The code throws an exception.

14. Which of the following are true? (Choose all that apply.)

```
4: Stream<Integer> s = Stream.of(1);
5: IntStream is = s.boxed();
6: DoubleStream ds = s.mapToDouble(x -> x);
7: Stream<Integer> s2 = ds.mapToInt(x -> x);
8: s2.forEach(System.out::print);
```

A. Line 4 causes a compiler error.

B. Line 5 causes a compiler error.

C. Line 6 causes a compiler error.

D. Line 7 causes a compiler error.

E. Line 8 causes a compiler error.

F. The code compiles but throws an exception at runtime.

G. The code compiles and prints 1.

15. Given the generic type `String`, the `partitioningBy()` collector creates a `Map<Boolean, List<String>>` when passed to `collect()` by default. When a downstream collector is passed to `partitioningBy()`, which return types can be created? (Choose all that apply.)

A. `Map<boolean, List<String>>`

B. `Map<Boolean, List<String>>`

    C. Map<Boolean, Map<String>>

    D. Map<Boolean, Set<String>>

    E. Map<Long, TreeSet<String>>

    F. None of the above

16. Which of the following statements are true about this code? (Choose all that apply.)

```
20: Predicate<String> empty = String::isEmpty;
21: Predicate<String> notEmpty = empty.negate();
22:
23: var result = Stream.generate(() -> "")
24:     .limit(10)
25:     .filter(notEmpty)
26:     .collect(Collectors.groupingBy(k -> k))
27:     .entrySet()
28:     .stream()
29:     .map(Entry::getValue)
30:     .flatMap(Collection::stream)
31:     .collect(Collectors.partitioningBy(notEmpty));
32: System.out.println(result);
```

    A. It outputs {}.

    B. It outputs {false=[], true=[]}.

    C. If we changed line 31 from partitioningBy(notEmpty) to groupingBy(n -> n), it would output {}.

    D. If we changed line 31 from partitioningBy(notEmpty) to groupingBy(n -> n), it would output {false=[], true=[]}.

    E. The code does not compile.

    F. The code compiles but does not terminate at runtime.

17. What is the result of the following?

```
var s = DoubleStream.of(1.2, 2.4);
s.peek(System.out::println).filter(x -> x> 2).count();
```

    A. 1

    B. 2

    C. 2.4

    D. 1.2 and 2.4

    E. There is no output.

    F. The code does not compile.

    G. An exception is thrown.

18. What is the output of the following?

```
11: public class Paging {
12:     record Sesame(String name, boolean human)  {
13:         @Override public String toString() {
14:             return name();
15:         }
16:     }
17:     record Page(List<Sesame> list, long count)  {}
18:
19:     public static void main(String[] args) {
20:         var monsters = Stream.of(new Sesame("Elmo", false));
21:         var people = Stream.of(new Sesame("Abby", true));
22:         printPage(monsters, people);
23:     }
24:
25:     private static void printPage(Stream<Sesame> monsters,
26:             Stream<Sesame> people) {
27:         Page page = Stream.concat(monsters, people)
28:             .collect(Collectors.teeing(
29:                 Collectors.filtering(s -> s.name().startsWith("E"),
30:                     Collectors.toList()),
31:                 Collectors.counting(),
32:                 (l, c) -> new Page(l, c)));
33:         System.out.println(page);
34:     } }
```

A. `Page[list=[Abby], count=1]`

B. `Page[list=[Abby], count=2]`

C. `Page[list=[Elmo], count=1]`

D. `Page[list=[Elmo], count=2]`

E. The code does not compile due to `Stream.concat()`.

F. The code does not compile due to `Collectors.teeing()`.

G. The code does not compile for another reason.

19. What is the simplest way of rewriting this code?

```
List<Integer> x = IntStream.range(1, 6)
    .mapToObj(i -> i)
    .collect(Collectors.toList());
x.forEach(System.out::println);
```

A.
```
IntStream.range(1, 6);
```

B.
```
IntStream.range(1, 6)
   .forEach(System.out::println);
```

C.
```
IntStream.range(1, 6)
    .mapToObj(i -> i)
    .forEach(System.out::println);
```

D. None of the above is equivalent.

E. The provided code does not compile.

20. Which of the following throw an exception when an `Optional` is empty? (Choose all that apply.)

A. `opt.orElse("");`

B. `opt.orElseGet(() -> "");`

C. `opt.orElseThrow();`

D. `opt.orElseThrow(() -> throw new Exception());`

E. `opt.orElseThrow(RuntimeException::new);`

F. `opt.get();`

G. `opt.get("");`

21. What is the output of the following?

```
var spliterator = Stream.generate(() -> "x")
    .spliterator();

spliterator.tryAdvance(System.out::print);
var split = spliterator.trySplit();
split.tryAdvance(System.out::print);
```

A. x

B. xx

C. A long list of x's.

D. There is no output.

E. The code does not compile.

F. The code compiles but does not terminate at runtime.

Chapter

11

Exceptions and Localization

OCP EXAM OBJECTIVES COVERED IN THIS CHAPTER:

✓ **Handling Exceptions**

- Handle exceptions using try/catch/finally, try-with-resources, and multi-catch blocks, including custom exceptions.

✓ **Implementing Localization**

- Implement localization using locales and resource bundles. Parse and format messages, dates, times, and numbers, including currency and percentage values.

This chapter is about creating applications that adapt to change. What happens if a user enters invalid data on a web page? What if our connection to a database goes down in the middle of a sale? Finally, how do we build applications that can support multiple languages or geographic regions?

In this chapter, we discuss these problems and solutions to them using exceptions, formatting, and localization. One way to make sure your applications respond to change is to build in support early on. For example, supporting localization doesn't mean you actually need to support specific languages right away. It just means your application can be more easily adapted in the future. By the end of this chapter, we hope we've provided structure for designing applications that better adapt to change.

Understanding Exceptions

A program can fail for just about any reason. Here are just a few possibilities:

- The code tries to connect to a website, but the Internet connection is down.

- You made a coding mistake and tried to access an invalid index in an array.

- One method calls another with a value that the method doesn't support.

As you can see, some of these are coding mistakes. Others are completely beyond your control. Your program can't help it if the Internet connection goes down. What it *can* do is deal with the situation.

The Role of Exceptions

An *exception* is Java's way of saying "I give up. I don't know what to do right now. You deal with it." When you write a method, you can either deal with the exception or make it the calling code's problem.

As an example, think of Java as a child who visits the zoo. The *happy path* is when nothing goes wrong. The child continues to look at the animals until the program ends nicely. Nothing went wrong, and there were no exceptions to deal with.

This child's younger sister doesn't experience the happy path. In all the excitement, she trips and falls. Luckily, it isn't a bad fall. The little girl gets up and proceeds to look at more animals. She has handled the issue all by herself. Unfortunately, she falls again later in the day and starts crying. This time, she has declared that she needs help by crying. The story ends well. Her daddy rubs her knee and gives her a hug. Then they go back to seeing more animals and enjoy the rest of the day.

These are the two approaches Java uses when dealing with exceptions. A method can handle the exception case itself or make it the caller's responsibility.

 **Real World Scenario**

Return Codes vs. Exceptions

Exceptions are used when "something goes wrong." However, the word *wrong* is subjective. The following code returns –1 instead of throwing an exception if no match is found:

```java
public int indexOf(String[] names, String name) {
   for (int i = 0; i < names.length; i++) {
      if (names[i].equals(name)) { return i; }
   }
   return -1;
}
```

While common for certain tasks like searching, return codes should generally be avoided. After all, Java provided an exception framework, so you should use it!

Understanding Exception Types

An exception is an event that alters program flow. Java has a `Throwable` class for all objects that represent these events. Not all of them have the word *exception* in their class name, which can be confusing. Figure 11.1 shows the key subclasses of `Throwable`.

FIGURE 11.1   Categories of exception

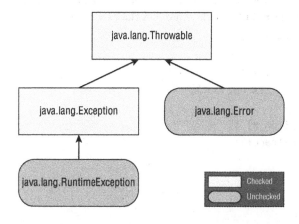

Make sure you memorize Figure 11.1 for the exam! We'll cover the details in this chapter, but it is very likely to come up on the exam.

Checked Exceptions

A *checked exception* is an exception that must be declared or handled by the application code where it is thrown. In Java, checked exceptions all inherit Exception but not RuntimeException. Checked exceptions tend to be more anticipated—for example, trying to read a file that doesn't exist.

Checked exceptions also include any class that inherits Throwable but not Error or RuntimeException, such as a class that directly extends Throwable. For the exam, you just need to know about checked exceptions that extend Exception.

Checked exceptions? What are we checking? Java has a rule called the handle or declare rule. The *handle or declare rule* means that all checked exceptions that could be thrown within a method are either wrapped in compatible try and catch blocks or declared in the method signature.

Because checked exceptions tend to be anticipated, Java enforces the rule that the programmer must do something to show that the exception was thought about. Maybe it was handled in the method. Or maybe the method declares that it can't handle the exception and someone else should.

Let's take a look at an example. The following fall() method declares that it might throw an IOException, which is a checked exception:

```java
void fall(int distance) throws IOException {
   if(distance > 10) {
      throw new IOException();
   }
}
```

Notice that you're using two different keywords here. The throw keyword tells Java that you want to throw an Exception, while the throws keyword simply declares that the method might throw an Exception. It also might not.

Now that you know how to declare an exception, how do you handle it? The following alternate version of the fall() method handles the exception:

```java
void fall(int distance) {
   try {
      if(distance > 10) {
         throw new IOException();
      }
   } catch (Exception e) {
      e.printStackTrace();
   }
}
```

Notice that the catch statement uses Exception, not IOException. Since IOException is a subclass of Exception, the catch block is allowed to catch it. We cover try and catch blocks in more detail later in this chapter.

Unchecked Exceptions

An *unchecked exception* is any exception that does not need to be declared or handled by the application code where it is thrown. Unchecked exceptions are often referred to as *runtime exceptions*, although in Java, unchecked exceptions include any class that inherits RuntimeException or Error.

It is permissible to handle or declare an unchecked exception. That said, it is better to document the unchecked exceptions callers should know about in a Javadoc comment rather than declaring an unchecked exception.

A *runtime exception* is defined as the RuntimeException class and its subclasses. Runtime exceptions tend to be unexpected but not necessarily fatal. For example, accessing an invalid array index is unexpected. Even though they do inherit the Exception class, they are not checked exceptions.

An unchecked exception can occur on nearly any line of code, as it is not required to be handled or declared. For example, a NullPointerException can be thrown in the body of the following method if the input reference is null:

```
void fall(String input) {
    System.out.println(input.toLowerCase());
}
```

We work with objects in Java so frequently that a NullPointerException can happen almost anywhere. If you had to declare unchecked exceptions everywhere, every single method would have that clutter! Remember, the code will still compile if you declare a redundant unchecked exception.

Error and *Throwable*

Error means something went so horribly wrong that your program should not attempt to recover from it. For example, the disk drive "disappeared" or the program ran out of memory. These are abnormal conditions that you aren't likely to encounter and cannot recover from.

For the exam, the only thing you need to know about Throwable is that it's the parent class of all exceptions, including the Error class. While you *can* handle Throwable and Error exceptions, it is not recommended you do so in your application code. When we refer to exceptions in this chapter, we generally mean any class that inherits Throwable, although we are almost always working with the Exception class or subclasses of it.

Reviewing Exception Types

Be sure to closely study everything in Table 11.1. For the exam, remember that a Throwable is either an Exception or an Error. You should not catch Throwable directly in your code.

TABLE 11.1 Types of exceptions and errors

Type	How to recognize	OK for program to catch?	Is program required to handle or declare?
Unchecked exception	Subclass of `RuntimeException`	Yes	No
Checked exception	Subclass of `Exception` but not subclass of `RuntimeException`	Yes	Yes
Error	Subclass of `Error`	No	No

Throwing an Exception

Any Java code can throw an exception; this includes code you write. Some exceptions are provided with Java. You might encounter an exception that was made up for the exam. This is fine. The question will make it obvious that this is an exception by having the class name end with `Exception`. For example, `MyMadeUpException` is clearly an exception.

It's common practice in Java to have exception classes end with the word `Exception`, but it is not required. You should follow this convention when creating your own exception classes, though!

On the exam, you will see two types of code that result in an exception. The first is code that's wrong. Here's an example:

```
String[] animals = new String[0];
System.out.println(animals[0]);  // ArrayIndexOutOfBoundsException
```

This code throws an `ArrayIndexOutOfBoundsException` since the array has no elements. That means questions about exceptions can be hidden in questions that appear to be about something else.

On the exam, some questions have a choice about not compiling and about throwing an exception. Pay special attention to code that calls a method on a null reference or that references an invalid array or `List` index. If you spot this, you know the correct answer is that the code throws an exception at runtime.

The second way for code to result in an exception is to explicitly request Java to throw one. Java lets you write statements like these:

```
throw new Exception();
throw new Exception("Ow! I fell.");
```

```
throw new RuntimeException();
throw new RuntimeException("Ow! I fell.");
```

The throw keyword tells Java that you want some other part of the code to deal with the exception. This is the same as the young girl crying for her daddy. Someone else needs to figure out what to do about the exception.

---

throw vs. _throws_

Anytime you see throw or throws on the exam, make sure the correct one is being used. The throw keyword is used as a statement inside a code block to throw a new exception or rethrow an existing exception, while the throws keyword is used only at the end of a method declaration to indicate what exceptions it supports.

When creating an exception, you can usually pass a String parameter with a message, or you can pass no parameters and use the defaults. We say *usually* because this is a convention. Someone has declared a constructor that takes a String. Someone could also create an exception class that does not have a constructor that takes a message.

Additionally, you should know that an Exception is an Object. This means you can store it in an object reference, and this is legal:

```
var e = new RuntimeException();
throw e;
```

The code instantiates an exception on one line and then throws on the next. The exception can come from anywhere, even passed into a method. As long as it is a valid exception, it can be thrown.

The exam might also try to trick you. Do you see why this code doesn't compile?

```
throw RuntimeException();   // DOES NOT COMPILE
```

If your answer is that there is a missing keyword, you're absolutely right. The exception is never instantiated with the new keyword.

Let's take a look at another place the exam might try to trick you. Can you see why the following does not compile?

```
3: try {
4:    throw new RuntimeException();
5:    throw new ArrayIndexOutOfBoundsException();  // DOES NOT COMPILE
6: } catch (Exception e) {}
```

Since line 4 throws an exception, line 5 can never be reached during runtime. The compiler recognizes this and reports an unreachable code error.

Calling Methods That Throw Exceptions

When you're calling a method that throws an exception, the rules are the same as those for handling an exception within the method. Do you see why the following doesn't compile?

```
class NoMoreCarrotsException extends Exception {}
```

```
public class Bunny {
    private void eatCarrot() throws NoMoreCarrotsException {}
    public void hopAround() {
        eatCarrot();  // DOES NOT COMPILE
    }
}
```

The problem is that NoMoreCarrotsException is a checked exception. Checked exceptions must be handled or declared. The code would compile if you changed the hopAround() method to either of these:

```
// Option 1
public void hopAround() throws NoMoreCarrotsException {
    eatCarrot();
}
```

```
// Option 2
public void hopAround() {
    try {
        eatCarrot();
    } catch (NoMoreCarrotsException e) {
        System.out.print("sad rabbit");
    }
}
```

You might have noticed that eatCarrot() didn't throw an exception; it just declared that it could. This is enough for the compiler to require the caller to handle or declare the exception.

The compiler is still on the lookout for unreachable code. Declaring an unused exception isn't considered unreachable code. It gives the method the option to change the implementation to throw that exception in the future. Do you see the issue here?

```
public class Bunny {
    private void eatCarrot() {}
    public void bad() {
        try {
            eatCarrot();
        } catch (NoMoreCarrotsException e) {  // DOES NOT COMPILE
```

```
        System.out.print("sad rabbit");
    }
  } }
```

Java knows that eatCarrot() can't throw a checked exception—which means there's no way for the catch block in bad() to be reached.

 When you see a checked exception declared inside a catch block on the exam, make sure the code in the associated try block is capable of throwing the exception or a subclass of the exception. If not, the code is unreachable and does not compile. Remember that this rule does not extend to unchecked exceptions or exceptions declared in a method signature.

Overriding Methods with Exceptions

When we introduced overriding methods in Chapter 6, "Class Design," we included a rule related to exceptions. An overridden method may not declare any new or broader checked exceptions than the method it inherits. For example, this code isn't allowed:

```
class CanNotHopException extends Exception {}

class Hopper {
   public void hop() {}
}

public class Bunny extends Hopper {
   public void hop() throws CanNotHopException {}  // DOES NOT COMPILE
}
```

Java knows hop() isn't allowed to throw any checked exceptions because the hop() method in the superclass Hopper doesn't declare any. Imagine what would happen if the subclasses' versions of the method could add checked exceptions—you could write code that calls Hopper's hop() method and not handle any exceptions. Then, if Bunny were used in its place, the code wouldn't know to handle or declare CanNotHopException.

An overridden method in a subclass is allowed to declare fewer exceptions than the superclass or interface. This is legal because callers are already handling them.

```
class Hopper {
   public void hop() throws CanNotHopException {}
}
public class Bunny extends Hopper {
   public void hop() {}  // This is fine
}
```

An overridden method not declaring one of the exceptions thrown by the parent method is similar to the method declaring that it throws an exception it never actually throws. This is perfectly legal. Similarly, a class is allowed to declare a subclass of an exception type. The idea is the same. The superclass or interface has already taken care of a broader type.

Printing an Exception

There are three ways to print an exception. You can let Java print it out, print just the message, or print where the stack trace comes from. This example shows all three approaches:

```
5:  public static void main(String[] args) {
6:      try {
7:          hop();
8:      } catch (Exception e) {
9:          System.out.println(e + "\n");
10:         System.out.println(e.getMessage()+ "\n");
11:         e.printStackTrace();
12:     }
13: }
14: private static void hop() {
15:     throw new RuntimeException("cannot hop");
16: }
```

This code prints the following:

```
java.lang.RuntimeException: cannot hop

cannot hop

java.lang.RuntimeException: cannot hop
    at Handling.hop(Handling.java:15)
    at Handling.main(Handling.java:7)
```

The first line shows what Java prints out by default: the exception type and message. The second line shows just the message. The rest shows a stack trace. The stack trace is usually the most helpful because it shows the hierarchy of method calls that were made to reach the line that threw the exception.

Recognizing Exception Classes

You need to recognize three groups of exception classes for the exam: RuntimeException, checked Exception, and Error. We look at common examples of each type. For the exam, you'll need to recognize which type of an exception it is and whether it's thrown by the Java

Virtual Machine (JVM) or by a programmer. For some exceptions, you also need to know which are inherited from one another.

RuntimeException Classes

RuntimeException and its subclasses are unchecked exceptions that don't have to be handled or declared. They can be thrown by the programmer or the JVM. Common unchecked exception classes are listed in Table 11.2.

TABLE 11.2   Unchecked exceptions

Unchecked exception	Description
ArithmeticException	Thrown when code attempts to divide by zero.
ArrayIndexOutOfBoundsException	Thrown when code uses illegal index to access array.
ClassCastException	Thrown when attempt is made to cast object to class of which it is not an instance.
NullPointerException	Thrown when there is a null reference where an object is required.
IllegalArgumentException	Thrown by programmer to indicate that method has been passed illegal or inappropriate argument.
NumberFormatException	Subclass of IllegalArgumentException. Thrown when attempt is made to convert String to numeric type but String doesn't have appropriate format.

ArithmeticException

Trying to divide an int by zero gives an undefined result. When this occurs, the JVM will throw an ArithmeticException.

```
int answer = 11 / 0;
```

Running this code results in the following output:

```
Exception in thread "main" java.lang.ArithmeticException: / by zero
```

Java doesn't spell out the word *divide*. That's OK, though, because we know that / is the division operator and that Java is trying to tell you division by zero occurred.

The thread "main" is telling you the code was called directly or indirectly from a program with a main method. On the exam, this is all the output you will see. Next comes the name of the exception, followed by extra information (if any) that goes with the exception.

ArrayIndexOutOfBoundsException

You know by now that array indexes start with 0 and go up to one less than the length of the array—which means this code will throw an `ArrayIndexOutOfBoundsException`.

```
int[] countsOfMoose = new int[3];
System.out.println(countsOfMoose[-1]);
```

This is a problem because there's no such thing as a negative array index. Running this code yields the following output:

```
Exception in thread "main" java.lang.ArrayIndexOutOfBoundsException:
   Index -1 out of bounds for length 3
```

ClassCastException

Java tries to protect you from impossible casts. This code doesn't compile because `Integer` is not a subclass of `String`:

```
String type = "moose";
Integer number = (Integer) type;  // DOES NOT COMPILE
```

More complicated code thwarts Java's attempts to protect you. When the cast fails at runtime, Java will throw a `ClassCastException`.

```
String type = "moose";
Object obj = type;
Integer number = (Integer) obj;  // ClassCastException
```

The compiler sees a cast from `Object` to `Integer`. This could be OK. The compiler doesn't realize there's a `String` in that `Object`. When the code runs, it yields the following output:

```
Exception in thread "main" java.lang.ClassCastException:
   java.base/java.lang.String cannot be cast to
   java.lang.base/java.lang.Integer
```

Java tells you both types that were involved in the problem, making it apparent what's wrong.

NullPointerException

Instance variables and methods must be called on a non-`null` reference. If the reference is `null`, the JVM will throw a `NullPointerException`.

```
public class Frog {
   static String name;
   public void hop() {
```

```
        System.out.print(name.toLowerCase() + " is hopping");
    }
    public static void main(String[] args) {
        new Frog().hop();
    }
}
```

Remember from Chapter 5, "Methods," that static variables are initialized as null. Running this code results in the following output:

```
Exception in thread "main" java.lang.NullPointerException:
    Cannot invoke "String.toLowerCase()" because "Frog.name" is null
```

Notice anything special about this output? Java includes a feature called *Helpful NullPointerExceptions*, in which the JVM tells you the object reference that triggered the NullPointerException.

On instance and static variables, the JVM will tell you the name of the variable in the nice, easy-to-read format as we just saw. On local variables (including method parameters), it is not as friendly. Let's try an example:

```
public class Frog {
    public void hop(String name) {
        System.out.print(name.toLowerCase() + " is hopping");
    }
    public static void main(String[] args) {
        new Frog().hop(null);
    }
}
```

This program prints the following:

```
Exception in thread "main" java.lang.NullPointerException:
    Cannot invoke "String.toLowerCase()" because "<parameter1>" is null
```

Wait, what's <parameter1>? On method parameters it prints <parameterX>, while on local variables it prints <localX>, where X is the order in which the variable appears in the method. The reason for this is that the name of the variable is lost when the code is compiled.

Not very helpful is it? Fret not, there is a fix! If the class is *compiled* with the -g:vars argument, then the code will print the variable name at runtime:

```
javac -g:vars Frog.java
java Frog
```

This is a debug argument, meant to provide additional information in the case that the code is behaving unexpectedly. This code now prints the following at runtime:

```
Exception in thread "main" java.lang.NullPointerException:
    Cannot invoke "String.toLowerCase()" because "name" is null
```

Remember, this argument applies only to local variables and method parameters and has to be used when the code is compiled.

 If you're using an IDE such as Eclipse or IntelliJ, they often have the -g:vars parameter enabled by default.

IllegalArgumentException

IllegalArgumentException is a way for your program to protect itself. You want to tell the caller that something is wrong—preferably in an obvious way that the caller can't ignore so the programmer will fix the problem. Seeing the code end with an exception is a great reminder that something is wrong. Consider this example when called as setNumberEggs(-2):

```
public void setNumberEggs(int numberEggs) {
    if (numberEggs < 0)
        throw new IllegalArgumentException("# eggs must not be negative");
    this.numberEggs = numberEggs;
}
```

The program throws an exception when it's not happy with the parameter values. The output looks like this:

```
Exception in thread "main" java.lang.IllegalArgumentException:
    # eggs must not be negative
```

Clearly, this is a problem that must be fixed if the programmer wants the program to do anything useful.

NumberFormatException

Java provides methods to convert strings to numbers. When these are passed an invalid value, they throw a NumberFormatException. The idea is similar to IllegalArgumentException. Since this is a common problem, Java gives it a separate class. In fact, NumberFormatException is a subclass of IllegalArgumentException. Here's an example of trying to convert something non-numeric into an int:

```
Integer.parseInt("abc");
```

The output looks like this:

```
Exception in thread "main" java.lang.NumberFormatException:
    For input string: "abc"
```

For the exam, you need to know that NumberFormatException is a subclass of IllegalArgumentException. We cover more about why that is important later in the chapter.

Checked *Exception* Classes

Checked exceptions have `Exception` in their hierarchy but not `RuntimeException`. They must be handled or declared. Common checked exceptions are listed in Table 11.3.

TABLE 11.3 Checked exceptions

Checked exception	Description
`FileNotFoundException`	Subclass of `IOException`. Thrown programmatically when code tries to reference file that does not exist.
`IOException`	Thrown programmatically when problem reading or writing file.
`NotSerializableException`	Subclass of `IOException`. Thrown programmatically when attempting to serialize or deserialize non-serializable class.
`ParseException`	Indicates problem parsing input.

For the exam, you need to know that these are all checked exceptions that must be handled or declared. You also need to know that `FileNotFoundException` and `NotSerializableException` are subclasses of `IOException`. You'll see `ParseException` later in this chapter and the other three classes in Chapter 14, "I/O."

Error Classes

Errors are unchecked exceptions that extend the `Error` class. They are thrown by the JVM and should not be handled or declared. Errors are rare, but you might see the ones listed in Table 11.4.

TABLE 11.4 Errors

Error	Description
`ExceptionInInitializerError`	Thrown when `static` initializer throws exception and doesn't handle it
`StackOverflowError`	Thrown when method calls itself too many times (called *infinite recursion* because method typically calls itself without end)
`NoClassDefFoundError`	Thrown when class that code uses is available at compile time but not runtime

For the exam, you just need to know that these errors are unchecked and the code is often unable to recover from them.

Handling Exceptions

What do you do when you encounter an exception? How do you handle or recover from the exception? In this section, we show the various statements in Java that support handling exceptions.

Using *try* and *catch* Statements

Now that you know what exceptions are, let's explore how to handle them. Java uses a `try` statement to separate the logic that might throw an exception from the logic to handle that exception. Figure 11.2 shows the syntax of a *try statement*.

FIGURE 11.2   The syntax of a `try` statement

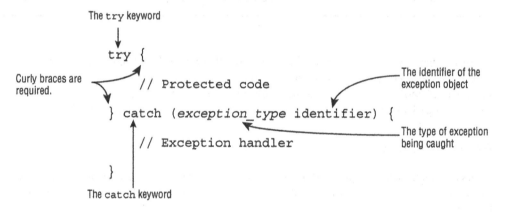

The code in the `try` block is run normally. If any of the statements throws an exception that can be caught by the exception type listed in the `catch` block, the `try` block stops running, and execution goes to the `catch` statement. If none of the statements in the `try` block throws an exception that can be caught, the *catch clause* is not run.

You probably noticed the words *block* and *clause* used interchangeably. The exam does this as well, so get used to it. Both are correct. *Block* is correct because there are braces present. *Clause* is correct because it is part of a `try` statement.

There aren't a ton of syntax rules here. The braces are required for `try` and `catch` blocks. In our example, the little girl gets up by herself the first time she falls. Here's what this looks like:

```
3:  void explore() {
4:     try {
```

```
5:         fall();
6:         System.out.println("never get here");
7:      } catch (RuntimeException e) {
8:         getUp();
9:      }
10:     seeAnimals();
11: }
12: void fall() {  throw new RuntimeException(); }
```

First, line 5 calls the fall() method. Line 12 throws an exception. This means Java jumps straight to the catch block, skipping line 6. The girl gets up on line 8. Now the try statement is over, and execution proceeds normally with line 10.

Now let's look at some invalid try statements that the exam might try to trick you with. Do you see what's wrong with this one?

```
try  // DOES NOT COMPILE
   fall();
catch (Exception e)
   System.out.println("get up");
```

The problem is that the braces {} are missing. The try statements are like methods in that the braces are required even if there is only one statement inside the code blocks, while if statements and loops are special and allow you to omit the braces.

What about this one?

```
try {  // DOES NOT COMPILE
   fall();
}
```

This code doesn't compile because the try block doesn't have anything after it. Remember, the point of a try statement is for something to happen if an exception is thrown. Without another clause, the try statement is lonely. As you see shortly, there is a special type of try statement that includes an implicit finally block, although the syntax is quite different from this example.

Chaining *catch* Blocks

For the exam, you may be given exception classes and need to understand how they function. Here's how to tackle them. First, you must be able to recognize if the exception is a checked or an unchecked exception. Second, you need to determine whether any of the exceptions are subclasses of the others.

```
class AnimalsOutForAWalk extends RuntimeException {}

class ExhibitClosed extends RuntimeException {}

class ExhibitClosedForLunch extends ExhibitClosed {}
```

In this example, there are three custom exceptions. All are unchecked exceptions because they directly or indirectly extend `RuntimeException`. Now we chain both types of exceptions with two `catch` blocks and handle them by printing out the appropriate message:

```java
public void visitPorcupine() {
    try {
        seeAnimal();
    } catch (AnimalsOutForAWalk e) {  // first catch block
        System.out.print("try back later");
    } catch (ExhibitClosed e) {       // second catch block
        System.out.print("not today");
    }
}
```

There are three possibilities when this code is run. If `seeAnimal()` doesn't throw an exception, nothing is printed out. If the animal is out for a walk, only the first `catch` block runs. If the exhibit is closed, only the second `catch` block runs. It is not possible for both `catch` blocks to be executed when chained together like this.

A rule exists for the order of the `catch` blocks. Java looks at them in the order they appear. If it is impossible for one of the `catch` blocks to be executed, a compiler error about unreachable code occurs. For example, this happens when a superclass `catch` block appears before a subclass `catch` block. Remember, *we warned you to pay attention to any subclass exceptions!*

In the porcupine example, the order of the `catch` blocks could be reversed because the exceptions don't inherit from each other. And yes, we have seen a porcupine be taken for a walk on a leash.

The following example shows exception types that do inherit from each other:

```java
public void visitMonkeys() {
    try {
        seeAnimal();
    } catch (ExhibitClosedForLunch e) { // Subclass exception
        System.out.print("try back later");
    } catch (ExhibitClosed e) {         // Superclass exception
        System.out.print("not today");
    }
}
```

If the more specific `ExhibitClosedForLunch` exception is thrown, the first `catch` block runs. If not, Java checks whether the superclass `ExhibitClosed` exception is thrown and catches it. This time, the order of the `catch` blocks does matter. The reverse does not work.

```java
public void visitMonkeys() {
    try {
        seeAnimal();
    } catch (ExhibitClosed e) {
        System.out.print("not today");
```

```
    } catch (ExhibitClosedForLunch e) {  // DOES NOT COMPILE
        System.out.print("try back later");
    }
}
```

If the more specific `ExhibitClosedForLunch` exception is thrown, the `catch` block for `ExhibitClosed` runs—which means there is no way for the second `catch` block to ever run. Java correctly tells you there is an unreachable `catch` block.

Let's try this one more time. Do you see why this code doesn't compile?

```
public void visitSnakes() {
    try {
    } catch (IllegalArgumentException e) {
    } catch (NumberFormatException e) {  // DOES NOT COMPILE
    }
}
```

Remember we said earlier that you needed to know that `NumberFormatException` is a subclass of `IllegalArgumentException`? This example is the reason why. Since `NumberFormatException` is a subclass, it will always be caught by the first `catch` block, making the second `catch` block unreachable code that does not compile. Likewise, for the exam, you need to know that `FileNotFoundException` is a subclass of `IOException` and cannot be used in a similar manner.

To review multiple `catch` blocks, remember that at most one `catch` block will run, and it will be the first `catch` block that can handle the exception. Also, remember that an exception defined by the `catch` statement is only in scope for that `catch` block. For example, the following causes a compiler error since it tries to use the exception object reference outside the block for which it was defined:

```
public void visitManatees() {
    try {
    } catch (NumberFormatException e1) {
        System.out.println(e1);
    } catch (IllegalArgumentException e2) {
        System.out.println(e1);  // DOES NOT COMPILE
    }
}
```

Applying a Multi-catch Block

Often, we want the result of an exception that is thrown to be the same, regardless of which particular exception is thrown. For example, take a look at this method:

```
public static void main(String args[]) {
    try {
```

```
      System.out.println(Integer.parseInt(args[1]));
   } catch (ArrayIndexOutOfBoundsException e) {
      System.out.println("Missing or invalid input");
   } catch (NumberFormatException e) {
      System.out.println("Missing or invalid input");
   }
}
```

Notice that we have the same `println()` statement for two different `catch` blocks. We can handle this more gracefully using a *multi-catch* block. A multi-catch block allows multiple exception types to be caught by the same `catch` block. Let's rewrite the previous example using a multi-catch block:

```
public static void main(String[] args) {
   try {
      System.out.println(Integer.parseInt(args[1]));
   } catch (ArrayIndexOutOfBoundsException | NumberFormatException e) {
      System.out.println("Missing or invalid input");
   }
}
```

This is much better. There's no duplicate code, the common logic is all in one place, and the logic is exactly where you would expect to find it. If you wanted, you could still have a second `catch` block for `Exception` in case you want to handle other types of exceptions differently.

Figure 11.3 shows the syntax of multi-catch. It's like a regular `catch` clause, except two or more exception types are specified, separated by a pipe. The pipe (|) is also used as the "or" operator, making it easy to remember that you can use either/or of the exception types. Notice how there is only one variable name in the `catch` clause. Java is saying that the variable named e can be of type `Exception1` or `Exception2`.

FIGURE 11.3 The syntax of a multi-catch block

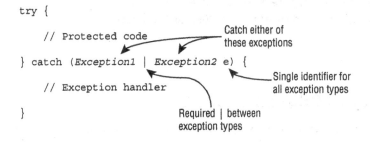

The exam might try to trick you with invalid syntax. Remember that the exceptions can be listed in any order within the `catch` clause. However, the variable name must appear only once and at the end. Do you see why these are valid or invalid?

```
catch(Exception1 e | Exception2 e | Exception3 e)      // DOES NOT COMPILE
```

```
catch(Exception1 e1 | Exception2 e2 | Exception3 e3) // DOES NOT COMPILE
```

```
catch(Exception1 | Exception2 | Exception3 e)
```

The first line is incorrect because the variable name appears three times. Just because it happens to be the same variable name doesn't make it OK. The second line is incorrect because the variable name again appears three times. Using different variable names doesn't make it any better. The third line does compile. It shows the correct syntax for specifying three exception types.

Java intends multi-catch to be used for exceptions that aren't related, and it prevents you from specifying redundant types in a multi-catch. Do you see what is wrong here?

```
try {
    throw new IOException();
} catch (FileNotFoundException | IOException p) {} // DOES NOT COMPILE
```

Specifying related exceptions in the multi-catch is redundant, and the compiler gives a message such as this:

```
The exception FileNotFoundException is already caught
  by the alternative IOException
```

Since `FileNotFoundException` is a subclass of `IOException`, this code will not compile. A multi-catch block follows rules similar to chaining `catch` blocks together, which you saw in the previous section. For example, both trigger compiler errors when they encounter unreachable code or duplicate exceptions being caught. The one difference between multi-catch blocks and chaining `catch` blocks is that order does not matter for a multi-catch block within a single `catch` expression.

Getting back to the example, the correct code is just to drop the extraneous subclass reference, as shown here:

```
try {
    throw new IOException();
} catch (IOException e) {}
```

Adding a *finally* Block

The `try` statement also lets you run code at the end with a *finally clause*, regardless of whether an exception is thrown. Figure 11.4 shows the syntax of a `try` statement with this extra functionality.

FIGURE 11.4   The syntax of a try statement with finally

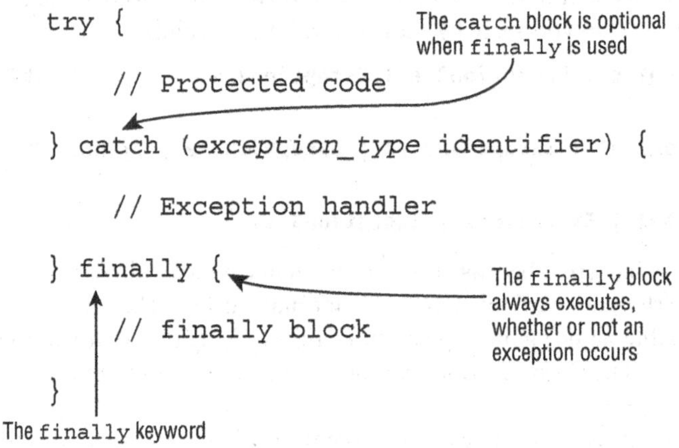

```
try {
                              The catch block is optional
                              when finally is used
    // Protected code

} catch (exception_type identifier) {

    // Exception handler

} finally {
                              The finally block
                              always executes,
    // finally block          whether or not an
                              exception occurs

}
```
The finally keyword

There are two paths through code with both a catch and a finally. If an exception is thrown, the finally block is run after the catch block. If no exception is thrown, the finally block is run after the try block completes.

Let's go back to our young girl example, this time with finally:

```
12: void explore() {
13:     try {
14:         seeAnimals();
15:         fall();
16:     } catch (Exception e) {
17:         getHugFromDaddy();
18:     } finally {
19:         seeMoreAnimals();
20:     }
21:     goHome();
22: }
```

The girl falls on line 15. If she gets up by herself, the code goes on to the finally block and runs line 19. Then the try statement is over, and the code proceeds on line 21. If the girl doesn't get up by herself, she throws an exception. The catch block runs, and she gets a hug on line 17. With that hug, she is ready to see more animals on line 19. Then the try statement is over, and the code proceeds on line 21. Either way, the ending is the same. The finally block is executed, and execution continues after the try statement.

The exam will try to trick you with missing clauses or clauses in the wrong order. Do you see why the following do or do not compile?

```
25: try { // DOES NOT COMPILE
26:     fall();
```

```
27: } finally {
28:     System.out.println("all better");
29: } catch (Exception e) {
30:     System.out.println("get up");
31: }
32:
33: try {  // DOES NOT COMPILE
34:     fall();
35: }
36:
37: try {
38:     fall();
39: } finally {
40:     System.out.println("all better");
41: }
```

The first example (lines 25–31) does not compile because the catch and finally blocks are in the wrong order. The second example (lines 33–35) does not compile because there must be a catch or finally block. The third example (lines 37–41) is just fine. The catch block is not required if finally is present.

Most of the examples you encounter on the exam with finally are going to look contrived. For example, you'll get asked questions such as what this code outputs:

```
public static void main(String[] unused) {
    StringBuilder sb = new StringBuilder();
    try {
        sb.append("t");
    } catch (Exception e) {
        sb.append("c");
    } finally {
        sb.append("f");
    }
    sb.append("a");
    System.out.print(sb.toString());
}
```

The answer is tfa. The try block is executed. Since no exception is thrown, Java goes straight to the finally block. Then the code after the try statement is run. We know that this is a silly example, but you can expect to see examples like this on the exam.

There is one additional rule you should know for finally blocks. If a try statement with a finally block is entered, then the finally block will always be executed, regardless of whether the code completes successfully. Take a look at the following goHome() method.

Assuming an exception may or may not be thrown on line 14, what are the possible values that this method could print? Also, what would the return value be in each case?

```
12: int goHome() {
13:     try {
14:         // Optionally throw an exception here
15:         System.out.print("1");
16:         return -1;
17:     } catch (Exception e) {
18:         System.out.print("2");
19:         return -2;
20:     } finally {
21:         System.out.print("3");
22:         return -3;
23:     } }
```

If an exception is not thrown on line 14, then line 15 will be executed, printing 1. Before the method returns, though, the finally block is executed, printing 3. If an exception is thrown, then lines 15 and 16 will be skipped and lines 17–19 will be executed, printing 2, followed by 3 from the finally block. While the first value printed may differ, the method always prints 3 last since it's in the finally block.

What is the return value of the goHome() method? In this case, it's always -3. Because the finally block is executed shortly before the method completes, it interrupts the return statement from inside both the try and catch blocks.

For the exam, you need to remember that a finally block will always be executed. That said, it may not complete successfully. Take a look at the following code snippet. What would happen if info was null on line 32?

```
31: } finally {
32:     info.printDetails();
33:     System.out.print("Exiting");
34:     return "zoo";
35: }
```

If info was null, then the finally block would be executed, but it would stop on line 32 and throw a NullPointerException. Lines 33 and 34 would not be executed. In this example, you see that while a finally block will always be executed, it may not finish.

System.exit()

There is one exception to "the finally block will always be executed" rule: Java defines a method that you call as System.exit(). It takes an integer parameter that represents the status code that is returned.

```
try {
   System.exit(0);
} finally {
   System.out.print("Never going to get here");   // Not printed
}
```

System.exit() tells Java, "Stop. End the program right now. Do not pass Go. Do not collect $200." When System.exit() is called in the try or catch block, the finally block does not run.

Automating Resource Management

Often, your application works with files, databases, and various connection objects. Commonly, these external data sources are referred to as *resources*. In many cases, you *open* a connection to the resource, whether it's over the network or within a file system. You then *read/write* the data you want. Finally, you *close* the resource to indicate that you are done with it.

What happens if you don't close a resource when you are done with it? In short, a lot of bad things could happen. If you are connecting to a database, you could use up all available connections, meaning no one can talk to the database until you release your connections. Although you commonly hear about memory leaks causing programs to fail, a *resource leak* is just as bad and occurs when a program fails to release its connections to a resource, resulting in the resource becoming inaccessible. This could mean your program can no longer talk to the database—or, even worse, all programs are unable to reach the database!

For the exam, a *resource* is typically a file or database that requires some kind of stream or connection to read or write data. In Chapter 14, you will create numerous resources that will need to be closed when you are finished with them.

Introducing Try-with-Resources

Let's take a look at a method that opens a file, reads the data, and closes it:

```
4:  public void readFile(String file) {
5:     FileInputStream is = null;
6:     try {
7:        is = new FileInputStream("myfile.txt");
8:        // Read file data
9:     } catch (IOException e) {
10:       e.printStackTrace();
```

```
11:     } finally {
12:        if(is != null) {
13:           try {
14:              is.close();
15:           } catch (IOException e2) {
16:              e2.printStackTrace();
17:           }
18:        }
19:     }
20: }
```

Wow, that's a long method! Why do we have two `try` and `catch` blocks? Well, lines 7 and 14 both include checked `IOException` calls, and those need to be caught in the method or rethrown by the method. Half the lines of code in this method are just closing a resource. And the more resources you have, the longer code like this becomes. For example, you may have multiple resources that need to be closed in a particular order. You also don't want an exception caused by closing one resource to prevent the closing of another resource.

To solve this, Java includes the *try-with-resources* statement to automatically close all resources opened in a `try` clause. This feature is also known as *automatic resource management*, because Java automatically takes care of the closing.

Let's take a look at our same example using a try-with-resources statement:

```
4:  public void readFile(String file) {
5:     try (FileInputStream is = new FileInputStream("myfile.txt")) {
6:        // Read file data
7:     } catch (IOException e) {
8:        e.printStackTrace();
9:     }
10: }
```

Functionally, they are similar, but our new version has half as many lines. More importantly, though, by using a try-with-resources statement, we guarantee that as soon as a connection passes out of scope, Java will attempt to close it within the same method.

Behind the scenes, the compiler replaces a try-with-resources block with a `try` and `finally` block. We refer to this "hidden" `finally` block as an *implicit* `finally` block since it is created and used by the compiler automatically. You can still create a programmer-defined `finally` block when using a try-with-resources statement; just be aware that the implicit one will be called first.

Unlike garbage collection, resources are not automatically closed when they go out of scope. Therefore, it is recommended that you close resources in the same block of code that opens them. By using a try-with-resources statement to open all your resources, this happens automatically.

Basics of Try-with-Resources

Figure 11.5 shows what a try-with-resources statement looks like. Notice that one or more resources can be opened in the try clause. When multiple resources are opened, they are closed in the *reverse* of the order in which they were created. Also, notice that parentheses are used to list those resources, and semicolons are used to separate the declarations. This works just like declaring multiple indexes in a for loop.

FIGURE 11.5   The syntax of a basic try-with-resources statement

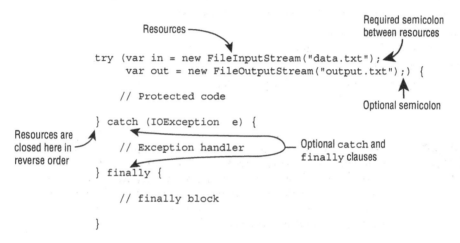

What happened to the catch block in Figure 11.5? Well, it turns out a catch block is *optional* with a try-with-resources statement. For example, we can rewrite the previous readFile() example so that the method declares the exception to make it even shorter:

```
4: public void readFile(String file) throws IOException {
5:     try (FileInputStream is = new FileInputStream("myfile.txt")) {
6:         // Read file data
7:     }
8: }
```

Earlier in the chapter, you learned that a try statement must have one or more catch blocks or a finally block. A try-with-resources statement differs from a try statement in that neither of these is required, although a developer may add both. For the exam, you need to know that the implicit finally block runs *before* any programmer-coded ones.

Constructing Try-with-Resources Statements

Only classes that implement the AutoCloseable interface can be used in a try-with-resources statement. For example, the following does not compile as String does not implement the AutoCloseable interface:

```
try (String reptile = "lizard") {}
```

Inheriting `AutoCloseable` requires implementing a compatible `close()` method.

```
interface AutoCloseable {
    public void close() throws Exception;
}
```

From your studies of method overriding, this means that the implemented version of `close()` can choose to throw `Exception` or a subclass or not throw any exceptions at all.

Throughout the rest of this section, we use the following custom resource class that simply prints a message when the `close()` method is called:

```
public class MyFileClass implements AutoCloseable {
    private final int num;
    public MyFileClass(int num) { this.num = num; }
    @Override public void close() {
        System.out.println("Closing: " + num);
    } }
```

> In Chapter 14, you encounter resources that implement `Closeable` rather than `AutoCloseable`. Since `Closeable` extends `AutoCloseable`, they are both supported in try-with-resources statements. The only difference between the two is that `Closeable`'s `close()` method declares `IOException`, while `AutoCloseable`'s `close()` method declares `Exception`.

Declaring Resources

While try-with-resources does support declaring multiple variables, each variable must be declared in a separate statement. For example, the following do not compile:

```
try (MyFileClass is = new MyFileClass(1),  // DOES NOT COMPILE
    os = new MyFileClass(2)) {
}
```

```
try (MyFileClass ab = new MyFileClass(1),  // DOES NOT COMPILE
    MyFileClass cd = new MyFileClass(2)) {
}
```

The first example does not compile because it is missing the data type, and it uses a comma (,) instead of a semicolon (;). The second example does not compile because it also uses a comma (,) instead of a semicolon (;). Each resource must include the data type and be separated by a semicolon (;).

You can declare a resource using `var` as the data type in a try-with-resources statement, since resources are local variables.

```
try (var f = new BufferedInputStream(new FileInputStream("it.txt"))) {
    // Process file
}
```

Declaring resources is a common situation where using var is quite helpful, as it shortens the already long line of code.

Scope of Try-with-Resources

The resources created in the try clause are in scope only within the try block. This is another way to remember that the implicit finally runs before any catch/finally blocks that you code yourself. The implicit close has run already, and the resource is no longer available. Do you see why lines 6 and 8 don't compile in this example?

```
3: try (Scanner s = new Scanner(System.in)) {
4:     s.nextLine();
5: } catch(Exception e) {
6:     s.nextInt(); // DOES NOT COMPILE
7: } finally {
8:     s.nextInt(); // DOES NOT COMPILE
9: }
```

The problem is that Scanner has gone out of scope at the end of the try clause. Lines 6 and 8 do not have access to it. This is a nice feature. You can't accidentally use an object that has been closed. In a traditional try statement, the variable has to be declared before the try statement so that both the try and finally blocks can access it, which has the unpleasant side effect of making the variable in scope for the rest of the method, just inviting you to call it by accident.

Following Order of Operations

When working with try-with-resources statements, it is important to know that resources are closed in the reverse of the order in which they are created. Using our custom MyFileClass, can you figure out what this method prints?

```
public static void main(String... xyz) {
    try (MyFileClass bookReader = new MyFileClass(1);
        MyFileClass movieReader = new MyFileClass(2)) {
        System.out.println("Try Block");
        throw new RuntimeException();
    } catch (Exception e) {
        System.out.println("Catch Block");
    } finally {
        System.out.println("Finally Block");
    } }
```

While this example may look a bit convoluted in practice, questions like this are common on the exam. It output is as follows:

```
Try Block
Closing: 2
```

```
Closing: 1
Catch Block
Finally Block
```

For the exam, make sure you understand why the method prints the statements in this order. Remember, the resources are closed in the reverse of the order in which they are declared, and the implicit `finally` is executed before the programmer-defined `finally`.

Applying Effectively Final

While resources are often created in the try-with-resources statement, it is possible to declare them ahead of time, provided they are marked `final` or are effectively final. See Chapter 5 if you'd like to review what effectively final means.

The syntax uses the resource name in place of the resource declaration, separated by a semicolon (;). Let's try another example:

```
11: public static void main(String... xyz) {
12:     final var bookReader = new MyFileClass(4);
13:     MyFileClass movieReader = new MyFileClass(5);
14:     try (bookReader;
15:          var tvReader = new MyFileClass(6);
16:          movieReader) {
17:        System.out.println("Try Block");
18:     } finally {
19:        System.out.println("Finally Block");
20:     } }
```

Let's take this one line at a time. Line 12 declares a `final` variable `bookReader`, while line 13 declares an effectively final variable `movieReader`. Both of these resources can be used in a try-with-resources statement. We know `movieReader` is effectively final because it is a local variable that is assigned a value only once. Remember, the test for effectively final is that if we insert the `final` keyword when the variable is declared, the code still compiles.

Lines 14 and 16 use the new syntax to declare resources in a try-with-resources statement, using just the variable name and separating the resources with a semicolon (;). Line 15 uses the normal syntax for declaring a new resource within the `try` clause.

On execution, the code prints the following:

```
Try Block
Closing: 5
Closing: 6
Closing: 4
Finally Block
```

If you come across a question on the exam that uses a try-with-resources statement with a variable not declared in the try clause, make sure it is effectively final. For example, the following does not compile:

```
31: var writer = Files.newBufferedWriter(path);
32: try (writer) {  // DOES NOT COMPILE
33:    writer.append("Welcome to the zoo!");
34: }
35: writer = null;
```

The writer variable is reassigned on line 35, resulting in the compiler not considering it effectively final. Since it is not an effectively final variable, it cannot be used in a try-with-resources statement on line 32.

The other place the exam might try to trick you is accessing a resource after it has been closed. Consider the following:

```
41: var writer = Files.newBufferedWriter(path);
42: writer.append("This write is permitted but a really bad idea!");
43: try (writer) {
44:    writer.append("Welcome to the zoo!");
45: }
46: writer.append("This write will fail!");  // IOException
```

This code compiles but throws an exception on line 46 with the message Stream closed. While it is possible to write to the resource before the try-with-resources statement, it is not afterward.

Understanding Suppressed Exceptions

We conclude our discussion of exceptions with probably the most confusing topic: suppressed exceptions. What happens if the close() method throws an exception? Let's try an illustrative example:

```
public class TurkeyCage implements AutoCloseable {
   public void close() {
      System.out.println("Close gate");
   }
   public static void main(String[] args) {
      try (var t = new TurkeyCage()) {
         System.out.println("Put turkeys in");
      }
} }
```

If the TurkeyCage doesn't close, the turkeys could all escape. Clearly, we need to handle such a condition. We already know that the resources are closed before any programmer-coded catch blocks are run. This means we can catch the exception thrown by close() if we want to. Alternatively, we can allow the caller to deal with it.

Let's expand our example with a new `JammedTurkeyCage` implementation, shown here:

```
1:  public class JammedTurkeyCage implements AutoCloseable {
2:      public void close() throws IllegalStateException {
3:          throw new IllegalStateException("Cage door does not close");
4:      }
5:      public static void main(String[] args) {
6:          try (JammedTurkeyCage t = new JammedTurkeyCage()) {
7:              System.out.println("Put turkeys in");
8:          } catch (IllegalStateException e) {
9:              System.out.println("Caught: " + e.getMessage());
10:         }
11: } }
```

The `close()` method is automatically called by try-with-resources. It throws an exception, which is caught by our `catch` block and prints the following:

```
Caught: Cage door does not close
```

This seems reasonable enough. What happens if the `try` block also throws an exception? When multiple exceptions are thrown, all but the first are called *suppressed exceptions*. The idea is that Java treats the first exception as the primary one and tacks on any that come up while automatically closing.

What do you think the following implementation of our `main()` method outputs?

```
5:      public static void main(String[] args) {
6:          try (JammedTurkeyCage t = new JammedTurkeyCage()) {
7:              throw new IllegalStateException("Turkeys ran off");
8:          } catch (IllegalStateException e) {
9:              System.out.println("Caught: " + e.getMessage());
10:             for (Throwable t: e.getSuppressed())
11:                 System.out.println("Suppressed: "+t.getMessage());
12: } }
```

Line 7 throws the primary exception. At this point, the `try` clause ends, and Java automatically calls the `close()` method. Line 3 of `JammedTurkeyCage` throws an `IllegalStateException`, which is added as a suppressed exception. Then line 8 catches the primary exception. Line 9 prints the message for the primary exception. Lines 10 and 11 iterate through any suppressed exceptions and print them. The program prints the following:

```
Caught: Turkeys ran off
Suppressed: Cage door does not close
```

Keep in mind that the `catch` block looks for matches on the primary exception. What do you think this code prints?

```
5:      public static void main(String[] args) {
6:          try (JammedTurkeyCage t = new JammedTurkeyCage()) {
```

```
7:            throw new RuntimeException("Turkeys ran off");
8:        } catch (IllegalStateException e) {
9:            System.out.println("caught: " + e.getMessage());
10:       } }
```

Line 7 again throws the primary exception. Java calls the close() method and adds a suppressed exception. Line 8 would catch the IllegalStateException. However, we don't have one of those. The primary exception is a RuntimeException. Since this does not match the catch clause, the exception is thrown to the caller. Eventually, the main() method would output something like the following:

```
Exception in thread "main" java.lang.RuntimeException: Turkeys ran off
    at JammedTurkeyCage.main(JammedTurkeyCage.java:7)
    Suppressed: java.lang.IllegalStateException:
        Cage door does not close
    at JammedTurkeyCage.close(JammedTurkeyCage.java:3)
    at JammedTurkeyCage.main(JammedTurkeyCage.java:8)
```

Java remembers the suppressed exceptions that go with a primary exception even if we don't handle them in the code.

> If more than two resources throw an exception, the first one to be thrown becomes the primary exception, and the rest are grouped as suppressed exceptions. And since resources are closed in the reverse of the order in which they are declared, the primary exception will be on the last declared resource that throws an exception.

Keep in mind that suppressed exceptions apply only to exceptions thrown in the try clause. The following example does not throw a suppressed exception:

```
5:    public static void main(String[] args) {
6:        try (JammedTurkeyCage t = new JammedTurkeyCage()) {
7:            throw new IllegalStateException("Turkeys ran off");
8:        } finally {
9:            throw new RuntimeException("and we couldn't find them");
10:       } }
```

Line 7 throws an exception. Then Java tries to close the resource and adds a suppressed exception to it. Now we have a problem. The finally block runs after all this. Since line 9 also throws an exception, the previous exception from line 7 is lost, with the code printing the following:

```
Exception in thread "main" java.lang.RuntimeException:
    and we couldn't find them
    at JammedTurkeyCage.main(JammedTurkeyCage.java:9)
```

This has always been and continues to be bad programming practice. We don't want to lose exceptions! Although out of scope for the exam, the reason for this has to do with backward compatibility. This behavior existed before automatic resource management was added.

Formatting Values

We now shift gears a bit and talk about how to format data for users. In this section, we're going to be working with numbers, dates, and times. This is especially important in the next section when we expand customization to different languages and locales. You may want to review Chapter 4, "Core APIs," if you need a refresher on creating various date/time objects.

Formatting Numbers

In Chapter 4, you saw how to control the output of a number using the `String.format()` method. That's useful for simple stuff, but sometimes you need finer-grained control. With that, we introduce the `NumberFormat` abstract class, which has two commonly used methods:

```
public final String format(double number)
public final String format(long number)
```

Since `NumberFormat` is an abstract class, we need the concrete `DecimalFormat` class to use it. It includes a constructor that takes a pattern `String`:

```
public DecimalFormat(String pattern)
```

The patterns can get quite complex. But luckily, for the exam you only need to know about two formatting characters, shown in Table 11.5.

TABLE 11.5   DecimalFormat symbols

Symbol	Meaning	Examples
#	Omit position if no digit exists for it.	$2.2
0	Put 0 in position if no digit exists for it.	$002.20

These examples should help illuminate how these symbols work:

```
12: double d = 1234.567;
13: NumberFormat f1 = new DecimalFormat("###,###,###.0");
14: System.out.println(f1.format(d));   // 1,234.6
15:
16: NumberFormat f2 = new DecimalFormat("000,000,000.00000");
```

```
17: System.out.println(f2.format(d));  // 000,001,234.56700
18:
19: NumberFormat f3 = new DecimalFormat("Your Balance $#,###,###.##");
20: System.out.println(f3.format(d));  // Your Balance $1,234.57
```

Line 14 displays the digits in the number, rounding to the nearest 10th after the decimal. The extra positions to the left are omitted because we used #. Line 17 adds leading and trailing zeros to make the output the desired length. Line 20 shows prefixing a nonformatting character along with rounding because fewer digits are printed than available. Notice that the commas are automatically removed if they are used between # symbols.

As you shall see in the localization section of this chapter, there's a second concrete class that inherits NumberFormat called CompactNumberFormat, which you'll need to know for the exam.

Formatting Dates and Times

The date and time classes support many methods to get data out of them.

```
LocalDate date = LocalDate.of(2025, Month.OCTOBER, 20);
System.out.println(date.getDayOfWeek());  // MONDAY
System.out.println(date.getMonth());      // OCTOBER
System.out.println(date.getYear());       // 2025
System.out.println(date.getDayOfYear());  // 293
```

Java provides a class called DateTimeFormatter to display standard formats.

```
LocalDate date = LocalDate.of(2025, Month.OCTOBER, 20);
LocalTime time = LocalTime.of(11, 12, 34);
LocalDateTime dt = LocalDateTime.of(date, time);

System.out.println(date.format(DateTimeFormatter.ISO_LOCAL_DATE));
System.out.println(time.format(DateTimeFormatter.ISO_LOCAL_TIME));
System.out.println(dt.format(DateTimeFormatter.ISO_LOCAL_DATE_TIME));
```

The code snippet prints the following:

```
2025-10-20
11:12:34
2025-10-20T11:12:34
```

The DateTimeFormatter will throw an exception if it encounters an incompatible type. For example, each of the following will produce an exception at runtime since it attempts to format a date with a time value, and vice versa:

```
date.format(DateTimeFormatter.ISO_LOCAL_TIME);  // RuntimeException
time.format(DateTimeFormatter.ISO_LOCAL_DATE);  // RuntimeException
```

Customizing the Date/Time Format

If you don't want to use one of the predefined formats, `DateTimeFormatter` supports a custom format using a date format `String`.

```
var f = DateTimeFormatter.ofPattern("MMMM dd, yyyy 'at' hh:mm");
System.out.println(dt.format(f));  // October 20, 2025 at 11:12
```

Let's break this down a bit. Java assigns each letter or symbol a specific date/time part. For example, `M` is used for month, while `y` is used for year. And case matters! Using `m` instead of `M` means it will return the minute of the hour, not the month of the year.

What about the number of symbols? The number often dictates the format of the date/time part. Using `M` by itself outputs the minimum number of characters for a month, such as `1` for January, while using `MM` always outputs two digits, such as `01`. Furthermore, using `MMM` prints the three-letter abbreviation, such as `Jul` for July, while `MMMM` prints the full month name.

> It's possible, albeit unlikely, to come across questions on the exam that use `SimpleDateFormat` rather than the more useful `DateTimeFormatter`. If you do see it on the exam used with an older `java.util.Date` object, just know that the custom formats that are likely to appear on the exam will be compatible with both.

Learning the Standard Date/Time Symbols

For the exam, you should be familiar enough with the various symbols that you can look at a date/time `String` and have a good idea of what the output will be. Table 11.6 includes the symbols you should be familiar with for the exam.

TABLE 11.6   Common date/time symbols

Symbol	Meaning	Examples
y	Year	25, 2025
M	Month	1, 01, Jan, January
d	Day	5, 05
H	24 Hour	15
h	12 Hour	9, 09
m	Minute	45
s	Second	52

Symbol	Meaning	Examples
a	a.m./p.m.	AM, PM
z	Time zone name	`Eastern Standard Time, EST`
Z	Time zone offset	`-0400`

 You may find it difficult to remember the differences between upper and lower case letters in Table 11.6. As a tip, you can remember H is 24 hours and h is 12 hours because uppercase is bigger. Similarly, M is month and m is minute because M is bigger.

Let's try some examples. What do you think the following prints?

```
var dt = LocalDateTime.of(2025, Month.OCTOBER, 20, 6, 15, 30);

var formatter1 = DateTimeFormatter.ofPattern("MM/dd/yyyy hh:mm:ss");
System.out.println(dt.format(formatter1));  // 10/20/2025 06:15:30

var formatter2 = DateTimeFormatter.ofPattern("MM_yyyy_-_dd");
System.out.println(dt.format(formatter2));  // 10_2025_-_20

var formatter3 = DateTimeFormatter.ofPattern("hh:mm:z");
System.out.println(dt.format(formatter3));  // DateTimeException
```

The first example prints the date, with the month before the day, followed by the time. The second example prints the date in a weird format with extra characters that are just displayed as part of the output.

The third example throws an exception at runtime because the underlying `LocalDateTime` does not have a time zone specified. If `ZonedDateTime` were used instead, the code would complete successfully and print something like `06:15 EDT`, depending on the time zone.

As you saw in the previous example, you need to make sure the format `String` is compatible with the underlying date/time type. Table 11.7 shows which symbols you can use with each of the date/time objects.

TABLE 11.7 Supported date/time symbols

Symbol	LocalDate	LocalTime	LocalDateTime	ZonedDateTime
y	√		√	√
M	√		√	√

TABLE 11.7 Supported date/time symbols *(continued)*

Symbol	LocalDate	LocalTime	LocalDateTime	ZonedDateTime
d	√		√	√
h		√	√	√
m		√	√	√
s		√	√	√
a		√	√	√
z				√
Z				√

Make sure you know which symbols are compatible with which date/time types. For example, trying to format a month for a LocalTime or an hour for a LocalDate will result in a runtime exception.

Selecting a *format()* Method

The date/time classes contain a format() method that will take a formatter, while the for-matter classes contain a format() method that will take a date/time value. The result is that either of the following is acceptable:

```
var dateTime = LocalDateTime.of(2025, Month.OCTOBER, 20, 6, 15, 30);
var formatter = DateTimeFormatter.ofPattern("MM/dd/yyyy hh:mm:ss");

System.out.println(dateTime.format(formatter));  // 10/20/2025 06:15:30
System.out.println(formatter.format(dateTime));  // 10/20/2025 06:15:30
```

These statements print the same value at runtime. Which syntax you use is up to you.

Adding Custom Text Values

What if you want your format to include some custom text values? If you just type them as part of the format String, the formatter will interpret each character as a date/time symbol. In the best case, it will display weird data based on extra symbols you enter. In the worst case, it will throw an exception because the characters contain invalid symbols. Neither is desirable!

One way to address this would be to break the formatter into multiple smaller formatters and then concatenate the results.

```
var dt = LocalDateTime.of(2025, Month.OCTOBER, 20, 6, 15, 30);

var f1 = DateTimeFormatter.ofPattern("MMMM dd, yyyy ");
var f2 = DateTimeFormatter.ofPattern(" hh:mm");
System.out.println(dt.format(f1) + "at" + dt.format(f2));
```

This prints `October 20, 2025 at 06:15` at runtime.

While this works, it could become difficult if a lot of text values and date symbols are intermixed. Luckily, Java includes a much simpler solution. You can *escape* the text by surrounding it with a pair of single quotes (`'`). Escaping text instructs the formatter to ignore the values inside the single quotes and just insert them as part of the final value.

```
var f = DateTimeFormatter.ofPattern("MMMM dd, yyyy 'at' hh:mm");
System.out.println(dt.format(f));   // October 20, 2025 at 06:15
```

But what if you need to display a single quote in the output, too? Welcome to the fun of escaping characters! Java supports this by putting two single quotes next to each other.

We conclude our discussion of date formatting with some examples of formats and their output that rely on text values, shown here:

```
var g1 = DateTimeFormatter.ofPattern("MMMM dd', Party''s at' hh:mm");
System.out.println(dt.format(g1));   // October 20, Party's at 06:15


var g2 = DateTimeFormatter.ofPattern("'System format, hh:mm: 'hh:mm");
System.out.println(dt.format(g2));   // System format, hh:mm: 06:15


var g3 = DateTimeFormatter.ofPattern("'NEW! 'yyyy', yay!'");
System.out.println(dt.format(g3));   // NEW! 2025, yay!
```

If you don't escape the text values with single quotes, an exception will be thrown at runtime if the text cannot be interpreted as a date/time symbol.

```
DateTimeFormatter.ofPattern("The time is hh:mm");   // IllegalArgumentException
```

This line throws an exception since T is an unknown symbol. The exam might also present you with an incomplete escape sequence.

```
DateTimeFormatter.ofPattern("'Time is: hh:mm: ");   // IllegalArgumentException
```

Failure to terminate an escape sequence will trigger an exception at runtime.

Supporting Internationalization and Localization

Many applications need to work in different countries and with different languages. For example, consider the sentence "The zoo is holding a special event on 4/1/25 to look at animal behaviors." When is the event? In the United States, it is on April 1. However, a

British reader would interpret this as January 4. A British reader might also wonder why we didn't write "behaviours." If we are making a website or program that will be used in multiple countries, we want to use the correct language and formatting.

Internationalization is the process of designing your program so it can be adapted. This involves placing strings in a properties file and ensuring that the proper data formatters are used. *Localization* means supporting multiple locales or geographic regions. You can think of a locale as being like a language and country pairing. Localization includes translating strings to different languages. It also includes outputting dates and numbers in the correct format for that locale.

> Initially, your program does not need to support multiple locales. The key is to future-proof your application by using these techniques. This way, when your product becomes successful, you can add support for new languages or regions without rewriting everything.

In this section, we look at how to define a locale and use it to format dates, numbers, and strings.

Picking a Locale

While Oracle defines a locale as "a specific geographical, political, or cultural region," you'll only see languages and countries on the exam. Oracle certainly isn't going to delve into political regions that are not countries. That's too controversial for an exam!

The `Locale` class is in the `java.util` package. The first useful `Locale` to find is the user's current locale. Try running the following code on your computer:

```
Locale locale = Locale.getDefault();
System.out.println(locale);
```

When we run it, it prints en_US. It might be different for you. This default output tells us that our computers are using English and are sitting in the United States.

Notice the format. First comes the lowercase language code. The language is always required. Then comes an underscore followed by the uppercase country code. The country is optional. Figure 11.6 shows the two formats for `Locale` objects that you are expected to remember.

FIGURE 11.6 Locale formats

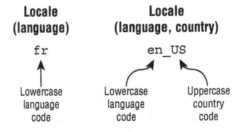

As practice, make sure that you understand why each of these Locale identifiers is invalid:

```
US      // Cannot have country without language
enUS    // Missing underscore
US_en   // The country and language are reversed
EN      // Language must be lowercase
```

The corrected versions are en and en_US.

 You do not need to memorize language or country codes. The exam will let you know about any that are being used. You do need to recognize valid and invalid formats. Pay attention to uppercase/lowercase and the underscore. For example, if you see a locale expressed as es_CO, then you should know that the language is es and the country is CO, even if you didn't know that they represent Spanish and Colombia, respectively.

As a developer, you often need to write code that selects a locale other than the default one. There are three common ways of doing this. The first is to use the built-in constants in the Locale class, available for some common locales.

```
System.out.println(Locale.GERMAN);    // de
System.out.println(Locale.GERMANY);   // de_DE
```

The first example selects the German language, which is spoken in many countries, including Austria (de_AT) and Liechtenstein (de_LI). The second example selects both German the language and Germany the country. While these examples may look similar, they are not the same. Only one includes a country code.

The second way of selecting a Locale is to use the factory Locale.of() methods. You can pass just a language, or both a language and country:

```
System.out.println(Locale.of("fr"));        // fr
System.out.println(Locale.of("hi", "IN"));  // hi_IN
```

The first is the language French, and the second is Hindi in India. Again, you don't need to memorize the codes. Java will let you create a Locale with an invalid language or country, such as xx_XX. However, it will not match the Locale that you want to use, and your program will not behave as expected.

There's a third way to create a Locale that is more flexible. The builder design pattern lets you set all of the properties that you care about and then build the Locale at the end. This means you can specify the properties in any order. The following two Locale values both represent en_US:

```
Locale l1 = new Locale.Builder()
    .setLanguage("en")
    .setRegion("US")
    .build();
```

```
Locale l2 = new Locale.Builder()
    .setRegion("US")
    .setLanguage("en")
    .build();
```

There's actually a fourth way to create a Locale instance, using a Locale constructor, such as new Locale("en") or new Locale("en", "US"). These constructors are now deprecated, so use one of the three previous techniques instead.

When testing a program, you might need to use a Locale other than your computer's default.

```
System.out.println(Locale.getDefault());  // en_US
Locale locale = Locale.of("fr");
Locale.setDefault(locale);
System.out.println(Locale.getDefault());  // fr
```

Try it, and don't worry—the Locale changes for only that one Java program. It does not change any settings on your computer. It does not even change future executions of the same program.

The exam may use setDefault() because it can't make assumptions about where you are located. In practice, we rarely write code to change a user's default locale.

Localizing Numbers

It might surprise you that formatting or parsing currency and number values can change depending on your locale. For example, in the United States, the dollar sign is prepended before the value along with a decimal point for values less than one dollar, such as $2.15. In Germany, though, the euro symbol is appended to the value along with a comma for values less than one euro, such as 2,15 €.

Luckily, the java.text package includes classes to save the day. The following sections cover how to format numbers, currency, and dates based on the locale.

The first step to formatting or parsing data is the same: obtain an instance of a NumberFormat. Table 11.8 shows the available factory methods.

TABLE 11.8   Factory methods to get a NumberFormat

Description	Using default Locale and a specified Locale
General-purpose formatter	NumberFormat.getInstance() NumberFormat.getInstance(Locale locale)
Same as getInstance	NumberFormat.getNumberInstance() NumberFormat.getNumberInstance(Locale locale)

Description	Using default `Locale` and a specified `Locale`
For formatting monetary amounts	`NumberFormat.getCurrencyInstance()` `NumberFormat.getCurrencyInstance(Locale locale)`
For formatting percentages	`NumberFormat.getPercentInstance()` `NumberFormat.getPercentInstance(Locale locale)`
Rounds decimal values before displaying	`NumberFormat.getIntegerInstance()` `NumberFormat.getIntegerInstance(Locale locale)`

Returns compact number formatter	`NumberFormat.getCompactNumberInstance()`
	`NumberFormat.getCompactNumberInstance(`
	`Locale locale, NumberFormat.Style formatStyle)`

Once you have the `NumberFormat` instance, you can call `format()` to turn a number into a `String`, or you can use `parse()` to turn a `String` into a number.

The format classes are not thread-safe. Do not store them in instance variables or `static` variables. You learn more about thread-safety in Chapter 13, "Concurrency."

Formatting Numbers

When we format data, we convert it from a structured object or primitive value into a `String`. The `NumberFormat.format()` method formats the given number based on the locale associated with the `NumberFormat` object.

Let's go back to our zoo for a minute. For marketing literature, we want to share the average monthly number of visitors to the San Diego Zoo. The following shows printing out the same number in three different locales:

```
int attendeesPerYear = 3_200_000;
int attendeesPerMonth = attendeesPerYear / 12;

var us = NumberFormat.getInstance(Locale.US);
System.out.println(us.format(attendeesPerMonth));  // 266,666

var gr = NumberFormat.getInstance(Locale.GERMANY);
System.out.println(gr.format(attendeesPerMonth));  // 266.666

var ca = NumberFormat.getInstance(Locale.CANADA_FRENCH);
System.out.println(ca.format(attendeesPerMonth));  // 266 666
```

This shows how our U.S., German, and French Canadian guests can all see the same information in the number format they are accustomed to using. In practice, we would just call NumberFormat.getInstance() and rely on the user's default locale to format the output.

Formatting currency works the same way.

```
double price = 48;
var myLocale = NumberFormat.getCurrencyInstance();
System.out.println(myLocale.format(price));
```

When run with the default locale of en_US for the United States, this code outputs $48.00. On the other hand, when run with the default locale of en_GB for Great Britain, it outputs £48.00.

 In the real world, use int or BigDecimal for money and not double. Doing math on amounts with double is dangerous because the values are stored as floating-point numbers. Your boss won't appreciate it if you lose pennies or fractions of pennies during transactions!

Finally, the exam may have examples that show formatting percentages:

```
double successRate = 0.802;
var us = NumberFormat.getPercentInstance(Locale.US);
System.out.println(us.format(successRate));  // 80%

var gr = NumberFormat.getPercentInstance(Locale.GERMANY);
System.out.println(gr.format(successRate));  // 80 %
```

Not much difference, we know, but you should at least be aware that the ability to print a percentage is locale-specific for the exam!

Parsing Numbers

When we parse data, we convert it from a String to a structured object or primitive value. The NumberFormat.parse() method accomplishes this and takes the locale into consideration.

For example, if the locale is the English/United States (en_US) and the number contains commas, the commas are treated as formatting symbols. If the locale relates to a country or language that uses commas as a decimal separator, the comma is treated as a decimal point.

Let's look at an example. The following code parses a discounted ticket price with different locales. The parse() method throws a checked ParseException, so make sure to handle or declare it in your own code.

```
String s = "40.45";

var en = NumberFormat.getInstance(Locale.US);
System.out.println(en.parse(s));  // 40.45
```

```
var fr = NumberFormat.getInstance(Locale.FRANCE);
System.out.println(fr.parse(s));   // 40
```

In the United States, a dot (.) is part of a number, and the number is parsed as you might expect. France does not use a decimal point to separate numbers. Java parses it as a formatting character, and it stops looking at the rest of the number. The lesson is to make sure that you parse using the right locale!

The parse() method is also used for parsing currency. For example, we can read in the zoo's monthly income from ticket sales:

```
String income = "$92,807.99";
var cf = NumberFormat.getCurrencyInstance();
double value = (Double) cf.parse(income);
System.out.println(value);   // 92807.99
```

The currency string "$92,807.99" contains a dollar sign and a comma. The parse method strips out the characters and converts the value to a number. The return value of parse is a Number object. Number is the parent class of all the java.lang wrapper classes, so the return value can be cast to its appropriate data type. The Number is cast to a Double and then automatically unboxed into a double.

Formatting with *CompactNumberFormat*

The second class that inherits NumberFormat that you need to know for the exam is CompactNumberFormat. If you haven't seen it before, don't worry, we'll cover it in this section.

CompactNumberFormat is similar to DecimalFormat, but it is designed to be used in places where print space may be limited. It is opinionated in the sense that it picks a format for you, and locale-specific in that output can change depending on your location.

Consider the following sample code that applies a CompactNumberFormat to a group of locales, using a static import for Style (an enum with value SHORT or LONG):

```
var formatters = Stream.of(
    NumberFormat.getCompactNumberInstance(),
    NumberFormat.getCompactNumberInstance(Locale.getDefault(), Style.SHORT),
    NumberFormat.getCompactNumberInstance(Locale.getDefault(), Style.LONG),

    NumberFormat.getCompactNumberInstance(Locale.GERMAN, Style.SHORT),
    NumberFormat.getCompactNumberInstance(Locale.GERMAN, Style.LONG),

    NumberFormat.getNumberInstance());

formatters.map(s -> s.format(7_123_456)).forEach(System.out::println);
```

The following is printed by this code when run in the en_US locale (line breaks added for readability):

```
7M
7M
```

```
7 million
```

```
7 Mio.
7 Millionen
```

```
7,123,456
```

Notice that the first two lines are the same. If you don't specify a style, SHORT is used by default. Next, notice that the values except the last one (which doesn't use a compact number formatter) are truncated. There's a reason it's called a compact number formatter! Also, notice that the short form uses common labels for large values, such as K for thousand. Last but not least, the output may differ for you when you run this, as it was run in an en_US locale.

Using the same formatters, let's try another example:

```
formatters.map(s -> s.format(314_900_000)).forEach(System.out::println);
```

This prints the following when run in the en_US locale:

```
315M
315M
315 million
```

```
315 Mio.
315 Millionen
```

```
314,900,000
```

Notice that the third digit is automatically rounded up for the entries that use a CompactNumberFormat. The following summarizes the rules for CompactNumberFormat:

- First it determines the highest range for the number, such as thousand (K), million (M), billion (B), or trillion (T).
- It then returns up to the first three digits of that range, rounding the last digit as needed.
- Finally, it prints an identifier. If SHORT is used, a symbol is returned. If LONG is used, a space followed by a word is returned.

For the exam, make sure you understand the difference between the SHORT and LONG formats and common symbols like M for million.

 While certainly out of scope for the exam, some CompactNumberFormat instances will display more than three digits if the value is higher than the supported range. For example, using Long.MAX_VALUE will display seven digits (9223372T) in the previous example, as trillion (10^{12}) is the highest range that the instance will use.

CompactNumberFormat can also be used for parsing, although not always in the way you might expect! Consider this example:

```
20: var locale = Locale.of("en", "US");
21: var compact = NumberFormat.getCompactNumberInstance(
22:    locale, Style.SHORT);
23: System.out.println(compact.format(1_000_000));  // 1M
24: System.out.println(compact.parse("1M"));         // 1000000
25: System.out.println(compact.parse("1000000"));    // 1000000
26: System.out.println(compact.parse("1,000,000"));  // 1
27: System.out.println(compact.parse("$1000000"));   // ParseException
```

Lines 20-23 should look familiar. They print a million using the short format of 1M. Lines 24 and 25 shows that the format is flexible in taking the original or shortened format. Line 26 might surprise you as Java stops at the initial punctuation and only prints 1. By contrast, line 27 is a road too far. Java doesn't know what to do with the $ and throws a ParseException.

Localizing Dates

Like numbers, date formats can vary by locale. Table 11.9 shows methods used to retrieve an instance of a DateTimeFormatter using the default locale.

TABLE 11.9   Factory methods to get a DateTimeFormatter

Description	Using default Locale
For formatting dates	DateTimeFormatter.ofLocalizedDate(FormatStyle dateStyle)
For formatting times	DateTimeFormatter.ofLocalizedTime(FormatStyle timeStyle)
For formatting dates and times	DateTimeFormatter.ofLocalizedDateTime(FormatStyle dateStyle, FormatStyle timeStyle) DateTimeFormatter.ofLocalizedDateTime(FormatStyle dateTimeStyle)

Each method in the table takes a FormatStyle parameter (or two) with possible values SHORT, MEDIUM, LONG, and FULL. For the exam, you are not required to know the format of each of these styles.

What if you need a formatter for a specific locale? Easy enough—just append withLocale(locale) to the method call.

Let's put it all together. Take a look at the following code snippet:

```
public static void print(DateTimeFormatter dtf,
      LocalDateTime dateTime, Locale locale) {
   System.out.println(dtf.format(dateTime) + " --- "
      + dtf.withLocale(locale).format(dateTime));
}

public static void main(String[] args) {
   Locale.setDefault(Locale.of("en", "US"));
   var italy = Locale.of("it", "IT");
   var dt = LocalDateTime.of(2025, Month.OCTOBER, 20, 15, 12, 34);

   // 10/20/25 --- 20/10/25
   print(DateTimeFormatter.ofLocalizedDate(FormatStyle.SHORT), dt, italy);

   // 3:12 PM --- 15:12
   print(DateTimeFormatter.ofLocalizedTime(FormatStyle.SHORT), dt, italy);

   // 10/20/25, 3:12 PM --- 20/10/25, 15:12
   print(DateTimeFormatter.ofLocalizedDateTime(
      FormatStyle.SHORT, FormatStyle.SHORT), dt, italy);
}
```

First we establish en_US as the default locale, with it_IT as the requested locale. We then output each value using the two locales. As you can see, applying a locale has a big impact on the built-in date and time formatters.

Specifying a Locale Category

When you call Locale.setDefault() with a locale, several display and formatting options are internally selected. If you require finer-grained control of the default locale, Java subdivides the underlying formatting options into distinct categories with the Locale.Category enum.

The Locale.Category enum is a nested element in Locale that supports distinct locales for displaying and formatting data. For the exam, you should be familiar with the two enum values in Table 11.10.

TABLE 11.10   Locale.Category values

Value	Description
DISPLAY	Category used for displaying data about locale
FORMAT	Category used for formatting dates, numbers, or currencies

When you call `Locale.setDefault()` with a locale, the DISPLAY and FORMAT are set together. Let's take a look at an example:

```
public static void printCurrency(Locale locale, double money) {
   System.out.println(
      NumberFormat.getCurrencyInstance().format(money)
      + ", " + locale.getDisplayLanguage());
}

public static void main(String[] args) {
   var spain = Locale.of("es", "ES");
   var money = 1.23;

   // Print with default locale
   Locale.setDefault(Locale.of("en", "US"));
   printCurrency(spain, money);   // $1.23, Spanish

   // Print with selected locale display
   Locale.setDefault(Category.DISPLAY, spain);
   printCurrency(spain, money);   // $1.23, español

   // Print with selected locale format
   Locale.setDefault(Category.FORMAT, spain);
   printCurrency(spain, money);   // 1,23 €, español
}
```

The code prints the same data three times. First it prints the money variable and the language value of spain using the locale en_US. Then it prints it using the DISPLAY category of es_ES, while the FORMAT category remains en_US. Finally, it prints the data using both categories set to es_ES.

For the exam, you do not need to memorize the various display and formatting options for each category. You just need to know that you can set parts of the locale independently. You should also know that calling `Locale.setDefault(Locale.US)` after the previous code snippet will change both locale categories to en_US.

Loading Properties with Resource Bundles

Up until now, we've kept all of the text strings displayed to our users as part of the program inside the classes that use them. Localization requires externalizing them to elsewhere.

A *resource bundle* contains the locale-specific objects to be used by a program. It is like a map with keys and values. The resource bundle is commonly stored in a properties file. A *properties file* is a text file in a specific format with key/value pairs.

Our zoo program has been successful. We are now getting requests to use it at three more zoos! We already have support for U.S.-based zoos. We now need to add Zoo de La Palmyre in France, the Greater Vancouver Zoo in English-speaking Canada, and Zoo de Granby in French-speaking Canada.

We immediately realize that we are going to need to internationalize our program. Resource bundles will be quite helpful. They will let us easily translate our application to multiple locales or even support multiple locales at once. It will also be easy to add more locales later if zoos in even more countries are interested. We thought about which locales we need to support, and we came up with these four:

```
Locale us           = Locale.of("en", "US");
Locale france       = Locale.of("fr", "FR");
Locale englishCanada = Locale.of("en", "CA");
Locale frenchCanada = Locale.of("fr", "CA");
```

In the next sections, we create a resource bundle using properties files. It is conceptually similar to a `Map<String,String>`, with each line representing a different key/value. The key and value are separated by an equal sign (=) or colon (:). To keep things simple, we use an equal sign throughout this chapter. We also look at how Java determines which resource bundle to use.

Creating a Resource Bundle

We're going to update our application to support the four locales listed previously. Luckily, Java doesn't require us to create four different resource bundles. If we don't have a country-specific resource bundle, Java will use a language-specific one. It's a bit more involved than this, but let's start with a simple example.

For now, we need English and French properties files for our Zoo resource bundle. First, create two properties files.

Zoo_en.properties
```
hello=Hello
open=The zoo is open
```

Zoo_fr.properties
```
hello=Bonjour
open=Le zoo est ouvert
```

The filenames match the name of our resource bundle, Zoo. They are then followed by an underscore (_), target locale, and `.properties` file extension. We can write our very first program that uses a resource bundle to print this information.

```
10: public static void printWelcomeMessage(Locale locale) {
11:     var rb = ResourceBundle.getBundle("Zoo", locale);
12:     System.out.println(rb.getString("hello")
13:         + ", " + rb.getString("open"));
```

```
14: }
15: public static void main(String[] args) {
16:     var us = Locale.of("en", "US");
17:     var france = Locale.of("fr", "FR");
18:     printWelcomeMessage(us);      // Hello, The zoo is open
19:     printWelcomeMessage(france); // Bonjour, Le zoo est ouvert
20: }
```

Lines 16 and 17 create the two locales that we want to test, but the method on lines 10–14 does the actual work. Line 11 calls a factory method on ResourceBundle to get the right resource bundle. Lines 12 and 13 retrieve the right string from the resource bundle and print the results.

Since a resource bundle contains key/value pairs, you can even loop through them to list all of the pairs. The ResourceBundle class provides a keySet() method to get a set of all keys.

```
var us = Locale.of("en", "US");
ResourceBundle rb = ResourceBundle.getBundle("Zoo", us);
rb.keySet().stream()
    .map(k -> k + ": " + rb.getString(k))
    .forEach(System.out::println);
```

This example goes through all of the keys. It maps each key to a String with both the key and the value before printing everything.

```
hello: Hello
open: The zoo is open
```

 Real World Scenario

Loading Resource Bundle Files at Runtime

For the exam, you don't need to know where the properties files for the resource bundles are stored. If the exam provides a properties file, it is safe to assume that it exists and is loaded at runtime.

In your own applications, though, the resource bundles can be stored in a variety of places. While they can be stored inside the JAR that uses them, doing so is not recommended. This approach forces you to rebuild the application JAR any time some text changes. One of the benefits of using resource bundles is to decouple the application code from the locale-specific text data.

Another approach is to have all of the properties files in a separate properties JAR or folder and load them in the classpath at runtime. In this manner, a new language can be added without changing the application JAR.

Picking a Resource Bundle

There are two methods for obtaining a resource bundle that you should be familiar with for the exam.

```
ResourceBundle.getBundle("name");
ResourceBundle.getBundle("name", locale);
```

The first uses the default locale. You are likely to use this one in programs that you write. Either the exam tells you what to assume as the default locale or it uses the second approach.

Java handles the logic of picking the best available resource bundle for a given key. It tries to find the most specific value. Table 11.11 shows what Java goes through when asked for resource bundle Zoo with the locale `Locale.of("fr", "FR")` when the default locale is U.S. English.

TABLE 11.11   Picking a resource bundle for French/France with default locale English/US

Step	Looks for file	Reason
1	Zoo_fr_FR.properties	Requested locale
2	Zoo_fr.properties	Language we requested with no country
3	Zoo_en_US.properties	Default locale
4	Zoo_en.properties	Default locale's language with no country
5	Zoo.properties	No locale at all—default bundle
6	If still not found, throw MissingResourceException	No locale or default bundle available

As another way of remembering the order of Table 11.11, learn these steps:

1. Look for the resource bundle for the requested locale, followed by the one for the default locale.

2. For each locale, check the language/country, followed by just the language.

3. Use the default resource bundle if no matching locale can be found.

As we mentioned earlier, Java supports resource bundles from Java classes and properties alike. When Java is searching for a matching resource bundle, it will first check for a resource bundle file with the matching class name. For the exam, you just need to know how to work with properties files.

Let's see if you understand Table 11.11. What is the maximum number of files that Java would need to consider in order to find the appropriate resource bundle with the following code?

```
Locale.setDefault(Locale.of("hi"));
ResourceBundle rb = ResourceBundle.getBundle("Zoo", Locale.of("en"));
```

The answer is three. They are listed here:

1. `Zoo_en.properties`
2. `Zoo_hi.properties`
3. `Zoo.properties`

The requested locale is en, so we start with that. Since the en locale does not contain a country, we move on to the default locale, hi. Again, there's no country, so we end with the default bundle.

Selecting Resource Bundle Values

Got all that? Good—because there is a twist. The steps that we've discussed so far are for finding the matching resource bundle to use as a base. Java isn't required to get all of the keys from the same resource bundle. It can get them from *any parent of the matching resource bundle*. A parent resource bundle in the hierarchy just removes components of the name until it gets to the top. Table 11.12 shows how to do this.

TABLE 11.12   Selecting resource bundle properties

Matching resource bundle	Properties files keys can come from
Zoo_fr_FR	Zoo_fr_FR.properties Zoo_fr.properties Zoo.properties

Once a resource bundle has been selected, *only properties along a single hierarchy will be used*. Contrast this behavior with Table 11.11, in which the default en_US resource bundle is used if no other resource bundles are available.

What does this mean, exactly? Assume the requested locale is fr_FR and the default is en_US. The JVM will provide data from en_US *only if there is no matching fr_FR or fr resource bundle*. If it finds a fr_FR or fr resource bundle, then only those bundles, along with the default bundle, will be used.

Let's put all of this together and print some information about our zoos. We have a number of properties files this time.

Zoo.properties
```
name=Vancouver Zoo
```

Zoo_en.properties
```
hello=Hello
open=is open
```

Zoo_en_US.properties
```
name=The Zoo
```

Zoo_en_CA.properties
```
visitors=Canada visitors
```

Suppose that we have a visitor from Québec (which has a default locale of French Canada) who has asked the program to provide information in English. What do you think this outputs?

```
10: Locale.setDefault(Locale.of("en", "US"));
11: var locale = Locale.of("en", "CA");
12: ResourceBundle rb = ResourceBundle.getBundle("Zoo", locale);
13:
14: System.out.print(rb.getString("hello"));
15: System.out.print(". ");
16: System.out.print(rb.getString("name"));
17: System.out.print(" ");
18: System.out.print(rb.getString("open"));
19: System.out.print(" ");
20: System.out.print(rb.getString("visitors"));
```

The program prints the following:

Hello. Vancouver Zoo is open Canada visitors

The default locale is en_US, and the requested locale is en_CA. First, Java goes through the available resource bundles to find a match. It finds one right away with Zoo_en_CA.properties. This means the default locale of en_US is irrelevant.

After line 12, the resource bundle is selected, and Java will only consider files it finds that are part of this resource bundle, namely Zoo_en_CA.properties, Zoo_en.properties, and Zoo.properties, in this order.

Line 14 doesn't find a match for the key hello in Zoo_en_CA.properties, so it goes up the hierarchy to Zoo_en.properties. Line 16 doesn't find a match for name in either of the first two properties files, so it has to go all the way to the top of the hierarchy to Zoo .properties. Line 18 has the same experience as line 14, using Zoo_en.properties. Finally, line 20 has an easier job of it and finds a matching key in Zoo_en_CA.properties.

In this example, only three properties files were used. Even when the property wasn't found in en_CA or en resource bundles, the program preferred using Zoo.properties (the default resource bundle) rather than Zoo_en_US.properties (the default locale).

What if a property is not found in any resource bundle? Then an exception is thrown. For example, attempting to retrieve a non-existent property results in an exception:

```
System.out.print(rb.getString("close"));   // MissingResourceException
```

Formatting Messages

Often we just want to output the text data from a resource bundle, but sometimes you want to format that data with parameters. In real programs, it is common to substitute variables in the middle of a resource bundle string. The convention is to use a number inside braces such as {0}, {1}, etc. The number indicates the order in which the parameters will be passed. Although resource bundles don't support this directly, the MessageFormat class does.

For example, suppose that we had this property defined:

```
helloGreeting=Hello, {0} and {1}
```

In Java, we can read in the value normally. After that, we can run it through the MessageFormat class to substitute the parameters. The second parameter to format() is a vararg, allowing you to specify any number of input values.

Suppose we have a resource bundle rb:

```
String greeting = rb.getString("helloGreeting");
System.out.print(MessageFormat.format(greeting, "Tammy", "Henry"));
```

This will print the following:

```
Hello, Tammy and Henry
```

Using the *Properties* Class

When working with the ResourceBundle class, you may also come across the Properties class. It functions like the HashMap class that you learned about in Chapter 9, "Collections and Generics," except that it uses String values for the keys and values. Let's create one and set some values.

```
import java.util.Properties;
public class ZooOptions {
   public static void main(String[] args) {
      var props = new Properties();
      props.setProperty("name", "Our zoo");
      props.setProperty("open", "10am");
   }
}
```

The Properties class is commonly used in handling values that may not exist.

```
System.out.println(props.getProperty("camel"));           // null
System.out.println(props.getProperty("camel", "Bob"));   // Bob
```

If a key were passed that actually existed, both statements would print it. This is commonly referred to as providing a default, or a backup value, for a missing key.

The `Properties` class also includes a `get()` method, but only `getProperty()` allows for a default value. For example, the following call is invalid since `get()` takes only a single parameter:

```
props.get("open");                                        // 10am
```

```
props.get("open", "The zoo will be open soon");  // DOES NOT COMPILE
```

Summary

This chapter covered a wide variety of topics centered around building applications that respond well to change. We started our discussion with exception handling. Exceptions can be divided into two categories: checked and unchecked. In Java, checked exceptions inherit `Exception` but not `RuntimeException` and must be handled or declared. Unchecked exceptions inherit `RuntimeException` or `Error` and do not need to be handled or declared. It is considered a poor practice to catch an `Error`.

You can create your own checked or unchecked exceptions by extending `Exception` or `RuntimeException`, respectively. You can also define custom constructors and messages for your exceptions, which will show up in stack traces.

Automatic resource management can be enabled by using a try-with-resources statement to ensure that the resources are properly closed. Resources are closed at the conclusion of the `try` block, in the reverse of the order in which they are declared. A suppressed exception occurs when more than one exception is thrown, often as part of a `finally` block or try-with-resources `close()` operation.

Java includes a number of built-in classes to format numbers and dates. We reviewed how to create custom formatters for each. You should be able to read these custom formats when you encounter them on the exam.

Localization involves creating programs that adapt to change. You can create a `Locale` class with a required lowercase language code and optional uppercase country code. For example, en and en_US are locales for English and U.S. English, respectively. You need to know how to format number and date/time values based on locale, including the new `CompactNumberFormat` class.

A `ResourceBundle` allows specifying key/value pairs in a properties file. Java goes through candidate resource bundles from the most specific to the most general to find a match. If no matches are found for the requested locale, Java switches to the default locale and then finally the default resource bundle. Once a matching resource bundle is found, Java looks only in the hierarchy of that resource bundle to select values.

By applying the principles you learned about in this chapter to your own projects, you can build applications that last longer, with built-in support for whatever unexpected events may arise.

Exam Essentials

Understand the various types of exceptions.   All exceptions are subclasses of java.lang.Throwable. Subclasses of java.lang.Error should never be caught. Only subclasses of java.lang.Exception should be handled in application code.

Differentiate between checked and unchecked exceptions.   Unchecked exceptions do not need to be caught or handled and are subclasses of java.lang.RuntimeException or java.lang.Error. All other subclasses of java.lang.Exception are checked exceptions and must be handled or declared.

Understand the flow of a *try* statement.   A try statement must have a catch or a finally block. Multiple catch blocks can be chained together, provided no superclass exception type appears in an earlier catch block than its subclass. A multi-catch expression may be used to handle multiple exceptions in the same catch block, provided one exception is not a subclass of another. The finally block runs last regardless of whether an exception is thrown.

Be able to follow the order of a try-with-resources statement.   A try-with-resources statement is a special type of try block in which one or more resources are declared and automatically closed in the reverse of the order in which they are declared. It can be used with or without a catch or finally block, with the implicit finally block always executed first.

Be able to write methods that declare exceptions.   Understand the difference between the throw and throws keywords and how to declare methods with exceptions. Know how to correctly override a method that declares exceptions.

Identify valid locale strings.   Know that the language code is lowercase and mandatory, while the country code is uppercase and optional. Be able to select a locale using a built-in constant, factory method, or builder class.

Format dates, numbers, and messages.   Be able to format dates, numbers, and messages into various String formats, and know how locale influences these formats. Know how the various number formatters (currency, percent, compact) differ. Be able to write a custom date or number formatter using symbols, including knowing how to escape literal values.

Determine which resource bundle Java will use to look up a key.   Be able to create resource bundles for a set of locales using properties files. Know the search order that Java uses to select a resource bundle and how the default locale and default resource bundle are considered. Once a resource bundle is found, recognize the hierarchy used to select values.

Review Questions

The answers to the chapter review questions can be found in the Appendix.

1. Which of the following can be inserted on line 8 to make this code compile? (Choose all that apply.)

```
7: public void whatHappensNext() throws IOException {
8:    // INSERT CODE HERE
9: }
```

   A. `System.out.println("it's ok");`

   B. `throw new Exception();`

   C. `throw new IllegalArgumentException();`

   D. `throw new java.io.IOException();`

   E. `throw new RuntimeException();`

   F. None of the above

2. Which statement about the following class is correct?

```
1:  class Problem extends Exception {
2:     public Problem() {}
3:  }
4:  class YesProblem extends Problem {}
5:  public class MyDatabase {
6:     public static void connectToDatabase() throw Problem {
7:        throws new YesProblem();
8:     }
9:     public static void main(String[] c) throw Exception {
10:       connectToDatabase();
11:    }
12: }
```

   A. The code compiles and prints a stack trace for `YesProblem` at runtime.

   B. The code compiles and prints a stack trace for `Problem` at runtime.

   C. The code does not compile because `Problem` defines a constructor.

   D. The code does not compile because `YesProblem` does not define a constructor.

   E. The code does not compile but would if `Problem` and `YesProblem` were switched on lines 6 and 7.

   F. None of the above.

3. Which of the following are common types to localize? (Choose all that apply.)

   A. Dates

   B. Lambda expressions

   C. Class names

   D. Currency

   E. Numbers

   F. Variable names

4. What is the output of the following snippet, assuming a and b are both 0?

```
3:  try {
4:      System.out.print(a / b);
5:  } catch (RuntimeException e) {
6:      System.out.print(-1);
7:  } catch (ArithmeticException e) {
8:      System.out.print(0);
9:  } finally {
10:     System.out.print("done");
11: }
```

   A. -1

   B. 0

   C. done-1

   D. done0

   E. The code does not compile.

   F. An uncaught exception is thrown.

   G. None of the above.

5. Assuming the current locale uses dollars ($) and the following method is called with a double value of 100_102.2, which of the following values are printed? (Choose all that apply.)

```
public void print(double t) {
   System.out.print(NumberFormat.getCompactNumberInstance().format(t));

   System.out.print(
      NumberFormat.getCompactNumberInstance(
         Locale.getDefault(), Style.SHORT).format(t));

   System.out.print(NumberFormat.getCurrencyInstance().format(t));
}
```

   A. 100

   B. $100,000.00

    C. 100K

    D. 100 thousand

    E. 100M

    F. $100,102.20

    G. None of the above

6. What is the output of the following code?

```
LocalDate date = LocalDate.parse("2025-04-30",
   DateTimeFormatter.ISO_LOCAL_DATE_TIME);
System.out.println(date.getYear() + " "
   + date.getMonth() + " "+ date.getDayOfMonth());
```

    A. 2025 APRIL 2

    B. 2025 APRIL 30

    C. 2025 MAY 2

    D. The code does not compile.

    E. A runtime exception is thrown.

7. What does the following method print?

```
11: public void tryAgain(String s) {
12:    try (FileReader r = null, p = new FileReader("")) {
13:       System.out.print("X");
14:       throw new IllegalArgumentException();
15:    } catch (Exception s) {
16:       System.out.print("A");
17:       throw new FileNotFoundException();
18:    } finally {
19:       System.out.print("O");
20:    }
21: }
```

    A. XAO

    B. XOA

    C. One line of this method contains a compiler error.

    D. Two lines of this method contain compiler errors.

    E. Three or more lines of this method contain compiler errors.

    F. The code compiles, but a NullPointerException is thrown at runtime.

    G. None of the above.

8. Assume that all of the files mentioned in the answer choices exist and define the same keys. Which one will be used to find the key in line 8?

```
6: Locale.setDefault(Locale.of("en", "US"));
7: var b = ResourceBundle.getBundle("Dolphins");
8: System.out.println(b.getString("name"));
```

   A. Dolphins.properties

   B. Dolphins_US.properties

   C. Dolphins_en.properties

   D. Whales.properties

   E. Whales_en_US.properties

   F. The code does not compile.

9. For what value of `pattern` will the following print `<005.21>` `<008.49>` `<1,234.0>`?

```
String pattern = "_____";
var message = DoubleStream.of(5.21, 8.49, 1234)
    .mapToObj(v -> new DecimalFormat(pattern).format(v))
    .collect(Collectors.joining("> <"));
System.out.println("<"+message+">");
```

   A. ##.#

   B. 0,000.0#

   C. #,###.0

   D. #,###,000.0#

   E. The code does not compile regardless of what is placed in the blank.

   F. None of the above.

10. Which scenario is the best use of an exception?

   A. An element is not found when searching a list.

   B. An unexpected parameter is passed into a method.

   C. The computer caught fire.

   D. You want to loop through a list.

   E. You don't know how to code a method.

11. Which of the following exceptions must be handled or declared in the method in which they are thrown? (Choose all that apply.)

```
class Apple extends RuntimeException {}
class Orange extends Exception {}
class Banana extends Error {}
```

```
class Pear extends Apple {}
class Tomato extends Orange {}
class Peach extends Throwable {}
```

A. Apple

B. Orange

C. Banana

D. Pear

E. Tomato

F. Peach

12. Which of the following changes, when made independently, would make this code compile? (Choose all that apply.)

```
1:  import java.io.*;
2:  public class StuckTurkeyCage implements AutoCloseable {
3:     public void close() throws IOException {
4:        throw new FileNotFoundException("Cage not closed");
5:     }
6:     public static void main(String[] args) {
7:        try (StuckTurkeyCage t = new StuckTurkeyCage()) {
8:           System.out.println("put turkeys in");
9:        }
10:   } }
```

A. Remove `throws IOException` from the declaration on line 3.

B. Add `throws Exception` to the declaration on line 6.

C. Change line 9 to `} catch (Exception e) {}`.

D. Change line 9 to `} finally {}`.

E. The code compiles as is.

F. None of the above.

13. Which of the following are true statements about exception handling in Java? (Choose all that apply.)

A. A traditional `try` statement without a `catch` block requires a `finally` block.

B. A traditional `try` statement without a `finally` block requires a `catch` block.

C. A traditional `try` statement with only one statement can omit the {}.

D. A try-with-resources statement without a `catch` block requires a `finally` block.

E. A try-with-resources statement without a `finally` block requires a `catch` block.

F. A try-with-resources statement with only one statement can omit the {}.

14. Assuming -g:vars is used when the code is compiled to include debug information, what is the output of the following code snippet?

```
var huey = (String)null;
Integer dewey = null;
Object louie = null;
if(louie == huey.substring(dewey.intValue())) {
    System.out.println("Quack!");
}
```

A. A NullPointerException that does not include any variable names in the stack trace

B. A NullPointerException naming huey in the stack trace

C. A NullPointerException naming dewey in the stack trace

D. A NullPointerException naming louie in the stack trace

E. A NullPointerException naming huey and louie in the stack trace

F. A NullPointerException naming huey and dewey in the stack trace

G. None of the above

15. Which of the following, when inserted independently in the blank, use locale parameters that are properly formatted? (Choose all that apply.)

```
import java.util.Locale;
public class ReadMap implements AutoCloseable {
    private Locale locale;
    private boolean closed = false;
    @Override public void close() {
        System.out.println("Folding map");
        locale = null;
        closed = true;
    }
    public void open() {
        this.locale = _____;
    }
    public void use() {
        // Implementation omitted
    }
}
```

A. Locale.of("xM")

B. Locale.of("MQ", "ks")

C. Locale.of("qw")

D. Locale.of("wp", "VW")

  E. `Locale.create("zp")`

  F. `new Locale.Builder().setLanguage("yw").setRegion("PM")`

  G. The code does not compile regardless of what is placed in the blank.

16. Which of the following can be inserted into the blank to allow the code to compile and run without throwing an exception?

```
var f = DateTimeFormatter.ofPattern("hh o'clock");
System.out.println(f.format(_____.now()));
```

  A. `ZonedTime`

  B. `LocalDate`

  C. `LocalTimestamp`

  D. `LocalTime`

  E. The code does not compile regardless of what is placed in the blank.

  F. None of the above.

17. Which of the following statements about resource bundles are correct? (Choose all that apply.)

  A. All keys must be in the same resource bundle to be used.

  B. A resource bundle is loaded by calling the `new ResourceBundle()` constructor.

  C. Resource bundle values are always read using the `Properties` class.

  D. Changing the default locale lasts for only a single run of the program.

  E. If a resource bundle for a specific locale is requested, then the resource bundle for the default locale will not be used.

  F. It is possible to use a resource bundle for a locale without specifying a default locale.

18. What is the output of the following code?

```
import java.io.*;
public class FamilyCar {
    static class Door implements AutoCloseable {
        public void close() {
            System.out.print("D");
    } }
    static class Window implements Closeable {
        public void close() {
            System.out.print("W");
            throw new RuntimeException();
    } }
    public static void main(String[] args) {
        var d = new Door();
        try (d; var w = new Window()) {
```

```
      System.out.print("T");
    } catch (Exception e) {
      System.out.print("E");
    } finally {
      System.out.print("F");
    } } }
```

A. TWF

B. TWDF

C. TWDEF

D. TWF followed by an exception

E. TWDF followed by an exception

F. TWEF followed by an exception

G. The code does not compile.

19. Suppose that we have the following three properties files and code. Which bundles are used on lines 8 and 9, respectively?

Dolphins.properties
```
name=The Dolphin
age=0
```

Dolphins_en.properties
```
name=Dolly
age=4
```

Dolphins_fr.properties
```
name=Dolly
```

```
5: var fr = Locale.of("fr");
6: Locale.setDefault(Locale.of("en", "US"));
7: var b = ResourceBundle.getBundle("Dolphins", fr);
8: b.getString("name");
9: b.getString("age");
```

A. Dolphins.properties and Dolphins.properties

B. Dolphins.properties and Dolphins_en.properties

C. Dolphins_en.properties and Dolphins_en.properties

D. Dolphins_fr.properties and Dolphins.properties

E. Dolphins_fr.properties and Dolphins_en.properties

F. The code does not compile.

G. None of the above.

20. What is printed by the following program?

```
1:  public class DriveBus {
2:     public void go() {
3:        System.out.print("A");
4:        try {
5:           stop();
6:        } catch (ArithmeticException e) {
7:           System.out.print("B");
8:        } finally {
9:           System.out.print("C");
10:       }
11:       System.out.print("D");
12:    }
13:    public void stop() {
14:       System.out.print("E");
15:       Object x = null;
16:       x.toString();
17:       System.out.print("F");
18:    }
19:    public static void main(String n[]) {
20:       new DriveBus().go();
21:    } }
```

A. AE

B. AEBCD

C. AEC

D. AECD

E. AE followed by a stack trace

F. AEBCD followed by a stack trace

G. AEC followed by a stack trace

H. A stack trace with no other output

21. Which change allows the following program to compile?

```
1: public class AhChoo {
2:    static class SneezeException extends Exception {}
3:    static class SniffleException extends SneezeException {}
4:    public static void main(String[] args) {
5:       try {
6:          throw new SneezeException();
7:       } catch (SneezeException | SniffleException e) {
```

```
8:        } finally {}
9:    } }
```

A. Add throws `SneezeException` to the declaration on line 4.

B. Add throws `Throwable` to the declaration on line 4.

C. Change line 7 to `} catch (SneezeException e) {`.

D. Change line 7 to `} catch (SniffleException e) {`.

E. Remove line 7.

F. The code compiles correctly as is.

G. None of the above.

22. What is the output of the following code?

```
try {
    LocalDateTime book = LocalDateTime.of(2025, 4, 5, 12, 30, 20);
    System.out.print(book.format(DateTimeFormatter.ofPattern("m")));
    System.out.print(book.format(DateTimeFormatter.ofPattern("z")));
    System.out.print(DateTimeFormatter.ofPattern("y").format(book));
} catch (Throwable e) {}
```

A. 4

B. 30

C. 402

D. 3002

E. 3002025

F. 402025

G. None of the above

23. Fill in the blank: A class that implements _____ may be in a try-with-resources statement. (Choose all that apply.)

A. `AutoCloseable`

B. `Resource`

C. `Exception`

D. `AutomaticResource`

E. `Closeable`

F. `RuntimeException`

G. `Serializable`

24. What is the output of the following program?

```
public class SnowStorm {
    static class WalkToSchool implements AutoCloseable {
        public void close() {
```

```
            throw new RuntimeException("flurry");
      } }
   public static void main(String[] args) {
      WalkToSchool walk1 = new WalkToSchool();
      try (walk1; WalkToSchool walk2 = new WalkToSchool()) {
         throw new RuntimeException("blizzard");
      } catch(Exception e) {
         System.out.println(e.getMessage()
            + " " + e.getSuppressed().length);
      }
      walk1 = null;
   } }
```

A. blizzard 0

B. blizzard 1

C. blizzard 2

D. flurry 0

E. flurry 1

F. flurry 2

G. None of the above

25. Assuming U.S. currency is in dollars ($) and German currency is in euros (€), what is the output of the following program?

```
import java.text.NumberFormat;
import java.util.Locale;
import java.util.Locale.Category;
public record Wallet(double money) {
   private String openWallet() {
      Locale.setDefault(Category.DISPLAY,
         new Locale.Builder().setRegion("us").build());
      Locale.setDefault(Category.FORMAT,
         new Locale.Builder().setLanguage("en").build());
      return NumberFormat.getCurrencyInstance(Locale.GERMANY)
         .format(money);
   }
   public void printBalance() {
      System.out.println(openWallet());
   }
   public static void main(String... unused) {
      new Wallet(2.4).printBalance();
   } }
```

A. 2,40 €
B. $2.40
C. 2.4
D. The code does not compile.
E. None of the above.

26. Which lines can fill in the blank to make the following code compile? (Choose all that apply.)

```
void rollOut() throws ClassCastException {}
```

```
public void transform(String c) {
   try {
      rollOut();
   } catch (IllegalArgumentException | _____) {
   }
}
```

A. IOException a
B. Error b
C. NullPointerException c
D. RuntimeException d
E. NumberFormatException e
F. ClassCastException f
G. None of the above. The code contains a compiler error regardless of what is inserted into the blank.

Chapter

12

Modules

OCP EXAM OBJECTIVES COVERED IN THIS CHAPTER:

✓ **Packaging and Deploying Java Code**

- Define modules and expose module content, including that by reflection, and declare module dependencies, define services, providers, and consumers.

- Compile Java code, create modular and non-modular jars, runtime images, and implement migration to modules using unnamed and automatic modules.

Packages can be grouped into modules. In this chapter, we explain the purpose of modules and how to build your own. We also show how to run them and how to discover existing modules. Next, we cover strategies for migrating an application to use modules, running a partially modularized application, and dealing with dependencies. We then move on to discuss services and service locators. Finally, we show how to create a runtime image.

We've made the code in this chapter available online. Since it can be tedious to create the directory structure, this will save you some time. Additionally, the commands need to be exactly right, so we've included those online so you can copy and paste them and compare them with what you typed. Both are available in our GitHub repo, linked from:

www.selikoff.net/ocp21

Introducing Modules

When writing code for the exam, you generally see small classes. After all, exam questions have to fit on a single screen! When you work on real programs, they are much bigger. A real project will consist of hundreds or thousands of classes grouped into packages. These packages are grouped into Java archive (JAR) files. A JAR is a zip file with some extra information, and the extension is .jar.

In addition to code written by your team, most applications also use code written by others. *Open source* is software with the code supplied and is often free to use. Java has a vibrant open-source software (OSS) community, and those libraries are also supplied as JAR files. For example, there are libraries to read files, connect to a database, and much more.

Some open-source projects even depend on functionality in other open-source projects. For example, Spring is a commonly used framework, and JUnit is a commonly used testing library. To use either, you need to make sure you have compatible versions of all the relevant JARs available at runtime. This complex chain of dependencies and minimum versions is often referred to by the community as *JAR hell*. Hell is an excellent way of describing the wrong version of a class being loaded or even a ClassNotFoundException at runtime.

The *Java Platform Module System* (JPMS) groups code at a higher level. The main purpose of a module is to provide groups of related packages that offer developers a particular set of functionality. It's like a JAR file, except a developer chooses which packages are accessible outside the module. Let's look at what modules are and what problems they are designed to solve.

The Java Platform Module System includes the following:

- A format for module JAR files
- Partitioning of the JDK into modules
- Additional command-line options for Java tools

Exploring a Module

In Chapter 1, "Building Blocks," we had a small Zoo application. It had only one class and just printed out one thing. Now imagine that we had a whole staff of programmers and were automating the operations of the zoo. Many things need to be coded, including the interactions with the animals, visitors, the public website, and outreach.

A *module* is a group of one or more packages plus a special file called module-info.java. The contents of this file are the *module declaration*. Figure 12.1 lists just a few of the modules a zoo might need. We decided to focus on the animal interactions in our example. The full zoo could easily have a dozen modules. In Figure 12.1, notice that there are arrows between many of the modules. These represent *dependencies*, where one module relies on code in another. The staff needs to feed the animals to keep their jobs. The line from zoo.staff to zoo.animal.feeding shows that the former depends on the latter.

FIGURE 12.1 Design of a modular system

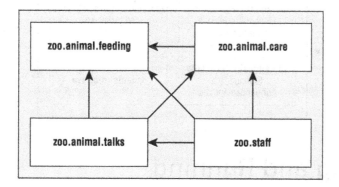

Now let's drill down into one of these modules. Figure 12.2 shows what is inside the zoo.animal.talks module. There are three packages with two classes each. (It's a small zoo.) There is also a strange file called module-info.java. This file is required to be inside all modules. We explain this in more detail later in the chapter.

Benefits of Modules

Modules look like another layer of things you need to know in order to program. While using modules is optional, it is important to understand the problems they are designed to solve.

- **Better access control:** In addition to the levels of access control covered in Chapter 5, "Methods," you can have packages that are only accessible to other packages in the module.

- **Clearer dependency management:** Since modules specify what they rely on, Java can complain about a missing JAR when starting up the program rather than when it is first accessed at runtime.

- **Custom Java builds:** You can create a Java runtime that has only the parts of the JDK that your program needs rather than the full one at over 150 MB.

- **Improved security:** Since you can omit parts of the JDK from your custom build, you don't have to worry about vulnerabilities discovered in a part you don't use.

- **Improved performance:** Another benefit of a smaller Java package is improved startup time and a lower memory requirement.

- **Unique package enforcement:** Since modules specify exposed packages, Java can ensure that each package comes from only one module and avoid confusion about what is being run.

FIGURE 12.2   Looking inside a module

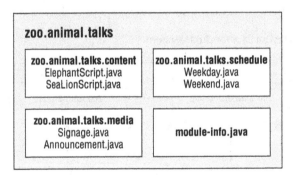

Creating and Running a Modular Program

In this section, we create, build, and run the `zoo.animal.feeding` module. We chose this one to start with because all the other modules depend on it. Figure 12.3 shows the design of this module. In addition to the `module-info.java` file, it has one package with one class inside.

In the next sections, we create, compile, run, and package the `zoo.animal.feeding` module.

FIGURE 12.3 Contents of zoo.animal.feeding

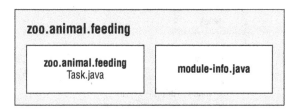

Creating the Files

First we have a really simple class that prints one line in a main() method. We know, that's not much of an implementation. All those programmers we hired can fill it in with business logic. In this book, we focus on what you need to know for the exam. So, let's create a simple class.

```
package zoo.animal.feeding;

public class Task {
   public static void main(String... args) {
      System.out.println("All fed!");
   }
}
```

Next comes the module-info.java file. This is the simplest possible one:

```
module zoo.animal.feeding {
}
```

There are a few key differences between a module declaration and a regular Java class declaration:

- The module-info.java file must be in the root directory of your module. Regular Java classes should be in packages.

- The module declaration must use the keyword module instead of class, interface, or enum.

- The module name follows the naming rules for package names. It often includes periods (.) in its name. Regular class and package names are not allowed to have dashes (-). Module names follow the same rule.

That's a lot of rules for the simplest possible file. There will be many more rules when we flesh out this file later in the chapter.

The next step is to make sure the files are in the right directory structure. Figure 12.4 shows the expected directory structure.

FIGURE 12.4   Module `zoo.animal.feeding` directory structure

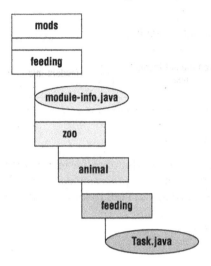

In particular, `feeding` is the module directory, and the `module-info.java` file is directly under it. Just as with a regular JAR file, we also have the `zoo.animal.feeding` package with one subfolder per portion of the name. The `Task` class is in the appropriate subfolder for its package.

Also, note that we created a directory called `mods` at the same level as the module. We use it to store the module artifacts a little later in the chapter. This directory can be named anything, but `mods` is a common name. If you are following along with the online code example, note that the `mods` directory is not included, because it is empty.

Compiling Our First Module

Before we can run modular code, we need to compile it. Other than the `module-path` option, this code should look familiar from Chapter 1:

```
javac --module-path mods
   -d feeding
   feeding/zoo/animal/feeding/*.java feeding/module-info.java
```

 When you're entering commands at the command line, they should be typed all on one line. We use line breaks in the book to make the commands easier to read and study. If you want to use multiple lines at the command prompt, the approach varies by operating system. Linux uses a backslash (\) as the line break.

As a review, the `-d` option specifies the directory to place the class files in. The end of the command is a list of the `.java` files to compile. You can list the files individually or use a wildcard for all `.java` files in a subdirectory.

The new part is module-path. This option indicates the location of any custom module files. In this example, module-path could have been omitted since there are no dependencies. You can think of module-path as replacing the classpath option when you are working on a modular program.

What About the *classpath*?

The classpath option has three possible forms: -cp, --class-path, and -classpath. You can still use these options. In fact, it is common to do so when writing nonmodular programs.

Just like classpath, you can use an abbreviation in the command. The syntax --module-path and -p are equivalent. That means we could have written many other commands in place of the previous command. The following four commands show alternatives if you choose the -p option:

```
javac -p mods -d feeding
    feeding/zoo/animal/feeding/*.java feeding/*.java

javac -p mods -d feeding
    feeding/zoo/animal/feeding/*.java feeding/module-info.java

javac -p mods -d feeding
    feeding/zoo/animal/feeding/Task.java feeding/module-info.java

javac -p mods -d feeding
    feeding/zoo/animal/feeding/Task.java feeding/*.java
```

While you can use whichever you like best, be sure that you can recognize all valid forms for the exam. Table 12.1 lists the options you need to know well when compiling modules. There are many more options you can pass to the javac command, but these are the ones you can expect to be tested on.

TABLE 12.1 Options you need to know for using modules with javac

Use for	Abbreviation	Long form
Directory for class files	-d \<dir>	n/a
Module path	-p \<path>	--module-path \<path>

Real World Scenario

Building Modules

Even without modules, it is rare to run java and java commands manually on a real project. They get long and complicated very quickly. Most developers use a build tool such as Maven or Gradle. These build tools suggest directories in which to place the class files, like target/classes.

It is likely that the only time you need to know the syntax of these commands is when you take the exam. The concepts themselves are useful, regardless.

Be sure to memorize the module command syntax. You will be tested on it on the exam. We give you a lot of practice questions on the syntax to reinforce it.

Running Our First Module

Before we package our module, we should make sure it works by running it. To do that, we need to learn the full syntax. Suppose there is a module named book.module. Inside that module is a package named com.sybex, which has a class named OCP with a main() method. Figure 12.5 shows the syntax for running a module. Pay special attention to the book.module/com.sybex.OCP part. It is important to remember that you specify the module name followed by a slash (/) followed by the fully qualified class name.

FIGURE 12.5   Running a module using java

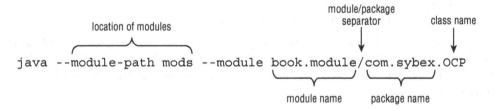

Now that we've seen the syntax, we can write the command to run the Task class in the zoo.animal.feeding package. In the following example, the package name and module name are the same. It is common for the module name to match either the full package name or the beginning of it.

```
java --module-path feeding
    --module zoo.animal.feeding/zoo.animal.feeding.Task
```

Since you already saw that --module-path uses the short form of -p, we bet you won't be surprised to learn there is a short form of --module as well. The short option is -m. That means the following command is equivalent:

```
java -p feeding
    -m zoo.animal.feeding/zoo.animal.feeding.Task
```

In these examples, we used feeding as the module path because that's where we compiled the code. This will change once we package the module and run that.

Table 12.2 lists the options you need to know for the java command.

TABLE 12.2   Options you need to know for using modules with java

Use for	Abbreviation	Long form
Module name	-m <name>	--module <name>
Module path	-p <path>	--module-path <path>

Packaging Our First Module

A module isn't much use if we can run it only in the folder it was created in. Our next step is to package it. Be sure to create a mods directory before running this command:

```
jar -cvf mods/zoo.animal.feeding.jar -C feeding/.
```

There's nothing module-specific here. We are packaging everything under the feeding directory and storing it in a JAR file named zoo.animal.feeding.jar under the mods folder. This represents how the module JAR will look to other code that wants to use it.

Now let's run the program again, but this time using the mods directory instead of the loose classes:

```
java -p mods
    -m zoo.animal.feeding/zoo.animal.feeding.Task
```

You might notice that this command looks identical to the one in the previous section except for the directory. In the previous example, it was feeding. In this one, it is the module path of mods. Since the module path is used, a module JAR is being run.

Updating Our Example for Multiple Modules

Now that our zoo.animal.feeding module is solid, we can start thinking about our other modules. As you can see in Figure 12.6, all three of the other modules in our system depend on the zoo.animal.feeding module.

FIGURE 12.6   Modules depending on `zoo.animal.feeding`

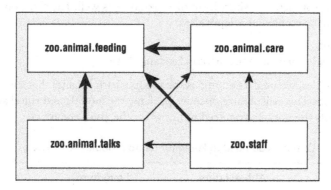

Updating the Feeding Module

Since we will be having our other modules call code in the `zoo.animal.feeding` package, we need to declare this intent in the module declaration.

The `exports` directive is used to indicate that a module intends for those packages to be used by Java code outside the module. As you might expect, without an `exports` directive, the module is only available to be run from the command line on its own. In the following example, we export one package:

```
module zoo.animal.feeding {
    exports zoo.animal.feeding;
}
```

Recompiling and repackaging the module will update the `module-info.class` inside our `zoo.animal.feeding.jar` file. These are the same `javac` and `jar` commands you ran previously:

```
javac -p mods
   -d feeding
   feeding/zoo/animal/feeding/*.java feeding/module-info.java

jar -cvf mods/zoo.animal.feeding.jar -C feeding/ .
```

Creating a Care Module

Next, let's create the `zoo.animal.care` module. This time, we are going to have two packages. The `zoo.animal.care.medical` package will have the classes and methods that are intended for use by other modules. The `zoo.animal.care.details` package is only going to be used by this module. It will not be exported from the module. Think of it as healthcare privacy for the animals.

Figure 12.7 shows the contents of this module. Remember that all modules must have a module-info.java file.

FIGURE 12.7   Contents of zoo.animal.care

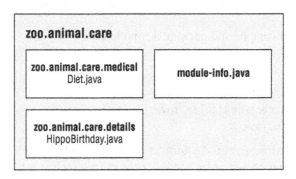

The module contains two basic packages and classes in addition to the module-info.java file:

```
// HippoBirthday.java
package zoo.animal.care.details;
import zoo.animal.feeding.*;
public class HippoBirthday {
    private Task task;
}
```

```
// Diet.java
package zoo.animal.care.medical;
public class Diet { }
```

This time the module-info.java file specifies three things:

```
1: module zoo.animal.care {
2:     exports zoo.animal.care.medical;
3:     requires zoo.animal.feeding;
4: }
```

Line 1 specifies the name of the module. Line 2 lists the package we are exporting so it can be used by other modules. So far, this is similar to the zoo.animal.feeding module.

On line 3, we see a new directive. The requires statement specifies that a module is needed. The zoo.animal.care module depends on the zoo.animal.feeding module.

Next, we need to figure out the directory structure. We will create two packages. The first is zoo.animal.care.details and contains one class named HippoBirthday. The second is zoo.animal.care.medical, which contains one class named Diet. Try to draw the directory structure on paper or create it on your computer. If you are trying to run these examples without using the online code, just create classes without variables or methods for everything except the module-info.java files.

You might have noticed that the packages begin with the same prefix as the module name. This is intentional. You can think of it as if the module name "claims" the matching package and all subpackages.

To review, we now compile and package the module:

```
javac -p mods
  -d care
  care/zoo/animal/care/details/*.java
  care/zoo/animal/care/medical/*.java
  care/module-info.java
```

We compile both packages and the module-info.java file. In the real world, you'll use a build tool rather than doing this by hand. For the exam, you just list all the packages and/ or files you want to compile.

Now that we have compiled code, it's time to create the module JAR:

```
jar -cvf mods/zoo.animal.care.jar -C care/ .
```

Creating the Talks Module

So far, we've used only one exports and requires statement in a module. Now you'll learn how to handle exporting multiple packages or requiring multiple modules. In Figure 12.8, observe that the zoo.animal.talks module depends on two modules: zoo.animal.feeding and zoo.animal.care. This means that there must be two requires statements in the module-info.java file.

FIGURE 12.8   Dependencies for zoo.animal.talks

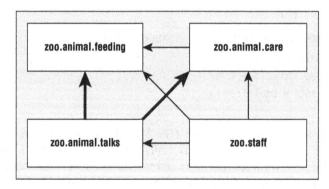

Figure 12.9 shows the contents of this module. We are going to export all three packages in this module.

FIGURE 12.9   Contents of zoo.animal.talks

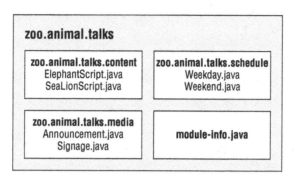

First let's look at the module-info.java file for zoo.animal.talks:

```
1: module zoo.animal.talks {
2:     exports zoo.animal.talks.content;
3:     exports zoo.animal.talks.media;
4:     exports zoo.animal.talks.schedule;
5:
6:     requires zoo.animal.feeding;
7:     requires zoo.animal.care;
8: }
```

Line 1 shows the module name. Lines 2–4 allow other modules to reference all three packages. Lines 6 and 7 specify the two modules that this module depends on.

Then we have the six classes, as shown here:

```
// ElephantScript.java
package zoo.animal.talks.content;
public class ElephantScript { }


// SeaLionScript.java
package zoo.animal.talks.content;
public class SeaLionScript { }


// Announcement.java
package zoo.animal.talks.media;
public class Announcement {
   public static void main(String[] args) {
      System.out.println("We will be having talks");
   }
}
```

```
// Signage.java
package zoo.animal.talks.media;
public class Signage { }
```

```
// Weekday.java
package zoo.animal.talks.schedule;
public class Weekday { }
```

```
// Weekend.java
package zoo.animal.talks.schedule;
public class Weekend {}
```

If you are still following along on your computer, create these classes in the packages. The following are the commands to compile and build the module:

```
javac -p mods
   -d talks
   talks/zoo/animal/talks/content/*.java talks/zoo/animal/talks/media/*.java
   talks/zoo/animal/talks/schedule/*.java talks/module-info.java

jar -cvf mods/zoo.animal.talks.jar -C talks/ .
```

Creating the Staff Module

Our final module is zoo.staff. Figure 12.10 shows that there is only one package inside. We will not be exposing this package outside the module.

FIGURE 12.10   Contents of zoo.staff

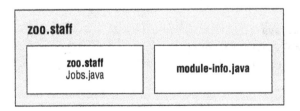

Based on Figure 12.11, do you know what should go in the module-info.java?

There are three arrows in Figure 12.11 pointing from zoo.staff to other modules. These represent the three modules that are required. Since no packages are to be exposed from zoo.staff, there are no exports statements. This gives us the following:

```
module zoo.staff {
    requires zoo.animal.feeding;
    requires zoo.animal.care;
    requires zoo.animal.talks;
}
```

FIGURE 12.11   Dependencies for `zoo.staff`

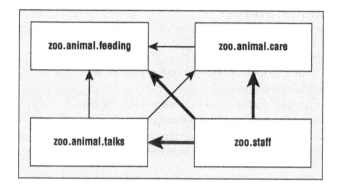

In this module, we have a single class in the `Jobs.java` file:

```
package zoo.staff;
public class Jobs { }
```

For those of you following along on your computer, create a class in the package. The following are the commands to compile and build the module:

```
javac -p mods
    -d staff
    staff/zoo/staff/*.java staff/module-info.java

jar -cvf mods/zoo.staff.jar -C staff/.
```

Diving into the Module Declaration

Now that we've successfully created modules, we can learn more about the module declaration. In these sections, we look at `exports`, `requires`, and `opens`. In the following section on services, we explore `provides` and `uses`. Now would be a good time to mention that these directives can appear in any order in the module declaration.

Exporting a Package

We've already seen how `exports` *packageName* exports a package to other modules. It's also possible to export a package to a specific module. Suppose the zoo decides that only staff members should have access to the talks. We could update the module declaration as follows:

```
module zoo.animal.talks {
    exports zoo.animal.talks.content to zoo.staff;
    exports zoo.animal.talks.media;
    exports zoo.animal.talks.schedule;

    requires zoo.animal.feeding;
    requires zoo.animal.care;
}
```

From the zoo.staff module, nothing has changed. However, no other modules would be allowed to access that package.

You might have noticed that none of our other modules requires zoo.animal.talks in the first place. However, we don't know what other modules will exist in the future. It is important to consider future use when designing modules. Since we want only the one module to have access, we only allow access for that module.

Exported Types

We've been talking about exporting a package. But what does that mean, exactly? All public classes, interfaces, enums, and records are exported. Further, any public and protected fields and methods in those files are visible.

Fields and methods that are private are not visible because they are not accessible outside the class. Similarly, package fields and methods are not visible because they are not accessible outside the package.

The exports directive essentially gives us more levels of access control. Table 12.3 lists the full access control options.

TABLE 12.3 Access control with modules

Level	Within module code	Outside module
private	Available only within class	No access
Package	Available only within package	No access
protected	Available only within package or to subclasses	Accessible to subclasses only if package is exported
public	Available to all classes	Accessible only if package is exported

Requiring a Module Transitively

As you saw earlier in this chapter, requires *moduleName* specifies that the current module depends on moduleName. There's also a requires transitive *moduleName*, which means that any module that requires this module will also depend on moduleName.

Well, that was a mouthful. Let's look at an example. Figure 12.12 shows the modules with dashed lines for the redundant relationships and solid lines for relationships specified in the module-info.java. This shows how the module relationships would look if we were to only use transitive dependencies.

For example, zoo.animal.talks depends on zoo.animal.care, which depends on zoo.animal.feeding. That means the arrow between zoo.animal.talks and zoo.animal.feeding no longer appears in Figure 12.12.

FIGURE 12.12   Transitive dependency version of our modules

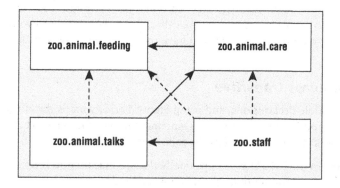

Now let's look at the four module declarations. The first module remains unchanged. We are exporting one package to any packages that use the module.

```
module zoo.animal.feeding {
    exports zoo.animal.feeding;
}
```

The zoo.animal.care module is the first opportunity to improve things. Rather than forcing all remaining modules to explicitly specify zoo.animal.feeding, the code uses requires transitive.

```
module zoo.animal.care {
    exports zoo.animal.care.medical;
    requires transitive zoo.animal.feeding;
}
```

In the zoo.animal.talks module, we make a similar change and don't force other modules to specify zoo.animal.care. We also no longer need to specify zoo.animal.feeding, so that line is commented out.

```
module zoo.animal.talks {
    exports zoo.animal.talks.content to zoo.staff;
```

```
    exports zoo.animal.talks.media;
    exports zoo.animal.talks.schedule;
    // no longer needed requires zoo.animal.feeding;
    // no longer needed requires zoo.animal.care;
    requires transitive zoo.animal.care;
}
```

Finally, in the `zoo.staff` module, we can get rid of two `requires` statements.

```
module zoo.staff {
    // no longer needed requires zoo.animal.feeding;
    // no longer needed requires zoo.animal.care;
    requires zoo.animal.talks;
}
```

The more modules you have, the greater the benefits of the `requires transitive` compound. It is also more convenient for the caller. If you were trying to work with this zoo, you could just require `zoo.staff` and have the remaining dependencies automatically inferred.

Effects of *requires transitive*

Given our new module declarations, and using Figure 12.12, what is the effect of applying the `transitive` modifier to the `requires` statement in our `zoo.animal.care` module? Applying the `transitive` modifier has the following effects:

- Module `zoo.animal.talks` can optionally declare that it `requires` the `zoo.animal.feeding` module, but it is not required.
- Module `zoo.animal.care` cannot be compiled or executed without access to the `zoo.animal.feeding` module.
- Module `zoo.animal.talks` cannot be compiled or executed without access to the `zoo.animal.care` module.

These rules hold even if the `zoo.animal.care` and `zoo.animal.talks` modules do not explicitly reference any packages in the `zoo.animal.feeding` module. On the other hand, without the `transitive` modifier in our module declaration of `zoo.animal.care`, the other modules would have to explicitly use `requires` in order to reference any packages in the `zoo.animal.feeding` module.

Duplicate *requires* Statements

One place the exam might try to trick you is mixing `requires` and `requires transitive`. Can you think of a reason this code doesn't compile?

```
module bad.module {
    requires zoo.animal.talks;
    requires transitive zoo.animal.talks;
}
```

Java doesn't allow you to repeat the same module in a `requires` clause. It is redundant and most likely an error in coding. Keep in mind that `requires transitive` is like `requires` plus some extra behavior.

Opening a Package

Java allows callers to inspect and call code at runtime with a technique called *reflection*. This is a powerful approach that allows calling code that might not be available at compile time. It can even be used to subvert access control! Don't worry—you don't need to know how to write code using reflection for the exam.

The opens directive is used to enable reflection of a package within a module. You only need to be aware that the opens directive exists rather than understanding it in detail for the exam.

Since reflection can be dangerous, the module system requires developers to explicitly allow reflection in the module declaration if they want calling modules to be allowed to use it. The following shows how to enable reflection for two packages in the `zoo.animal.talks` module:

```
module zoo.animal.talks {
    opens zoo.animal.talks.schedule;
    opens zoo.animal.talks.media to zoo.staff;
}
```

The first example allows any module using this one to use reflection. The second example gives that privilege only to the `zoo.staff` module. There are two more directives you need to know for the exam—`provides` and `uses`—which are covered in the following section.

 Real World Scenario

Opening an Entire Module

In the previous example, we opened two packages in the `zoo.animal.talks` module, but suppose we instead wanted to open all packages for reflection. No problem. We can use the open module modifier, rather than the opens directive (notice the s difference):

```
open module zoo.animal.talks {
}
```

With this module modifier, Java knows we want all the packages in the module to be open. What happens if you apply both together?

```
open module zoo.animal.talks {
    opens zoo.animal.talks.schedule;   // DOES NOT COMPILE
}
```

This does not compile because a module that uses the open modifier is not permitted to use the opens directive. After all, the packages are already open!

Creating a Service

In this section, you learn how to create a service. A *service* is composed of an interface, any classes the interface references, and a way of looking up implementations of the interface. The implementations are not part of the service.

We will be using a tour application in the services section. It has four modules shown in Figure 12.13. In this example, the zoo.tours.api and zoo.tours.reservations modules make up the service since they consist of the interface and lookup functionality.

FIGURE 12.13   Modules in the tour application

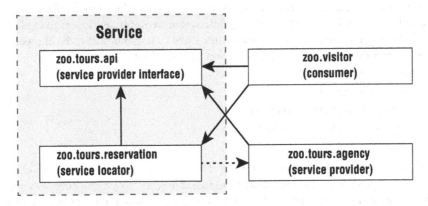

    You aren't required to have four separate modules. We do so to illustrate the concepts. For example, the service provider interface and service locator could be in the same module.

Declaring the Service Provider Interface

First, the zoo.tours.api module defines a Java object called Souvenir. It is considered part of the service because it will be referenced by the interface.

// Souvenir.java
```
package zoo.tours.api;

public record Souvenir(String description) { }
```

Next, the module contains a Java interface type. This interface is called the *service provider interface* because it specifies what behavior our service will have. In this case, it is a simple API with three methods.

```
// Tour.java
package zoo.tours.api;

public interface Tour {
   String name();
   int length();
   Souvenir getSouvenir();
}
```

All three methods use the implicit `public` modifier. Since we are working with modules, we also need to create a `module-info.java` file so our module definition exports the package containing the interface.

```
// module-info.java
module zoo.tours.api {
   exports zoo.tours.api;
}
```

Now that we have both files, we can compile and package this module.

```
javac -d serviceProviderInterfaceModule
   serviceProviderInterfaceModule/zoo/tours/api/*.java
   serviceProviderInterfaceModule/module-info.java

jar -cvf mods/zoo.tours.api.jar -C serviceProviderInterfaceModule/ .
```

A service provider "interface" can be an abstract class rather than an actual `interface`. Since you will only see it as an `interface` on the exam, we use that term in the book.

To review, the service includes the service provider interface and supporting classes it references. The service also includes the lookup functionality, which we define next.

Creating a Service Locator

To complete our service, we need a service locator. A *service locator* can find any classes that implement a service provider interface.

Luckily, Java provides a `ServiceLoader` class to help with this task. You pass the service provider interface type to its `load()` method, and Java will return any implementation services it can find. The following class shows it in action:

```
// TourFinder.java
package zoo.tours.reservations;

import java.util.*;
import zoo.tours.api.*;
```

```java
public class TourFinder {

   public static Tour findSingleTour() {
      ServiceLoader<Tour> loader = ServiceLoader.load(Tour.class);
      for (Tour tour : loader)
         return tour;
      return null;
   }
   public static List<Tour> findAllTours() {
      List<Tour> tours = new ArrayList<>();
      ServiceLoader<Tour> loader = ServiceLoader.load(Tour.class);
      for (Tour tour : loader)
         tours.add(tour);
      return tours;
   }
}
```

As you can see, we provided two lookup methods. The first is a convenience method if you are expecting exactly one Tour to be returned. The other returns a List, which accommodates any number of service providers. At runtime, there may be many service providers (or none) that are found by the service locator.

The ServiceLoader call is relatively expensive. If you are writing a real application, it is best to cache the result.

Our module definition exports the package with the lookup class TourFinder. It requires the service provider interface package. It also has the uses directive since it will be looking up a service.

// module-info.java
```java
module zoo.tours.reservations {
   exports zoo.tours.reservations;
   requires zoo.tours.api;
   uses zoo.tours.api.Tour;
}
```

Remember that both requires and uses are needed, one for compilation and one for lookup. Finally, we compile and package the module.

```
javac -p mods -d serviceLocatorModule
   serviceLocatorModule/zoo/tours/reservations/*.java
   serviceLocatorModule/module-info.java

jar -cvf mods/zoo.tours.reservations.jar -C serviceLocatorModule/ .
```

Now that we have the interface and lookup logic, we have completed our service.

Using *ServiceLoader*

There are two methods in `ServiceLoader` that you need to know for the exam. The declaration is as follows, sans the full implementation:

```java
public final class ServiceLoader<S> implements Iterable<S> {

    public static <S> ServiceLoader<S> load(Class<S> service) { ... }

    public Stream<Provider<S>> stream() { ... }

    // Additional methods
}
```

As we already saw, calling `ServiceLoader.load()` returns an object that you can loop through normally. However, requesting a `Stream` gives you a different type. The reason for this is that a `Stream` controls when elements are evaluated. Therefore, a `ServiceLoader` returns a `Stream` of `Provider` objects. You have to call `get()` to retrieve the value you wanted out of each `Provider`, such as in this example:

```java
ServiceLoader.load(Tour.class)
    .stream()
    .map(Provider::get)
    .mapToInt(Tour::length)
    .max()
    .ifPresent(System.out::println);
```

Invoking from a Consumer

Next up is to call the service locator by a consumer. A *consumer* (or *client*) refers to a module that obtains and uses a service. Once the consumer has acquired a service via the service locator, it is able to invoke the methods provided by the service provider interface.

```java
// Tourist.java
package zoo.visitor;

import java.util.*;
import zoo.tours.api.*;
import zoo.tours.reservations.*;

public class Tourist {
    public static void main(String[] args) {
```

```
        Tour tour = TourFinder.findSingleTour();
        System.out.println("Single tour: " + tour);

        List<Tour> tours = TourFinder.findAllTours();
        System.out.println("# tours: " + tours.size());
    }
}
```

Our module definition doesn't need to know anything about the implementations since the zoo.tours.reservations module is handling the lookup.

// module-info.java
```
module zoo.visitor {
    requires zoo.tours.api;
    requires zoo.tours.reservations;
}
```

This time, we get to run a program after compiling and packaging.

```
javac -p mods -d consumerModule
    consumerModule/zoo/visitor/*.java consumerModule/module-info.java

jar -cvf mods/zoo.visitor.jar -C consumerModule/ .

java -p mods -m zoo.visitor/zoo.visitor.Tourist
```

The program outputs the following:

```
Single tour: null
# tours: 0
```

Well, that makes sense. We haven't written a class that implements the interface yet.

Adding a Service Provider

A *service provider* is the implementation of a service provider interface. As we said earlier, at runtime it is possible to have multiple implementation classes or modules. We will stick to one here for simplicity.

Our service provider is the zoo.tours.agency package because we've outsourced the running of tours to a third party.

// TourImpl.java
```
package zoo.tours.agency;

import zoo.tours.api.*;
```

```java
public class TourImpl implements Tour {
    public String name() {
        return "Behind the Scenes";
    }
    public int length() {
        return 120;
    }
    public Souvenir getSouvenir() {
        return new Souvenir("stuffed animal");
    }
}
```

Again, we need a `module-info.java` file to create a module.

```java
// module-info.java
module zoo.tours.agency {
    requires zoo.tours.api;
    provides zoo.tours.api.Tour with zoo.tours.agency.TourImpl;
}
```

The module declaration requires the module containing the interface as a dependency. We don't export the package that implements the interface since we don't want callers referring to it directly. Instead, we use the `provides` directive. This allows us to specify that we provide an implementation of the interface with a specific implementation class. The syntax looks like this:

```java
provides interfaceName with className;
```

We have not exported the package containing the implementation. Instead, we have made the implementation available to a service provider using the interface.

Finally, we compile it and package it up.

```
javac -p mods -d serviceProviderModule
    serviceProviderModule/zoo/tours/agency/*.java
    serviceProviderModule/module-info.java
```

```
jar -cvf mods/zoo.tours.agency.jar -C serviceProviderModule/ .
```

Now comes the cool part. We can run the Java program again.

```
java -p mods -m zoo.visitor/zoo.visitor.Tourist
```

This time, we see output like the following:

```
Single tour: zoo.tours.agency.TourImpl@1936f0f5
# tours: 1
```

Notice how we didn't recompile the `zoo.tours.reservations` or `zoo.visitor` package. The service locator was able to observe that there was now a service provider implementation available and find it for us.

This is useful when you have functionality that changes independently of the rest of the code base. For example, you might have custom reports or logging.

 In software development, the concept of separating different components into stand-alone pieces is referred to as *loose coupling*. One advantage of loosely coupled code is that it can be easily swapped out or replaced with minimal (or zero) changes to code that uses it. Relying on a loosely coupled structure allows service modules to be easily extensible at runtime.

Reviewing Directives and Services

Table 12.4 summarizes what we've covered in the section about services. We recommend learning really well what is needed when each artifact is in a separate module. That is most likely what you will see on the exam and will ensure that you understand the concepts. Table 12.5 lists all the directives you need to know for the exam.

TABLE 12.4 Reviewing services

Artifact	Part of the service	Directives required
Service provider interface	Yes	`exports`
Service provider	No	`requires` `provides`
Service locator	Yes	`exports` `requires` `uses`
Consumer	No	`requires`

TABLE 12.5 Reviewing directives

Directive	Description
exports *package*; **exports** *package* **to** *module*;	Makes package available outside module
requires *module*; **requires transitive** *module*;	Specifies another module as dependency

Directive	Description
opens *package*; **opens** *package* **to** *module*;	Allows package to be used with reflection
provides *serviceInterface* **with** *implName*;	Makes service available
uses *serviceInterface*;	References service

Discovering Modules

So far, we've been working with modules that we wrote. Even the classes built into the JDK are modularized. In this section, we show you how to use commands to learn about modules.

You do not need to know the output of the commands in this section. You do, however, need to know the syntax of the commands and what they do. We include the output where it facilitates remembering what is going on. But you don't need to memorize that (which frees up more space in your head to memorize command-line options).

Identifying Built-in Modules

The most important module to know is java.base. It contains most of the packages you have been learning about for the exam. In fact, it is so important that you don't even have to use the requires directive; it is available to all modular applications. Your module-info.java file will still compile if you explicitly require java.base. However, it is redundant, so it's better to omit it. Table 12.6 lists some common modules and what they contain.

TABLE 12.6 Common modules

Module name	What it contains	Coverage in book
java.base	Collections, math, IO, NIO.2, concurrency, etc.	Most of this book
java.desktop	Abstract Windows Toolkit (AWT) and Swing	Not on exam beyond module name
java.logging	Logging	Not on exam beyond module name

TABLE 12.6   Common modules *(continued)*

Module name	What it contains	Coverage in book
java.sql	JDBC	Not on exam beyond module name
java.xml	Extensible Markup Language (XML)	Not on exam beyond module name

The exam creators feel it is important to recognize the names of modules supplied by the JDK. While you don't need to know the names by heart, you do need to be able to pick them out of a lineup.

For the exam, you need to know that module names begin with java for APIs you are likely to use and with jdk for APIs that are specific to the JDK. Table 12.7 lists all the modules that begin with java.

TABLE 12.7   Java modules prefixed with java

java.base	java.naming	java.smartcardio
java.compiler	java.net.http	java.sql
java.datatransfer	java.prefs	java.sql.rowset
java.desktop	java.rmi	java.transaction.xa
java.instrument	java.scripting	java.xml
java.logging	java.se	java.xml.crypto
java.management	java.security.jgss	
java.management.rmi	java.security.sasl	

Table 12.8 lists all the modules that begin with jdk. We recommend reviewing this right before the exam to increase the chances of them sounding familiar. Remember that you don't have to memorize them.

TABLE 12.8   Java modules prefixed with jdk

jdk.accessibility	jdk.jcmd	jdk.management.agent
jdk.attach	jdk.jconsole	jdk.management.jfr
jdk.charsets	jdk.jdeps	jdk.naming.dns
jdk.compiler	jdk.jdi	jdk.naming.rmi
jdk.crypto.cryptoki	jdk.jdwp.agent	jdk.net
jdk.crypto.ec	jdk.jfr	jdk.nio.mapmode
jdk.dynalink	jdk.jlink	jdk.sctp
jdk.editpad	jdk.jpackage	jdk.security.auth
jdk.hotspot.agent	jdk.jshell	jdk.security.jgss
jdk.httpserver	jdk.jsobject	jdk.xml.dom
jdk.incubator.vector	jdk.jstatd	jdk.zipfs
jdk.jartool	jdk.localedata	
jdk.javadoc	jdk.management	

Getting Details with *java*

The java command has three module-related options. One describes a module, another lists the available modules, and the third shows the module resolution logic.

 It is also possible to add modules, exports, and more at the command line. But please don't. It's confusing and hard to maintain. Note that these flags are available on java but not all commands.

Describing a Module

Suppose you are given the zoo.animal.feeding module JAR file and want to know about its module structure. You could "unjar" it and open the module-info.java file. This would show you that the module exports one package and doesn't explicitly require any modules.

```
module zoo.animal.feeding {
    exports zoo.animal.feeding;
}
```

However, there is an easier way. The `java` command has an option to describe a module. The following two commands are equivalent:

```
java -p mods
  -d zoo.animal.feeding
```

```
java -p mods
  --describe-module zoo.animal.feeding
```

Each prints information about the module. For example, it might print this:

```
zoo.animal.feeding file:///absolutePath/mods/zoo.animal.feeding.jar
exports zoo.animal.feeding
requires java.base mandated
```

The first line is the module we asked about: `zoo.animal.feeding`. The second line starts with information about the module. In our case, it is the same package `exports` statement we had in the module declaration file.

On the third line, we see `requires java.base mandated`. Now, wait a minute. The module declaration very clearly does not specify any modules that `zoo.animal.feeding` has as dependencies.

Remember, the `java.base` module is special. It is automatically added as a dependency to all modules. This module has frequently used packages like `java.util`. That's what the `mandated` is about. You get `java.base` regardless of whether you asked for it.

In classes, the `java.lang` package is automatically imported whether you type it or not. The `java.base` module works the same way. It is automatically available to all other modules.

More About Describing Modules

You only need to know how to run `--describe-module` for the exam rather than interpret the output. However, you might encounter some surprises when experimenting with this feature, so we describe them in a bit more detail here.

Assume the following are the contents of `module-info.java` in `zoo.animal.care`:

```
module zoo.animal.care {
    exports zoo.animal.care.medical to zoo.staff;
    requires transitive zoo.animal.feeding;
}
```

Now we have the command to describe the module and the output.

```
java -p mods -d zoo.animal.care
```

```
zoo.animal.care file:///absolutePath/mods/zoo.animal.care.jar
requires zoo.animal.feeding transitive
requires java.base mandated
qualified exports zoo.animal.care.medical to zoo.staff
contains zoo.animal.care.details
```

The first line of the output is the absolute path of the module file. The two `requires` lines should look familiar as well. The first is in the `module-info.java`, and the other is added to all modules. Next comes something new. The `qualified exports` is the full name of the package we are exporting to a specific module.

Finally, the `contains` means that there is a package in the module that is not exported at all. This is true. Our module has two packages, and one is available only to code inside the module.

Listing Available Modules

In addition to describing modules, you can use the `java` command to list the modules that are available. The simplest form lists the modules that are part of the JDK.

```
java --list-modules
```

When we ran it, the output went on for about 70 lines and starts with this:

```
java.base@21
java.compiler@21
java.datatransfer@21
```

This is a listing of all the modules that come with Java and their version numbers. You can tell that we were using Java 21 when testing this example.

More interestingly, you can use this command with custom code. Let's try again with the directory containing our zoo modules.

```
java -p mods --list-modules
```

How many extra lines do you expect to be in the output this time? There are eight more; the ones we've created in this chapter. Two of the custom lines look like this:

```
zoo.animal.care file:///absolutePath/mods/zoo.animal.care.jar
zoo.animal.feeding file:///absolutePath/mods/zoo.animal.feeding.jar
```

Since these are custom modules, we get a location on the file system. If the project had a module version number, it would have both the version number and the file system path.

Note that `--list-modules` exits as soon as it prints the observable modules. It does not run the program.

Showing Module Resolution

If listing the modules doesn't give you enough output, you can also use the
--show-module-resolution option. You can think of it as a way of debugging modules.
It spits out a lot of output when the program starts up. Then it runs the program.

```
java --show-module-resolution
   -p feeding
   -m zoo.animal.feeding/zoo.animal.feeding.Task
```

Luckily, you don't need to understand this output. That said, having seen it will make it
easier to remember. Here's a snippet of the output:

```
root zoo.animal.feeding file:///absolutePath/feeding/
java.base binds java.desktop jrt:/java.desktop
java.base binds jdk.jartool jrt:/jdk.jartool
...
jdk.security.auth requires java.naming jrt:/java.naming
jdk.security.auth requires java.security.jgss jrt:/java.security.jgss
...
All fed!
```

It starts by listing the root module. That's the one we are running:
zoo.animal.feeding. Then it lists many lines of packages included by the mandatory
java.base module. After a while, it lists modules that have dependencies. Finally, it outputs
the result of the program: All fed!.

Describing with *jar*

Like the java command, the jar command can describe a module. These commands are
equivalent:

```
jar -f mods/zoo.animal.feeding.jar -d
```

```
jar --file mods/zoo.animal.feeding.jar --describe-module
```

The output is slightly different from when we used the java command to describe the
module. With jar, it outputs the following:

```
zoo.animal.feeding jar:file:///absolutePath/mods/zoo.animal.feeding.jar
/!module-info.class
exports zoo.animal.feeding
requires java.base mandated
```

The JAR version includes the module-info.class in the filename, which is not a particularly significant difference in the scheme of things. You don't need to know this difference.
You do need to know that both commands can describe a module.

Learning About Dependencies with *jdeps*

The jdeps command gives you information about dependencies within a module. Unlike describing a module, it looks at the code in addition to the module declaration. This tells you what dependencies are actually used rather than simply declared. Luckily, you are not expected to memorize all the options for the exam.

You are expected to understand how to use jdeps with projects that have not yet been modularized to assist in identifying dependencies and problems. First, we will create a JAR file from this class. If you are following along, feel free to copy the class from the online examples referenced at the beginning of the chapter rather than typing it in.

```
// Animatronic.java
package zoo.dinos;

import java.time.*;
import java.util.*;
import sun.misc.Unsafe;

public class Animatronic {
    private List<String> names;
    private LocalDate visitDate;

    public Animatronic(List<String> names, LocalDate visitDate) {
        this.names = names;
        this.visitDate = visitDate;
    }
    public void unsafeMethod() {
        Unsafe unsafe = Unsafe.getUnsafe();
    }
}
```

This example is silly. It uses a number of unrelated classes. The Bronx Zoo really did have electronic moving dinosaurs for a while, so at least the idea of having dinosaurs in a zoo isn't beyond the realm of possibility.

Now we can compile this file. You might have noticed that there is no module-info.java file. That is because we aren't creating a module. We are looking into what dependencies we will need when we do modularize this JAR.

```
javac zoo/dinos/*.java
```

Compiling works, but it gives you some warnings about Unsafe being an internal API. Don't worry about those for now—we discuss that shortly. (Maybe the dinosaurs went extinct because they did something unsafe.)

Next, we create a JAR file.

```
jar -cvf zoo.dino.jar .
```

We can run the `jdeps` command against this JAR to learn about its dependencies. First, let's run the command without any options. On the first two lines, the command prints the modules that we would need to add with a `requires` directive to migrate to the module system. It also prints a table showing what packages are used and what modules they correspond to.

```
jdeps zoo.dino.jar

zoo.dino.jar -> java.base
zoo.dino.jar -> jdk.unsupported
   zoo.dinos     -> java.lang     java.base
   zoo.dinos     -> java.time     java.base
   zoo.dinos     -> java.util     java.base
   zoo.dinos     -> sun.misc      JDK internal API (jdk.unsupported)
```

Note that `java.base` is always included. It also says which modules contain packages used by the JAR. If we run in summary mode, we only see just the first part where `jdeps` lists the modules. There are two formats for the summary flag:

```
jdeps -s zoo.dino.jar
jdeps -summary zoo.dino.jar

zoo.dino.jar -> java.base
zoo.dino.jar -> jdk.unsupported
```

For a real project, the dependency list could include dozens or even hundreds of packages. It's useful to see the summary of just the modules. This approach also makes it easier to see whether `jdk.unsupported` is in the list.

There is also a `--module-path` option that you can use if you want to look for modules outside the JDK. Unlike other commands, there is no short form for this option on `jdeps`.

 You might have noticed that jdk.unsupported is not in the list of modules you saw in Table 12.8. It's special because it contains internal libraries that developers in previous versions of Java were discouraged from using, although many people ignored this warning. You should not reference it, as it may disappear in future versions of Java.

Using the *--jdk-internals* Flag

The `jdeps` command has an option to provide details about these unsupported APIs. The output looks something like this:

```
jdeps --jdk-internals zoo.dino.jar
```

```
zoo.dino.jar -> jdk.unsupported
   zoo.dinos.Animatronic  -> sun.misc.Unsafe
      JDK internal API (jdk.unsupported)

Warning: <omitted warning>

JDK Internal API      Suggested Replacement
_____         _____

sun.misc.Unsafe       See http://openjdk.java.net/jeps/260
```

The --jdk-internals option lists any classes you are using that call an internal API along with which API. At the end, it provides a table suggesting what you should do about it. If you wrote the code calling the internal API, this message is useful. If not, the message would be useful to the team that did write the code. You, on the other hand, might need to update or replace that JAR file entirely with one that fixes the issue. Note that -jdkinternals is equivalent to --jdk-internals.

 Real World Scenario

About *sun.misc.Unsafe*

Prior to the Java Platform Module System, classes had to be public if you wanted them to be used outside the package. It was reasonable to use the class in JDK code since that is low-level code that is already tightly coupled to the JDK. Since it was needed in multiple packages, the class was made public. Sun even named it Unsafe, figuring that would prevent anyone from using it outside the JDK.

However, developers are clever and used the class since it was available. A number of widely used open-source libraries started using Unsafe. While it is quite unlikely that you are using this class in your project directly, you probably use an open-source library that is using it.

The jdeps command allows you to look at these JARs to see whether you will have any problems when Oracle finally prevents the usage of this class. If you find any uses, you can look at whether there is a later version of the JAR that you can upgrade to.

Using Module Files with *jmod*

The next command you need to know for the exam is jmod. You might think a JMOD file is a Java module file. Not quite. Oracle recommends using JAR files for most modules. JMOD files are recommended only when you have native libraries or something that can't go inside a JAR file. This is unlikely to affect you in the real world.

The most important thing to remember is that jmod is only for working with the JMOD files. Conveniently, you don't have to memorize the syntax for jmod. Table 12.9 lists the common modes.

TABLE 12.9   Modes using jmod

Operation	Description
create	Creates JMOD file.
extract	Extracts all files from JMOD. Works like unzipping.
describe	Prints module details such as requires.
list	Lists all files in JMOD file.
hash	Prints or records hashes.

Creating Java Runtime Images with *jlink*

One of the benefits of modules is being able to supply just the parts of Java you need. Our zoo example from the beginning of the chapter doesn't have many dependencies. If the user already doesn't have Java or is on a device without much memory, downloading a JDK that is more than 150 MB is a big ask. Let's see how big the package actually needs to be! This command creates our smaller distribution, referred to as a *runtime image*:

```
jlink --module-path mods --add-modules zoo.animal.talks --output zooApp
```

First we specify where to find the custom modules with -p or --module-path. Then we specify our module names with --add-modules. This will include the dependencies it requires as long as they can be found. Finally, we specify the folder name of our smaller JDK with --output.

Our runtime image is stored in the output directory, which contains the bin, conf, include, legal, lib, and man directories along with a release file. These should look familiar as you find them in the full JDK as well.

When we run this command and zip up the zooApp directory, the file is only 15 MB. This is an order of magnitude smaller than the full JDK. Where did this space savings come from? There are many modules in the JDK we don't need. Additionally, development tools like javac don't need to be in a runtime image.

There are a lot more items to customize this process that you don't need to know for the exam. For example, you can skip generating the help documentation and save even more space.

Remember that a Java runtime image, like the ones jlink creates, is a folder that contains multiple folders, libraries, and executables. It is not packaged as a single "image file". As we'll see in the next section, we can use jpackage to create a single executable package.

Creating Self-Contained Java Applications with *jpackage*

Unlike jlink which can only create a *runtime image*, the jpackage command can create an *application image*. An application image is a single executable file capable of running your application on a specific platform. For example, you get an .exe file for Windows or a .dmg file for Mac.

Both jlink and jpackage provide the parts of Java you need in order to run. And for both, you do not need a JDK to already be installed on the system you want to run the application on.

Besides output formats, a big difference between jlink and jpackage is that jpackage can package both modular and non-modular applications while jlink is limited to modular applications.

A command to create a modular application for the zoo.animal.feeding module from this chapter is:

```
jpackage --name feedingTask --module-path mods
    --module zoo.animal.feeding/zoo.animal.feeding.Task
```

On Mac, this creates the file feedingTask-1.0.dmg. Let's take a look at the options. First --name or -n gives the name of the application in the created filename. You can pass --app-version if you want a version other than 1.0, the default. The --module-path (or -p) and --module (or -m) parameters should look familiar from running a modular application. You can even call --add-modules like in jlink to add extra modules that aren't in your module-info file.

You don't have to know this for the exam, but you can even run jlink to create a runtime image and use that as input to create an application image with jpackage!

Using *jpackage* with Non-Modular Applications

You can create a run the jpackage command against a non-modular jar. For example:

```
jpackage --name myApp --input myDir --main-class com.wiley.java.Cat
    --main-jar myApp.jar
```

Like the modular example, --name or -n are used for the name of the application in the created filename. Either of --input or -i specify the directory where the files to package are located. The --main-class option specifies the fully qualified class name to run and the --main-jar option specifies where to find that class.

Reviewing Command-Line Options

This section presents a number of tables that cover what you need to know about running command-line options for the exam.

Table 12.10 shows the command-line operations you should expect to encounter on the exam. There are many more options in the documentation. For example, there is a --module option on javac that limits compilation to that module. Luckily, you don't need to know those for the exam.

TABLE 12.10   Comparing command-line operations

Description	Syntax

Compile nonmodular code	`javac -cp` *classpath* `-d` *directory classesToCompile*
	`javac --class-path` *classpath* `-d` *directory*
	   classesToCompile
	`javac -classpath` *classpath* `-d` *directory*
	   classesToCompile

Run nonmodular code	`java -cp` *classpath package.className* `java -classpath` *classpath package.className* `java --class-path` *classpath package.className*

Compile module	`javac -p` *moduleFolderName* `-d` *directory*
	   classesToCompileIncludingModuleInfo
	`javac --module-path` *moduleFolderName* `-d` *directory*
	   classesToCompileIncludingModuleInfo

Run module	`java -p` *moduleFolderName*
	   `-m` *moduleName/package.className*
	`java --module-path` *moduleFolderName*
	   `--module` *moduleName/package.className*

Describe module	`java -p` *moduleFolderName* `-d` *moduleName*
	`java --module-path` *moduleFolderName*
	   `--describe-module` *moduleName*
	`jar --file` *jarName* `--describe-module`
	`jar -f` *jarName* `-d`

Description	Syntax
List available modules	**java** --module-path *moduleFolderName* --list-modules **java** -p *moduleFolderName* --list-modules **java** --list-modules
View dependencies	**jdeps** -summary --module-path *moduleFolderName* *jarName* **jdeps** -s --module-path *moduleFolderName* *jarName* **jdeps** --jdk-internals *jarName* **jdeps** -jdkinternals *jarName*

Show module resolution	**java** --show-module-resolution -p *moduleFolderName*
	   -m *moduleName*
	java --show-module-resolution
	   --module-path *moduleFolderName* --module *moduleName*

Create runtime JAR	**jlink** -p *moduleFolderName*
	   --add-modules *moduleName* --output *zooApp*
	jlink --module-path *moduleFolderName*
	   --add-modules *moduleName* --output *zooApp*

Create a self-contained Java application	**jpackage** -n *name* -p *moduleFolderName*
	   -m *moduleName/package.className*
	jpackage --name *name*
	   --module-path *moduleFolderName*
	   --module *moduleName/package.className*
	jpackage -n *myApp* -i *myDir*
	   --main class *package.className*
	   --main-jar *appJar.jar*
	jpackage --name *myApp* --input *myDir*
	   --main class *package.className*
	   --main-jar *appJar.jar*

Table 12.11 shows the options for javac, Table 12.12 shows the options for java, Table 12.13 shows the options for jar, and Table 12.14 shows the options for jdeps. Finally, Table 12.15 shows the options for jlink and Table 12.16 shows the options for jpackage.

TABLE 12.11 Options you need to know for the exam: `javac`

Option	Description

`-cp <classpath>`
`-classpath <classpath>`
`--class-path <classpath>`
	Location of JARs in nonmodular program

`-d <dir>`	Directory in which to place generated class files
`-p <path>` `--module-path <path>`	Location of JARs in modular program

TABLE 12.12 Options you need to know for the exam: `java`

Option	Description

`-cp <classpath>`
`-classpath <classpath>`
`--class-path <classpath>`
	Location of JARs in nonmodular program

`-p <path>` `--module-path <path>`	Location of JARs in modular program
`-m <name>` `--module <name>`	Module name to run
`-d` `--describe-module`	Describes details of module
`--list-modules`	Lists observable modules without running program
`--show-module-resolution`	Shows modules when running program

TABLE 12.13 Options you need to know for the exam: `jar`

Option	Description
`-c` `--create`	Creates new JAR file
`-v` `--verbose`	Prints details when working with JAR files

Option	Description
-f --file	JAR filename
-C <dir>	Directory containing files to be used to create JAR
-d --describe-module	Describes details of module

TABLE 12.14   Options you need to know for the exam: jdeps

Option	Description
--module-path <path>	Location of JARs in modular program
-s -summary	Summarizes output
--jdk-internals -jdkinternals	Lists uses of internal APIs

TABLE 12.15   Options you need to know for the exam: jlink

Option	Description
-p <path> --module-path <path>	Location of JARs in modular program
--add-modules <name>	List of modules to package
--output	Name of output directory

TABLE 12.16   Options you need to know for the exam: jpackage

Option	Description
-n <name> --name <name>	Prefix of the output file. Will be combined with a version number and suffix.

TABLE 12.16   Options you need to know for the exam: jpackage *(continued)*

Option	Description
-p <path> --module-path <path>	Location of JARs in modular program.
--add-modules <name>	List of modules to package.
--app-version	Optional version number for the output file name. Will default to 1.0 if not specified.
--i <dir> --input <dir>	Input directory containing files to package for non-modular app.
--main-class	Fully qualified class name to run in non-modular jar.
--main-jar	Non modular jar containing class to run.

Comparing Types of Modules

All the modules we've used so far in this chapter are called named modules. There are two other types of modules: automatic modules and unnamed modules. In this section, we describe these three types of modules. On the exam, you will need to be able to compare them.

Named Modules

A *named module* is one containing a module-info.java file. To review, this file appears in the root of the JAR alongside one or more packages. Unless otherwise specified, a module is a named module. Named modules appear on the module path rather than the classpath. Later, you learn what happens if a JAR containing a module-info.java file is on the classpath. For now, just know it is not considered a named module because it is not on the module path.

As a way of remembering this, a named module has the *name* inside the module-info.java file and is on the module path.

Remember from Chapter 7, "Beyond Classes," that the only way for sub-classes of sealed classes to be in a different package is to be within the same-named module.

Automatic Modules

An *automatic module* appears on the module path but does not contain a
`module-info.java` file. It is simply a regular JAR file that is placed on the module path
and gets treated as a module.

As a way of remembering this, Java *automatically* determines the module name. The code
referencing an automatic module treats it as if there is a `module-info.java` file present. It
automatically exports all packages. It also determines the module name. How does it
determine the module name, you ask? Excellent question.

To answer this, we need to provide a bit of history on JAR files and module adoption.
Every JAR file contains a special folder called `META-INF` and, within it, a text file called
`MANIFEST.MF`. It can be created automatically when the JAR is created or by hand by the
JAR's author. Getting back to modules, many Java libraries weren't quite ready to modularize when the feature was introduced. The authors were encouraged to declare the name they
intended to use for the module by adding a property named `Automatic-Module-Name` into
their `MANIFEST.MF` file.

About the *MANIFEST.MF* File

A JAR file contains a special text file called `META-INF/MANIFEST.MF` that contains
information about the JAR. It's been around significantly longer than modules—since the
early days of Java and JARs, to be exact. The figure shows how the manifest fits into the
directory structure of a JAR file.

The manifest contains extra information about the JAR file. For example, it often
contains the version of Java used to build the JAR file. For command-line programs,
the class with the `main()` method is commonly specified.

Each line in the manifest is a key/value pair separated by a colon. You can think of the manifest as a map of property names and values. The default manifest in Java 21 looks like this:

```
Manifest-Version: 1.0
Created-By: 21 (Oracle Corporation)
```

Specifying a single property in the manifest allowed library providers to make things easier for applications that wanted to use their library in a modular application. You can think of it as a promise that when the library becomes a named module, it will use the specified module name.

If the JAR file does not specify an automatic module name, Java will still allow you to use it in the module path. In this case, Java will determine the module name for you. We'd say that this happens automatically, but the joke is probably wearing thin by now.

Java determines the automatic module name by basing it on the filename of the JAR file. Let's go over the rules by starting with an example. Suppose we have a JAR file named `holiday-calendar-1.0.0.jar`.

First Java will remove the extension `.jar` from the name. Then Java will remove the version from the end of the JAR filename. This is important because we want module names to be consistent. Having a different automatic module name every time you upgraded to a new version would not be good! After all, this would force you to change the module declaration of your nice, clean, modularized application every time you pulled in a later version of the holiday calendar JAR.

Removing the version and extension gives us `holiday-calendar`. This leaves us with a problem. Dashes (-) are not allowed in module names. Java solves this problem by converting any special characters in the name to dots (.). As a result, the module name is `holiday.calendar`. Any characters other than letters and numbers are considered special characters in this replacement. Finally, any adjacent dots or leading/trailing dots are removed.

Since that's a number of rules, let's review the algorithm in a list for determining the name of an automatic module:

- If the `MANIFEST.MF` specifies an `Automatic-Module-Name`, use that. Otherwise, proceed with the remaining rules.

- Remove the file extension from the JAR name.

- Remove any version information from the end of the name. A version is digits and dots with possible extra information at the end: for example, `-1.0.0` or `-1.0-RC`.

- Replace any remaining characters other than letters and numbers with dots.

- Replace any sequences of dots with a single dot.

- Remove the dot if it is the first or last character of the result.

Table 12.17 shows how to apply these rules to two examples where there is no automatic module name specified in the manifest.

TABLE 12.17   Practicing with automatic module names

#	Description	Example 1	Example 2
1	Beginning JAR name	`commons2-x-1.0.0-SNAPSHOT` `.jar`	`mod_$-1.0.jar`
2	Remove file extension	`commons2-x-1.0.0-SNAPSHOT`	`mod_$-1.0`
3	Remove version information	`commons2-x`	`mod_$`
4	Replace special characters	`commons2.x`	`mod..`
5	Replace sequence of dots	`commons2.x`	`mod.`
6	Remove leading/trailing dots (results in the automatic module name)	`commons2.x`	`mod`

While the algorithm for creating automatic module names does its best, it can't always come up with a good name. For example, `1.2.0-calendar-1.2.2-good-1.jar` isn't conducive. Luckily, such names are rare and out of scope for the exam.

Unnamed Modules

An *unnamed module* appears on the classpath. Like an automatic module, it is a regular JAR. Unlike an automatic module, it is on the classpath rather than the module path. This means an unnamed module is treated like old code and a second-class citizen to modules.

An unnamed module does not usually contain a `module-info.java` file. If it happens to contain one, that file will be ignored since it is on the classpath.

Unnamed modules do not export any packages to named modules. The unnamed module can read from any JARs on the classpath or module path. You can think of an unnamed module as code that works the way Java worked before modules. Yes, we know it is confusing for something that isn't really a module to have the word *module* in its name.

Reviewing Module Types

You can expect to get questions on the exam comparing the three types of modules. Please study Table 12.18 thoroughly and be prepared to answer questions about these items in any combination. A key point to remember is that code on the classpath can access the module path. By contrast, code on the module path is unable to read from the classpath.

TABLE 12.18   Properties of module types

Property	Named	Automatic	Unnamed
Does a _____ module contain a `module-info.java` file?	Yes	No	Ignored if present
Which packages does a _____ module export to named modules?	Those in `module-info.java` file	All packages	No packages
Which packages does a _____ module export to automatic modules?	Those in `module-info.java` file	All packages	All packages
Is a _____ module readable by other modules on the module path?	Yes	Yes	No
Is a _____ module readable by other JARs on the classpath?	Yes	Yes	Yes

Migrating an Application

Many applications were not designed to use the Java Platform Module System because they were written before it was created or chose not to use it. Ideally, they were at least designed with projects instead of as a big ball of mud. This section gives you an overview of strategies for migrating an existing application to use modules. We cover ordering modules, bottom-up migration, top-down migration, and how to split up an existing project.

 **Real World Scenario**

Migrating Your Applications at Work

The exam exists in a pretend universe where there are no open-source dependencies and applications are very small. These scenarios make learning and discussing migration far easier. In the real world, applications have libraries that haven't been updated in 10 or more years, complex dependency graphs, and all sorts of surprises.

Note that you can use all the features of Java 21 without converting your application to modules (except the features in this module chapter, of course!). Please make sure you have a reason for migration and don't think it is required.

This chapter does a great job teaching you what you need to know for the exam. However, it does not adequately prepare you to convert real applications to use modules. If you find yourself in that situation, consider reading *The Java Module System* by Nicolai Parlog (Manning Publications, 2019).

Determining the Order

Before we can migrate our application to use modules, we need to know how the packages and libraries in the existing application are structured. Suppose we have a simple application with three JAR files, as shown in Figure 12.14. The dependencies between projects form a graph. Both of the representations in Figure 12.14 are equivalent. The arrows show the dependencies by pointing from the project that will require the dependency to the one that makes it available. In the language of modules, the arrow will go from `requires` to `exports`.

FIGURE 12.14 Determining the order

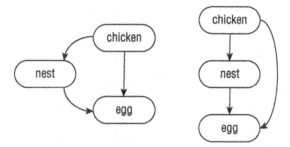

The right side of the diagram makes it easier to identify the top and bottom that top-down and bottom-up migration refer to. Projects that do not have any dependencies are at the bottom. Projects that do have dependencies are at the top.

In this example, there is only one order from top to bottom that honors all the dependencies. Figure 12.15 shows that the order is not always unique. Since two of the projects do not have an arrow between them, either order is allowed when deciding migration order.

Exploring a Bottom-Up Migration Strategy

The easiest approach to migration is a bottom-up migration. This approach works best when you have the power to convert any JAR files that aren't already modules. For a bottom-up migration, you follow these steps:

1. Pick the lowest-level project that has not yet been migrated. (Remember the way we ordered them by dependencies in the previous section?)

2. Add a module-info.java file to that project. Be sure to add any exports to expose any package used by higher-level JAR files. Also, add a requires directive for any modules this module depends on.

3. Move this newly migrated named module from the classpath to the module path.

4. Ensure that any projects that have not yet been migrated stay as unnamed modules on the classpath.

5. Repeat with the next-lowest-level project until you are done.

FIGURE 12.15   Determining the order when not unique

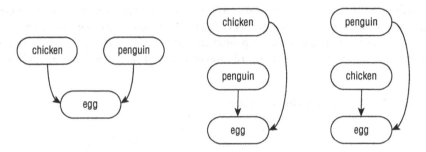

You can see this procedure applied to migrate three projects in Figure 12.16. Notice that each project is converted to a module in turn.

With a bottom-up migration, you are getting the lower-level projects in good shape. This makes it easier to migrate the top-level projects at the end. It also encourages care in what is exposed.

During migration, you have a mix of named modules and unnamed modules. The named modules are the lower-level ones that have been migrated. They are on the module path and not allowed to access any unnamed modules.

The unnamed modules are on the classpath. They can access JAR files on both the classpath and the module path.

Exploring a Top-Down Migration Strategy

A top-down migration strategy is most useful when you don't have control of every JAR file used by your application. For example, suppose another team owns one project. They are just too busy to migrate. You wouldn't want this situation to hold up your entire migration.

For a top-down migration, you follow these steps:

1. Place all projects on the module path.

2. Pick the highest-level project that has not yet been migrated.

3. Add a `module-info.java` file to that project to convert the automatic module into a named module. Again, remember to add any `exports` or `requires` directives. You can use the automatic module name of other modules when writing the `requires` directive since most of the projects on the module path do not have names yet.

4. Repeat with the next-highest-level project until you are done.

FIGURE 12.16   Bottom-up migration

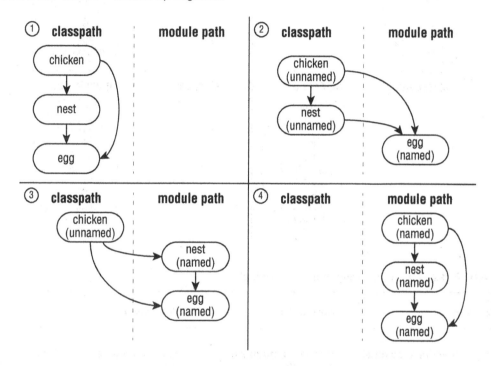

You can see this procedure applied in order to migrate three projects in Figure 12.17. Notice that each project is converted to a module in turn.

With a top-down migration, you are conceding that all of the lower-level dependencies are not ready but that you want to make the application itself a module.

During migration, you have a mix of named modules and automatic modules. The named modules are the higher-level ones that have been migrated. They are on the module path and have access to the automatic modules. The automatic modules are also on the module path.

Table 12.19 reviews what you need to know about the two main migration strategies. Make sure you know it well.

FIGURE 12.17   Top-down migration

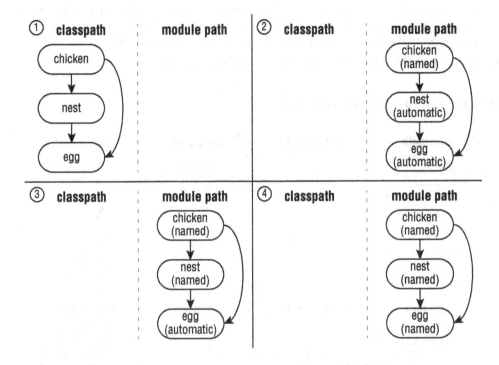

TABLE 12.19   Comparing migration strategies

Category	Bottom-Up	Top-Down
Project that depends on all others	Unnamed module on classpath	Named module on module path
Project that has no dependencies	Named module on module path	Automatic module on module path

Splitting a Big Project into Modules

For the exam, you need to understand the basic process of splitting a big project into modules. You won't be given a big project, of course. After all, there is only so much space to ask a question. Luckily, the process is the same for a small project.

Suppose you start with an application that has a number of packages. The first step is to break them into logical groupings and draw the dependencies between them. Figure 12.18 shows an imaginary system's decomposition. Notice that there are seven packages on both the left and right sides. There are fewer modules because some packages share a module.

There's a problem with this decomposition. Do you see it? The Java Platform Module System does not allow for *cyclic dependencies*. A cyclic dependency, or *circular dependency*, is when two things directly or indirectly depend on each other. If the zoo.tickets.delivery module requires the zoo.tickets.discount module, zoo.tickets.discount is not allowed to require the zoo.tickets.delivery module.

FIGURE 12.18   First attempt at decomposition

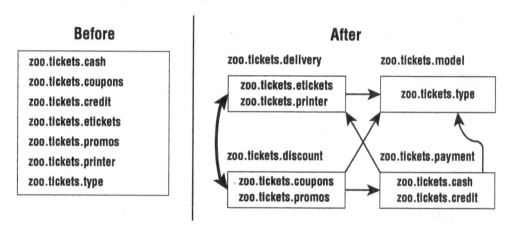

Now that we know that the decomposition in Figure 12.18 won't work, what can we do about it? A common technique is to introduce another module. That module contains the code that the other two modules share. Figure 12.19 shows the new modules without any cyclic dependencies. Notice the new module zoo.tickets.etech. We created new packages to put in that module. This allows the developers to put the common code in there and break the dependency. No more cyclic dependencies!

FIGURE 12.19   Removing the cyclic dependencies

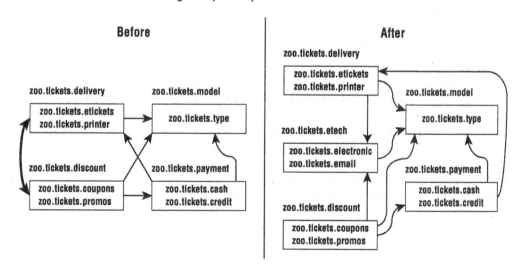

Failing to Compile with a Cyclic Dependency

It is extremely important to understand that Java will not allow you to compile modules that have circular dependencies. In this section, we look at an example leading to that compiler error.

Consider the `zoo.butterfly` module described here:

```
// Butterfly.java
package zoo.butterfly;
public class Butterfly {
   private Caterpillar caterpillar;
}
```

```
// module-info.java
module zoo.butterfly {
    exports zoo.butterfly;
    requires zoo.caterpillar;
}
```

We can't compile this yet as we need to build `zoo.caterpillar` first. After all, our butterfly `requires` it. Now we look at `zoo.caterpillar`:

```
// Caterpillar.java
package zoo.caterpillar;
public class Caterpillar {
   Butterfly emergeCocoon() {
      // logic omitted
   }
}
```

```
// module-info.java
module zoo.caterpillar {
    exports zoo.caterpillar;
    requires zoo.butterfly;
}
```

We can't compile this yet as we need to build `zoo.butterfly` first. Uh-oh! Now we have a stalemate. Neither module can be compiled. This is our circular dependency problem at work.

This is one of the advantages of the module system. It prevents you from writing code that has a cyclic dependency. Such code won't even compile!

You might be wondering what happens if three modules are involved. Suppose module `ballA` requires module `ballB` and `ballB` requires module `ballC`. Can module `ballC` require module `ballA`? No. This would create a cyclic dependency. Don't believe us? Try drawing it. You can follow your pencil around the circle from ballA to ballB to ballC to ballA to. . .well, you get the idea. There are just too many balls in the air!

 Java will still allow you to have a cyclic dependency between packages within a module. It enforces that you do not have a cyclic dependency between modules.

Summary

The Java Platform Module System organizes code at a higher level than packages. Each module contains one or more packages and a module-info.java file. The java.base module is most common and is automatically supplied to all modules as a dependency.

The process of compiling and running modules uses the -module-path, also known as -p. Running a module uses the --module option, also known as -m. The class to run is specified in the format moduleName/className.

The module declaration file supports a number of directives. The exports directive specifies that a package should be accessible outside the module. It can optionally restrict that export to a specific module. The requires directive is used when a module depends on code in another module. Additionally, requires transitive can be used when all modules that require one module should always require another. The provides and uses directives are used when sharing and consuming a service. Finally, the opens directive is used to allow access via reflection.

Both the java and jar commands can be used to describe the contents of a module. The java command can additionally list available modules and show module resolution. The jdeps command prints information about packages used in addition to module-level information. The jmod command is used when dealing with files that don't meet the requirements for a JAR. The jlink command creates a smaller Java runtime image. The jpackage command creates an application image, which is a self-contained, operating system specific file.

There are three types of modules. Named modules contain a module-info.java file and are on the module path. They can read only from the module path. Automatic modules are also on the module path but have not yet been modularized. They might have an automatic module name set in the manifest. Unnamed modules are on the classpath.

The two most common migration strategies are top-down and bottom-up migration. Top-down migration starts migrating the module with the most dependencies and places all other modules on the module path. Bottom-up migration starts migrating a module with no dependencies and moves one module to the module path at a time. Both of these strategies require ensuring that you do not have any cyclic dependencies since the Java Platform Module System will not allow cyclic dependencies to compile.

Exam Essentials

Create _module-info.java_ files.   Place the module-info.java file in the root directory of the module. Know how to code exports, requires, provides, and uses directives. Additionally, be familiar with the opens directive.

Use command-line operations with modules.   The java command can describe a module, list available modules, or show the module resolution. The jar command can describe a module similar to how the java command does. The jdeps command prints details about a module and packages. The jmod command provides various modes for working with JMOD files rather than JAR files. The jlink command creates custom Java images. The jpackage command creates an executable file.

Identify the three types of modules.   Named modules are JARs that have been modularized. Unnamed modules have not been modularized. Automatic modules are in between. They are on the module path but do not have a module-info.java file.

List built-in JDK modules.   The java.base module is available to all modules. There are about 20 other modules provided by the JDK that begin with java.* and about 30 that begin with jdk.*.

Explain top-down and bottom-up migration.   A top-down migration places all JARs on the module path, making them automatic modules while migrating from top to bottom. A bottom-up migration leaves all JARs on the classpath, making them unnamed modules while migrating from bottom to top.

Differentiate the four main parts of a service.   A service provider interface declares the interface that a service must implement. The service locator looks up the service, and a consumer calls the service. Finally, a service provider implements the service.

Review Questions

The answers to the chapter review questions can be found in the Appendix.

1. Which statement is true of the following module?

```
|---zoo
   |-- staff
      |-- Vet.java
```

   A. The directory structure shown is a valid module.
   B. The directory structure would be a valid module if `module.java` were added directly underneath `zoo/staff`.
   C. The directory structure would be a valid module if `module.java` were added directly underneath `zoo`.
   D. The directory structure would be a valid module if `module-info.java` were added directly underneath `zoo/staff`.
   E. The directory structure would be a valid module if `module-info.java` were added directly underneath `zoo`.
   F. None of these changes would make this directory structure a valid module.

2. Suppose module `puppy` depends on module `dog` and module `dog` depends on module `animal`. Fill in the blank so that code in module `dog` can access the `animal.behavior` package in module `animal`.

```
module animal {
    _____ animal.behavior;
}
```

   A. `export`
   B. `exports`
   C. `require`
   D. `requires`
   E. `require transitive`
   F. `requires transitive`
   G. None of the above

3. Fill in the blanks so this command to run the program is correct:

```
java
_____ modules
_____ zoo.animal.talks/zoo/animal/talks/Peacocks
```

   A. `-d` and `-m`
   B. `-d` and `-p`
   C. `-m` and `-d`

   D. −m and −p

   E. −p and −d

   F. −p and −m

   G. None of the above

4. Which of the following pairs make up a service?

   A. Consumer and service locator

   B. Consumer and service provider interface

   C. Service locator and service provider

   D. Service locator and service provider interface

   E. Service provider and service provider interface

5. A(n) _____ module is on the classpath while a(n) _____ module is on the module path. (Choose all that apply.)

   A. automatic, named

   B. automatic, unnamed

   C. named, automatic

   D. named, unnamed

   E. unnamed, automatic

   F. unnamed, named

   G. None of the above

6. Which of the following statements are true in a `module-info.java` file? (Choose all that apply.)

   A. The opens directive allows the use of reflection.

   B. The opens directive declares that an API is called.

   C. The use directive allows the use of reflection.

   D. The use directive declares that an API is called.

   E. The uses directive allows the use of reflection.

   F. The uses directive declares that an API is called.

7. An automatic module name is generated if one is not supplied. Which of the following JAR filenames and generated automatic module name pairs are correct? (Choose all that apply.)

   A. `emily-1.0.0.jar` and `emily`

   B. `emily-1.0.0-SNAPSHOT.jar` and `emily`

   C. `emily_the_cat-1.0.0.jar` and `emily_the_cat`

   D. `emily_the_cat-1.0.0.jar` and `emily-the-cat`

   E. `emily.$.jar` and `emily`

   F. `emily.$.jar` and `emily.`

   G. `emily.$.jar` and `emily..`

8. Which of the following statements are true? (Choose all that apply.)

   A. Modules with cyclic dependencies will not compile.

   B. Packages with a cyclic dependency will not compile.

   C. A cyclic dependency always involves exactly two modules.

   D. A cyclic dependency always involves at least two `requires` statements.

   E. An unnamed module can be involved in a cyclic dependency with an automatic module.

9. Suppose you are creating a service provider that contains the following class. Which line of code needs to be in your `module-info.java`?

```
package dragon;
import magic.*;
public class Dragon implements Magic {
   public String getPower() {
     return "breathe fire";
   }
}
```

   A. `provides dragon.Dragon by magic.Magic;`

   B. `provides dragon.Dragon using magic.Magic;`

   C. `provides dragon.Dragon with magic.Magic;`

   D. `provides magic.Magic by dragon.Dragon;`

   E. `provides magic.Magic using dragon.Dragon;`

   F. `provides magic.Magic with dragon.Dragon;`

10. What is true of a module containing a file named `module-info.java` with the following contents? (Choose all that apply.)

```
module com.food.supplier {}
```

   A. All packages inside the module are automatically exported.

   B. No packages inside the module are automatically exported.

   C. A main method inside the module can be run.

   D. A main method inside the module cannot be run since the class is not exposed.

   E. The `module-info.java` file contains a compiler error.

   F. The `module-info.java` filename is incorrect.

11. Suppose module `puppy` depends on module `dog` and module `dog` depends on module `animal`. Which lines allow module `puppy` to access the `animal.behavior` package in module `animal`? (Choose all that apply.)

```
module animal {
   exports animal.behavior;
}
module dog {
```

```
_____ animal;   // line S
}
module puppy {
    _____ dog;        // line T
}
```

   A. require on line S
   B. require on line T
   C. requires on line S
   D. requires on line T
   E. require transitive on line S
   F. require transitive on line T
   G. requires transitive on line S
   H. requires transitive on line T

12. Which of the following modules are provided by the JDK? (Choose all that apply.)
   A. java.base
   B. java.desktop
   C. java.logging
   D. java.util
   E. jdk.base
   F. jdk.compiler
   G. jdk.xerces

13. Which of the following compiles and is equivalent to this loop?

```
List<Unicorn> all  = new ArrayList<>();
for (Unicorn current : ServiceLoader.load(Unicorn.class))
   all.add(current);
```

   A.
```
List<Unicorn> all = ServiceLoader.load(Unicorn.class)
.getStream()
.toList();
```

   B.
```
List<Unicorn> all = ServiceLoader.load(Unicorn.class)
.stream()
.toList();
```

   C.
```
List<Unicorn> all = ServiceLoader.load(Unicorn.class)
.getStream()
.map(Provider::get)
.toList();
```

D.
```
List<Unicorn> all = ServiceLoader.load(Unicorn.class)
.stream()
.map(Provider::get)
.toList();
```
E. None of the above

14. Which of the following is a legal command to run a modular program where n is the module name and c is the fully qualified class name?

   A. `java --module-path x -m n.c`

   B. `java --module-path x -p n.c`

   C. `java --module-path x-x -m n/c`

   D. `java --module-path x -p n/c`

   E. `java --module-path x-x -m n-c`

   F. `java --module-path x -p n-c`

   G. None of the above

15. For a top-down migration, all modules other than named modules are _____ modules and are on the _____.

   A. automatic, classpath

   B. automatic, module path

   C. unnamed, classpath

   D. unnamed, module path

   E. None of the above

16. Suppose you have separate modules for a service provider interface, service provider, service locator, and consumer. If you add a second service provider module, how many of the existing modules do you need to recompile?

   A. Zero

   B. One

   C. Two

   D. Three

   E. Four

17. Suppose we have a JAR file named `cat-1.2.3-RC1.jar`, and `Automatic-Module-Name` in the `MANIFEST.MF` is set to dog. What should an unnamed module referencing this automatic module include in `module-info.java`?

   A. `requires cat;`

   B. `requires cat.RC;`

   C. `requires cat-RC;`

   D. `requires dog;`

   E. None of the above

18. Two commands create artifacts that include smaller versions of the JDK. Which are used to create an `.exe` file and a directory, respectively?

   A. `jimage` and `jlink`

   B. `jimage` and `jpackage`

   C. `jlink` and `jimage`

   D. `jlink` and `jpackage`

   E. `jpackage` and `jimage`

   F. `jpackage` and `jlink`

19. Which is a true statement about the following module?

```
class dragon {
    exports com.dragon.fire;
    exports com.dragon.scales to castle;
}
```

   A. All modules can reference the `com.dragon.fire` package.

   B. All modules can reference the `com.dragon.scales` package.

   C. Only the `castle` module can reference the `com.dragon.fire` package.

   D. Only the `castle` module can reference the `com.dragon.scales` package.

   E. None of the above.

20. Which would you expect to see when describing any module?

   A. `requires java.base mandated`

   B. `requires java.core mandated`

   C. `requires java.lang mandated`

   D. `requires mandated java.base`

   E. `requires mandated java.core`

   F. `requires mandated java.lang`

   G. None of the above

21. Suppose you have separate modules for a service provider interface, service provider, service locator, and consumer. Which module(s) need to specify a `requires` directive on the service provider?

   A. Service locator

   B. Service provider interface

   C. Consumer

   D. Consumer and service locator

   E. Consumer and service provider

   F. Service locator and service provider interface

   G. Consumer, service locator, and service provider interface

   H. None of the above

22. Which are true statements? (Choose all that apply.)

A. An automatic module exports all packages to named modules.

B. An automatic module exports only the specified packages to named modules.

C. An automatic module exports no packages to named modules.

D. An unnamed module exports only the named packages to named modules.

E. An unnamed module exports all packages to named modules.

F. An unnamed module exports no packages to named modules.

23. Which is the first line to contain a compiler error?

```
1: module snake {
2:     exports com.snake.tail;
3:     exports com.snake.fangs to bird;
4:     requires skin;
5:     requires transitive skin;
6: }
```

A. Line 1.

B. Line 2.

C. Line 3.

D. Line 4.

E. Line 5.

F. The code does not contain any compiler errors.

24. Which is a true statement about a package in a JAR on the classpath containing a `module-info.java` file?

A. It is possible to make the package available to all other modules on the classpath.

B. It is possible to make the package available to all other modules on the module path.

C. It is possible to make the package available to exactly one other specific module on the classpath.

D. It is possible to make the package available to exactly one other specific module on the module path.

E. It is possible to make sure the package is not available to any other modules on the classpath.

25. Suppose you have separate modules for a service provider interface, service provider, service locator, and consumer. Which statements are true about the directives you need to specify? (Choose all that apply.)

A. The consumer must use the `requires` directive.

B. The consumer must use the `uses` directive.

C. The service locator must use the `requires` directive.

D. The service locator must use the `uses` directive.

E. None of the above.

Chapter

13

Concurrency

OCP EXAM OBJECTIVES COVERED IN THIS CHAPTER:

✓ **Managing Concurrent Code Execution**

- Create both platform and virtual threads. Use both Runnable and Callable objects, manage the thread lifecycle, and use different Executor services and concurrent API to run tasks.

- Develop thread-safe code, using locking mechanisms and concurrent API.

- Process Java collections concurrently and utilize parallel streams.

✓ **Working with Streams and Lambda expressions**

- Perform decomposition, concatenation, and reduction, and grouping and partitioning on sequential and parallel streams.

As you will learn in Chapter 14, "I/O," computers are capable of reading and writing data. Unfortunately, these disk/network operations are much slower than CPU operations. In fact, if your computer's operating system were to stop and wait for every disk or network operation to finish, your computer would appear to freeze constantly.

Luckily, all operating systems support what is known as *multithreaded processing* where an application or group of applications can execute multiple tasks at the same time. This allows tasks waiting to give way to other processing requests.

In this chapter, we introduce threads and provide numerous ways to manage threads using the Concurrency API. Threads and concurrency are challenging topics for many programmers to grasp, as problems with threads can be frustrating even for veteran developers. In practice, concurrency issues are among the most difficult problems to diagnose and resolve.

Introducing Threads

We begin this chapter by reviewing common terminology associated with threads. A *thread* is the smallest unit of execution that can be scheduled by the operating system. A *process* is a group of associated threads that execute in the same shared environment. It follows, then, that a *single-threaded process* is one that contains exactly one thread, whereas a *multi-threaded process* contains one or more threads.

By *shared environment*, we mean that the threads in the same process share the same memory space and can communicate directly with one another.

Within a computer, an Operating System (OS) manages the operating system threads using the underlying CPU hardware. Java executes processes using *platform threads*, which have a one-to-one mapping with operating system threads, as shown in Figure 13.1.

This figure shows a single process with three platform threads. It also shows how they are mapped to an arbitrary number of *n* CPUs available within the system.

The Java Virtual Machine (JVM) creates and manages two different types of platform threads. A *system thread* is created by the JVM and runs in the background of the application. For example, garbage collection is managed by a system thread created by the JVM. Alternatively, a *user-defined thread* is created by the application developer.

In this chapter, we talk a lot about tasks and their relationships to threads. A *task* is a single unit of work performed by a thread. A thread can complete multiple independent tasks but only one task at a time.

FIGURE 13.1   Platform threads

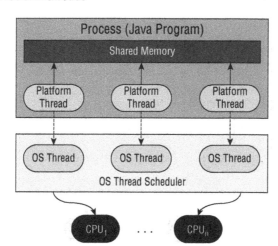

By *shared memory* in Figure 13.1, we are generally referring to `static` variables as well as instance and local variables passed to a thread. Yes, you finally see how `static` variables can be useful for performing complex, multithreaded tasks! Remember from Chapter 5, "Methods," that `static` methods and variables are defined on a single class object. For example, if one thread updates the value of a `static` variable, this information is immediately available for other threads within the process to read.

Comparing to Virtual Threads

Platform threads are often inefficient. They are like having a personal butler who stands around in case you need something. If you constantly need things, this is a good use of the butler's time. For a platform thread to be efficient, you need to be heavily using the CPU.

By contrast, when we go to a restaurant, there is a server who is assigned to many tables. Since we don't need someone to stand there while the food is cooking and when we eat, this is a more efficient use of the server's time. The Java equivalent of a single server handling multiple tables is a *carrier thread*. The tables correspond to *virtual threads*, which are less resource intensive than platform threads, making virtual threads a good choice when you expect to wait for I/O or network resources.

Each time the virtual thread is ready to run, it waits for a carrier thread to be available. The virtual thread does not automatically get the same carrier thread. It's like when a server walks by and refills your coffee or water. They don't tell you that only your original server can do it! Figure 13.2 shows a virtual thread running on a carrier thread.

Notice how the other carrier thread is not currently running a virtual thread. The three blocked virtual threads are not ready to continue, so they don't need a carrier thread at the moment. They are not tied to specific OS threads, which frees the OS threads to work on other tasks. (Thanks to Venkat Subramaniam for the waiter analogy. The butler extension is all ours!)

FIGURE 13.2 Virtual threads

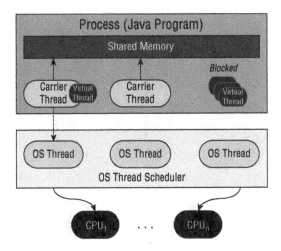

In documentation, you may see a carrier thread referenced as a type of platform thread. This is intending to convey that it runs on the operating system. From a code point of view, platform threads and carrier threads are different things.

 **Real World Scenario**

Platform vs. Virtual Threads

To see how lightweight virtual threads are, let's compare them to platform threads. Don't worry if you haven't seen these methods before. You'll learn about them later in this chapter. Suppose we have a task that takes a second to run:

```java
public class PlatformVsVirtual {
   static void waitUp() {
      try {
         Thread.sleep(1_000);
      } catch (InterruptedException e) {
         throw new RuntimeException(e);
      }
} }
```

Now we try to run a million platform threads. How long do you think it takes?

```java
   public static void main(String[] args) throws InterruptedException {
      var threads = Stream.generate(() -> Thread.ofPlatform()
         .unstarted(PlatformVsVirtual::waitUp))
```

```
            .limit(1_000_000)
            .toList();
        threads.forEach(Thread::start);
        for (var t : threads)
            t.join();
    }
```

The answer is that it may not even run. Platform threads are resource intensive enough that the program likely fails.

```
Exception in thread "main" java.lang.OutOfMemoryError:
unable to create native thread: possibly out of memory
or process/resource limits reached
```

Changing `Thread.ofPlatform()` to `Thread.ofVirtual()` allows the program to run. The program was pretty fast when we tested it. That's pretty good for a million threads!

Understanding Thread Concurrency

The property of executing multiple threads and processes at the same time is referred to as *concurrency*. A *thread scheduler* determines which threads should be currently executing. For example, a thread scheduler may employ a *round-robin schedule* in which each available thread receives an equal number of CPU cycles with which to execute, with threads visited in a circular order.

When a thread's allotted time is complete but the thread has not finished processing, a *context switch* occurs. A *context switch* is the process of storing a thread's current state and later restoring the state of the thread to continue execution. Since there's a cost to context switch due to lost time and having to reload a thread's state, intelligent thread schedulers do their best to minimize the number of context switches while keeping an application running smoothly.

Finally, a thread can interrupt or supersede another thread if it has a higher thread priority. A *thread priority* is a numeric value associated with a thread that the thread scheduler considers when determining which threads should execute. The priority can be set from 1 (`Thread.MIN_PRIORITY`) to 10 (`Thread.MAX_PRIORITY`), either before a thread is started or while it is running.

```
var thread1 = new Thread(() -> System.out.print("Super Important"));
thread1.setPriority(Thread.MAX_PRIORITY);
thread1.start();

var thread2 = new Thread(() -> System.out.print("Less Important"));
thread2.start();
thread2.setPriority(2);
```

Note that thread priority is just a suggestion and the JVM does not guarantee the order that the threads will execute. For example, if there are enough thread resources available for all processes, then all threads will run at the same time.

Creating a Thread

One of the most common ways to define a task for a thread is by using the Runnable interface, which takes no arguments and returns no data.

```
@FunctionalInterface public interface Runnable {
    void run();
}
```

With this, it's easy to create and start a thread. In fact, you can do so in one line of code using the Thread class:

```
Thread.ofPlatform().start(() -> System.out.print("Hello"));
System.out.print("World");
```

The first line creates a new platform thread builder object with the ofPlatform() method. It then starts the thread with the start() method, while also passing in a Runnable task, aka the work to be done, as a lambda expression. Does this code print HelloWorld or WorldHello? The answer is that we don't know. Depending on the thread priority/scheduler, either is possible. Remember that order of thread execution is not often guaranteed. The exam commonly presents questions in which multiple tasks are started at the same time, and you must determine the result.

There are a number of ways to create a thread, as shown in Table 13.1. Pay attention to which are platform threads and which are virtual threads.

TABLE 13.1   Creating and starting a Thread

Code	Type	Description
`var builder = Thread.ofPlatform();` `Thread thread = builder.start(runnable);`	Platform	Factory
`var builder = Thread.ofVirtual();` `Thread thread = builder.start(runnable);`	Virtual	Factory
`Thread thread = new Thread(runnable);` `thread.start();`	Platform	Constructor

Prior to Java 21, it was advisable to create a thread with the new Thread() constructor call, in which the task is defined when the thread is created. Starting with Java 21, the factory method is preferable since it is clearer which type of thread you are getting. The factory method creates a builder, which allows you to call other methods to set attributes like the name.

For platform threads, you can set a priority via the builder object by calling `priority()`. The priority for virtual threads is always 5 (`Thread.NORM_PRIORITY`) and cannot be changed. Calling `setPriority()` on the newly created virtual `Thread` has no effect.

Deferring the Task

Notice that `Thread.ofPlatform()` and `Thread.ofVirtual()` create a builder that you use to create a `Thread`. You pass a `Runnable` using the `start()` or `unstarted()` method depending on whether you want the thread to run now or later. Take a look at the following code snippet, which starts the thread after the task has been set:

```
Thread t = Thread.ofVirtual().unstarted(task);

// Do some other stuff

t.start();
```

Let's take a look at a more complex example. What is the output of this?

```
12: public static void main(String[] args)
13:        throws InterruptedException {
14:     Runnable printInventory =
15:         () -> System.out.println("Printing zoo inventory");
16:     Runnable printRecords = () -> {
17:         for (int i = 0; i < 3; i++)
18:             System.out.println("Printing record: " + i);
19:     };
20:     System.out.println("begin");
21:     var platformThread = Thread.ofPlatform()
22:         .priority(10)
23:         .start(printInventory);
24:     var virtualThread = Thread.ofVirtual()
25:         .start(printRecords);
26:     var constructorThread = new Thread(printInventory);
27:     constructorThread.start();
28:     System.out.println("end");
29:     platformThread.join();
30:     virtualThread.join();
```

```
31:     constructorThread.join();
32: }
```

The answer is that the order is unknown until runtime. The following is just one possible output:

```
begin
Printing record: 0
Printing zoo inventory
end
Printing record: 1
Printing zoo inventory
Printing record: 2
```

This sample uses a total of four threads: the main() user thread and three additional threads created on lines 21–25. Each thread created on these lines is executed as an asynchronous task. By *asynchronous*, we mean that the thread executing the main() method does not wait for the results of each newly created thread before continuing. The opposite of this behavior is a *synchronous* task in which the program waits (or *blocks*) on line 20 for the thread to finish executing before moving on to the next line. So far, the vast majority of method calls used in this book have been synchronous. Remember that the priority() call is a suggestion, so you cannot assume it influences the order of the threads.

While the order of thread execution is indeterminate once the threads have been started, the order within a single thread is still linear. In particular, the for() loop is still ordered. Also, begin always appears before end.

The join() methods on lines 29–31 tell the main() method not to end before the three threads have completed. The join() method throws an InterruptedException if it fails, which the main() method declares.

Calling *run()* instead of *start()*

On the exam, be mindful of code that attempts to start a thread by calling run() instead of start(). Calling run() on a Thread or a Runnable *does not start a new thread*. While the following code snippet will compile, it runs synchronously rather than starting a thread:

```
new Thread(printInventory).run();
```

Working with Daemon Threads

A *daemon thread* is one that will not prevent the JVM from exiting when the program finishes. A Java application terminates when the only threads that are running are daemon threads. For example, if garbage collection is the only thread left running, the JVM will automatically shut down.

Let's take a look at an example. What do you think this outputs?

```
1:  public class Zoo {
2:      public static void pause() {                    // Defines the thread task
3:          try {
4:              Thread.sleep(10_000);                   // Wait for 10 seconds
5:          } catch (InterruptedException e) {}
6:          System.out.println("Thread finished!");
7:      }
8:
9:      public static void main(String[] unused) {
10:         var job = Thread.ofPlatform().start(Zoo::pause);
11:         System.out.println("Main method finished!");
12:     } }
```

The program will output two statements roughly 10 seconds apart:

```
Main method finished!
< 10 second wait >
Thread finished!
```

That's right. Even though the main() method is done, the JVM will wait for the user thread to be done before ending the program. What if we change job to be a daemon thread by adding this to line 11?

```
10: var job = Thread.ofPlatform().daemon(true).start(Zoo::pause);
```

The program will print the first statement and terminate without ever printing the second line.

```
Main method finished!
```

Virtual threads are always daemons. Platform threads default to non-daemon but can be changed.

Managing a Thread's Life Cycle

After a Thread object has been created, it is in one of six states, shown in Figure 13.3. You can query a thread's state by calling getState() on the thread object.

Every thread is initialized with a NEW state. As soon as start() is called, the thread is moved to a RUNNABLE state. Does that mean it is actually running? Not exactly: it may be running, or it may not be. The RUNNABLE state just means the thread is able to be run. Once the work for the thread is completed or an uncaught exception is thrown, the thread state becomes TERMINATED, and no more work is performed.

FIGURE 13.3 Thread states

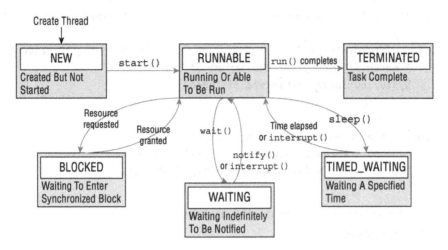

While in a RUNNABLE state, the thread may transition to one of three states where it pauses its work: BLOCKED, WAITING, or TIMED_WAITING. In these states, a thread is not using any CPU resources (other than keeping track of a timer for TIMED_WAITING). Figure 13.3 includes common transitions between thread states, but there are other possibilities. For example, a thread in a WAITING state might be triggered by notifyAll().

Once a thread enters a waiting state, another thread can call interrupt() on the thread, causing it to move back to a RUNNABLE state. Most methods that cause a thread to wait also declare InterruptedException.

```
var thread = Thread.ofPlatform().start(() -> {
   try {
      Thread.sleep(1000);
   } catch (InterruptedException e) {
      System.out.println("Interrupted!");
   }});
thread.interrupt();
```

This code prints Interrupted! and then resumes running. What if interrupt() is called on a thread that is already in the RUNNABLE state? In this case, an exception won't be thrown. The thread can periodically check Thread.interrupted() to determine if an interrupt has been sent recently.

```
var thread = Thread.ofPlatform().start(() -> {
   while(true) {
```

```
    if(Thread.interrupted())
        System.out.println("Someone interrupted us!");
    }});
thread.interrupt();
```

We cover some (but not all) of the transitions in Figure 13.3 in this chapter. If an operation that is not supported is called on a thread, such as interrupting a suspended thread, an `IllegalThreadStateException` will be thrown. Some thread-related methods—such as `wait()` and `notify()`—are beyond the scope of the exam and, frankly, difficult to use well. You should avoid them and use the Concurrency API as much as possible. It takes a large amount of skill (and some luck!) to use these methods correctly.

Reviewing Thread Concepts

We conclude this section with the list of terminology that you should know in Table 13.2. Pay close attention to the different types of threads, as we'll be using them throughout the chapter.

TABLE 13.2   Java thread terminology

Term	Description
Carrier thread	System thread that runs virtual threads when they are not blocked
Daemon thread	Thread that will not prevent the JVM from exiting when the program finishes
Platform thread	Thread that is scheduled by the operating system
Process	Group of associated threads that execute in the same shared environment
System thread	Thread created by the JVM that runs in the background of the application, such as the garbage collector
Task	Single unit of work performed by a thread
Thread	Smallest unit of execution that can be scheduled
User-defined thread	Thread created by the application developer to accomplish a specific task
Virtual thread	Lightweight thread that is mapped to a carrier thread when needed to run

Creating Threads with the Concurrency API

Java includes the java.util.concurrent package, which we refer to as the Concurrency API, to handle the complicated work of managing threads for you. The Concurrency API includes the ExecutorService interface, which defines services that create and manage threads.

You first obtain an instance of an ExecutorService interface, and then you send the service tasks to be processed. The framework includes numerous useful features, such as thread pooling and scheduling. It is recommended that you use this framework any time you need to create and execute a separate task, even if you need only a single thread.

Introducing the Single-Thread Executor

Since ExecutorService is an interface, how do you obtain an instance of it? The Concurrency API includes the Executors factory class that can be used to create instances of the ExecutorService object. Let's rewrite our earlier example with the two Runnable instances to using an ExecutorService.

```
try (ExecutorService service = Executors.newSingleThreadExecutor()) {
    System.out.println("begin");
    service.execute(printInventory);
    service.execute(printRecords);
    service.execute(printInventory);
    System.out.println("end");
}
```

In this example, we use the newSingleThreadExecutor() method to create the service. Unlike our earlier example, in which we had four threads (one main() and three new threads), we have only two threads (one main() and one new thread). This means that the output, while still unpredictable, will have less variation than before. For example, the following is one possible output:

```
begin
Printing zoo inventory
Printing record: 0
Printing record: 1
end
Printing record: 2
Printing zoo inventory
```

Notice that the printRecords loop is no longer interrupted by other Runnable tasks sent to the thread executor. With a single-thread executor, tasks are guaranteed to be executed sequentially. Notice that the end text is output while our thread executor tasks are still running. This is because the main() method is still an independent thread from the ExecutorService.

Submitting Tasks

You can submit tasks to an ExecutorService instance multiple ways. The execute() method takes a Runnable instance and completes the task asynchronously. Because the return type of the method is void, it does not tell us anything about the result of the task. It is considered a "fire-and-forget" method, as once it is submitted, the results are not directly available to the calling thread.

Fortunately, the writers of Java added submit() methods to the ExecutorService interface, which, like execute(), can be used to complete tasks asynchronously. Unlike execute(), though, submit() returns a Future instance that can be used to determine whether the task is complete. It can also be used to return a generic result object after the task has been completed.

Table 13.3 shows the five methods, including execute() and two submit() methods, that you should know for the exam. Don't worry if you haven't seen Future or Callable before; we discuss them in detail in the next section.

TABLE 13.3 ExecutorService methods

Method name	Description
void **execute**(Runnable command)	Executes Runnable task at some point in future.
Future<?> **submit**(Runnable task)	Executes Runnable task at some point in future and returns Future representing task.
<T> Future<T> **submit**(Callable<T> task)	Executes Callable task at some point in future and returns Future representing pending results of task.
<T> List<Future<T>> **invokeAll**(Collection<? extends Callable<T>> tasks)	Executes given tasks and waits for all tasks to complete. Returns List of Future instances in the same order in which they were in original collection.
<T> T **invokeAny**(Collection<? extends Callable<T>> tasks)	Executes given tasks and waits for at least one to complete.

> For the exam, you need to be familiar with both execute() and
> submit(), but in your own code we recommend submit() over
> execute() whenever possible since it supports Callable and therefore
> an optional return value.

Waiting for Results

How do we know when a task submitted to an ExecutorService is complete? As mentioned in the previous section, the submit() method returns a Future<?> instance that can be used to determine this result.

```java
Future<?> future = service.submit(() -> System.out.println("Hello"));
```

The Future type is actually an interface. For the exam, you don't need to know any of the classes that implement Future, just that a Future instance is returned by various API methods. Table 13.4 includes the most useful methods.

TABLE 13.4   Future methods

Method name	Description
boolean isDone()	Returns true if task was completed, threw exception, or was cancelled.
boolean isCancelled()	Returns true if task was cancelled before it completed normally.
boolean cancel(boolean mayInterruptIfRunning)	Attempts to cancel execution of task and returns true if it was successfully cancelled or false if it could not be cancelled or is complete.
V get()	Retrieves result of task, waiting endlessly if it is not yet available.
V get(long timeout, TimeUnit unit)	Retrieves result of task, waiting specified amount of time. If result is not ready by time timeout is reached, checked TimeoutException will be thrown.

The following uses a Future instance to wait for the results:

```java
import java.util.concurrent.*;
public class CheckResults {
    private static int counter = 0;
    public static void main(String[] unused) throws Exception {
        try (var service = Executors.newSingleThreadExecutor()) {
            Future<?> result = service.submit(() -> {
                for (int i = 0; i < 1_000_000; i++) counter++;
            });
```

```
    result.get(10, TimeUnit.SECONDS);  // Returns null for Runnable
    System.out.println("Reached!");
  } catch (TimeoutException e) {
    System.out.println("Not reached in time");
} } }
```

Note this example does not use the Thread class directly. In part, this is the essence of the Concurrency API: to do complex things with threads without having to manage threads directly. This code also waits at most 10 seconds, throwing a TimeoutException on the call to result.get() if the task is not done.

What is the return value of this task? As Future<V> is a generic interface, the type V is determined by the return type of the Runnable method. Since the return type of Runnable.run() is void, the get() method always returns null when working with Runnable expressions.

The Future.get() method can take an optional value and enum type java.util.concurrent.TimeUnit. Table 13.5 lists the full list of TimeUnit values since numerous methods in the Concurrency API use this enum.

TABLE 13.5 TimeUnit values

Enum name	Description
TimeUnit.NANOSECONDS	Time in one-billionths of a second (1/1,000,000,000)
TimeUnit.MICROSECONDS	Time in one-millionths of a second (1/1,000,000)
TimeUnit.MILLISECONDS	Time in one-thousandths of a second (1/1,000)
TimeUnit.SECONDS	Time in seconds
TimeUnit.MINUTES	Time in minutes
TimeUnit.HOURS	Time in hours
TimeUnit.DAYS	Time in days

Polling with Sleep

Polling is the process of intermittently checking data at some fixed interval. You might see code using Thread.sleep() inside of a loop for this purpose in older code. It is much better to use a Future and let Java handle the checking for you!

Investigating Callable

The java.util.concurrent.Callable functional interface is similar to Runnable except that its call() method returns a value and can throw a checked exception. The following is the definition of the Callable interface:

```
@FunctionalInterface public interface Callable<V> {
   V call() throws Exception;
}
```

When Callable<V> is passed to an ExecutorService via submit(), a Future<V> object is returned. Once the task is complete, calling get() on the Future<V> will return the result of type V. This allows you to find out a lot of information about the results of the task.

> The ExecutorService submit() method takes a Runnable and returns a Future<?> object. This object can be used to check if the thread is done. But, since Runnable tasks have a return type of void, calling get() on such a Future will always return null upon successful completion of the task.

The Callable interface is often preferable over Runnable, since it allows more details to be retrieved easily from the task after it is completed. That said, we use both interfaces, as they are interchangeable in situations where the lambda does not throw an exception, and there is no return type. Luckily, the ExecutorService includes an overloaded version of the submit() method that takes a Callable object and returns a generic Future<T> instance.

Let's take a look at an example using Callable:

```
try (var service = Executors.newSingleThreadExecutor()) {
   Future<Integer> result = service.submit(() -> 30 + 11);
   System.out.println(result.get());    // 41
}
```

This implementation is easier to code and understand than if we had used a Runnable, some shared object, and an interrupt() or timed wait. In essence, that's the spirit of the Concurrency API, giving you the tools to write multithreaded code that is thread-safe, performant, and easy to follow.

Shutting Down a Thread Executor

You might have noticed the ExecutorService has been declared in a try-with-resources block like you learned about in Chapter 11, "Exceptions and Localization." A thread executor creates a *non-daemon* thread on the first task that is executed, so forgetting to do this will result in your application *never terminating*. Don't believe us? Try executing the following:

```
public class MissingClose {
   public static void main(String[] args) {
```

```
    var service = Executors.newSingleThreadExecutor();
    service.submit(() -> System.out.println("Never stops"));
} }
```

This code runs but never terminates, because the ExecutorService is never shut down or closed. The fix is to always use an ExecutorService with a try-with-resources block. The try-with-resources block automatically calls close(), which shuts down the executor service so no more tasks get accepted. It then waits until they all complete execution.

Using an ExecutorService in a try-with-resources takes care of ensuring the tasks complete. However, the close() method was only added to this API in Java 19. In older code, you'd see an explicit shutdown() call. Or perhaps you want to tell tasks to end with shutdownNow(). In these scenarios, you wouldn't use the try-with-resources. Table 13.6 describes the behavior of these options.

TABLE 13.6   ExecutorService states

Scenario	Description	More tasks allowed	isShutdown()	isTerminated()
Active	Accepts tasks	Yes	false	false
shutdown()	Runs waiting tasks to completion, but doesn't accept more	No	true	false while tasks running true when tasks complete
close()	Calls shutdown() and then awaits termination of executing tasks	No	true	true
shutdownNow()	Stops executing tasks and cancels waiting tasks	No	true	false while tasks running true when tasks complete

Figure 13.4 shows how ExecutorService separates the states of shutdown and terminated.

When it's winding down and tasks are running, isShutdown() can return true, while isTerminated() can return false. Once the tasks complete, both methods return true.

Scheduling Tasks

Often in Java, we need to schedule a task to happen at some future time. We might even need to schedule the task to happen repeatedly, at some set interval. For example, imagine that we want to check the supply of food for zoo animals once an hour and fill it as needed.

ScheduledExecutorService, which is a subinterface of ExecutorService, can be used for just such a task.

FIGURE 13.4 Thread Executor Lifecycle

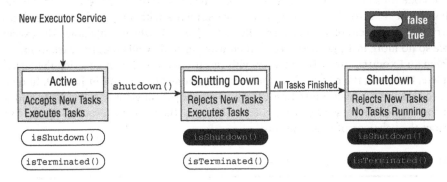

Like ExecutorService, we obtain an instance of ScheduledExecutorService using a factory method in the Executors class, as shown in the following snippet:

```
ScheduledExecutorService service
  = Executors.newSingleThreadScheduledExecutor();
```

Refer to Table 13.7 for our summary of ScheduledExecutorService methods. Each of these methods returns a ScheduledFuture object.

TABLE 13.7 ScheduledExecutorService methods

Method name	Description
schedule(Callable<V> callable, long delay, TimeUnit unit)	Creates and executes Callable task after given delay
schedule(Runnable command, long delay, TimeUnit unit)	Creates and executes Runnable task after given delay
scheduleAtFixedRate(Runnable command, long initialDelay, long period, TimeUnit unit)	Creates and executes Runnable task after given initial delay, creating new task every period value that passes
scheduleWithFixedDelay(Runnable command, long initialDelay, long delay, TimeUnit unit)	Creates and executes Runnable task after given initial delay and subsequently with given delay between termination of one execution and commencement of next

In practice, these methods are among the most convenient in the Concurrency API, as they perform relatively complex tasks with a single line of code. The delay and period parameters rely on the TimeUnit argument to determine the format of the value, such as seconds or milliseconds.

The first two schedule() methods in Table 13.7 take a Callable or Runnable, respectively; perform the task after some delay; and return a ScheduledFuture instance. The ScheduledFuture interface is identical to the Future interface, except that it includes a getDelay() method that returns the remaining delay. The following uses the schedule() method with Callable and Runnable tasks:

```
try (var service = Executors.newSingleThreadScheduledExecutor()) {
    Runnable task1 = () -> System.out.println("Hello Zoo");
    Callable<String> task2 = () -> "Monkey";
    ScheduledFuture<?> r1 = service.schedule(task1, 10, TimeUnit.SECONDS);
    ScheduledFuture<?> r2 = service.schedule(task2, 8,  TimeUnit.MINUTES);
}
```

The first task is scheduled 10 seconds in the future, whereas the second task is scheduled 8 minutes in the future.

While these tasks are scheduled in the future, the actual execution may be delayed. For example, there may be no threads available to perform the tasks, at which point they will just wait in the queue. Also, if the ScheduledExecutorService has completely shut down by the time the scheduled task execution time is reached, then these tasks will be discarded.

Each of the ScheduledExecutorService methods is important and has real-world applications. For example, you can use the schedule() command to check on the state of cleaning a lion's cage. It can then send out notifications if it is not finished or even call schedule() to check again later.

The last two methods in Table 13.7 might be a little confusing if you have not seen them before. Conceptually, they are similar as they both perform the same task repeatedly after an initial delay. The difference is related to the timing of the process and when the next task starts.

The scheduleAtFixedRate() method creates a new task and submits it to the executor every period, regardless of whether the previous task finished. The following example executes a Runnable task every minute, following an initial five-minute delay:

```
service.scheduleAtFixedRate(task1, 5, 1, TimeUnit.MINUTES);
```

The scheduleAtFixedRate() method is useful for tasks that need to be run at specific intervals, such as checking the health of the animals once a day. Even if it takes two hours to examine an animal on Monday, this doesn't mean that Tuesday's exam should start any later in the day.

Bad things can happen with scheduleAtFixedRate() if each task consistently takes longer to run than the execution interval. Imagine if your boss came by your desk every minute and dropped off a piece of paper. Now imagine that it took you five minutes to read each piece of paper. Before long, you would be drowning in piles of paper. This is how an executor feels. Given enough time, the program would submit more tasks to the executor service than could fit in memory, causing the program to crash.

On the other hand, the scheduleWithFixedDelay() method creates a new task only after the previous task has finished. For example, if a task runs at 12:00 and takes five minutes to finish, with a period between executions of two minutes, the next task will start at 12:07.

```
service.scheduleWithFixedDelay(task1, 0, 2, TimeUnit.MINUTES);
```

The scheduleWithFixedDelay() method is useful for processes that you want to happen repeatedly but whose specific time is unimportant. For example, imagine that we have a zoo cafeteria worker who periodically restocks the salad bar throughout the day. The process can take 20 minutes or more, since it requires the worker to haul a large number of items from the back room. Once the worker has filled the salad bar with fresh food, they don't need to check at some specific time, just after enough time has passed for it to become low on stock again.

Increasing Concurrency with Pools

All of our examples up until now have been with a single-thread executor, which, while interesting, weren't particularly useful. After all, the name of this chapter is "Concurrency," and you can't do a lot of that with a single-thread executor!

Luckily, the Executors class includes a variety of methods that act on a pool of threads. A *thread pool* is a group of pre-instantiated reusable threads that are available to perform a set of arbitrary tasks. Table 13.8 includes our two previous single-thread executor methods, along with the new ones that you should know for the exam.

TABLE 13.8   Executors factory methods

Method name	Description
ExecutorService **newSingleThreadExecutor()**	Creates single-threaded executor that uses single worker platform thread operating off unbounded queue. Results are processed sequentially in the order in which they are submitted.
ScheduledExecutorService **newSingleThreadScheduledExecutor()**	Creates single-threaded executor for platform threads that can schedule commands to run after given delay or to execute periodically.

Method name	Description
`ExecutorService` `newCachedThreadPool()`	Creates platform thread pool that creates new threads as needed but reuses previously constructed threads when they are available.
`ExecutorService` `newFixedThreadPool(int)`	Creates platform thread pool that reuses fixed number of threads operating off shared unbounded queue.
`ScheduledExecutorService` `newScheduledThreadPool(int)`	Creates platform thread pool that can schedule commands to run after given delay or execute periodically.
`ExecutorService` `newVirtualThreadPerTaskExecutor()`	Creates thread pool that creates a new virtual thread for each task.

As shown in Table 13.8, these methods return the same instance types, `ExecutorService` and `ScheduledExecutorService`, that we used earlier in this chapter. In other words, all of our previous examples are compatible with these new pooled-thread executors!

The difference between a single-thread and a pooled-thread executor is what happens when a task is already running. While a single-thread executor will wait for the thread to become available before running the next task, a pooled-thread executor can execute the next task concurrently. If the pool runs out of available threads, the task will be queued by the thread executor and wait to be completed.

All but the last row in Table 13.8 are for platform threads. Virtual threads have their own factory method `newVirtualThreadPerTaskExecutor`. They are not pooled since they are so lightweight. This allows a new virtual thread to be used for each task.

Writing Thread-Safe Code

Thread-safety is the property of an object that guarantees safe execution by multiple threads at the same time. Since threads run in a shared environment and memory space, how do we prevent two threads from interfering with each other? We must organize access to data so that we don't end up with invalid or unexpected results.

In this part of the chapter, we show how to use a variety of techniques to protect data, including atomic classes, `synchronized` blocks, the `Lock` framework, and cyclic barriers.

Understanding Thread-Safety

Imagine that our zoo has a program to count sheep, preferably one that won't put the zoo workers to sleep! Each zoo worker runs out to a field, adds a new sheep to the flock, counts the total number of sheep, and runs back to us to report the results. The following shows this conceptually, choosing a thread pool size so that all tasks can be run concurrently:

```
1:  import java.util.concurrent.*;
2:  public class SheepManager {
3:     private int sheepCount = 0;
4:     private void incrementAndReport() {
5:        System.out.print((++sheepCount) + " ");
6:     }
7:     public static void main(String[] args) {
8:        try (var service = Executors.newFixedThreadPool(20)) {
9:           SheepManager manager = new SheepManager();
10:          for (int i = 0; i < 10; i++)
11:             service.submit(() -> manager.incrementAndReport());
12:  } } }
```

What does this program output? You might think it will output numbers from 1 to 10, in order, but that is far from guaranteed. It may output in a different order. Worse yet, it may print some numbers twice and not print some numbers at all! The following are possible outputs of this program:

```
1 2 3 4 5 6 7 8 9 10
1 9 8 7 3 6 6 2 4 5
1 8 7 3 2 6 5 4 2 9
```

So, what went wrong? In this example, we use the pre-increment (++) operator to update the sheepCount variable. A problem occurs when two threads both read the "old" value before either thread writes the "new" value of the variable. The two assignments become redundant; they both assign the same new value, with one thread overwriting the results of the other. Figure 13.5 demonstrates this problem with two threads, assuming that sheepCount has a starting value of 1.

You can see in Figure 13.5 that both threads read and write the same values, causing one of the two ++sheepCount operations to be lost. Therefore, the increment operator ++ is not thread-safe. As you will see later in this chapter, the unexpected result of two or more tasks executing at the same time is referred to as a *race condition*.

Conceptually, the idea here is that some zoo workers may run faster on their way to the field but more slowly on their way back and report late. Other workers may get to the field last but somehow be the first ones back to report the results.

The volatile modifier can be used on an instance variable to ensure a thread does not see any intermediary values while an operation is being performed. Unfortunately, adding it to the sheepCount variable in our

previous example is insufficient for thread-safety since ++sheepCount
is really two separate read and write operations. In practice, volatile is
rarely used. We only mention it because it has been known to show up on
the exam from time to time.

FIGURE 13.5   Lack of thread synchronization

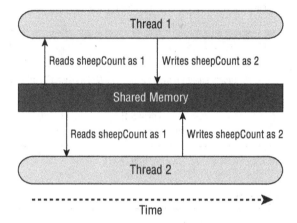

Protecting Data with Atomic Classes

In our previous SheepManager application, the same values were sometimes printed twice,
with the highest counter being 9 instead of 10. As we saw, the increment operator ++ is not
thread-safe because the operation is not atomic, carrying out two tasks, read and write, that
can be interrupted by other threads.

Atomic is the property of an operation to be carried out as a single unit of execution
without any interference from another thread. A thread-safe atomic version of the increment
operator would perform the read and write of the variable as a single operation, not
allowing any other threads to access the variable during the operation. Figure 13.6 shows
the result of making the sheepCount variable atomic.

In this case, any thread trying to access the sheepCount variable while an atomic operation is in process will have to wait until the atomic operation on the variable is complete.
Conceptually, this is like setting a rule for our zoo workers that there can be only one
employee in the field at a time, although they may not each report their results in order.

Since accessing primitives and references is common in Java, the Concurrency API
includes numerous useful classes in the java.util.concurrent.atomic package.
Table 13.9 lists the atomic classes with which you should be familiar for the exam. As with
many of the classes in the Concurrency API, these classes exist to make your life easier.

FIGURE 13.6   Thread synchronization using atomic operations

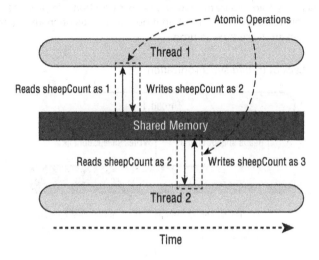

TABLE 13.9   Atomic classes

Class name	Description
AtomicBoolean	A boolean value that may be updated atomically
AtomicInteger	An int value that may be updated atomically
AtomicLong	A long value that may be updated atomically

How do we use an atomic class? Each class includes numerous methods that are equivalent to many of the built-in operators that we use on primitives, such as the assignment operator (=) and the increment operators (++). We describe the common atomic methods that you should know for the exam in Table 13.10. The *type* is determined by the class.

TABLE 13.10   Common atomic methods

Method name	Description
get()	Retrieves current value
set(*type* newValue)	Sets given value, equivalent to assignment = operator
getAndSet(*type* newValue)	Atomically sets new value and returns old value

Method name	Description
`incrementAndGet()`	For numeric classes, atomic pre-increment operation equivalent to ++value
`getAndIncrement()`	For numeric classes, atomic post-increment operation equivalent to value++
`decrementAndGet()`	For numeric classes, atomic pre-decrement operation equivalent to --value
`getAndDecrement()`	For numeric classes, atomic post-decrement operation equivalent to value--

In the following example, assume we import the `atomic` package and then update our `SheepManager` class with an `AtomicInteger`:

```
3:     private AtomicInteger sheepCount = new AtomicInteger(0);
4:     private void incrementAndReport() {
5:         System.out.print(sheepCount.incrementAndGet() + " ");
6:     }
```

How does this implementation differ from our previous examples? When we run this modification, we get varying output, such as the following:

```
2 3 1 4 5 6 7 8 9 10
1 4 3 2 5 6 7 8 9 10
1 4 3 5 6 2 7 8 10 9
```

Unlike our previous sample output, the numbers 1 through 10 will always be printed, although the order is still not guaranteed. Don't worry; we address that issue shortly. The key in this section is that using the atomic classes ensures that the data is consistent between workers and that no values are lost due to concurrent modifications.

Improving Access with *synchronized* Blocks

While atomic classes are great at protecting a single variable, they aren't particularly useful if you need to execute a series of commands or call a method. For example, we can't use them to update two atomic variables at the same time. How do we improve the results so that each worker is able to increment and report the results in order?

The most common technique is to use a monitor to synchronize access. A *monitor*, also called a *lock*, is a structure that supports *mutual exclusion*, which is the property that at most one thread is executing a particular segment of code at a given time.

In Java, any `Object` can be used as a monitor, along with the `synchronized` keyword, as shown in the following example:

```
var manager = new SheepManager();
synchronized(manager) {
    // Work to be completed by one thread at a time
}
```

This example is referred to as a *synchronized block*. Each thread that arrives will first check if any threads are already running the block. If the lock is not available, the thread will transition to a BLOCKED state until it can "acquire the lock." If the lock is available (or the thread already holds the lock), the single thread will enter the block, preventing all other threads from entering. Once the thread finishes executing the block, it will release the lock, allowing one of the waiting threads to proceed.

> To synchronize access across multiple threads, each thread must have access to the *same* `Object`. If each thread synchronizes on different objects, the code is not thread-safe.

Let's revisit our `SheepManager` example that used `++sheepCount` and see whether we can improve the results so that each worker increments and outputs the counter in order. Let's say that we replaced our `for()` loop with the following implementation:

```
10: for (int i = 0; i < 10; i++) {
11:     synchronized(manager) {
12:         service.submit(() -> manager.incrementAndReport());
13:     }
14: }
```

Does this solution fix the problem? No, it does not! Can you spot the problem? We've synchronized the *creation* of the threads but not the *execution* of the threads. In this example, the threads would be created one at a time, but they might all still execute and perform their work simultaneously, resulting in the same type of output that you saw earlier. We did say diagnosing and resolving thread problems is difficult in practice!

This is a corrected version of the `SheepManager` class that orders the workers:

```
1:  import java.util.concurrent.*;
2:  public class SheepManager {
3:      private int sheepCount = 0;
4:      private void incrementAndReport() {
5:          synchronized(this) {
6:              System.out.print((++sheepCount) + " ");
7:          }
8:      }
9:      public static void main(String[] args) {
```

```
10:        try (var service = Executors.newFixedThreadPool(20)) {
11:            var manager = new SheepManager();
12:            for (int i = 0; i < 10; i++)
13:                service.submit(() -> manager.incrementAndReport());
14:        } } }
```

When this code executes, it will consistently output the following:

```
1 2 3 4 5 6 7 8 9 10
```

Although all threads are still created and executed at the same time, they each wait at the `synchronized` block for the worker to increment and report the result before entering. In this manner, each zoo worker waits for the previous zoo worker to come back before running out on the field. While it's random which zoo worker will run out next, it is guaranteed that there will be at most one on the field and that the results will be reported in order.

We could have synchronized on any object, as long as it was the same object. For example, the following code snippet would also work:

```
4:    private final Object herd = new Object();
5:    private void incrementAndReport() {
6:        synchronized(herd) {
7:            System.out.print((++sheepCount) + " ");
8:        }
9:    }
```

Although we didn't need to make the `herd` variable `final`, doing so ensures that it is not reassigned after threads start using it.

Synchronizing Methods

In the previous example, we established our monitor using `synchronized(this)` around the body of the method. Java provides a more convenient syntax for doing so. We can add the `synchronized` modifier to any instance method to synchronize automatically on the object itself. For example, the following two method definitions are equivalent:

```
void sing() {
    synchronized(this) {
        System.out.print("La la la!");
    }
}
synchronized void sing() {
    System.out.print("La la la!");
}
```

The first uses a synchronized block, whereas the second uses the synchronized method modifier. Which you use is completely up to you.

We can also apply the synchronized modifier to static methods. What object is used as the monitor when we synchronize on a static method? The class object, of course! For example, the following two methods are equivalent for static synchronization inside our SheepManager class:

```java
static void dance() {
    synchronized(SheepManager.class) {
        System.out.print("Time to dance!");
    }
}
static synchronized void dance() {
    System.out.print("Time to dance!");
}
```

As before, the first uses a synchronized block, with the second example using the synchronized modifier. You can use static synchronization if you need to order thread access across all instances rather than a single instance.

Understanding the Lock Framework

A synchronized block supports only a limited set of functionality. For example, what if we want to check whether a lock is available and, if it is not, perform some other task? Furthermore, if the lock is never available and we synchronize on it, we might wait forever.

The Concurrency API includes the Lock interface, which is conceptually similar to using the synchronized keyword but with a lot more bells and whistles.

Applying a *ReentrantLock*

The Lock interface is pretty easy to use. When you need to protect a piece of code from multithreaded processing, create an instance of Lock that all threads have access to. Each thread then calls lock() before it enters the protected code and calls unlock() before it exits the protected code.

For contrast, the following shows two implementations, one with a synchronized block and one with a Lock instance. While longer, the Lock solution has a number of features not available to the synchronized block.

```java
// Implementation #1 with a synchronized block
var object = new Object();
synchronized(object) {
    // Protected code
}


// Implementation #2 with a Lock
var myLock = new ReentrantLock();
```

```
try {
    myLock.lock();
    // Protected code
} finally {
    myLock.unlock();
}
```

These two implementations are conceptually equivalent. The ReentrantLock class is a simple monitor that implements the Lock interface and supports mutual exclusion. In other words, at most one thread is allowed to hold a lock at any given time.

 While certainly not required, it is a good practice to use a try/finally block with Lock instances to ensure that any acquired locks are properly released. This can help prevent a resource leak in practice.

The ReentrantLock class ensures that once a thread has called lock() and obtained the lock, all other threads that call lock() will wait until the first thread calls unlock(). Which thread gets the lock next depends on the parameters used to create the Lock object.

If you need to control the order threads run, you can use the ReentrantLock constructor that takes a single boolean "fairness" parameter. In practice, you should enable fairness only when ordering is absolutely required, as it could lead to a significant slowdown.

Besides always making sure to release a lock, you also need to be sure that you only release a lock that you have. If you attempt to release a lock that you do not have, you will get an exception at runtime.

```
var lock = new ReentrantLock();
lock.unlock();  // IllegalMonitorStateException
```

The Lock interface includes four methods you should know for the exam, as listed in Table 13.11.

TABLE 13.11   Lock methods

Method name	Description
void **lock()**	Requests lock and blocks until lock is acquired.
void **unlock()**	Releases lock.
boolean **tryLock()**	Requests lock and returns immediately. Returns boolean indicating whether lock was successfully acquired.
boolean **tryLock(** long timeout, TimeUnit unit)	Requests lock and blocks for specified time or until lock is acquired. Returns boolean indicating whether lock was successfully acquired.

Attempting to Acquire a Lock

While the ReentrantLock class allows you to wait for a lock, it so far suffers from the same problem as a synchronized block. A thread could end up waiting forever to obtain a lock. Luckily, Table 13.11 includes two additional methods that make the Lock interface a lot safer to use than a synchronized block.

For convenience, we use the following printHello() method for the code in this section:

```
static void printHello(Lock myLock) {
   try {
      myLock.lock();
      System.out.println("Hello");
   } finally {
      myLock.unlock();
   } }
```

The tryLock() method will attempt to acquire a lock and immediately return a boolean result indicating whether the lock was obtained. Unlike the lock() method, it does not wait if another thread already holds the lock. It returns immediately, regardless of whether a lock is available.

The following is a sample implementation using the tryLock() method:

```
var myLock = new ReentrantLock();
Thread.ofPlatform().start(() -> printHello(myLock));
if (myLock.tryLock()) {
   try {
      System.out.println("Lock obtained, entering protected code");
   } finally {
      myLock.unlock();
   }
} else {
   System.out.println("Unable to acquire lock, doing something else");
}
```

When you run this code, it could produce either the if or else message, depending on the order of execution. It will always print Hello, though, as the call to lock() in printHello() will wait indefinitely for the lock to become available. A fun exercise is to insert some Thread.sleep() delays into this snippet to encourage a particular message to be displayed.

Like lock(), the tryLock() method should be used with a try/finally block. Fortunately, you need to release the lock only if it was successfully acquired. For this reason, it is common to use the output of tryLock() in an if statement, so that unlock() is called only when the lock is obtained.

It is imperative that your program always check the return value of the `tryLock()` method. It tells your program whether it is safe to proceed with the operation and whether the lock needs to be released later.

The Lock interface includes an overloaded version of `tryLock(long, TimeUnit)` that acts like a hybrid of `lock()` and `tryLock()`. Like the other two methods, if a lock is available, it will immediately return with it. If a lock is unavailable, though, it will wait up to the specified time limit for the lock.

Acquiring the Same Lock Twice

The `ReentrantLock` class maintains a counter of the number of times a lock has been successfully granted to a thread. To release the lock for other threads to use, `unlock()` must be called the same number of times the lock was granted. The following code snippet contains an error. Can you spot it?

```
var myLock = new ReentrantLock();
if (myLock.tryLock()) {
   try {
      myLock.lock();
      System.out.println("Lock obtained, entering protected code");
   } finally {
      myLock.unlock();
   } }
```

The thread obtains the lock twice but releases it only once. You can verify this by spawning a new thread after this code runs that attempts to obtain a lock. The following prints `false`:

```
Thread.ofPlatform().start(() -> System.out.print(myLock.tryLock()));
```

It is critical that you release a lock the same number of times it is acquired! For calls with `tryLock()`, you need to call `unlock()` only if the method returned `true`.

Reviewing the *Lock* Framework

To review, the `ReentrantLock` class supports the same features as a `synchronized` block while adding a number of improvements:

- Ability to request a lock without blocking.
- Ability to request a lock while blocking for a specified amount of time.
- A lock can be created with a `fairness` property, in which the lock is granted to threads in the order in which it was requested.

Introducing *ReentrantReadWriteLock*

When working with shared data, reading data is often far more common than writing data. For example, a single operator at the zoo might be updating the lunch menu that thousands of patrons are reading from their phone.

For this reason, ReentrantReadWriteLock is a really useful class. It includes separate locks for reading and writing data. At runtime, only one thread can hold the write lock at a time, but many threads can hold the read lock. Having separate locks can help you maximize concurrent access.

```java
var lock = new ReentrantReadWriteLock();
lock.writeLock().lock();
lock.readLock().lock();
System.out.println(lock.isWriteLocked());     // true
System.out.println(lock.getReadLockCount());  // 1

lock.writeLock().unlock();
System.out.println(lock.isWriteLocked());     // false
System.out.println(lock.getReadLockCount());  // 1

lock.readLock().unlock();
System.out.println(lock.getReadLockCount());  // 0
```

On the exam, you are likely to see it used within a single class. You need to know that you can trivially get a read lock after acquiring a write lock because reading is a subset of write. However, if you attempt to get the read lock first, the code will hang as you can't upgrade to a write lock.

```java
var lock = new ReentrantReadWriteLock();
lock.readLock().lock();
lock.writeLock().lock();  // Wait forever
```

Orchestrating Tasks with a *CyclicBarrier*

We started the thread-safety topic by discussing protecting individual variables and then moved on to blocks of code and locks. We complete our discussion of thread-safety by showing how to orchestrate complex tasks with many steps.

Our zoo workers are back, and this time they are cleaning pens. Imagine a lion pen that needs to be emptied, cleaned, and then refilled with the lions. To complete the task, we have assigned four zoo workers. Obviously, we don't want to start cleaning the cage while a lion is roaming in it, lest we end up losing a zoo worker! Furthermore, we don't want to let the lions back into the pen while it is still being cleaned.

We could have all of the work completed by a single worker, but this would be slow and ignore the fact that we have three zoo workers standing by to help. A better solution would be to have all four zoo employees work concurrently, pausing between the end of one set of tasks and the start of the next.

To coordinate these tasks, we can use the `CyclicBarrier` class:

```java
import java.util.concurrent.*;
public class LionPenManager {
    private void removeLions() { System.out.println("Removing lions");   }
    private void cleanPen()    { System.out.println("Cleaning the pen"); }
    private void addLions()    { System.out.println("Adding lions");     }
    public void performTask() {
        removeLions();
        cleanPen();
        addLions();
    }
    public static void main(String[] args) {
        try (var service = Executors.newFixedThreadPool(4)) {
            var manager = new LionPenManager();
            for (int i = 0; i < 4; i++)
                service.submit(() -> manager.performTask());
    } } }
```

The following is sample output based on this implementation:

```
Removing lions
Removing lions
Cleaning the pen
Adding lions
Removing lions
Cleaning the pen
Adding lions
Removing lions
Cleaning the pen
Adding lions
Cleaning the pen
Adding lions
```

Although the results are ordered within a single thread, the output is entirely random among multiple workers. We see that some lions are still being removed while the cage is being cleaned, and other lions are added before the cleaning process is finished. Let's hope none of the zoo workers get eaten!

We can improve these results by using the `CyclicBarrier` class. The `CyclicBarrier` class takes in its constructors a `limit` value, indicating the number of threads to wait for. As each thread finishes, it calls the `await()` method on the cyclic barrier. Once the specified number of threads have each called `await()`, the barrier is released, and all threads can continue.

```java
import java.util.concurrent.*;
public class LionPenManager {
    private void removeLions() { System.out.println("Removing lions");   }
    private void cleanPen()    { System.out.println("Cleaning the pen"); }
    private void addLions()    { System.out.println("Adding lions");     }
    public void performTask(CyclicBarrier c1, CyclicBarrier c2) {
        try {
            removeLions();
            c1.await();
            cleanPen();
            c2.await();
            addLions();
        } catch (InterruptedException | BrokenBarrierException e) {
            // Handle checked exceptions here
        }
    }
    public static void main(String[] args) {
        try (var service = Executors.newFixedThreadPool(4)) {
            var manager = new LionPenManager();
            var c1 = new CyclicBarrier(4);
            var c2 = new CyclicBarrier(4,
                () -> System.out.println("*** Pen Cleaned!"));
            for (int i = 0; i < 4; i++)
                service.submit(() -> manager.performTask(c1, c2));
} } }
```

The following is sample output based on this revised implementation of our `LionPenManager` class:

```
Removing lions
Removing lions
Removing lions
Removing lions
Cleaning the pen
Cleaning the pen
Cleaning the pen
Cleaning the pen
```

```
*** Pen Cleaned!
Adding lions
Adding lions
Adding lions
Adding lions
```

As you can see, all of the results are now organized. Removing the lions happens in one step, as does cleaning the pen and adding the lions back in. In this example, we used two different constructors for our `CyclicBarrier` objects, the latter of which executes a `Runnable` instance upon completion.

The `CyclicBarrier` class allows us to perform complex, multithreaded tasks while all threads stop and wait at logical barriers. This solution is superior to a single-threaded solution, as the individual tasks, such as removing the lions, can be completed in parallel by all four zoo workers.

Reusing *CyclicBarrier*

After a CyclicBarrier limit is reached (aka the barrier is broken), all threads are released, and the number of threads waiting on the CyclicBarrier goes back to zero. At this point, the CyclicBarrier may be used again for a new set of waiting threads. For example, if our CyclicBarrier limit is 5 and we have 15 threads that call await(), the CyclicBarrier will be activated a total of three times.

Using Concurrent Collections

Besides managing threads, the Concurrency API includes interfaces and classes that help you coordinate access to collections shared by multiple tasks. By collections, we are of course referring to the Java Collections Framework that we introduced in Chapter 9, "Collections and Generics." In this section, we demonstrate many of the concurrent classes available to you when using the Concurrency API.

Understanding Memory Consistency Errors

The purpose of the concurrent collection classes is to solve common memory consistency errors. A *memory consistency error* occurs when two threads have inconsistent views of what should be the same data. Conceptually, we want writes on one thread to be available to another thread if it accesses the concurrent collection after the write has occurred.

When two threads try to modify the same nonconcurrent collection, the JVM may throw a ConcurrentModificationException at runtime. In fact, it can happen with a single thread. Take a look at the following code snippet:

```
11: var foodData = new HashMap<String, Integer>();
12: foodData.put("penguin", 1);
13: foodData.put("flamingo", 2);
14: for (String key : foodData.keySet())
15:     foodData.remove(key);
```

This snippet will throw a ConcurrentModificationException during the second iteration of the loop, since the iterator on keySet() is not properly updated after the first element is removed. Changing the first line to use a ConcurrentHashMap will prevent the code from throwing an exception at runtime.

```
11: var foodData = new ConcurrentHashMap<String, Integer>();
```

Although we don't usually modify a loop variable, this example highlights the fact that the ConcurrentHashMap is ordering read/write access such that all access to the class is consistent. In this code snippet, the iterator created by keySet() is updated as soon as an object is removed from the Map.

The concurrent classes were created to help avoid common issues in which multiple threads are adding and removing objects from the same collections. At any given instance, all threads should have the same consistent view of the structure of the collection.

Working with Concurrent Classes

You should use a concurrent collection class any time you have multiple threads modify a collection outside a synchronized block or method, even if you don't expect a concurrency problem. Without the concurrent collections, multiple threads accessing a collection could result in an exception being thrown or, worse, corrupt data!

> If the collection is immutable (and contains immutable objects), the concurrent collections are not necessary. Immutable objects can be accessed by any number of threads and do not require synchronization. By definition, they do not change, so there is no chance of a memory consistency error.

Table 13.12 lists the common concurrent classes with which you should be familiar for the exam.

TABLE 13.12   Concurrent collection classes

Class name	Java Collections interfaces	Sorted?	Blocking?
ConcurrentHashMap	Map ConcurrentMap	No	No
ConcurrentLinkedQueue	Queue	No	No

Class name	Java Collections interfaces	Sorted?	Blocking?
ConcurrentSkipListMap	Map SequencedMap SortedMap NavigableMap ConcurrentMap ConcurrentNavigableMap	Yes	No
ConcurrentSkipListSet	Set SequencedSet SortedSet NavigableSet	Yes	No
CopyOnWriteArrayList	List SequencedCollection	No	No
CopyOnWriteArraySet	Set	No	No
LinkedBlockingQueue	Queue BlockingQueue	No	Yes

Most of the classes in Table 13.12 are just concurrent versions of their nonconcurrent counterpart classes, such as ConcurrentHashMap vs. HashMap, or ConcurrentLinkedQueue vs. LinkedList. For the exam, you don't need to know any class-specific concurrent methods. You just need to know the inherited methods, such as get() and set() for List instances.

The Skip classes might sound strange, but they are just "sorted" versions of the associated concurrent collections. When you see a class with Skip in the name, just think "sorted concurrent" collections, and the rest should follow naturally.

The CopyOnWrite classes behave a little differently than the other concurrent data structures you have seen. These classes create a copy of the collection any time a reference is added, removed, or changed in the collection and then update the original collection reference to point to the copy. These classes are commonly used to ensure an iterator doesn't see modifications to the collection.

Let's take a look at how this works with an example:

```
List<Integer> favNumbers = new CopyOnWriteArrayList<>(List.of(4, 3, 42));
for (var n : favNumbers) {
    System.out.print(n + " ");  // 4 3 42
    favNumbers.add(n + 1);
}
System.out.println();
System.out.println("Size: " + favNumbers.size());  // Size: 6
```

Despite adding elements, the iterator is not modified, and the loop executes exactly three times. Alternatively, if we had used a regular ArrayList object, a ConcurrentModificationException would have been thrown at runtime. The CopyOnWrite classes can use a lot of memory, since a new collection structure is created any time the collection is modified. Therefore, they are commonly used in multithreaded environment situations where reads are far more common than writes.

Finally, Table 13.12 includes LinkedBlockingQueue, which implements the concurrent BlockingQueue interface. This class is just like a regular Queue, except that it includes overloaded versions of offer() and poll() that take a timeout. These methods wait (or block) up to a specific amount of time to complete an operation.

Obtaining Synchronized Collections

Besides the concurrent collection classes that we have covered, the Concurrency API also includes methods for obtaining synchronized versions of existing nonconcurrent collection objects. These synchronized methods are defined in the Collections class. They operate on the inputted collection and return a reference that is the same type as the underlying collection. We list these static methods in Table 13.13.

TABLE 13.13   Synchronized Collections methods

synchronizedCollection(Collection<T> c)
synchronizedList(List<T> list)
synchronizedMap(Map<K,V> m)
synchronizedNavigableMap(NavigableMap<K,V> m)
synchronizedNavigableSet(NavigableSet<T> s)
synchronizedSet(Set<T> s)
synchronizedSortedMap(SortedMap<K,V> m)
synchronizedSortedSet(SortedSet<T> s)

If you're writing code to create a collection and it requires synchronization, you should use the classes defined in Table 13.12. On the other hand, if you are passed a nonconcurrent collection and need synchronization, use the methods in Table 13.13.

Identifying Threading Problems

Now that you know how to write thread-safe code, let's talk about what qualifies as a threading problem. A threading problem can occur in multithreaded applications when two or more threads interact in an unexpected and undesirable way. For example, two threads may block each other from accessing a particular segment of code.

The Concurrency API was created to help eliminate potential threading issues common to all developers. As you have seen, the Concurrency API creates threads and manages complex thread interactions for you, often in just a few lines of code.

Although the Concurrency API reduces the potential for threading issues, it does not eliminate them. In practice, finding and identifying threading issues within an application is often one of the most difficult tasks a developer can undertake.

Understanding Liveness

As you have seen in this chapter, many thread operations can be performed independently, but some require coordination. For example, synchronizing on a method requires all threads that call the method to wait for other threads to finish before continuing. You also saw earlier in the chapter that threads in a CyclicBarrier will each wait for the barrier limit to be reached before continuing.

What happens to the application while all of these threads are waiting? In many cases, the waiting is ephemeral, and the user has very little idea that any delay has occurred. In other cases, though, the waiting may be extremely long, perhaps infinite.

Liveness is the ability of an application to be able to execute in a timely manner. Liveness problems, then, are those in which the application becomes unresponsive or is in some kind of "stuck" state. More precisely, liveness problems are often the result of a thread entering a BLOCKING or WAITING state forever, or repeatedly entering/exiting these states. For the exam, there are three types of liveness issues with which you should be familiar: deadlock, starvation, and livelock.

Deadlock

Deadlock occurs when two or more threads are blocked forever, each waiting on the other. We can illustrate this principle with the following example. Imagine that our zoo has two foxes: Foxy and Tails. Foxy likes to eat first and then drink water, while Tails likes to drink water first and then eat. Furthermore, neither animal likes to share, and they will finish their meal only if they have exclusive access to both food and water.

The zookeeper places the food on one side of the environment and the water on the other side. Although our foxes are fast, it still takes them 100 milliseconds to run from one side of the environment to the other.

What happens if Foxy gets the food first and Tails gets the water first? The following application models this behavior:

```java
class Food {}
class Water {}
public record Fox(String name) {
   public void eatAndDrink(Food food, Water water) {
      synchronized(food) {
         System.out.println(name() + " Got Food!");
         move();
         synchronized(water) {
            System.out.println(name() + " Got Water!");
      } } }
   public void drinkAndEat(Food food, Water water) {
      synchronized(water) {
         System.out.println(name() + " Got Water!");
         move();
         synchronized(food) {
            System.out.println(name() + " Got Food!");
      } } }
   public void move() {
      try { Thread.sleep(100); } catch (InterruptedException e) {}
   }
   public static void main(String[] args) {
      // Create participants and resources
      var foxy = new Fox("Foxy");
      var tails = new Fox("Tails");
      var food = new Food();
      var water = new Water();
      // Process data
      try (var service = Executors.newScheduledThreadPool(10)) {
         service.submit(() -> foxy.eatAndDrink(food,water));
         service.submit(() -> tails.drinkAndEat(food,water));
   } } }
```

In this example, Foxy obtains the food and then moves to the other side of the environment to obtain the water. Unfortunately, Tails already drank the water and is waiting for the food to become available. The result is that our program outputs the following, and it hangs indefinitely:

```
Foxy Got Food!
Tails Got Water!
```

This example is considered a deadlock because both participants are permanently blocked, waiting on resources that will never become available.

Starvation

Starvation occurs when a single thread is perpetually denied access to a shared resource or lock. The thread is still active, but it is unable to complete its work as a result of other threads constantly taking the resource that it is trying to access.

In our fox example, imagine that we have a pack of very hungry, very competitive foxes in our environment. Every time Foxy stands up to go get food, one of the other foxes sees her and rushes to eat before her. Foxy is free to roam around the enclosure, take a nap, and howl for a zookeeper but is never able to obtain access to the food. In this example, Foxy literally and figuratively experiences starvation. It's a good thing that this is just a theoretical example!

Livelock

Livelock occurs when two or more threads are conceptually blocked forever, although they are each still active and trying to complete their task. Livelock is a special case of resource starvation in which two or more threads actively try to acquire a set of locks, are unable to do so, and restart part of the process.

Livelock is often a result of two threads trying to resolve a deadlock. Returning to our fox example, imagine that Foxy and Tails are both holding their food and water resources, respectively. They each realize that they cannot finish their meal in this state, so they both let go of their food and water, run to the opposite side of the environment, and pick up the other resource. Now Foxy has the water, Tails has the food, and neither is able to finish their meal!

If Foxy and Tails continue this process forever, it is referred to as *livelock*. Both Foxy and Tails are active, running back and forth across their area, but neither can finish their meal. Foxy and Tails are executing a form of failed deadlock recovery. Each fox notices that they are potentially entering a deadlock state and responds by releasing all of its locked resources. Unfortunately, the lock and unlock process is cyclical, and the two foxes are conceptually deadlocked.

In practice, livelock is often a difficult issue to detect. Threads in a livelock state appear active and able to respond to requests, even when they are stuck in an endless cycle.

Managing Race Conditions

A *race condition* is an undesirable result that occurs when two tasks that should be completed sequentially are completed at the same time. We encountered examples of race conditions earlier in the chapter when we introduced synchronization.

While Figure 13.5 shows a classical thread-based example of a race condition, we now provide a more illustrative example. Imagine that two zoo patrons, Olivia and Sophia, are signing up for an account on the zoo's new visitor website. Both of them want to use the same username, ZooFan, and each sends a request to create the account at the same time, as shown in Figure 13.7.

What result does the web server return when both users attempt to create an account with the same username in Figure 13.7?

FIGURE 13.7 Race condition on user creation

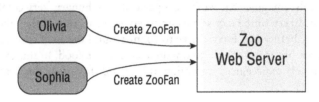

Possible Outcomes for This Race Condition

- Both users are able to create accounts with the username ZooFan.

- Neither user is able to create an account with the username ZooFan, and an error message is returned to both users.

- One user is able to create an account with the username ZooFan, while the other user receives an error message.

The first outcome is *really bad*, as it leads to users trying to log in with the same username. Whose data do they see when they log in? The second outcome causes both users to have to try again, which is frustrating but at least doesn't lead to corrupt or bad data.

The third outcome is often considered the best solution. Like the second situation, we preserve data integrity; but unlike the second situation, at least one user is able to move forward on the first request, avoiding additional race condition scenarios.

For the exam, you should understand that race conditions lead to invalid data if they are not properly handled. Even the solution where both participants fail to proceed is preferable to one in which invalid data is permitted to enter the system.

Working with Parallel Streams

We conclude this chapter by combining what you learned in Chapter 10, "Streams," with the concepts you learned about in this chapter. One of the most powerful features of the Stream API is built-in concurrency support. Up until now, all of the streams you have worked with have been serial streams. A *serial stream* is a stream in which the results are ordered, with only one entry being processed at a time.

A *parallel stream* is capable of processing results concurrently, using multiple threads. For example, you can use a parallel stream and the map() operation to operate concurrently on the elements in the stream, vastly improving performance over processing a single element at a time.

Using a parallel stream can change not only the performance of your application but also the expected results. As you shall see, some operations also require special handling to be able to be processed in a parallel manner.

Generating Random Numbers

In Chapter 4, "Core APIs," you learned about generating random numbers for a single-threaded program. To generate random numbers in a multithreaded program, you use the `ThreadLocalRandom` class instead. To start out, you get an instance using `current()`. Then all the instance methods are available to you.

```
ThreadLocalRandom.current()
    .ints()
    .limit(5)
    .forEach(System.out::println);  // Prints 5 random ints
```

There are six methods available for working with ints:

- **ints()**: Infinite stream of any `int` values

- **ints(lowestInclusive, highestExclusive)**: Unlimited stream of `int` values between the two parameters, excluding the second one

- **ints(numberIntsToInclude)**: Finite stream of the requested number of `int` values

- **ints(numberIntsToInclude, lowestInclusive, highestExclusive)**: Finite stream of the requested number of `int` values between the two parameters, excluding the second one

- **nextInt(highestExclusive)**: Single `int` between 0 and the parameter, not including the parameter

- **nextInt(lowestInclusive, highestExclusive)**: Single `int` between the first parameter and the second parameter, not including the second parameter

Similar methods are available for doubles and longs, such `doubles()`, `nextDouble()`, `longs()`, `nextLong()`, etc.

Creating Parallel Streams

The Stream API was designed to make creating parallel streams quite easy. For the exam, you should be familiar with two ways of creating a parallel stream.

```
Collection<Integer> collection = List.of(1, 2);

Stream<Integer> p1 = collection.stream().parallel();
Stream<Integer> p2 = collection.parallelStream();
```

The first way to create a parallel stream is from an existing stream. Isn't this cool? Any stream can be made parallel! The second way to create a parallel stream is from a Java Collection class. We use both of these methods throughout this section.

 The Stream interface includes a method isParallel() that can be used to test whether the instance of a stream supports parallel processing. Some operations on streams preserve the parallel attribute, while others do not.

Performing a Parallel Decomposition

A *parallel decomposition* is the process of taking a task, breaking it into smaller pieces that can be performed concurrently, and then reassembling the results. The more concurrent a decomposition, the greater the performance improvement of using parallel streams.

Let's try it out. First, let's define a reusable function that "does work" just by waiting for five seconds.

```
private static int doWork(int input) {
   try {
      Thread.sleep(5000);
   } catch (InterruptedException e) {}
   return input;
}
```

We can pretend that in a real application, this work might involve calling a database or reading a file. Now let's use this method with a serial stream.

```
10: long start = System.currentTimeMillis();
11: List.of(1, 2, 3, 4, 5)
12:    .stream()
13:    .map(w -> doWork(w))
14:    .forEach(s -> System.out.print(s + " "));
15:
16: System.out.println();
17: var timeTaken = (System.currentTimeMillis()-start)/1000;
18: System.out.println("Time: " + timeTaken + " seconds");
```

What do you think this code will output when executed as part of a main() method? Let's take a look:

```
1 2 3 4 5
Time: 25 seconds
```

As you might expect, the results are ordered and predictable because we are using a serial stream. It also took around 25 seconds to process all five results, one at a time. What happens if we replace line 12 with one that uses a `parallelStream()`? The following is some sample output:

```
3 2 1 5 4
Time: 5 seconds
```

As you can see, the results are no longer ordered or predictable. The `map()` and `forEach()` operations on a parallel stream are equivalent to submitting multiple `Runnable` lambda expressions to a pooled thread executor and then waiting for the results.

What about the time required? In this case, our system had enough CPUs for all of the tasks to be run concurrently. If you ran this same code on a computer with fewer processors, it might output 10 seconds, 15 seconds, or some other value. The key is that we've written our code to take advantage of parallel processing when available, so our job is done.

Ordering Results

If your stream operation needs to guarantee ordering and you're not sure if it is serial or parallel, you can replace line 14 with one that uses `forEachOrdered()`:

```
14:      .forEachOrdered(s -> System.out.print(s + " "));
```

This outputs the results in the order in which they are defined in the stream:

```
1 2 3 4 5
Time: 5 seconds
```

While we've lost some of the performance gains of using a parallel stream, our `map()` operation can still take advantage of the parallel stream.

Processing Parallel Reductions

Besides potentially improving performance and modifying the order of operations, using parallel streams can impact how you write your application. A *parallel reduction* is a reduction operation applied to a parallel stream. The results for parallel reductions can differ from what you expect when working with serial streams.

Performing Order-Based Tasks

Since order is not guaranteed with parallel streams, methods such as findAny() on parallel streams may result in unexpected behavior. Consider the following example:

```
System.out.print(List.of(1, 2, 3, 4, 5, 6)
    .parallelStream()
    .findAny()
    .get());
```

The JVM allocates a number of threads and returns the value of the first one to return a result, which could be 4, 2, and so on. While *neither* the serial nor the parallel stream is guaranteed to return the first value, the serial stream often does. With a parallel stream, the results are likely to be more random.

What about operations that consider order, such as findFirst(), limit(), and skip()? Order is still preserved, but performance may *suffer* on a parallel stream as a result of a parallel processing task being forced to coordinate all of its threads in a synchronized-like fashion.

Sorting a Parallel Stream

It's possible to sort a parallel stream, although the results might not be what you expect. The following prints the numbers from 1 to 99 in a stochastic, or random, ordering:

```
IntStream.range(1,100).parallel().sorted().forEach(System.out::println);
```

After the call to sorted(), the stream is still considered parallel, resulting in the forEach() method printing the values in a stochastic ordering. Remember to use an ordered method such as forEachOrdered() if you need to guarantee ordering on a parallel stream.

On the plus side, the results of ordered operations on a parallel stream will be consistent with a serial stream. For example, calling skip(5).limit(2).findFirst() will return the same result on ordered serial and parallel streams.

 Real World Scenario

Creating Unordered Streams

All of the streams you have been working with are considered ordered by default. It is possible to create an unordered stream from an ordered stream, similar to how you create a parallel stream from a serial stream.

```
List.of(1, 2, 3, 4, 5, 6).stream().unordered();
```

This method does not reorder the elements; it just tells the JVM that if an order-based stream operation is applied, the order can be ignored. For example, calling skip(5) on an unordered stream will skip any 5 elements, not necessarily the first 5 required on an ordered stream.

For serial streams, using an unordered version has no effect. But on parallel streams, the results can greatly improve performance.

```
List.of(1, 2, 3, 4, 5, 6).stream().unordered().parallel();
```

Even though unordered streams will not be on the exam, if you are developing applications with parallel streams, you should know when to apply an unordered stream to improve performance.

Combining Results with *reduce()*

As you learned in Chapter 10, the stream operation reduce() combines a stream into a single object. Recall that the first parameter to the reduce() method is called the *identity*, the second parameter is called the *accumulator*, and the third parameter is called the *combiner*. The following is the signature for the method:

```
<U> U reduce(U identity,
    BiFunction<U,? super T,U> accumulator,
    BinaryOperator<U> combiner)
```

We can concatenate a list of char values using the reduce() method, as shown in the following example:

```
System.out.println(List.of('w', 'o', 'l', 'f')
    .parallelStream()
    .reduce("",
      (s1, c) -> s1 + c,
      (s2, s3) -> s2 + s3));  // wolf
```

 The naming of the variables in this stream example is not accidental. We used c for char, whereas s1, s2, and s3 are String values.

On parallel streams, the reduce() method works by applying the reduction to pairs of elements within the stream to create intermediate values and then combining those intermediate values to produce a final result. Put another way, in a serial stream, wolf is built one character at a time. In a parallel stream, the intermediate values wo and lf are created and then combined.

With parallel streams, we now have to be concerned about order. What if the elements of a string are combined in the wrong order to produce wlfo or flwo? The Stream API prevents this problem while still allowing streams to be processed in parallel, as long as you follow one simple rule: make sure that the accumulator and combiner produce the same result regardless of the order they are called in.

> While this is not in scope for the exam, the accumulator and combiner must be associative, non-interfering, and stateless. Don't panic; you don't need to know advanced math terms for the exam!

While the requirements for the input arguments to the reduce() method hold true for both serial and parallel streams, you may not have noticed any problems in serial streams because the result was always ordered. With parallel streams, though, order is no longer guaranteed, and any argument that violates these rules is much more likely to produce side effects or unpredictable results.

Let's take a look at an example using a problematic accumulator. In particular, order matters when subtracting numbers; therefore, the following code can output different values depending on whether you use a serial or parallel stream. We can omit a combiner parameter in these examples, as the accumulator can be used when the intermediate data types are the same.

```
System.out.println(List.of(1, 2, 3, 4, 5, 6)
    .parallelStream()
    .reduce(0, (a, b) -> (a - b)));  // PROBLEMATIC ACCUMULATOR
```

It may output -21, 3, or some other value.

You can see other problems if we use an identity parameter that is not truly an identity value. For example, what do you expect the following code to output?

```
System.out.println(List.of("w","o","l","f")
    .parallelStream()
    .reduce("X", String::concat));  // XwXoXlXf
```

On a serial stream, it prints Xwolf, but on a parallel stream, the result is XwXoXlXf. As part of the parallel process, the identity is applied to multiple elements in the stream, resulting in very unexpected data.

Selecting a *reduce()* Method

Although the one- and two-argument versions of reduce() support parallel processing, it is recommended that you use the three-argument version of reduce() when working with parallel streams. Providing an explicit combiner method allows the JVM to partition the operations in the stream more efficiently.

Combining Results with *collect()*

Like reduce(), the Stream API includes a three-argument version of collect() that takes *accumulator* and *combiner* operators along with a *supplier* operator instead of an identity.

```
<R> R collect(Supplier<R> supplier,
   BiConsumer<R, ? super T> accumulator,
   BiConsumer<R, R> combiner)
```

Also, like reduce(), the accumulator and combiner operations must be able to process results in any order. In this manner, the three-argument version of collect() can be performed as a parallel reduction, as shown in the following example:

```
Stream<String> stream = Stream.of("w", "o", "l", "f").parallel();
SortedSet<String> set = stream.collect(ConcurrentSkipListSet::new,
   Set::add,
   Set::addAll);
System.out.println(set);  // [f, l, o, w]
```

Recall that elements in a ConcurrentSkipListSet are sorted according to their natural ordering. You should use a concurrent collection to combine the results, ensuring that the results of concurrent threads do not cause a ConcurrentModificationException.

Performing parallel reductions with a collector requires additional considerations. For example, if the collection into which you are inserting is an ordered data set, such as a List, the elements in the resulting collection must be in the same order, regardless of whether you use a serial or parallel stream. This may reduce performance, though, as some operations cannot be completed in parallel.

Performing a Parallel Reduction on a Collector

While we covered the Collector interface in Chapter 10, we didn't go into detail about its properties. Every Collector instance defines a characteristics() method that returns a set of Collector.Characteristics attributes. When using a Collector to perform a parallel reduction, a number of properties must hold true. Otherwise, the collect() operation will execute in a single-threaded fashion.

Requirements for Parallel Reduction with *collect()*

- The stream is parallel.
- The parameter of the collect() operation has the Characteristics.CONCURRENT characteristic.
- Either the stream is unordered or the collector has the characteristic Characteristics.UNORDERED.

For example, while Collectors.toSet() does have the UNORDERED characteristic, it does not have the CONCURRENT characteristic. Therefore, the following is not a parallel reduction even with a parallel stream:

```
parallelStream.collect(Collectors.toSet());  // Not a parallel reduction
```

The Collectors class includes two sets of static methods for retrieving collectors, toConcurrentMap() and groupingByConcurrent(), both of which are UNORDERED and CONCURRENT. These methods produce Collector instances capable of performing parallel reductions efficiently. Like their nonconcurrent counterparts, there are overloaded versions that take additional arguments.

Here is a rewrite of an example from Chapter 10 to use a parallel stream and parallel reduction:

```
Stream<String> ohMy = Stream.of("lions", "tigers", "bears").parallel();
ConcurrentMap<Integer, String> map = ohMy
   .collect(Collectors.toConcurrentMap(String::length,
      k -> k,
      (s1, s2) -> s1 + "," + s2));
System.out.println(map);              // {5=lions,bears, 6=tigers}
System.out.println(map.getClass());  // java.util.concurrent.ConcurrentHashMap
```

We use a ConcurrentMap reference, although the actual class returned is likely ConcurrentHashMap. The particular class is not guaranteed; it will just be a class that implements the interface ConcurrentMap.

Finally, we can rewrite our groupingBy() example from Chapter 10 to use a parallel stream and parallel reduction.

```
var ohMy = Stream.of("lions", "tigers", "bears").parallel();
ConcurrentMap<Integer, List<String>> map = ohMy.collect(
   Collectors.groupingByConcurrent(String::length));
System.out.println(map);              // {5=[lions, bears], 6=[tigers]}
```

As before, the returned object can be assigned to a ConcurrentMap reference.

 Real World Scenario

Avoiding Stateful Streams

Side effects can appear in parallel streams if your lambda expressions are stateful. A *stateful lambda expression* is one whose result depends on any state that might change during the execution of a pipeline. For example, the following method that filters out even numbers is stateful:

```
public List<Integer> addValues(IntStream source) {
   var data = Collections.synchronizedList(new ArrayList<Integer>());
   source.filter(s -> s % 2 == 0)
      .forEach(i -> { data.add(i); });  // STATEFUL: DON'T DO THIS!
   return data;
}
```

Let's say this method is executed with a serial stream:

```
var list = addValues(IntStream.range(1, 11));
System.out.print(list);                    // [2, 4, 6, 8, 10]
```

Great, the results are in the same order that they were entered. But what if someone else passes in a parallel stream?

```
var list = addValues(IntStream.range(1, 11).parallel());
System.out.print(list);                    // [6, 8, 10, 2, 4]
```

Oh, no: our results no longer match our input order! The problem is that our lambda expression is stateful and modifies a list that is outside our stream. We can fix this solution by rewriting our stream operation to be stateless:

```
public List<Integer> addValuesBetter(IntStream source) {
    return source.filter(s -> s % 2 == 0)
        .boxed()
        .collect(Collectors.toList());
}
```

This method processes the stream and then collects all the results into a new list. It produces the same ordered result on both serial and parallel streams. It is strongly recommended that you avoid stateful operations when using parallel streams to remove any potential data side effects. In fact, they should be avoided in serial streams since doing so limits the code's ability to someday take advantage of parallelization.

Summary

This chapter introduced you to both platform and virtual threads and outlined some of the key concurrency concepts you need to know for the exam (and to be a better software developer!). You should know how to create and define the thread's work using a Runnable instance. When working with the Concurrency API, you should also know how to create threads using Callable lambda expressions.

At this point, you should know how to concurrently execute tasks using ExecutorService like a pro. You should also know which ExecutorService instances are available, including scheduled and pooled services.

Thread-safety is about protecting data from being corrupted by multiple threads modifying it at the same time. Java offers many tools to keep data safe, including atomic classes, synchronized methods/blocks, the Lock framework, and CyclicBarrier. The Concurrency API also includes numerous collection classes that handle multithreaded access for you. You should be familiar with the concurrent collections, including the CopyOnWrite classes, which create a new underlying structure any time the collection is modified.

When processing tasks concurrently, a variety of potential threading issues can arise. Deadlock, starvation, and livelock can result in programs that appear stuck, while race conditions can result in unpredictable data. For the exam, you need to know only the basic theory behind these concepts. In professional software development, however, finding and resolving such problems is a valuable skill.

Finally, we discussed parallel streams and showed you how to use them to perform parallel decompositions and reductions. Parallel streams can greatly improve the performance of your application. They can also cause unexpected results since the processing is no longer ordered. Remember to avoid stateful lambda expressions, especially when working with parallel streams.

Exam Essentials

Identify the differences between platform threads and virtual threads. Platform threads map to the underlying operating system threads. Virtual threads are lighter weight using a carrier thread only when they need to run. A carrier thread runs on an operating system thread as well. Virtual threads can be run on Executors.newVirtualThreadPerTaskExecutor(). Since they are so lightweight, they don't need to be pooled.

Be able to write thread-safe code. Thread-safety is about protecting shared data from concurrent access. A monitor can be used to ensure that only one thread processes a particular section of code at a time. In Java, monitors can be implemented with a synchronized block or method or using an instance of Lock. ReentrantLock has a number of advantages over using a synchronized block, including the ability to check whether a lock is available without blocking it, as well as supporting the fair acquisition of locks. To achieve synchronization, two or more threads must coordinate on the same shared object.

Be able to apply the atomic classes. An atomic operation is one that occurs without interference from another thread. The Concurrency API includes a set of atomic classes that are similar to the primitive classes, except that they ensure that operations on them are performed atomically. Know the difference between an atomic variable and one marked with the volatile modifier.

Create concurrent tasks with a thread executor service using *Runnable* and *Callable*. An ExecutorService creates and manages a single thread or a pool of threads. Instances of Runnable and Callable can both be submitted to a thread executor and will be completed using the available threads in the service. Callable differs from Runnable in that Callable returns a generic data type and can throw a checked exception.

A ScheduledExecutorService can be used to schedule tasks at a fixed rate or with a fixed interval between executions.

Be able to use the concurrent collection classes.   The Concurrency API includes numerous collection classes that include built-in support for multithreaded processing, such as ConcurrentHashMap. It also includes a class CopyOnWriteArrayList that creates a copy of its underlying list structure every time it is modified and is useful in highly concurrent environments.

Identify potential threading problems.   Deadlock, starvation, and livelock are three threading problems that can occur and result in threads never completing their task. Deadlock occurs when two or more threads are blocked forever. Starvation occurs when a single thread is perpetually denied access to a shared resource. Livelock is a form of starvation where two or more threads are active but conceptually blocked forever. Finally, race conditions occur when two threads execute at the same time, resulting in an unexpected outcome.

Understand the impact of using parallel streams.   The Stream API allows for the easy creation of parallel streams. Using a parallel stream can cause unexpected results, since the order of operations may no longer be predictable. Some operations, such as reduce() and collect(), require special consideration to achieve optimal performance when applied to a parallel stream.

Review Questions

The answers to the chapter review questions can be found in the Appendix.

1. Given the following code snippet, which options correctly create a parallel stream? (Choose all that apply.)

    ```
    var c = List.of(19, 66);
    var s = ThreadLocalRandom.current().doubles();
    var p = _____;
    ```

    A. new ParallelStream(s)

    B. c.parallel()

    C. s.parallelStream()

    D. c.parallelStream()

    E. new ParallelStream(c)

    F. s.parallel()

2. Given that the sum of the numbers from 1 (inclusive) to 10 (exclusive) is 45, what are the possible results of executing the following program? (Choose all that apply.)

    ```
    1:  import java.util.concurrent.locks.*;
    2:  import java.util.stream.*;
    3:  public class Bank {
    4:      private Lock vault = new ReentrantLock();
    5:      private int total = 0;
    6:      public void deposit(int value) {
    7:          try {
    8:              vault.tryLock();
    9:              total += value;
    10:         } finally { vault.unlock(); }
    11:     }
    12:     public static void main(String[] unused) {
    13:         var bank = new Bank();
    14:         IntStream.range(1, 10).parallel()
    15:             .forEach(s -> bank.deposit(s));
    16:         System.out.println(bank.total);
    17:     } }
    ```

    A. 45 is printed.

    B. A number less than 45 is printed.

    C. A number greater than 45 is printed.

    D. An exception is thrown.

    E. None of the above, as the code does not compile.

3. Which of the following statements about the `Callable call()` and `Runnable run()` methods are correct? (Choose all that apply.)

A. Both methods return `void`.

B. Both can throw unchecked exceptions.

C. Both can be implemented with lambda expressions.

D. `Runnable` returns a generic type.

E. Both can throw checked exceptions.

F. `Callable` returns a generic type.

4. Which lines need to be changed to make the code compile?

```
try (ExecutorService service =          // w1
   Executors.newSingleThreadScheduledExecutor()) {
   service.scheduleWithFixedDelay(() -> {
      System.out.println("Open Zoo");
      return null;                       // w2
   }, 0, 1, TimeUnit.MINUTES);
   var result = service.submit(() ->     // w3
      System.out.println("Wake Staff"));
   System.out.println(result.get());
}
```

A. Only line w1.

B. Only line w2.

C. Only line w3.

D. Line w1 and w2.

E. Line w1 and w2.

F. Line w1 and w3.

G. None of the above; the code compiles.

5. What statement about the following code is true?

```
var value1 = new AtomicLong(0);
final long[] value2 = {0};
IntStream.iterate(1, i -> 1).limit(100).parallel()
   .forEach(i -> value1.incrementAndGet());
IntStream.iterate(1, i -> 1).limit(100).parallel()
   .forEach(i -> ++value2[0]);
System.out.println(value1 + " " + value2[0]);
```

A. It outputs 100 100.

B. It outputs 100 99.

C. The output cannot be determined ahead of time.

D. The code does not compile.

E. It compiles but throws an exception at runtime.

F. It compiles but enters an infinite loop at runtime.

G. None of the above.

6. Which statements about the following code are correct? (Choose all that apply.)

```
var data = List.of(2, 5, 1, 9, 8);
data.stream().parallel()
    .mapToInt(s -> s)
    .peek(System.out::print)
    .forEachOrdered(System.out::print);
```

A. The peek() method will print the entries in the sorted order: 12589.

B. The peek() method will print the entries in the original order: 25198.

C. The peek() method will print the entries in an order that cannot be determined ahead of time.

D. The forEachOrdered() method will print the entries in the sorted order: 12589.

E. The forEachOrdered() method will print the entries in the original order: 25198.

F. The forEachOrdered() method will print the entries in an order that cannot be determined ahead of time.

G. The code does not compile.

7. Fill in the blanks: _____ occur(s) when two or more threads are blocked forever but both appear active. _____ occur(s) when two or more threads try to complete a related task at the same time, resulting in invalid or unexpected data.

A. Livelock, Deadlock

B. Deadlock, Starvation

C. Race conditions, Deadlock

D. Livelock, Race conditions

E. Starvation, Race conditions

F. Deadlock, Livelock

8. Assuming this class is accessed by only a single thread at a time, what is the result of calling the countIceCreamFlavors() method?

```
import java.util.stream.LongStream;
public class Flavors {
    private static int counter;
    public static void countIceCreamFlavors() {
        counter = 0;
        Runnable task = () -> counter++;
        LongStream.range(0, 500)
```

```
      .forEach(m -> Thread.ofPlatform()
        .priority(1)
        .unstarted(task)
        .run());
    System.out.println(counter);
  } }
```

A. The method consistently prints a number less than 500.

B. The method consistently prints 500.

C. The method compiles and prints a value, but that value cannot be determined ahead of time.

D. The method does not compile.

E. The method compiles but throws an exception at runtime.

F. None of the above.

9. Which are true of `ExecutorService`? (Choose all that apply.)

   A. If a task is submitted when no threads are available, the executor discards the task without completing it.

   B. If a task is submitted when no threads are available, the executor adds the task to an internal queue and completes when there is an available thread.

   C. If a task is submitted when no threads are available, the thread submitting the task waits on the submit call until a thread is available before continuing.

   D. Platform threads can be pooled using `ExecutorService`, but not virtual threads.

   E. Virtual threads can be pooled using `ExecutorService`, but not platform threads.

   F. Both platform threads and virtual threads can be pooled using `ExecutorService`.

10. What is the result of executing the following code snippet?

```
SequencedCollection<Integer> lions = new ArrayList<>(List.of(1, 2, 3));
SequencedCollection<Integer> tigers = new CopyOnWriteArrayList<>(lions);
Set<Integer> bears = new ConcurrentSkipListSet<>();
bears.addAll(lions);
for (Integer item: tigers) tigers.add(4); // x1
for (Integer item: bears) bears.add(5);   // x2
System.out.println(lions.size() + " " + tigers.size()
   + " " + bears.size());
```

   A. It outputs 3 6 4.

   B. It outputs 6 6 6.

   C. It outputs 6 3 4.

   D. The code does not compile.

   E. It compiles but throws an exception at runtime on line x1.

    F.   It compiles but throws an exception at runtime on line x2.

    G. It compiles but enters an infinite loop at runtime.

11. What statement about the following code is true?

```
Integer i1 = List.of(1, 2, 3, 4, 5).stream().findAny().get();
synchronized(i1) { // y1
    Integer i2 = List.of(6, 7, 8, 9, 10)
        .parallelStream()
        .sorted()
        .findAny().get(); // y2
    System.out.println(i1 + " " + i2);
}
```

    A.   The first value printed is always 1.

    B.   The second value printed is always 6.

    C.   The code will not compile because of line y1.

    D.   The code will not compile because of line y2.

    E.   The code compiles but throws an exception at runtime.

    F.   The output cannot be determined ahead of time.

    G. It compiles but waits forever at runtime.

12. Assuming each call to takeNap() takes five seconds to execute without throwing an exception, what is the expected result of executing the following code snippet? (Choose all that apply.)

```
public void shutdown() throws InterruptedException {
    var service = Executors.newFixedThreadPool(4);
    try {
        service.execute(() -> takeNap());
        service.execute(() -> takeNap());
        service.execute(() -> takeNap());
    } finally {
        service.shutdown();
    }
    service.awaitTermination(2, TimeUnit.SECONDS);
    System.out.println("DONE!");
}
public void refactored() {
    try (var service = Executors.newFixedThreadPool(4)) {
        service.execute(() -> takeNap());
        service.execute(() -> takeNap());
        service.execute(() -> takeNap());
```

```
        }
    System.out.println("DONE!");
    }
```

A. `shutdown()` will pause for approximately 2 seconds and then print DONE!.

B. `shutdown()` will pause for approximately 5 seconds and then print DONE!.

C. `shutdown()` will pause for approximately 15 seconds and then print DONE!.

D. `refactored()` will pause for approximately 2 seconds and then print DONE!.

E. `refactored()` will pause for approximately 5 seconds and then print DONE!.

F. `refactored()` will pause for approximately 15 seconds and then print DONE!.

G. One of the methods returns the result immediately.

H. One of the methods throws an exception.

13. What statement about the following code is true?

```
System.out.print(List.of("duck","flamingo","pelican")
    .parallelStream().parallel()    // q1
    .reduce(0,
        (c1, c2) -> c1.length() + c2.length(),  // q2
        (s1, s2) -> s1 + s2));       // q3
```

A. It compiles and runs without issue, outputting the total length of all strings in the stream.

B. The code will not compile because of line q1.

C. The code will not compile because of line q2.

D. The code will not compile because of line q3.

E. It compiles but throws an exception at runtime.

F. None of the above.

14. What statements about the following code snippet are true? (Choose all that apply.)

```
Object o1 = new Object();
Object o2 = new Object();
try (var service = Executors.newFixedThreadPool(2)) {
    var f1 = service.submit(() -> {
        synchronized (o1) {
            synchronized (o2) { System.out.print("Tortoise"); }
        }
    });
    var f2 = service.submit(() -> {
        synchronized (o2) {
            synchronized (o1) { System.out.print("Hare"); }
        }
```

```
  });
  f1.get();
  f2.get();
}
```

- **A.** The code will always output `Tortoise` followed by `Hare`.
- **B.** The code will always output `Hare` followed by `Tortoise`.
- **C.** If the code does output anything, the order cannot be determined.
- **D.** The code does not compile.
- **E.** The code compiles but may produce a deadlock at runtime.
- **F.** The code compiles but may produce a livelock at runtime.
- **G.** It compiles but throws an exception at runtime.

15. Which statement about the following code snippet is correct?

```
2: var cats = Stream.of("leopard", "lynx", "ocelot", "puma")
3:    .parallel();
4: var bears = Stream.of("panda","grizzly","polar").parallel();
5: var data = Stream.of(cats,bears).flatMap(s -> s)
6:    .collect(Collectors.groupingByConcurrent(
7:       s -> !s.startsWith("p")));
8: System.out.println(data.get(false).size()
9:    + " " + data.get(true).size());
```

- **A.** It outputs 3 4.
- **B.** It outputs 4 3.
- **C.** The code will not compile because of line 6.
- **D.** The code will not compile because of line 7.
- **E.** The code will not compile because of line 8.
- **F.** It compiles but throws an exception at runtime.

16. Which APIs exist for creating or working with platform threads? (Choose all that apply.)

- **A.** `Executors.newCachedThreadPool()`
- **B.** `Executors.newPlatformThreadPool()`
- **C.** `Executors.newPlatformThreadPerTaskExecutor()`
- **D.** `new Thread()`
- **E.** `Thread.ofPlatform()`
- **F.** `Thread.ofPlatformThread()`

17. Which statement about methods in `ReentrantLock` is correct?

- **A.** The `lock()` method will attempt to acquire a lock without waiting indefinitely for it.
- **B.** The `testLock()` method will attempt to acquire a lock without waiting indefinitely for it.

C. The `attemptLock()` method will attempt to acquire a lock without waiting indefinitely for it.

D. By default, a `ReentrantLock` fairly releases to each thread in the order in which it was requested.

E. Calling the `unlock()` method once will release a resource so that other threads can obtain the lock.

F. None of the above.

18. Which of the following lambda expressions are valid `Callable` expressions? (Choose all that apply.)

A. `a -> {return 10;}`

B. `() -> {String s = "";}`

C. `() -> 5`

D. `() -> {return null}`

E. `() -> "The" + "Zoo"`

F. `(int count) -> count+1`

G. `() -> {System.out.print("Giraffe"); return 10;}`

19. What is the result of executing the following application? (Choose all that apply.)

```java
import java.util.concurrent.*;
import java.util.stream.*;
public class PrintConstants {
   public static void main(String[] args) {
      var s = Executors.newVirtualThreadPerTaskExecutor();
      DoubleStream.of(3.14159, 2.71828)    // b1
         .forEach(c -> s.submit(           // b2
            () -> System.out.println(10 * c))); // b3
      s.execute(() -> System.out.println("Printed"));
   } }
```

A. It compiles and outputs the two numbers followed by `Printed`.

B. The code will not compile because of line b1.

C. The code will not compile because of line b2.

D. The code will not compile because of line b3.

E. It compiles, but the output cannot be determined ahead of time.

F. It compiles but throws an exception at runtime.

G. It compiles but waits forever at runtime.

20. What is the result of executing the following program?

```java
import java.util.*;
import java.util.concurrent.*;
import java.util.stream.*;
```

```
public class PrintCounter {
    static int count = 0;
    public static void main(String[] args) throws
                    InterruptedException, ExecutionException {
        try (var service = Executors.newSingleThreadExecutor()) {
            var r = new ArrayList<Future<?>>();
            IntStream.iterate(0,i -> i + 1).limit(5).forEach(
                i -> r.add(service.execute(() -> {count++;}))) // n1
            );
            for (Future<?> result : r) {
                System.out.print(result.get() + " "); // n2
            }
        }
    }
} }
```

A. It prints 0 1 2 3 4

B. It prints 1 2 3 4 5

C. It prints null null null null null

D. It hangs indefinitely at runtime.

E. The output cannot be determined.

F. The code will not compile because of line n1.

G. The code will not compile because of line n2.

21. Given the following code snippet and blank lines on p1 and p2, which values guarantee that 1 is printed at runtime? (Choose all that apply.)

```
var data = List.of(List.of(1, 2),
    List.of(3, 4),
    List.of(5, 6));
data._____ // p1
    .flatMap(s -> s.stream())
    ._____ // p2
    .ifPresent(System.out::print);
```

A. stream() on line p1, findFirst() on line p2.

B. stream() on line p1, findAny() on line p2.

C. parallelStream() on line p1, findAny() on line p2.

D. parallelStream() on line p1, findFirst() on line p2.

E. The code does not compile regardless of what is inserted into the blanks.

F. None of the above.

22. Assuming one minute is enough time for the tasks submitted to the service executor to complete, what is the result of executing `countSheep()`?

```java
import java.util.concurrent.*;
import java.util.concurrent.atomic.*;
public class BedTime {
   private AtomicInteger s1 = new AtomicInteger(0); // w1
   private int s2 = 0;

   private void countSheep() throws InterruptedException {
      try (var service = Executors.newSingleThreadExecutor()) { // w2
         for (int i = 0; i < 100; i++)
         service.execute(() -> {
            s1.getAndIncrement(); s2++; }); // w3
         Thread.sleep(60_000);
         System.out.println(s1 + " " + s2);
      }
   }
   public static void main(String... nap)
     throws InterruptedException {
      new BedTime().countSheep();
   } }
```

A. The method consistently prints 100 99.

B. The method consistently prints 100 100.

C. The output cannot be determined ahead of time.

D. The code will not compile because of line w1.

E. The code will not compile because of line w2.

F. The code will not compile because of line w3.

G. It compiles but throws an exception at runtime.

23. What is the result of executing the following application?

```java
import java.util.concurrent.*;
import java.util.stream.*;
public class StockRoomTracker {
   public static void await(CyclicBarrier cb) { // j1
      try { cb.await(); } catch (Exception e) {}
   }
   public static void main(String[] args) {
      var cb = new CyclicBarrier(10,
         () -> System.out.println("Stock Room Full!")); // j2
```

```
IntStream.iterate(1, i -> 1).limit(9).parallel()
    .forEach(i -> await(cb)); // j3
} }
```

A. It outputs Stock Room Full!

B. The code will not compile because of line j1.

C. The code will not compile because of line j2.

D. The code will not compile because of line j3.

E. It compiles but throws an exception at runtime.

F. It compiles but waits forever at runtime.

24. What statements about the following class definition are true? (Choose all that apply.)

```
public final class TicketManager {
    private int tickets;
    private static TicketManager instance;
    private TicketManager() {}
    static synchronized TicketManager getInstance() {      // k1
        if (instance==null) instance = new TicketManager(); // k2
        return instance;
    }

    public int getTicketCount() { return tickets; }
    public void addTickets(int value) {tickets += value;}  // k3
    public void sellTickets(int value) {
        synchronized (this) {                              // k4
            tickets -= value;
    } } }
```

A. It compiles without issue.

B. The code will not compile because of line k2.

C. The code will not compile because of line k3.

D. The locks acquired on k1 and k4 are on the same object.

E. The class correctly protects the tickets data from race conditions.

F. At most one instance of TicketManager will be created in an application that uses this class.

25. Assuming an implementation of the performCount() method is provided prior to runtime, which of the following are possible results of executing the following application? (Choose all that apply.)

```
import java.util.*;
import java.util.concurrent.*;
```

```
public class CountZooAnimals {
   public static void performCount(int animal) {
      // IMPLEMENTATION OMITTED
   }
   public static void printResults(Future<?> f) {
      try {
         System.out.println(f.get(1, TimeUnit.DAYS)); // o1
      } catch (Exception e) {
         System.out.println("Exception!");
      }
   }
   public static void main(String[] args) throws Exception {
      final var r = new ArrayList<Future<?>>();
      try (var s = Executors.newSingleThreadExecutor()) {
         for (int i = 0; i < 10; i++) {
            final int animal = i;
            r.add(s.submit(() -> performCount(animal))); // o2
         }
         r.forEach(f -> printResults(f));
      }
   } }
```

A. It outputs a number 10 times.

B. It outputs a Boolean value 10 times.

C. It outputs a null value 10 times.

D. It outputs Exception! 10 times.

E. The code will not compile because of line o1.

F. The code will not compile because of line o2.

Chapter

14

I/O

OCP EXAM OBJECTIVES COVERED IN THIS CHAPTER:

✓ **Using Java I/O API**

- Read and write console and file data using I/O streams.

- Serialize and de-serialize Java objects.

- Construct, traverse, create, read, and write Path objects and their properties using the java.nio.file API.

What can Java applications do outside the scope of managing objects and attributes in memory? How can they save data so that information is not lost every time the program is terminated? They use files, of course! You can design code that writes the current state of an application to a file every time the application is closed and then reloads the data when the application is executed the next time. In this manner, information is preserved between program executions.

This chapter focuses on using I/O (input/output) and NIO.2 (non-blocking I/O) APIs to interact with files and I/O streams. The preferred approach for working with files and directories with newer software applications is to use NIO.2 rather than I/O where possible. However, you'll see that the two relate, and both are in wide use.

We start by describing how files and directories are organized within a file system and show how to access them with the File class and Path interface. Then we show how to work with files and directories. We conclude this chapter with advanced topics like serializing data, reading user input at runtime using the Console class, and interacting with file attributes.

NIO stands for non-blocking input/output API and is sometimes referred to as *new I/O*. The exam covers NIO version 2. There was a version 1 that covered channels, but it is not on the exam.

Referencing Files and Directories

We begin this chapter by reviewing what files and directories are within a file system. We also present the File class and Path interface along with how to create them.

Conceptualizing the File System

We start with the basics. Data is stored on persistent storage devices, such as hard disk drives and memory cards. A *file* within the storage device holds data. Files are organized into hierarchies using directories. A *directory* is a location that can contain files as well as other directories.

When working with directories in Java, we often treat them like files. In fact, we use many of the same classes and interfaces to operate on files and directories. For example, a file and directory both can be renamed with the same Java method. In this chapter, we often say *file* to mean *file or directory*.

To interact with files, we need to connect to the file system. The *file system* is in charge of reading and writing data within a computer. Different operating systems use different file systems to manage their data. For example, Windows-based systems use a different file system than Unix-based ones. For the exam, you just need to know how to issue commands using the Java APIs. The JVM will automatically connect to the local file system, allowing you to perform the same operations across multiple platforms.

Next, the *root directory* is the topmost directory in the file system, from which all files and directories inherit. In Windows, it is denoted with a drive letter such as C:\, while on Linux, it is denoted with a single forward slash, /.

A *path* is a representation of a file or directory within a file system. Each file system defines its own path separator character that is used between directory entries. The value to the left of a separator is the parent of the value to the right of the separator. For example, the path value /user/home/zoo.txt means that the file zoo.txt is inside the home directory, with the home directory inside the user directory.

Operating System File Separators

Different operating systems vary in their format of pathnames. For example, Unix-based systems use the forward slash, /, for paths, whereas Windows-based systems use the back-slash, \, character. That said, many programming languages and file systems support both types of slashes when writing path statements. Java offers a system property to retrieve the local separator character for the current environment:

```
System.out.print(System.getProperty("file.separator"));
```

We show how a directory and file system is organized in a hierarchical manner in Figure 14.1.

FIGURE 14.1 Directory and file hierarchy

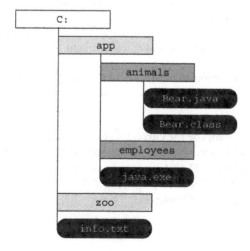

This diagram shows the root directory, C:, as containing two directories, app and zoo, along with the file info.txt. Within the app directory, there are two more folders, animals and employees, along with the file java.exe. Finally, the animals directory contains two files, Bear.java and Bear.class.

We use both absolute and relative paths to the file or directory within the file system. The *absolute path* of a file or directory is the full path from the root directory to the file or directory, including all subdirectories that contain the file or directory. Alternatively, the *relative path* of a file or directory is the path from the current working directory to the file or directory. For example, the following is an absolute path to the Bear.java file:

C:\app\animals\Bear.java

The following is a relative path to the same file, assuming the user's current directory is set to C:\app:

animals\Bear.java

Determining whether a path is relative or absolute is file system dependent. To match the exam, we adopt the following conventions:

- If a path starts with a forward slash (/), it is absolute, with / as the root directory, such as /bird/parrot.png.
- If a path starts with a drive letter (C:), it is absolute, with the drive letter as the root directory, such as C:/bird/info.
- Otherwise, it is a relative path, such as bird/parrot.png.

Absolute and relative paths can contain path symbols. A *path symbol* is one of a reserved series of characters with special meaning in some file systems. For the exam, there are two path symbols you need to know, as listed in Table 14.1.

TABLE 14.1 File system symbols

Symbol	Description
.	A reference to the current directory
..	A reference to the parent of the current directory

Looking at Figure 14.2, suppose the current directory is /fish/shark/hammerhead. In this case, ../swim.txt is a valid relative path equivalent to /fish/shark/swim.txt. Likewise, ./play.png refers to play.png in the current directory. These symbols can also be combined for greater effect. For example, ../../clownfish is a relative path equivalent to /fish/clownfish within the file system.

FIGURE 14.2   Relative paths using path symbols

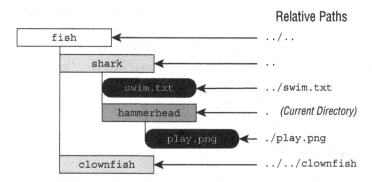

Sometimes you'll see path symbols that are redundant or unnecessary. For example, the absolute path /fish/clownfish/../shark/./swim.txt can be simplified to /fish/shark/swim.txt. We see how to handle these redundancies later in the chapter when we cover normalize().

A *symbolic link* is a special file within a file system that serves as a reference or pointer to another file or directory. Suppose we have a symbolic link from /zoo/user/favorite to /fish/shark. The shark folder and its elements can be accessed directly or via the symbolic link. For example, the following two paths reference the same file:

/fish/shark/swim.txt
/zoo/user/favorite/swim.txt

In general, symbolic links are transparent to the user, as the operating system takes care of resolving the reference to the actual file. While the I/O APIs do not support symbolic links, NIO.2 includes full support for creating, detecting, and navigating symbolic links within the file system.

Creating a *File* or *Path*

To do anything useful, you first need an object that represents the path to a particular file or directory on the file system. Using legacy I/O, this is the java.io.File class, whereas with NIO.2, it is the java.nio.file.Path interface. The File class and Path interface cannot read or write data within a file, although they are passed as a reference to other classes, as you see in this chapter.

Remember, a File or Path can represent a file or a directory.

Creating a *File*

The File class is created by calling its constructor. This code shows three different constructors:

```
File zooFile1 = new File("/home/tiger/data/stripes.txt");
File zooFile2 = new File("/home/tiger", "data/stripes.txt");

File parent = new File("/home/tiger");
File zooFile3 = new File(parent, "data/stripes.txt");

System.out.println(zooFile1.exists());
```

All three create a File object that points to the same location on disk. If we passed null as the parent to the final constructor, it would be ignored, and the method would behave the same way as the single String constructor. For fun, we also show how to tell if the file exists on the file system.

Creating a *Path*

Since Path is an interface, we can't create an instance directly. After all, interfaces don't have constructors! The most common way to create a Path is the following:

```
public static Path of(String first, String... more)
```

The following two examples reference the same file on disk:

```
Path zooPath1 = Path.of("/home/tiger/data/stripes.txt");
Path zooPath2 = Path.of("/home", "tiger", "data", "stripes.txt");

System.out.println(Files.exists(zooPath1));
```

The method allows passing a varargs parameter to pass additional path elements. The values are combined and automatically separated by the operating system–dependent file separator. We also show the Files helper class, which can check if the file exists on the file system. More on the Files class shortly!

Other Ways to Create a Path

There are three other ways to create a Path that might show up on the exam. An older way to create a Path is to use the Paths helper class.

```
Path zooPath1 = Paths.get("/home", "tiger", "data", "stripes.txt");
```

This method has the exact same signature as the Path.of() method, which means it takes a varargs parameter. From the Javadoc, the Paths class may be deprecated in the future, so you should use Path.of() instead.

Behind the scenes, Path.of() actually uses the FileSystems helper class to create a Path, which means you can call it directly:

```
Path zooPath2 = FileSystems.getDefault().getPath("/home/tiger/data/stripes.txt");
```

Finally, a Path can also be created using a uniform resource identifier (URI). It begins with a schema that indicates the resource type, followed by a path value, such as file:// for local file systems and https:// for remote file systems.

```
Path zooPath3 = Path.of(URI.create("https://www.selikoff.net"));
```

Switching Between *File* and *Path*

Since File and Path both reference locations on disk, it is helpful to be able to convert between them. Luckily, Java makes this easy by providing methods to do just that:

```
File file = new File("rabbit");
Path newPath = file.toPath();
File backToFile = newPath.toFile();
```

Many older libraries use File, making it convenient to be able to get a File from a Path and vice versa. When working with newer applications, you should rely on NIO.2's Path interface, as it contains a lot more features.

Operating on *File* and *Path*

Now that we know how to create File and Path objects, we can start using them to do useful things. In this section, we explore the functionality available to us that involves directories.

Using Shared Functionality

Many operations can be done using both the I/O and NIO.2 libraries. We present many common APIs in Table 14.2 and Table 14.3. Although these tables may seem like a lot of methods to learn, many of them are self-explanatory. You can ignore the vararg parameters for now. We explain those later in the chapter.

TABLE 14.2   Common File and Path operations

Description	I/O *File* instance method	NIO.2 *Path* instance method
Gets name of file/directory	getName()	getFileName()
Retrieves parent directory or null if there is none	getParent()	getParent()
Checks if file/directory is absolute path	isAbsolute()	isAbsolute()
Retrieves absolute path of file/directory	getAbsolutePath()	toAbsolutePath()

TABLE 14.3 Common `File` and `Files` operations

Description	I/O *File* instance method	NIO.2 *Files* static method
Deletes file/directory	`delete()`	`deleteIfExists(Path p) throws IOException`
Checks if file/directory exists	`exists()`	`exists(Path p, LinkOption... o)`
Checks if resource is directory	`isDirectory()`	`isDirectory(Path p, LinkOption... o)`
Checks if resource is file	`isFile()`	`isRegularFile(Path p, LinkOption... o)`
Returns the time the file was last modified	`lastModified()`	`getLastModifiedTime(Path p, LinkOption... o) throws IOException`
Retrieves number of bytes in file	`length()`	`size(Path p) throws IOException`
Lists contents of directory	`listFiles()`	`list(Path p) throws IOException`
Creates directory	`mkdir()`	`createDirectory(Path p, FileAttribute... a) throws IOException`
Creates directory including any nonexistent parent directories	`mkdirs()`	`createDirectories(Path p, FileAttribute... a) throws IOException`
Renames file/directory denoted	`renameTo(File dest)`	`move(Path src, Path dest, CopyOption... o) throws IOException`

The `java.io.File` is the I/O class, while `Files` is an NIO.2 helper class. `Files` operates on `Path` instances, not `java.io.File` instances. We know this is confusing, but they are from completely different APIs!

Now let's try to use some of these APIs. The following is a sample program using only legacy I/O APIs. Given a file path, it outputs information about the file or directory, such as whether it exists, what files are contained within it, and so forth:

```
11: public void io(File file) {
```

```
12:    if (file.exists()) {
13:        System.out.println("Absolute Path: " + file.getAbsolutePath());
14:        System.out.println("Is Directory: " + file.isDirectory());
15:        System.out.println("Parent Path: " + file.getParent());
16:        if (file.isFile()) {
17:            System.out.println("Size: " + file.length());
18:            System.out.println("Last Modified: " + file.lastModified());
19:        } else {
20:            for (File subfile : file.listFiles()) {
21:                System.out.println("   " + subfile.getName());
22:    } } } }
```

If the path provided points to a valid file, the program outputs something similar to the following due to the if statement on line 16:

```
Absolute Path: C:\data\zoo.txt
Is Directory: false
Parent Path: C:\data
Size: 12382
Last Modified: 1650610000000
```

Finally, if the path provided points to a valid directory, such as C:\data, the program outputs something similar to the following, thanks to the else block:

```
Absolute Path: C:\data
Is Directory: true
Parent Path: C:\
   employees.txt
   zoo.txt
   zoo-backup.txt
```

In these examples, you see that the output of an I/O-based program is completely dependent on the directories and files available at runtime in the underlying file system.

On the exam, you might see paths that look like files but are directories or vice versa. For example, /data/zoo.txt could be a file or a directory, even though it has a file extension. Don't assume it is either unless the question tells you it is!

NOTE   In the previous example, we used two backslashes (\\) in the path String, such as C:\\data\\zoo.txt. When the compiler sees a \\ inside a String expression, it interprets it as a single \ value.

Now, let's write that same program using only NIO.2 and see how it differs:

```
26: public void nio(Path path) throws IOException {
27:     if (Files.exists(path)) {
```

```
28:        System.out.println("Absolute Path: " + path.toAbsolutePath());
29:        System.out.println("Is Directory: " + Files.isDirectory(path));
30:        System.out.println("Parent Path: " + path.getParent());
31:        if (Files.isRegularFile(path)) {
32:           System.out.println("Size: " + Files.size(path));
33:           System.out.println("Last Modified: "
34:               + Files.getLastModifiedTime(path));
35:        } else {
36:           try (Stream<Path> stream = Files.list(path)) {
37:              stream.forEach(p ->
38:                  System.out.println("   " + p.getFileName()));
39:        } } } }
```

Most of this example is equivalent and replaces the I/O method calls in the previous tables with the NIO.2 versions. However, there are key differences. First, line 25 declares a checked exception. More APIs in NIO.2 throw IOException than the I/O APIs did. In this case, Files.size(), Files.getLastModifiedTime(), and Files.list() throw an IOException.

Second, lines 36–39 use a Stream and a lambda instead of a loop. Since streams use lazy evaluation, this means the method will load each path element as needed, rather than the entire directory at once.

Closing the Stream

Did you notice that in the last code sample, we put our Stream object inside a try-with-resources? The NIO.2 stream-based methods open a connection to the file system *that must be properly closed*; otherwise, a resource leak could ensue. A resource leak within the file system means the path may be locked from modification long after the process that used it is completed.

If you assumed that a stream's terminal operation would automatically close the underlying file resources, you'd be wrong. There was a lot of debate about this behavior when it was first presented; in short, requiring developers to close the stream won out.

On the plus side, not all streams need to be closed: only those that open resources, like the ones found in NIO.2. For instance, you didn't need to close any of the streams you worked with in Chapter 10, "Streams."

Finally, the exam doesn't always properly close NIO.2 resources. To match the exam, we sometimes skip closing NIO.2 resources in review and practice questions. Always use try-with-resources statements with these NIO.2 methods in your own code.

For the remainder of this section, we only discuss the NIO.2 methods, because they are more important. There is also more to know about them, and they are more likely to come up on the exam.

Handling Methods That Declare *IOException*

Many of the methods presented in this chapter declare IOException. Common causes of a method throwing this exception include the following:

- Loss of communication to the underlying file system.
- File or directory exists but cannot be accessed or modified.
- File exists but cannot be overwritten.
- File or directory is required but does not exist.

Methods that access or change files and directories, such as those in the Files class, often declare IOException. There are exceptions to this rule, as we will see. For example, the method Files.exists() does not declare IOException. If it did throw an exception when the file did not exist, it would never be able to return false! As a rule of thumb, if an NIO.2 method declares an IOException, it *usually* requires the paths it operates on to exist.

Providing NIO.2 Optional Parameters

Many of the NIO.2 methods in this chapter include a varargs that takes an optional list of values. Table 14.4 presents the arguments you should be familiar with for the exam.

TABLE 14.4   Common NIO.2 method arguments

Enum type	Interface inherited	Enum value	Details
LinkOption	CopyOption OpenOption	NOFOLLOW_LINKS	Do not follow symbolic links.
Standard CopyOption	CopyOption	ATOMIC_MOVE	Move file as atomic file system operation.
		COPY_ATTRIBUTES	Copy existing attributes to new file.
		REPLACE_EXISTING	Overwrite file if it already exists.

TABLE 14.4   Common NIO.2 method arguments *(continued)*

Enum type	Interface inherited	Enum value	Details
Standard OpenOption	OpenOption	APPEND	If file is already open for write, append to the end.
		CREATE	Create new file if it does not exist.
		CREATE_NEW	Create new file only if it does not exist; fail otherwise.
		READ	Open for read access.
		TRUNCATE_EXISTING	If file is already open for write, erase file and append to beginning.
		WRITE	Open for write access.
FileVisit Option	N/A	FOLLOW_LINKS	Follow symbolic links.

With the exceptions of `Files.copy()` and `Files.move()`, we won't discuss these varargs parameters each time we present a method. Their behavior should be straightforward, though. For example, can you figure out what the following call to `Files.exists()` with the `LinkOption` does in the following code snippet?

```
Path path = Path.of("schedule.xml");
boolean exists = Files.exists(path, LinkOption.NOFOLLOW_LINKS);
```

The `Files.exists()` simply checks whether a file exists. But if the parameter is a symbolic link, the method checks whether the target of the symbolic link exists, instead. Providing `LinkOption.NOFOLLOW_LINKS` means the default behavior will be overridden, and the method will check whether the symbolic link itself exists.

Note that some of the enums in Table 14.4 inherit an interface. That means some methods accept a variety of enum types. For example, the `Files.move()` method takes a `CopyOption` vararg so it can take enums of different types, and more options can be added over time.

```
void move(Path source, Path target) throws IOException {
    Files.move(source, target,
        LinkOption.NOFOLLOW_LINKS,
        StandardCopyOption.ATOMIC_MOVE);
}
```

Interacting with NIO.2 Paths

Just like `String` values, `Path` instances are immutable. In the following example, the `Path` operation on the second line is lost since p is immutable:

```
Path p = Path.of("whale");
p.resolve("krill");
System.out.println(p);  // whale
```

Many of the methods available in the `Path` interface transform the path value in some way and return a new `Path` object, allowing the methods to be chained. We demonstrate chaining in the following example, the details of which we discuss in this section of the chapter:

```
Path.of("/zoo/../home").getParent().normalize().toAbsolutePath();
```

Viewing the Path

The `Path` interface contains three methods to retrieve basic information about the path representation. The `toString()` method returns a `String` representation of the entire path. In fact, it is the only method in the `Path` interface to return a `String`. Many of the other methods in the `Path` interface return `Path` instances.

The `getNameCount()` and `getName()` methods are often used together to retrieve the number of elements in the path and a reference to each element, respectively. These two methods do not include the root directory as part of the path.

```
Path path = Path.of("/land/hippo/harry.happy");
System.out.println("The Path is: " + path);
for(int i=0; i<path.getNameCount(); i++)
    System.out.println("   Element " + i + " is: " + path.getName(i));
```

Notice that we didn't call `toString()` explicitly on the second line. Remember, Java calls `toString()` on any `Object` as part of string concatenation. We use this feature throughout the examples in this chapter.

The code prints the following:

```
The Path is: /land/hippo/harry.happy
   Element 0 is: land
   Element 1 is: hippo
   Element 2 is: harry.happy
```

Even though this is an absolute path, the root element is not included in the list of names. As we said, these methods do not consider the root part of the path.

```
var p = Path.of("/");
System.out.print(p.getNameCount()); // 0
System.out.print(p.getName(0));     // IllegalArgumentException
```

Notice that if you try to call `getName()` with an invalid index, it will throw an exception at runtime.

Our examples print / as the file separator character because of the system we are using. Your actual output may vary throughout this chapter.

Creating Part of the Path

The Path interface includes the subpath() method to select portions of a path. It takes two parameters: an inclusive beginIndex and an exclusive endIndex. This should sound familiar as it is how String's substring() method works, as you saw in Chapter 4, "Core APIs."

The following code snippet shows how subpath() works. We also print the elements of the Path using getName() so that you can see how the indices are used.

```java
var p = Path.of("/mammal/omnivore/raccoon.image");
System.out.println("Path is: " + p);
for (int i = 0; i < p.getNameCount(); i++) {
    System.out.println("   Element " + i + " is: " + p.getName(i));
}
System.out.println();
System.out.println("subpath(0,3): " + p.subpath(0, 3));
System.out.println("subpath(1,2): " + p.subpath(1, 2));
System.out.println("subpath(1,3): " + p.subpath(1, 3));
```

The output of this code snippet is the following:

```
Path is: /mammal/omnivore/raccoon.image
   Element 0 is: mammal
   Element 1 is: omnivore
   Element 2 is: raccoon.image

subpath(0,3): mammal/omnivore/raccoon.image
subpath(1,2): omnivore
subpath(1,3): omnivore/raccoon.image
```

Like getNameCount() and getName(), subpath() is zero-indexed and does not include the root. Also like getName(), subpath() throws an exception if invalid indices are provided.

```java
var q = p.subpath(0, 4); // IllegalArgumentException
var x = p.subpath(1, 1); // IllegalArgumentException
```

The first example throws an exception at runtime, since the maximum index value allowed is 3. The second example throws an exception since the start and end indexes are the same, leading to an empty path value.

Accessing Path Elements

The Path interface contains numerous methods for retrieving particular elements of a Path, returned as Path objects themselves. The getFileName() method returns the Path element of the current file or directory, while getParent() returns the full path of the containing directory. The getParent() method returns null if operated on the root path or at the top of a relative path. The getRoot() method returns the root element of the file within the file system, or null if the path is a relative path.

Consider the following method, which prints various Path elements:

```
public void printPathInformation(Path path) {
    System.out.println("Filename is: " + path.getFileName());
    System.out.println("   Root is: " + path.getRoot());
    Path currentParent = path;
    while((currentParent = currentParent.getParent()) != null)
        System.out.println("   Current parent is: " + currentParent);
    System.out.println();
}
```

The while loop in the printPathInformation() method continues until getParent() returns null. We apply this method to the following three paths:

```
printPathInformation(Path.of("zoo"));
printPathInformation(Path.of("/zoo/armadillo/shells.txt"));
printPathInformation(Path.of("./armadillo/../shells.txt"));
```

This sample application produces the following output:

```
Filename is: zoo
   Root is: null

Filename is: shells.txt
   Root is: /
   Current parent is: /zoo/armadillo
   Current parent is: /zoo
   Current parent is: /

Filename is: shells.txt
   Root is: null
   Current parent is: ./armadillo/..
   Current parent is: ./armadillo
   Current parent is: .
```

Reviewing the sample output, you can see the difference in the behavior of getRoot() on absolute and relative paths. As you can see in the first and last examples, the getParent() method does not traverse relative paths outside the current working directory.

You also see that these methods do not resolve the path symbols and treat them as a distinct part of the path. While most of the methods in this part of the chapter treat path symbols as part of the path, we present one shortly that cleans up path symbols.

Resolving Paths

Suppose you want to concatenate paths in a manner similar to how we concatenate strings. The `resolve()` method provides overloaded versions that let you pass either a `Path` or `String` parameter. The object on which the `resolve()` method is invoked becomes the basis of the new `Path` object, with the input argument being appended onto the `Path`. Let's see what happens if we apply `resolve()` to an absolute path and a relative path:

```
Path path1 = Path.of("/cats/../panther");
Path path2 = Path.of("food");
System.out.println(path1.resolve(path2));
```

The code snippet generates the following output:

```
/cats/../panther/food
```

Like the other methods we've seen, `resolve()` does not clean up path symbols. In this example, the input argument to the `resolve()` method was a relative path, but what if it had been an absolute path?

```
Path path3 = Path.of("/turkey/food");
System.out.println(path3.resolve("/tiger/cage"));
```

Since the input parameter is an absolute path, the output would be the following:

```
/tiger/cage
```

For the exam, you should be cognizant of mixing absolute and relative paths with the `resolve()` method. If an absolute path is provided as input to the method, that is the value returned. Simply put, you cannot combine two absolute paths using `resolve()`.

On the exam, when you see `resolve()`, think concatenation.

Relativizing a Path

The `Path` interface includes a `relativize()` method for constructing the relative path from one `Path` to another, often using path symbols. What do you think the following examples will print?

```
var path1 = Path.of("fish.txt");
var path2 = Path.of("friendly/birds.txt");
System.out.println(path1.relativize(path2));
System.out.println(path2.relativize(path1));
```

The examples print the following:

```
../friendly/birds.txt
../../fish.txt
```

The idea is this: if you are pointed at a path in the file system, what steps would you need to take to reach the other path? For example, to get to fish.txt from friendly/birds.txt, you need to go up two levels (the file itself counts as one level) and then select fish.txt.

If both path values are relative, the relativize() method computes the paths as if they are in the same current working directory. Alternatively, if both path values are absolute, the method computes the relative path from one absolute location to another, regardless of the current working directory. The following example demonstrates this property when run on a Windows computer:

```
var path3 = Path.of("E:\\habitat");
var path4 = Path.of("E:\\sanctuary\\raven\\poe.txt");
System.out.println(path3.relativize(path4));
System.out.println(path4.relativize(path3));
```

This code snippet produces the following output:

```
..\sanctuary\raven\poe.txt
..\..\..\habitat
```

The relativize() method requires both paths to be absolute or relative and throws an exception if the types are mixed.

```
var path1 = Path.of("/primate/chimpanzee");
var path2 = Path.of("bananas.txt");
path1.relativize(path2); // IllegalArgumentException
```

On Windows-based systems, it also requires that if absolute paths are used, both paths must have the same root directory or drive letter. For example, the following would also throw an IllegalArgumentException on a Windows-based system:

```
var path3 = Path.of("C:\\primate\\chimpanzee");
var path4 = Path.of("D:\\storage\\bananas.txt");
path3.relativize(path4); // IllegalArgumentException
```

Normalizing a Path

So far, we've presented a number of examples that included path symbols that were unnecessary. Luckily, Java provides the normalize() method to eliminate unnecessary redundancies in a path.

Remember, the path symbol .. refers to the parent directory, while the path symbol . refers to the current directory. We can apply normalize() to some of our previous paths.

```
var p1 = Path.of("./armadillo/../shells.txt");
System.out.println(p1.normalize()); // shells.txt
```

```
var p2 = Path.of("/cats/../panther/food");
System.out.println(p2.normalize()); // /panther/food
```

```
var p3 = Path.of("../../fish.txt");
System.out.println(p3.normalize()); // ../../fish.txt
```

The first two examples apply the path symbols to remove the redundancies, but what about the last one? That is as simplified as it can be. The normalize() method does not remove all of the path symbols, only the ones that can be reduced.

The normalize() method also allows us to compare equivalent paths. Consider the following example:

```
var p1 = Path.of("/pony/../weather.txt");
var p2 = Path.of("/weather.txt");
System.out.println(p1.equals(p2));                         // false
System.out.println(p1.normalize().equals(p2.normalize())); // true
```

The equals() method returns true if two paths represent the same value. In the first comparison, the path values are different. In the second comparison, the path values have both been reduced to the same normalized value, /weather.txt. This is the primary function of the normalize() method: to allow us to better compare different paths.

Retrieving the Real File System Path

While working with theoretical paths is useful, sometimes you want to verify that the path exists within the file system using toRealPath(). This method is similar to normalize() in that it eliminates any redundant path symbols. It is also similar to toAbsolutePath(), in that it will join the path with the current working directory if the path is relative.

Unlike those two methods, though, toRealPath() will throw an exception if the path does not exist. In addition, it will follow symbolic links, with an optional LinkOption varargs parameter to ignore them.

Let's say that we have a file system in which we have a symbolic link from /zebra to /horse. What do you think the following will print, given a current working directory of /horse/schedule?

```
System.out.println(Path.of("/zebra/food.txt").toRealPath());
System.out.println(Path.of(".././food.txt").toRealPath());
```

The output of both lines is the following:

```
/horse/food.txt
```

In this example, the absolute and relative paths both resolve to the same absolute file, as the symbolic link points to a real file within the file system. We can also use the toRealPath() method to gain access to the current working directory as a Path object.

```
System.out.println(Path.of(".").toRealPath());
```

Reviewing NIO.2 Path APIs

We've covered a lot of instance methods on Path in this section. Table 14.5 lists them for review.

TABLE 14.5   Path API

Description	*Path* instance method
File path as string	String **toString**()
Single segment	Path **getName**(int index)
Number of segments	int **getNameCount**()
Segments in range	Path **subpath**(int beginIndex, int endIndex)
Final segment	Path **getFileName**()
Immediate parent	Path **getParent**()
Top-level segment	Path **getRoot**()
Concatenate paths	Path **resolve**(String p) Path **resolve**(Path p)
Construct path to one provided	Path **relativize**(Path p)
Remove redundant parts of path	Path **normalize**()
Follow symbolic links to find path on file system	Path **toRealPath**()

Creating, Moving, and Deleting Files and Directories

Since creating, moving, and deleting have some nuance, we flesh them out in this section.

Making Directories

To create a directory, we use these Files methods:

```
public static Path createDirectory(Path dir,
    FileAttribute<?>... attrs) throws IOException

public static Path createDirectories(Path dir,
    FileAttribute<?>... attrs) throws IOException
```

The `createDirectory()` method will create a directory and throw an exception if it already exists or if the paths leading up to the directory do not exist. The `createDirectories()` method creates the target directory along with any nonexistent parent directories leading up to the path. If all of the directories already exist, `createDirectories()` will simply complete without doing anything. This is useful in situations where you want to ensure a directory exists and create it if it does not.

Both of these methods also accept an optional list of `FileAttribute<?>` values to apply to the newly created directory or directories. We discuss file attributes toward the end of the chapter.

The following shows how to create directories:

```
Files.createDirectory(Path.of("/bison/field"));
Files.createDirectories(Path.of("/bison/field/pasture/green"));
```

The first example creates a new directory, `field`, in the directory `/bison`, assuming `/bison` exists; otherwise, an exception is thrown. Contrast this with the second example, which creates the directory green along with any of the following parent directories if they do not already exist, including `bison`, `field`, and `pasture`.

Copying Files

The `Files` class provides a method for copying files and directories within the file system.

```
public static Path copy(Path source, Path target,
    CopyOption... options) throws IOException
```

The method copies a file or directory from one location to another using `Path` objects. The following shows an example of copying a file and a directory:

```
Files.copy(Path.of("/panda/bamboo.txt"),    Path.of("/panda-save/bamboo.txt"));

Files.copy(Path.of("/turtle"), Path.of("/turtleCopy"));
```

When directories are copied, the copy is shallow. A *shallow copy* means that the files and subdirectories within the directory are not copied. A *deep copy* means that the entire tree is copied, including all of its content and subdirectories. A deep copy typically requires *recursion*, where a method calls itself.

```
public void copyPath(Path source, Path target) {
    try {
        Files.copy(source, target);
        if(Files.isDirectory(source))
            try (Stream<Path> s = Files.list(source)) {
                s.forEach(p -> copyPath(p,
                    target.resolve(p.getFileName())));
            }
    } catch(IOException e) {
        // Handle exception
    }
}
```

The method first copies the path, whether a file or a directory. If it is a directory, only a shallow copy is performed. Next, it checks whether the path is a directory and, if it is, performs a recursive copy of each of its elements.

Copying and Replacing Files

By default, if the target already exists, the copy() method will throw an exception. You can change this behavior by providing the StandardCopyOption enum value REPLACE_EXISTING to the method. The following method call will overwrite the movie.txt file if it already exists:

```
Files.copy(Path.of("book.txt"), Path.of("movie.txt"),
   StandardCopyOption.REPLACE_EXISTING);
```

For the exam, you need to know that without the REPLACE_EXISTING option, this method will throw an exception if the file already exists.

Copying Files with I/O Streams

The Files class includes two copy() methods that operate with I/O streams.

```
public static long copy(InputStream in, Path target,
   CopyOption... options) throws IOException
```

```
public static long copy(Path source, OutputStream out)
   throws IOException
```

The first method reads the contents of an I/O stream and writes the output to a file. The second method reads the contents of a file and writes the output to an I/O stream. These methods are quite convenient if you need to quickly read/write data from/to disk.

The following are examples of each copy() method:

```
try (var is = new FileInputStream("source-data.txt")) {
   // Write I/O stream data to a file
   Files.copy(is, Path.of("/mammals/wolf.txt"));
}
```

```
Files.copy(Path.of("/fish/clown.xsl"), System.out);
```

While we used FileInputStream in the first example, the I/O stream could have been any valid I/O stream including website connections, in-memory stream resources, and so forth. The second example prints the contents of a file directly to the System.out stream.

Copying Files into a Directory

For the exam, it is important that you understand how the copy() method operates on both files and directories. For example, let's say we have a file, food.txt, and a directory, /enclosure. Both the file and directory exist. What do you think is the result of executing the following process?

```
var file = Path.of("food.txt");
var directory = Path.of("/enclosure");
Files.copy(file, directory);
```

If you said it would create a new file at /enclosure/food.txt, you're way off. It throws an exception. The command tries to create a new file named /enclosure. Since the path /enclosure already exists, an exception is thrown at runtime.

On the other hand, if the directory did not exist, the process would create a new file with the contents of food.txt, but the file would be called /enclosure. Remember, we said files may not need to have extensions, and in this example, it matters.

This behavior applies to both the copy() and move() methods, the latter of which we cover next. In case you're curious, the correct way to copy the file into the directory is to do the following:

```
var file = Path.of("food.txt");
var directory = Path.of("/enclosure/food.txt");
Files.copy(file, directory);
```

Moving or Renaming Paths with *move()*

The Files class provides a useful method for moving or renaming files and directories.

```
public static Path move(Path source, Path target,
    CopyOption... options) throws IOException
```

The following sample code uses the move() method:

```
Files.move(Path.of("C:\\zoo"), Path.of("C:\\zoo-new"));

Files.move(Path.of("C:\\user\\addresses.txt"),
    Path.of("C:\\zoo-new\\addresses2.txt"));
```

The first example renames the zoo directory to a zoo-new directory, keeping all of the original contents from the source directory. The second example moves the addresses.txt file from the directory user to the directory zoo-new and renames it addresses2.txt.

Similarities between *move()* and *copy()*

Like copy(), move() requires REPLACE_EXISTING to overwrite the target if it exists; otherwise, it will throw an exception. Also like copy(), move() will not put a file in a directory if the source is a file and the target is a directory. Instead, it will create a new file with the name of the directory.

Performing an Atomic Move

Another enum value that you need to know for the exam when working with the move() method is the StandardCopyOption value ATOMIC_MOVE.

```
Files.move(Path.of("mouse.txt"), Path.of("gerbil.txt"),
    StandardCopyOption.ATOMIC_MOVE);
```

You may remember the atomic property from Chapter 13, "Concurrency," and the principle of an atomic move is similar. An atomic move is one in which a file is moved within the file system as a single indivisible operation. Put another way, any process monitoring the file system never sees an incomplete or partially written file. If the file system does not support this feature, an `AtomicMoveNotSupportedException` will be thrown.

Note that while `ATOMIC_MOVE` is available as a member of the `StandardCopyOption` type, it will likely throw an exception if passed to a `copy()` method.

Deleting a File with *delete()* and *deleteIfExists()*

The `Files` class includes two methods that delete a file or empty directory within the file system.

```
public static void delete(Path path) throws IOException
```

```
public static boolean deleteIfExists(Path path) throws IOException
```

To delete a directory, it must be empty. Both of these methods throw an exception if operated on a nonempty directory. In addition, if the path is a symbolic link, the symbolic link will be deleted, not the path that the symbolic link points to.

The methods differ on how they handle a path that does not exist. The `delete()` method throws an exception if the path does not exist, while the `deleteIfExists()` method returns `true` if the delete was successful or `false` otherwise. Similar to `createDirectories()`, `deleteIfExists()` is useful in situations where you want to ensure that a path does not exist and delete it if it does.

Here we provide sample code that performs `delete()` operations:

```
Files.delete(Path.of("/vulture/feathers.txt"));
Files.deleteIfExists(Path.of("/pigeon"));
```

The first example deletes the `feathers.txt` file in the `vulture` directory, and it throws a `NoSuchFileException` if the file or directory does not exist. The second example deletes the `pigeon` directory, assuming it is empty. If the `pigeon` directory does not exist, the second line will not throw an exception.

Comparing Files with *isSameFile()* and *mismatch()*

Since a path may include path symbols and symbolic links within a file system, the `equals()` method can't be relied on to know if two `Path` instances refer to the same file. Luckily, there is the `isSameFile()` method. This method takes two `Path` objects as input, resolves all path symbols, and follows symbolic links. Despite the name, the method can also be used to determine whether two `Path` objects refer to the same directory.

While most uses of `isSameFile()` will trigger an exception if the paths do not exist, there is a special case in which it does not. If the two path objects are equal in terms of `equals()`, the method will just return `true` without checking whether the file exists.

Assume that the file system exists, as shown in Figure 14.3, with a symbolic link from /animals/snake to /animals/cobra.

FIGURE 14.3   Comparing file uniqueness

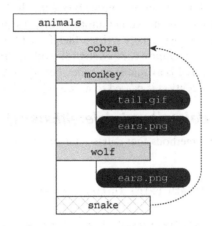

Given the structure defined in Figure 14.3, what does the following output?

```
System.out.println(Files.isSameFile(
   Path.of("/animals/cobra"),
   Path.of("/animals/snake")));
```

```
System.out.println(Files.isSameFile(
   Path.of("/animals/monkey/ears.png"),
   Path.of("/animals/wolf/ears.png")));
```

Since snake is a symbolic link to cobra, the first example outputs true. In the second example, the paths refer to different files, so false is printed.

Sometimes you want to compare the contents of the file rather than whether it is physically the same file. For example, we could have two files with text hello. The mismatch() method was introduced in Java 12 to help us out here. It takes two Path objects as input. The method returns −1 if the files are the same; otherwise, it returns the index of the first position in the file that differs.

```
System.out.println(Files.mismatch(
   Path.of("/animals/monkey.txt"),
   Path.of("/animals/wolf.txt")));
```

Suppose monkey.txt contains the name Harold and wolf.txt contains the name Howler. The previous code prints 1 in that case because the second position is different, and we use zero-based indexing in Java. Given those values, what do you think this code prints?

```
System.out.println(Files.mismatch(
   Path.of("/animals/wolf.txt"),
   Path.of("/animals/monkey.txt")));
```

The answer is the same as the previous example. The code prints 1 again. The mismatch() method is symmetric and returns the same result regardless of the order of the parameters.

Introducing I/O Streams

Now that we have the basics out of the way, let's move on to I/O streams, which are far more interesting. In this section, we show you how to use I/O streams to read and write data. The "I/O" refers to the nature of how data is accessed, either by reading the data from a resource (input) or by writing the data to a resource (output).

> When we refer to *I/O streams* in this chapter, we are referring to the ones found in the java.io API. If we just say *streams*, it means the ones from Chapter 10. We agree that the naming can be a bit confusing!

Understanding I/O Stream Fundamentals

The contents of a file may be accessed or written via an I/O *stream*, which is a list of data elements presented sequentially. An I/O stream can be conceptually thought of as a long, nearly never-ending stream of water with data presented one wave at a time.

We demonstrate this principle in Figure 14.4. The I/O stream is so large that once we start reading it, we have no idea where the beginning or the end is. We just have a pointer to our current position in the I/O stream and read data one block at a time.

FIGURE 14.4   Visual representation of an I/O stream

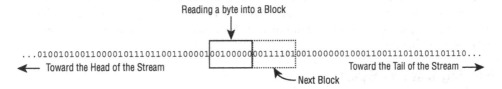

Each type of I/O stream segments data into a wave or block in a particular way. For example, some I/O stream classes read or write data as individual bytes. Other I/O stream classes read or write individual characters or strings of characters. On top of that, some I/O stream classes read or write larger groups of bytes or characters at a time, specifically those with the word Buffered in their name.

> Although the java.io API is full of I/O streams that handle characters, strings, groups of bytes, and so on, nearly all are built on top of reading or writing an individual byte or an array of bytes at a time. Higher-level I/O streams exist for convenience as well as performance.

Although I/O streams are commonly used with file I/O, they are more generally used to handle the reading/writing of any sequential data source. For example, you might construct a Java application that submits data to a website using an output stream and reads the result via an input stream.

I/O Streams Can Be Big

When writing code where you don't know what the I/O stream size will be at runtime, it may be helpful to visualize an I/O stream as being so large that all of the data contained in it could not possibly fit into memory. For example, a 1 TB file could not be stored entirely in memory by most computer systems (at the time this book is being written). The file can still be read and written by a program with very little memory, since the I/O stream allows the application to focus on only a small portion of the overall I/O stream at any given time.

Learning I/O Stream Nomenclature

The java.io API provides numerous classes for creating, accessing, and manipulating I/O streams—so many that it tends to overwhelm many new Java developers. Stay calm! We review the major differences between each I/O stream class and show you how to distinguish between them.

Even if you come across a particular I/O stream on the exam that you do not recognize, the name of the I/O stream often gives you enough information to understand exactly what it does.

The goal of this section is to familiarize you with common terminology and naming conventions used with I/O streams. Don't worry if you don't recognize the particular stream class names used in this section or their function; we cover how to use them in detail in this chapter.

Storing Data as Bytes

Data is stored in a file system (and memory) as a 0 or 1, called a *bit*. Since it's really hard for humans to read/write data that is just 0s and 1s, they are grouped into a set of 8 bits, called a *byte*.

What about the Java byte primitive type? As you learn later, when we use I/O streams, values are often read or written using byte values and arrays.

Byte Streams vs. Character Streams

The java.io API defines two sets of I/O stream classes for reading and writing I/O streams: byte I/O streams and character I/O streams. We use both types of I/O streams throughout this chapter.

Differences Between Byte and Character I/O Streams

- Byte I/O streams read/write binary data (0s and 1s) and have class names that end in InputStream or OutputStream.

- Character I/O streams read/write text data and have class names that end in Reader or Writer.

The API frequently includes similar classes for both byte and character I/O streams, such as FileInputStream and FileReader. The difference between the two classes is based on how the bytes are read or written.

It is important to remember that even though character I/O streams do not contain the word Stream in their class name, they are still I/O streams. The use of Reader/Writer in the name is just to distinguish them from byte streams.

 Throughout the chapter, we refer to both InputStream and Reader as *input streams*, and we refer to both OutputStream and Writer as *output streams*.

The byte I/O streams are primarily used to work with binary data, such as an image or executable file, while character I/O streams are used to work with text files. For example, you can use a Writer class to output a String value to a file without necessarily having to worry about the underlying character encoding of the file.

The *character encoding* determines how characters are encoded and stored in bytes in an I/O stream and later read back or decoded as characters. Although this may sound simple, Java supports a wide variety of character encodings, ranging from ones that may use one byte for Latin characters, UTF-8 and ASCII for example, to using two or more bytes per character, such as UTF-16. For the exam, you don't need to memorize the character encodings, but you should be familiar with the names.

Character Encoding in Java

In Java, the character encoding can be specified using the Charset class by passing a name value to the static Charset.forName() method, such as in the following examples:

```
Charset usAsciiCharset = Charset.forName("US-ASCII");
Charset utf8Charset = Charset.forName("UTF-8");
Charset utf16Charset = Charset.forName("UTF-16");
```

Java supports numerous character encodings, each specified by a different standard name value.

Input vs. Output Streams

Most InputStream classes have a corresponding OutputStream class, and vice versa. For example, the FileOutputStream class writes data that can be read by a

`FileInputStream`. If you understand the features of a particular `Input` or `Output` stream class, you should naturally know what its complementary class does.

It follows, then, that most `Reader` classes have a corresponding `Writer` class. For example, the `FileWriter` class writes data that can be read by a `FileReader`.

There are some exceptions to this rule. For the exam, you should know that `PrintWriter` has no accompanying `PrintReader` class. Likewise, the `PrintStream` is an `OutputStream` that has no corresponding `InputStream` class. It also does not have `Output` in its name. We discuss these classes later in this chapter.

Low-Level vs. High-Level Streams

Another way that you can familiarize yourself with the `java.io` API is by segmenting I/O streams into low-level and high-level streams.

A *low-level stream* connects directly with the source of the data, such as a file, an array, or a `String`. Low-level I/O streams process the raw data or resource and are accessed in a direct and unfiltered manner. For example, a `FileInputStream` is a class that reads file data one byte at a time.

Alternatively, a *high-level stream* is built on top of another I/O stream using wrapping. *Wrapping* is the process by which an instance is passed to the constructor of another class, and operations on the resulting instance are filtered and applied to the original instance. For example, take a look at the `FileReader` and `BufferedReader` objects in the following sample code:

```
try (var br = new BufferedReader(new FileReader("zoo-data.txt"))) {
   System.out.println(br.readLine());
}
```

In this example, `FileReader` is the low-level I/O stream, whereas `BufferedReader` is the high-level I/O stream that takes a `FileReader` as input. Many operations on the high-level I/O stream pass through as operations to the underlying low-level I/O stream, such as `read()` or `close()`. Other operations override or add new functionality to the low-level I/O stream methods. The high-level I/O stream may add new methods, such as `readLine()`, as well as performance enhancements for reading and filtering the low-level data.

High-level I/O streams can also take other high-level I/O streams as input. For example, although the following code might seem a little odd at first, the style of wrapping an I/O stream is quite common in practice:

```
try (var ois = new ObjectInputStream(
     new BufferedInputStream(
        new FileInputStream("zoo-data.ser")))) {
   System.out.print(ois.readObject());
}
```

In this example, the low-level `FileInputStream` interacts directly with the file, which is wrapped by a high-level `BufferedInputStream` to improve performance. Finally, the entire object is wrapped by another high-level ObjectInputStream, which allows us to interpret the data as a Java object.

For the exam, the only low-level stream classes you need to be familiar with are the ones that operate on files. The rest of the nonabstract stream classes are all high-level streams.

Stream Base Classes

The java.io library defines four abstract classes that are the parents of all I/O stream classes defined within the API: InputStream, OutputStream, Reader, and Writer.

The constructors of high-level I/O streams often take a reference to the abstract class. For example, BufferedWriter takes a Writer object as input, which allows it to take any subclass of Writer.

One common area where the exam likes to play tricks on you is mixing and matching I/O stream classes that are not compatible with each other. For example, take a look at each of the following examples and see whether you can determine why they do not compile:

```
new BufferedInputStream(new FileReader("z.txt"));  // DOES NOT COMPILE
new BufferedWriter(new FileOutputStream("z.txt")); // DOES NOT COMPILE
new ObjectInputStream(
    new FileOutputStream("z.txt"));                // DOES NOT COMPILE
new BufferedInputStream(new InputStream());        // DOES NOT COMPILE
```

The first two examples do not compile because they mix Reader/Writer classes with InputStream/OutputStream classes, respectively. The third example does not compile because we are mixing an OutputStream with an InputStream. Although it is possible to read data from an InputStream and write it to an OutputStream, wrapping the I/O stream is not the way to do so. As you see later in this chapter, the data must be copied over. Finally, the last example does not compile because InputStream is an abstract class, and therefore you cannot create an instance of it.

Like we saw with input vs output streams, there are a few exceptions. InputStreamReader is a Reader that takes an InputStream, while OutputStreamWriter is a Writer that takes an OutputStream. While unlikely to be on the exam, these convenience classes allow you to convert one stream type to another, which is why they have both types in their names. The PrintWriter class is also special in that it can take an OutputStream or a Writer. We'll cover PrintWriter more later in the chapter.

Decoding I/O Class Names

Pay close attention to the name of the I/O class on the exam, as decoding it often gives you context clues as to what the class does. For example, without needing to look it up, it should be clear that FileReader is a class that reads data from a file as characters or strings. Furthermore, ObjectOutputStream sounds like a class that writes object data to a byte stream.

Table 14.6 lists the abstract base classes that all I/O streams inherit from.

TABLE 14.6 The java.io abstract stream base classes

Class name	Description
InputStream	Abstract class for all input byte streams
OutputStream	Abstract class for all output byte streams
Reader	Abstract class for all input character streams
Writer	Abstract class for all output character streams

Table 14.7 lists the concrete I/O streams that you should be familiar with for the exam. Note that most of the information about each I/O stream, such as whether it is an input or output stream or whether it accesses data using bytes or characters, can be decoded by the name alone.

TABLE 14.7 The java.io concrete I/O stream classes

Class name	Low/High level	Description
FileInputStream	Low	Reads file data as bytes
FileOutputStream	Low	Writes file data as bytes
FileReader	Low	Reads file data as characters
FileWriter	Low	Writes file data as characters
BufferedInputStream	High	Reads byte data from existing InputStream in buffered manner, which improves efficiency and performance
Buffered OutputStream	High	Writes byte data to existing OutputStream in buffered manner, which improves efficiency and performance
BufferedReader	High	Reads character data from existing Reader in buffered manner, which improves efficiency and performance
BufferedWriter	High	Writes character data to existing Writer in buffered manner, which improves efficiency and performance
ObjectInputStream	High	Deserializes primitive Java data types and graphs of Java objects from existing InputStream

Class name	Low/High level	Description
ObjectOutputStream	High	Serializes primitive Java data types and graphs of Java objects to existing OutputStream
PrintStream	High	Writes formatted representations of Java objects to binary stream
PrintWriter	High	Writes formatted representations of Java objects to character stream

Keep Table 14.6 and Table 14.7 handy as you learn more about I/O streams in this chapter. We discuss these in more detail, including examples of each.

Reading and Writing Files

There are a number of ways to read and write from a file. We show them in this section by copying one file to another.

Using I/O Streams

I/O streams are all about reading/writing data, so it shouldn't be a surprise that the most important methods are read() and write(). Both InputStream and Reader declare a read() method to read byte data from an I/O stream. Likewise, OutputStream and Writer both define a write() method to write a byte to the stream.

The following copyStream() methods show an example of reading all of the values of an InputStream and Reader and writing them to an OutputStream and Writer, respectively. In both examples, -1 is used to indicate the end of the stream.

```
void copyStream(InputStream in, OutputStream out) throws IOException {
    int b;
    while ((b = in.read()) != -1) {
        out.write(b);
    }
}

void copyStream(Reader in, Writer out) throws IOException {
    int b;
```

```
    while ((b = in.read()) != -1) {
       out.write(b);
    }
}
```

Hold on. We said we are reading and writing bytes, so why do the methods use `int` instead of `byte`? Remember, the `byte` data type has a range of 256 characters. They needed an extra value to indicate the end of an I/O stream. The authors of Java decided to use a larger data type, `int`, so that special values like -1 would indicate the end of an I/O stream. The output stream classes use `int` as well, to be consistent with the input stream classes.

Reading and writing one byte at a time isn't a particularly efficient way of doing this. Luckily, there are overloaded methods for reading and writing multiple bytes at a time. The `offset` and `length` values are applied to the array itself. For example, an `offset` of 3 and `length` of 5 indicates that the stream should read up to five bytes/characters of data and put them into the array starting with position 3. Let's look at an example:

```
10: void copyStream(InputStream in, OutputStream out) throws IOException {
11:     int batchSize = 1024;
12:     var buffer = new byte[batchSize];
13:     int lengthRead;
14:     while ((lengthRead = in.read(buffer, 0, batchSize)) > 0) {
15:        out.write(buffer, 0, lengthRead);
16:        out.flush();
17:     }
```

Instead of reading the data one byte at a time, we read and write up to 1024 bytes at a time on lines 14–15. The return value `lengthRead` is critical for determining whether we are at the end of the stream and knowing how many bytes we should write into our output stream.

Unless our file happens to be a multiple of 1024 bytes, the last iteration of the `while` loop will write some value less than 1024 bytes. For example, if the buffer size is 1,024 bytes and the file size is 1,054 bytes, the last read will be only 30 bytes. If we ignored this return value and instead wrote 1,024 bytes, 994 bytes from the previous loop would be written to the end of the file.

We also added a `flush()` method on line 16 to reduce the amount of data lost if the application terminates unexpectedly. When data is written to an output stream, the underlying operating system does not guarantee that the data will make it to the file system immediately. The `flush()` method requests that all accumulated data be written immediately to disk. It is not without cost, though. Each time it is used, it may cause a noticeable delay in the application, especially for large files. Unless the data that you are writing is extremely critical, the `flush()` method should be used only intermittently. For example, it should not necessarily be called after every write, as it is in this example.

Equivalent methods exist on `Reader` and `Writer`, but they use char rather than byte, making the equivalent `copyStream()` method very similar.

The previous example makes reading and writing a file look like a lot to think about. That's because it uses only low-level I/O streams. Let's try again using high-level streams.

```
26: void copyTextFile(File src, File dest) throws IOException {
27:    try (var reader = new BufferedReader(new FileReader(src));
28:        var writer = new BufferedWriter(new FileWriter(dest))) {
29:        String line = null;
30:        while ((line = reader.readLine()) != null) {
31:            writer.write(line);
32:            writer.newLine();
33:        } } }
```

The key is to choose the most useful high-level classes. In this case, we are dealing with a File, so we want to use a FileReader and FileWriter. Both classes have constructors that can take either a String representing the location or a File directly.

If the source file does not exist, a FileNotFoundException, which inherits IOException, will be thrown. If the destination file already exists, this implementation will overwrite it. We can pass an optional boolean second parameter to FileWriter for an append flag if we want to change this behavior.

We also chose to use a BufferedReader and BufferedWriter so we can read a whole line at a time. This gives us the benefits of reading batches of characters on line 30 without having to write custom logic. Line 31 writes out the whole line of data at once. Since reading a line strips the line breaks, we add those back on line 32. Lines 27 and 28 demonstrate chaining constructors. The try-with-resources takes care of closing all the objects in the chain.

Now imagine that we wanted byte data instead of characters. We would need to choose different high-level classes: BufferedInputStream, BufferedOutputStream, File InputStream, and FileOuputStream. We would call readAllBytes() instead of read Line() and store the result in a byte[] instead of a String. Finally, we wouldn't need to handle new lines since the data is binary.

We can do a little better than BufferedOutputStream and BufferedWriter by using a PrintStream and PrintWriter. These classes contain four key methods. The print() and println() methods print data with and without a new line, respectively. There are also the format() and printf() methods, which we describe in the section on user interactions.

```
void copyTextFile(File src, File dest) throws IOException {
    try (var reader = new BufferedReader(new FileReader(src));
        var writer = new PrintWriter(new FileWriter(dest))) {
        String line = null;
        while ((line = reader.readLine()) != null)
            writer.println(line);
    }
}
```

While we used a String, there are numerous overloaded versions of println(), which take everything from primitives and String values to objects. Under the covers, these methods often just perform String.valueOf().

The print stream classes have the distinction of being the only I/O stream classes we cover that do not have corresponding input stream classes. And unlike other OutputStream classes, PrintStream does not have Output in its name.

NOTE   It may surprise you that you've been regularly using a PrintStream throughout this book. Both System.out and System.err are PrintStream objects. Likewise, System.in, often useful for reading user input, is an InputStream.

Unlike the majority of the other I/O streams we've covered, the methods in the print stream classes do not throw any checked exceptions. If they did, you would be required to catch a checked exception any time you called System.out.print()!

The line separator is \n or \r\n, depending on your operating system. The println() method takes care of this for you. If you need to get the character directly, either of the following will return it for you as a String:

```
System.getProperty("line.separator");
System.lineSeparator();
```

Enhancing with *Files*

The NIO.2 APIs provide even easier ways to read and write a file using the Files class. Let's start by looking at three ways of copying a file by reading in the data and writing it back:

```
private void copyPathAsString(Path input, Path output) throws IOException {
   String string = Files.readString(input);
   Files.writeString(output, string);
}
private void copyPathAsBytes(Path input, Path output) throws IOException {
   byte[] bytes = Files.readAllBytes(input);
   Files.write(output, bytes);
}
private void copyPathAsLines(Path input, Path output) throws IOException {
   List<String> lines = Files.readAllLines(input);
   Files.write(output, lines);
}
```

That's pretty concise! You can read a Path as a String, a byte array, or a List. Be aware that the entire file is read at once for all three of these, thereby storing all of the contents of the file in memory at the same time. If the file is significantly large, you may trigger an OutOfMemoryError when trying to load all of it into memory. Luckily, there is an alternative. This time, we print out the file as we read it.

```
private void readLazily(Path path) throws IOException {
   try (Stream<String> s = Files.lines(path)) {
      s.forEach(System.out::println);
   }
}
```

Now the contents of the file are read and processed lazily, which means that only a small portion of the file is stored in memory at any given time. Taking things one step further, we can leverage other stream methods for a more powerful example.

```
try (var s = Files.lines(path)) {
   s.filter(f -> f.startsWith("WARN:"))
      .map(f -> f.substring(5))
      .forEach(System.out::println);
}
```

This sample code searches a log for lines that start with WARN:, outputting the text that follows. Assuming that the input file sharks.log is as follows:

```
INFO:Server starting
DEBUG:Processes available = 10
WARN:No database could be detected
DEBUG:Processes available reset to 0
WARN:Performing manual recovery
INFO:Server successfully started
```

Then the sample output would be the following:

```
No database could be detected
Performing manual recovery
```

As you can see, we have the ability to manipulate files in complex ways, often with only a few short expressions.

Files.readAllLines() vs. Files.lines()

For the exam, you need to know the difference between readAllLines() and lines(). Both of these examples compile and run.

```
Files.readAllLines(Path.of("birds.txt")).forEach(System.out::println);
Files.lines(Path.of("birds.txt")).forEach(System.out::println);
```

The first line reads the entire file into memory and performs a print operation on the result, while the second line lazily processes each line and prints it as it is read. The advantage of the second code snippet is that it does not require the entire file to be stored in memory at any time.

You should also be aware of when they are mixing incompatible types on the exam. Do you see why the following does not compile?

```
Files.readAllLines(Path.of("birds.txt"))
    .filter(s -> s.length()> 2)
    .forEach(System.out::println);
```

The readAllLines() method returns a List, not a Stream, so the filter() method is
not available.

Combining with *newBufferedReader()* and *newBufferedWriter()*

Sometimes you need to mix I/O streams and NIO.2. Conveniently, Files includes two
convenience methods for getting I/O streams.

```
private void copyPath(Path input, Path output) throws IOException {
    try (var reader = Files.newBufferedReader(input);
        var writer = Files.newBufferedWriter(output)) {

        String line = null;
        while ((line = reader.readLine()) != null) {
            writer.write(line);
            writer.newLine();
        } } }
```

You can wrap I/O stream constructors to produce the same effect, although it's a lot
easier to use the factory method. The first method, newBufferedReader(), reads the file
specified at the Path location using a BufferedReader object.

Reviewing Common Read and Write Methods

Table 14.8 reviews the public common I/O stream methods you should know for reading
and writing. We also include close() and flush() since they are used when performing
these actions. Table 14.9 does the same for common public NIO.2 read and write methods.

TABLE 14.8   Common I/O read and write instance methods

Class	Method name	Description
All input streams	int **read**()	Reads single byte or returns −1 if no bytes available.
InputStream	int **read**(byte[] b)	Reads values into buffer and returns number of bytes or characters read.
Reader	int **read**(char[] c)	

Class	Method name	Description
InputStream Reader	int **read**(byte[] b, int offset, int length) int **read**(char[] c, int offset, int length)	Reads up to length values into buffer starting from position offset and returns number of bytes or characters read.
All output streams	void **write**(int b)	Writes single byte.
OutputStream Writer	void **write**(byte[] b) void **write**(char[] c)	Writes array of values into stream.
OutputStream Writer	void **write**(byte[] b, int offset, int length) void **write**(char[] c, int offset, int length)	Writes length values from array into stream, starting with offset index.
InputStream	byte[] **readAllBytes**()	Reads data in bytes.
BufferedReader	String **readLine**()	Reads line of data.
Writer	void **write**(String line)	Writes line of data.
BufferedWriter	void **newLine**()	Writes new line.
All output streams	void **flush**()	Flushes buffered data through stream.
All streams	void **close**()	Closes stream and releases resources.

TABLE 14.9 Common Files NIO.2 read and write static methods

Method Name	Description
byte[] **readAllBytes**(Path path)	Reads all data as bytes
String **readString**(Path path)	Reads all data into String
List<String> **readAllLines**(Path path)	Read all data into List
Stream<String> **lines**(Path path)	Lazily reads data

TABLE 14.9   Common Files NIO.2 read and write static methods *(continued)*

Method Name	Description
void **write**(Path path, byte[] bytes)	Writes array of bytes
void **writeString**(Path path, String string)	Writes String
void **write**(Path path, List<String> list)	Writes list of lines (technically, an Iterable of CharSequence, but you don't need to know that for the exam)

Serializing Data

Throughout this book, we have been managing our data model using classes, so it makes sense that we would want to save these objects between program executions. Data about our zoo animals' health wouldn't be particularly useful if it had to be entered every time the program runs!

You can certainly use the I/O stream classes you've learned about so far to store text and binary data, but you still have to figure out how to put the data in the I/O stream and then decode it later. There are various file formats like XML and CSV you can standardize to, but you often have to build the translation yourself.

Alternatively, we can use serialization to solve the problem of how to convert objects to/from an I/O stream. *Serialization* is the process of converting an in-memory object to a byte stream. Likewise, *deserialization* is the process of converting from a byte stream into an object. Serialization often involves writing an object to a stored or transmittable format, while deserialization is the reciprocal process.

Figure 14.5 shows a visual representation of serializing and deserializing a Giraffe object to and from a giraffe.ser file.

FIGURE 14.5   Serialization process

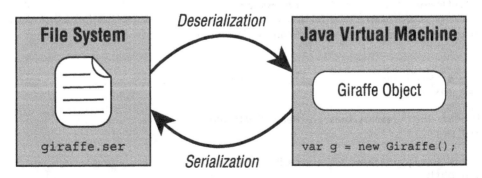

In this section, we show you how Java provides built-in mechanisms for serializing and deserializing I/O streams of objects directly to and from disk, respectively.

Applying the *Serializable* Interface

To serialize an object using the I/O API, the object must implement the java.io .Serializable interface. The Serializable interface is a marker interface, which means it does not have any methods. Any class can implement the Serializable interface since there are no required methods to implement.

Since Serializable is a marker interface with no abstract members, why not just apply it to every class? Generally speaking, you should only mark data-oriented classes serializable. Process-oriented classes, such as the I/O streams discussed in this chapter or the Thread instances you learned about in Chapter 13, are often poor candidates for serialization, as the internal state of those classes tends to be ephemeral or short-lived.

The purpose of using the Serializable interface is to inform any process attempting to serialize the object that you have taken the proper steps to make the object serializable. All Java primitives and many of the built-in Java classes that you have worked with throughout this book are Serializable. For example, this class can be serialized:

```java
import java.io.Serializable;
public class Gorilla implements Serializable {
    private static final long serialVersionUID = 1L;
    private String name;
    private int age;
    private Boolean friendly;
    private transient String favoriteFood;

    // Constructors/Getters/Setters/toString() omitted
}
```

In this example, the Gorilla class contains three instance members (name, age, friendly) that will be saved to an I/O stream if the class is serialized. Note that since Serializable is not part of the java.lang package, it must be imported or referenced with the package name.

What about the favoriteFood field that is marked transient? Any field that is marked transient will not be saved to an I/O stream when the class is serialized. We discuss that in more detail next.

 Real World Scenario

Maintaining a *serialVersionUID*

It's a good practice to declare a static serialVersionUID variable in every class that implements Serializable. The version is stored with each object as part of serialization. Then, every time the class structure changes, this value is updated or incremented.

> Perhaps our Gorilla class receives a new instance member Double banana, or maybe the age field is renamed. The idea is a class could have been serialized with an older version of the class and deserialized with a newer version of the class.
>
> The serialVersionUID helps inform the JVM that the stored data may not match the new class definition. If an older version of the class is encountered during deserialization, a java.io.InvalidClassException may be thrown. Alternatively, some APIs support converting data between versions.

Marking Data *transient*

The transient modifier can be used for sensitive data of the class, like a password. There are other objects it does not make sense to serialize, like the state of an in-memory Thread. If the object is part of a serializable object, we just mark it transient to ignore these select instance members.

What happens to data marked transient on deserialization? It reverts to its default Java values, such as 0.0 for double, or null for an object. You see examples of this shortly when we present the object stream classes.

 Marking static fields transient has little effect on serialization. Other than the serialVersionUID, only the instance members of a class are serialized. A static variable keeps it state as long as the JVM is running, so transient is ignored.

Ensuring That a Class Is Serializable

Since Serializable is a marker interface, you might think there are no rules to using it. Not quite! Any process attempting to serialize an object will throw a NotSerializableException if the class does not implement the Serializable interface properly.

How to Make a Class Serializable

- The class must be marked Serializable.
- Every instance member of the class must be serializable, marked transient, or have a null value at the time of serialization.

Be careful with the second rule. For a class to be serializable, we must apply the second rule recursively. Do you see why the following Cat class is not serializable?

```
public class Cat implements Serializable {
    private Tail tail = new Tail();
}
```

```
public class Tail implements Serializable {
    private Fur fur = new Fur();
}
```

```
public class Fur {}
```

Cat contains an instance of Tail, and both of those classes are marked Serializable, so no problems there. Unfortunately, Tail contains an instance of Fur that is not marked Serializable.

Either of the following changes fixes the problem and allows Cat to be serialized:

```
public class Tail implements Serializable {
    private transient Fur fur = new Fur();
}
```

```
public class Fur implements Serializable {}
```

We could also make our tail or fur instance members null, although this would make Cat serializable only for particular instances, rather than all instances.

Serializing Records

Do you think this record is serializable?

```
record Record(String name) {}
```

It is not serializable because it does not implement Serializable. A record follows the same rules as other types of classes with respect to whether it can be serialized. Therefore, this one can be:

```
record Record(String name) implements Serializable {}
```

Storing Data with *ObjectOutputStream* and *ObjectInputStream*

The ObjectInputStream class is used to deserialize an object, while the ObjectOutputStream is used to serialize an object. They are high-level streams that operate on existing I/O streams. While both of these classes contain a number of methods for built-in data types like primitives, the two methods you need to know for the exam are the ones related to working with objects.

```
// ObjectInputStream
public Object readObject() throws IOException, ClassNotFoundException
```

```
// ObjectOutputStream
public void writeObject(Object obj) throws IOException
```

Note the parameters, return types, and exceptions thrown. We now provide a sample method that serializes a List of Gorilla objects to a file:

```
void saveToFile(List<Gorilla> gorillas, File dataFile)
        throws IOException {
    try (var out = new ObjectOutputStream(
            new BufferedOutputStream(
                new FileOutputStream(dataFile)))) {
        for (Gorilla gorilla : gorillas)
            out.writeObject(gorilla);
    }
}
```

Pretty easy, right? Notice that we start with a file stream, wrap it in a buffered I/O stream to improve performance, and then wrap that with an object stream. Serializing the data is as simple as passing it to writeObject().

Once the data is stored in a file, we can deserialize it by using the following method:

```
List<Gorilla> readFromFile(File dataFile) throws IOException,
        ClassNotFoundException {
    var gorillas = new ArrayList<Gorilla>();
    try (var in = new ObjectInputStream(
            new BufferedInputStream(new FileInputStream(dataFile)))) {
        while (true) {
            var object = in.readObject();
            if (object instanceof Gorilla g)
                gorillas.add(g);
        }
    } catch (EOFException e) {
        // File end reached
    }
    return gorillas;
}
```

Ah, not as simple as our save method, was it? When calling readObject(), null and -1 do not have any special meaning, as someone might have serialized objects with those values. Unlike our earlier techniques for reading methods from an input stream, we need to use an infinite loop to process the data, which throws an EOFException when the end of the I/O stream is reached.

> If your program happens to know the number of objects in the I/O stream, you can call readObject() a fixed number of times, rather than using an infinite loop.

Since the return type of readObject() is Object, we need to check the type before obtaining access to our Gorilla properties. Notice that readObject() declares a checked ClassNotFoundException since the class might not be available on deserialization.

The following code snippet shows how to call the serialization methods:

```
var gorillas = new ArrayList<Gorilla>();
gorillas.add(new Gorilla("Grodd", 5, false));
gorillas.add(new Gorilla("Ishmael", 8, true));
File dataFile = new File("gorilla.ser");

saveToFile(gorillas, dataFile);
var gorillasFromDisk = readFromFile(dataFile);
System.out.print(gorillasFromDisk);
```

Assuming that the toString() method was properly overridden in the Gorilla class, this prints the following at runtime:

```
[[name=Grodd, age=5, friendly=false],
 [name=Ishmael, age=8, friendly=true]]
```

 ObjectInputStream inherits an available() method from InputStream that you might think can be used to check for the end of the I/O stream rather than throwing an EOFException. Unfortunately, this only tells you the number of blocks that can be read without blocking another thread. In other words, it can return 0 even if there are more bytes to be read.

Understanding the Deserialization Creation Process

For the exam, you need to understand how a deserialized object is created. When you deserialize an object, *the constructor of the serialized class, along with any instance initializers, is not called when the object is created.* Java will call the no-arg constructor of the first nonserializable parent class it can find in the class hierarchy. In our Gorilla example, this would just be the no-arg constructor of Object.

As we stated earlier, any static or transient fields are ignored. Values that are not provided will be given their default Java value, such as null for String, or 0 for int values.

Let's take a look at a new Chimpanzee class which has a parent class that is not Serializable. This time we do list the constructors to illustrate which is used on deserialization.

```
// Mammal.java
public class Mammal {
    private int id;
```

```java
    public Mammal() {
        this.id = 4;
    }

    // Getters/Setters/toString() omitted
}


// Chimpanzee.java
import java.io.Serializable;
public class Chimpanzee extends Mammal implements Serializable {
    private static final long serialVersionUID = 2L;
    private transient String name;
    private transient int age = 10;
    private static char type = 'C';
    { this.age = 14; }

    public Chimpanzee() {
        this("Unknown", 12, 'Q');
    }

    public Chimpanzee(String name, int age, char type) {
        this.name = name;
        this.age = age;
        this.type = type;
        setId(9);
    }

    // Getters/Setters/toString() omitted
}
```

Assuming we rewrite our previous serialization and deserialization methods to process a Chimpanzee object instead of a Gorilla object, what do you think the following prints?

```java
var chimpanzees = List.of(new Chimpanzee("Ham", 2, 'A'),
    new Chimpanzee("Enos", 3, 'B'));
File dataFile = new File("chimpanzee.ser");
System.out.println("Original:  " + chimpanzees);

saveToFile(chimpanzees, dataFile);
var chimpanzeesFromDisk = readFromFile(dataFile);
System.out.println("From Disk: " + chimpanzeesFromDisk);
```

Think about it. Go on, we'll wait.

Ready for the answer? Well, for starters, none of the instance members is serialized to a file. The name and age variables are both marked transient, while the type variable is static. We purposely accessed the type variable using this to see whether you were paying attention.

Upon deserialization, none of the constructors in Chimpanzee is called. Even the no-arg constructor that sets the values [name=Unknown, age=12, type=Q, id=8] is ignored. The instance initializer that sets age to 14 is also not executed.

In this case, the name variable is initialized to null since that's the default value for String in Java. Likewise, the age variable is initialized to 0.

However, the superclass of Mammal is not Serializable so the default constructor is called and id is set to 4. The program prints the following, assuming the toString() method is implemented:

```
Original:  [[name=Ham, age=2, type=B, id=9,
   [name=Enos, age=3, type=B, id=9]

From Disk: [[name=null, age=0, type=B, id=4,
   [name=null, age=0, type=B, id=4]
```

What about the type variable? Since it's static, it will display whatever value was set last. If the data is serialized and deserialized within the same execution, it will display B, since that was the last Chimpanzee we created. On the other hand, if the program performs the deserialization and print on startup, it will print C, since that is the value the class is initialized with.

For the exam, make sure you understand that the constructor and any instance initializations defined in the serialized class are ignored during the deserialization process. Java only calls the constructor of the first non-serializable parent class in the class hierarchy.

Finally, let's add a subclass:

```java
public class BabyChimpanzee extends Chimpanzee {
    private static final long serialVersionUID = 3L;

    private String mother = "Mom";

    public BabyChimpanzee() { super(); }

    public BabyChimpanzee(String name, char type) {
        super(name, 0, type);
    }
    // Getters/Setters/toString() omitted
}
```

Notice that this subclass BabyChimpanzee is serializable because the superclass Chimpanzee has implemented Serializable. We now have an additional instance variable. The code to serialize and deserialize remains the same. We can even still cast to Chimpanzee because this is a subclass.

Customizing Serialization

Normally, the rules that you get out of the box for serialization are good enough. However, you can control the serialization process in finer grained detail.

To customize serialization, just define `private` methods in your `Serializable` class with specific signatures. These methods are not actually overrides, but are called as part of the serialization process automatically. It is common to start by calling `defaultReadObject()` at the beginning of the `readObject()` method, and `defaultWriteObject()` at the end of the `writeObject()` method. These handle the default serialization behaviors.

```java
public class Fish implements Serializable {
    private String name;
    private transient int fins;
    ...
    private void readObject(ObjectInputStream in)
            throws ClassNotFoundException, IOException {
        in.defaultReadObject();

        // custom logic
        this.fins = 10;
    }
    private void writeObject(ObjectOutputStream out)
            throws IOException {
        // custom logic
        this.name = "Nemo";

        out.defaultWriteObject();
    } }
```

In this example, the `transient` variable `fins` is given a default value of 10 anytime it is read from disk. When writing to disk, the name value is replaced within the object with "Nemo", which is then saved to disk.

Interacting with Users

Java includes numerous classes for interacting with the user. For example, you might want to write an application that asks a user to log in and then prints a success message. This section contains numerous techniques for handling and responding to user input.

Printing Data to the User

Java includes two PrintStream instances for providing information to the user: System.out and System.err. While System.out should be old hat to you, System.err might be new to you. The syntax for calling and using System.err is the same as for System.out, but it is used to report errors to the user in a separate I/O stream from the regular output information.

```
try (var in = new FileInputStream("zoo.txt")) {
    System.out.println("Found file!");
} catch (FileNotFoundException e) {
    System.err.println("File not found!");
}
```

How do they differ in practice? In part, that depends on what is executing the program. For example, if you are running from a command prompt, they will likely print text in the same format. On the other hand, if you are working in an integrated development environment (IDE), they might print the System.err text in a different color. Finally, if the code is being run on a server, the System.err stream might write to a different log file.

 Real World Scenario

Using Logging APIs

While System.out and System.err are incredibly useful for debugging stand-alone or simple applications, they are rarely used in professional software development. Most applications rely on a logging service or API.

While many logging APIs are available, they tend to share a number of similar attributes. First you create a static logging object in each class. Then you log a message with an appropriate logging level: debug(), info(), warn(), or error(). The debug() and info() methods are useful as they allow developers to log things that aren't errors but may be useful. For example:

```
var logger = Logger.getLogger("errors");
logger.info("Code is running");
logger.warning("Code shouldn't have done that");
```

You can also use the log() method and provide the level programmatically:

```
logger.log(Level.SEVERE, "You should worry");
```

Reading Input as an I/O Stream

The System.in returns an InputStream and is used to retrieve text input from the user. It is commonly wrapped with a BufferedReader via an InputStreamReader to use the readLine() method.

```
var reader = new BufferedReader(new InputStreamReader(System.in));
String userInput = reader.readLine();
System.out.println("You entered: " + userInput);
```

When executed, this application first fetches text from the user until the user presses the Enter key. It then outputs the text the user entered to the screen.

Closing System Streams

You might have noticed that we never created or closed System.out, System.err, and System.in when we used them. In fact, these are the only I/O streams in the entire chapter that we did not use a try-with-resources block on!

Because these are static objects, the System streams are shared by the entire application. The JVM creates and opens them for us. They can be used in a try-with-resources statement or by calling close(), although *closing them is not recommended*. Closing the System streams makes them permanently unavailable for all threads in the remainder of the program.

What do you think the following code snippet prints?

```
try (var out = System.out) {}
System.out.println("Hello");
```

Nothing. It prints nothing. The methods of PrintStream do not throw any checked exceptions and rely on the checkError() to report errors, so they fail silently.

What about this example?

```
try (var err = System.err) {}
System.err.println("Hello");
```

This one also prints nothing. Like System.out, System.err is a PrintStream. Even if it did throw an exception, we'd have a hard time seeing it since our I/O stream for reporting errors is closed! Closing System.err is a particularly bad idea, since the stack traces from all exceptions will be hidden.

Finally, what do you think this code snippet does?

```
var reader = new BufferedReader(new InputStreamReader(System.in));
try (reader) {}
String data = reader.readLine();   // IOException
```

It prints an exception at runtime. Unlike the PrintStream class, most InputStream implementations will throw an exception if you try to operate on a closed I/O stream.

Acquiring Input with *Console*

The java.io.Console class is specifically designed to handle user interactions. After all, System.in and System.out are just raw streams, whereas Console is a class with numerous methods centered around user input.

The `Console` class is a singleton because it is accessible only from a factory method and only one instance of it is created by the JVM. For example, if you come across code on the exam such as the following, it does not compile, since the constructors are all `private`:

```
Console c = new Console();   // DOES NOT COMPILE
```

The following snippet shows how to obtain a `Console` and use it to retrieve user input:

```
Console console = System.console();
if (console != null) {
   String userInput = console.readLine();
   console.writer().println("You entered: " + userInput);
   console.flush();
} else {
   System.err.println("Console not available");
}
```

 The Console object may not be available, depending on where the code is being called. If it is not available, `System.console()` returns `null`. It is imperative that you check for a `null` value before attempting to use a `Console` object!

This program first retrieves an instance of the `Console` and verifies that it is available, outputting a message to `System.err` if it is not. If it is available, the program retrieves a line of input from the user and prints the result. The `flush()` is to ensure the output gets written. As you might have noticed, this example is similar to our earlier example of reading user input with `System.in` and `System.out`.

Obtaining Underlying I/O Streams

The `Console` class includes access to two streams for reading and writing data.

```
public Reader reader()
public PrintWriter writer()
```

Accessing these classes is analogous to calling `System.in` and `System.out` directly, although they use character streams rather than byte streams. In this manner, they are more appropriate for handling text data.

Formatting Console Data

In Chapter 4, you learned about the `format()` method on `String`; and in Chapter 11, "Exceptions and Localization," you worked with formatting using locales. Conveniently, each print stream class includes a `format()` method, which includes an overloaded version that takes a `Locale` to combine both of these:

```
// PrintStream
public PrintStream format(String format, Object... args)
```

```
public PrintStream format(Locale loc, String format, Object... args)

// PrintWriter
public PrintWriter format(String format, Object... args)
public PrintWriter format(Locale loc, String format, Object... args)
```

 For convenience (as well as to make C developers feel more at home), Java includes printf() methods, which function identically to the format() methods. The only thing you need to know about these methods is that they are interchangeable with format().

Let's take a look at using multiple methods to print information for the user:

```
Console console = System.console();
if (console == null) {
    throw new RuntimeException("Console not available");
} else {
    console.writer().println("Welcome to Our Zoo!");
    console.format("It has %d animals and employs %d people", 391, 25);
    console.writer().println();
    console.printf("The zoo spans %5.1f acres", 128.91);
    console.flush();
}
```

Assuming the Console is available at runtime, it prints the following:

```
Welcome to Our Zoo!
It has 391 animals and employs 25 people
The zoo spans 128.9 acres.
```

 PrintStream and PrintWriter are similar, as they both support a lot of the same overridden methods. One difference is that PrintStream will convert characters into bytes using the provided (or default charset) encoding. Also, only PrintStream supports working directly with the raw bytes.

Reading Console Data

The Console class includes four methods for retrieving regular text data from the user.

```
public String readLine()
public String readLine(String fmt, Object... args)

public char[] readPassword()
public char[] readPassword(String fmt, Object... args)
```

Like using `System.in` with a `BufferedReader`, the `Console readLine()` method reads input until the user presses the Enter key. The overloaded version of `readLine()` displays a formatted message prompt prior to requesting input.

The `readPassword()` methods are similar to the `readLine()` method, with two important differences.

- The text the user types is not echoed back and displayed on the screen as they are typing. Note that the password is not encrypted.

- The data is returned as a `char[]` instead of a `String`.

The first feature improves security by not showing the password on the screen if someone happens to be sitting next to you. The second feature involves preventing passwords from entering the `String` pool.

Reviewing Console Methods

The last code sample we present asks the user a series of questions and prints results based on this information using many of various methods we learned in this section:

```
Console console = System.console();
if (console == null) {
    throw new RuntimeException("Console not available");
} else {
    String name = console.readLine("Please enter your name: ");
    console.writer().format("Hi %s", name);
    console.writer().println();

    console.format("What is your address? ");
    String address = console.readLine();

    char[] password = console.readPassword("Enter a password "
        + "between %d and %d characters: ", 5, 10);
    char[] verify = console.readPassword("Enter the password again: ");
    console.printf("Passwords "
        + (Arrays.equals(password, verify) ? "match" : "do not match"));
    console.flush();
}
```

Assuming the `Console` is available, the output should resemble the following:

```
Please enter your name: Max
Hi Max
What is your address? Spoonerville
Enter a password between 5 and 10 characters:
Enter the password again:
Passwords match
```

Working with Advanced APIs

Files, paths, I/O streams: you've worked with a lot this chapter! In this final section, we cover some advanced features of I/O streams and NIO.2 that can be quite useful in practice—and have been known to appear on the exam from time to time!

Manipulating Input Streams

All input stream classes include the following methods to manipulate the order in which data is read from an I/O stream:

```
// InputStream and Reader
public boolean markSupported()
public void mark(int readLimit)
public void reset() throws IOException
public long skip(long n) throws IOException
```

The mark() and reset() methods return an I/O stream to an earlier position. Before calling either of these methods, you should call the markSupported() method, which returns true only if mark() is supported. The skip() method is pretty simple; it basically reads data from the I/O stream and discards the contents.

Not all input stream classes support mark() and reset(). Make sure to call markSupported() on the I/O stream before calling these methods, or an exception will be thrown at runtime.

Marking Data

Assume that we have an InputStream instance whose next values are LION. Consider the following code snippet:

```
public void readData(InputStream is) throws IOException {
    System.out.print((char) is.read());      // L
    if (is.markSupported()) {
        is.mark(100);  // Marks up to 100 bytes
        System.out.print((char) is.read());  // I
        System.out.print((char) is.read());  // O
        is.reset();      // Resets stream to position before I
    }
    System.out.print((char) is.read());      // I
    System.out.print((char) is.read());      // O
    System.out.print((char) is.read());      // N
}
```

The code snippet will output LIOION if mark() is supported and LION otherwise. It's a good practice to organize your read() operations so that the I/O stream ends up at the same position regardless of whether mark() is supported.

What about the value of 100 that we passed to the mark() method? This value is called the readLimit. It instructs the I/O stream that we expect to call reset() after at most 100 bytes. If our program calls reset() after reading more than 100 bytes from calling mark(100), it may throw an exception, depending on the I/O stream class.

In actuality, mark() and reset() are not putting the data back into the I/O stream but are storing the data in a temporary buffer in memory to be read again. Therefore, you should not call the mark() operation with too large a value, as this could take up a lot of memory.

Skipping Data

Assume that we have an InputStream instance whose next values are TIGERS. Consider the following code snippet:

```
System.out.print ((char)is.read()); // T
is.skip(2);   // Skips I and G
is.read();    // Reads E but doesn't output it
System.out.print((char)is.read());  // R
System.out.print((char)is.read());  // S
```

This code prints TRS at runtime. We skipped two characters, I and G. We also read E but didn't use it anywhere, so it behaved like calling skip(1).

The return parameter of skip() tells us how many values were skipped. For example, if we are near the end of the I/O stream and call skip(1000), the return value might be 20, indicating that the end of the I/O stream was reached after 20 values were skipped. Using the return value of skip() is important if you need to keep track of where you are in an I/O stream and how many bytes have been processed.

Reviewing Manipulation APIs

Table 14.10 reviews these APIs related to manipulating I/O input streams. While you may not have used these in practice, you need to know them for the exam.

TABLE 14.10   Common I/O stream methods

Method name	Description
boolean **markSupported()**	Returns true if stream class supports mark()
void **mark**(int readLimit)	Marks current position in stream
void **reset()**	Attempts to reset stream to mark() position
long **skip**(long n)	Reads and discards specified number of characters

Discovering File Attributes

We begin our discussion by presenting the basic methods for reading file attributes. These methods are usable within any file system, although they may have limited meaning in some file systems.

Checking for Symbolic Links

Earlier, we saw that the Files class has methods called isDirectory() and isRegularFile(), which are similar to the isDirectory() and isFile() methods on File. While the File object can't tell you if a reference is a symbolic link, the isSymbolicLink() method on Files can.

It is possible for isDirectory() or isRegularFile() to return true for a symbolic link, as long as the link resolves to a directory or regular file, respectively. Let's take a look at some sample code:

```
System.out.print(Files.isDirectory(Path.of("/canine/fur.jpg")));
System.out.print(Files.isSymbolicLink(Path.of("/canine/coyote")));
System.out.print(Files.isRegularFile(Path.of("/canine/types.txt")));
```

The first example prints true if fur.jpg is a directory or a symbolic link to a directory and false otherwise. The second example prints true if /canine/coyote is a symbolic link, regardless of whether the file or directory it points to exists. The third example prints true if types.txt points to a regular file or a symbolic link that points to a regular file.

Checking File Accessibility

In many file systems, it is possible to set a boolean attribute to a file that marks it hidden, readable, or executable. The Files class includes methods that expose this information: isHidden(), isReadable(), isWriteable(), and isExecutable().

A hidden file can't normally be viewed when listing the contents of a directory. The readable, writable, and executable flags are important in file systems where the filename can be viewed, but the user may not have permission to open the file's contents, modify the file, or run the file as a program, respectively.

Here we present an example of each method:

```
System.out.print(Files.isHidden(Path.of("/walrus.txt")));
System.out.print(Files.isReadable(Path.of("/seal/baby.png")));
System.out.print(Files.isWritable(Path.of("dolphin.txt")));
System.out.print(Files.isExecutable(Path.of("whale.png")));
```

If the walrus.txt file exists and is hidden within the file system, the first example prints true. The second example prints true if the baby.png file exists and its contents are readable. The third example prints true if the dolphin.txt file can be modified. Finally, the last example prints true if the file can be executed within the operating system. Note that the file extension does not necessarily determine whether a file is executable. For example, an image file that ends in .png could be marked executable in some file systems.

With the exception of the isHidden() method, these methods do not declare any checked exceptions and return false if the file does not exist.

Improving Attribute Access

Up until now, we have been accessing individual file attributes with multiple method calls. While this is functionally correct, there is often a cost each time one of these methods is called. Put simply, it is far more efficient to ask the file system for all of the attributes at once rather than performing multiple round trips to the file system. Furthermore, some attributes are file system–specific and cannot be easily generalized for all file systems.

NIO.2 addresses both of these concerns by allowing you to construct views for various file systems with a single method call. A *view* is a group of related attributes for a particular file system type. That's not to say that the earlier attribute methods that we just finished discussing do not have their uses. If you need to read only one attribute of a file or directory, requesting a view is unnecessary.

Understanding Attribute and View Types

NIO.2 includes two methods for working with attributes in a single method call: a read-only attributes method and an updatable view method. For each method, you need to provide a file system type object, which tells the NIO.2 method which type of view you are requesting. By updatable view, we mean that we can both read and write attributes with the same object.

Table 14.11 lists the commonly used attributes and view types. For the exam, you only need to know about the basic file attribute types. The other views are for managing operating system–specific information.

TABLE 14.11   The attributes and view types

Attributes interface	View interface	Description
BasicFileAttributes	BasicFileAttributeView	Basic set of attributes supported by all file systems
DosFileAttributes	DosFileAttributeView	Basic set of attributes along with those supported by DOS/Windows-based systems
PosixFileAttributes	PosixFileAttributeView	Basic set of attributes along with those supported by POSIX systems, such as Unix, Linux, Mac, etc.

Retrieving Attributes

The Files class includes the following method to read attributes of a class in a read-only capacity:

```
public static <A extends BasicFileAttributes> A readAttributes(
   Path path,
   Class<A> type,
   LinkOption... options) throws IOException
```

Applying it requires specifying the Path and BasicFileAttributes.class parameters.

```
var path = Path.of("/turtles/sea.txt");
BasicFileAttributes data = Files.readAttributes(path,
   BasicFileAttributes.class);

System.out.println("Is a directory? " + data.isDirectory());
System.out.println("Is a regular file? " + data.isRegularFile());
System.out.println("Is a symbolic link? " + data.isSymbolicLink());
System.out.println("Size (in bytes): " + data.size());
System.out.println("Last modified: " + data.lastModifiedTime());
```

The BasicFileAttributes class includes many values with the same name as the attribute methods in the Files class. The advantage of using this method, though, is that all of the attributes are retrieved at once for some operating systems.

Modifying Attributes

The following Files method returns an updatable view:

```
public static <V extends FileAttributeView> V getFileAttributeView(
   Path path,
   Class<V> type,
   LinkOption... options)
```

We can use the updatable view to increment a file's last modified date/time value by 10,000 milliseconds, or 10 seconds.

```
// Read file attributes
var path = Path.of("/turtles/sea.txt");
BasicFileAttributeView view = Files.getFileAttributeView(path,
   BasicFileAttributeView.class);
BasicFileAttributes attributes = view.readAttributes();

// Modify file last modified time
FileTime lastModifiedTime = FileTime.fromMillis(
```

```
      attributes.lastModifiedTime().toMillis() + 10_000);
view.setTimes(lastModifiedTime, null, null);
```

After the updatable view is retrieved, we need to call readAttributes() on the view to obtain the file metadata. From there, we create a new FileTime value and set it using the setTimes() method:

```
// BasicFileAttributeView instance method
public void setTimes(FileTime lastModifiedTime,
   FileTime lastAccessTime, FileTime createTime)
```

This method allows us to pass null for any date/time value that we do not want to modify. In our sample code, only the last modified date/time is changed.

Not all file attributes can be modified with a view. For example, you cannot set a property that changes a file into a directory. Likewise, you cannot change the size of the object without modifying its contents.

Traversing a Directory Tree

While the Files.list() method is useful, it traverses the contents of only a single directory. What if we want to visit all of the paths within a directory tree? Before we proceed, we need to review some basic concepts about file systems. Remember that a directory is organized in a hierarchical manner. For example, a directory can contain files and other directories, which can in turn contain other files and directories. Every record in a file system has exactly one parent, with the exception of the root directory, which sits atop everything.

A file system is commonly visualized as a tree with a single root node and many branches and leaves. In this model, a directory is a branch or internal node, and a file is a leaf node.

A common task in a file system is to iterate over the descendants of a path, either recording information about them or, more commonly, filtering them for a specific set of files. For example, you may want to search a folder and print a list of all of the .java files. Furthermore, file systems store file records in a hierarchical manner. Generally speaking, if you want to search for a file, you have to start with a parent directory, read its child elements, then read their children, and so on.

Traversing a directory, also referred to as walking a directory tree, is the process by which you start with a parent directory and iterate over all of its descendants until some condition is met or there are no more elements over which to iterate. For example, if we're searching for a single file, we can end the search when the file is found or we've checked all files and come up empty. The starting path is usually a specific directory; after all, it would be time-consuming to search the entire file system on every request!

Selecting a Search Strategy

Two common strategies are associated with walking a directory tree: a depth-first search and a breadth-first search. A *depth-first search* traverses the structure from the root to an arbitrary leaf and then navigates back up toward the root, traversing fully any paths it skipped along the way. The *search depth* is the distance from the root to current node. To prevent endless searching, Java includes a search depth that is used to limit how many levels (or hops) from the root the search is allowed to go.

Alternatively, a *breadth-first search* starts at the root and processes all elements of each particular depth before proceeding to the next depth level. The results are ordered by depth, with all nodes at depth 1 read before all nodes at depth 2, and so on. While a breadth-first search tends to be balanced and predictable, it also requires more memory since a list of visited nodes must be maintained.

For the exam, you don't have to understand the details of each search strategy that Java employs; you just need to be aware that the NIO.2 Stream API methods use depth-first searching with a depth limit, which can be optionally changed.

Walking a Directory

That's enough background information; let's get to more Stream API methods. The `Files` class includes two methods for walking the directory tree using a depth-first search.

```
public static Stream<Path> walk(Path start,
    FileVisitOption... options) throws IOException
```

```
public static Stream<Path> walk(Path start, int maxDepth,
    FileVisitOption... options) throws IOException
```

Like our other stream methods, walk() uses lazy evaluation and evaluates a Path only as it gets to it. This means that even if the directory tree includes hundreds or thousands of files, the memory required to process a directory tree is low. The first walk() method relies on a default maximum depth of Integer.MAX_VALUE, while the overloaded version allows the user to set a maximum depth. This is useful in cases where the file system might be large and we know the information we are looking for is near the root.

Rather than just printing the contents of a directory tree, we can again do something more interesting. The following getPathSize() method walks a directory tree and returns the total size of all the files in the directory:

```
private long getSize(Path p) {
    try {
        return Files.size(p);
    } catch (IOException e) {
        throw new UncheckedIOException(e);
    }
}
```

```
public long getPathSize(Path source) throws IOException {
    try (var s = Files.walk(source)) {
        return s.parallel()
```

```
    .filter(p -> !Files.isDirectory(p))
    .mapToLong(this::getSize)
    .sum();
  }
}
```

The getSize() helper method is needed because Files.size() declares IOException, and we'd rather not put a try/catch block inside a lambda expression. Instead, we wrap it in the unchecked exception class UncheckedIOException. We can print the data using the format() method:

```
var size = getPathSize(Path.of("/fox/data"));
System.out.format("Total Size: %.2f megabytes", (size/1000000.0));
```

Depending on the directory you run this on, it will print something like this:

```
Total Size: 15.30 megabytes
```

Applying a Depth Limit

Let's say our directory tree is quite deep, so we apply a depth limit by changing one line of code in our getPathSize() method.

```
try (var s = Files.walk(source, 5)) {
```

This new version checks for files only within five steps of the starting node. A depth value of 0 indicates the current path itself. Since the method calculates values only on files, you'd have to set a depth limit of at least 1 to get a nonzero result when this method is applied to a directory tree.

Avoiding Circular Paths

Many of our earlier NIO.2 methods traverse symbolic links by default, with a NOFOLLOW_LINKS used to disable this behavior. The walk() method is different in that it does *not* follow symbolic links by default and requires the FOLLOW_LINKS option to be enabled. We can alter our getPathSize() method to enable following symbolic links by adding the FileVisitOption:

```
try (var s = Files.walk(source,
    FileVisitOption.FOLLOW_LINKS)) {
```

When traversing a directory tree, your program needs to be careful of symbolic links, if enabled. For example, if our process comes across a symbolic link that points to the root directory of the file system, every file in the system will be searched!

Worse yet, a symbolic link could lead to a cycle in which a path is visited repeatedly. A *cycle* is an infinite circular dependency in which an entry in a directory tree points to one of its ancestor directories. Let's say we had a directory tree as shown in Figure 14.6 with the symbolic link /birds/robin/allBirds that points to /birds.

FIGURE 14.6   File system with cycle

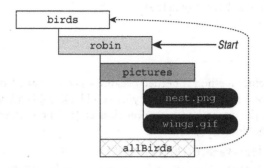

What happens if we try to traverse this tree and follow all symbolic links, starting with /birds/robin? Table 14.12 shows the paths visited after walking a depth of 3. For simplicity, we walk the tree in a breadth-first ordering, *although a cycle occurs regardless of the search strategy used.*

TABLE 14.12   Walking a directory with a cycle using breadth-first search

Depth	Path reached
0	/birds/robin
1	/birds/robin/pictures
1	/birds/robin/allBirds ➤ /birds
2	/birds/robin/pictures/nest.png
2	/birds/robin/pictures/wings.gif
2	**/birds/robin/allBirds/robin** **➤ /birds/robin**
3	/birds/robin/allBirds/robin/pictures ➤ /birds/robin/pictures
3	/birds/robin/allBirds/robin/allBirds ➤ /birds

After walking a distance of 1 from the start, we hit the symbolic link /birds/robin/allBirds and go back to the top of the directory tree /birds. That's OK because we haven't visited /birds yet, so there's no cycle yet!

Unfortunately, at depth 2, we encounter a cycle. We've already visited the /birds/robin directory on our first step, and now we're encountering it again. If the process continues, we'll be doomed to visit the directory over and over again.

Be aware that when the FOLLOW_LINKS option is used, the walk() method will track all of the paths it has visited, throwing a FileSystemLoopException if a path is visited twice.

Searching a Directory

In the previous example, we applied a filter to the Stream<Path> object to filter the results, although there is a more convenient method.

```
public static Stream<Path> find(Path start,
    int maxDepth,
    BiPredicate<Path, BasicFileAttributes> matcher,
    FileVisitOption... options) throws IOException
```

The find() method behaves in a similar manner as the walk() method, except that it takes a BiPredicate to filter the data. It also requires a depth limit to be set. Like walk(), find() also supports the FOLLOW_LINK option.

The two parameters of the BiPredicate are a Path object and a BasicFileAttributes object, which you saw earlier in the chapter. In this manner, Java automatically retrieves the basic file information for you, allowing you to write complex lambda expressions that have direct access to this object. We illustrate this with the following example:

```
var path = Path.of("/bigcats");
long minSize = 1_000;
try (var s = Files.find(path, 10,
        (p, a) -> a.isRegularFile()
            && p.toString().endsWith(".java")
            && a.size() > minSize)) {
    s.forEach(System.out::println);
}
```

This example searches a directory tree and prints all .java files with a size of at least 1,000 bytes, using a depth limit of 10. While we could have accomplished this using the walk() method along with a call to readAttributes(), this implementation is a lot shorter and more convenient than those would have been. We also don't have to worry about any methods within the lambda expression declaring a checked exception, as we saw in the getPathSize() example.

Using *DirectoryStream*

An older way of getting the contents of a directory is with `DirectoryStream`. The following gets all the files in a directory ending in `.txt` and `.java`.

```
try (DirectoryStream<Path> dirStream = Files
      .newDirectoryStream(path, "*.{txt,java}")) {
   for (Path entry: dirStream)
      System.out.println(entry);
}
```

It's better to use `Files.find()` in new code, but you might see either approach on the exam.

Review of Key APIs

Table 14.13 lists the key APIs you need to know for the exam. We know some of the classes look similar. You need to know this table really well before taking the exam.

TABLE 14.13   Key APIs

Class	Purpose
File	I/O representation of location in file system
Files	Helper methods for working with Path
Path	NIO.2 representation of location in file system
Paths	Contains factory methods to get Path
InputStream	Superclass for reading files based on bytes
OuputStream	Superclass for writing files based on bytes
Reader	Superclass for reading files based on characters
Writer	Superclass for writing files based on characters

Additionally, Figure 14.7 shows all of the I/O stream classes that you should be familiar with for the exam, with the exception of the filter streams. `FilterInputStream` and `FilterOutputStream` are high-level superclasses that filter or transform data. They are rarely used directly.

FIGURE 14.7 Diagram of I/O stream classes

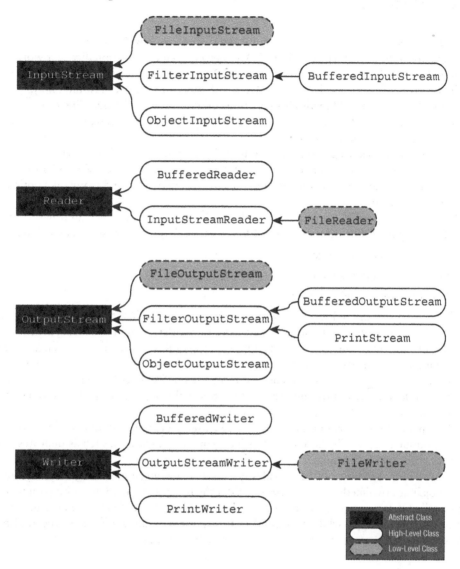

The InputStreamReader and OutputStreamWriter are incredibly convenient and are also unique in that they are the only I/O stream classes to have both InputStream/OutputStream and Reader/Writer in their name.

Summary

This chapter is all about reading and writing data. We started by showing you how to create `File` from I/O and `Path` from NIO.2. We then covered the functionality that works with both I/O and NIO.2 before getting into NIO.2-specific APIs. You should be familiar with how to combine or resolve `Path` objects with other `Path` objects. Additionally, NIO.2 includes Stream API methods that can be used to process files and directories. We discussed methods for listing a directory, walking a directory tree, searching a directory tree, and reading the lines of a file.

We spent time reviewing various methods available in the `Files` helper class. As discussed, the name of the function often tells you exactly what it does. We explained that most of these methods are capable of throwing an `IOException`, and many take optional varargs enum values.

We then introduced I/O streams and explained how they are used to read or write large quantities of data. While there are a lot of I/O streams, they differ on some key points:

- Byte versus character streams
- Input versus output streams
- Low-level versus high-level streams

Often, the name of the I/O stream can tell you a lot about what it does. We visited many of the I/O stream classes that you will need to know for the exam in increasing order of complexity. A common practice is to start with a low-level resource or file stream and wrap it in a buffered I/O stream to improve performance. You can also apply a high-level stream to manipulate the data, such as an object or print stream. We described what it means to be serializable in Java, and we showed you how to use the object stream classes to persist objects directly to and from disk.

We explained how to read input data from the user using both the system stream objects and the `Console` class. The `Console` class has many useful features, such as built-in support for passwords and formatting.

We also discussed how NIO.2 provides methods for reading and writing file metadata. NIO.2 includes two methods for retrieving all of the file system attributes for a path in a single call without numerous round trips to the operating system. One method returns a read-only attribute type, while the second method returns an updatable view type. It also allows NIO.2 to support operating system–specific file attributes.

Exam Essentials

Understand files and directories. Files are records that store data within a persistent storage device, such as a hard disk drive, that is available after the application has finished executing. Files are organized within a file system in directories, which in turn may contain other directories. The root directory is the topmost directory in a file system.

Be able to use *File* and *Path*.   An I/O File instance is created by calling the constructor. It contains a number of instance methods for creating and manipulating a file or directory. An NIO.2 Path instance is an immutable object that is created from the factory method Path.of(). The Path interface includes many instance methods for reading and manipulating the path value.

Distinguish between types of I/O streams.   I/O streams are categorized by byte/character, input/output, and low-level/high-level. Byte streams operate on binary data and have names that end with Stream, while character streams operate on text data and have names that end in Reader or Writer. The InputStream and Reader classes are the topmost abstract classes that receive data, while the OutputStream and Writer classes are the topmost abstract classes that send data. A low-level stream is one that operates directly on the under-lying resource, such as a file or network connection. A high-level stream operates on a low-level or other high-level stream to filter data, convert data, or improve performance.

Understand how to use Java serialization.   A class is considered serializable if it implements the java.io.Serializable interface and contains instance members that are either serializable or marked transient. All Java primitives and the String class are serializable. The ObjectInputStream and ObjectOutputStream classes can be used to read and write a Serializable object from and to an I/O stream, respectively.

Be able to interact with the user.   Be able to interact with the user using the system streams (System.out, System.err, and System.in) as well as the Console class. The Console class includes special methods for formatting data and retrieving complex input such as passwords.

Manage file attributes.   The NIO.2 Files class includes many methods for reading single file attributes, such as its size or whether it is a directory, a symbolic link, hidden, etc. NIO.2 also supports reading all of the attributes in a single call. An attribute type is used to support operating system–specific views. Finally, NIO.2 supports updatable views for modifying selected attributes.

Review Questions

The answers to the chapter review questions can be found in the Appendix.

1. Which class would be best to use to read a binary file into a Java object?

    A. `BufferedStream`

    B. `FileReader`

    C. `ObjectInputStream`

    D. `ObjectReader`

    E. `ObjectOutputStream`

    F. `ObjectWriter`

    G. None of the above

2. Assuming that / is the root directory within the file system, which of the following are true statements? (Choose all that apply.)

    A. `/home/parrot` is an absolute path.

    B. `/home/parrot` is a directory.

    C. `/home/parrot` is a relative path.

    D. `new File("/home")` will throw an exception if `/home` does not exist.

    E. `new File("/home").delete()` will throw an exception if `/home` does not exist.

    F. A `Reader` offers character encoding, making it more useful when working with `String` data than an `InputStream`.

    G. A `Reader` offers multithreading support, making it more useful than an `InputStream`.

3. What are possible results of executing the following code? (Choose all that apply.)

    ```java
    public static void main(String[] args) throws IOException {
        String line;
        var c = System.console();
        Writer w = c.writer();
        try (w) {
            if ((line = c.readLine("Enter your name: ")) != null)
                w.append(line);
            w.flush();
        }
    }
    ```

    A. The code runs, but nothing is printed.

    B. The code prints what was entered by the user.

    C. The code behaves the same if `throws IOException` is removed.

    D. A `NullPointerException` may be thrown.

E. A `NullPointerException` will always be thrown.

F. A `NullPointerException` will never be thrown.

G. The code does not compile.

4. For which value of `path` sent to this method would it be guaranteed for the following code to output `Success`?

```
public void removeBadFile(Path path) {
   if(Files.isDirectory(path))
      System.out.println(Files.deleteIfExists(path)
         ? "Success": "Try Again");
}
```

A. `path` refers to a regular file in the file system.

B. `path` refers to a symbolic link in the file system.

C. `path` refers to an empty directory in the file system.

D. `path` refers to a directory with content in the file system.

E. `path` does not refer to a record that exists within the file system.

F. The code does not compile.

5. Assume that the directory `/animals` exists and is empty. What is the result of executing the following code?

```
Path path = Path.of("/animals");
try (var z = Files.walk(path)) {
   boolean b = z
      .filter((p,a) -> a.isDirectory() && !path.equals(p)) // x
      .findFirst().isPresent();  // y
   System.out.print(b ? "No Sub": "Has Sub");
}
```

A. It prints `No Sub`.

B. It prints `Has Sub`.

C. The code will not compile because of line x.

D. The code will not compile because of line y.

E. The output cannot be determined.

F. It produces an infinite loop at runtime.

6. What would be the value of `name` if the instance of `Eagle` created in the `main()` method were serialized and then deserialized?

```
import java.io.Serializable;
class Bird {
   protected transient String name;
   public void setName(String name) { this.name = name; }
```

```
         public String getName() { return name; }
         public Bird() {
            this.name = "Matt";
         }
      }
   public class Eagle extends Bird implements Serializable {
      { this.name = "Olivia"; }
      public Eagle() {
         this.name = "Bridget";
      }
      public static void main(String[] args) {
         var e = new Eagle();
         e.name = "Adeline";
      }
   }
```

A. Adeline

B. Bridget

C. Matt

D. Olivia

E. null

F. The code does not compile.

G. The code compiles but throws an exception at runtime.

7. Assume that /kang exists as a symbolic link to the directory /mammal/kangaroo within the file system. Which of the following statements are correct about this code snippet? (Choose all that apply.)

```
var path = Path.of("/kang");
if(Files.isDirectory(path) && Files.isSymbolicLink(path))
   Files.createDirectory(path.resolve("joey"));
```

A. A new directory will always be created.

B. A new directory may be created.

C. If the code creates a directory, it will be reachable at /kang/joey.

D. If the code creates a directory, it will be reachable at /mammal/joey.

E. The code does not compile.

F. The code will compile but will always throw an exception at runtime.

8. Assuming that the /fox/food-schedule.csv file exists with the specified contents, what is the expected output of calling printData() on it?

/fox/food-schedule.csv

```
6am,Breakfast
9am,SecondBreakfast
```

```
12pm,Lunch
6pm,Dinner

void printData(Path path) throws IOException {
   Files.readAllLines(path) // r1
      .flatMap(p -> Stream.of(p.split(","))) // r2
      .map(q -> q.toUpperCase())  // r3
      .forEach(System.out::println);
}
```

A. The code will not compile because of line r1.

B. The code will not compile because of line r2.

C. The code will not compile because of line r3.

D. It throws an exception at runtime.

E. It does not print anything at runtime.

F. None of the above.

9. Given the following method and file1 data, which statements are correct? (Choose all that apply.)

```
// file1 data
ABCDEF

public void copyFile(File file1, File file2) throws Exception {
   var reader = new InputStreamReader(new FileInputStream(file1));
   try (var writer = new FileWriter(file2)) {
      char[] buffer = new char[5];
      while(reader.read(buffer) != -1) {
         writer.write(buffer);
         // n1
      }
   }
}
```

A. The code does not compile because reader is not a buffered stream.

B. The code does not compile because writer is not a buffered stream.

C. The contents of the copied file are: ABCDEF

D. The contents of the copied file are: ABCDEFBCDE

E. The contents of the copied file cannot be determined.

F. If we check file2 on line n1 within the file system after five iterations of the while loop, it may be empty.

G. If we check file2 on line n1 within the file system after five iterations, it will contain exactly 50 characters.

H. This method contains a resource leak.

10. Which of the following correctly create `Path` instances? (Choose all that apply.)

   A. `new Path("jaguar.txt")`

   B. `Path.get("cats","lynx.txt")`

   C. `new java.io.File("tiger.txt").toPath()`

   D. `Paths.get("ocelot.txt")`

   E. `Path.of(".")`

11. Which classes will allow the following to compile? (Choose all that apply.)

```
var is = new BufferedInputStream(new FileInputStream("z.txt"));
InputStream wrapper = new _____ (is);
try (wrapper) {}
```

   A. `BufferedInputStream`

   B. `BufferedReader`

   C. `BufferedWriter`

   D. `FileInputStream`

   E. `ObjectInputStream`

   F. `ObjectOutputStream`

   G. None of the above, as the first line does not compile

12. What is the result of executing the following code? (Choose all that apply.)

```
4: var p = Path.of("sloth.schedule");
5: var a = Files.readAttributes(p, BasicFileAttributes.class);
6: Files.mkdir(p.resolve(".backup"));
7: if(a.size()>0 && a.isDirectory()) {
8:    a.setTimes(null,null,null);
9: }
```

   A. It compiles and runs without issue.

   B. The code will not compile because of line 5.

   C. The code will not compile because of line 6.

   D. The code will not compile because of line 7.

   E. The code will not compile because of line 8.

   F. None of the above.

13. Which of the following are true statements about serialization in Java? (Choose all that apply.)

   A. All non-`null` instance members of the class must be serializable or marked `transient`.

   B. Records are automatically serializable.

   C. Serialization involves converting data into Java objects.

   D. `Serializable` is a functional interface.

E. The class must declare a `static serialVersionUID` variable.

F. The class must extend the `Serializable` class.

G. The class must implement the `Serializable` interface.

14. What is the output of the following code? (Choose three.)

```
22: var p1 = Path.of("/zoo/./bear","../food.txt");
23: p1.normalize().relativize(Path.of("/lion"));
24: System.out.println(p1);
25:
26: var p2 = Path.of("/zoo/animals/bear/koala/food.txt");
27: System.out.println(p2.subpath(1,3).getName(1));
28:
29: var p3 = Path.of("/pets/../cat.txt");
30: var p4 = Path.of("./dog.txt");
31: System.out.println(p4.resolve(p3));
```

A. `../../lion`

B. `/zoo/./bear/../food.txt`

C. `animal`

D. `bear`

E. `/pets/../cat.txt`

F. `/pets/../cat.txt/./dog.txt`

15. Suppose that the working directory is /weather and the absolute path /weather/winter/snow.dat represents a file that exists within the file system. Which of the following lines of code create an object that represents the file? (Choose all that apply.)

A. `new File("/weather", "winter", "snow.dat")`

B. `new File("/weather/winter/snow.dat")`

C. `new File("/weather/winter", new File("snow.dat"))`

D. `new File("weather", "/winter/snow.dat")`

E. `new File(new File("/weather/winter"), "snow.dat")`

F. `Path.of("/weather/winter/snow.dat").toFile()`

G. None of the above

16. Assuming `zoo-data.txt` exists and is not empty, what statements about the following method are correct? (Choose all that apply.)

```
private void echo() throws IOException {
    var o = new FileWriter("new-zoo.txt");
    try (var f = new FileReader("zoo-data.txt");
        var b = new BufferedReader(f); o) {
```

```
        o.write(b.readLine());
    }
    o.write("");
}
```

A. When run, the method creates a new file with one line of text in it.

B. When run, the method creates a new file with two lines of text in it.

C. When run, the method creates a new file with the same number of lines as the original file.

D. The method compiles but will produce an exception at runtime.

E. The method does not compile.

F. The method uses byte stream classes.

17. Which are true statements? (Choose all that apply.)

   A. NIO.2 includes a method to delete an entire directory tree.

   B. NIO.2 includes a method to traverse a directory tree.

   C. NIO.2 includes methods that are aware of symbolic links.

   D. `Files.readAttributes()` cannot access file system dependent attributes.

   E. `Files.readAttributes()` is often more performant since it reads multiple attributes rather than accessing individual attributes.

   F. `Files.readAttributes()` works with the `File` object.

18. Assume that `reader` is a valid stream whose next characters are PEACOCKS. Which is true about the output of the following code snippet?

```
var sb = new StringBuilder();
sb.append((char)reader.read());
reader.mark(10);
for(int i=0; i<2; i++) {
    sb.append((char)reader.read());
    reader.skip(2);
}
reader.reset();
reader.skip(0);
sb.append((char)reader.read());
System.out.println(sb.toString());
```

   A. The code may print PEAE.

   B. The code may print PEOA.

   C. The code may print PEOE.

   D. The code may print PEOS.

   E. The code will always print PEAE.

   F. The code will always print PEOA.

   G. The code will always print PEOE.

   H. The code will always print PEOS.

19. Assuming that the directories and files referenced exist and are not symbolic links, what is the result of executing the following code?

```
var p1 = Path.of("/lizard",".").resolve(Path.of("walking.txt"));
var p2 = new File("/lizard/././actions/../walking.txt").toPath();
System.out.print(Files.isSameFile(p1,p2));
System.out.print(" ");
System.out.print(p1.equals(p2));
System.out.print(" ");
System.out.print(Files.mismatch(p1,p2));
```

   A. `true true -1`

   B. `true true 0`

   C. `true false -1`

   D. `true false 0`

   E. `false true -1`

   F. `false true 0`

   G. The code does not compile.

   H. The result cannot be determined.

20. Assume that `monkey.txt` is a file that exists in the current working directory. Which statement about the following code snippet is correct?

```
Files.move(Path.of("monkey.txt"), Path.of("/animals"),
    StandardCopyOption.ATOMIC_MOVE);
```

   A. If `/animals/monkey.txt` exists, it will be overwritten at runtime.

   B. If `/animals` exists as an empty directory, `/animals/monkey.txt` will be the new location of the file.

   C. If the move is successful and another process is monitoring the file system, it will not see an incomplete file at runtime.

   D. None of the above.

21. Assume that `/monkeys` exists as a directory containing multiple files, symbolic links, and subdirectories. Which statement about the following code is correct?

```
var f = Path.of("/monkeys");
try (var m =
    Files.find(f, 0, (p,a) -> a.isSymbolicLink())) { // y1
        m.map(s -> s.toString())
            .collect(Collectors.toList())
```

```
        .stream()
        .filter(s -> s.toString().endsWith(".txt")) // y2
        .forEach(System.out::println);
}
```

A. It will print all symbolic links in the directory tree ending in `.txt`.

B. It will print the target of all symbolic links in the directory ending in `.txt`.

C. It will print nothing.

D. It does not compile because of line `y1`.

E. It does not compile because of line `y2`.

F. It compiles but throws an exception at runtime.

22. Which of the following fields will be `null` after an instance of the class created on line 17 is serialized and then deserialized using `ObjectOutputStream` and `ObjectInputStream`?

```
1:   import java.io.Serializable;
2:   import java.util.List;
3:   public class Zebra implements Serializable {
4:       private transient String name = "George";
5:       private static String birthPlace = "Africa";
6:       private transient Integer age;
7:       List<Zebra> friends = new java.util.ArrayList<>();
8:       private Object stripes = new Object();
9:       { age = 10;}
10:      public Zebra() {
11:          this.name = "Sophia";
12:      }
13:      static Zebra writeAndRead(Zebra z) {
14:          // Implementation omitted
15:      }
16:      public static void main(String[] args) {
17:          var zebra = new Zebra();
18:          zebra = writeAndRead(zebra);
19:      } }
```

A. age

B. birthplace

C. friends

D. name

E. stripes

F. The code does not compile.

G. The code compiles but throws an exception at runtime.

23. What are some possible results of executing the following code? (Choose all that apply.)

```
var x = Path.of("/animals/fluffy/..");
Files.walk(x.toRealPath().getParent())        // u1
    .map(p -> p.toAbsolutePath().toString()) // u2
    .filter(s -> s.endsWith(".java"))
    .forEach(System.out::println);
```

A. It prints some files in the root directory.

B. It prints all files in the root directory.

C. `FileSystemLoopException` is thrown at runtime.

D. Another exception is thrown at runtime.

E. The code will not compile because of line u1.

F. The code will not compile because of line u2.

24. Assume that the `source` instance passed to the following method represents a file that exists. Also assume that `/flip/sounds.txt` exists as a file prior to executing this method. When this method is executed, which statement correctly copies the file to the path specified by `/flip/sounds.txt`?

```
void copyIntoFlipDirectory(Path source) throws IOException {
    var dolphinDir = Path.of("/flip");
    dolphinDir = Files.createDirectories(dolphinDir);
    var n = Path.of("sounds.txt");
    Files.copy(source,_____);
}
```

A. `dolphinDir`

B. `dolphinDir.resolve(n), StandardCopyOption.REPLACE_EXISTING`

C. `dolphinDir, StandardCopyOption.REPLACE_EXISTING`

D. `dolphinDir.resolve(n)`

E. The method does not compile, regardless of what is placed in the blank.

F. The method compiles but throws an exception at runtime, regardless of what is placed in the blank.

25. Suppose that you need to read text data from a file and want the data to be performant on large files. Which two `java.io` stream classes can be chained together to best achieve this result? (Choose two.)

A. `BufferedInputStream`

B. `BufferedReader`

C. `FileInputStream`

D. `FileReader`

E. `PrintInputStream`

F. `ObjectInputStream`

G. `PrintReader`

Appendix

Answers to Review Questions

Chapter 1: Building Blocks

1. D, E. Option E is the canonical `main()` method signature. You need to memorize it. Option D is an alternate form with the redundant `final`. Option A is incorrect because the `main()` method must be public. Options B and F are incorrect because the `main()` method must have a `void` return type. Option C is incorrect because the `main()` method must be `static`.

2. C, D, E. The `package` and `import` statements are both optional. If both are present, the order must be `package`, then `import`, and then `class`. Option A is incorrect because `class` is before `package` and `import`. Option B is incorrect because `import` is before `package`. Option F is incorrect because `class` is before `package`.

3. A, E. Bunny is a class, which can be seen from the declaration: `public class Bunny`. The variable bun is a reference to an object. The method `main()` is the standard entry point to a program. Option G is incorrect because the parameter type matters, not the parameter name.

4. B, E, G. Option A is invalid because a single underscore is not allowed. Option C is not a valid identifier because `true` is a Java reserved word. Option D is not valid because a period (`.`) is not allowed in identifiers. Option F is not valid because the first character is not a letter, dollar sign (`$`), or underscore (`_`). Options B, E, and G are valid because they contain only valid characters.

5. A, D, F. Garbage collection is never guaranteed to run, making option F correct and option E incorrect. Next, the class compiles and runs without issue, so option G is incorrect. The `Bear` object created on line 9 is accessible until line 13 via the `brownBear` reference variable, which is option A. The `Bear` object created on line 10 is accessible via both the `polarBear` reference and the `brownBear.pandaBear` reference. After line 12, the object is still accessible via `brownBear.pandaBear`. After line 13, though, it is no longer accessible since `brownBear` is no longer accessible, which makes option D the final correct answer.

6. F. To solve this problem, you need to trace the braces (`{}`) and see when variables go in and out of scope. The variables on lines 2 and 7 are only in scope for a single line block. The variable on line 12 is only in scope for the `for` loop. None of these is in scope on line 14. By contrast, the three instance variables on lines 3 and 4 are available in all instance methods. Additionally, the variables on lines 6, 9, and 10 are available since the method and `while` loop are still in scope. This is a total of 7 variables, which is option F.

7. C, E. The first thing to recognize is that this is a text block and the code inside the `"""` is just text. Options A and B are incorrect because the `numForks` and `numKnives` variables are not used. This is convenient since `numKnives` is not initialized and would not compile if it were referenced. Option C is correct as it is matching text. Option D is incorrect because the text block does not have a trailing blank line. Finally, option E is also an answer since `"   # knives` is indented.

8. B, D, E, H. A `var` cannot be initialized with a `null` value without a type, but it can be assigned a `null` value later if the underlying type is not a primitive. For these reasons, option H is correct, but options A and C are incorrect. Options B and D are correct as the

underlying types are `String` and `Integer`, respectively. Option E is correct as this is a valid numeric expression. You might know that dividing by zero produces a runtime exception, but the question was only about whether the code compiled. Finally, options F and G are incorrect as `var` cannot be used in a multiple-variable assignment.

9. E. Options C and D are incorrect because local variables don't have default values. Option A is incorrect because `float` should have a decimal point. Option B is incorrect because primitives do not default to `null`. Option E is correct and option F incorrect because reference types in class variables default to `null`.

10. A, E, F. An underscore (`_`) can be placed in any numeric literal, as long as it is not at the beginning, at the end, or next to a decimal point (`.`). Underscores can even be placed next to each other. For these reasons, options A, E, and F are correct. Options B and D are incorrect as the underscore (`_`) is next to a decimal point (`.`). Options C and G are incorrect because an underscore (`_`) cannot be placed at the beginning or end of the literal.

11. E. The first two imports can be removed because `java.lang` is automatically imported. The following two imports can be removed because `Tank` and `Water` are in the same package, making the correct option E. If `Tank` and `Water` were in different packages, exactly one of these two imports could be removed. In that case, the answer would be option D.

12. A, C, D. Line 2 does not compile as only one type should be specified, making option A correct. Line 3 compiles without issue as it declares a local variable inside an instance initializer that is never used. Line 4 does not compile because Java does not support setting default method parameter values, making option C correct. Finally, line 7 does not compile because `fins` is in scope and accessible only inside the instance initializer on line 3, making option D correct.

13. A, B, C. Option A is correct because it imports all the classes in the `aquarium` package including `aquarium.Water`. Options B and C are correct because they import `Water` by class name. Since importing by class name takes precedence over wildcards, these compile. Option D is incorrect because Java doesn't know which of the two wildcard `Water` classes to use. Option E is incorrect because you cannot specify the same class name in two imports.

14. A, B, D, E. Line 3 does not compile because the `L` suffix makes the literal value a `long`, which cannot be stored inside a `short` directly, making option A correct. Line 4 does not compile because `int` is an integral type, but `2.0` is a `double` literal value, making option B correct. Line 5 compiles without issue. Lines 6 and 7 do not compile because `numPets` and `numGrains` are both primitives, and you can call methods only on reference types, not primitive values, making options D and E correct, respectively. Finally, line 8 compiles because there is a `length()` method defined on `String`.

15. C, E, F. In Java, there are no guarantees about when garbage collection will run. The JVM is free to ignore calls to `System.gc()`. For this reason, options A, B, and D are incorrect. Option C is correct as the purpose of garbage collection is to reclaim used memory. Option E is also correct that an object may never be garbage collected, such as if the program ends before garbage collection runs. Option F is correct and is the primary means by which garbage collection algorithms determine whether an object is eligible for garbage collection. Finally, option G is incorrect as marking a variable `final` means it is constant within its own scope. For example, a local variable marked `final` will be eligible for garbage collection after the method ends, assuming there are no other references to the object that exist outside the method.

16. A, D. Option A is correct. There are two lines. One starts with squirrel, and the other starts with pigeon. Remember that a backslash means to skip the line break. Option D is also correct as \s means to keep whitespace. In a text block, incidental indentation is ignored, making option F incorrect.

17. D, F, G. The code compiles and runs without issue, so options A and B are incorrect. A boolean field initializes to false, making option D correct with Empty = false being printed. Object references initialize to null, not the empty String, so option F is correct with Brand = null being printed. Finally, the default value of floating-point numbers is 0.0. Although float values can be declared with an f suffix, they are not printed with an f suffix. For these reasons, option G is correct and Code = 0.0 is printed.

18. B, C, F. A var cannot be used for a constructor or method parameter or for an instance or class variable, making option A incorrect and option C correct. The type of a var is known at compile time, and the type cannot be changed at runtime, although its value can change at runtime. For these reasons, options B and F are correct, and option E is incorrect. Option D is incorrect, as var is not permitted in multiple-variable declarations. Finally, option G is incorrect, as var is not a reserved word in Java.

19. A, D. The first two lines provide a way to convert a String into a number. The first is a int primitive, and the second is a Integer reference object, making option D one of the answers. Remember that B is 11 in base 16. The code is correct, and the maximum is 11, which is option A.

20. C. The key thing to notice is that line 4 does not define a constructor but instead a method named PoliceBox(), since it has a return type of void. This method is never executed during the program run, and color and age are assigned the default values null and 0L, respectively. Lines 11 and 12 change the values for an object associated with p, but then, on line 13, the p variable is changed to point to the object associated with q, which still has the default values. For this reason, the program prints Q1=null, Q2=0, P1=null, and P2=0, making option C the only correct answer.

21. D. We start with the main() method, which prints 7- on line 10. Next, a new Salmon instance is created on line 11. This causes the two instance initializers on lines 3 and 4 to be executed in order. The default value of an instance variable of type int is 0, so 0- is printed next, and count is assigned a value of 1. Next, the constructor is called. This assigns a value of 4 to count and prints 2-. Finally, line 12 prints 4-, since that is the value of count. Putting it all together, we have 7-0-2-4-, making option D the correct answer.

22. C, F, G. First, 0b is the prefix for a binary value, and 0x is the prefix for a hexadecimal value. These values can be assigned to many primitive types, including int and double, making options C and F correct. Option A is incorrect because naming the variable Amount will cause the System.out.print(amount) call on the next line to not compile. Option B is incorrect because 9L is a long value. If the type was changed to long amount = 9L, then it would compile. Option D is incorrect because 1_2.0 is a double value. If the type was changed to double amount = 1_2.0, then it would compile. Options E and H are incorrect because the underscore (_) appears next to the decimal point (.), which is not allowed. Finally, option G is correct, and the underscore and assignment usage is valid.

23. A, D. The first compiler error is on line 3. The variable `temp` is declared as a `float`, but the assigned value is `50.0`, which is a `double` without the F/f postfix. Since a `double` doesn't fit inside a `float`, line 3 does not compile. Next, `depth` is declared inside the `for` loop and has scope only inside this loop. Therefore, reading the value on line 10 triggers a compiler error. For these reasons, options A and D are the correct answers.

Chapter 2: Operators

1. A, D, G. Option A is the equality operator and can be used on primitives and object references. Options B and C are both arithmetic operators and cannot be applied to a `boolean` value. Option D is the logical complement operator and is used exclusively with `boolean` values. Option E is the modulus operator, which can be used only with numeric primitives. Option F is a negation/subtraction operator and can be applied only to numeric values. Finally, option G is correct, as you can cast a `boolean` variable since `boolean` is a type.

2. A, B, D. The expression `apples + oranges` is automatically promoted to `int`, so `int` and data types that can be promoted automatically from `int` will work, making options A, B, and D correct. Option C will not work because `boolean` is not a numeric data type. Options E and F will not work without an explicit cast to a smaller data type.

3. B, C, D, F. The code will not compile as is, so option A is not correct. The value `2 * ear` is automatically promoted to `long` and cannot be automatically stored in `hearing`, which is an `int` value. Options B, C, and D solve this problem by reducing the `long` value to `int`. Option E does not solve the problem and actually makes it worse by attempting to place the value in a smaller data type. Option F solves the problem by increasing the data type of the declaration so that `long` is allowed.

4. B. The code compiles and runs without issue, so option E is not correct. This example is tricky because of the second assignment operator embedded in line 5. The expression `(wolf=false)` assigns the value `false` to `wolf` and returns `false` for the entire expression. Since `teeth` does not equal `10`, the left side returns `true`; therefore, the exclusive or (`^`) of the entire expression assigned to `canine` is `true`. The output reflects these assignments, with no change to `teeth`, so option B is the only correct answer.

5. A, C. Options A and C are correct, as they show operators in increasing or the same order of precedence. Options B and E are in decreasing or the same order of precedence. Options D, F, and G are in neither increasing nor decreasing order of precedence. In option D, the assignment operator (`=`) is between two unary operators, with the multiplication operator (`*`) incorrectly being in place of highest precedence. In option F, the logical complement operator (`!`) has the highest order of precedence, so it should be last. In option G, the assignment operators have the lowest order of precedence, not the highest, so the last two operators should be first.

6. F. The code does not compile because line 3 contains a compilation error. The cast (`int`) is applied to `fruit`, not the expression `fruit+vegetables`. Since the cast operator has a higher operator precedence than the addition operator, it is applied to `fruit`, but the expression is promoted to a `float`, due to `vegetables` being `float`. The result cannot be returned as `long` in the `addCandy()` method without a cast. For this reason, option F is correct. If parentheses were added around `fruit+vegetables`, then the output would be 3, 5, 6, and option B would be correct. Remember that casting floating-point numbers to integral values results in truncation, not rounding.

7. D. In the first `boolean` expression, `vis` is 2 and `ph` is 7, so this expression evaluates to `true & (true || false)`, which reduces to `true`. The second `boolean` expression uses the conditional operator, and since `(vis > 2)` is `false`, the right side is not evaluated, leaving `ph` at 7. In the last assignment, `ph` is 7, and the pre-decrement operator is applied first, reducing the expression to `7 <= 6` and resulting in an assignment of `false`. For these reasons, option D is the correct answer.

8. A. The code compiles and runs without issue, so option E is incorrect. Line 7 does not produce a compilation error since the compound operator applies casting automatically. Line 5 increments `pig` by 1, but it returns the original value of 4 since it is using the post-increment operator. The `pig` variable is then assigned this value, and the increment operation is discarded. Line 7 just reduces the value of `goat` by 1, resulting in an output of 4 - 1 and making option A the correct answer.

9. A, D, E. The code compiles without issue, so option G is incorrect. In the first expression, `a > 2` is `false`, so b is incremented to 5; but since the post-increment operator is used, 4 is printed, making option D correct. The `--c` was not applied, because only one of the right-hand expressions was evaluated. In the second expression, `a!=c` is `false` since c was never modified. Since b is 5 due to the previous line and the post-increment operator is used, `b++` returns 5. The result is then assigned to b using the assignment operator, overriding the incremented value for b and printing 5, making option E correct. In the last expression, parentheses are not required, but lack of parentheses can make ternary expressions difficult to read. From the previous lines, a is 2, b is 5, and c is 2. We can rewrite this expression with parentheses as `(2 > 5 ? (5 < 2 ? 5 : 2) : 1)`. The second ternary expression is never evaluated since `2 > 5` is `false`, and the expression returns 1, making option A correct.

10. E. The code does not compile due to an error on the second line, making option E correct. Even though both `height` and `weight` are cast to `byte`, the multiplication operator automatically promotes them to `int`, resulting in an attempt to store an `int` in a `short` variable.

11. D. First, `*` and `%` have the same operator precedence, so the expression is evaluated from left to right unless parentheses are present. The first expression evaluates to `8 % 3`, which leaves a remainder of 2. The second expression is evaluated left to right since `*` and `%` have the same operator precedence, and it reduces to `6 % -3`, which is 0. The last expression reduces to `5 * 1`, which is 5. Therefore, the output on line 14 is 2, 0, 5, making option D the correct answer.

12. D. The *pre-* prefix indicates the operation is applied first, and the new value is returned, while the *post-* prefix indicates the original value is returned prior to the operation. Next, increment increases the value, while decrement decreases the value. For these reasons, option D is the correct answer.

13. F. The first expression is evaluated from left to right, letting us reduce it to
`false ^ sunday`, which is `true`, because `sunday` is `true`. In the second expression, we
apply the negation operator (`!`) first, reducing the expression to `sunday && true`, which
evaluates to `true`. In the last expression, both variables are `true`, so they reduce to
`!(true && true)`, which further reduces to `!true`, aka `false`. For these reasons, option
F is the correct answer.

14. B, E, G. The return value of an assignment operation in the expression is the same as the
value of the newly assigned variable. For this reason, option A is incorrect, and option E is
correct. Option B is correct, as the equality (`==`) and inequality (`!=`) operators can both be
used with objects. Option C is incorrect, as `boolean` and numeric types are not comparable.
For example, you can't say `true == 3` without a compilation error. Option D is incorrect,
as logical operators evaluate both sides of the expression. Option F is incorrect, as Java does
not accept numbers for `boolean` values. Finally, option G is correct, as you need to use
the negation operator (`-`) to flip or negate numeric values, not the logical complement
operator (`!`).

15. D. The ternary operator is the only operator that takes three values, making option D the
only correct choice. Options A, B, C, E, and G are all binary operators. While they can be
strung together in longer expressions, each operation uses only two values at a time. Option
F is a unary operator and takes only one value.

16. B. The first line contains a compilation error. The value 3 is cast to `long`. The `1 * 2`
value is evaluated as `int` but promoted to `long` when added to the 3. Trying to store a
`long` value in an `int` variable triggers a compiler error. The other lines do not contain any
compilation errors, as they store smaller values in larger or same-size data types, with lines 2
and 4 using casting to do so. Since only one line does not compile, option B is correct.

17. C, F. The starting values of `ticketsTaken` and `ticketsSold` are 1 and 3, respectively.
After the first compound assignment, `ticketsTaken` is incremented to 2. The
`ticketsSold` value is increased from 3 to 5; since the post-increment operator was used,
the value of `ticketsTaken++` returns 1. On the next line, `ticketsTaken` is doubled to
4. On the final line, `ticketsSold` is increased by 1 to 6. The final values of the variables
are 4 and 6, for `ticketsTaken` and `ticketsSold`, respectively, making options C and F
the correct answers. Note the last line does not trigger a compilation error as the compound
operator automatically casts the right-hand operand.

18. C. Only parentheses, ( ), can be used to change the order of operation in an expression,
making option C correct. The other operators, such as [ ], < >, and { }, cannot be used to
change the order of precedence in Java.

19. B, F. The code compiles and runs successfully, so options G and H are incorrect. On line 5,
the pre-increment operator is executed first, so `start` is incremented to 8, and the new value
is returned as the right side of the expression. The value of `end` is computed by adding 8 to
the original value of 4, leaving a new value of 12 for `end` and making option F a correct
answer. On line 6, we are incrementing one past the maximum `byte` value. Due to overflow,
this will result in a negative number, making option B the correct answer. Even if you didn't

know the maximum value of byte, you should have known the code compiles and runs and looked for the answer for start with a negative number.

20. A, D, E. Unary operators have the highest order of precedence, making option A correct. The negation operator (-) is used only for numeric values, while the logical complement operator (!) is used exclusively for boolean values. For these reasons, option B is incorrect, and option E is correct. Finally, the pre-increment/pre-decrement operators return the new value of the variable, while the post-increment/post-decrement operators return the original variable. For these reasons, option C is incorrect, and option D is correct.

Chapter 3: Making Decisions

1. F. Lines 34 and 35 do not compile because they are missing the pattern variable type, making option F correct. If a supported type, such as Integer, were added between the case and variable on each line, then the code would compile and print 4.

2. A, B, C. A switch expression supports enum values, making option A correct. It also supports int and byte primitives, including their wrapper classes Integer and Byte, making options B and C correct. It does not support the other types.

3. B. The code compiles and runs without issue, so options D, E, and F are incorrect. Even though two consecutive else statements on lines 7 and 8 look a little odd, they are associated with separate if statements on lines 5 and 6, respectively. The value of humidity on line 4 is equal to −4 + 12, which is 8. The first if statement evaluates to true on line 5, so line 6 is executed and evaluates to false. This causes the else statement on line 7 to run, printing Just Right and making option B the correct answer.

4. A, D, F. A for-each loop supports arrays, making options A and F correct. For Double[][], each element of the for-each loop would be a Double[]. A for-each also supports classes that implement java.lang.Iterable. Although this includes many of the Collections Framework classes, not all of them implement java.lang.Iterable. For this reason, option C is incorrect, and option D is correct. Options B, E, and G are incorrect, as they do not implement java.lang.Iterable. Although a String is a list of ordered characters, the class does not implement the required interface for a for-each loop.

5. F. The code does not compile because the switch expression requires all possible case values to be handled, making option F correct. If a valid default clause was added, then the code would compile and print Turtle at runtime.

6. E. The second for-each loop contains a continue followed by a print() statement. Because the continue is not conditional and always included as part of the body of the for-each loop, the print() statement is not reachable. For this reason, the print() statement does not compile. As this is the only compilation error, option E is correct. The other lines of code compile without issue.

7. B, D. Option A is incorrect because on the first iteration, it attempts to access weather[weather.length] of the nonempty array, which causes an

ArrayIndexOutOfBoundsException to be thrown. Option B is correct and will print the elements in order. Option C doesn't compile as i is undefined in weather[i]. For this to work, the body of the for-each loop would have to be updated as well. Option D is also correct and is a common way to print the elements of an array in reverse order. Option E does not compile and is therefore incorrect. You can declare multiple elements in a for loop, but the data type must be listed only once, such as in for (int i=0, j=3; ...). Finally, option F is incorrect because the first element of the array is skipped. Since the conditional expression is checked before the loop is executed the first time, the first value of i used inside the body of the loop will be 1.

8. G. The first two pattern matching statements compile without issue. The variable bat is allowed to be used again, provided it is no longer in scope. Line 36 does not compile, though. Due to flow scoping, if o is not a Long, then bat is not in scope in the expression bat <= 20. Line 38 also does not compile as default cannot be used as part of an if/else statement. For these two reasons, option G is correct.

9. B, C, E. The code contains a nested loop and a conditional expression that is executed if the sum of col + row is an even number; otherwise, count is incremented. Note that options E and F are equivalent to options B and D, respectively, since unlabeled statements apply to the most inner loop. Studying the loops, the first time the condition is true is in the second iteration of the inner loop, when row is 1 and col is 1. Option A is incorrect because this causes the loop to exit immediately with count only being set to 1. Options B, C, and E follow the same pathway. First, count is incremented to 1 on the first inner loop, and then the inner loop is exited. On the next iteration of the outer loop, row is 2 and col is 0, so execution exits the inner loop immediately. On the third iteration of the outer loop, row is 3 and col is 0, so count is incremented to 2. In the next iteration of the inner loop, the sum is even, so we exit, and our program is complete, making options B, C, and E each correct. Options D and F are both incorrect, as they cause the inner and outer loops to execute multiple times, with count having a value of 5 when done. You don't need to trace through all the iterations; just stop when the value of count exceeds 2.

10. E. This code contains numerous compilation errors, making options A and H incorrect. Line 15 does not compile, as continue cannot be used inside a switch statement like this. Line 16 is not a compile-time constant since any int value can be passed as a parameter. Marking it final does not change this, so it doesn't compile. Line 18 does not compile because Sunday is not marked as final. Being effectively final is insufficient. Finally, line 19 does not compile because DayOfWeek.MONDAY is not an int value. While switch statements do support enum values, each case clause must have the same data type as the switch variable otherDay, which is int. The rest of the lines do compile. Since exactly four lines do not compile, option E is the correct answer.

11. A. The code compiles and runs without issue, printing 3 at runtime and making option A correct. The default clause on line 17 is optional since all the enum values are accounted for and can be removed without changing the output.

12. C. Prior to the first iteration, sing = 8, squawk = 2, and notes = 0. After the iteration of the first loop, sing is updated to 7, squawk to 4, and notes to the sum of the new values for sing + squawk, 7 + 4 = 11. After the iteration of the second loop, sing is

updated to 6, squawk to 6, and `notes` to the sum of itself plus the new values for `sing` + `squawk`, 11 + 6 + 6 = 23. On the third iteration of the loop, `sing` > `squawk` evaluates to `false`, as 6 > 6 is `false`. The loop ends and the most recent value of `sing`, 23, is output, so the correct answer is option C.

13. F. The code does not compile because `case` clause uses the logical complement operator (!), which is not permitted with pattern matching. If this was removed, then the code would still not compile, as this clause would dominate the `case` on line 15, leading to unreachable code on line 15. For this reason, option F is correct.

14. G. This example may look complicated, but the code does not compile. Line 8 is missing the required parentheses around the `boolean` conditional expression. Since the code does not compile and it is not because of line 6, option G is the correct answer. If line 8 was corrected with parentheses, then the loop would be executed twice, and the output would be 11.

15. B, D, F. The code does compile, making option G incorrect. In the first for-each loop, the right side of the for-each loop has a type of `int[]`, so each element `penguin` has a type of `int`, making option B correct. In the second for-each loop, `ostrich` has a type of `Character[]`, so `emu` has a data type of `Character`, making option D correct. In the last for-each loop, `parrots` has a data type of `List<Integer>`. Since the generic type of `Integer` is used in the `List`, `macaw` will have a data type of `Integer`, making option F correct.

16. F. The code does not compile, although not for the reason specified in option E. The second `case` clause contains invalid syntax. Each `case` clause must have the keyword `case`—in other words, you cannot chain them with a colon (:). For this reason, option F is the correct answer. This line could have been fixed to say `case 'B', 'C'` or by adding the `case` keyword before `'C'`; then the rest of the code would have compiled and printed `great good` at runtime.

17. A, B, D. To print items in the `wolf` array in reverse order, the code needs to start with `wolf[wolf.length-1]` and end with `wolf[0]`. Option A accomplishes this and is the first correct answer. Option B is also correct and is one of the most common ways a reverse loop is written. The termination condition is often `m>=0` or `m>-1`, and both are correct. Options C and F each cause an `ArrayIndexOutOfBoundsException` at runtime since both read from `wolf[wolf.length]` first, with an index that is passed the length of the 0-based array `wolf`. The form of option C would be successful if the value was changed to `wolf[wolf.length-z-1]`. Option D is also correct, as the `j` is extraneous and can be ignored in this example. Finally, option E is incorrect and produces an infinite loop, as `w` is repeatedly set to `r-1`, in this case 4, on every loop iteration. Since the update statement has no effect after the first iteration, the condition is never met, and the loop never terminates.

18. B, E. The code compiles without issue and prints two distinct numbers at runtime, so options G and H are incorrect. The first loop executes a total of five times, with the loop ending when `participants` has a value of 10. For this reason, option E is correct. In the second loop, `animals` starts out not less than or equal to 1, but since it is a do/while loop, it executes at least once. In this manner, `animals` takes on a value of 3 and the loop terminates, making option B correct. Finally, the last loop executes a total of two times, with `performers` starting with -1, going to 1 at the end of the first loop, and then ending with

a value of 3 after the second loop, which breaks the loop. This makes option B a correct answer twice over.

19. E. The variable `snake` is declared within the body of the do/while statement, so it is out of scope on line 7. For this reason, option E is the correct answer. If `snake` were declared before line 3 with a value of 1, then the output would have been 1 2 3 4 5 -5.0, and option G would have been the correct answer.

20. A, E. The most important thing to notice when reading this code is that the innermost loop is an infinite loop. Therefore, you are looking for solutions that skip the innermost loop entirely or that exit that loop. Option A is correct, as `break` L2 on line 8 causes the second inner loop to exit every time it is entered, skipping the innermost loop entirely. For option B, the first `continue` on line 8 causes the execution to skip the innermost loop on the first iteration of the second loop but not the second iteration of the second loop. The innermost loop is executed, and with `continue` on line 12, it produces an infinite loop at runtime, making option B incorrect. Option C is incorrect because it contains a compiler error. The label L3 is not visible outside its loop. Option D is incorrect, as it is equivalent to option B since the unlabeled `break` and `continue` apply to the nearest loop and therefore produce an infinite loop at runtime. Like option A, the `continue` L2 on line 8 allows the innermost loop to be executed the second time the second loop is called. The `continue` L2 on line 12 exits the infinite loop, though, causing control to return to the second loop. Since the first and second loops terminate, the code terminates, and option E is a correct answer.

21. D. Line 23 does not compile because it is missing a `yield` statement. Line 24 does not compile because it contains an extra semicolon at the end. Finally, lines 25 and 26 do not compile because they use the same `case` value. At least one of them would need to be changed for the code to compile. Since three lines need to be corrected, option D is correct.

22. E. The code compiles without issue, making options F and G incorrect. Remember, `var` is supported in both `switch` and `while` loops, provided the compiler determines that the type is compatible with these statements. In addition, the variable `one` is allowed in a `case` clause because it is a `final` local variable, making it a compile-time constant. The value of `tailFeathers` is 3, which matches the second `case` clause, making 5 the first output. The `while` loop is executed twice, with the pre-decrement operator (`--`) modifying the value of `tailFeathers` from 3 to 2 and then to 1 on the second loop. For this reason, the final output is 5 2 1, making option E the correct answer.

23. F. Line 19 starts with an `else` statement, but there is no preceding `if` statement that it matches. For this reason, line 19 does not compile, making option F the correct answer. If the `else` keyword was removed from line 19, then the code snippet would print `Success`.

24. B. Since this is a pattern matching `switch` statement, the `case` branches are evaluated in the order in which they appear. In particular, each branch does not dominate the ones after it, so the code compiles without issue. If either of the `when` clauses were removed from their accompanying `case` clause, then the code would not compile. The first branch is skipped because `Closed` does not match `Open`. The second one matches, resulting in 20 being printed at runtime and making option B correct.

25. D. The code compiles without issue, so option F is incorrect. The `viola` variable created on line 8 is never used and can be ignored. If it had been used as the `case` value on line 15, it would have caused a compilation error since it is not marked `final`. Since "violin" and "VIOLIN" are not an exact match, the `default` branch of the `switch` statement is executed at runtime. This execution path increments p a total of three times, bringing the final value of p to 2 and making option D the correct answer.

26. F. The code snippet does not contain any compilation errors, so options D and E are incorrect. There is a problem with this code snippet, though. While it may seem complicated, the key is to notice that the variable r is updated outside of the `do/while` loop. This is allowed from a compilation standpoint, since it is defined before the loop, but it means the innermost loop never breaks the termination condition `r <= 1`. At runtime, this will produce an infinite loop the first time the innermost loop is entered, making option F the correct answer.

27. D. The code compiles and runs without issue, as every case block contains a `yield` statement. The second case block contains two paths which both end in a `yield` statement. At runtime, the code prints `Blue`, making option D correct.

28. F. Based on flow scoping, guppy is in scope after lines 41–42 if the type is not a `String`. In this case, line 43 declares a variable `guppy` that is a duplicate of the previously defined local variable defined on line 41. For this reason, the code does not compile, and option F is correct. If a different variable name was used on line 43, then the code would compile and print `Swim!` at runtime with the specified input.

29. C. Since the pre-increment operator was used, the first value that will be displayed is −1, so options A and B are incorrect. On the second-to-last iteration of the loop, y will be incremented to 5, and the loop will output 5. The loop will continue since `5 <= 5` is `true`, and on the last iteration, 6 will be output. At the end of this last iteration, the `boolean` expression `6 <= 5` will evaluate to `false`, and the loop will terminate. Since 6 was the last value output by the loop, the answer is option C.

30. E. On line 43, the semicolon should be after the `yield` statement, not outside the brace. Line 48 is missing a semicolon after the `return` statement containing the `switch` expression. For these reasons, at least two lines must be corrected. Next, lines 43, 44, and 45 do not compile because the numeric values are not compatible with the reference type for `Object`. We can fix this by changing line 41 to pass `speed` as a compatible type, such as `Integer`. Finally, the `default` clause on line 46 dominates the proceeding `case null` on line 47. Removing line 47 fixes this issue, as `case null` is not required. Since we can get the code to compile by changing or removing four lines, option E is the correct answer.

Chapter 4: Core APIs

1. F. Line 5 does not compile. This question is checking to see whether you are paying attention to the types. numFish is an `int`, and 1 is an `int`. Therefore, we use numeric addition and get 5. The problem is that we can't store an `int` in a `String` variable. Suppose line 5 said `String anotherFish = numFish + 1 + "";`. In that case, the answers would be option A and option C. The variable defined on line 5 would be the string "5", and both output statements would use concatenation.

2.   C, E, F. Option C uses the variable name as if it were a type, which is clearly illegal. Options E and F don't specify any size. Although it is legal to leave out the size for later dimensions of an array of arrays, the first one is required. Option A declares a legal 2D array. Option B declares a legal 3D array. Option D declares a legal 2D array. Remember that it is normal to see classes on the exam you might not have learned. You aren't expected to know anything about them.

3.   A, C, D. Option B throws an exception because there is no March 40. Option E also throws an exception because 2029 isn't a leap year and therefore has no February 29. Option F doesn't compile because the enum should be named Month, rather than MonthEnum. Option D is correct because it is just a regular date and has nothing to do with daylight saving time. Options A and C are correct because Java is smart enough to adjust for daylight saving time.

4.   A, C, D. The code compiles fine. Line 3 points to the String in the string pool. Line 4 calls the String constructor explicitly and is therefore a different object than s. Line 5 checks for object equality, which is true, and so it prints one. Line 6 uses object reference equality, which is not true since we have different objects. Line 7 calls intern(), which returns the value from the string pool and is therefore the same reference as s. Line 8 also compares references but is true since both references point to the object from the string pool. Finally, line 9 is a trick. The string Hello is already in the string pool, so calling intern() does not change anything. The reference t is a different object, so the result is still false. Therefore, options A, C, and D are correct.

5.   B. This example uses method chaining. After the call to append(), sb contains "aaa". That result is passed to the first insert() call, which inserts at index 1. At this point, sb contains abbaa. That result is passed to the final insert(), which inserts at index 4, resulting in abbaccca. Therefore, option B is the answer.

6.   C. Remember to watch return types on math operations. One of the tricks is line 24. The round() method returns an int when called with a float. However, we are calling it with a double, so it returns a long. The other trick is line 25. The random() method returns a double. Since two lines have a compiler error, option C is the answer.

7.   A, E. When dealing with time zones, it is best to convert to GMT first by subtracting the time zone. Remember that subtracting a negative is like adding. The first date/time is 9:00 GMT, and the second is 15:00 GMT. Therefore, the first one is earlier by six hours. Therefore, options A and E are correct.

8.   A, B, F. Remember that indexes are zero-based, which means index 4 corresponds to 5, and option A is correct. For option B, the replace() method starts the replacement at index 2 and ends before index 4. This means two characters are replaced, and charAt(3) is called on the intermediate value of 1265. The character at index 3 is 5, making option B correct. Option C is similar, making the intermediate value 126 and returning 6.

Option D results in an exception since there is no character at index 5. Option E is incorrect. It does not compile because the parentheses for the length() method are missing. Finally, option F's replace results in the intermediate value 145. The character at index 2 is 5, so option F is correct.

9. A, C, F. Arrays are zero-indexed, making option A correct and option B incorrect. They are not able to change size, which is option C. The values can be changed, making option D incorrect. An array does not override `equals()`, so it uses object equality. Since two different objects are not equal, option F is correct, and options E and G are incorrect.

10. A. All of these lines compile. The `min()` and `floor()` methods return the same type passed in: `int` and `double`, respectively. The `round()` method returns a `long` when called with a `double`. Option A is correct since the code compiles.

11. E. A `LocalDate` does not have a time element. Therefore, there is no method to add hours, making option E the answer.

12. A, D, E. First, notice that the `indent()` call adds a blank space to the beginning of `numbers`, and `stripLeading()` immediately removes it. The `substring()` method has two forms. The first takes the index to start with and the index to stop immediately before. The second takes just the index to start with and goes to the end of the `String`. Remember that indexes are zero-based. The first call starts at index 1 and ends with index 2 since it needs to stop before index 3. This gives us option A. The second call starts at index 7 and ends in the same place, resulting in an empty `String`, which is option E. This prints out a blank line. The final call starts at index 7 and goes to the end of the `String` finishing up with option D.

13. B. A `String` is immutable. Calling `concat()` returns a new `String` but does not change the original. A `StringBuilder` is mutable. Calling `append()` adds characters to the existing character sequence along with returning a reference to the same object. Therefore, option B is correct.

14. B, F. Options A and C are incorrect because there is no `asTime()` or `withTime()` method defined on `LocalDate`. Option B correctly creates a `LocalDateTime` from a `LocalDate` and `LocalTime`. Option E is incorrect because `Instant`, like other date/time classes, does not have a `public` constructor and is instantiated via methods. Option F is the proper conversion. Option D is incorrect because the source object does not represent a point in time. Without a time zone, Java doesn't know what moment in time to use for the `Instant`.

15. C, E. Numbers sort before letters, and uppercase sorts before lowercase. This makes option C one of the answers. The `binarySearch()` method looks at where a value would be inserted, which is before the second element for `Pippa`. It then negates it and subtracts one, which is option E.

16. A, G. The `substring()` method includes the starting index but not the ending index. When called with 1 and 2, it returns a single-character `String`, making option A correct and option E incorrect. Calling `substring()` with 2 as both parameters is legal. It returns an empty `String`, making options B and F incorrect. Java does not allow the indexes to be specified in reverse order. Option G is correct because it throws a `StringIndexOutOfBoundsException`. Finally, option H is incorrect because it returns an empty `String`.

17. C, F. This question is tricky because it has several parts. First, you have to know that the text block on lines 13 and 14 is equivalent to a regular `String`. Since there is no line break at the end, this is four characters. Then, you have to know that `String` objects are immutable, which means the results of lines 17–19 are ignored. Finally, on line 20, something happens. We concatenate three new characters to s1 and now have a String of length 7, making option C correct.

Next, s2 += 2 expands to s2 = s2 + 2. A String concatenated with any other type gives a String. Lines 22, 23, and 24 all append to s2, giving a result of "2cfalse". The if statement on line 27 returns true because the values of the two String objects are the same using object equality. For this reason, option F is correct. The if statement on line 26 returns false because the two String objects are not the same in memory. One comes directly from the string pool, and the other comes from building using String operations.

18. A, B, D. The compare() method returns a positive integer when the arrays are different and the first is larger. This is the case for option A since the s2 element at index 1 comes first alphabetically. It is not the case for option C because the s4 is longer or for option E because the arrays are the same.

The mismatch() method returns a positive integer when the arrays are different in a position index 1 or greater. This is the case for options B and D since the difference is at index 1. It is not the case for option F because there is no difference.

19. A, D. The dateTime1 object has a time of 1:30 per initialization. The dateTime2 object is an hour later. However, there is no 2:30 when springing ahead, setting the time to 3:30. Option A is correct because it is an hour later. Option D is also correct because the hour of the new time is 3. Option E is not correct because we have changed the time zone offset due to daylight saving time.

20. A, C. The reverse() method is the easiest way of reversing the characters in a String Builder; therefore, option A is correct. In option B, substring() returns a String, which is not stored anywhere. Option C uses method chaining. First, it creates the value "JavavaJ$". Then, it removes the first three characters, resulting in "avaJ$". Finally, it removes the last character, resulting in "avaJ". Option D throws an exception because you cannot delete the character after the last index. Remember that deleteCharAt() uses indexes that are zero-based, and length() counts the number of characters rather than the index.

21. A. The date starts out as April 30, 2025. Since dates are immutable and the plus methods' return values are ignored, the result is unchanged. Therefore, option A is correct.

22. E. The code first creates a date of 2025-10-31. The chaining in the output is valid resulting in interim states of 2026-10-31, followed by 2026-05-31, then 2026-06-30, then 2026-06-30, and finally the result of 2026-06-30T13:04.

Chapter 5: Methods

1. A, E. Instance and static variables can be marked final, making option A correct. Effectively final means a local variable is not marked final but whose value does not change after it is set, making option B incorrect. Option C is incorrect, as final refers only to the reference to an object, not its contents. Option D is incorrect, as `var` and `final` can be used together. Finally, option E is correct: once a primitive is marked `final`, it cannot be modified.

2. B, C. The keyword `void` is a return type. Only the access modifier or optional specifiers are allowed before the return type. Option C is correct, creating a method with `private` access. Option B is also correct, creating a method with package access and the optional specifier `final`. Since package access does not use a modifier, we get to jump right to `final`. Option A is incorrect because package access omits the access modifier rather than specifying `default`. Option D is incorrect because Java is case sensitive. It would have been correct if `public` were the choice. Option E is incorrect because the method already has a `void` return type. Option F is incorrect because labels are not allowed for methods.

3. A, D. Options A and D are correct because the optional specifiers are allowed in any order. Options B and C are incorrect because they each have two return types. Options E and F are incorrect because the return type is before the optional specifier and access modifier, respectively.

4. A, B, C, E. The value 6 can be implicitly promoted to any of the primitive types, making options A, C, and E correct. It can also be autoboxed to `Integer`, making option B correct. It cannot be both promoted and autoboxed, making options D and F incorrect.

5. A, C, D. Options A and C are correct because a `void` method is optionally allowed to have a `return` statement as long as it doesn't try to return a value. Option B does not compile because `null` requires a reference object as the return type. Since `int` is primitive, it is not a reference object. Option D is correct because it returns an `int` value. Option E does not compile because it tries to return a `double` when the return type is `int`. Since a `double` cannot be assigned to an `int`, it cannot be returned as one either. Option F does not compile because no value is actually returned.

6. A, B, F. Options A and B are correct because the single varargs parameter is the last parameter declared. Option F is correct because it doesn't use any varargs parameters. Option C is incorrect because the varargs parameter is not last. Option D is incorrect because two varargs parameters are not allowed in the same method. Option E is incorrect because the `...` for a varargs must be after the type, not before it.

7. D, F. Options D and F are correct. Option D passes the initial parameter plus two more to turn into a varargs array of size 2. Option F passes the initial parameter plus an array of size 2. Option A does not compile because it does not pass the initial parameter. Option E does not compile because it does not declare an array properly. It should be `new boolean[] {true, true}`. Option B creates a varargs array of size 0, and option C creates a varargs array of size 1.

8. D. Option D is correct. A common practice is to set all fields to be `private` and all methods to be `public`. Option A is incorrect because `protected` access allows everything that package access allows and additionally allows subclasses access. Option B is incorrect because the class is `public`. This means that other classes can see the class. However, they cannot call any of the methods or read any of the fields. It is essentially a useless class. Option C is incorrect because package access applies to the whole package. Option E is incorrect because Java has no such wildcard access capability.

9. B, C, D, F. The two classes are in different packages, which means `private` access and package access will not compile. This causes compiler errors on lines 5, 6, and 7, making options B, C, and D correct answers. Additionally, `protected` access will not compile since `School` does not inherit from `Classroom`. This causes the compiler error on line 9, making option F a correct answer as well.

10. B. `Rope` runs line 3, setting `LENGTH` to 5, and then immediately after that runs the `static` initializer, which sets it to 10. Line 5 in the `Chimp` class calls the `static` method normally and prints `swing` and a space. Line 6 also calls the `static` method. Java allows calling a `static` method through an instance variable, although it is not recommended. Line 7 uses the `static` import on line 2 to reference `LENGTH`. For these reasons, option B is correct.

11. B, E. Line 10 does not compile because `static` methods are not allowed to call instance methods. Even though we are calling `play()` as if it were an instance method and an instance exists, Java knows `play()` is really a `static` method and treats it as such. Since this is the only line that does not compile, option B is correct. If line 10 is removed, the code prints `swing-swing`, making option E correct. It does not throw a `NullPointerException` on line 17 because `play()` is a `static` method. Java looks at the type of the reference for `rope2` and translates the call to `Rope.play()`.

12. B. The test for effectively final is if the `final` modifier can be added to the local variable and the code still compiles. The `monkey` variable declared on line 11 is not effectively final because it is modified on line 13. The `giraffe` and `name` variables declared on lines 13 and 14, respectively, are effectively final and not modified after they are set. The `name` variable declared on line 17 is not effectively final since it is modified on line 22. Finally, the `food` variable on line 18 is not effectively final since it is modified on line 20. Since there are two effectively final variables, option B is correct.

13. D. There are two details to notice in this code. First, note that `RopeSwing` has an instance initializer and not a `static` initializer. Since `RopeSwing` is never constructed, the instance initializer does not run. The other detail is that `length` is `static`. Changes from any object update this common `static` variable. The code prints 8, making option D correct.

14. E. If a variable is `static final`, it must be set exactly once, and it must be in the declaration line or in a `static` initialization block. Line 4 doesn't compile because `bench` is not set in either of these locations. Line 15 doesn't compile because `final` variables are not allowed to be set after that point. Line 11 doesn't compile because `name` is set twice: once in the declaration and again in the `static` block. Line 12 doesn't compile because `rightRope` is set twice as well. Both are in `static` initialization blocks. Since four lines do not compile, option E is correct.

15. B. The two valid ways to do this are `import static java.util.Collections.*;` and `import static java.util.Collections.sort;`, making option B correct. Option A is incorrect because you can do a static import only on `static` members. Classes such as `Collections` require a regular `import`. Option C is nonsense as method parameters have no business in an import. Options D, E, and F try to trick you into reversing the syntax of `import static`.

16. E. The argument on line 17 is a `short`. It can be promoted to an `int`, so `print()` on line 5 is invoked. The argument on line 18 is a `boolean`. It can be autoboxed to a `Boolean`, so `print()` on line 11 is invoked. The argument on line 19 is a `double`. It can be autoboxed to a `Double`, so `print()` on line 11 is invoked. Therefore, the output is `int-Object-Object-`, and the correct answer is option E.

17. B. Since Java is pass-by-value and the variable on line 8 never gets reassigned, it stays as 9. In the method `square`, x starts as 9. The y value becomes 81, and then x gets set to –1. Line 9 does set `result` to 81. However, we are printing out `value`, and that is still 9, making option B correct.

18. B, D, E. Since Java is pass-by-value, assigning a new object to a does not change the caller. Calling `append()` does affect the caller because both the method parameter and the caller have a reference to the same object. Finally, returning a value does pass the reference to the caller for assignment to s3. For these reasons, options B, D, and E are correct.

19. B, C, E. The variable `value1` is a `final` instance variable. It can be set only once: in the variable declaration, an instance initializer, or a constructor. Option A does not compile because the `final` variable was already set in the declaration. The variable `value2` is a `static` variable. Both instance and `static` initializers are able to access `static` variables, making options B and E correct. The variable `value3` is an instance variable, making option C correct. Options D and F do not compile because a `static` initializer does not have access to instance variables.

20. A, E. The `100` parameter is an `int` and so calls the matching `int` method, making option A correct. When this method is removed, Java looks for the next most specific constructor. Java prefers autoboxing to varargs, so it chooses the `Integer` constructor. The `100L` parameter is a `long`. Since it can't be converted into a smaller type, it is autoboxed into a `Long`, and then the method for `Object` is called, making option E correct.

21. B, D. Option A is incorrect because it has the same parameter list of types and therefore the same signature as the original method. Options B and D are the correct answers, as they are valid method overloads in which the types of parameters change. When overloading methods, the return type and access modifiers do not need to be the same. Options C and E are incorrect because the method name is different. Options F and G do not compile. There can be at most one varargs parameter, and it must be the last element in the parameter list.

Chapter 6: Class Design

1. E. Options A and B will not compile because constructors cannot be called without new. Options C and D will compile but will create a new object rather than setting the fields in this one. The result is the program will print 0, not 2, at runtime. Calling an overloaded constructor, using `this()`, or a parent constructor, using `super()`, is allowed only on the first line of the constructor, making option E correct and option F incorrect. Finally, option G is incorrect because the program prints 0 without any changes, not 2.

2. A, B, F. The final modifier can be used with `private` and `static`, making options A and F correct. Marking a `private` method `final` is redundant but allowed. A `private` method may also be marked `static`, making option B correct. Options C, D, and E are incorrect because methods marked `static`, `private`, or `final` cannot be overridden; therefore, they cannot be marked `abstract`.

3. B, C. Overloaded methods have the same method name but a different signature (the method parameters differ), making option A incorrect. Overridden instance methods and hidden `static` methods must have the same signature (the name and method parameters must match), making options B and C correct. Overloaded methods can have different return types, while overridden and hidden methods can have covariant return types. None of these methods is required to use the same return type, making options D, E, and F incorrect.

4. F. The code will not compile as is, because the parent class `Mammal` does not define a no-argument constructor. For this reason, the first line of a `Platypus` constructor should be an explicit call to `super(int)`, making option F the correct answer. Option E is incorrect, as line 7 compiles without issue. The `sneeze()` method in the `Mammal` class is marked `private`, meaning it is not inherited and therefore is not overridden in the `Platypus` class. For this reason, the `sneeze()` method in the `Platypus` class is free to define the same method with any return type.

5. E. The code compiles, making option F incorrect. An instance variable with the same name as an inherited instance variable is hidden, not overridden. This means that both variables exist, and the one that is used depends on the location and reference type. Because the `main()` method uses a reference type of `Speedster` to access the `numSpots` variable, the variable in the `Speedster` class, not the `Cheetah` class, must be set to 50. Option A is incorrect, as it reassigns the method parameter to itself. Option B is incorrect, as it assigns the method parameter the value of the instance variable in `Cheetah`, which is 0. Option C is incorrect, as it assigns the value to the instance variable in `Cheetah`, not `Speedster`. Option D is incorrect, as it assigns the method parameter the value of the instance variable in `Speedster`, which is 0. Options A, B, C, and D all print 0 at runtime. Option E is the correct answer, as it assigns the instance variable `numSpots` in the `Speedster` class a value of 50. The `numSpots` variable in the `Speedster` class is then correctly referenced in the `main()` method, printing 50 at runtime.

6. D, E. The `Moose` class doesn't compile, as the `final` variable `antlers` is not initialized when it is declared, in an instance initializer, or in a constructor. `Caribou` and `Reindeer` are not immutable because they are not marked `final`, which means a subclass could extend them and add mutable fields. `Elk` and `Deer` are both immutable classes since they are marked `final` and only include `private final` members, making options D and E correct. As shown with `Elk`, a class doesn't need to declare any fields to be considered immutable.

7. A. The code compiles and runs without issue, so options E and F are incorrect. The `Arthropod` class defines two overloaded versions of the `printName()` method. The `printName()` method that takes an `int` value on line 5 is correctly overridden in the `Spider` class on line 9. Remember, an overridden method can have a broader access modifier, and `protected` access is broader than package access. Because of polymorphism, the overridden method replaces the method on all calls, even if an Arthropod reference variable is used, as is done in the main() method. For these reasons, the overridden method is called on lines 14 and 15, printing Spider twice. Note that the short value is automatically cast to the larger type of int, which then uses the overridden method. Line 16 calls the overloaded method in the Arthropod class, as the long value 5L does not match the overridden method, resulting in Arthropod being printed. Therefore, option A is the correct answer.

8. D. The code compiles without issue. The question is making sure you know that superclass constructors are called in the same manner in abstract classes as they are in non-abstract classes. Line 9 calls the constructor on line 6. The compiler automatically inserts super() as the first line of the constructor defined on line 6. The program then calls the constructor on line 3 and prints Wow-. Control then returns to line 6, and Oh- is printed. Finally, the method call on line 10 uses the version of fly() in the Pelican class, since it is marked private and the reference type of var is resolved as Pelican. The final output is Wow-Oh-Pelican, making option D the correct answer. Remember that private methods cannot be overridden. If the reference type of chirp was Bird, then the code would not compile as it would not be accessible outside the class.

9. B, E. The signature must match exactly, making option A incorrect. There is no such thing as a covariant signature. An overridden method must not declare any new checked exceptions or a checked exception that is broader than the inherited method. For this reason, option B is correct, and option D is incorrect. Option C is incorrect because an overridden method may have the same access modifier as the version in the parent class. Finally, overridden methods must have covariant return types, and only void is covariant with void, making option E correct.

10. A, C. Option A is correct, as this(3) calls the constructor declared on line 5, while this("") calls the constructor declared on line 10. Option B does not compile, as inserting this() at line 3 results in a compiler error, since there is no matching constructor. Option C is correct, as short can be implicitly cast to int, resulting in this((short)1) calling the constructor declared on line 5. In addition, this(null) calls the String constructor declared on line 10. Option D does not compile because inserting super() on line 14 results in an invalid constructor call. The Howler class does not contain a no-argument constructor. Option E is also incorrect. Inserting this(2L) at line 3 results in a recursive constructor definition. The compiler detects this and reports an error. Option F is incorrect, as using super(null) on line 14 does not match any parent constructors. If an explicit cast was used, such as super((Integer)null), then the code would have compiled but would throw an exception at runtime during unboxing. Finally, option G is incorrect because the superclass Howler does not contain a no-argument constructor. Therefore, the constructor declared on line 13 will not compile without an explicit call to an overloaded or parent constructor.

11. C. The code compiles and runs without issue, making options F and G incorrect. Line 16 initializes a PolarBear instance and assigns it to the bear reference. The variable declaration and instance initializers are run first, setting value to tac. The constructor declared on line 5 is called, resulting in value being set to tacb. Remember, a static main() method can access private constructors declared in the same class. Line 17 creates another PolarBear instance, replacing the bear reference declared on line 16. First, value is initialized to tac

as before. Line 17 calls the constructor declared on line 8, since `String` is the narrowest match of a `String` literal. This constructor then calls the overloaded constructor declared on line 5, resulting in `value` being updated to `tacb`. Control returns to the previous constructor, with line 10 updating `value` to `tacbf`, and making option C the correct answer. Note that if the constructor declared on line 8 did not exist, then the constructor on line 12 would match. Finally, the `bear` reference is properly cast to `PolarBear` on line 18, making the `value` parameter accessible.

12. C. The code doesn't compile, so option A is incorrect. The first compilation error is on line 8. Since `Rodent` declares at least one constructor, and it is not a no-argument constructor, `Beaver` must declare a constructor with an explicit call to a `super()` constructor. Line 9 contains two compilation errors. First, the return types are not covariant since `Number` is a supertype, not a subtype, of `Integer`. Second, the inherited method is `static`, but the overridden method is not, making this an invalid override. The code contains three compilation errors, although they are limited to two lines, making option C the correct answer.

13. A, G. The compiler will insert a default no-argument constructor if the class compiles and does not define any constructors. Options A and G fulfill this requirement, making them the correct answers. The `bird()` declaration in option G is a method declaration, not a constructor. Options B and C do not compile. Since the constructor name does not match the class name, the compiler treats these as methods with missing return types. Options D, E, and F all compile, but since they declare at least one constructor, the compiler does not supply one.

14. B, E, F. A class can only directly extend a single class, making option A incorrect. A class can implement any number of interfaces, though, making option B correct. Option C is incorrect because primitive variables types do not inherit `java.lang.Object`. If a class extends another class, then it is a subclass, not a superclass, making option D incorrect. A class that implements an interface is a subtype of that interface, making option E correct. Finally, option F is correct as it is an accurate description of multiple inheritance, which is not permitted in Java.

15. C. The code does not compile because the `isBlind()` method in `Nocturnal` is not marked `abstract` and does not contain a method body. The rest of the lines compile without issue, making option C the correct answer. If the `abstract` modifier was added to line 2, then the code would compile and print `false` at runtime, making option B the correct answer.

16. D. The code compiles, so option G is incorrect. Based on order of initialization, the `static` components are initialized first, starting with the `Arachnid` class, since it is the parent of the `Scorpion` class, which initializes the `StringBuilder` to u. The `static` initializer in `Scorpion` then updates `sb` to contain uq, which is printed twice by lines 13 and 14 along with spaces separating the values. Next, an instance of `Arachnid` is initialized on line 15. There are two instance initializers in `Arachnid`, and they run in order, appending cr to the `StringBuilder`, resulting in a value of uqcr. An instance of `Scorpion` is then initialized on line 16. The instance initializers in the superclass `Arachnid` run first, appending cr again and updating the value of `sb` to uqcrcr. Finally, the instance initializer in `Scorpion` runs and appends m. The program completes with the final value printed being uq uq uqcrcrm, making option D the correct answer.

17. C, F. Calling an overloaded constructor with this() may be used only as the first line of a constructor, making options A and B incorrect. Accessing this.variableName can be performed from any instance method, constructor, or instance initializer, but not from a static method or static initializer. For this reason, option C is correct, and option D is incorrect. Option E is tricky. The default constructor is written by the compiler only if no user-defined constructors were provided. And this() can only be called from a constructor in the same class. Since there can be no user-defined constructors in the class if a default constructor was created, it is impossible for option E to be true. Since the main() method is in the same class, it can call private methods in the class, making option F correct.

18. D, F. The eat() method is private in the Mammal class. Since it is not inherited in the Primate class, it is neither overridden nor overloaded, making options A and B incorrect. The drink() method in Mammal is correctly hidden in the Monkey class, as the signature is the same and both are static, making option D correct and option C incorrect. The version in the Monkey class throws a new exception, but it is unchecked; therefore, it is allowed. The dance() method in Mammal is correctly overloaded in the Monkey class because the signatures are not the same, making option E incorrect and option F correct. For methods to be overridden, the signatures must match exactly. Finally, line 12 is an invalid override and does not compile, as int is not covariant with void, making options G and H both incorrect.

19. F. The Reptile class defines a constructor, but it is not a no-argument constructor. Therefore, the Lizard constructor must explicitly call super(), passing in an int value. For this reason, line 9 does not compile, and option F is the correct answer. If the Lizard class were corrected to call the appropriate super() constructor, then the program would print BALizard at runtime, with the static initializer running first, followed by the instance initializer, and finally the method call using the overridden method.

20. E. The program compiles and runs without issue, making options A through D incorrect. The fly() method is correctly overridden in each subclass since the signature is the same, the access modifier is less restrictive, and the return types are covariant. For covariance, Macaw is a subtype of Parrot, which is a subtype of Bird, so overridden return types are valid. Likewise, the constructors are all implemented properly, with explicit calls to the parent constructors as needed. Line 19 calls the overridden version of fly() defined in the Macaw class, as overriding replaces the method regardless of the reference type. This results in feathers being assigned a value of 3. The Macaw object is then cast to Parrot, which is allowed because Macaw inherits Parrot. The feathers variable is visible since it is defined in the Bird class, and line 19 prints 3, making option E the correct answer.

21. B, G. Immutable objects do not include setter methods, making option A incorrect. An immutable class must be marked final or contain only private constructors, so no subclass can extend it and make it mutable, making option B correct. Options C and E are incorrect, as immutable classes can contain both instance and static variables. Option D is incorrect, as marking a class static is not a property of immutable objects. Option F is incorrect. While an immutable class may contain only private constructors, this is not a requirement. Finally, option G is correct. It is allowed for the caller to access data in mutable elements of an immutable object, provided they have no ability to modify these elements.

22. D. The code compiles and runs without issue, making option E incorrect. The Child class overrides the setName() method and hides the static name variable defined in the inherited Person class. Since variables are only hidden, not overridden, there are two distinct name variables accessible, depending on the location and reference type. Line 8 creates a Child instance, which is implicitly cast to a Person reference type on line 9. Line 10 uses the Child reference type, updating Child.name to Elysia. Line 11 uses the Person reference type, updating Person.name to Sophia. Lines 12 and 13 both call the overridden setName() instance method declared on line 6. This sets Child.name to Webby on line 12 and then to Olivia on line 13. The final values of Child.name and Person.name are Olivia and Sophia, respectively, making option D the correct answer.

23. B. The program compiles, making option F incorrect. The constructors are called from the child class upward, but since each line of a constructor is a call to another constructor, via this() or super(), they are ultimately executed in a top-down manner. On line 29, the main() method calls the Fennec() constructor declared on line 19. Remember, integer literals in Java are considered int by default. This constructor calls the Fox() constructor defined on line 12, which in turn calls the overloaded Fox() constructor declared on line 11. Since the constructor on line 11 does not explicitly call a parent constructor, the compiler inserts a call to the no-argument super() constructor, which exists on line 3 of the Canine class. Line 3 is then executed, adding q to the output, and the compiler chain is unwound. Line 11 then executes, adding p, followed by line 14, adding z. Finally, line 21 is executed, and j is added, resulting in a final value for logger of qpzj and making option B correct. For the exam, remember to follow constructors from the lowest level upward to determine the correct pathway, but then execute them from the top down using the established order.

24. C. The code compiles and runs without issue, making options E and F incorrect. First, the class is initialized, starting with the superclass Antelope and then the subclass Gazelle. This involves invoking the static variable declarations and static initializers. The program first prints 1, followed by 8. Then we follow the constructor pathway from the object created on line 14 upward, initializing each class instance using a top-down approach. Within each class, the instance initializers are run, followed by the referenced constructors. The Antelope instance is initialized, printing 24, followed by the Gazelle instance, printing 93. The final output is 182493, making option C the correct answer.

25. B, C. Concrete classes are, by definition, not abstract, so option A is incorrect. A concrete class must implement all inherited abstract methods, so option B is correct. Concrete classes can be optionally marked final, so option C is correct. Option D is incorrect; concrete classes need not be immutable. A concrete subclass only needs to override the inherited abstract method, not match the declaration exactly. For example, a covariant return type can be used. For this reason, option E is incorrect.

26. D. The classes are structured correctly, but the body of the main() method contains a compiler error. The Orca object is implicitly cast to a Whale reference on line 7. This is permitted because Orca is a subclass of Whale. By performing the cast, the whale reference on line 8 does not have access to the dive(int... depth) method. For this reason, line 8 does not compile, making option D correct.

Chapter 7: Beyond Classes

1. B, D, E. Iguana does not compile, as it declares a static field with the same name as an instance field. Records are implicitly final and cannot be marked abstract, which is why Gecko compiles and Chameleon does not, making option B correct. Notice in Gecko that records are not required to declare any fields. BeardedDragon also compiles, as records may override any accessor methods, making option D correct. Reptile compiles as it contains a valid compact constructor, making option E correct. Newt does not compile because it cannot extend another record. It also does not compile because the compact constructor tries to read this.age, which is not permitted.

2. A, B, D, E. The code compiles without issue, so option G is incorrect. The blank can be filled with any class or interface that is a supertype of TurtleFrog. Option A is the direct superclass of TurtleFrog, and option B is the same class, so both are correct. BrazilianHornedFrog is not a superclass of TurtleFrog, so option C is incorrect. TurtleFrog inherits the CanHop interface, so option D is correct. Option E is also correct, as var is permitted when the type is known. Finally, Long is an unrelated class that is not a superclass of TurtleFrog and is therefore incorrect.

3. D. When an enum contains only a list of values, the semicolon (;) after the list is optional. When an enum contains any other members, such as a constructor or variable, the semicolon is required. For this reason, line 13 does not compile. Line 14 also does not compile, as enum constructors are implicitly private and cannot be declared as public or protected. For this reason, option D is correct. If these two issues were corrected, then the program would print 0 1 0 at runtime.

4. C. A class extending a sealed class must be marked final, sealed, or non-sealed. Since Armadillo is missing a modifier, the code does not compile, and option C is correct.

5. E. First, the declarations of HasExoskeleton and Insect are correct and do not contain any errors, making options C and D incorrect. The concrete class Beetle extends Insect and inherits two abstract methods, getNumberOfSections() and getNumberOfLegs(). The Beetle class includes an overloaded version of getNumberOfSections() that takes an int value. The method declaration is valid, making option F incorrect, although it does not satisfy the abstract method requirement inherited from HasExoskeleton. For this reason, only one of the two abstract methods is properly overridden. The Beetle class therefore does not compile, and option E is correct.

6. D, E. Line 4 does not compile, since an abstract method cannot include a body. Line 7 also does not compile because the wrong keyword is used. A class implements an interface; it does not extend it. For these reasons, options D and E are correct.

7. E. The inherited interface method getNumOfGills(int) is implicitly public; therefore, it must be declared public in any concrete class that implements the interface. Since the method uses the package (default) modifier in the ClownFish class, line 6 does not compile, making option E the correct answer. If the method declaration were corrected to include public on line 6, then the program would compile and print 15 at runtime, and option B would be the correct answer.

8. B, E, G. Options A and F do not compile because they are not compatible with List<String>. Option C does not compile because the reference type of w is Object, which doesn't have an animal() method. Option D does not compile because the variable i is used twice in the same pattern matching statement. Option H does not compile because you can't use null in a pattern matching statement. Options B, E, and G correctly compile and print true at runtime.

9. A, E, F. The setSnake() method requires an instance of Snake. Cobra is a direct subclass, while GardenSnake is an indirect subclass. For these reasons, options A and E are correct. Option B is incorrect because Snake is abstract and requires a concrete subclass for instantiation. Option C is incorrect because Object is a supertype of Snake, not a subtype. Option D is incorrect as String is an unrelated class and does not inherit Snake. Finally, a null value can always be passed as an object value, regardless of type, so option F is also correct.

10. A, B, C, E. Walk declares a private method that is not inherited in any of its subtypes. For this reason, any valid class is supported on line X, making options A, B, and C correct. Line Z is more restrictive, with only ArrayList or subtypes of ArrayList supported, making option E correct.

11. B. Inner classes can contain static variables, so the code compiles. Remember that private constructors can be used by any methods within the outer class. The butter reference on line 8 refers to the inner class variable defined on line 6, with the output being 10 at runtime, and making option B correct.

12. A, D, E, F. The code compiles, making options G, H, and I incorrect. The hiss() method is an instance member, so it can access any visible static members inside itself or the outer class, making option F correct. It can also access instance variables and methods within the record, making options A, D, and E correct. Because nested records are inherently static, it cannot access body or tail, which are instance members of the outer class, making options B and C incorrect.

13. G. The code compiles without issue, so options E and F are incorrect. It prints a NullPointerException at runtime, making option G correct.

14. A, C, E. A sealed interface restricts which interfaces may extend it, or which classes may implement it, making options A and E correct. Option B is incorrect. For example, a non-sealed subclass allows classes not listed in the permits clause to indirectly extend the sealed class. Option C is correct. While a sealed class is commonly extended by a subclass marked final, it can also be extended by a sealed or non-sealed subclass marked abstract. Option D is incorrect, as the modifier is non-sealed, not nonsealed. Finally, option F is incorrect, as sealed classes can contain nested subclasses.

15. F. Trick question—the code does not compile! For this reason, option F is correct. The Spirit class is marked final, so it cannot be extended. The main() method uses an anonymous class that inherits from Spirit, which is not allowed. If Spirit were not marked final, then option C would be correct. Option A would print Booo!!!, while options B, D, and E would not compile for various reasons.

16. E. The OstrichWrangler class is a static nested class; therefore, it cannot access the instance member count. For this reason, line 5 does not compile, and option E is correct.

17. E, G. Lines 2 and 3 compile with interface variables implicitly public, static, and final. Line 4 also compiles, as static methods are implicitly public. Line 5 does not compile, making option E correct. Non-static interface methods with a body must be explicitly marked private or default. Line 6 compiles, with the public modifier being added by the compiler. Line 7 does not compile, as interfaces do not have protected members, making option G correct. Finally, line 8 compiles without issue.

18. E. Diet is an inner class, which requires an instance of Deer to instantiate. Since the main() method is static, there is no such instance. Therefore, the main() method does not compile, and option E is correct. If a reference to Deer were used, such as calling new Deer().new Diet(), then the code would compile and print b at runtime.

19. F. The isHealthy() method is marked abstract in the enum; therefore, it must be implemented in each enum value declaration. Since only INSECTS implements it, the code does not compile, making option F correct.

20. H. The record declarations compile but the switch expression does not, making option H correct. First, the second case statement does not compile, as double is not compatible with Double. Next, the pattern matching case statement on line 22 dominates the ones on lines 23–25. If three of them were to be removed (including the second one), then the code would compile and print the value associated with the remaining one.

21. F. The record defines an overloaded constructor using parentheses, not a compact one. For this reason, the first line must be a call to another constructor, such as this(500, "Acme", LocalDate.now()). For this reason, the code does not compile and option F is correct.

22. C, D, G. Option C correctly creates an instance of an inner class Cub using an instance of the outer class Lion. Options A, B, E, and H use incorrect syntax for creating an instance of the Cub class. Options D and G correctly create an instance of the static nested Den class, which does not require an instance of Lion, while option F uses invalid syntax.

23. D. First, if a class or interface inherits two interfaces containing default methods with the same signature, it must override the method with its own implementation. The Penguin class does this correctly, so option E is incorrect. The way to access an inherited default method is by using the syntax Swim.super.perform(), making option D correct. We agree that the syntax is bizarre, but you need to learn it. Options A, B, and C are incorrect and result in compiler errors.

24. B, E. Line 3 does not compile because the static method hunt() cannot access an abstract instance method getName(), making option B correct. Line 6 does not compile because the private static method sneak() cannot access the private instance method roar(), making option E correct. The rest of the lines compile without issue.

25. B. Zebra.this.x is the correct way to refer to x in the Zebra class. Line 5 defines an abstract local class within a method, while line 11 defines a concrete anonymous class that extends the `Stripes` class. The code compiles without issue and prints x is 24 at runtime, making option B the correct answer.

26. C. The code compiles and runs without issue. The `stand()` method is overridden on line 24, so the code prints 3 (-1 + 4) at runtime, making option C correct. Note that unlike records, enums can have mutable members, so the modification of `legs` on line 34 is permitted (albeit not recommended!).

27. B, C, D, G. The compiler inserts an accessor for each field, a constructor containing all of the fields in the order they are declared, and useful implementations of `equals()`, `hashCode()`, and `toString()`, making options B, C, D, and G correct. Option A is incorrect, as the compiler would only insert a no-argument constructor if the record had no fields. Option E is incorrect, as records are immutable. Option F is also incorrect and not a property of records.

28. A, B, D. `Camel` does not compile because the `travel()` method does not declare a body, nor is it marked `abstract`, making option A correct. `EatsGrass` also does not compile because an interface method cannot be marked both `private` and `abstract`, making option B correct. Finally, `Eagle` does not compile because it declares an abstract method `soar()` in a concrete class, making option D correct. The other classes compile without issue.

29. F. The code does not compile, so options A through options C are incorrect. Both lines 5 and 12 do not compile, as `this()` is used instead of `this`. Remember, `this()` refers to calling a constructor, whereas `this` is a reference to the current instance. Next, the compiler does not allow casting to an unrelated class type. Since `Orangutan` is not a subclass of `Primate`, the cast on line 15 is invalid, and the code does not compile. Due to these three lines containing compilation errors, option F is the correct answer.

30. C, E. `Bird` and its nested `Flamingo` subclass compile without issue. The `permits` clause is optional if the subclass is nested or declared in the same file. For this reason, `Monkey` and its subclass `Mandrill` also compile without issue. `EmperorTamarin` does not compile, as it is missing a `non-sealed`, `sealed`, or `final` modifier, making option C correct. `Friendly` also does not compile, since it lists a subclass `Silly` that does not extend it, making option E correct. While the `permits` clause is optional, the `extends` clause is not. `Silly` compiles just fine. Even though it does not extend `Friendly`, the compiler error is in the sealed class.

Chapter 8: Lambdas and Functional Interfaces

1. A. This code is correct. Line 8 creates a lambda expression that checks whether the age is less than 5, making option A correct. Since there is only one parameter and it does not specify a type, the parentheses around the parameter are optional. Lines 11 and 13 use the `Predicate` interface, which declares a `test()` method.

2. C. The interface takes two `int` parameters. The code on line 7 attempts to use them as if h is a `StringBuilder`, making option C correct. It is tricky to use types in a lambda when they are implicitly specified. Remember to check the interface for the real type.

3. A, C. A functional interface can contain any number of nonabstract methods, including `default`, `private`, `static`, and `private static`. For this reason, option A is correct, and option D is incorrect. Option B is incorrect, as classes are never considered functional interfaces. A functional interface contains exactly one abstract method, although methods that have matching signatures as `public` methods in `java.lang.Object` do not count toward the single method test. For these reasons, option C is correct. Finally, option E is incorrect. While a functional interface can be marked with the `@FunctionalInterface` annotation, it is not required.

4. A, F. Option B is incorrect because it does not use the `return` keyword. Options C, D, and E are incorrect because the variable `e` is already in use from the lambda and cannot be redefined. Additionally, option C is missing the `return` keyword, and option E is missing the semicolon. Therefore, options A and F are correct.

5. A, C, E. Java includes support for three primitive streams, along with numerous functional interfaces to go with them: `int`, `double`, and `long`. For this reason, options C and E are correct. Additionally, there is a `BooleanSupplier` functional interface, making option A correct. Java does not include primitive streams or related functional interfaces for other numeric data types, making options B and D incorrect. Option F is incorrect because `String` is not a primitive but an object. Only primitives have custom suppliers.

6. A, C. `Predicate<String>` takes a parameter list of one parameter using the specified type. Options E and F are incorrect because they specify the wrong type. Options B, D, and F are incorrect because they use the wrong syntax for the arrow operator. This leaves us with options A and C as the answers.

7. E. While there appears to have been a variable name shortage when this code was written, it does compile. Lambda variables and method names are allowed to be the same. The `x` lambda parameter is scoped to within each lambda, so it is allowed to be reused. The type is inferred by the method it calls. The first lambda maps `x` to a `String` and the second to a `Boolean`. Therefore, option E is correct.

8. E. The question starts with a `UnaryOperator<Integer>`, which takes one parameter and returns a value of the same type. Therefore, option E is correct, as `UnaryOperator` extends `Function`. Notice that other options don't even compile because they have the wrong number of generic types for the functional interface provided. You should know that a `BiFunction<T,U,R>` takes three generic arguments, a `BinaryOperator<T>` takes one generic argument, and a `Function<T,R>` takes two generic arguments.

9. A, F. Option A is correct, and option B is incorrect because a `Supplier` returns a value while a `Consumer` takes one and acts on it. Option C is tricky. `IntSupplier` does return an `int`. However, the option asks about `IntegerSupplier`, which doesn't exist. Option D is incorrect because a `Predicate` returns a `boolean`. It does have a method named `test()`, making option F correct. Finally, option E is incorrect because `Function` has an `apply()` method.

10. A, B, C. Since the scope of `start` and `c` is within the lambda, the variables can be declared or updated after it without issue, making options A, B, and C correct. Option D is incorrect because setting `end` prevents it from being effectively final.

11. D. The code does not compile because the lambdas are assigned to `var`. The compiler does not have enough information to determine they are of type `Predicate<String>`. Therefore, option D is correct.

12. A. The `a.compose(b)` method calls the `Function` parameter b before the reference `Function` variable `a`. In this case, that means we multiply by 3 before adding 4. This gives a result of 7, making option A correct.

13. E. Lambdas are only allowed to reference `final` or effectively final variables. You can tell the variable j is effectively final because adding a `final` keyword before it wouldn't introduce a compiler error. Each time the **else** statement is executed, the variable is redeclared and goes out of scope. Therefore, it is not reassigned. Similarly, `length` is effectively final. There are no compiler errors, and option E is correct.

14. B, D. Option B is a valid functional interface, one that could be assigned to a `Consumer<Camel>` reference. Notice that the `final` modifier is permitted on variables in the parameter list. Option D is correct, as the exception is being returned as an object and not thrown. This would be compatible with a `BiFunction` that included `RuntimeException` as its return type.

Options A and G are incorrect because they mix format types for the parameters. Option C is invalid because the variable b is used twice. Option E is incorrect, as a `return` statement is permitted only inside braces (`{}`). Option F is incorrect because the variable declaration requires a semicolon (`;`) after it.

15. A, F. Option A is a valid lambda expression. While `main()` is a `static` method, it can access `age` since it is using a reference to an instance of `Hyena`, which is effectively final in this method. Since `var` is not a reserved word, it may be used for variable names. Option F is also correct, with the lambda variable being a reference to a `Hyena` object. The variable is processed using deferred execution in the `testLaugh()` method.

Options B and E are incorrect; since the local variable `age` is not effectively final, this would lead to a compilation error. Option C would also cause a compilation error, since the expression uses the variable name p, which is already declared within the method. Finally, option D is incorrect, as this is not even a lambda expression.

16. C. Lambdas are not allowed to redeclare local variables, making options A and B incorrect. Option D is incorrect because setting `end` prevents it from being effectively final. Lambdas are only allowed to reference `final` or effectively final variables. Option C compiles since `chars` is not used.

17. C. Line 8 uses braces around the body. This means the `return` keyword and semicolon are required. Since the code doesn't compile, option C is the answer.

18. B, F, G. We can eliminate four choices right away. Options A and C are there to mislead you; these interfaces don't exist. Option D is incorrect because a `BiFunction<T,U,R>` takes three generic arguments, not two. Option E is incorrect because none of the examples returns a `boolean`.

The declaration on line 6 doesn't take any parameters, and it returns a String, so a Supplier<String> can fill in the blank, making option F correct. The declaration on line 7 requires you to recognize that Consumer and Function, along with their binary equivalents, have an andThen() method. This makes option B correct. Finally, line 8 takes a single parameter, and it returns the same type, which is a UnaryOperator. Since the types are the same, only one generic parameter is needed, making option G correct.

19. F. While there is a lot in this question trying to confuse you, note that there are no options about the code not compiling. This allows you to focus on the lambdas and method references. Option A is incorrect because a Consumer requires one parameter. Options B and C are close. The syntax for the lambda is correct. However, s is already defined as a local variable, and therefore the lambda can't redefine it. Options D and E use incorrect syntax for a method reference. Option F is correct.

20. E. Option A does not compile because the second statement within the block is missing a semicolon (;) at the end. Option B is an invalid lambda expression because t is defined twice: in the parameter list and within the lambda expression. Options C and D are both missing a return statement and semicolon. Options E and F are both valid lambda expressions, although only option E matches the behavior of the Sloth class. In particular, option F only prints Sleep:, not Sleep: 10.0.

21. A, E, F. A valid functional interface is one that contains a single abstract method, excluding any public methods that are already defined in the java.lang.Object class. Transport and Boat are valid functional interfaces, as they each contain a single abstract method: go() and hashCode(String), respectively. This gives us options A and E. Since the other methods are part of Object, they do not count as abstract methods. Train is also a functional interface since it extends Transport and does not define any additional abstract methods. This adds option F as the final correct answer.

Car is not a functional interface because it is an abstract class. Locomotive is not a functional interface because it includes two abstract methods, one of which is inherited. Finally, Spaceship is not a valid interface, let alone a functional interface, because a default method must provide a body. A quick way to test whether an interface is a functional interface is to apply the @FunctionalInterface annotation and check if the code still compiles.

Chapter 9: Collections and Generics

1. A, F. Option E is incorrect for both scenarios, as SequencedTreeSet does not exist. For the first scenario, the answer needs to implement List because the scenario allows duplicates, narrowing it down to options A and D. Option A is a better answer than option D because LinkedList is both a List and a Queue, and you just need a regular List. For the second scenario, the answer needs to implement Map because you are dealing with key/value pairs per the unique id field. This narrows it down to options B and F. Since the question talks about ordering, you need the TreeMap. Therefore, the answer is option F.

2. C, G. Line 12 creates a `List<?>`, which means it is treated as if all the elements are of type `Object` rather than `String`. Lines 15 and 16 do not compile since they call the `String` methods `isEmpty()` and `length()`, which are not defined on `Object`. Line 13 creates a `List<String>` because `var` uses the type that it deduces from the context. Lines 17 and 18 do compile. However, `List.of()` creates an immutable list, so both of those lines would throw an `UnsupportedOperationException` if run. Therefore, options C and G are correct.

3. B. This is a double-ended queue. On lines 4 and 5, we add to the back, giving us `[hello, hi]`. On line 6, we add to the front and have `[ola, hello, hi]`. On line 7, we remove the first element, which is `"ola"`. On line 8, we look at the new first element (`"hello"`) but don't remove it. On lines 9 and 10, we remove each element in turn until no elements are left, printing `hello` and `hi` together, which makes option B the answer.

4. B, F. Option A does not compile because the generic types are not compatible. We could say `HashSet<? extends Number> hs2 = new HashSet<Integer>();`. Option B uses a lower bound, so it allows superclass generic types. Option C does not compile because the diamond operator is allowed only on the right side. Option D does not compile because a `Set` is not a `List`. Option E does not compile because upper bounds are not allowed when instantiating the type. Finally, option F does compile because the upper bound is on the correct side of the `=`.

5. B. The record compiles and runs without issue. Line 8 gives a compiler warning for not using generics but not a compiler error. Line 7 creates the `Hello` class with the generic type `String`. It also passes an `int` to the `println()` method, which gets autoboxed into an `Integer`. While the `println()` method takes a generic parameter of type T, it is not the same `<T>` defined for the class on line 1. Instead, it is a different T defined as part of the method declaration on line 3. Therefore, the `String` argument on line 7 applies only to the class. The method can take any object as a parameter, including autoboxed primitives. Line 8 creates the `Hello` class with the generic type `Object` since no type is specified for that instance. It passes a `boolean` to `println()`, which gets autoboxed into a `Boolean`. The result is that `hi-1hola-true` is printed, making option B correct.

6. B, F. We're looking for a `Comparator` definition that sorts in descending order by `beakLength`. Option A is incorrect because it sorts in ascending order by `beakLength`. Similarly, option C is incorrect because it sorts by `beakLength` in ascending order within those matches that have the same `name`. Option E is incorrect because there is no `thenComparingNumber()` method.

Option B is a correct answer, as it sorts by `beakLength` in descending order. Options D and F are trickier. First, notice that we can call either `thenComparing()` or `thenComparingInt()` because the former will simply autobox the `int` into an `Integer`. Then observe what `reversed()` applies to. Option D is incorrect because it sorts by name in ascending order and only reverses the beak length of those with the same name. Option F creates a comparator that sorts by name in ascending order and then by beak size in ascending order. Finally, it reverses the result. This is just what we want, so option F is correct.

7. B, F. A valid override of a method with generic arguments must have a return type that is covariant, with matching generic type parameters. Options D and E are incorrect because the return type is too broad. Additionally, the generic arguments must have the same signature with the same generic types. This eliminates options A and C. The remaining options are correct, making the answer options B and F.

8. E. There is no `get(int)` method defined in `SequencedCollection`, meaning line 16 does not compile, regardless of what is placed in the blank. For this reason, option E is correct. If line 16 was removed or corrected to use `getFirst()`, then `LinkedList` would be the correct answer.

9. A. The array is sorted using `MyComparator`, which sorts the elements in reverse alphabetical order in a case-insensitive fashion. Normally, numbers sort before letters. This code reverses that by calling the `compareTo()` method on `b` instead of `a`. Therefore, option A is correct.

10. A, B, D. The generic type must be `Exception` or a subclass of `Exception` since this is an upper bound, making options A and B correct. Options C and E are wrong because `Throwable` is a superclass of `Exception`. Additionally, option D is correct despite the odd syntax by explicitly listing the type. You should still be able to recognize it as acceptable.

11. A, B, E, F. The `forEach()` method works with a `Collection`, such as `List` or a `Set`. Therefore, options A and B are correct. Additionally, options E and F return a `Set` and `Collection`, respectively, and can be used as well. Options D and G refer to methods that do not exist. Option C is tricky because a `Map` does have a `forEach()` method. However, it uses two lambda parameters rather than one. Since there is no matching `System.out.println` method, it does not compile.

12. B, E. The `showSize()` method can take any type of `List` since it uses an unbounded wildcard. Option A is incorrect because it is a `Set` and not a `List`. Option C is incorrect because the wildcard is not allowed to be on the right side of an assignment. Option D is incorrect because the generic types are not compatible.

Option B is correct because a lower-bounded wildcard allows that same type to be the generic. Option E is correct because `Integer` is a subclass of `Number`.

13. C. This question is difficult because it defines both `Comparable` and `Comparator` on the same object. The `t1` object doesn't specify a `Comparator`, so it uses the `Comparable` object's `compareTo()` method. This sorts by the `text` instance variable. The `t2` object does specify a `Comparator` when calling the constructor, so it uses the `compare()` method, which sorts by the `int`. This gives us option C as the answer. Note that the `SequencedSet` reference on line 16 does not change the ordering, as the underlying object is still a `TreeSet`.

14. A. When using `binarySearch()`, the `List` must be sorted in the same order that the `Comparator` uses. Since the `binarySearch()` method does not specify a `Comparator` explicitly, the default sort order is used. Only `c2` uses that sort order and correctly identifies that the value 2 is at index 0. Therefore, option A is correct. The other two comparators sort in descending order. Therefore, the precondition for `binarySearch()` is not met, and the result is undefined for those two. The two calls to `reverse()` are just there to distract you; they cancel each other out.

15. A, B. `Y` is both a class and a type parameter. This means that within the class `Z`, when we refer to `Y`, it uses the type parameter. All of the choices that mention class `Y` are incorrect because it no longer means the class `Y`. Only options A and B are correct.

16. A, C. A `LinkedList` implements both `List` and `Queue`. The `List` interface has a method to remove by index. Since this method exists, Java does not autobox to call the other method, making the output [10] and option A correct. Similarly, option C is correct because the method to remove an element by index is available on a `LinkedList<Object>` (which is what `var` represents here). By contrast, `Queue` has only the remove by object method, so Java does autobox there. Since the number 1 is not in the list, Java does not remove anything for the `Queue`, and the output is [10, 12]. The `unmodifiableCollection()` call is a distractor as it is an unmodifiable view and the underlying connection can be changed.

17. E. This question looks like it is about generics, but it's not. It is trying to see whether you noticed that `Map` does not have a `contains()` method. It has `containsKey()` and `containsValue()` instead, making option E the answer. If `containsKey()` were called, the answer would be `false` because 123 is an `Integer` key in the `Map`, rather than a `String`.

18. A, E. The key to this question is keeping track of the types. Line 48 is a `Map<Integer, Integer>`. Line 49 builds a `List` out of a `Set` of `Entry` objects, giving us `List<Entry<Integer, Integer>>`. This causes a compiler error on line 56 since we can't multiply an `Entry` object by two.

Lines 51–54 are all of type `List<Integer>`. The first three are immutable, and the one on line 54 is mutable. This means line 57 throws an `UnsupportedOperationException` since we attempt to modify the list. Line 58 would work if we could get to it. Since there is one compiler error and one runtime error, options A and E are correct.

19. B. When using generic types in a method, the generic specification goes before the return type, so option B is correct.

20. F. The first call to `merge()` calls the mapping function and adds the numbers to get 13. It then updates the map. The second call to `merge()` sees that the map currently has a `null` value for that key. It does not call the mapping function but instead replaces it with the new value of 3. Therefore, option F is correct.

21. B, D, F. The `java.lang.Comparable` interface is implemented on the object to compare. It specifies the `compareTo()` method, which takes one parameter. The `java.util.Comparator` interface specifies the `compare()` method, which takes two parameters. This gives us options B, D, and F as the answers.

22. B. The code compiles and runs without issue, so options D and E are incorrect. A `TreeMap` sorts its items in the natural order of keys (not the values). Therefore, lines 25 and 27 remove [1, Minnie Mouse] and [2, Sugar], respectively. Line 26 has no impact on the map. On line 28, Snowball is printed, making option B correct. If line 26 were changed to use `pollLastEntry()`, then the map would be empty and line 28 would throw a `NullPointerException` trying to call `getValue()`.

23. H. `TreeSet` is a `SequencedSet`, so it does have an `addFirst()` method. For this reason, the code does compile. Unfortunately, `addFirst()` is not supported at runtime, as inserting an element at the front of the `TreeSet` could violate the `Comparator` of the `TreeSet`. For this reason, the code program throws an `UnsupportedOperationException` on the third line.

Chapter 10: Streams

1. D. No terminal operation is called, so the stream never executes. The first line creates an infinite stream reference. If the stream were executed on the second line, it would get the first two elements from that infinite stream, "" and "1", and add an extra character, resulting in "2" and "12", respectively. Since the stream is not executed, the reference is printed instead, giving us option D.

2. F. Both streams created in this code snippet are infinite streams. The variable b1 is set to true since anyMatch() terminates. Even though the stream is infinite, Java finds a match on the first element and stops looking. However, when allMatch() runs, it needs to keep going until the end of the stream since it keeps finding matches. Since all elements continue to match, the program hangs, making option F the answer.

3. E. An infinite stream is generated where each element is twice as long as the previous one. While this code uses the three-parameter iterate() method, the condition is never false. The variable b1 is set to false because Java finds an element that matches when it gets to the element of length 4. However, the next line tries to operate on the same stream. Since streams can be used only once, this throws an exception that the "stream has already been operated upon or closed," making option E the answer. If two different streams were used, the result would be option B.

4. A, B. Terminal operations are the final step in a stream pipeline. Exactly one is required, because it triggers the execution of the entire stream pipeline. Therefore, options A and B are correct. Option C is true of intermediate operations rather than terminal operations. Option D is incorrect because peek() is an intermediate operation. Finally, option E is incorrect because once a stream pipeline is run, the Stream is marked invalid.

5. C, F. Yes, we know this question is a lot of reading. Remember to look for the differences between options rather than studying each line. These options all have much in common. All of them start out with a LongStream and attempt to convert it to an IntStream. However, options B and E are incorrect because they do not cast the long to an int, resulting in a compiler error on the mapToInt() calls.

   Next, we hit the second difference. Options A and D are incorrect because they are missing boxed() before the collect() call. Since groupingBy() is creating a Collection, we need a nonprimitive Stream. The final difference is that option F specifies the type of Collection. This is allowed, though, meaning both options C and F are correct.

6. A. The anyMatch() and noneMatch() methods run infinitely. The stream has no way to know that a match won't show up later. Option A is correct because only allMatch() makes it safe to return false as soon as one element passes through the stream that doesn't match.

7. F. There is no Stream<T> method called compare() or compareTo(), so options A through D can be eliminated. The sorted() method is correct to use in a stream pipeline to return a sorted Stream and fills in the first blank. Either toList() or collect(Collectors.toList()) can fill in the second blank. Only one answer correctly fills in both blanks, and therefore option F is correct.

8. D, E. The `average()` method returns an `OptionalDouble` since averages of any type can result in a fraction. Therefore, options A and B are both incorrect. The `findAny()` method returns an `OptionalInt` because there might not be any elements to find. Therefore, option D is correct. The `sum()` method returns an `int` rather than an `OptionalInt` because the sum of an empty stream is zero. Therefore, option E is correct.

9. B, D. Lines 4–6 compile and run without issue, making options E and F incorrect. Line 4 creates a stream of elements [1, 2, 3]. Line 5 maps the stream to a new stream with values [10, 20, 30]. Line 6 filters out all items not less than 5, which in this case results in an empty stream. For this reason, `findFirst()` returns an empty `Optional`.

Option A does not compile. It would work for a `Stream<T>` object, but we have a `LongStream` and therefore need to call `getAsLong()`. Option C also does not compile, as it is missing the : : that would make it a method reference. Options B and D both compile and run without error, although neither produces any output at runtime since the stream is empty.

10. F. Only one of the method calls, `forEach()`, is a terminal operation, so any answer in which M is not the last line will not execute the pipeline. This eliminates all but options C, E, and F. Option C is incorrect because `filter()` is called before `limit()`. Since none of the elements of the stream meets the requirement for the `Predicate<String>`, the `filter()` operation will run infinitely, never passing any elements to `limit()`. Option E is incorrect because there is no `limit()` operation, which means that the code would run infinitely. Option F is correct. It first limits the infinite stream to a finite stream of 10 elements and then prints the result.

11. B, C, E. As written, the code doesn't compile because the `Collectors.joining()` expects to get a `Stream<String>`. Option B fixes this, at which point nothing is output because the collector creates a `String` without outputting the result. Option E fixes this and causes the output to be 11111. Since the post-increment operator is used, the stream contains an infinite number of the character 1. Option C fixes this and causes the stream to contain increasing numbers.

12. F. The code does not compile because `Stream.concat()` takes two parameters, not the three provided. This makes the answer option F.

13. F. If the `map()` and `flatMap()` calls were reversed, option B would be correct. In this case, the `Stream` created from the source is of type `Stream<List>`. Trying to use the addition operator (+) on a `List` is not supported in Java. Therefore, the code does not compile, and option F is correct.

14. B, D. Line 4 creates a `Stream` and uses autoboxing to put the `Integer` wrapper of 1 inside. Line 5 does not compile because `boxed()` is available only on primitive streams like `IntStream`, not `Stream<Integer>`. This makes option B one answer. Line 6 converts to a `double` primitive, which works since `Integer` can be unboxed to a value that can be implicitly cast to a `double`. Line 7 does not compile for two reasons, making option D the second answer. First, converting from a `double` to an `int` would require an explicit cast. Also, `mapToInt()` returns an `IntStream`, so the data type of s2 is incorrect. The rest of the lines compile without issue.

15. B, D. Options A and C do not compile because they are invalid generic declarations. Primitives are not allowed as generics, and Map must have two generic type parameters. Option E is incorrect because partitioning only gives a Boolean key. Options B and D are correct because they return a Map with a Boolean key and a value type that can be customized to any Collection.

16. B, C. First, this mess of code does compile. While it starts with an infinite stream on line 23, it becomes finite on line 24 thanks to limit(), making option F incorrect. The pipeline preserves only nonempty elements on line 25. Since there aren't any of those, the pipeline is empty. Line 26 converts this to an empty map.

Lines 27 and 28 create a Set with no elements and then another empty stream. Lines 29 and 30 convert the generic type of the Stream to List<String> and then String. Finally, line 31 gives us another Map<Boolean, List<String>>.

The partitioningBy() operation always returns a map with two Boolean keys, even if there are no corresponding values. Therefore, option B is correct if the code is kept as is. By contrast, groupingBy() returns only keys that are actually needed, making option C correct if the code is modified on line 31.

17. D. The terminal operation is count(). Since there is a terminal operation, the intermediate operations run. The peek() operation comes before the filter(), so both numbers are printed, making option D the answer. After the filter(), the count() happens to be 1 since one of the numbers is filtered out. However, the result of the stream pipeline isn't stored in a variable or printed, and it is ignored.

18. D. This compiles, ruling out options E, F, and G. Since line 29 filters by names starting with E, that rules out options A and B. Finally, line 31 counts the entire list, which is of size 2, giving us option D as the answer.

19. B. Both lists and streams have forEach() methods. There is no reason to collect into a list just to loop through it. Option A is incorrect because it does not contain a terminal operation or print anything. Options B and C both work. However, the question asks about the simplest way, which is option B.

20. C, E, F. Options A and B compile and return an empty string without throwing an exception, using a String and Supplier parameter, respectively. Option G does not compile as the get() method does not take a parameter. Options C and F throw a NoSuchElementException. Option E throws a RuntimeException. Option D looks correct but will compile only if the throw is removed. Remember, the orElseThrow() should get a lambda expression or method reference that returns an exception, not one that throws an exception.

21. B. We start with an infinite stream where each element is x. The spliterator() method is a terminal operation since it returns a Spliterator rather than a Stream. The tryAdvance() method gets the first element and prints a single x. The trySplit() method takes a large number of elements from the stream. Since this is an infinite stream, it doesn't attempt to take half. Then tryAdvance() is called on the new split variable, and another x is printed. Since there are two values printed, option B is correct.

Chapter 11: Exceptions and Localization

1. **A, C, D, E.** A method that declares an exception isn't required to throw one, making option A correct. Unchecked exceptions can be thrown in any method, making options C and E correct. Option D matches the exception type declared, so it's also correct. Option B is incorrect because a broader exception is not allowed.

2. **F.** The code does not compile because the `throw` and `throws` keywords are incorrectly used on lines 6, 7, and 9. If the keywords were fixed, the rest of the code would compile and print a stack trace with `YesProblem` at runtime. For this reason, option F is correct.

3. **A, D, E.** Localization refers to user-facing elements. Dates, currency, and numbers are commonly used in different formats for different countries, making options A, D, and E correct. Class and variable names, along with lambda expressions, are internal to the application, so there is no need to translate them for users.

4. **E.** The order of `catch` blocks is important because they're checked in the order they appear after the `try` block. Because `ArithmeticException` is a child class of `RuntimeException`, the `catch` block on line 7 is unreachable (if an `ArithmeticException` is thrown in the `try` block, it will be caught on line 5). Line 7 generates a compiler error because it is unreachable code, making option E correct.

5. **C, F.** The code compiles and runs without issue. When a `CompactNumberFormat` instance is requested without a style, it uses the SHORT style by default. This results in both of the first two statements printing `100K`, making option C correct. If the LONG style were used, then `100 thousand` would be printed. Option F is also correct, as the full value is printed with a currency formatter.

6. **E.** A `LocalDate` does not have a time element. Therefore, a date/time formatter is not appropriate. The code compiles but throws an exception at runtime, making option E correct. If `ISO_LOCAL_DATE` were used, the code would print `2025 APRIL 30`.

7. **E.** The first compiler error is on line 12 because each resource in a try-with-resources statement must have its own data type and be separated by a semicolon (`;`). Line 15 does not compile because the variable s is already declared in the method. Line 17 also does not compile. The `FileNotFoundException`, which inherits from `IOException` and `Exception`, is a checked exception, so it must be handled or declared by the method. Because these three lines of code do not compile, option E is the correct answer.

8. **C.** Java will first look for the most specific matches it can find, starting with `Dolphins_en_US.properties`. Since that is not an answer choice, it drops the country and looks for `Dolphins_en.properties`, making option C correct. Option B is incorrect because a country without a language is not a valid locale.

9. **D.** When working with a custom number formatter, the 0 symbol displays the digit as 0, even if it's not present, while the # symbol omits the digit from the start or end of the `String` if it is not present. Based on the requested output, a format that displays at least three digits before the decimal (including a comma) and at least one after the decimal is required.

It should display a second digit after the decimal if one is available. For this reason, option D is the correct answer.

10. B. An `IllegalArgumentException` is used when an unexpected parameter is passed into a method, making option B correct. Option A is incorrect because returning `null` or `-1` is a common return value for searching for data. Option D is incorrect because a `for` loop is typically used for this scenario. Option E is incorrect because you should find out how to code the method and not leave it for the unsuspecting programmer who calls your method. Option C is incorrect because you should run!

11. B, E, F. An exception that must be handled or declared is a checked exception. A checked exception inherits `Exception` but not `RuntimeException`. The entire hierarchy counts, so options B and E are both correct. Option F is also correct, as a class that inherits `Throwable` but not `RuntimeException` or `Error` is also checked.

12. B, C. The code does not compile as is because the exception declared by the `close()` method must be handled or declared. Option A is incorrect because removing the exception from the declaration causes a compilation error on line 4, as `FileNotFoundException` is a checked exception that must be handled or declared. Option B is correct because the unhandled exception within the `main()` method becomes declared. Option C is also correct because the exception becomes handled. Option D is incorrect because the exception remains unhandled.

13. A, B. A try-with-resources statement does not require a `catch` or `finally` block. A traditional `try` statement requires at least one of the two. Neither statement can be written without a body encased in braces, {}. For these reasons, options A and B are correct.

14. C. `NullPointerException` stack traces include the name of the variable that is `null` by default, making option A incorrect. The first `NullPointerException` encountered at runtime is when `dewey.intValue()` is called, making option C correct. Options E and F are incorrect as only one `NullPointerException` exception can be thrown at a time.

15. C, D. The code compiles with the appropriate locale, so option G is incorrect. A locale consists of a required lowercase language code and optional uppercase country code. In the `Locale.of()` method, the language code is provided first. For these reasons, options C and D are correct. Option E is incorrect because a `Locale` is created using the `Locale.of()` method or `Locale.Builder` class. Option F is really close but is missing `build()` at the end. Without that, option F does not compile.

16. F. When creating a custom formatter, any nonsymbol code must be properly escaped using pairs of single quotes (`'`). In this case, it fails because o is not a symbol. Even if you didn't know o wasn't a symbol, the code contains an unmatched single quote. If the properly escaped value of `"hh' o''clock'"` were used, then the correct answer would be option D, `LocalTime`. Without this change, though, the code throws an exception at runtime, making option F the correct answer. Option B would not be correct because `LocalDate` values do not have an hour part. Options A and C are incorrect because `ZonedTime` and `LocalTimestamp` are not valid date/time classes.

17. D, F. Option A is incorrect because Java will look at parent bundles if a key is not found in a specified resource bundle. Option B is incorrect because resource bundles are loaded from

static factory methods. Option C is incorrect, as resource bundle values are read from the ResourceBundle object directly. Option D is correct because the locale is changed only in memory. Option E is incorrect, as the resource bundle for the default locale may be used if there is no resource bundle for the specified locale (or its locale without a country code). Finally, option F is correct. The JVM will set a default locale automatically.

18. C. After both resources are declared and created in the try-with-resources statement, T is printed as part of the body. Then the try-with-resources completes and closes the resources in the reverse of the order in which they were declared. After W is printed, an exception is thrown. However, the remaining resource still needs to be closed, so D is printed. Once all the resources are closed, the exception is thrown and swallowed in the catch block, causing E to be printed. Last, the finally block is run, printing F. Therefore, the answer is TWDEF and option C is correct.

19. D. Java will use Dolphins_fr.properties as the matching resource bundle on line 7 because it is an exact match on the language of the requested locale. Line 8 finds a matching key in this file. Line 9 does not find a match in that file; therefore, it has to look higher up in the hierarchy. Once a bundle is chosen, only resources in that hierarchy are allowed. It cannot use the default locale anymore, but it can use the default resource bundle specified by Dolphins.properties. For these reasons, option D is correct.

20. G. The main() method invokes go(), and A is printed on line 3. The stop() method is invoked, and E is printed on line 14. Line 16 throws a NullPointerException, so stop() immediately ends, and line 17 doesn't execute. The exception isn't caught in go(), so the go() method ends as well, but not before its finally block executes and C is printed on line 9. Because main() doesn't catch the exception, the stack trace displays, and no further output occurs. For these reasons, AEC is printed followed by a stack trace for a NullPointerException, making option G correct.

21. C. The code does not compile because the multi-catch block on line 7 cannot catch both a superclass and a related subclass. Options A and B do not address this problem, so they are incorrect. Since the try body throws SneezeException, it can be caught in a catch block, making option C correct. Option D allows the catch block to compile but causes a compiler error on line 6. Both of the custom exceptions are checked and must be handled or declared in the main() method. A SneezeException is not a SniffleException, so the exception is not handled. Likewise, option E leads to an unhandled exception compiler error on line 6.

22. B. For this question, the date used is April 5, 2025, at 12:30:20 p.m. The code compiles, and either form of the formatter is correct: dateTime.format(formatter) or formatter.format(dateTime). The custom format m returns the minute, so 30 is output first. The next line throws an exception as z relates to time zone, and date/time does not have a zone component. This exception is then swallowed by the try/catch block. Since this is the only value printed, option B is correct. If the code had not thrown an exception, the last line would have printed 2025.

23. A, E. Resources must inherit AutoCloseable to be used in a try-with-resources block. Since Closeable, which is used for I/O classes, extends AutoCloseable, both may be used, making options A and E correct.

24. G. The code does not compile because the resource walk1 is not final or effectively final and cannot be used in the declaration of a try-with-resources statement. For this reason, option G is correct. If the line that set walk1 to null were removed, then the code would compile and print blizzard 2 at runtime, with the exception inside the try block being the primary exception since it is thrown first. Then two suppressed exceptions would be added to it when trying to close the AutoCloseable resources.

25. A. The code compiles and prints the value for Germany, 2,40 €, making option A the correct answer. Note that the default locale category is ignored since an explicit currency locale is selected.

26. B, F. The try block is not capable of throwing an IOException, making the catch block unreachable code and option A incorrect. Options B and F are correct, as both are unchecked exceptions that do not extend or inherit from IllegalArgumentException. Remember, it is not a good idea to catch Error in practice, although because it is possible, it may come up on the exam. Option C is incorrect because the variable c is declared already in the method declaration. Option D is incorrect because the IllegalArgumentException inherits from RuntimeException, making the first declaration unnecessary. Similarly, option E is incorrect because NumberFormatException inherits from IllegalArgumentException, making the second declaration unnecessary. Since options B and F are correct, option G is incorrect.

Chapter 12: Modules

1. E. Modules are required to have a module-info.java file at the root directory of the module. Option E matches this requirement.

2. B. Options A, C, and E are incorrect because they refer to directives that don't exist. The exports directive is used when allowing a package to be called by code outside of the module, making option B the correct answer. Notice that options D and F are incorrect because requires is the wrong keyword to use.

3. G. The -p or --module-path option is used to specify the location of the modules. The -m or --module option is used to specify the module and class name. However, running a program requires the package name to be specified with periods (.) instead of slashes. Since the command is incorrect, option G is correct.

4. D. A service consists of the service provider interface and logic to look up implementations using a service locator. This makes option D correct. Make sure you know that the service provider itself is the implementation, which is not considered part of the service.

5. E, F. Automatic modules are on the module path but do not have a module-info.java file. Named modules are on the module path and do have a module-info.java. Unnamed modules are on the classpath. Therefore, options E and F are correct.

6. A, F. Options C and D are incorrect because there is no use directive. Options A and F are correct because opens is for reflection and uses declares that an API consumes a service.

7. A, B, E. Any version information at the end of the JAR filename is removed, making options A and B correct. Underscores (_) are turned into dots (.), making options C and D incorrect. Other special characters like a dollar sign ($) are also turned into dots. However, adjacent dots are merged, and leading/trailing dots are removed. Therefore, option E is also correct.

8. A, D. A cyclic dependency is when a module graph forms a circle. Option A is correct because the Java Platform Module System does not allow cyclic dependencies between modules. No such restriction exists for packages, making option B incorrect. A cyclic dependency can involve two or more modules that require each other, making option D correct, while option C is incorrect. Finally, option E is incorrect because unnamed modules cannot be referenced from an automatic module.

9. F. The `provides` directive takes the interface name first and the implementing class name second and also uses `with`. Only option F meets these two criteria, making it the correct answer.

10. B, C. Packages inside a module are not exported by default, making option B correct and option A incorrect. Exporting is necessary for other code to use the packages; it is not necessary to call the `main()` method at the command line, making option C correct and option D incorrect. The `module-info.java` file has the correct name and compiles, making options E and F incorrect.

11. D, G, H. Options A, B, E, and F are incorrect because they refer to directives that don't exist. The `requires transitive` directive is used when specifying a module to be used by the requesting module and any other modules that use the requesting module. Therefore, `dog` needs to specify the transitive relationship, and option G is correct. The module `puppy` just needs `requires dog`, and it gets the transitive dependencies, making option D correct. However, `requires transitive` does everything `requires` does and more, which makes option H the final correct answer.

12. A, B, C, F. Option D is incorrect because it is a package name rather than a module name. Option E is incorrect because `java.base` is the module name, not `jdk.base`. Option G is wrong because we made it up. Options A, B, C, and F are correct.

13. D. There is no `getStream()` method on a `ServiceLoader`, making options A and C incorrect. Option B does not compile because the `stream()` method returns a list of `Provider` interfaces and needs to be converted to the `Unicorn` interface we are interested in. Therefore, option D is correct.

14. C. The `-p` option is a shorter form of `--module-path`. Since the same option cannot be specified twice, options B, D, and F are incorrect. The module name and class name are separated with a slash, making option C the answer. Note that `x-x` is legal because the module path is a folder name, so dashes are allowed.

15. B. A top-down migration strategy first places all JARs on the module path. Then it migrates the top-level module to be a named module, leaving the other modules as automatic modules. Option B is correct as it matches both of those characteristics.

16. A. Since this is a new module, you need to compile it. However, none of the existing modules needs to be recompiled, making option A correct. The service locator will see the new service provider simply by having that new service provider on the module path.

17. E. Trick question! An unnamed module doesn't use a `module-info.java` file. Therefore, option E is correct. An unnamed module can access an automatic module. The unnamed module would simply treat the automatic module as a regular JAR without involving the `module-info.java` file.

18. F. The `jpackage` command creates self-contained application such as an `.exe`. The `jlink` command creates a directory with a smaller Java runtime containing just what is needed. The `jimage` command is used to inspect a Java image file. Therefore, option F is correct.

19. E. There is a trick here. A module definition uses the keyword `module` rather than `class`. Since the code does not compile, option E is correct. If the code did compile, options A and D would be correct.

20. A. When running `java` with the `-d` option, all the required modules are listed. Additionally, the `java.base` module is listed since it is included automatically. The line ends with `mandated`, making option A correct. The `java.lang` is a trick since it is a package that is imported by default in a class rather than a module.

21. H. This question is tricky. The service locator must have a `uses` directive, but that is on the service provider interface. No modules need to specify `requires` on the service provider since that is the implementation. Since none of the options are correct, option H is the answer.

22. A, F. An automatic module exports all packages, making option A correct. An unnamed module is not available to any modules on the module path. Therefore, it doesn't export any packages, and option F is correct.

23. E. The module name is valid, as are the `exports` statements. Lines 4 and 5 are tricky because each is valid independently. However, the same module name is not allowed to be used in two `requires` statements. The second one fails to compile on line 5, making option E the answer.

24. A. Since the JAR is on the classpath, it is treated as a regular unnamed module even though it has a `module-info.java` file inside. Remember from learning about top-down migration that modules on the module path are not allowed to refer to the classpath, making options B and D incorrect. The classpath does not have a facility to restrict packages, making option A correct and options C and E incorrect.

25. A, C, D. Options A and C are correct because both the consumer and the service locator depend on the service provider interface. Additionally, option D is correct because the service locator must specify that it `uses` the service provider interface to look it up.

Chapter 13: Concurrency

1. D, F. There is no such class within the Java API called `ParallelStream`, so options A and E are incorrect. The method defined in the `Stream` class to create a parallel stream from an existing stream is `parallel()`; therefore, option F is correct, and option C is incorrect. The method defined in the `Collection` class to create a parallel stream from a collection is `parallelStream()`; therefore, option D is correct, and option B is incorrect.

2. A, D. The `tryLock()` method returns immediately with a value of `false` if the lock cannot be acquired. Unlike `lock()`, it does not wait for a lock to become available. This code fails to check the return value on line 8, resulting in the protected code being entered regardless of whether the lock is obtained. In some executions (when `tryLock()` returns `true` on every call), the code will complete successfully and print 45 at runtime, making option A correct. On other executions (when `tryLock()` returns `false` at least once), the `unlock()` method on line 10 will throw an `IllegalMonitorStateException` at runtime, making option D correct. Option B would be possible if line 10 did not throw an exception.

3. B, C, F. `Runnable` returns `void` and `Callable` returns a generic type, making options A and D incorrect and option F correct. All methods are capable of throwing unchecked exceptions, so option B is correct. Only `Callable` is capable of throwing checked exceptions, so option E is incorrect. Both `Runnable` and `Callable` are functional interfaces that can be implemented with a lambda expression, so option C is also correct.

4. D. The first problem is that although a `ScheduledExecutorService` is created, it is assigned to an `ExecutorService`. The type of the variable on line w1 would have to be updated to `ScheduledExecutorService` for the code to compile. The second problem is that `scheduleWithFixedDelay()` supports only `Runnable`, not `Callable`, and any attempt to return a value is invalid in a `Runnable` lambda expression; therefore, line w2 will also not compile, and option D is correct.

5. C. The code compiles and runs without throwing an exception or entering an infinite loop, so options D, E, and F are incorrect. The key here is that the increment operator `++` is not atomic. While the first part of the output will always be 100, the second part is nondeterministic. It may output any value from 1 to 100, because the threads can overwrite each other's work. Therefore, option C is the correct answer, and options A and B are incorrect.

6. C, E. The code compiles, so option G is incorrect. The `peek()` method on a parallel stream will process the elements concurrently, so the order cannot be determined ahead of time, and option C is correct. The `forEachOrdered()` method will process the elements in the order in which they are stored in the stream, making option E correct. None of the methods sort the elements, so options A and D are incorrect.

7. D. Livelock occurs when two or more threads are conceptually blocked forever, although they are each still active and trying to complete their task. A race condition is an undesirable result that occurs when two tasks that should have been completed sequentially are completed at the same time. For these reasons, option D is correct.

8. B. Be wary of run() vs. start() on the exam! The method looks like it executes a task concurrently, but it runs synchronously. In each iteration of the forEach() loop, the process waits for the run() method to complete before moving on. For this reason, the code is thread-safe. Since the program consistently prints 500 at runtime, option B is correct. Note that if start() had been used instead of run() (or the stream was parallel), then the output would be indeterminate, and option C would have been correct.

9. B, D. If a task is submitted to a thread executor and the thread executor does not have any available threads, the call to the task will return immediately with the task being queued internally by the thread executor. For this reason, option B is correct. Additionally, only platform threads can be pooled, making option D correct as well. Virtual threads are lightweight so they don't benefit from pooling.

10. A. The code compiles without issue, so option D is incorrect. The CopyOnWriteArrayList class is designed to preserve the original list on iteration, so the first loop will be executed exactly three times and, in the process, will increase the size of tigers to six elements. The ConcurrentSkipListSet class allows modifications, and since it enforces the uniqueness of its elements, the value 5 is added only once, leading to a total of four elements in bears. Finally, despite using the elements of lions to populate the collections, tigers and bears are not backed by the original list, so the size of lions is 3 throughout this program. For these reasons, the program prints 3 6 4, and option A is correct.

11. F. The code compiles and runs without issue, so options C, D, E, and G are incorrect. There are two important things to notice. First, synchronizing on the first variable doesn't impact the results of the code. Second, sorting on a parallel stream does not mean that findAny() will return the first record. The findAny() method will return the value from the first thread that retrieves a record. Therefore, the output is not guaranteed, and option F is correct. Option A looks correct, but even on serial streams, findAny() is free to select any element.

12. A, E. The shutdown() method submits three tasks to an ExecutorService, shuts it down, and then waits for the results. The awaitTermination() method waits a specified amount of time for all tasks to complete and the service to finish shutting down. Since each five-second task is still executing, the awaitTermination() method will return with a value of false after two seconds but not throw an exception making option A correct. The refactored() method uses a try-with-resources, which allows the tasks to gracefully finish and option E to be the other answer.

13. C. The code does not compile, so options A and E are incorrect. The problem here is that c1 is an Integer and c2 is a String, so the code fails to combine on line q2, since calling length() on an Integer is not allowed, and option C is correct. The rest of the lines compile without issue. Note that calling parallel() on an already parallel stream is allowed, and it may return the same object.

14. C, E. The code compiles without issue, so option D is incorrect. Since both tasks are submitted to the same thread executor pool, the order cannot be determined, so options A and B are incorrect, and option C is correct. The key here is that the order in which the resources o1 and o2 are synchronized could result in a deadlock. For example, if the first thread gets a lock on o1 and the second thread gets a lock on o2 before either thread can get their second lock, the code will hang at runtime, making option E correct. The code cannot produce a livelock, since both threads are waiting, so option F is incorrect. Finally, if a deadlock does occur, an exception will not be thrown, so option G is incorrect.

15. A. The code compiles and runs without issue, so options C, D, E, and F are incorrect. The `collect()` operation groups the animals into those that do and do not start with the letter p. Note that there are four animals that do not start with the letter p and three animals that do. Therefore, the output is 3 4, and option A is correct, making option B incorrect.

16. A, D, E. All the factory methods on `Executors` work with platform threads except `newVirtualThreadPerTaskExecutor()`, making option A correct. You can also create a platform thread using the constructor or factory method `Thread.ofPlatform()`, making options D and E the other answers.

17. F. The `lock()` method will wait indefinitely for a lock, so option A is incorrect. Options B and C are also incorrect, as the correct method name to attempt to acquire a lock is `tryLock()`. Option D is incorrect, as fairness is set to `false` by default and must be enabled by using an overloaded constructor. Finally, option E is incorrect because a thread that holds the lock may have called `lock()` or `tryLock()` multiple times. A thread needs to call `unlock()` once for each call to `lock()` and successful `tryLock()`. Option F is the correct answer since none of the other options is a valid statement.

18. C, E, G. A `Callable` lambda expression takes no values and returns a generic type; therefore, options C, E, and G are correct. Options A and F are incorrect because they both take an input parameter. Option B is incorrect because it does not return a value. Option D is not a valid lambda expression, because it is missing a semicolon at the end of the `return` statement, which is required when inside braces, `{}`.

19. E, G. The application compiles and does not throw an exception. Even though the stream is processed in sequential order, the tasks are submitted to a thread executor, which may complete the tasks in any order. Therefore, the output cannot be determined ahead of time, and option E is correct. Finally, the thread executor is never shut down; therefore, the code will run but never terminate, making option G also correct.

20. F. The key to solving this question is to remember that the `execute()` method returns `void`, not a `Future` object. Therefore, line n1 does not compile, and option F is the correct answer. If the `submit()` method had been used instead of `execute()`, option C would have been the correct answer, as the output of the `submit(Runnable)` task is a `Future<?>` object that can only return `null` on its `get()` method.

21. A, D. The `findFirst()` method guarantees the first element in the stream will be returned, whether it is serial or parallel, making options A and D correct. While option B may consistently print 1 at runtime, the behavior of `findAny()` on a serial stream is not guaranteed, so option B is incorrect. Option C is likewise incorrect, with the output being random at runtime.

22. B. The code compiles and runs without issue. The key aspect to notice in the code is that a single-thread executor is used, meaning that no task will be executed concurrently. Therefore, the results are valid and predictable, with 100 100 being the output, and option B is the correct answer. If a thread executor with more threads was used, then the `s2++` operations could overwrite each other, making the second value indeterminate at the end of the program. In this case, option C would be the correct answer.

23. F. The code compiles without issue, so options B, C, and D are incorrect. The limit on the cyclic barrier is 10, but the stream can generate only up to 9 threads that reach the barrier; therefore, the limit can never be reached, and option F is the correct answer, making options A and E incorrect. Even if the `limit(9)` statement was changed to `limit(10)`, the program could still hang since the JVM might not allocate 10 threads to the parallel stream.

24. A, F. The class compiles without issue, so option A is correct. Since `getInstance()` is a `static` method and `sellTickets()` is an instance method, lines k1 and k4 synchronize on different objects, making option D incorrect. The class is not thread-safe because the `addTickets()` method is not synchronized, and option E is incorrect. One thread could call `sellTickets()` while another thread calls `addTickets()`, possibly resulting in bad data. Finally, option F is correct because the `getInstance()` method is `synchronized`. Since the constructor is `private`, this method is the only way to create an instance of `TicketManager` outside the class. The first thread to enter the method will set the `instance` variable, and all other threads will use the existing value. This is a singleton pattern.

25. C, D. The code compiles and runs without issue, so options F and G are incorrect. The return type of `performCount()` is `void`, so `submit()` is interpreted as being applied to a `Runnable` expression. While `submit(Runnable)` does return a `Future<?>`, calling `get()` on it always returns `null`. For this reason, options A and B are incorrect, and option C is correct. The `performCount()` method can also throw a runtime exception, which will then be thrown by the `get()` call as an `ExecutionException`; therefore, option D is also a correct answer.

Chapter 14: I/O

1. C. Since the question asks about putting data into a structured object, the best class would be one that deserializes the data. Therefore, `ObjectInputStream` is the best choice, which is option C. `ObjectWriter`, `BufferedStream`, and `ObjectReader` are not I/O stream classes. `ObjectOutputStream` is an I/O class but is used to serialize data, not deserialize it. `FileReader` can be used to read text file data and construct an object, but the question asks what would be the best class to use for binary data.

2. A, F. Paths that begin with the root directory are absolute paths, so option A is correct, and option C is incorrect. Option B is incorrect because the path could be a file or directory within the file system. There is no rule that files have to end with a file extension. Option D is incorrect, as it is possible to create a `File` reference to files and directories that do not exist. Option E is also incorrect. The `delete()` method returns `false` if the file or directory cannot be deleted. Character stream classes often include built-in convenience methods for working with `String` data, so option F is correct. There is no such optimization for multi-threading, making option G incorrect.

3. B, D. If the console is unavailable, `System.console()` will return `null`, making option D correct and options E and F incorrect. The `writer` methods throw a checked `IOException`, making option C incorrect. The code works correctly, prompting for input and printing it. Therefore, option A is incorrect and option B is correct.

4. F. The code does not compile, as `Files.deleteIfExists()` declares the checked `IOException` that must be handled or declared. Remember, most `Files` methods declare `IOException`, especially the ones that modify a file or directory. For this reason, option F is correct.

5. C. The `filter()` operation applied to a `Stream<Path>` takes only one parameter, not two, so the code does not compile, and option C is correct. If the code were rewritten to use the `Files.find()` method with the `BiPredicate` as input (along with a `maxDepth` value), the output would be option B, `Has Sub`, since the directory is given to be empty. For fun, we reversed the expected output of the ternary operation.

6. C. The code compiles and runs without issue, so options F and G are incorrect. The key here is that while `Eagle` is serializable, its parent class, `Bird`, is not. Therefore, none of the members of `Bird` will be serialized. Even if you didn't know that, you should know what happens on deserialization. During deserialization, Java calls the constructor of the first nonserializable parent. In this case, the `Bird` constructor is called, with `name` being set to `Matt`, making option C correct. Note that none of the constructors or instance initializers in `Eagle` is executed as part of deserialization.

7. B, C. The code snippet will attempt to create a directory if the target of the symbolic link exists and is a directory. If the directory already exists, though, it will throw an exception. For this reason, option A is incorrect, and option B is correct. It will be created in `/mammal/kangaroo/joey` and also reachable at `/kang/joey` because of the symbolic link, making option C correct.

8. B. The `readAllLines()` method returns a `List`, not a `Stream`. Therefore, the call to `flatMap()` is invalid, and option B is correct. If the `Files.lines()` method were used instead, it would print the contents of the file one capitalized word at a time with the commas removed.

9. D, F, H. First, the method does compile, so options A and B are incorrect. Methods to read/write `byte[]` values exist in the abstract parent of all I/O stream classes. This implementation is not correct, though, as the return value of `read(buffer)` is not used properly. It will only correctly copy files whose character count is a multiple of 5, making option D correct and options C and E incorrect. Option F is also correct as the data may not have made it to disk yet. Option G would be correct if the `flush()` method were called after every write. Finally, option H is correct as the `reader` stream is never closed.

10. C, D, E. Option A is incorrect because `Path` is an abstract type so there is no constructor. Option B is incorrect because the `static` method in the `Path` interface is `of()`, not `get()`. Options C, D, and E are correct ways to obtain a `Path` instance.

11. A, E. The code will compile if the correct classes are used, so option G is incorrect. Remember, a try-with-resources statement can use resources declared before the start of the statement. The reference type of `wrapper` is `InputStream`, so we need a class that inherits `InputStream`. We can eliminate `BufferedWriter`, `ObjectOutputStream`, and `BufferedReader` since their names do not end in `InputStream`. Next, we see the class must take another stream as input, so we need to choose the remaining streams that are high-level streams. `BufferedInputStream` is a high-level stream, so option A is correct. Even though the instance is already a `BufferedInputStream`, there's no rule that it can't be wrapped multiple times by a high-level stream. Option D is incorrect, as `FileInputStream` operates on a file, not another stream. Finally, option E is correct—an `ObjectInputStream` is a high-level stream that operates on other streams.

12. C, E. The method to create a directory in the `Files` class is `createDirectory()`, not `mkdir()`. For this reason, line 6 does not compile, and option C is correct. In addition, the `setTimes()` method is available only on `BasicFileAttributeView`, not the read-only `BasicFileAttributes`, so line 8 will also not compile, making option E correct.

13. A, G. For a class to be serialized, it must implement the `Serializable` interface and contain instance members that are serializable or marked `transient`. For these reasons, options A and G are correct, and option F is incorrect. Option B is incorrect because even records are required to implement `Serializable` to be serialized. Option C is incorrect because it describes deserialization. The `Serializable` interface is a marker interface that does not contain any abstract methods, making option D incorrect. While it is a good practice for a serializable class to include a `static serialVersionUID` variable, it is not required. Therefore, option E is incorrect as well.

14. B, D, E. `Path` is immutable, so line 23 is ignored. If it were assigned to `p1`, option A would be correct. Since it is not assigned, the original value is still present, which is option B. Moving on to the second section, the `subpath()` method on line 27 is applied to the absolute path, which returns the relative path `animals/bear`. Next, the `getName()` method is applied to the relative path, and since this is indexed from 0, it returns the relative path `bear`. Therefore, option D is correct. Finally, remember calling `resolve()` with an absolute path as a parameter returns the absolute path, so option E is correct.

15. B, E, F. Option A does not compile, as there is no `File` constructor that takes three parameters. Option B is correct and is the proper way to create a `File` instance with a single `String` parameter. Option C is incorrect, as there is no constructor that takes a `String` followed by a `File`. There is a constructor that takes a `File` followed by a `String`, making option E correct. Option D is incorrect because the first parameter is missing a slash (`/`) to indicate it is an absolute path. Since it's a relative path, it is correct only when the user's current directory is the root directory. Finally, option F is correct as it creates a `File` from a `Path`.

16. A, D. The method compiles, so option E is incorrect. The method creates a new-zoo.txt file and copies the first line from zoo-data.txt into it, making option A correct. The try-with-resources statement closes all of the declared resources, including the FileWriter o. For this reason, the Writer is closed when the last o.write() is called, resulting in an IOException at runtime and making option D correct. Option F is incorrect because this implementation uses the character stream classes, which inherit from Reader or Writer.

17. B, C, E. Options B and C are properties of NIO.2 and are good reasons to use it over the java.io.File class. Option A is incorrect as both APIs can delete only empty directories, not a directory tree. Using a view to read multiple attributes leads to fewer round-trips between the process and the file system and better performance, making option E correct. Views can be used to access file system–specific attributes that are not available in Files methods; therefore, option D is incorrect. Files is part of NIO.2, whereas File is part of java.io, which means option F is incorrect.

18. C. To begin with, P is added to the StringBuilder first. Next, assuming mark() is supported, the position in the stream is marked before E. The E is added to the StringBuilder, with AC being skipped, and then the O is added to the StringBuilder, with CK being skipped. The stream is then reset() to the position before the E. The call to skip(0) doesn't do anything since there are no characters to skip, so E is added onto the StringBuilder in the next read() call. The value PEOE is printed, and option C is correct. Option G is incorrect because mark() may not be supported.

19. C. The code compiles and runs without issue, so option G is incorrect. If you simplify the redundant path symbols, p1 and p2 represent the same path, /lizard/walking.txt. Therefore, isSameFile() returns true. The second output is false, because equals() checks only if the path values are the same, without reducing the path symbols. Finally, mismatch() sees that the contents are the same and returns −1. For these reasons, option C is correct.

20. C. The target path of the file after the move() operation is /animals, not /animals/monkey.txt, so options A and B are both incorrect. Both will throw an exception at runtime since /animals already exists and is a directory. The option ATOMIC_MOVE means that any process monitoring the file system will not see an incomplete file during the move, so option C is correct.

21. C. The code compiles and runs without issue, so options D, E, and F are incorrect. The most important thing to notice is that the depth parameter specified as the second argument to find() is 0, meaning the only record that will be searched is the top-level directory. Since we know that the top directory is a directory and not a symbolic link, no other paths will be visited, and nothing will be printed. For these reasons, option C is the correct answer.

22. G. The code compiles, so option F is incorrect. To be serializable, a class must implement the Serializable interface, which Zebra does. It must also contain instance members that either are marked transient or are serializable. The instance member stripes is of type Object, which is not serializable. If Object implemented Serializable, all objects would be serializable by default, defeating the purpose of having the Serializable interface. Therefore, the Zebra class is not serializable, with the program throwing an exception at runtime if serialized and making option G correct. If `stripes` were removed from the class, options A and D would be the correct answers, as `name` and `age` are both marked `transient`.

23. A, D. The code compiles without issue, so options E and F are incorrect. The `toRealPath()` method will simplify the path to `/animals` and throw an exception if it does not exist, making option D correct. If the path does exist, calling `getParent()` on it returns the root directory. Walking the root directory with the filter expression will print all `.java` files in the root directory (along with all `.java` files in the directory tree), making option A correct. Option B is incorrect because it will skip files and directories that do not end in the `.java` extension. Option C is also incorrect as `Files.walk()` does not follow symbolic links by default. Only if the `FOLLOW_LINKS` option is provided and a cycle is encountered will the exception be thrown.

24. B. The method compiles without issue, so option E is incorrect. Option F is also incorrect. Even though `/flip` exists, `createDirectories()` does not throw an exception if the path already exists. If `createDirectory()` were used instead, option F would be correct. Next, the `copy()` command takes a target that is the path to the new file location, not the directory to be copied into. Therefore, the target path should be `/flip/sounds.txt`, not `/flip`. For this reason, options A and C are incorrect. Since the question says the file already exists, the `REPLACE_EXISTING` option must be specified or an exception will be thrown at runtime, making option B the correct answer.

25. B, D. Since you need to read characters, the `Reader` classes are appropriate. Therefore, you can eliminate options A, C, and F. Additionally, options E and G are incorrect, as they reference classes that do not exist. Options B and D are correct since they read from a file and buffer for performance.

Index

M

S

Online Test Bank

To help you study for your OCP Oracle Professional Certified Java SE 21 Developer certification exam, register to gain one year of FREE access after activation to the online interactive test bank—included with your purchase of this book!

To access our learning environment, simply visit www.wiley.com/go/sybextest prep, follow the instructions to register your book, and instantly gain one year of FREE access after activation to:

- Hundreds of practice test questions, so you can practice in a timed and graded setting.
- Flashcards
- A searchable glossary